GOVERNMENT AND BUSINESS

GOVERNMENT AND BUSINESS

Damodar Gujarati

Professor of Economics and Finance
Bernard Baruch College
City University of New York

McGRAW-HILL BOOK COMPANY

New York   St. Louis   San Francisco   Auckland   Bogotá
Hamburg   Johannesburg   London   Madrid   Mexico   Montreal   New Delhi
Panama   Paris   São Paulo   Singapore   Sydney   Tokyo   Toronto

This book was set in Optima by University Graphics, Inc.
The editors were Patricia A. Mitchell and Peggy Rehberger;
the production supervisor was Charles Hess.
The drawings were done by ECL Art.
The cover was designed by James Handloser.
R. R. Donnelley & Sons Company was printer and binder.

GOVERNMENT AND BUSINESS

2 3 4 5 6 7 8 9 0 D O C D O C 8 9 8 7 6 5 4

ISBN 0-07-025186-X

Library of Congress Cataloging in Publication Data

Gujarati, Damodar.
    Government and business.

    Includes bibliographical references and indexes.
    1. Industry and state—United States—History.
2. Industrial laws and legislation—United States—
History.   3. Commercial law—United States—History.
I. Title.
HD3616.U47G84   1984   338.973   83-24889
ISBN 0-07-025186-X

To my admirers,
Pushpa, Joan, and Diane

CONTENTS

PREFACE

Government and Business is written primarily for upper-level undergraduates and beginning graduate students in business and economics. The course for which this text is designed is described variously in school catalogues. Some representative titles are: *Government Policies toward Business, Business and Society, Business and Public Policy, Social Control of Business,* the *Economics of Government Regulation,* and *Government and Business Relations.* Whatever the title, such courses discuss the role of the government in a free-enterprise or a free-market economy, that is, an economy in which decisions about what to produce, how to produce, and for whom to produce are made by the actions of individuals and firms in the marketplace rather than by the government. The American economy is often cited as an example of a free-market economy, although the description is not quite correct because since late in the nineteenth century there has been a steady increase in the influence of the government in the marketplace. It is perhaps better to describe our economy as a *mixed economy* in which both the government and private institutions exercise economic control.

In writing this book my major aim has been to trace the growing influence of the government in the marketplace by considering several important questions, such as the following:

- When and under what circumstances should the government intervene in the marketplace?
- Even if theoretically it is desirable for the government to intervene, is it practically desirable to do so?
- If it can be shown that it is theoretically desirable as well as practically necessary to regulate business, what is the best form of such intervention? Is it through subsidy, taxation, government ownership of business, or simply as a watchdog agency — a kind of ombudsman?
- What is the best mode of regulation? A department, an agency within the executive branch, or an independent regulatory commission?
- What is the actual experience of government regulation of business?
- How does the performance of a regulatory agency measure against the purpose(s) for which it was created?

- How does one measure the benefits and the costs of regulation?
- Is there a tendency for a regulatory agency to be "captured" by the regulated?
- Why is it that once a regulatory agency is established it generally does not go out of business?
- What are the general accomplishments of business regulation in terms of the twin economic criteria of efficiency (efficient allocation of resources) and equity (equitable distribution of income)?
- If a particular regulation creates conflict between efficiency and equity, which criterion is preferable and why?
- Is there too much regulation? Can a strong case be made for deregulating some of the existing heavily regulated industries?
- If total deregulation is not feasible for whatever reasons, how can the existing regulation be made more effective so as to strike a proper balance between efficiency and equity?
- Considering the highly interdependent nature of the world economy, should the U.S. government enact rules and regulations that put the domestic producer at a competitive disadvantage vis-à-vis producers in other countries? For example, should the U.S. government enforce its antitrust laws rigorously even if the other countries are very lax in their antitrust enforcement?

To answer these and related questions, I have divided this text into five parts and eighteen chapters. Part One, *Regulation: An Overview,* provides a general introduction to the nature, the significance, the theories, and the structure of economic and social regulation in the United States and thereby sets the stage for the discussion of the various regulatory experiences discussed in the remainder of the text. Part Two, *General Purpose Regulation: The U.S. Antitrust Laws and How They Work,* discusses the omnipresent and omnipotent U.S. antitrust laws whose overall goal is to make and keep the American economy competitive. Through the presentation of several leading case studies, it shows the extent to which this goal has been achieved and with what consequences. Part Three, *Economic Regulation,* considers economic regulation in five major industries — railroad and trucking, civil aeronautics, energy, securities markets, and communications. The major objective of economic regulation is to regulate price and entry conditions in an industry either to alleviate a market failure or to redistribute income in favor of certain interest groups or both. In each of the regulatory episodes considered here I discuss the reason for the regulation, the methods of regulation, and the consequences of regulation. Also discussed are the recent deregulatory moves in many of these industries. Part Four, *Social Regulation,* discusses the new breed of social regulation started in the 1960s and covers regulation in the areas of environmental pollution and occupational health and safety. Unlike the price/entry type economic regulation, the primary objective of social regulation is to improve the overall quality of life. I illustrate with many examples why such regulation came about and with what consequence. Part Five, *The Nature and Significance of Regulatory Reform,* raises the question of the need for regulatory reform and considers the various reform measures that have been proposed by academic scholars, legal experts, governmental agencies and the Congress. An attempt has been made to evaluate the pros and cons of the proposed measures.

Because of frequent technological innovations and the changing loyalties of interest group pressures, the field of government regulation of business is vast, complex, and continuously evolving. In view of the introductory nature of the text, however, I have tried to keep the level of discussion as simple as possible. A distinguishing feature of the text is that it tries to integrate the historical, legal, institutional, economic, and empirical aspect of each regulatory experience in a manner that will be most accessible to the beginner. Wherever possible, I have introduced case studies bearing on one or more aspects of regulation. In my view, in the area of regulation the case studies are a valuable adjunct to the text.

Another distinguishing feature of *Government and Business* is the end-of-chapter questions, which are an integral part of the text. The questions are generally challenging and often raise some controversial issues in the area of government and business relations. Some of the questions require the student to refer to material not directly covered in the chapter, but with the hints and references provided the reader should be able to track them down.

The field of government regulation of business is dynamic. In the wake of the deregulation of the airline industry in 1978, the mood in Washington is toward more deregulation. Therefore, some of the regulatory experiences discussed in the text might become obsolete. But that should not diminish their importance, for each experience has a lesson or two to offer for future regulatory activity by the government. A study of the history of regulation, like any other history, is therefore extremely valuable.

In writing this text I have received help from several people. In particular, I am most indebted to my colleague Steven Lustgarten for his painstaking reading of the entire manuscript and for making very valuable suggestions that have materially improved the text. I would also like to acknowledge the following reviewers for their many helpful comments and suggestions: John D. Blackburn, Ohio State University; James R. Chelius, Rutgers University, Cook Campus; Kenneth G. Elzinga, University of Virginia; W. Bruce Erickson, University of Minnesota; William H. Greene, New York University; John Jordan, Seton Hall University; Steven Klepper, Carnegie-Mellon University; William Shepherd, University of Michigan; George Strauss, University of California at Berkeley; and Pauline Weber-Fox, Southeast Missouri State University. Of course, I alone am responsible for any deficiencies that remain. I hope the reader will let me know about them.

Damodar Gujarati

PART ONE

REGULATION: AN OVERVIEW

This part, consisting of five chapters, discusses the growth of government regulation of business in the United States, the various theories of government intervention in the marketplace, the administrative structure of the regulatory agencies, the various methods used to regulate social and economic activities, and the costs and benefits of regulation.

Chapter 1 provides a historical perspective on regulation in the United States and points out the dimensions of the phenomenal growth in regulation in the past several years. Chapter 2 discusses the major theories of government intervention in the marketplace and considers their relative merits and demerits. Wherever possible, empirical evidence supporting or refuting the theories is also adduced. The main thrust of this chapter is that there are clear situations in which government intervention is theoretically as well as practically justifiable from the viewpoint of economic efficiency. Whether such intervention is also justifiable from equity (i.e., equitable distribution of income) viewpoint is a very difficult question to decide since it involves interpersonal comparison of satisfactions. In Chapter 3 we discuss the various administrative structures that have been created to carry out the various regulations, with special emphasis on the independent regulatory commissions which seem to be the preferred means of government regulation in many areas of social and economic activity. Chapter 4 studies the various methods the government has adopted to achieve regulatory goals. They range from the very informal method of "jawboning" to direct entry into production via the public enterprises. In between are the standards approach, licensing, certification and registration, economic incentives via subsidies or disincentives via taxation, and the rate of return regulation of the public utilities. We discuss the relative advantages and disadvantages of the various methods and point out why economists generally prefer the incentives methods (taxes or subsidies). Chapter 5 considers the difficult topic of evaluating the costs and benefits of public regulation, pointing out the conceptual as well as the practical difficulties in obtaining reliable estimates of the two.

These five chapters and Chapter 6 on monopoly from Part Two provide a general framework against which we will examine specific regulatory experiences in the rest of the text. Therefore, we will refer to them frequently.

CHAPTER 1

REGULATION AS A GROWTH INDUSTRY

The primary purpose of this chapter is to provide a historical perspective on regulation in the United States and to lay the groundwork for the topics to be discussed in the ensuing chapters.

1.1 THE ROLE OF GOVERNMENT IN A MIXED ECONOMY

Although characterized as "free enterprise" or "competitive private capitalism,"[1] the United States is in fact a mixed economy in which the government plays an important role. As a matter of fact, since late in the nineteenth century, and especially since the great depression, there has been such a steady increase in the economic role of the government that the dictum "that government governs best which governs least" seems no longer true in this and other capitalist countries.

The government's role in economic activity is multifarious and can be schematized as shown in Figure 1.1. The figure shows that there are three major ways the government can affect the economy: through fiscal policy, monetary policy, and regulation.

The government affects the economy directly by its purchase of goods and services (e.g., hardware for the military) and indirectly by transfer payments either to individuals (Social Security, Medicare, and Medicaid) or to state and

---

[1]Capitalism may be broadly defined as the political economic system which is based on private property and private profit.

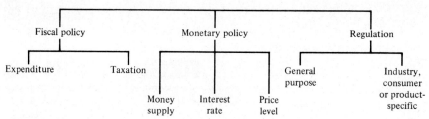

FIGURE 1.1
The role of government in a mixed economy.

local governments via grants-in-aid (e.g., federal revenue sharing). In 1981, for example, these expenditures amounted to about $657 billion, which is about 22 percent of the gross national product (GNP) of about $2937 billion for that year. To pay for these expenditures, the government collects revenues from personal, corporate, and indirect taxes. In 1981 it collected some $599 billion from individual, corporate, Social Security, excise, gift, and custom taxes, or about 19 percent of the 1981 GNP.

Government's monetary policy via the Federal Reserve System also affects the economy, for it influences money supply, which influences prices, interest rates, and credit availability. As a matter of fact, the monetarists, led by the Nobel laureate Milton Friedman, believe that monetary policy is more important than fiscal policy. But this is a minority view; most economists agree that both monetary and fiscal policies are important, their relative importance changing from time to time.

The instrument of government influence that has become more active and very potent in the recent past is the instrument of regulation whereby the government tries to control the actions of individuals and institutions in the private sector. In this text we are primarily concerned with this instrument of government control.

1.2 THE NATURE OF GOVERNMENT REGULATION

Broadly speaking, there are two types of regulation: (1) general purpose and (2) industry, consumer or product-specific.

General Purpose Regulation

This kind of regulation is typified by the U.S. antitrust laws, whose general thrust is to preserve competition in the economy as a whole. These antitrust laws, which are discussed in Part Two, cut across industries and are not designed against a particular industry or product.

Specific Purpose Regulation

This form of regulation is devised to regulate a particular industry or a particular product or to protect the consumer directly. An example is the Motor Vehicle

Air Pollution Control Act of 1965, which was the first major environmental law to prescribe minimum auto emission standards. Such specific purpose regulations have been categorized into two groups: economic and social regulation.

Economic Regulation   The determination of prices, output level, entry into the industry, and rate of return on capital are the main concerns of economic regulation. For example, until the 1978 Airline Deregulation Act, the Civil Aeronautics Board (CAB) was solely responsible for promoting and regulating the civil air transport industry within the United States. It had absolute powers to grant licenses to provide air transportation services, to approve or disapprove proposed rates and fares, and to approve or disapprove proposed agreements and corporate relationships involving air carriers.

Social Regulation   It has been said that social regulation "affects the conditions under which goods and services are produced and the physical characteristics of products that are manufactured."[2] The Environmental Protection Agency (EPA), for example, sets standards on the amounts of pollution a manufacturer may create in the conduct of its business, thus determining the conditions under which goods may be produced. The Consumer Product Safety Commission (CPSC) establishes minimum safety standards for products that in its judgment are potentially unsafe, thus affecting the physical characteristic of the product.

A General Definition of Regulation

From the preceding discussion one can define regulation as follows. Regulation includes those activities which:

Impact on the operating business environment of broad sectors of private enterprise, including market entry and exit; rate, price, and profit structures; and competition;

impact on specific commodities, products, or services through permit, certification, or licensing requirements; and

involve the development, administration and enforcement of national standards, violations of which could result in civil or criminal penalties, or which result in the types of impact described above.[3]

From this definition it is clear that *regulation* encompasses both social and economic aspects.

---

[2]William Lilley III and James C. Miller III, *The New "Social Regulation,"* reprint no. 66, The American Enterprise Institute, 1977, p. 53.

[3]Congressional Budget Office, "The Number of Federal Employees Engaged in Regulated Activities," *Subcommittee Print of the Subcommittee on Oversight and Investigations of the Committee on Interstate and Foreign Commerce,* House of Representatives, August 1976, pp. 15–16.

1.3 A BRIEF HISTORY OF REGULATION IN THE UNITED STATES[4]

Although regulation in the United States is as old as the Constitution itself (which gave to Congress the right to regulate interstate commerce), real economic regulation began in 1887 with the establishment of the Interstate Commerce Commission (ICC). The ICC was created to deal with the anticompetitive practices then prevailing in the railroad industry, especially the practices of price discrimination and rebates to certain types of customers.[5] Then came the Sherman (antitrust) Act of 1890, which made illegal "every contract, combination in the form of a trust or otherwise, or conspiracy, in restraint of trade or commerce among several states, or within foreign nations." In short, it outlawed monopoly. This was followed by the Federal Trade Commission Act of 1914, which established the Federal Trade Commission (FTC). The chief function of the FTC is to prohibit "unfair methods of competition" and "unfair or deceptive acts or practices" (more on this will be said in Part Two). In the same year the Clayton Act was passed, which outlawed four specific business practices, namely, price discrimination, exclusive and tying contracts, mergers, and interlocking directorates — topics discussed in Part Two.

The real spurt to regulation however came during the great depression of the 1930s; during the period 1929–1933 total output in the United States fell by about 30 percent, spending for new buildings and equipment decreased by about 80 percent, and by 1933 the unemployment rate reached the astronomical figure of 25 percent. The depression produced a fundamental change in the American attitude toward the role of the government in the economy. The philosophy that government should be seen and not heard was discarded in favor of active participation by the government in the affairs of business. In the famous 100 days following the swearing in of President Franklin Roosevelt in March 1933, the President asked for and the Congress readily granted an unprecedented list of emergency legislation which put the federal government deeply and permanently into the business of regulating the economy (see Table 1.1).

Since the New Deal legislation of the great depression, the history of regulation in the United States is a history of continually increasing government intervention in the affairs of society and the economy. To see this, Table 1.1 gives in capsule the growth of regulation in the United States since 1932 (the table gives only some major pieces of legislation and the list is by no means exhaustive).

---

[4]The following discussion leans heavily on Steven Ratner's "Regulating the Regulators," *The New York Times Magazine,* June 10, 1979, pp. 102–109 and 113–121; and the 50th anniversary issue of *Business Week,* Sept. 3, 1979.

[5]The topics of monopoly and price discrimination are discussed in Chapter 6. More details on the ICC can be found in Chapter 11.

TABLE 1.1
GROWTH OF REGULATION IN THE UNITED STATES: SOME HIGHLIGHTS

Year	Name of act or amendment	What it accomplished
1932	Federal Home Loan Bank	Regulation of home financing institutions
	Reconstruction Finance Corporation	Use of government credit to help troubled private companies
1933	Agricultural Adjustment	Agricultural price and production supports (declared unconstitutional)
	Glass-Steagall	Created bank deposit insurance, prohibited interest on checking accounts, separated banking from underwriting, strengthened Federal Reserve's ability to stabilize the economy through open market operations
	National Industrial Recovery	First major attempt to plan and regulate the economy, first collective bargaining and wage and hour regulation (parts of the act declared unconstitutional)
	Securities	Required full disclosure of companies wishing to sell securities to the public
	Tennessee Valley Authority	First direct government involvement in energy production and marketing
1934	Communications	Centralized regulation of broadcasting, telephone, and telegraph
	National Housing	Provided for federal mortgage insurance, put government into secondary mortgage market, and provided for regulation of housing standards
	Securities Exchange	Extended full disclosure to all listed companies, provided for securities registration, regulated insider trading and stock exchange trading practices
1935	National Labor Relations (Wagner Act)	Promoted collective bargaining and prohibited unfair labor practices by employers
	Social Security	Created national retirement system
1936	Commodity Exchange	First regulation of commodity exchanges
	Robinson-Patman	Antiprice discrimination law designed to protect small retailers from chain competition
1938	Agricultural Adjustment	Extended price supports, instituted parity payments, and launched wide federal management of agriculture
	Food, Drug and Cosmetic	Established predistribution safety clearance of new drugs
	Fair Labor Standards	Provided for minimum wage, 40-hour week, overtime, and control of child labor
	Natural Gas	Regulated natural gas pipeline rates
	Wheeler-Lea	Banned false and deceptive advertising

TABLE 1.1
GROWTH OF REGULATION IN THE UNITED STATES: SOME HIGHLIGHTS (*continued*)

Year	Name of act or amendment	What it accomplished
1939	Wool Products Labeling	Prohibited sale of mislabeled goods
1947	Taft-Hartley	Extended prohibition of unfair labor practices to union activities
1953	Flammable Fabrics	Authorized control of sale of dangerous fabrics and apparel
	Outer Continental Shelf	Established jurisdiction over oil and gas exploration in federal offshore waters
1954	Atomic Energy	Opened nuclear technology, under regulation, to private industry
1956	Interstate and Defense Highway	Provided for interstate highway system
	Spence-Robertson	First comprehensive regulation of bank holding companies
1958	Federal Aviation	Centralized regulation of air safety
	Food Additives Amendment	Extended preclearance requirement to food as well as drugs
	Textile Fiber Products Identification	Controlled misbranding and false advertising
1962	All-Channel Receiver	Required all TV sets to be able to receive UHF channels
	Drug Amendments	Required proof of effectiveness as well as safety before marketing of new drugs and labeling of drugs by generic names
	Air Pollution Control	First act to control the quality of air
1963	Equal Pay	First key antidiscrimination act; eliminated wage differentials based on sex alone
1964	Civil Rights	Banned discrimination in private employment on account of race, sex or national origin; Established the Equal Employment Opportunity Commission
1965	Medicare	First major federal regulation of health care
	Motor Vehicle Air Pollution Control	First major environmental law to establish auto emissions standards
1966	Highway Safety	Set uniform safety standards for state highways
	National Traffic and Motor Vehicle Safety	Established vehicle and equipment safety standards
	Fair Packaging and Labeling	Required producers to disclose the contents of packages
1967	Wholesome Meat Act	Federal assistance in interstate meat inspection system
1968	Consumer Credit Protection (Truth in Lending)	First federal regulation of consumer borrowing requiring full disclosure of terms of credit

8

TABLE 1.1
GROWTH OF REGULATION IN THE UNITED STATES: SOME HIGHLIGHTS (*continued*)

Year	Name of act or amendment	What it accomplished
1969	National Environmental Policy	Required environmental impact statements for federal agencies and projects
1970	Clean Air	Established basic standards and time tables for air pollution abatement
	Occupational Safety and Health (OSHA)	Provided for regulation of safety and health standards in workplace
1972	Consumer Product Safety	Provided for mandatory product safety standards and for banning of hazardous substances
	Water Pollution Control	Established standards for federal regulation of water pollution
	Noise Pollution Control	Regulated noise limits of products and transportation of vehicles
1973	Emergency Petroleum Allocation	First price control and allocation systems for oil
1974	Commodity Futures Trading Commission	Extended federal control to all contracts on all exchanges
	Employee Retirement Income and Security (ERISA)	Established federal regulation of private pension plans
	Motor Vehicle and Schoolbus Safety	Established auto recall and defect notification
	Federal Energy Administration	Provided authority for mandatory conservation programs
1975	Federal Trade Commission Improvement	Funded public participation in rule making, added requirement for refunds and corrective advertising
	Securities Act Amendments	Ended fixed brokerage commissions and launched planning for national securities market
1977	Surface Mining Control and Reclamation	Provided for regulation of coal strip-mining
1978	Airline Deregulation	Required all pricing, entry, and route regulations of domestic airlines to cease completely by 1985
	Natural Gas Pricing	Required elimination of all inter- and intrastate gas price controls by 1989
1980	Staggers Rail	Permitted railroads greater flexibility in pricing and in abandoning uneconomical rail routes
	Motor Carrier	Permitted substantial freedom of pricing and new entry into the trucking industry
1982	Bus Deregulation	Allowed price and entry competition in passenger bus transportation

Source: 50th anniversary issue, *Business Week,* Sept. 3, 1979, (adapted and updated).

1.4   REGULATION: THE "FOURTH BRANCH" OF GOVERNMENT

To the executive, legislative, and judiciary branches of our government we may add the "fourth branch," which consists of a vast network of regulatory agencies, boards, and commissions that have been created to administer various regulatory programs. The table in the appendix to this chapter gives the list of the various regulatory bodies and the areas in which they operate and also gives some idea about the enormity of the fourth branch. Incidentally, notice the overlapping jurisdiction of some of the agencies.

It is important to point out that very often the fourth branch is not answerable, or answerable only to a limited extent, to the executive, legislative, or judiciary branches, although it wields enormous power (more on this in Section 3.5). An example of this power is the FTC. In its mission "to prevent the free enterprise system from being stifled, substantially lessened or fettered by monopoly or restraint of trade, or corrupted by unfair and deceptive trade practices,"[6] the FTC has from time to time promulgated regulations which, according to some interest groups, are excessive. For example, in August 1981 the commission issued rules which required the used-car dealers to disclose major known defects on the used cars they sell and the extent of any outstanding warranties. The used-car dealers felt this to be an undue interference in their trade practices and the Congress itself believed that such rules would lead to costly inspections and repairs that would raise the price of used cars. Therefore, using its recently acquired legislative veto power over FTC regulations, Congress vetoed the used-car regulations in May 1982 by a vote of 286 to 133 in the House and 69 to 27 in the Senate.

As we will see in Chapter 18, the constitutionality of such a veto over the rulings of an independent regulatory commission is of questionable validity, and in October 1982 the U.S. Court of Appeals for the District of Columbia Circuit held such veto to be unconstitutional and specifically upheld the FTC used-car regulations. In a dramatic decision on June 23, 1983, the Supreme Court ruled that such legislative veto is unconstitutional as it exceeds consitutional limits designed to preserve the separation of powers. It seems that this decision has curbed Congress's power over some of the regulatory agencies (we will discuss this topic thoroughly in Chapter 18). Whether this is good or bad will be discussed in subsequent chapters, especially in Chapter 18.

The growth of regulatory legislation has brought in its wake a dramatic increase in the number of regulations issued by the regulatory agencies. As an index of the growth of the "regulation industry," consider the *Federal Register,*[7]

---

[6]*U.S. Government Manual,* 1978–1979, p. 546 (issued by the *Federal Register,* National Archives and Records Service, a division of the General Services Administration).

[7]*Federal Register* is published daily, Monday through Friday. Some of the recent issues contain well over 400 pages.

TABLE 1.2
FEDERAL REGULATORY EXPENDITURES, 1974–1979

Area	1974	1975	1976	1977	1978	1979	1974–1979
Consumer safety & health							
$(million)	1,302	1,463	1.613	1.985	2,582	2,671	
% change		12	10	23	30	3	105
Job safety & working conditions							
$(million)	310	379	446	492	562	626	
% change		22	18	10	14	11	102
Environment & energy							
$(million)	347	527	682	870	989	1,116	
% change		52	29	28	14	13	222
Financial reporting & other financial							
$(million)	36	45	53	58	70	69	
% change		25	18	9	21	−5	92
Industry-specific regulation							
$(million)	245	269	270	309	340	341	
% change		10	—	14	10	—	39
Totals							
$(million)	2,240	2.683	3,064	3,714	4,543	4,823	
% change		20	14	21	22	6	115

Source: Federal Reserve Bank of Philadelphia, *Business Review,* September–October 1978, figure 1, p. 4. The above estimates were originally made by Robert DeFina and Murray Weidenbaum of the Center for the Study of American Business, Washington University.

which publishes the rules and procedures promulgated by the various agencies. Between 1955 and 1975 the number of pages published in the register rose from about 10,000 to well over 60,000. But most of the growth is recent, since about 1970. It has been estimated that between 1955 and 1970 the number of pages in the register increased at the compound annual rate of about 5 percent, whereas between 1970 and 1975 the corresponding rate was about 25 percent, a five-fold jump.

Another index of growth of the regulation industry can be found in the federal expenditure on regulation. Although this topic will be studied more exhaustively in Chapter 5, it may be helpful to note here a few statistics, which are given in Table 1.2. It should be emphasized that the data given in Table 1.2 pertain only to direct federal expenditures on certain regulatory activities and do not include the costs borne by the affected parties in carrying out the mandate of the various legislations. (This topic will be considered further in Chapter 5.) What the data reveal is a dramatic increase in the federal regulatory expenditures, especially those relating to social regulation. It has been estimated that for fiscal year 1979 about 92 percent of the federal regulatory expenditure was devoted to social regulation, particularly regulation pertaining to consumer safety and health, job safety and other working conditions, and the environment.

1.5 WHY GROWTH? THE NEW SOCIAL REGULATION

As the preceding discussion shows, there has been a vast increase in the scope and detail of government regulation over the years. But the pace of growth has quickened since the mid-1960s, especially in the area of social regulation such as air pollution, water pollution, job safety, drug safety, Medicare, etc. Why this growth in social regulation? Perhaps in the 1960s and 1970s the failure of business to protect the safety and health of its workers, but more importantly the public's concern for a better environment, fueled by environmental lobbyists, may very well account for the growth. (We shall provide some of the theoretical reasons for government intervention in Chapter 2.) The matter has been put succinctly by John T. Dunlop of Harvard, as follows:

> The rapid expansion of government regulation in recent years and specifically government's penchant for rigid, bureaucratic "command and control" regulations, even when ineffective or counterproductive, have arisen in part from a lack of coherence and consensus within the business community about more constructive choices for achieving social purposes.[8]

The same theme is echoed by Irwin S. Shapiro, former chairperson of the board and chief executive officer of E. I. du Pont de Nemours & Company, when he states that

> Business, particularly big business, is seen as an uncontrolled power that bends the political process to its will and is not sincerely concerned with the quality of its products or the safety of the people whose lives it affects — which is to say, just about everybody.[9]

The fact that there has been an increase in government's regulatory activity does not mean that each government regulation can be necessarily justified either in theory or in practice. An example will drive home the point. In the United States during 1976 to 1978 an average of thirteen major explosions occurred at grain elevators, a rise from an average of eight in earlier years. Why? The EPA prohibited the grain companies from allowing grain dust to escape into the atmosphere but probably forgot the fact that the retained grain dust becomes extremely explosive. Thus the protection of the environment came at the cost of more explosions![10]

---

[8]"Business and Public Policy Symposium," *Harvard Business Review,* November–December 1979, p. 86.
[9]Ibid., p. 98.
[10]See Murray L. Weidenbaum, *The Future of Business Regulation,* American Management Association, New York, 1979.

The preceding example raises the important question of the costs and benefits of government regulation. As we shall see in Chapter 5, very often the (direct or administrative) costs of government regulation can be identified, but the benefits may not be so readily identifiable. As a result, oftentimes it is not easy to find out whether the benefits of an intended regulation justify the costs such regulation may involve. The reader should keep this point in mind when examining any regulation, economic or social.

1.6   REGULATION AT THE STATE AND LOCAL LEVEL

The focus of this textbook is on federal regulatory activity. But it should be noted that regulation is not a monopoly of the federal government; state and local governments also engage in regulatory activities. Some of these activities parallel the federal efforts and some are peculiar to local interests (e.g., licensing of doctors and lawyers, and public utility rate regulation). For example, New York State has its own antimonopoly law which is administered by the Anti-Monopoly Bureau. Similarly, it has the Consumer Fraud and Protection Bureau, the Securities Bureau, the Civil Rights Bureau, the Environmental Protection Bureau, and the Water and Air Resources Bureau. New York City has its own regulatory network, which is often patterned after the state regulatory machinery.

Although state and local regulatory activities have increased along with federal activities, there is very little information about how much the state and local agencies spend on regulation. Perhaps the budgets of state and local governments could be examined to learn about the costs of regulation; this may provide some useful data for comparative purposes. But that calls for another book!

1.7   SUMMARY AND CONCLUSIONS

The main purpose of this chapter was to discuss the origin, nature, and growth of regulation in the United States. Although regulation in the United States dates back to at least 1887, when the ICC was created, it has become more pronounced in the recent past, since about the mid-1960s. The growth is largely in the area of social regulation — regulation that deals with health, job security, job safety, environmental protection, and product safety — although traditional economic types of regulation persist (perhaps with added vigor, as in the case of SEC's quest for more and more information from the companies listed on the stock exchanges). The concern with social regulation perhaps stems from the failure of business to pay adequate attention to the security and safety of workers and workplaces. The passage of the Employee Retirement Income and Security Act (ERISA) (see Table 1.1) and the various job safety and health care regulations are indications of this failure.

This chapter also discussed the vast growth in the regulatory network that is created to administer the various laws, and it pointed out the concern of business as well as the Congress over the ever-increasing power of some regulatory agencies such as the FTC.

QUESTIONS

1-1 According to the Nobel laureate economist Milton Friedman the basic roles of government in a free society are as follows: `` . . . to provide a means whereby we can modify the rules, to mediate differences among us on the meaning of the rules, and to enforce compliance with the rules on the part of those few who would otherwise not play the game.'' (Milton Friedman, *Capitalism and Freedom,* The University of Chicago Press, 1962, p. 25). Is this too narrow a view of the government's role in a mixed economy? (The rules Friedman refers to are the general conditions that govern relationships among people in a free society and pertain to the maintenance of law and order, enforcement of contracts voluntarily entered into, and interpretation and enforcement of property rights.)

1-2 Is the distinction between social and economic regulation meaningful? Isn't all regulation social in the sense that it affects human welfare?

1-3 From library sources trace the historical development of the Glass-Steagall Act. What was the significance of the creation of the bank deposit insurance scheme? Could the bank failures that heralded the great depression have been avoided if such a scheme had been in existence?

1-4 What accounts for the growth of social regulation during the Nixon-Ford period of 1968–1976?

1-5 The Equal Pay Act of 1963 outlawed wage differentials based on sex alone. In a suit brought under this act, how would the judge decide whether the observed differences in wages are due to sex alone? What factors might influence his decision?

1-6 If you look at your TV set, you will find somewhere between seventy to eighty-three UHF channels and about twelve VHF channels, although in most areas very few UHF channels are functional. Why? Also, of the twelve VHF channels, only a few are operative in any given area. Why is this so?

1-7 Following the Truth in Lending Act, would you vote for a Truth in Testing Act so that students appearing for various entrance examinations (e.g., law school admission test) are assured that answers to the questions represent nothing but the truth? What would be the consequences of such an act for the students, the colleges, and the test-administering institutions?

1-8 Are you familiar with the Privacy Act of 1974? If not, find out the main provisions of the act. What is the significance of the act for confidential information provided to governmental agencies, such as the IRS, the Census Bureau, etc.?

1-9 What do you know about the Freedom of Information Act? Under the act can you force the government to divulge any information it may have about you?

1-10 A Harvard Business School professor of finance taught his class a method of predicting short-term interest rates based on a regression model. The model worked well for the period 1960–1968. A 1969 graduate of the school who was exposed to the method subsequently applied it while working for a respected company. The model did not predict well for 1969 and 1970, and the 1969 graduate lost his job. He thereupon sued his alma mater as well as the professor, charging that the professor had taught him something that was demonstrably false. The lower court ruled in favor of the school and the professor, citing the First Amendment (academic freedom). On appeal, however, the decision was overruled by the presiding justice, who stated that: "It seems paradoxical beyond endurance to rule that a manufacturer of shampoos may not endanger a student's scalp but a premier educational institution is free to stuff his skull with nonsense." On further appeal, however, the case was decided in favor of the school and the professor. (For details, see George J. Stigler, *The Citizen and the State: Essay on Regulation,* The Univeristy of Chicago Press, Chicago, 1975, pp. 189–191).

In view of the preceding (apocryphal) case, would you recommend that the government pass a law requiring universities to teach nothing but the truth — call it the Truth in Teaching Act? What would be the consequences of such an act for the students, the professors, and society at large?

APPENDIX: Inventory of Authorizing Legislation and Programs by Agency

CATEGORY 1   REGULATION OF ENERGY, ENVIRONMENT, HOUSING, AND OCCUPATIONAL HEALTH AND SAFETY

Substantive areas

Power and energy

Agencies:
Federal Power Commission
Tennessee Valley Authority
Bonneville Power Administration
Southeastern, Alaska, Southwestern Power Administrations
Energy Research and Development Administration
Nuclear Regulatory Commission
Federal Energy Administration
Federal Trade Commission
Antitrust Division
National Bureau of Standards

Natural resources and environment

Agencies:
U.S. Fish and Wildlife Service
Appalachian Regional Commission
Delaware River Basin Commission
Susquehanna River Basin Commission
National Oceanic and Atmospheric Administration
Environmental Protection Agency
Nuclear Regulatory Commission
U.S. Forest Service
Army Corps of Engineers
U.S. Geological Survey
Bureau of Land Management
Bureau of Reclamation
Coast Guard

Housing and Community development

Agencies:
Federal Housing Administration
Office for Consumer Affairs and Regulatory Functions
Office for Fair Housing and Equal Opportunity
Federal Insurance Administration
Federal Trade Commission
Farmers Home Administration
Veterans Administration

Occupational health and safety

Agencies:
Mining Enforcement and Safety Administration
Center for Disease Control, Public Health Service
Occupational Safety and Health Review Commission
Occupational Safety and Health Administration

CATEGORY 2   REGULATION OF TRANSPORTATION AND COMMUNICATION

Substantive areas

Transportation

Agencies:
Civil Aeronautics Board
National Transportation Safety Board
Tennessee Valley Authority
Interstate Commerce Commission
Federal Maritime Commission
National Highway Traffic Safety Administration
Federal Highway Administration
Federal Aviation Administration
Urban Mass Transportation Administration
Materials Transportation Bureau
St. Lawrence Seaway Development Corporation
Federal Railroad Administration
U.S. Coast Guard
Antitrust Division
Federal Trade Commission

Communication

Agencies:
Federal Communications Commission
U.S. Postal Service
Postal Rate Commission
Office of Telecommunications Policy

CATEGORY 3   REGULATION OF BANKING, FINANCE, INTERNATIONAL TRADE, AND GOVERNMENT PROCUREMENT

Substantive areas

Economic regulation – banking

Agencies:
Comptroller of the Currency
Federal Deposit Insurance Corporation
Federal Home Loan Bank Board
Federal Savings and Loan Insurance Corporation
National Credit Union Administration
Board of Governors of the Federal Reserve System
Farm Credit Administration
Antitrust Division
Veterans Administration

Economic regulation – commodities

Agencies:
Commodity Futures Trading Commission

Economic regulation – securities

Agencies:
Securities and Exchange Commission

Economic regulation – public finance

Agencies:
Internal Revenue Service
Customs Service
Bureau of Alcohol, Tobacco and Firearms

Economic regulation – international trade

Agencies:
Office of Munitions Control
Foreign Agricultural Service
Foreign Trade Zones Board
International Trade Commission
Commodity Credit Corporation
U.S. Customs Service
Office of Tariff Affairs
Federal Trade Commission
Maritime Administration

Procurement

Agencies:
Federal Supply Service, General Services Administration
Cost Accounting Standards Board

CATEGORY 4 REGULATION OF FOOD, CONSUMER HEALTH AND SAFETY, ECONOMIC TRADE PRACTICES AND LABOR-MANAGEMENT CONCERNS

Substantive areas

Food resources

Agencies:
Agricultural Stabilization and Conservation Service
Agricultural Marketing Service
Animal and Plant Health Inspection Service
Packers and Stockyards Administration
Federal Grain Inspection Service
Federal Trade Commission

Consumer protection and safety

Agencies:
Consumer Product Safety Commission
Federal Trade Commission
Board of Governors of the Federal Reserve System
Federal Highway Administration
Federal Aviation Administration
Civil Aeronautics Board
Center for Disease Control, Public Health Service
Food and Drug Administration, Public Health Service
Food Safety and Quality Service
Office for Consumer Affairs and Regulatory Functions
Federal Insurance Administration
Environmental Protection Agency
Nuclear Regulatory Commission
National Bureau of Standards

Economic regulation — commerce and trade

Agencies:
Small Business Administration
Institute for Basic Standards, National Bureau of Standards
Institute of Materials Research, National Bureau of Standards
Institute for Applied Technology, National Bureau of Standards
Economic Developmnt Administration
Patent Office
Federal Trade Commission
Commodity Credit Corporation
Bureau of Alcohol, Tobacco, and Firearms
Drug Enforcement Administration

Economic regulation — antitrust

Agencies:
Antitrust Division
Federal Trade Commission

Comptroller of the Currency
Board of Governors of the Federal Reserve System

Economic regulation — income security

Agencies:
Social Security Administration
Railroad Retirement Board
Pension Benefit Guaranty Corporation
Public Safety Officers' Benefits Program
Office of Workers Compensation Programs
Labor Management Services Administration
Employment and Training Administration
Economic Development Administration
Food and Nutrition Service
Compensation and Pension Service, Veterans Administration
Education and Rehabilitation Service, Veterans Administration

Human resources — labor management

Agencies:
National Labor Relations Board
National Mediation Board
National Air Transport Adjustment Board, National Mediation Board
National Railroad Adjustment Board, National Mediation Board
Labor Management Services Administration
Employment Standards Administration
Employment and Training Administration

CATEGORY 5   CIVIL RIGHTS, INDIANS, ALIENS AND NATIONALITY, AND CANAL ZONE GOVERNMENT

Substantive areas

Human resources — civil rights

Agencies:
Equal Employment Opportunity Commission
Board of Governors of the Federal Reserve System
Commission on Civil Rights
Office for Civil Rights, Office of the Secretary (HEW)
U.S. Civil Service Commission
Employment Standards Administration
Office of Human Development
Architectural and Transportation Barriers Compliance Board
Civil Rights Division
Office of Civil Rights Compliance, Law Enforcement Assistance Administration
National Criminal Justice Information Statistics Service, Law Enforcement Assistance
  Administration
Community Relations Service
Education and Rehabilitation Service, Veterans Administration

Office for Fair Housing and Equal Opportunity
Urban Mass Transportation Administration

Human resources — Indian affairs

Agencies:
Bureau of Indian Affairs

Aliens and nationality

Agencies:
U.S. Department of State
Visa Office, Bureau of Consular Affairs
Consular Offices
Passport Office, Bureau of Consular Affairs
Immigration and Naturalization Service

The Panama Canal

Agencies:
Canal Zone Government

Source: "Federal Regulatory Programs and Activities," *Report of the Comptroller General of the United States,* March 16, 1978.

CHAPTER 2

THEORIES OF REGULATION

The vast increase in the nature and scope of federal government's regulatory activity cannot be explained by a single, unanimously accepted theory. As a matter of fact, several theories have been proposed to account for government's intervention in the marketplace. In this chapter we consider specifically the following four theories of regulation:

1 The public interest theory
2 The self-interest or capture theory
3 Stigler's economic theory
4 Posner's theory of indirect taxation

We discuss these theories in the hope that they may provide some rationale for the various regulatory acts enacted over the past 50 years. Consider, for example, the 1970 Clean Air Act, which established basic standards and timetables for air pollution abatement. The importance of clean air from a health viewpoint is beyond doubt. But the question is: Why did the government have to pass the act? Could the private market not be trusted to provide clean air without government intervention? Here the explanation can be found in the public interest theory of externality discussed in Section 2.2, which states why the marketplace may not be able to provide the optimum or the best amount of clean air and why government intervention may be necessary.[1] On the other hand, one would be hard-pressed to give a public interest rationale for the Interstate Commerce Commission's (ICC) regulation of the trucking industry, an

---

[1]The term *optimum* means the maximal level of achievement of a particular objective or goal, be it profit, gross national product, prevention of a disease or whatever.

industry that can be competitive if left to itself. But here the capture theory or George J. Stigler's economic theory of regulation may provide some explanation. With the knowledge of the theories discussed in this chapter the reader may want to find out which of the acts mentioned in Table 1.1 or the ones to be discussed in Parts Three and Four can be explained by one or more of these theories.

2.1 THE IDEALIZED WORLD OF PERFECT COMPETITION AND THE THEOREM OF THE "INVISIBLE HAND"

These days one increasingly hears that there is too much government regulation and that things will be better if they are left to the "market." For example, there are economists who strongly believe that our energy crisis is due to excessive regulation of the oil industry, and that if the government left the matter to the market, the "invisible hand" of self-interest, to use Adam Smith's phrase, would resolve the crisis in due course (see Chapter 13 for the energy crisis and the government's role it it). The term *market* refers to the competitive market or more accurately to the perfectly competitive market.[2]

Although perfect competition in its strict sense does not exist in the United States or elsewhere, why does one hear so frequently about it and why do prominent economists such as Milton Friedman and his disciples at the "Chicago School" of economics advocate it so strongly?

To understand this, let us assume that society's goal is to obtain maximum social welfare or maximum social satisfaction — the greatest good of the greatest numbers — at the least possible economic cost. Now social welfare can be said to have reached a maximum when it is not possible to make one person better off (in terms of utility or satisfaction) without making someone else worse off (again in terms of utility or satisfaction). This condition is known as *Pareto optimality* or the *Pareto efficiency* principle, named after the Italian economist Vilfredo Pareto, who argued that the only objective basis for saying that society is better off is when some people are made better off and no one is made worse off (see the appendix to this chapter for a technical discussion of the Pareto principle). In judging the efficacy of any public policy measure, economists often discuss it in terms of the Pareto-optimality criterion.

When can one say that an economy is in a Pareto-optimality situation? Economic theory shows that to reach Pareto optimality the following conditions must be satisfied:[3] (1) prices of all goods must equal their marginal costs;

[2]Recall from elementary microeconomics that perfect competition is said to exist when:

1 There are large numbers of buyers and sellers so that no single buyer or seller can affect the market price or output or both. This rules out monopoly.

2 There is product homogeneity: A seller in a given market sells a product which is identical to the one sold by another seller in the same market.

3 There is free mobility of resources; that is, there are no artificial restrictions on entry into or exit from an industry or a market.

4 There is complete and perfect knowledge on the parts of the buyers and sellers.

[3]For a rigorous treatment of these conditions, see Jack Hirshleifer, *Price Theory and Applications,* 2d ed., Prentice-Hall, Englewood Cliffs, N.J., 1980, ch. 17. For an informal discussion, see Paul A. Samuelson, *Economics,* 10th ed., McGraw-Hill, New York, pp. 460–462.

(2) prices of all factors of production or inputs (land, labor, and capital) must equal their marginal products, and the total costs of production are minimized; and (3) the desires and well-being of individuals are all represented by their marginal utilities as expressed in their dollar voting (i.e., as represented by the demand curves).

The question then is: What kind of economic system will guarantee such a Pareto-optimal outcome? A branch of economics, known as "welfare economics," shows that under some ideal assumptions the perfectly competitive market system can assure such an outcome. In the economics literature this finding is known as the "theorem of the invisible hand," where the term *invisible hand* refers to Adam Smith's invisible hand of self-interest.[4]

It is important to emphasize that the "invisible hand" will lead to maximum social welfare only if the following conditions are satisfied: (1) An individual derives satisfaction from the goods and services he or she consumes and this satisfaction is not dependent on the goods and services consumed by others. In short, there is no "catching up with the Joneses" phenomenon. More technically, there are no consumption externalities (externalities or external effects are discussed in Section 2.2); (2) there are constant returns to scale, which means doubling the inputs doubles the output, tripling the inputs triples the output, and so on; and (3) the distribution of income or wealth in society is what Samuelson calls, "ethically" correct or is to be made so by ideal lump-sum transfer payments.

Given the preceding conditions (about which something will be said shortly), how does the competitive economy achieve maximum social welfare? That is, how does one prove the theorem of the invisible hand? We will not give the entire proof, which is somewhat involved.[5] Rather, we will concentrate on one aspect, namely, why the equality of prices and marginal costs leads to efficient allocation of resources or why "price equal to marginal cost" has become the golden rule of pricing under competitive conditions.

To fix the ideas, consider Figure 2.1, which depicts the short-run supply and demand curves facing three sample firms in a hypothetical competitive industry producing a homogenous product, and the industry supply and demand curves. This diagram should be familiar to the student from elementary price theory. On the far right we have the industry supply curve (obtained by horizontally summing the firm marginal cost curves) and the industry demand curve (obtained by horizontally summing the demand curves of each individual consumer). The intersection of the industry supply and demand curves establishes the equilibrium price and quantity at P and Q, respectively. Since in a competitive market

---

[4]In his celebrated book, *The Wealth of Nations,* Adam Smith wrote,
Every individual endeavors to employ his capital so that its produce may be of greatest value. He generally neither intends to promote the public interest, nor knows how much he is promoting it. He intends only his own security, only his own gain. And he is in this led by an *invisible hand* to promote an end which was no part of his intention. By pursuing his own interest he frequently promotes that of society more effectually than when he really intends to promote it. (Quote reproduced from Samuelson, op. cit., p. 41).
[5]For proof, see Hirshleifer, op. cit., ch. 17.

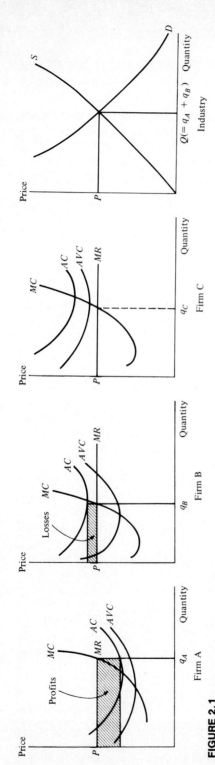

FIGURE 2.1
Short-run supply and demand curves in a competitive industry.

any single firm is a price-taker, the demand curve it faces is horizontal at the industry price level P. Since this demand curve is horizontal, the marginal revenue curve is also horizontal and coincident with the demand curve.

Now consider firm A. Since it is a price-taker, the only decision it has to make is about the level of its output. Now the best or optimum level of output for A is q_A, that is, at the point where its marginal cost curve intersects its marginal revenue (= price) curve. Why? Because to the right of q_A the cost of producing an additional unit of output (i.e., marginal cost) exceeds what that additional unit will bring in terms of additional revenue (i.e., marginal revenue). No sensible producer acting in her self-interest will produce the additional unit. Likewise, she will not produce any output less than q_A, for then the marginal cost is less than the marginal revenue (= price); by producing an extra unit she can add more to her revenue than to her cost. It is only at q_A that the cost of producing an extra unit of output is just balanced by the revenue that the additional unit brings in. At this level the producer is making a profit shown by the striped area. This is the maximum profit she can make; any other level of output will reduce her profits. Thus we have seen that for firm A, $MC = MR(= P)$ gives the maximum profit. Incidentally, if we include a reasonable rate of return on the capital supplied by the owner in the average cost curve, the profits shown in the diagram will be what are called *pure* profits.

What about firm B? Should it also produce at the level at which its marginal cost is equal to marginal revenue (= price), that is, at the level q_B? If it does, does it not incur a loss, for the price does not cover the average cost of production. But in this situation, too, the MC = MR rule applies; a moment's reflection will show that at this level of output the price more than covers the average variable cost and minimizes the overall losses. In other words, producing at a level other than q_B will increase the producer's losses more than at level q_B. And considering the fact that this is a short-run situation, this is the best that the producer can accomplish.

What about firm C? Should it adopt the same $MC = MR$ rule? In this case the answer is no because if it were to do that and produce output q_C, the price would not cover even the out-of-pocket or variable cost of production. For this firm the best decision is to close down.

The general rule then is that in the short run a competitive firm should produce that level of output at which its marginal cost is equal to the marginal revenue, which happens to be equal to the industry price (in view of the price-taking nature of a competitive firm), provided that at that level of output the price exceeds the average variable cost.

The situation depicted in Figure 2.1 will not continue forever. In the long run, because of free entry into and exit from the industry, firms such as B will tend to leave the industry and others outside the industry with a cost situation similar to that of firm A will tend to move in to take advantage of the pure economic profits, profits over and above a reasonable rate of return on capital included in the average cost curve. With such in-and-out movements, eventually the situation that will emerge in the long run will be as shown in Figure 2.2.

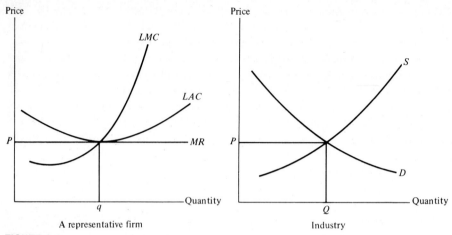

FIGURE 2.2
Long-run equilibrium in a competitive industry.

Figure 2.2 shows that in the long run a competitive firm will produce at the level at which the following equality is satisfied:

$$MR = P = LMC = LAC$$

That is, the firm will produce at the level where marginal revenue, price, long-run marginal cost, and long-run average cost are all equal (at this level, the short-run marginal and average cost will also equal their long-run counterparts. Why?). At this level of output, the firm is making only normal profits or a normal rate of return on capital included in the average cost curve, that is, that rate of return on capital which will leave total investment in the industry unchanged: If there are pure profits to be made, new firms will enter the industry and total investment will increase, which will put downward pressure on the pure profits and eventually wipe them out; in that case all the firms in the industry will be making the same normal rate of return on capital. If every industry in the economy reaches this situation, firms in all those industries too will be earning normal returns. If this happens, we can say that the economy's scarce resources are allocated most efficiently, that is, they are employed in their best-possible or most-valued uses. Given the distribution of income, we can say that such an outcome maximizes social welfare.

Although the preceding discussion is somewhat heuristic, it is sufficient to give the reader the flavor of the argument in support of the competitive model. As we will show in Chapter 6, in cases of imperfect competition, especially monopoly, there can be considerable misallocation of scarce resources.

To sum up, *under some idealized conditions,* perfect competition solves one of the twin problems of economics, namely, *allocative efficiency:* competitive markets are Pareto-efficient.

It is now time to probe critically into this competitive model. First, note that a Pareto optimum is so only in relation to the particular distribution of income (that is, rights to assets that generate income). Suppose that distribution of income is changed, say, by the government. Corresponding to the new income distribution there will be another Pareto optimum. Is the second Pareto optimum any better than the first one? Unfortunately, economic theory cannot answer this question because it involves comparing utilities or satisfactions of the gainers and losers before and after the change of income distribution. Economists have not yet found ways of comparing such satisfactions, nor have psychologists for that matter.

This is why economists are generally silent when it comes to the discussion of the other twin of the economic problem, namely, *distributive efficiency* or *distributive equity,* that is, how justly, or equitably, or equally, the income is distributed. To them there is no simple way to decide both the ideal output and its distribution among members of society. This is why Samuelson calls the issue of income distribution an ''ethical'' issue; it involves making value judgments.

Although the debate over efficiency versus equity is a never-ending one, economists such as Jack Hirshleifer argue that economists' preoccupation with allocative efficiency has played a useful social role. According to him:

> The political processes that determine social policy tend to overlook considerations of efficiency almost entirely. Whether the issue be the progressive income tax, the protection of some industries by tariffs and quotas, penalization of others for ''excessive'' profits, combating monopoly, or choosing the proper scale of government, it has become a function of the economist to point out that there are efficiency implications that need to be evaluated as one input into the social decision process.[6]

As we shall see in the chapters in Part Three, Hirshleifer has a very good point to make — under the guise of redressing inequities the government very often introduces allocative inefficiencies.

Even if we leave aside the question of income distribution, however, the theorem of the invisible hand is too good to be true, for the conditions requisite for its fulfillment are too ideal to be met in practice. Consider, for example, the requirement that there be no monopoly in the economy. The American economy is full of examples of monopolies of varying types: the utility industry (gas, electric, and telephone) is a legally recognized monopoly for reasons to be explained shortly, but a company such as IBM has de facto monopoly in certain areas of its operation. Then, the requirement that there be no externalities either in consumption or production is difficult to satisfy: My consumption is influenced by my friends' consumption; a firm located downstream finds its cost of production increased because a firm located upstream has polluted the water (further discussion of externalities is given in Section 2.2). In short, the conditions necessary for the satisfaction of the theorem of the invisible hand are so strict that, as Samuelson has put it, ''One would have thought that the elementary

---

[6]See Hirshleifer, op. cit., p. 548.

consideration that a line is infinitely thinner than a plane would make it a miracle for these conditions to be met."[7]

From the preceding discussion it is clear that according to economic theory it is only in the presence of market failure (or to correct income distribution) that government intervention is justified. The public interest theory of regulation that we are about to discuss is motivated by this philosophy, whereas the other theories we will discuss subsequently do not look upon government intervention necessarily to correct market failures, although that may be one of the objectives.

2.2 MARKET FAILURES AND THE PUBLIC INTEREST THEORY OF REGULATION

Broadly defined, the public interest (PI) theory of regulation holds that the government may intervene in the marketplace to correct market failures which prevent society from obtaining maximum or optimum welfare or satisfaction. In this view, regulation is strictly a remedial measure designed to reduce the costs associated with market failures. But what exactly are these market failures? Some of the important market failures are as follows.

Inadequate Supply of Public Goods

Even a perfectly competitive market may not supply pure public goods. *Pure public goods* or *collective consumption goods* are those goods and services whose benefits can be enjoyed by any individual without interfering in the enjoyment of the same goods and services by any other individual. Alternatively, these are goods and services which cannot be withheld from one individual without withholding them from all. The classic example is national defense. Other examples are: street lighting, police protection, recreational parks, fundamental knowledge (e.g., Newton's law of gravity), and so on. These goods have two main atttributes, namely, *nonexcludability* (no one can be excluded) and *nondepletability* (e.g., my enjoyment of Central Park in New York does not deplete the enjoyment of any one else in the park, assuming of course that the park is not very crowded).

Why can't the private market provide such goods and services? Why can't, for instance, national defense be supplied by a private corporation? The answer is implicit in the very nature of the public goods. Because of the nonexcludability character, no one can be excluded from the use of such public goods whether people pay for them or not. Thus, those who do not pay the income tax because of poverty or any other reason are still given police protection or national defense, whose costs are borne by those who pay the tax. In economics this is called the *free lunch* or the *free rider* problem; a free rider is one who enjoys the benefits of a good or service without paying for it. The private mar-

---

[7]Paul A. Samuelson, "The Economic Role of Private Activity," in Joseph E. Stiglitz (ed.), *The Collected Scientific Papers of Paul A. Samuelson,* vol. 2, Oxford & IBM, New York, 1966, p. 1422.

ket has no incentive to provide such a good, for no one will pay for it if it is accessible without payment (because of the nonexcludability feature); it is the essence of the market for ''private'' goods that one can be excluded from their consumption if they are not paid for. As a result, most pure public goods are generally supplied by the government.

Although the case for public supply of pure public goods can be made, there are nonpure or quasi-public goods which can be supplied privately. Some examples are: housing, education, and hospital services. Public housing can be replaced by private housing, public education by private education, and public hospitals by private hospitals. But these services are very often provided by local governments perhaps under the belief that the quality or quantity of these services may not be adequately supplied privately or the price charged for them may be beyond the means of some of the residents. The provision of quasi-public goods in this situation essentially amounts to income subsidies from the local authorities — subsidies which may be justifiable from an equity viewpoint. But this policy is open to debate.

Natural Monopoly and Economies of Scale

Traditionally, natural monopolies have been regulated in most countries. ''Natural monopoly occurs when the average cost of a single firm falls over such an extended range that one firm can produce the total quantity sold at a lower average cost than could two or more firms.''[8] When this happens, there are *economies of scale:* The larger the output, the lower the average cost of production. Some examples of natural monopolies are: electric, gas, and telephone utilities; cable TV and oil and gas pipelines. In case of the pipelines, for example, total pipeline construction costs are proportional to the circumference of the pipeline and therefore to its radius. Since the square of the radius increases more rapidly than the radius, it follows that cost per unit decreases continuously as the pipeline's capacity increases. Indeed, this understates the economies of large-diameter pipe because friction in transmitting oil and gas is also reduced as capacity grows, and because the amount of right-of-way needed is practically the same regardless of pipe capacity.

Why do the natural monopolies need to be regulated? Regulation usually controls the price these monopolies charge or the rate of return they can earn on their capital.[9] Why can there be no more than one electric or gas or telephone company in a given geographical area? Why not let competition determine the number of such companies in a given city or town? The answer is that from an efficiency (of resource allocation) viewpoint monopoly is preferable to competition in situations in which there are economies of scale (i.e., continuously declining average cost over a fairly wide range of output). To see this clearly, consider Figure 2.3.

Figure 2.3 gives the cost and demand curves of a hypothetical natural

---

[8]Paul Wonnacott and Ronald Wonnacott, *Economics,* McGraw-Hill, New York, 1979, p. 457.
[9]On the question of the economics of monopoly in general, see Ch. 6.

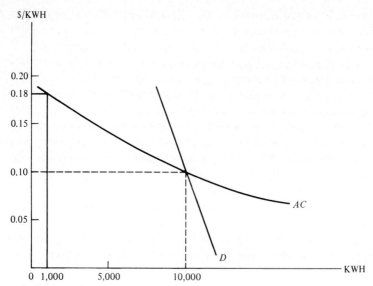

FIGURE 2.3
Hypothetical cost and demand curves of a natural monopoly.

monopoly, say, an electric utility. The equilibrium price and quantity are 10 cents
and 10,000 kilowatthours. Now suppose that we insist that there be ten electric
utilities in the industry, each producing 1000 killowatthours, which can be produced at 18 cents per kilowatthour. Obviously, in this case it is preferable to
have a single company than ten separate companies. This explains why in any
given geographical areas one does not find more than one gas or electric or
telephone company. Of course, as UCLA economist Harold Demsetz argues,
just because only one firm can efficiently provide the service does not mean
that there cannot be competition among firms for the franchise.

   It should be pointed out that a natural monopoly is only ''natural'' in a given
technological or economic environment: Technological advances may change
the character of a natural monopoly. Thus, at one stage the railroads were a
natural monopoly, but with the advent of the trucking industry its monopoly
power has been seriously eroded. Also, some monopolies are not natural,
although they are so treated and regulated by the government. Obvious examples are the airline and trucking industries. In both these industries, there is no
substantial evidence of economies of scale (this will be discussed more fully in
Chapters 11 and 12).

Externalities, Spillovers, or Neighborhood Effects

Externalities, spillovers, or neighborhood effects constitute another example of
market failure. An externality or ''an external effect of an economic decision is

an effect, whether beneficial or harmful, upon a person who was not a party to the decision."[10] A harmful external effect is called a *spillout* or *negative externality* and a beneficial external effect is called a *spillin* or *positive externality.*[11]

Examples of spillouts are air pollution, water pollution, noise pollution, congested highways, and umpteen other negative externalities. Examples of spillins are vaccines against diseases, clean and beautiful parks, and fundamental knowledge (e.g., the discovery of the normal distribution law).

More broadly, one can distinguish between *consumption externalities* and *production externalities.* In consumption externalities the consumption of a good by an individual may have an effect on the welfare or satisfaction of another consumer. In production externalities, the production technology used by one firm may have effects, good or bad, on another firm.

A consumption spillout occurs when, for example, your neighbor builds a high fence around his property which cuts sunshine from your trees. A consumption spillin occurs when, say, your neighbor keeps her lawn neat, which enhances the appearance of the neighborhood and thus increases your property value.

A production spillout occurs when, for instance, a firm located upstream discharges harmful effluent into the river. This greatly increases the cost of production of the firm located downstream. A production spillin occurs when, say, a firm introduces a technology which reduces the cost of production and which is available to another firm without charge.

Why do externalities constitute a market failure? To answer this question, we need to distinguish between *private costs* and *social costs,* a distinction originally introduced by the late Cambridge economist A. C. Pigou. Social costs are costs of some activity or output which are borne by society as a whole, and which need not be equal to the costs borne by the individual or firm carrying out that activity or producing that output; the latter are private costs. In other words, social costs equal private costs plus uncompensated damages to others.[12] Thus, if a factory produces smoke in the production process and that increases my laundry cost because I happen to live near the factory, the private cost of production does not reflect the additional laundry costs to me, a member of society at large. Hence, in this case the social cost of producing a unit of output is equal to the private cost (that was actually incurred by the polluting factory) plus my additional laundry cost. Of course, in the case of spillins, the social cost is less than the private cost.

Since the private market generally does not take into account social costs, its output may not be socially optimal in the sense that it produces more than the society desires (in case of spillouts) or produces less than the society wants (in case of spillins). In short, because of the divergence between social and private

---

[10]George J. Stigler, *The Citizen and the State: Essays on Regulation,* The University of Chicago Press, Chicago 1975, p. 104.

[11]To the best of my knowledge, the terms *spillout* and *spillin* are due to Robert Mundell. See his *Man and Economics,* McGraw-Hill, New York, 1968, ch. 19.

[12]In case of a spillin, social costs equal private costs minus uncompensated benefits.

costs, under externality, society's resources may not be allocated most efficiently.

To see this clearly, consider Figure 2.4. In Figure 2.4(a) because of spillout (say, air pollution), the social cost of production (represented by the supply curve S_2) is greater than the private cost (represented by the supply curve S_1) at each level of output. Given the demand curve D, the private market will produce Q_2 units of output, whereas from society's viewpoint the optimal output should be Q_1. In contrast, in Figure 2.4(b), because of spillin, the social cost is less than the private cost at each level of output. Here, the private market will produce q_1 units whereas society would prefer q_2 units. In other words, the private market underproduces the desirable good by the amount q_1q_2.

For the reasons just described, the private market may fail to allocate resources efficiently in cases of externalities. Therefore, there is a need for "internalizing" the externalities, that is, taking into account their effects. There are some who believe that government can do this in many ways, such as by instituting effluent taxes or charges (charges on polluting industries) or subsidies (to encourage the production of spillins), or establishing standards of performance (e.g., the maximum amount of air pollution or noise pollution that may be tolerated), etc. (These methods will be discussed in Chapter 4 and additionally in Chapter 17.)

Although a case can be made for government intervention in the marketplace to internalize the externalities, it does not necessarily mean that the government will actually achieve socially desirable output and allocate resources more efficiently. A priori, there is no reason to believe that the private market cannot internalize the externalities, as our discussion of the Coase theorem in Section

FIGURE 2.4
Effects of externalities on cost and output.

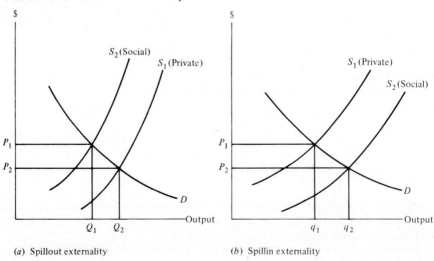

(a) Spillout externality   (b) Spillin externality

2.3 will reveal. (In Chapter 4 we will discuss the methods of taxes or subsidies, unitization, and property rights reassignment as some of the ways by which the government may try to internalize the externalities.)

Inadequate Information and Erroneous Decisions

Even if all other attributes of perfect competition are satisfied, lack of perfect information may lead to erroneous decisions and therefore to allocative inefficiency. This market failure (or failure of the market to obtain adequate information) can have serious consequences.

Consider, for example, the problem of job safety. If a worker is unaware of the hazards of his job, and the management makes no special effort to tell the worker about the full nature of his job, it is quite possible that the worker may expose himself to death or to serious injury which may incapacitate him for life. If this spillout is neglected, the private costs of production will be less than the social costs and the private market may overproduce commodities in an amount not desirable from society's viewpoint. Here some statistics may be useful. According to the National Safety Council, more than 14,000 workers are killed and over 2.2 million suffer serious injuries annually as a result of accidents on the job. According to the National Institute for Occupational Safety and Health, as many as 400,000 workers are disabled and as many as 100,000 workers are killed each year by occupational diseases resulting from exposure to toxic substances (the institute has compiled a list of such substances). The genesis of the Occupational Safety and Health Act of 1970 (OSHA) can be found in these statistics. (OSHA will be considered in detail in Chapter 16.)

As another example of the dangers of inadequate information, consider the drug industry. If a prospective customer is not warned about the possible effects of a drug or a medical device, the outcome can be very serious or fatal. The thalidomide case is well known; it was found in Europe that some mothers who took thalidomide during pregnancy gave birth to deformed babies. The case of the pacemakers, however, is perhaps not well known. Pacemakers are implanted in the chest by doctors to stimulate a regular heartbeat. Prompted by complaints from consumers and congressional investigations, the General Electric Company in 1972 recalled about 575 pacemakers because defects in its model were suspected of contributing to fatal heart failure in several users and to heart problems in many others. This subsequently led to the passage of the Medical Device Amendments of 1976.

Why is it difficult to obtain (perfect) information? There are several reasons. First, there is the question of cost; information is not a free good—time or money spent in acquiring it has an opportunity cost because that time or money could be spent on more tangible goods; information is "invisible." Stigler argues that some of the consequences arising from lack of information are due to "under-investment in information": people are not willing to spend enough time or money to acquire information. Sometimes this underinvestment may be deliberate. Consider, for instance, the case of job safety. Although the potential loss from a job injury could be substantial, individuals may not expend much time, effort, or money to seek information about the safety and health hazards they face if they perceive the risk as very small. (How many people carry accidental disability insurance on their own?)

Second, there is the problem of the free rider: You want a particular good or service but are not willing to pay for it in the hope that some other people who want that good or service will pay for it anyway. The private market may therefore have little incentive to provide information, for the producer of information may not be able to recoup its cost; once information becomes public it is freely available and because of the free rider problem the producers may not be able to charge all those who receive its benefits.

Third, sometimes information is very technical and the consumer may not be able to comprehend it (for example, how many people really know the mechanics of the car(s) they own?). Even magazines such as *Consumer Reports* may not provide the consumer with technical information in easily understandable form if the product is technically complex.

For all these reasons, some type of government intervention in the marketplace may be called for. In Chapter 4 we will examine the various means by which this can be done. Suffice it to note here that the government may insist on more information from the producers by requiring accurate labeling or prohibiting misleading statements in advertisements (e.g., the statement made by a credit card company in its advertising campaign: "You can get refund on your stolen traveller's checks more promptly from *us* than any other company") or it may lay down some performance standards (e.g., auto emission standards or auto safety-belt standards, etc.). As we will see in Chapter 14, on the securities industry, the government can go overboard and require overproduction of information.)

Conservation of Natural Resources

Natural resources such as rivers, mineral deposits, virgin farmland, fisheries, etc., can be divided into two groups: renewable and nonrenewable. Timber and fish are examples of renewable resources; oil, gas, and coal are examples of nonrenewable resources in the sense that their finite amount (proven resources) can be depleted. Obviously, nonrenewable resources pose a critical problem in terms of prices to be charged and the quantities to be produced now and in the future. For example, from a given oil well of known quantity, if you produce more now, you will have less left for the future. The late 1970s oil "crisis" in the United States very well reflects this concern; countries such as Saudi Arabia contend that the United States is consuming "too much" oil in the present and that unless oil prices rise there will not be much incentive to curtail current consumption (whether this really explains OPEC's pricing policy is of course open to question).

How does one optimally consume depletable, nonrenewable resources?

That is, how does one strike a balance between present needs and future needs? How should nonrenewable resources be priced so that the needs of both present and future generations are well balanced? The answer depends on who has the property right to the resource, that is, who owns it. If a non-renewable resource is privately owned (e.g., a private iron ore mine), the private market can determine the optimum present versus future use of the resource following the well-known economic technique of present value analysis. Given the expected rate of return on investment, if the value of the resource today exceeds the present value of it at any time in the future, then society's economic interest might be best served if that resource is used now; otherwise, it may be exploited at a future date.

But what happens if the property right is not well-defined and there is more than one producer using a "common pool" of a resource? The clearest example is that of the fishing industry. Since the sea is free to all, anyone can fish from this "common pool," the sea. This is known as the tragedy of the commons — everyone's property is no one's property. As a result, there is no incentive to conserve the fish and there is every likelihood that the fish may be decimated. This is where the government may step in to prevent excessive fishing by issuing fishing licenses or putting restrictions on the amount of fishing that can be done, say, in a day.

In this connection it is important to distinguish between defining and enforcing property rights to scarce resources and allocating such resources to alternative uses. The former is routinely done by government with respect to many resources, especially land, where there are cases of separate mineral rights, air rights, and easements. However, the FCC engages in the latter as well. As will be shown in Chapter 15, on the communications industry, the FCC decides who is entitled to use the resources (the nation's airways) and for what purposes.

Another example of the common pool or commonly owned resources is the electromagnetic spectrum (the nation's airways). In the absence of some kind of regulation, what prevents literally hundreds of TV and radio stations from jamming the nation's airways? That is why the Federal Communications Commission (FCC) has been given the responsibility of licensing radio and TV stations as to frequency, location, power, and time of day, in order to avoid interference from competing stations.

Although oil and gas wells are by and large privately owned in this country, the common pool problem applies to them too. Oil, for example, flows underground, and if two oil wells owned by A and B are located in close proximity to each other, more production by A would drain the supply of B and vice versa. This is why many states have passed prorationing laws which specify the maximum amount of oil that an owner may produce each month, and that is why the federal Connally Hot Oil Act prohibits interstate shipment of oil produced in violation of the state prorationing laws. (This is not to suggest that these laws are necessarily desirable or that other ways of accomplishing the same objective may not be found).

To sum up, in the case of nonrenewable resources with the "common pool" problem a case can be made for government efforts to conserve natural resources.

2.3 MARKET FAILURES AND THE COASE THEOREM

From the preceding discussion it is clear that because of market failure of one kind or another social welfare may not be maximum within the private market. Therefore, a case can be made for some kind of government intervention to remedy one or more market failures. But before accepting this conclusion let us raise a question: Are there situations in which despite the market failures it is possible for the affected parties to engage in private arrangements or contracts to alleviate the failures and thus not invite government intervention? Take, for instance, the spillout-type externality. Is it possible for me to negotiate with my neighbor who has put a fence around his property to take it out so that the sunshine on my property is not blocked out? Or, can I "bribe" my neighbor who plays loud music all the time and disturbs my peace? Similarly, can the firm located downstream enter into an agreement with the polluting firm located upstream so that it is assured of a water supply of some quality? If such arrangements can be made privately at a mutually agreeable price, then, despite the spillouts, will the final outcome be beneficial from society's viewpoint?

The answers to the above questions are a qualified yes and are given by the celebrated Coase theorem, whose gist is: Despite externalities, the private market will allocate resources efficiently if (1) property rights are well-defined, (2) the resources are marketable, and (3) there is no or very little transaction cost in carrying out negotiations between affected parties.[13] In other words, under the assumed conditions, bargaining by private parties will remove any misallocation of resources and there will be no divergence between private interest and social interest or between private cost and social cost. Thus, if the firm located upstream initially owned the right to pollute the river, the firm downstream can buy that right from that firm or offer it some financial reward for not exercising that right. If this can be done with little transaction cost, then, Coase's theorem says, the final outcome, through the invisible hand, will be efficient in the sense of a Pareto optimum.

Coase's theorem is too good to be true. The proviso that there are no transaction costs is simply unrealistic. For example, if there is more than one firm located upstream, how does the firm located downstream find out which firm is causing the pollution spillout? Acquiring such information is bound to cost some money (in the opportunity-cost sense). But the real problem with the Coase theorem is that it underplays the problems involved in negotiations to buy or sell the property rights in externalities. If there are, say, fifty downstream and fifty upstream firms, it may be practically impossible to achieve unanimity about the "equilibrium" prices of pollution permits. Unanimity is not easy to

[13]R. H. Coase, "The Problem of Social Cost," *Journal of Law and Economics,* vol. 3, October 1960.

achieve even when the numbers involved are small, for it leads to all kinds of game theory–oriented strategy problems so that it is difficult to tell, as a general rule, what the final outcome will be.[14] Perhaps more important than the bargaining problem, however, is the problem of identifying the parties who either benefit or are harmed from externalities and of measuring the benefits and the costs. It is important to note that these problems also prevent the government from figuring out the optimal allocation of resources. As a result, as we shall see in later chapters, the government sometimes makes things worse rather than better.

The real merit of Coase's theorem, however, lies in the suggestion that with proper institutional arrangements and legal practices about assigning exchangeable property rights unambiguously it is possible for private parties to take actions which are economically efficient in the Pareto-optimality sense.

To sum up the discussion about the public interest theory of regulation, it can be said that the theory has a good deal of merit and that government intervention may be justifiable in certain cases, such as natural monopoly, externalities, and provision of public goods, especially in view of the impracticability of the Coase theorem. In the next chapter we will examine the various methods by which government may remedy some market failures.

2.4   THE SELF-INTEREST, OR CAPTURE, THEORY OF REGULATION[15]

According to the self-interest, or capture, theory, regulation is not for the purpose of remedying one or more of the market failures discussed previously, but is solely for the furtherance of private gain of certain interest groups. This theory amounts to "letting the prisoners guard the prison," or letting the captured (i.e., the regulated) regulate the captors (i.e., the regulators). There are two versions of the theory.

The Marxian View of the Capture Theory

Marxists and certain consumer advocates contend that institutions in America are controlled by big business. And since regulation is an institution, it is also controlled by big business for its own good. This version of the capture theory is, however, naive; there are many small businesses such as dairy farming, trucking, barbering, etc., that are also regulated but do not fit the theory.

The Political Scientist's View of Regulation

Based upon the work in their own area, some political scientists have formulated theories which explain how certain interest groups use the legislative and admin-

---

[14]The problem is similar to that found in oligopoly (competition among a small number of firms in an industry), where each competitor is likely to be conscious of the effects its actions have on other competitors. The problem here is how to outwit each other. For details and the game theory-oriented approach to some pricing strategies, see Hirshleifer, op. cit., ch. 13.

[15]For details, see Richard A. Posner, "Theories of Economic Regulation," *Bell Journal of Economics and Management Science,* pp. 341–342.

istrative processes to further their own interests. One theory is that over time regulatory agencies come to be dominated by the industries regulated. It suggests the following sequence.[16] Initially the industry opposes regulation, but somehow it comes about. Once established, the regulated industry finds the regulated life comforting and therefore opposes any attempt at deregulation. The trucking industry followed this sequence quite closely. Originally, the truckers opposed regulation, but it came as a result of pressure from the railroad companies who felt threatened by competition from the truckers. But once established, the truckers developed mutuality of interest with the ICC to reap profits for themselves and were bitterly opposed to the passage of the Motor Carrier Act of 1980, which was the first congressional attempt in many a year to deregulate the trucking industry — there was fear that if competition were allowed in the industry, the monopoly profits resulting from government regulation would disappear, a fear that seems to be well-founded (see Chapter 11).

An implication of the self-interest theory is that the ''captured'' will always benefit themselves because they can influence their ''captors'' to pass legislation beneficial to them or use the administrative machinery of the captors (i.e., regulators) to get a higher price or a higher rate of return or restriction of entry. Whether this in fact happens is an empirical question, but the evidence is not very impressive, as the following case study reveals.

Public Regulation of National Securities Exchanges: A Test of the Capture Hypothesis

In an interesting study, G. William Schwert set out to test the capture hypothesis in the context of the securities brokerage industry. He postulated the following (capture) hypothesis:

> If securities brokers are able to capture the government agency which regulates them, the Securities and Exchange Commission (SEC), NYSE [New York Stock Exchange] and ASE [American Stock Exchange], brokers' profits should be higher with regulation than without it.[17]

To test this hypothesis, he examined the behavior of stock exchange seat (membership) prices (as a proxy for profits) in response to changes in the regulatory behavior of the SEC.[18] The period of the study was from 1926 to 1972. If the

[16]See Marver Bernstein, *Regulating Business by Independent Commissions,* Princeton University Press, Princeton, N.J., 1966.

[17]G. William Schwert, ''Public Regulation of National Securities Exchanges: A Test of the Capture Hypothesis,'' *Bell Journal of Economics and Management Science,* Spring 1977, p. 129.

[18]Note that the seat price represents the capitalized value of the expected future flow of profits or the present value of all future expected profits discounted at the expected rate of return. Thus if the brokerage firm expects a profit of $50,000 a year for perpetuity and the expected rate of return on investment into the seat (stock market membership) is 10%, then the maximum price the firm will be willing to pay for the seat will be $500,000; this is derived from the well-known formula from investment analysis, namely, for perpetuity the capitalized value = profit per period/rate of return. In our example this is $50,000/0.10 equal to $500,000.

capture hypothesis is true, the seat prices over the years should increase and therefore the profitability of the industry.

Before presenting the empirical evidence, a brief historical background is in order. Although the NYSE dates back to 1792, in its present form its organization dates to 1869 when three major securities exchanges merged and decided to sell 1060 seats in the newly formed NYSE. Over the years the membership increased, and now it stands at 1366. Membership in the NYSE is a valued asset, for it gives the member the right to trade at reduced costs. The brokerage industry was pretty much unregulated until the great (black October) crash of 1929; U.S. Steel, a bluechip stock, fell from $261 in 1929 to $21 in 1932! Largely in response to this crash, but also owing to the New Deal philosophy of the great depression, Congress passed the Securities Act of 1933 and the Securities Exchange Act of 1934. The latter established the SEC as an independent regulatory agency in charge of regulating the securities industry. (The workings of the SEC will be dealt with in Chapter 14.)

The advent of the SEC had an immediate impact on the stock exchange seat prices, as Table 2.1 reveals. (Note that the initial version of the 1934 act was announced on February 6, 1934, and the last "free market" seat was sold on February 3. Between February 3 and March 21 there was no trading in the seats, probably due to the uncertainty created by the act).

As Table 2.1 shows, the most severe impact of the 1934 act occurred in the month of March; seat prices fell by about 50 percent. This heavy capital loss would tend to refute the capture hypothesis that the captured benefit from regulation. But this may not be so because after the initial shock of regulation it is quite possible that the seat prices would bounce back and that in the long run

TABLE 2.1
NEW YORK STOCK EXCHANGE SEAT
TRANSACTIONS
(February and March 1934)

Date	Price
Feb. 3	$190,000 (two trades at this price)
Mar. 21	110,000
21	105,000
26	112,000
27	100,000
27	85,000
27	83,000
27	100,000
29	100,000

Source: G. William Schwert, "Public Regulation of National Securities Exchanges: A Test of the Capture Hypothesis," *Bell Journal of Economics and Management Science,* Spring 1977, table 4, p. 138.

the industry would benefit from regulation. But with some highly sophisticated statistical analysis Schwert concluded that there was no evidence that this initial capital loss was ever recouped after March 1934.

Up until 1968, the brokerage commission rates were rigidly fixed by the NYSE (with the blessing of the SEC), but since then, and especially since May 1975, the commission rates have become negotiable. Schwert also examined the impact of this change on the seat prices and found it was negative. Therefore, he concludes, "the capture hypothesis does not provide an appropriate description of the public regulation of the securities brokerage industry."

The capture theory, apart from the above negative empirical evidence, has other deficiencies. The regulators do not always support the regulated. For example, the ICC, which controls the railroad industry, did not always favor the industry; this is reflected in the Hepburn Act, which fixed the maximum (not the minimum) rates that the railroads can charge. Moreover, the theory does not predict the behavior of a regulatory agency if it is in charge of controlling more than one industry. The case in point is the ICC, which regulates the railroad, trucking, and barge line industries. How does the ICC balance the competing interests of these industries? The theory cannot tell.

2.5 THE ECONOMIC THEORY OF REGULATION

The economic theory of regulation, originally propounded by George J. Stigler, a Nobel laureate in economics, and subsequently refined by Sam Peltzman, both of the University of Chicago, regards regulation as an economic commodity or good.[19] Then, like any economic good, its equilibrium price and equilibrium output are determined by the demand for and supply of regulation. This is indeed a novel approach to regulation.

Regulation is an economic good because it confers some benefits on the demanders, that is, those who are interested in obtaining or procuring regulation to augment their income or wealth. What are these benefits? Stigler identified several:

Direct subsidy of money. For example, until 1968 the domestic airlines, a regulated industry, received airmail subsidies of $1.5 billion annually whether they carried mail or not.

Control over entry by new rivals. The Civil Aeronautics Board (CAB), for instance, has not allowed a new trunk line to be launched since it was created in 1938. The Federal Deposit Insurance Corporation (FDIC) (recall the signs in most banks which proclaim that your deposits are insured by the FDIC to the tune of $100,000) which has the power to insure banks, has reduced entry into commercial banking by about 60 percent. The SEC has put restrictions on the selling expenses that a mutual fund can charge, thus retarding the growth of the industry.

---

[19]Stigler, op. cit., ch. 8. Sam Paltzman, "Toward a More General Theory of Regulation," *Journal of Law and Economics,* vol. 19, no. 2, August 1976, pp. 211–240.

Effects on substitutions and complements. There are numerous examples of these effects. The building trade unions have opposed labor-saving material through building codes. The milk producers in Wisconsin have been able in past years to suppress the sale of margarine in that state. The commercial TV stations, thanks to the FCC, have until recently succeeded in suppressing or curtailing the introduction of pay TV. As an example of complementarity, the airlines have asked for and have successfully received subsidies from the government to build bigger and better airports.

Who are the suppliers of these and similar benefits? They are the politicians at various levels of government. And why are they interested in "supplying" regulation, the economic commodity? Obviously, to obtain the most political support (measured by the votes they get) and power and to be elected term after term. Of course, regulation is supplied for a "price," which usually means political contributions, lucrative jobs for relatives of the politicians, "free" time given by "volunteers" at the time of elections, and the like.

Although the demand for and supply of regulation, that is, interest group pressures, will determine its "equilibrium" price and "equilibrium" output, there are subtle points relating to the group behavior of the beneficiaries of regulation that need to be pointed out. Once regulation comes into being, it benefits *all* the firms in the regulated industry, including those who did not contribute time, money, or energy to acquire benefits of the regulation. In other words, there is the free rider problem; some firms reap the benefits of regulation for which they have done nothing (e.g., in the Right-to-Work Law states, those who do not join trade unions still receive the benefits negotiated by the unions for those who belong to them). This raises the question of how to avoid the free rider problem.

Alternatively, one can ask the question: In which industries or groups of producers is the free rider problem likely to be less serious? Since the acquisition of regulation is costly (e.g., lobbying costs), it is likely to succeed in those industries where the number of producers is reasonably small so that it is possible to police the actions of the various members. Moreover, it is probably easier to solicit lobbying funds from a smaller group than a larger group; the free rider problem becomes serious in larger groups. Also, increase in the size of the group will reduce the per capita benefits of the participants. Therefore, for regulation to be effective as well as most beneficial, there is a limit beyond which it will not pay to increase the number of beneficiaries, a kind of law of diminishing returns.

Empirical Evidence: Stigler's Study of Motor Truck Weight Limitations

As evidence of his economic theory of regulation, Stigler studied state limitations on motor truck weights. Until 1925, because of lack of both good roads and powerful trucks, the motor trucking industry was essentially operating within cities. But over time these deficiencies were removed, and by 1930 about 4 percent of ton-miles of intercity freight was carried by the industry. Concerned over this incipient competition, the railroad industry tried to stave it off by encouraging state regulation of maximum truck weights. By the early 1930s all states passed such regulation, limiting truck weight between 13,000 pounds (Louisiana) and 34,000 pounds (New York) on a four-wheel truck and between 20,000 pounds (New Hampshire) and 45,000 pounds (Michigan) on a six-wheel truck.

The empirical question that Stigler was trying to investigate was: What factors determine the intercity weight variations in weight limitations? To protect its self-interest, the railroad industry would obviously prefer that pattern of weight limitation that would benefit it most. Now the railroads found the trucks most competitive in the shorter hauls (distance) and in hauls of less than carload traffic; the trucks did not offer much competition in full carload and longer-haul traffic. If this is true, Stigler postulates, then, "the longer the average haul, the less the railroads will be opposed to trucks." He further postulates that, because of powerful agricultural interests, "heavy trucks would be allowed in states with a substantial number of farms."

Based on statistical data on truck weights in pounds for forty-eight states for the period 1932–1934, Stigler found that the above hypotheses were borne out. The actual empirical results are given in Question 2-12.

Critique of the Economic Theory of Regulation

Although intellectually novel and appealing, the economic theory of regulation is not without demerits. Richard A. Posner, in his article "Theories of Economic Regulation," contends that despite an important advance over competing theories, " . . . the economic theory has not been refined to the point where it enables us to predict specific industries in which regulation will be found. That is because the theory does not tell us what (under various conditions) is the number of members of a coalition that maximizes the likelihood of regulation."[20] He further contends that, " . . . the economic theory is still so spongy that virtually any observations can be reconciled with."[21] This can be seen from the fact that less concentrated industries such as agriculture (with farm price-support programs) as well as extremely concentrated industries such as local telephone or electric service are regulated.

It is true that the economic theory of regulation cannot yet predict which groups of producers or industries will be regulated. But some recent work by Sam Peltzman (see footnote #19) sheds some light on this question. Stigler himself does not buy Posner's criticism that the economic theory is spongy, if "sponginess" is to be judged by empirical evidence alone. In his words, "The economic theory tells us to look, as precisely and carefully as we can, at who gains and who loses, and how much, when we seek to explain a regulatory policy."

[20]Posner, op. cit., p. 347.
[21]Ibid., p. 348.

2.6 POSNER'S THEORY OF TAXATION BY REGULATION

A variant of the economic theory (i.e., interest group pressures) is Posner's theory of taxation by regulation.[22] To Posner, regulation is a form of (indirect) taxation by which the government taxes one group, say, A for the benefit of another group, say, B. The tax is not direct but indirect and is reflected in the higher (than average cost) price paid by A. The classic example is the U.S. Postal Service. It is well known that the postal service has been charging more (than the average cost) for first-class mail so as to subsidize third-class mail (magazines, newspapers, etc.) This practice is called *cross-subsidization* or *internal subsidization* — charging higher than average cost on one product or service but charging lower than average cost on another product or service, the philosophy being that without such help the other product or service will not be supplied. Another example of such cross-subsidization is that until 1975 the CAB permitted the airlines to charge higher (than average cost) fares on the long-distance flights to subsidize the unprofitable short-distance flights.

There is no doubt that cross-subsidization or internal subsidization, whatever its purpose, does involve redistribution of income in favor of those who receive the subsidy. There are two questions involved here. First: Is such a subsidy desirable? Second: If it is desirable, what is the best method of giving it? About the first question, the economist may not have much to say from the distributive equity viewpoint: In a democratic society, if the majority (through elected officials) decides that a group of people need a subsidy, the economist will take this as a datum or given. Thus, in the 1978 Airline Deregulation Act, the Congress decided on a 10-year guarantee of essential air service to small communities, and to this end devised a new cross-subsidization scheme. Once subsidy is deemed desirable the second question can be addressed, concerning the best way the subsidy can be given. One alternative to cross-subsidization is to provide some relief in the income tax, say, by instituting the negative income tax originally proposed by Milton Friedman — if the income of a person (or a corporate entity) falls below a certain level of income (say, the poverty-level income determined by the Department of Labor), the government would make good the difference between the two by a cash grant. If such a tax scheme is more conducive to (allocative) efficiency than cross-subsidization, one may opt for it. But Posner is not sure whether replacing cross-subsidization by income tax relief is any more efficient. He would not condemn cross-subsidization on efficiency grounds alone. (For a technical exposition of cross-subsidization, see Chapter 11.)

Posner, however, criticizes cross-subsidization as a costly method of taxation, for it encourages entry of inefficient firms into the industry. He gives the following example.

Suppose the regulated firm's costs in the high-price market are $2 but its price $3 — not because its profits are not effectively controlled by the regulatory agency but

[22]Richard A. Posner, "Taxation by Regulation," *Bell Journal of Economics and Management Science*, vol. 2, no. 1, Spring 1971, pp. 22–50.

because in another market it is selling the same $2 service at a price of only $1. A firm that could serve the high-price market at a cost of $2.50 would have an incentive to enter that market. To prevent the waste of resources that such entry would involve, as well as the collapse of the subsidy program, the regulatory agency must establish entry controls.[23]

In short, by encouraging the entry of an inefficient firm whose cost of production is $2.50 per unit as compared to the one whose cost is $2 but which is forced to charge $3 so that it can sell cheaply in another market, cross-subsidization leads to misallocation of resources.

Taxation By Regulation: The Case of Financial Intermediaries

As an empirical test of Posner's theory, John Tuccillo studied the effect of regulation on depository institutions (DIs) such as commercial banks. These DIs are subject to a variety of state and federal regulations. Some of these involve price (i.e., interest) restrictions or output restrictions (i.e., the types of services that can be offered) or both.

For example, until recently only commercial banks could offer full-service facilities; savings banks were not allowed to issue demand deposits (in some states the negotiable order of withdrawal (NOW) accounts, which are like demand deposits, are issued by some savings banks). On the other hand, savings accounts earned on the average a higher return in savings banks than in commercial banks. But in return, it would seem, the commercial banks do not by law pay any interest on demand deposits (this has changed recently and such interest is now allowed if the depositor keeps some minimum amount, ranging from $1000 to 3000, in the bank). This exemption from paying interest on demand deposits obviously has a beneficial effect on the commercial banks, for it reduces the overall cost of funds to the banks. But this amounts to a subsidy by the demand depositors to the commercial banks or, what amounts to the same thing, a tax on the depositors.

The whole area of banking regulation exhibits this kind of tax (or subsidy) on one group to the disadvantage (or advantage) of another group. Commercial banks are required to keep about 8 percent of their deposit amount in cash, whereas this figure ranges between 0.0098 percent and 0.122 percent for savings and loan associations. As a result, the commercial banks tie up more of their money in cash, on which they get no interest. (In principle, these reserve amounts are to be kept in the Federal Reserve System, in the case of commercial banks, or with the Federal Home Loan Board, in the case of savings and loan associations, and earn no interest).

Tuccillo tried to assess the overall effects of these taxes and subsidies on the DIs. These effects are measured in terms of the percentage reduction (in the case of a subsidy) or percentage increase (in the case of a tax) in the federal income tax the DIs pay. The empirical results for the year 1973 are given in Table 2.2.

[23]Richard A. Posner, *Economic Analysis of Law*, 2d ed., Little, Brown, Boston, 1977, pp. 266–

TABLE 2.2
IMPACT OF IMPLICIT TAXES (+) AND SUBSIDIES (−) ON EFFECTIVE FEDERAL TAX RATES:
SAVINGS AND LOAN ASSOCIATIONS, 1973

Asset size ($ million)	Prohibition of services*	Reserve structure*	Borrowing privilege*	Effect of mutual form of organization*	Total impact*†
Less than $10	+1.2	−0.7	−0.1	−0.2	+0.2
$10–$25	+1.3	−1.1	−0.1	−0.4	−0.3
$25–$50	+1.8	−1.3	−0.1	−0.3	+0.1
$50–$100	+2.2	−1.4	−0.1	−0.3	+0.4
$100–$250	+1.9	−1.7	−0.2	−0.4	−0.4
Over $250	+1.8	−0.6	−0.2	−0.4	+0.6

*These effects are in percentage points. One would adjust effective rates by adding or subtracting these figures.
†Total impact is the sum of the first four columns.
Source: J. Tuccillo, "Taxation by Regulation: The Case of Financial Intermediaries," *Bell Journal of Economics and Management Science,* Autumn 1977, table 4, p. 583.

To illustrate, consider the case of savings and loan associations in the $10 to $25 million asset category. Because these associations, unlike commercial banks, cannot offer full services, this restriction increases their income tax liability by about 1.3 percent. On the other hand, because their reserve requirements are lower than those for the commercial banks, their tax liability is reduced by about 1.1 percent. Table 2.2 shows the effects of other types of regulation. The total impact is given in the last column, which shows that for the asset category under consideration, this impact is a reduction of tax liability by about 0.3 percent. In short, for this particular category, compared to commercial banks, there is net subsidy from the various regulations. By contrast, for the asset category over $250 million, the net effect, again compared to commercial banks, is an increase in tax liability of about 0.6 percent. Therefore, this category suffers compared to the one just studied. Based on the results presented in Table 2.2 and other statistical analysis, Tuccillo concludes that compared to the commercial banks the thrift institutions (i.e., savings and loan associations) as a group suffer because they pay a comparatively higher tax due to the differential regulation. As Table 2.2 shows, four out of the six asset categories pay higher taxes and only two receive (implicit) subsidies. This amounts to a transfer of income from the thrifts to the commercial banks, thus providing some support to Posner's theory of "taxation by regulation." But this theory is not strong enough to suggest which asset category receives the subsidy and which pays higher taxes. Referring again to Table 2.2, we see that the asset categories of $10 to $25 and $100 to $250 million received (implicit) subsidies in 1973 but the others did not. What explains this pattern? The theory cannot tell a priori. Obviously, further careful empirical work is needed to answer this question.

2.7 SUMMARY AND CONCLUSIONS

The primary purpose of this chapter was to examine the various theories of regulation that have been advanced to justify government intervention in the marketplace. First we considered the public interest theory. The crux of this theory is that the idealized world of perfect competition does not exist because of various market failures, which make it impossible to attain the highest possible social welfare. Some of the important market failures we discussed were inadequate supply of public goods, natural monopolies, externalities, lack of perfect information, and inadequate conservation of natural resources. The public interest theory contends that the government can legitimately intervene in the marketplace to remedy one or more of these failures and thereby protect and improve consumer welfare. Although the case for government intervention in the marketplace can be made, it does not necessarily follow that the government should actually do so; Coase's theorem states that with appropriate institutional arrangements the alleged market failures can be corrected by private negotiations among the affected parties. In reality, though, the conditions for the satisfaction of the Coase Theorem are simply unrealistic, especially the requirement that there be no or very little transaction cost. And even if the transaction costs are minimal, private negotiations are difficult to conduct if the number of parties involved is large. Therefore, the public interest theory has considerable merit; there is no question that in the supply of pure public goods or in alleviating negative externalities the government can play a useful role. (As we will see in Chapters 16 and 17, in the areas of health, safety, and environmental pollution the government has a legitimate role to play, the only question being the form or the method of that intervention.)

We then examined the self-interest, or capture, theory of regulation. The thrust of this theory is that government regulation is not meant to correct one or more market failures but is solely for the benefit of interest or pressure groups, be they farmers, truckers, or barbers. These interest groups tend to initially oppose government regulation, but over time they develop mutuality of interest with the regulators; the groups ultimately wind up "capturing" the regulators and reaping substantial benefits for themselves. These benefits come in the form of higher prices, higher rates of return, or restriction of entry into the industry. As we will see in Chapter 11 (the ICC), Chapter 14 (the SEC) and Chapter 15 (the FCC), the capture theory may very well explain the behavior of these regulatory agencies. Note, however, that the capture theory is very often superimposed on the public interest theory in the sense that the initial push for regulation may be on account of the one or more market failures discussed earlier (e.g., the early monopoly power of the railroads), and once the regulation comes into being the regulated try to bend it to their own advantage. From this perspective, the capture theory is really not an explanation of regulation per se but of the behavior of the regulatory agencies once regulation is instituted.

We then considered Stigler's economic theory of regulation. To Stigler, regulation is an economic commodity, for it confers some valuable benefits on the regulated. Since regulation is an economic commodity, according to Stigler, its equilibrium price and equilibrium quantity are determined by the usual tools of supply and demand analysis, the demanders in this case being those who are seeking some benefits and the suppliers being the politicians at various levels of government. To gain maximum benefits, the demanders behave like a cartel by trying to restrict the number of members who receive the benefits. The economic theory is quite novel and, in conjunction with the capture theory, can explain many a regulatory phenomenon — the former explaining the passage of a regulatory bill and the latter explaining how the regulatory agencies created by such bills get manipulated by the regulated to their greatest advantage.

Finally we considered Posner's theory of taxation by regulation. Posner views regulation primarily as a means of transferring income from one group of consumers to another or from one group of producers to another or from producers to consumers or vice versa. This redistribution is accomplished by taxing one group and subsidizing the other. Regardless of the merit of the tax-subsidy mechanism to transfer income, from an efficiency viewpoint, such transfers can lead to misallocation of economic resources. But as we will learn throughout the remainder of the text, income redistribution considerations have often taken precedence over efficiency considerations.

In evaluating all these theories it should be remembered that no single theory can explain fully as important and as pervasive a phenomenon as regulation. Therefore, no single theory can claim superiority over the other. Readers should examine each regulatory experience and try to see for themselves whether it can be explained by one or more of the theories discussed in this chapter. Very often they will find that part of a regulatory experience can be explained by one of the theories considered here and another by one or more other theories, the relative importance of each theory varying from experience to experience.[24]

QUESTIONS

2-1 Evaluate the following statement:
When you hear people objecting to the market or to capitalism and you examine their objections, you will find that most of those objections are objections to freedom itself. What most people are objecting to is that the market gives people what the people want instead of what the person talking thinks the people ought to want. (Milton Friedman, "The Economics of Freedom," *Sohio,* 1978, p. 13.)

2-2 Are public libraries a pure or quasi-pure public good? What would be the consequences if public libraries were managed privately?

2-3 Are the following industries natural monopolies? Why? Airlines, trucking, long-line transmission, railroads, and cable TV.

2-4 What types of externalities are exhibited by the following phenomena? What costs or benefits do these phenomena confer on society?
  1 Brain-drain
  2 Reckless driving
  3 Pornographic districts
  4 Free museums

---

[24]For a critical appraisal of the various theories of regulation, see Paul L. Joskow and Roger G. Noll, "Regulation in Theory and Practice: An Overview," in Gary Fromm (ed.), *Studies in Public Regulation,* M.I.T., Cambridge, Mass., 1983, ch. 1.

2-5 What explains the ban on the public sale of heroin? What would happen if the ban were lifted?

2-6 Would OPEC's pricing policies lead to conservation of oil usage in this country? Why or why not?

2-7 In the "Fable of the Bees," the bee keeper provides pollination services for the neighborhood fruit growers who in turn provide nectar for the bees. How would you characterize the externalities involved in this case? How would the bee keeper induce the fruit growers to provide more nectar for the bees (to increase the output of honey) and how would the fruit growers induce the bee keeper to provide more pollination services? (Hint: Recall the Coase theorem.) See if your answer agrees with that of Steven N. S. Cheung, "The Fable of the Bees: An Economic Investigation," *Journal of Law and Economics*, vol. 16, April 1973, p. 23.

2-8 How would the CAB reconcile the interest of trunkline airlines with those of the regional or the local service lines? Which theory of regulation would help you in answering the question?

2-9 The telephone companies and Western Union provide competing services. Both are regulated by the FCC. How would the FCC reconcile their competing interests?

2-10 State the reasons why you agree or disagree with the following implications derived from the economic theory of regulation (quotes are from Donald J. Mullineaux, "Regulation: Whence It Came and Whether Its Here to Stay," *Federal Reserve Bank of Philadelphia*, September–October 1978, p. 8):

> ... since the reward for politicians in supplying regulation is an opportunity to increase political support, regulation is more likely to surface in monopolistic or competitive industries than in so-called oligopolistic ones (industries with a few highly independent firms).
>
> ... increases in productivity or growth in demand within an industry will boost the likelihood of regulation.
>
> When a regulated firm's costs increase, for example, price behaves as it would in a nonregulated environment — it goes up. But it goes up by more than it would if there were no regulation.

2-11 Comment: " ... Regulation is more likely to be imposed in a declining industry because adversity is a greater spur to effort than opportunity." (Posner, "Theories of Economic Regulation," p. 343.)

2-12 George Stigler's empirical study on motor truck weight limitations produced the following results:

Dependent variable	N	Constant	X_3	X_4	X_5	R^2
X_1	48	12.28 (4.87)	0.0336 (3.99)	0.0287 (2.77)	0.2641 (3.04)	0.502
X_2	46	10.34 (1.57)	0.0437 (2.01)	0.0788 (2.97)	0.2528 (1.15)	0.243

Where X_1 = Weight limit on 40-wheel trucks (thousands of pounds), 1932–1933
X_2 = Weight limit on 6-wheel trucks (thousands of pounds), 1932–1933
X_3 = Trucks on farms per 1000 agricultural labor force, 1930
X_4 = Average length of railroad haul of freight (miles), 1930
X_5 = Percent of state highways with high-type surface, Dec. 1930
N = Number of observations

The figures in parentheses are the estimated t values. How do the above results support Stigler's economic theory of regulation? Note: For the benefit of those who do not know regression analysis the above results are to be interpreted as follows. For the first equation in the above table, if, say, X_4 increases by a mile, then holding all other variables (i.e., X_3 and X_5, here) constant, X_1, the weight limit on a four-wheel truck, goes up on the average by 0.0287 per unit increase in X_4. Since X_1 is measured in thousands of pounds, this means it will increase by about 28.7 pounds. Similarly, holding all other variables constant, if X_3, the number of trucks on farms per 1000 labor force increases by 1, on the average X_1 goes up by about 33.6 pounds. R^2 of 0.502 means that X_3, X_4, and X_5 taken together explain about 50 percent of the variation in X_1. The other equation in the table is to be interpreted similarly. (For an elementary introduction to regression analysis, see the author's *Basic Econometrics,* McGraw-Hill, New York, 1978, chs. 1–5.)

2-13 The Interest Adjustment Act of 1966 introduced differential interest rate ceilings (the maximum interest rate that can be paid) on the interest rate that commercial banks and other thrift institutions (primarily savings and loan associations) can pay on the savings deposits kept with them — the ceiling was higher for the thrift institutions than for the commercial banks. What is the rationale for the differential interest rate ceilings? From an economic viewpoint, is this ceiling differential desirable? Which theory of regulation can explain this differential? In answering the questions keep in mind that traditionally the thrift institutions have been the prime lenders in the residential housing mortgage market, while the commercial banks have played a comparatively secondary role.

In 1980 the Congress passed the Depository Institutions Deregulation and Monetary Control Act of 1980, which calls for the elimination of ceilings on deposit interest rates (popularly known as Regulation Q) by 1986. What do you think was the reason behind this change? What would be the effect of this deregulation on the savers? And on the borrowers? See if your thinking agrees with the one discussed in R. Alton Gilbert, "Will the Removal of Regulation Q Raise Mortgage Interest Rates?" in *Review,* Federal Reserve Bank of St. Louis, December 1981, vol. 63, no. 10, pp. 3–12.

APPENDIX: A Graphic Presentation of Pareto Optimality

The following is a *very* heuristic explanation of Pareto optimality discussed in the text. Consider a community consisting of two individuals, A and B. Using the community's resources (labor, land, and capital), they produce some goods. (Let us not worry about the distribution of these resources between the two for now.) The consumption of these goods gives some utility or satisfaction to them. Let us represent A's satisfaction on the horizontal axis and B's on the vertical axis, satisfaction being measured somehow. Now consider Figure 2.5.

The curve shown in the figure may be called the social opportunity curve, or frontier, and the area bounded by this curve and the two axes the *social opportunity set.* The social opportunity frontier represents the *maximum* attainable satisfaction by the two. Point b_3 represents the maximum possible satisfaction attainable by B when he consumes all the goods produced by the community, while point a_3 represents the maximum possible satisfaction attainable by A when she consumes all the produced goods. Any other point on the frontier shows the combination of satisfactions obtained by the two when

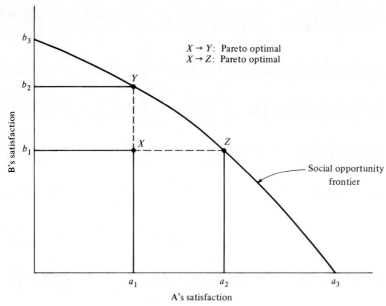

FIGURE 2.5
A graphic illustration of Pareto optimality.

each consumes some positive amounts of the goods. Points inside the opportunity set show the *attainable* (but not maximum attainable) combination of satisfactions derived by A and B.

Now consider the combination X inside the social opportunity set, which results from the satisfaction derived from a certain allocation of the goods between the two. Would a reallocation to point Y be socially desirable? Since at Y B's satisfaction has increased from b_1 to b_2 while that of A has remained the same, we can say that the move from X to Y is Pareto-optimal since the two parties are at least as well off as before and one party (B) is actually better off. Likewise, a move from X to Z is also Pareto-optimal, only that here B's satisfaction has remained the same, while A's has increased.

In short, a move from a point inside the social opportunity set to a point on the social opportunity frontier is Pareto-justified or Pareto-optimal, since none of the parties are worse off and some parties are actually better off.

But suppose we are at Y or Z to begin with. Can a move from Y to Z or vice versa be deemed Pareto-optimal? No, because a move from Y to Z, while making A better off makes B worse off. And likewise the move from Z to Y makes B better off but A worse off. Thus, on the social opportunity frontier itself one cannot say that one point is more Pareto-optimal than some other point.

In economics, when we talk about efficiency (that is, efficient allocation of economic resources) we have in mind a move from an interior point of the social opportunity set (such as point X) to a point on the social opportunity frontier (such as point Y or Z).

Incidentally, Figure 2.5 can be used to show why the question of distributive equity is difficult to deal with. Suppose we are at point Z on the opportunity frontier. Suppose we "ethically" feel that the income distribution represented by point Z is not "equitable" and that we should move to point Y, where it is more equitable. Now for reasons noted above, such a move will involve an increase in B's satisfaction but a decrease in A's satisfaction, a move not Pareto-preferred or Pareto-optimal. But if we still insist on such a move, it would imply the increase in B's satisfaction (resulting from the new income distribution) is more important than the decrease in A's satisfaction. Now unless we have some means of comparing the satisfactions of A and B, we cannot make such a statement. And economists have not yet developed methods of comparing interpersonal satisfactions (nor for that matter have psychologists). That is why economists have generally focused their attention on allocative efficiency (e.g., the move from X to Y or from X to Z).

CHAPTER 3

THE PROCESS OF GOVERNMENT REGULATION: THE ADMINISTRATIVE STRUCTURE

Once Congress passes a regulatory law, its actual implementation is left to one or more regulatory agencies. It is these agencies which can make or mar the success of any regulation. As the comptroller general of the United States has put it, "One approach to the study of regulatory activity is to evaluate the impact of the organization and structure of a regulatory agency on the nature of the regulation that occurs."[1]

In this chapter we examine the organizational network that has been established to carry out the goals of various legislative actions. Although there are various types of regulatory agencies, our emphasis will be on the independent regulatory commissions (IRC) that have been created by Congress with specific purposes in mind. We will see how these commissions, which have been called "miniature independent governments" or "the headless fourth branch of the government,"[2] are established, what their purposes are, what the nature of their membership is, how they work, to whom they are accountable, and whether there is any need for change. We will not discuss the actual working of the various IRCs; that task is left to subsequent chapters.

3.1 TYPES OF REGULATORY AGENCIES

Looking at various regulatory experiences, one can distinguish several types of regulatory agencies.

---

[1]The comptroller general of the United States, "Government Regulatory Activity: Justification, Process, Impacts, and Alternatives," *Report to the Congress*, June 3, 1977, p. 42.

[2]This characterization is due to the Brownlow Committee, more formally known as the *U.S. President's Committee on Administrative Management, Report with Special Studies*, U.S. Government Printing Press, 1937.

Executive Branch Agency

Although not as visible as the independent regulatory commissions, there are several regulatory agencies which are established in the executive branch of the government and are therefore under the direct control of the President. These agencies are generally located within the major administrative departments, such as the Department of Labor, the Department of Commerce, the Department of Agriculture, etc. Nominally, the secretary of the department is the head of such agencies, although the day-to-day operations of the agency are left to a specially appointed head of the agency. The heads of the agencies, through the secretary, are ultimately responsible to the President; very often these agency heads are political appointees of the President, perhaps people who have helped the President politically.

Some of the important executive branch agencies which are primarily or mostly regulatory in nature are listed in Table 3.1. These agencies literally administer hundreds of laws and issue hundreds of regulatory rules every year (which are published in the *Federal Register*) — rules which are far-reaching in character. Just to give the flavor of the job these agencies do, consider the Animal and Plant Health Inspection Service of the Department of Agriculture; it regulates, among other things, the following:

1 The process and distribution of reindeer meat

2 The movement into or from the United States and interstate of animals affected with or having been exposed to any communicable animal disease and sanitary conditions related to the movement of such animals

3 Transportation, purchase, sale, housing, care, handling, and treatment of certain animals used for research experiments or exhibition (under the federal laboratory Animal Welfare Act)

4 Movement in interstate or foreign commerce of stored horses (under the Horse Protection Act of 1970)

5 Sale and importation of viruses, serums, and toxins used in the treatment of domestic animals (under the Virus, Serum and Toxin Act)

6 Marketing of anti-hog-cholera serum and hog-cholera virus in interstate and foreign commerce (under the Anti Hog Cholera Serum and Virus Act)

Independent Agency within a Department

The recently created Federal Energy Regulatory Commission (FERC) typifies this form of organization (for details of FERC, see Chapter 13). Although created by Congress as an independent commission, it is not autonomous in that it is located within the Department of Energy (DEO), itself of recent origin. The reason for the creation of this kind of mixed independent–executive branch agency was due to the critical nature of the energy problem facing the country. It was thought that this form would stop the sometime procrastinating deliberations of the independent commissions while at the same time preventing arbitrary or summary action by a single agency administrator. This agency would therefore

TABLE 3.1
SELECTED EXECUTIVE BRANCH REGULATORY AGENCIES

Name of department	Name of agency
Department of Agriculture	Animal and Plant Health Inspection Service
	Commodity Credit Corporation Service
	Federal Grain Inspection Service
	Food Safety and Quality Service
	Packers and Stockyards Administration
Department of Health, Education, and Welfare	Social Security Administration Office for Civil Rights
Department of Housing and Urban Development	Office for Fair Housing and Equal Opportunity
	Office of Consumer Affairs and Regulatory Functions
Department of the Interior	Mining Enforcement and Safety Administration
	U.S. Fish and Wildlife Service
Department of Labor	Employment Standards Administration
	Employment and Training Administration
Department of Transportation	National Highway Traffic Safety Administration
	Federal Aviation Administration
	Federal Highway Administration
	Federal Railroad Administration
Department of Justice	Antitrust Division
	Drug Enforcement Administration
Department of Commerce	Patent Office
	National Oceanic and Atmospheric Administration
Department of the Treasury	Bureau of Alcohol, Tobacco and Firearms
	Customs Service

make it easier to coordinate the nation's energy policies as expeditiously as possible. The FERC and DEO have a concurrent relationship so far as rule making. Thus:

1 In matters within FERC's jurisdiction, the secretary of DEO may propose rules, regulations, and statements of policy and he may establish "reasonable" timetables for agency action on these proposals.

2 The secretary is authorized to participate and intervene, as a matter of right, in any proceeding before the commission.

3 In a "seesaw" fashion, the commission may, under certain circumstances, become involved in rules proposed by the secretary, and if the commission opposes a rule issued by the secretary, it cannot be adopted.

But in the important matter of price-setting (e.g., the well-head price of gas), the commission is to act independently of the DEO, and therefore of the White House.

Agency Located Outside the Executive Branch but not Independent of It

The Environmental Protection Agency (EPA), established in 1970, is an executive branch agency, although it is not located within any executive department. It is administered by a single administrator who is directly responsible to the President. The reason that it is outside any department can be found in the very nature of the job entrusted to it, namely, the abatement of air, water, and noise pollution, and the control of solid waste, pesticides, and radiation. Obviously, with such wide-ranging activities, it is difficult to assign the EPA to any single department.[3]

Independent Regulatory Commission (IRC)

By far the most popular and, in terms of visibility and impact, the most influential regulatory agency is the IRC. The Interstate Commerce Commission (ICC), the Civil Aeronautics Board (CAB), the Federal Power Commission (FPC), and the Securities and Exchange Commission (SEC) have now become quite familiar names. Because of their importance, IRCs are dealt with thoroughly in the rest of this chapter.

Specialized Agencies

Agencies such as the Federal Reserve System (FRS) and the Federal Deposit Insurance Corporation (FDIC) cannot be readily classified into any of the four categories just mentioned. The FRS, which serves as the nation's central bank, charged with the prime responsibility of managing the nation's monetary policy, consists of five parts: the Board of Governors in Washington, the twelve Federal Reserve Banks and their twenty-five branches, the Federal Open Market Committee (which buys and sells government securities, thereby affecting bank reserves and the money supply), the Federal Advisory Council (which advises the Board of Governors on general business conditions), and the Consumer Advisory Council (which advises the Board on consumer credit protection). The Board of Governors, consisting of seven members, is appointed by the President with the advice and consent of the Senate.

---

[3]The quasi-independent status of the EPA is also due to the environmental lobbyists as well as the general concern with the environment exhibited through most of the 1970s. (For details about the EPA, see Ch. 17.)

The FDIC, which was established to promote and preserve confidence in banks and to protect the money supply through provision of insurance coverage for bank deposits, is an independent agency within the executive branch. However, it is different from the second category of regulatory agency discussed in this chapter in that it does not operate on funds appropriated by Congress; its income, like that of the Federal Reserve System, comes from assessments on deposits held by insured banks and from interest on the required investment of its surplus funds in government securities.

3.2 INDEPENDENT REGULATORY COMMISSIONS (IRCs)[4]

The IRCs, such as the CAB, Commodity Futures Trading Commission(CFTC), Federal Communications Commission (FCC), Federal Maritime Commission (FMC), Federal Trade Commission (FTC), Interstate Commerce Commission (ICC), etc., are by far the most popular and more visible forms of organization for regulatory agencies. The IRCs are expressly created by Congress and are essentially an ''arm of the Congress.'' Some of the important IRCs will be discussed in detail in later chapters; here we will discuss them in broad terms.

The Nature of the IRC

The IRCs are multimember commissions whose members are nominated by the President and are subject to confirmation by the Senate. The ICC, established in 1887, was the first IRC, although in fact it did not become fully independent until 1889. In creating the ICC (and similar commissions), Congress wanted to create an organizational structure that would be insulated from presidential influence, and therefore from presidential politics. In this respect the IRCs are different from the executive branch agencies (located within or outside an executive department), which are directly responsible to the President, and the President can appoint or remove the heads of such agencies without congressional approval.

The IRCs, besides being administrative agencies administering the various laws, are quasi-judicial in nature; they hold courtlike hearings which carry the force of law and their decisions are binding on the affected parties, unless they are overturned by federal appeals courts.

As noted, these IRCs are essentially an ''arm of the Congress'' in that they are supposed to do things that ordinarily Congress is supposed to do but does not want to do because it lacks the time or the resources or the expertise that is required to administer the complex business of economic regulation. That this is the case can be seen from the following remarks made by the late Senator

---

[4]The following discussion draws heavily from the *Study on Federal Regulation*, vol. V, Committee on Government Affairs, U.S. Senate, December 1977 (hereafter, *Senate Study on Federal Regulation*). In all there are six volumes of the study.

TABLE 3.2
MEMBERSHIP SIZE OF SELECTED INDEPENDENT REGULATORY COMMISSIONS
AND SPECIALIZED AGENCIES

No. of members	Name of commission
5	CAB, CFTC, CPSC, FERC, FMC, FTC, NRC, SEC
7	FCC, FRS
11	ICC

Phillip Hart during the debate on a nominee to an IRC (the nominee was William Springer, for the FPC):

> Congress, and more specifically the Senate, is subject to criticism for loss of sight over the years as to the purpose for which we established these commissions. *The Commissions,* if I may risk over-simplification, *are ours.* We have concluded that certain regulatory activities have gotten to a point where, on a day-to-day basis, Congress itself is inept and ill-equipped to make decisions. So we create a commission . . . . In substance, we say to them, "Gentlemen . . . you do for us what we like to think we would do if we had your skill and the time to give attention to the problems that confront you.[5] [Emphasis added.]

Size of Membership

The size of the multimember IRCs varies from commission to commission, as can be seen from Table 3.2.

Term of Office

Like the membership size, the term of office varies from commission to commission, which can be seen from Table 3.3. A unique feature is that the membership term is staggered so that not all the commissioners retire at the same

TABLE 3.3
MEMBERSHIP TENURE OF INDEPENDENT
REGULATORY COMMISSIONS AND
SPECIALIZED AGENCIES

No. of years	Name of commission
4	FERC
5	CFTC, FMC, NRC, SEC
6	CAB
7	CPSC, FCC, FTC, ICC
14	FRS

[5]*Congressional Record,* May 21, 1973, p. S-16273.

time. This both ensures continuity in the working of the commissions and insulates them from presidential influence through the appointment process. In any single year, because of the staggered membership, the President has only a limited opportunity to affect the leadership of any given commission. As a result, most of the time, holdovers from a prior administration can be expected to be part of the commission membership.

Selection of Commissioners

The commissioners, as noted previously, are nominated by the President with the advice and consent of the Senate. To ensure independence of the commissions, Congress has put several restrictions on the President. First, the membership of the commissions must be bipartisan with no more than a simple majority coming from a single political party. Second, with certain exceptions, the decisions of the IRCs are not subject to clearance or approval by the President.[6] Finally, the President can remove a duly appointed commissioner only for "inefficiency, neglect of duty or malfeasance in office" and for no other reason. That this restriction has teeth in it can be seen from the following legal case.

HUMPREY'S EXECUTOR V. UNITED STATES

The case revolves around Mr. Humprey, who was a FTC commissioner. Mr. Humprey, a Coolidge appointee, was philosophically opposed to President Franklin Roosevelt's New Deal measures. Therefore, President Roosevelt removed him from office. Whereupon, Mr. Humprey sued the government for pay as well as for the return of his office. But he died before the case was resolved. The U.S. Supreme Court, however, upheld his estate's claim for back pay and affirmed unequivocally that a commissioner can be removed from office only for "inefficiency, neglect of duty or malfeasance." Thus, the court reaffirmed the independent status of the IRCs.

The President designates one commissioner as chairperson of the commission. The chairperson can be removed by the President without Senate approval, although he remains a member of the commission. In other words, the chairperson can be removed by the President as chairperson but not as a member of the commission.

How does the President select people for appointment to the IRC? This has usually been an extremely informal and often a haphazard process. Very often is follows the "BOGSAT" principle, BOGSAT being an acronym for a "Bunch of Guys Sitting Around the Table," and simply means that presidential advisors and

---

[6]For example, during national emergency or in times of war, the President can limit the construction permits for radio stations or require the CAB to seek his approval before issuing permits for foreign air transportation.

TABLE 3.4
MEMBERSHIP CHARACTERISTICS OF SELECTED AGENCIES

Characteristic	Agency											
	FPC	EPA	FTC	FAA	FMC	FDA	SEC	CAB	ICC	CPSC	FCC	NRC
1 Party affiliation:												
Republican	11	2	9	4	6	—	11	7	12	2	11	3
Democratic	10	—	6	1	5	—	8	4	8	3	11	1
Independent	1	—	2	1	0	5	0	2	7	1	1	1
2 Sex:												
Male	22	2	15	6	10	5	19	13	26	4	22	5
Female	—	—	2	—	1	—	—	—	1	2	1	—
3 Education:												
Some college	—	—	—	—	1	1	1	1	2	—	2	—
Bachelor's degree	2	—	—	3	4	—	2	2	3	2	8	—
Master's degree	3	—	—	1	—	—	—	—	—	1	—	2
Ph.D.	1	—	—	1	—	—	—	—	1	2	—	2
Law degree	16	2	17	1	6	—	16	9	20	1	13	1
Medical degree	—	—	—	—	—	4	—	—	—	—	—	—
Not known or high school	—	—	—	—	—	—	—	1	1	—	—	—
4 Major political positions held:												
Yes	9	2	9	—	8	—	4	10	19	1	14	—
No	13	—	8	6	3	5	15	3	8	5	9	5

Source: *Senate Study on Federal Regulation*, vol. I, *The Regulatory Appointments Process*, Appendix H. The information in this table is based on appointees from 1961 to June 1976.

confidants suggest some name as a commissioner and generally that person gets the job. Sometimes the process becomes ridiculous, as with the Butterfield appointment to the Federal Aviation Administration (FAA) (see Question 3-1).

What are the qualifications of the commissioners? There are no set qualifications. The *Senate Study on Federal Regulation,* after studying several regulatory agencies, found various characteristics of commissioners, presented in Table 3.4.

Some patterns that emerge from Table 3.4 are as follows. First, over the period of the study, there were more Republican than Democratic commissioners. Second, the regulatory commissions were dominated by lawyers; ironically, there were few professional economists, although a substantial amount of the commissions' work involves economic analysis. Third, women were just about conspicuous by their absence. Finally, a substantial number of commissioners were politically very active before their appointment to the IRCs.

3.3 ACCOUNTABILITY AND INDEPENDENCE: SOME PROBLEMS FACING THE IRCs

The fact that the IRCs are independent of presidential influence might give the impression that these agencies are not accountable to anyone. This is far from the truth. As a matter of fact, there are several checks on the IRCs, some of which are as follows.

Federal Judiciary Review

It was pointed out earlier that the IRCs are administrative and quasi-judicial bodies which are empowered to reach final decisions on adjudicatory matters and to issue rules and regulations which are generally not subject to approval by any government agency. But the decisions of the commissions can be appealed to the federal courts, which can set aside commission rulings. The Administrative Procedure Act provides that the reviewing court shall ''hold unlawful and set aside agency action, findings and conclusions'' which are found to be:

1 Arbitrary, capricious, and abusive of discretion, or otherwise not in accordance with law
2 Contrary to constitutional right, power, privilege, or immunity
3 In excess of statutory jurisdiction, authority, or limitation or short of statutory right
4 Without observance of procedure required by law
5 Unsupported by substantial evidence
6 Unwarranted by the facts to the extent that the facts are subject to trial *de novo* by the review court.

Although the reviewing court may not substitute its judgment on the merits for that of the regulatory agency, the above provisions were intended by Congress to assure a comprehensive review of a broad spectrum of agency administrative actions.

OMB Supervision of the Budget

The Office of Management and Budget (OMB), formerly the Bureau of the Budget, was established in the executive branch of the government in 1970. Among its other functions, it is responsible for the supervision and control of the budgets submitted by various governmental agencies as well as by the IRCs. Thus the OMB review of IRC actions is an indirect check on the activities of the commissions. It is here that the President can exert some influence on the working of the commissions; for example, he may not approve the budget for some items which are not to his liking.

OMB Clearance of Legislative Messages

As mentioned, the IRCs are administrative cum quasi-judicial agencies. They also initiate legislative proposals, which are sent to Congress. However, in most cases, before the legislative messages are sent to the Congress they need to be cleared by the OMB, the idea being that there should be some coordination between the legislative policies pursued by the President and those proposed by the commissions. Thus, this provision is another check on the independence of the commissions. Recently, though, Congress has tried to curtail the supervisory power of the OMB over the agency legislative proposals by requiring the OMB to show Congress these proposals, whether they are liked by the President or not. This, in the view of some members of Congress, will not only ensure the independence of the commissions but will also encourage them to submit legislative proposals which may be in the interest of the public, although not necessarily politically palatable to the President.

GAO Coordination of Information Gathering

The General Accounting Office (GAO), under the control and direction of the comptroller general, is an independent, nonpolitical watchdog agency which assists Congress in carrying out its legislative and oversight responsibilities. One of its important functions is the supervision of the data gathering activities of the various regulatory commissions – the IRCs in pursuit of their mission gather all sorts of data from the interested parties. The GAO supervision thus provides another check on the activities of the IRCs.

Supervision by the Justice Department

Another check on the IRCs is the limitation on their litigious power. As stated elsewhere, the rulings of the commissions have the force of law, but sometimes these agencies are forced to go to court to seek compliance with their rulings. Now any court action involves several steps, namely, (1) initiation of the suit, (2) legal theories to back up the suit, (3) strategies to follow in court proceedings, (4) settlement of the suit, and (5) appeals to higher courts in case the lower court turns down the suit. The important question is: Who can best perform the job of seeing the IRCs through these legal processes?

Traditionally, suits involving the federal government are handled by the Justice Department, with the attorney general serving as the chief lawyer for the government. Over the years, there has been a conflict as to whether legal suits involving the IRCs should be handled by the commissions themselves or be left to the resources of the Justice Department. And there is confusion about who has the final say in case there is a conflict between the IRCs and the Justice Department.

Examining historical experience, it seems that there are three aspects to the involvement of the commissions in litigious proceedings. First, most agencies are allowed to participate fully in court proceedings instituted by the Justice Department on behalf of these agencies or commissions. Second, the power to initiate lawsuits on their own is generally not available to all independent agencies. For example, the FTC, FERC, and SEC have complete or near complete authority to initiate and conduct lawsuits independent of the Justice Department. Five others, the CFTC (Commodity Futures Trading Commission), CPSC (Consumer Product Safety Commission), FMC, FRB (Federal Reserve Board), and ICC, have only partial or doubtful authority, but agencies such as the CAB, FCC, and NRC (Nuclear Regulatory Commission) may not sue in their own name without the approval of the attorney general. Third, in appeals before the U.S. Supreme Court — the final element of civil litigating authority — the attorney general and the solicitor general are by law the only authorities who can appear. Only the FTC, by a 1975 amendment to the FTC Act of 1914, can appear before the Supreme Court in certain cases — cases in which after the commission requests the Justice Department to take certain actions and the attorney general fails to do so within 60 days.

The Legislative Veto

Until the Supreme Court's decision in June 1983 declaring the congressional legislative veto power unconstitutional, such veto power was yet another check on the IRCs. It remains to be seen what the Congress does to regain such veto power.

To sum up, although the IRCs are independent of Presidential power, they are not autonomous in relation to the government. Their status has been well summarized by the *Senate Study on Federal Regulation* as follows:

> There are, . . . limitations on the independence of the commissions — some of which are necessary and appropriate. As to appointments, appropriations, personnel practices and other matters, they are integrated into the rest of government, and subject to the legislative, judicial and executive branches. Other restrictions, are imposed by budget and legislative message review, litigation control, coordination of information gathering; and clearance of certain top-level staff appointments. . . .
>
> But within those limits the commissions are independent if they choose to do so. Much depends on the self-image of the agency's leadership. If an independent commission conducts itself in the public view as subordinate to a branch of government, or to any other interest, then dependency will be the likely result. . . . Attitude can and does make a difference. If a commission asserts its proper independent status, the structure is there to support that objective.[7]

3.4   CRITICISM OF THE INDEPENDENT FORM OF ORGANIZATION

One of the greatest virtues claimed for the independent form of organization for regulatory agencies is that, because of their independence from political pressures, IRCs can discharge their administrative and judicial functions with the greatest possible neutrality; hence they can serve the public interest better. This very feature, however, has led almost all Presidents to dislike the IRCs.

President Roosevelt found these commissions an impediment to his New Deal economic policies. In his view, independence impairs the aggressiveness and

---

[7] *Senate Study on Federal Regulation,* vol. V, p. 67.

effectiveness of the President's regulatory program and obstructs coordination of national policy on those matters.

In the Truman administration, the Budget Bureau, after a study of the IRC operations, concluded that independence was a major source of weakness and ineffectiveness, which made coordination of policy on regulation very difficult.

The same view was expressed in a report submitted by James Landis to President-elect Kennedy.[8] Landis found that the IRCs posed serious questions regarding accountability and coordination of presidential regulatory policies.

The latest charge against the independent commissions came from the Ash Council report to President Nixon in 1970. It stated:

> The overseeing of economic regulation by responsible public officials, necessary to assure effective discharge of agency responsibilities, cannot exist if the decisionmakers are immune from public concerns as expressed through their elected representatives . . . commissioners have a degree of independence that may serve to protect them from improper influence but was not intended to allow them to become unresponsive.[9]

The Ash Council went so far as to recommend the replacement of the IRCs by a single administrator directly responsible to the President. The council found the independent regulatory commissions to be ineffective for three reasons: "Collegial organization, the judicial caste of agency activities, and the misalignment of certain functional responsibilities."[10]

Besides Presidents, opposition to the IRCs has come from independent scholars. For example, Marver Bernstein states:

> Maintenance of the myth of commission independence represents a conscious effort by regulated groups to confine regulatory authority to an agency that is somewhat more susceptible than an executive department to influence, persuasion, and, eventually, capture and control.[11]

In short, Bernstein seems to be supporting the capture theory of regulation discussed in Chapter 2.

It is also argued by some that since the commissions are independent of the President, they do not get as much budget support as they would if they were an executive branch agency. As a result, the IRCs are budgetarily weak, which is therefore to the advantage of those private interests who oppose regulation.

In sum, the main thrust of the criticism against the independent regulatory commissions is that being independent they do not lead to an integrated and

---

[8]James M. Landis, "Report on the Regulatory Agencies to the President-Elect," in *Separation of Powers and the Independent Agencies: Cases and Selected Readings,* Subcommittee on Separation of Powers, Committee on the Judiciary, U.S. Senate, 1969.

[9]U.S. President's Advisory Council on Executive Organization, *A New Regulatory Framework Report on Selected Independent Regulatory Agencies,* U.S. Government Printing Office, Washington, D.C., 1971 (hereafter *Ash Council Report*), p. 40.

[10]Ibid., p. 20.

[11]Marver H. Bernstein, *Regulating Business by Independent Commission,* Princeton University Press, Princeton, N.J., 1955, p. 146.

coordinated regulatory policy and therefore they are not as effective as they are supposed to be.

3.5 APPRAISAL OF THE ARGUMENTS AGAINST INDEPENDENCE

The *Senate Study on Federal Regulation* evaluated most of the above criticisms and found that they are not so substantial as to render the independent form inappropriate for regulatory agencies. In particular, it found that:

1 Private interests will monitor their interests no matter where the regulatory agency is located, within or outside the executive branch. In its words: "Every regulatory body, wherever it is located, will be subject to pressure from the regulated industries."

2 Part of the blame for the failures of the commissions lies with the Congress. It has not always exercised its overseer role properly.[12]

3 Neither have the Presidents used their appointment power wisely. Most often, selection of the commissioners is left to lower-echelon White House staff, who have often followed the BOGSAT principle discussed previously.

4 Since there is very little political gain to the President from properly functioning commissions, Presidents have traditionally exhibited very little interest in the working of these commissions. The President steps in when there has been a scandal or wide newspaper publicity about the working of a particular commission. (Recall the interest in the Nuclear Regulatory Commission following the near mishap at the Three Mile Island plant).

5 It is not true that the IRCs are "miniature independent governments" or the "headless fourth branch of the government," for there are several checks on these commissions, as discussed in Section 3.3.

The real problem is not with the independent form, or the executive agency form for that matter; it is with the lack of coherent national policy toward regulation itself. That this is the case will be seen when we discuss specific forms of regulation later in the text.

3.6 CHOICE OF APPROPRIATE FORM FOR REGULATORY AGENCIES

In this chapter we have examined various organizational structures that have been created to administer various regulatory activities. Are there any criteria as to when one form is more appropriate than another? For example, when is the independent regulatory commission more appropriate? The fact that the IRCs are quasi-judicial would imply that if a regulatory activity involves quasi-judicial decisions, the independent form is the most appropriate administrative structure. But this need not be the case, for the EPA, although an executive branch agency, performs such a quasi-judicial function.

[12]See *Senate Study on Federal Regulation,* vol. II.

The answer depends on who creates the administrative structure. If it is left to the President, he would obviously prefer an agency administered by a single administrator who is directly responsible to him. On the other hand, if it is left to the Congress, it would generally favor a multimember independent commission, an ''arm of the Congress.'' Ultimately, the nature of the agency created is a political issue, very much influenced by the prevailing political atmosphere, and that atmosphere cannot be quantified nor predicated.

However, if one were to look to the past for guidance, one could say that the independent commissions are more appropriate where great importance is attached to group decision making, which requires compromise and accommodation of varying viewpoints and opinions. By the same token, where the procrastination of group decision making might prove detrimental to effectively carrying out the goals of regulation, an executive-type agency might be more appropriate. Of course, in some cases a compromise between the two may be necessary, and that is possible. Thus, the FERC, although an independent commission, is not totally independent of the Department of Energy because of the critical nature of the energy problem facing the nation. On the other hand, even the Ash Council recommended the retention of the FCC as an independent regulatory commission; the work of the commission, such as allocating the nation's valuable airways to the radio or TV networks, is too important to be left to the discretion of a single administrator. As yet another example, because of the very nature of its work, the National Highway Traffic Safety Administration (NHTSA), overlooking the safety performance of motor vehicles and motor vehicle drivers, is better off as an executive branch agency within the Department of Transportation.

3.7   SUMMARY AND CONCLUSIONS

The success of any regulation critically depends on the organizational structure created to administer it. In this chapter we examined the various forms of organizations that have been used to administer various regulatory laws. At one extreme there is the executive branch agency, headed by a single administrator who is directly responsible to the President. At the other end of the spectrum is the independent regulatory commission (IRC), run by several commissioners who are not directly answerable to the President.

Because of their importance, the bulk of the chapter was devoted to the IRCs. In particular, we examined how these commissions are established, the nature of their membership, the term of office of the members, and the process of selecting commission members.

We then discussed some of the problems facing these commissions, problems which raise some questions about the accountability and independence of these commissions. It was seen that the IRCs, although supposedly independent of presidential politics, are not totally independent of the government at large. There are several checks on these commissions. These checks involve the federal judiciary review of commission rulings, OMB review of commission budgets, OMB clearance of legislative proposals emanating from the commissions,

GAO supervision of the data gathering activities of the commissions, control of the litigious powers of the commissions by the Department of Justice, and the legislative veto.

We also examined some of the criticism leveled against the IRCs. Most of the criticism hinges on the point that the independent form makes it difficult to coordinate the nation's regulatory policies; the policies pursued by the commissions may not coincide with those espoused by the President. We also noted that the problem of coordination is not due to the independent form per se, but is due to not only the lack of congressional oversight of commission workings but also the lack of interest on the part of the President, the latter evidenced by the lesser importance attached by Presidents in selecting commission members.

In this connection we raised the broader question of the proper form of organization for regulatory agencies. We pointed out that the IRC is most appropriate in situations where group decision making is important, whereas an executive branch agency may be desirable in situations where decisions need to be made expeditiously. Of course, a compromise between the forms is possible in some cases, such as that of the Federal Energy Regulatory Commission. Ultimately, however, the proper form of regulatory organization is a function of both who creates it (Congress or the President) as well as the prevailing political atmosphere.

QUESTIONS

3-1 *The Butterfield case:* From 1968 to 1972 Alexander Butterfield (whose disclosure of the existence of the White House tapes broke open the now well-known Watergate scandal) was a deputy assistant to President Nixon and was in charge of scheduling the President's official day. By December 1972 he was eager for a more responsible position in one of the federal agencies. After the 1972 elections, someone in the White House suggested his name to head the Federal Aviation Agency (FAA), which is charged with the regulation of air safety. Although Butterfield had been a command pilot with 20 years of experience in the Air Force, he did not know much about the FAA, not even the fact that it is part of the Department of Transportation. When John Ehrlichman, President Nixon's domestic affairs advisor, called Butterfield about the FAA job, Butterfield, while talking to Mr. Ehrlichman, was looking at the *United States Government Manual* to find out the functions of the FAA. By the end of the conversation, he decided to accept the job. President Nixon did not discuss the appointment with Butterfield. Apparently, either Bob Haldeman, special assistant to the president, or John Ehrlichman informed the President that Butterfield would be suitable for the job. Butterfield was nominated for the job and the Senate routinely approved his name, although he was not prepared to answer even the few substantive questions put to him concerning the FAA.

What is the moral of the Butterfield case? What does it say about the appointment process to the regulatory agencies? (Details from *Senate Study on Federal Regulation,* vol.I, op. cit. pp. 4–7.

3-2 Do you agree with the following quotation? Why or Why not? What is needed is "continuous political monitoring of all government regulation to ensure its responsiveness to changing economic and social needs that the political process reflects." (Lloyed N. Cutter and David R. Johnson, "Regulation and the Political Process, *Yale Law Journal, June 1975, p. 1395).*

3-3 Do you agree with the statement that the independent regulatory commissions are really "stepchildren whose custody is contested by both the Congress and the Executive, but without very much affection from either"? (The quote is from William L. Cary in his, *Politics and the Regulatory Agencies, The Senate Study on Federal Regulation,* vol. V. p. 8).

3-4 Present the arguments for and against the operation of the Nuclear Regulatory Commission (NRC) by a single administrator directly responsible to the President.

3-5 What would be the consequences of making membership terms of the IRCs coextensive with the term of office of the President?

3-6 Could the following agencies be made executive branch agencies directly responsible to the President? Present your arguments clearly.

    1 National Credit Union Administration (which regulates and insures all federal credit unions and is an independent agency of the executive branch).

    2 National Labor Relations Board (which is responsible for preventing and remedying unfair labor practices by employers and labor organizations and conducting secret ballot elections to determine whether or not a group of employees want to join a union).

    3 U.S. Postal Service (which is an independent agency within the executive branch.)

3-7 Find out the functions of the following regulatory agencies:

    1 Federal Highway Administration

    2 Federal Aviation Administration

    3 Patent and Trade Mark Office (Department of Commerce)

    4 Commodity Credit Corporation

3-8 In a survey of lawyers, administrative law judges, and members of the Administrative Conferences of the United States concerning their views of the performance of commissioners and board members of eight federal regulatory agencies, the Congressional Research Service of the Library of Congress, the sponsor of the survey, obtained the results shown in Table 3.5. What general conclusions can you draw from the data given in Table 3.5?

TABLE 3.5

OPINION OF CURRENT MEMBERS OF COMMISSION/BOARD

(Mean Scores*)

Opinion	CAB	FCC	FMC	FPC	FTC	ICC	NRC	SEC
Confidence in judgment	4.0	4.2	4.4	4.4	4.6	3.8	4.3	34.
Confidence in technical knowledge	4.4	5.0	4.8	4.9	4.9	43.	3.6	3.0
Confidence in impartiality	3.7	3.8	4.0	3.8	4.5	3.1	4.2	3.0
Confidence in legal ability	4.0	4.5	4.7	4.7	4.6	4.1	4.0	3.1
Confidence of integrity	2.7	2.8	2.9	2.8	2.7	2.5	2.7	1.9
Confidence in members working hard	4.0	3.8	4.6	3.3	4.4	3.9	3.3	2.7
Confidence in relationship with staff	4.2	3.4	4.0	4.3	4.3	4.0	4.0	3.5

*Values in each column represent mean across on a scale running from 1 to 7. The higher the score, the less confidence the respondents had in the commission.

Source: Senate Study on Federal Regulation, vol. I: *The Regulatory Appointment Process,* U.S. Government Printing Office, January 1977, table 4, p. 289.

3-9 The survey mentioned in Question 3-8 also obtained the results shown in Table 3.6. What do these data reveal?

TABLE 3.6
HOW MANY OF THE CURRENT COMMISSIONERS / BOARD MEMBERS . . .
(Mean Scores*)

	CAB	FCC	FMC	FPC	FTC	ICC	NRC	SEC
. . . have the necessary training and experience to be federal regulators?	70.35	60.60	50.72	61.81	50.54	56.42	63.78	83.12
. . . have a record of fair and impartial decisionmaking?	70.66	66.22	54.55	67.01	42.05	74.49	62.01	78.47
. . . have an understanding of laws they administer?	69.37	60.84	49.47	60.12	55.16	62.36	55.70	81.87
. . . exhibit a high level of interest and commitment to their word as regulators?	71.03	64.22	52.55	70.97	55.90	68.02	72.57	87.18
. . . would you recommend the President reappoint based on their record of accomplishments?	51.11	51.2	39.17	46.32	35.60	53.06	48.08	70.62
. . . are effective?	51.67	55.5	42.55	51.65	40.80	52.44	54.04	75.0

*Values within each column represent the mean percent or average percent of current commissioners / board members who have these characteristics.
Source: Senate Study on Federal Regulation, vol. I: *The Regulatory Appointment Process,* U.S. Government Printing Office, January 1977, table 3, p. 288.

3-10 The survey mentioned above obtained additional data, shown in Table 3.7. What do the statistics in Table 3.7 reveal?

TABLE 3.7
RESPONSIVENESS OF THE CURRENT COMMISSION/BOARD MEMBERS
(Mean Scores*)

Responsiveness to:	CAB	FCC	FMC	FPC	FTC	ICC	NRC	SEC
Needs of industry	−.10	.26	.17	.59	−1.2	−.35	.7	−.46
Consumers	−.47	−.52	−.61	−.73	−.77	−.29	−.86	.04
The President	.71	.34	.46	.55	−.02	.14	.56	.42
Congress	.06	.15	.11	.12	.30	.42	.03	.29

*Numbers in columns represent the mean scores of a 7-point scale scored from −3 (unresponsive) to +3 (too responsive). A zero (0) represents "right amount" of responsiveness. Thus, scores around 0 represent the "best" score a commission could have received.

*Source: Senate Study on Federal Regulation, vol. I: The Regulatory Appointment Process, U.S. Government Printing Office, January 1977, table 5, p. 291.

3-11 Do you agree with the Ash Council recommendation to replace the IRCs with agencies administered by a single administrator? Why or why not?

CHAPTER 4

THE PROCESS
OF GOVERNMENT
REGULATION: METHODS
OF REGULATION

Once a decision has been made to regulate an activity, and once the appropriate administrative structure has been established, the most important question that arises is: What method or methods may be used so that the goals of regulation can best be achieved? Broadly speaking, the methods fall into six categories: (1) informal methods, typified by government persuasion, or ''jawboning''; (2) the standards enforcement approach, which specifies certain standards of performance or ways in which certain activities may be conducted, or both; (3) licensing, which is often a complement of the standards approach; (4) the economic incentives or disincentives approach, which, by subsidies or taxation, rewards a socially beneficial activity and discourages a socially undesirable activity; (5) the rate of return regulation, mostly applied to natural monopolies; and (6) the formation of public enterprises, such as the Tennessee Valley Authority (TVA) and Veterans Administration hospitals. In this chapter we take a closer look at these categories, illustrating them with examples and studying their relative merits and demerits.

4.1 INFORMAL METHODS: GOVERNMENT PERSUASION, OR ''JAWBONING''

Regulation need not always take the form of a regulatory law with specific directives in terms of the dos and dont's. The government can use the technique of ''jawboning,'' or moral suasion, to exhort someone to do or not to do something. Sometimes this can work. The most celebrated example is President John Kennedy's confrontation with the steel industry in 1962. Irked by the steel industry's price increases despite an economic recession then prevailing, President Kennedy tongue-lashed the executives of the industry for the price rises and threatened to cancel the steel orders by the Department of Defense. Although this was not a realistic threat, the industry gave in and rescinded the price increases for fear of adverse public reaction.

Since then, jawboning has been used by all Presidents. The so-called wage-price guidelines — the maximum percentage amount of increase in wages and prices — introduced in the Kennedy administration persisted in the Johnson administration and continued during the Nixon administration under the watchful eye of the Cost of Living Council and later under the Council on Wage and Price Stability (COWPS).[1] The COWPS became very visible during the Carter administration because of the high rate of inflation then prevailing — in March 1980 inflation reached an annual rate of 18 percent. But soon after taking office in January 1981, President Reagan abolished the COWPS because he felt that the council was "unnecessarily" interfering in private wage and price determinations. This decision may be short-sighted because, if nothing else, the council was collecting some useful data on wages and prices and publicizing them. This information gathering mechanism is useful in its own right.

The Federal Reserve System (FRS), the nation's central banker, also has resorted to jawboning from time to time. In times of high inflation the FRS has advised the banks who are members of the system to reduce the amount of loans they make. If the banks refuse to cooperate, the FRS, through its twelve Federal Banks (FEDs), can use several methods of compliance. For example, a recalcitrant bank may find it difficult to borrow from the FED (the lender of last resort), for borrowing from the FED is a privilege and not a right. Historical record shows that the moral suasion power of the FRS in conjunction with its other tools of monetary policy has had some success in curtailing business loans during inflationary periods, thereby slowing the rate of inflation to some extent.

One great advantage of jawboning is that it is a relatively costless method of achieving a desired goal. Moreover, it does not involve direct government intervention in the marketplace. Its greatest drawback is that it has no legal teeth to it and may not always work. There is also the temptation on the part of the President to use jawboning for political reasons, thus not addressing the root cause of a given problem. A rise in the price of a good or service may very well be due to the underlying supply and demand conditions. Jawboning in this case may threaten a genuine price increase. Moreover, if used repeatedly, jawboning loses its persuasion power.

4.2   THE STANDARDS APPROACH[2]

In contrast to the informal method of moral suasion, the standards approach is formal and mandates how a certain regulated activity may be done. The stan-

---

[1]The Council on Wage and Price Stability was established within the executive office of the President in 1974. The mission of the council was to monitor the economy as a whole with respect to such key economic indicators as wages, costs, productivity, profits, and prices.

[2]The following discussion leans heavily on the *Senate Study on Federal Regulation,* vol. VI: *Framework for Regulation,* ch. V.

dards approach may take two forms, namely, (1) performance standards and (2) specification standards.

Performance Standards

Performance standards prescribe some level of performance without specifying how it is to be achieved. Thus, the Environmental Protection Agency (EPA) may state the maximum level of emission for automobiles, or the Food and Drug Administration (FDA) may lay down the minimum amounts of nutritional standards for breakfast cereals or vitamin tablets, or the Occupational Safety and Health Act (OSHA) may prescribe the maximum noise level permissible in a workplace.

As a concrete example of performance standards, consider Table 4.1, which gives EPA emission standards for automobiles. Note that the standards listed in Table 4.1 do not specify the method or methods by which the auto industry should accomplish said standards. Therefore, the auto industry has considerable leeway as well as incentive to look for the method(s) which will accomplish the mandated objectives at the least possible cost.

Specification Standards

By contrast, specification standards are much more stringent in that they prescribe the means or methods that must be used to achieve a goal, such as the height of railings in a workplace, the design of cars, or the type of pollution control equipment that may be used. For example, the OSHA standard for rail-

TABLE 4.1
U.S. AUTOMOBILE EMISSION STANDARDS
(Grams per Mile)

	Hydrocarbons	Carbon monoxide	Nitrogen oxides
Uncontrolled car	8.7	87.0	4.0
Interim federal standards for 1975 and 1976	1.5	15.0	3.1
Interim California standards for 1975 and 1976	0.9	9.0	2.0
Ultimate target federal standards (as defined in the 1970 amendments to the Clean Air Act)	0.41	3.4	0.4

Source: "Air Quality and Automobile Emission Control," *Environmental Quality, The Fifth Annual Report of the Council on Environmental Quality, and National Academy of Sciences and National Academy of Engineering,* prepared for the Committee on Public Works, U.S. Senate, September 1974, vol. 4, *The Costs and Benefits of Automobile Emission Control,* p. 57 (reproduced from William J. Baumol and Alan S. Blinder, *Economics: Principles and Policy,* Harcourt, Brace, New York, 1979, p. 678).

ings is very specific — it requires that standard railing should have a top and intermediate rail, a height of 42 inches from upper surface of top rail to floor or platform, as well as other detailed requirements. Similarly, many FDA standards for food safety are based on regulation of the production process in accordance with Good Manufacturing Practice (GMP) standards. These standards, which have the force of law, concern such matters as equipment design and materials, cooling time, and work practices. Food not prepared according to GMP standards is considered adulterated and is subject to seizure. Another area in which specification standards are rigidly adhered to is that of nuclear power: The Nuclear Regulatory Commission (NRC) has laid down quite rigid standards in the construction and operation of nuclear power generating plants.

Performance versus Specification Standards

In general, a standards approach may be necessary in situations where potential risks are grave and consequences are severe or irreversible, as in the occupational health area (see Chapter 16 for the reasons). In these situations the problem is one of deciding between performance standards and specification standards. Since performance standards usually specify the threshold level (either maximum or minimum) of performance, they are more flexible; given sufficient time, alternative methods can be devised to accomplish them. Thus, there will be incentive to innovate.

Specification standards, on the other hand, are definite; they do not give much leeway to the industry or activity affected. However, there can be scope for genuine differences between the regulating authority and the regulated over the best means of achieving the goals of regulation.

Broadly speaking, one can say that performance standards, because of their flexibility, should be preferred to specification standards wherever possible. In the nuclear power generating area perhaps specification standards are inevitable, although there is no guarantee that there will be no mishaps, as the Three Mile Island plant so well demonstrated in 1979. (We have a great deal to say about the standards approach in Chapters 16 and 17.)

4.3 LICENSING

A variant of the standards approach, applied especially in the context of occupation or profession, is licensing. Broadly defined, the term *licensing* includes registration, certification, and licensing proper or licensure.

Registration   Individuals engaged in certain activities or professions list their names in some official register. For example, most economists belong to the American Economic Association. Similarly, statisticians are often associated with the American Statistical Association. Likewise, local businesses are often registered with local better business bureaus.

Certification More formal than registration, certification implies that the person with a certificate from a constituted authority has some requisite quality or competence. The Ph.D. degree in economics, for instance, certifies that the person holding it is a trained economist (a good one, it is hoped). Note, however, that the fact that a person does not have a Ph.D in economics does not mean that he or she cannot pursue economic consulting or teaching or research. Of course, if a Ph.D. in economics becomes a prerequisite to teach economics; then certification in essence becomes licensure, as discussed below.

Licensure, or Licensing Proper This procedure goes beyond certification or registration and requires that a person cannot engage in an activity without a license from a duly recognized authority. Thus, lawyers and doctors are licensed by state authorities with the blessing of their respective professional bodies, namely, the American Bar Association (ABA) and the American Medical Association (AMA). Practicing without a license in these areas is an offense punishable by civil and/or criminal sanctions.

Registration, the mildest form of regulation, can be justified on several grounds.[3] First, as in the case of registration of firearms, registration is a device to safeguard the public — in case of a crime involving firearms, registration may help to track down the owner(s) of such firearms. Second, by requiring, say, that all stores or businesses register with local authorities, the local governments can collect sales taxes which these entities collect from their customers. Finally, registration is often a means of protecting the public against fraud. Thus the requirement that all taxicab drivers display their registration certificates with their pictures on them helps cab passengers in identifying their drivers in case some problem arises.

Certification, although not as easy to justify as registration, has been defended on grounds of assuring that the person possessing a given certificate has some minimum quality or competence so that any one who wants to engage his or her services may be assured of some quality. Thus, a certified public accountant (CPA) may be better prepared to handle your tax problems than a novice. So long as certification is voluntary, there should not be any objection to it. Very often, however, certification is the most important step to licensure.

Licensure, the most stringent form of control over some occupations, is justified in situations where it is difficult to obtain or appraise information, where potential risks of mistakes are great, and where the spillover or neighborhood effects are substantial. In the medical field, for instance, an average citizen may not be able to form an informed opinion about the nature of an illness without the help of a trained doctor. Similarly, in the legal field, it might be dangerous for an individual to depend on a novice for advice or to plead his or her own case. It is argued that a licensed doctor or lawyer has gone through the rigor of

---

[3]For further discussion, see Milton Friedman, *Capitalism and Freedom,* The University of Chicago Press, 1962, ch. IX.

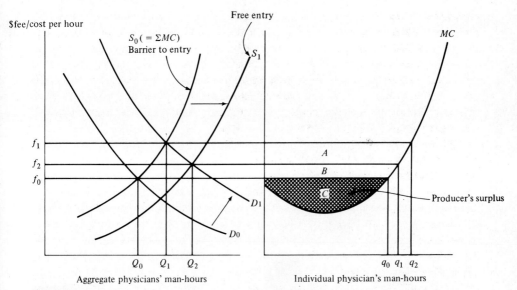

FIGURE 4.1
Demand and supply curves for physician's services under free entry and under barriers to entry conditions.

training and has passed the examination(s) given by the licensing board so that the dangers mentioned above may be minimized.

Although there may be certain advantages to licensing doctors and lawyers, there are also serious social costs that go with it. Very often, professional bodies such as the ABA or AMA use the licensing power as an entry-controlling device to assure a high level of income for the members of such bodies.[4] It has been argued by scholars that the AMA has restricted entry by first influencing the Council on Medical Education and Hospitals of the American Medical Association to approve medical schools and then determining how many students can enter medical schools. Those who finish medical training are later required to appear for examinations given by the licensing boards approved by the AMA. Interestingly enough, all this is done with the blessing of the local or state authorities (the capture theory?).

To see how by controlling the supply of physicians the AMA or any professional body can increase physicians' fees and thereby their income, consider Figure 4.1. Figure 4.1(b) shows the marginal cost curve of a single physician: After a certain number of hours worked per day (or per week), the MC curve slopes upward, reflecting the fact that the disutility of work increases as the

[4]But C. M. Lindsay in his article, "Real Returns to Medical Education", *Journal of Human Resources* (vol. 8, Summer 1973) argues that so far as the medical profession is concerned this may not be so when account is taken of the loss of leisure because doctors reportedly work 62 hours a week. This figure is subject to questions, however.

number of hours worked increases. The aggregate supply curve S_0 (and S_1) shown in panel (a) is obtained by summing such individual MCs (see any elementary microeconomics text on this). D_0 represents the aggregate demand curve for the physicians' services. Initially the equilibrium price (fee) and quantity are f_0 and Q_0, respectively. The individual physician, under competitive conditions, will take the fee f_0 as given and supply q_0 hours of work. The return over the cost (technically known as the producer's surplus) at this fee is given by the crosshatched area C.

Assume that the demand for physicians' services increases and is now given by the demand curve D_1. If there are no barriers to entry into the medical profession (via restrictions on the number of admissions to the medical schools or restrictive board examinations), eventually the supply curve will shift to the right, as shown by S_1 (why?). Therefore, the new equilibrium fee and quantity supplied will be f_2 and Q_2, the individual physician supplying the additional quantity q_0q_1 and earning additional producer's surplus of the area B. But suppose the AMA imposes entry barriers and does not let the supply curve shift to S_1 (i.e., keeps it at the level S_0). This has the effect of increasing the fees to f_1 and reducing the aggregate quantity supplied to the level Q_1. Because of the higher fee, however, the individual physician belonging to the AMA not only increases work by q_1q_2 hours but also adds to producer's surplus by the amount of the area A. Thus, the entry restriction has increased the fees as well as the income of those physicians who are fortunate enough to belong to the professional body with monopoly powers.

4.4   THE INCENTIVES APPROACH

Instead of relying on the standards approach discussed in Section 4.2 one may use economic incentives or disincentives to achieve the objectives of regulation. The incentives generally involve tax concessions, subsidies, fees, compliance penalties, etc. The general philosophy of these incentives is that they will propel the regulated party to take actions that will fulfill the stated goals of regulation as best as possible. For example, referring to Table 4.1: The federal government may devise a tax scheme such that if the auto industry does succeed in reducing the level of hydrocarbons from 8.7 grams per mile to 0.41 grams per mile, there will be no tax on the industry, but if it does not meet the target, it will pay a certain tax, say, so many cents per car-mile for so many additional units of hydrocarbon in excess of 0.41 grams per mile.

The crux of the incentives approach is that economically it may not always be feasible to meet either the performance or the specification standards. There is some trade-off involved between absolute adherence to the standards and the economic costs involved. As we shall show shortly, instead of insisting that the air be completely free from pollution, which can be obtained by abolishing all automobiles (or worse yet if we all stop breathing, for we exhale carbon dioxide which is a polluter), we can talk about the "optimal" or the "best" amount of pollution that we can tolerate without harming us unduly.

The optimal amount of, say, air pollution can be determined by the celebrated economic principle of cost-benefit analysis, which states that the benefit obtained from, say, reducing air pollution by a stated amount is just equal to the cost of that reduction. More technically, the optimal amount of air pollution is achieved when the marginal benefit of air pollution reduction by a given amount is equal to the marginal cost of that reduction. A further reduction from this level, although technically feasible, is not economically viable, for the additional cost involved in obtaining such a reduction means a decrease in other things (e.g., housing, education, clothing, travel, etc.) the consumer enjoys. The consumer does not want absolutely pure air, or absolutely pure water, at any cost. Unfortunately, this commonsensical principle is often neglected by the regulators. (For additional discussion, see Chapter 17.)

Let us look at some specific incentive mechanisms that have been used or have been recommended from time to time.

Direct Subsidies

By *subsidies* we mean cash or other valuable benefits given to an individual or a group of people or a business entity. It is a kind of negative income tax whereby the government instead of collecting money from taxes actually pays out money or similar benefits.

Cash Subsidies Subsidies can take many forms. Cash is the most visible of them. The best-known example of cash subsidy is the federal Aid to Families with Dependent Children (AFDC) program, which gives money to families in which there are dependent children but the father or mother or both do not or cannot work for a variety of reasons. Another well-known example is the government's farm price-support program. Since the great depression, the government has supported the price of many products. For example, in 1980 the government-supported price of wheat was $3.63 per bushel. If the market price of wheat was, say, $3.28, the government in effect would buy it from farmers at $3.63 and sell it for $3.28, thus subsidizing the farmers to the tune of $0.35 per bushel.[5] The avowed purpose of this subsidy was to guarantee the farmers some minimum level of income in view of the fluctuating nature of most agricultural prices. Yet another example is the cash subsidies granted the domestic airlines so that they can continue providing air services to economically unprofitable smaller-town and rural areas which would otherwise be without such service (see Chapter 12 for a further discussion of such subsidies to airlines).

Benefit-in-Kind Another type of subsidy is benefit-in-kind. The federal food stamps program is a case in point. Under this program, poor families buy food

---

[5]In the past, the Commodity Credit Corporation (CCC) purchased wheat from the farmers. The CCC was established in 1933 with the purpose of stabilizing and protecting farm income and farm prices.

stamps (vouchers) from the government at less than the face value of the stamps and redeem them at grocery stores. The difference between the face value of the vouchers and the cost the families incur to obtain them represents subsidy-in-kind. If this difference were to be given in cash, that would constitute cash subsidy. It was believed that such cash subsidies would not be utilized by the poor families for food purposes and might be dissipated on frivolous items. However, some families sell the food stamps for cash, thus defeating the purpose of the stamps.

Other examples of subsidy-in-kind are the government's Medicare and Medicaid programs. The Medicare program, passed by Congress in 1965, is a federal health insurance scheme for people over 65 who are covered by Social Security. It provides for compulsory hospital insurance covering up to 60 days for each occurrence of illness. The beneficiary pays a small amount toward the hospital cost ($104 in 1978), the rest being borne by the government. The government collects payroll taxes from employers of 1.8 percent of payroll, in addition to the Social Security payroll tax, to finance the cost of this program. The same act established the Medicaid program, which helps medically needy people. The cost of this program is shared equally by state and federal governments.

Loan Guarantee Yet another form of subsidy involves loan or credit guarantees by the government. A recent example is the $1.5 billion bank loan given the financially ailing Chrysler Corporation, guaranteed by federal government. The proponents of such aid to the Chrysler Corporation argued that without such a loan guarantee it would not be able to raise money in the private market, thus spelling bankruptcy for the corporation and all the consequences that follow from such a major bankruptcy, especially the loss of jobs for thousands of workers. This guarantee is an implicit subsidy, for without it the needy company would not have been able to secure the loan, or could secure it only at a prohibitively high rate of interest; a lender is bound to expect a high-risk premium from a borrower with financial difficulties. This guarantee seems to have helped Chrysler, for not only did the company pay back a substantial part of the guaranteed loan but has been able to record some impressive sales gains and gains for its stockholders. When things were grim, Chrylser stock dipped below $4 a share, but in June 1983 it bounced over $35 a share. Another example of such assistance is the Export-Import Bank of the United States (Eximbank), which provides below market rate loans to needy American exporters.

Such loan guarantees are not confined to the private sector. In the spring of 1975 New York City nearly went bankrupt. But at the last moment the federal government stepped in by providing the city with $1.26 billion in loans and promising an additional $2.3 billion for 1976 and 1977. These loan guarantees made it possible for New York State to borrow on behalf of the city to weather the crisis. — Like Chrysler, New York City has bounced back from its fiscal crisis.

Table 4.2 gives some idea about the magnitude of the government's subsidy program. The table shows that there has been a vast increase in the government's subsidy programs, direct as well as in-kind, in several important cate-

TABLE 4.2
SUMMARY OF FEDERAL SUBSIDY AND RELATED PROGRAM COSTS
(Billions)

	Direct cash subsidies			Credit subsidies			Benefit-in-kind subsidies			Total order of magnitude		
	1970	1975	1978	1970	1975	1978*	1970	1975	1978*	1970	1975	1978*
Agriculture	$4.4	$0.6	N/A	$0.4	$0.7	$1.7	—	—	—	$4.8	$1.4	$1.7
Food	—	0.6	—	—	—	—	1.5	5.9	8.8	1.5	5.9	8.8
Health	0.8	3.3	—	—	—	—	4.6	10.2	17.3	5.4	10.5	17.3
Manpower	2.0	5.0	—	0.1	0.1	—	0.1	0.1	—	2.0	3.4	0.0
Education	1.9	—	—	0.1	0.9	0.4	0.4	0.4	—	2.4	5.5	0.4
International	0.1	1.7	—	0.6	0.1	1.5	—	—	—	0.7	0.9	1.5
Housing	0.1	—	—	3.0	—	3.7	—	—	3.0	3.0	2.8	6.7
Natural resources and energy	0.1	0.1	—	—	—	0.1	0.1	0.1	—	0.1	0.3	0.0
Transportation	0.3	0.6	—	—	—	0.1	0.2	1.7	—	0.5	2.2	0.1
Commerce	2.0	0.3	—	0.1	0.1	0.6	1.8	1.9	—	3.9	2.2	0.6
Other	—	—	—	0.1	—	—	—	—	—	0.1	0.1	0.0
Total order of magnitude†	11.6	12.3	N/A	4.1	2.9	8.0	8.8	20.2	29.1	24.5	35.4	37.1

*Estimate based on incomplete data.

†Individual items may not add to totals because of rounding error. The total order of magnitude for 1978 will be greater than $37.1 billion when direct cash subsidies are included.

Source: Joint Economic Committee, U.S. Congress, *Federal Subsidy Programs: A Staff Study* (Washington, D.C.: Oct. 18, 1974), p. 5. The data for fiscal years 1970 and 1975 are taken directly from the 1974 JEC staff study. The data have been updated to 1978. The inclusion of benefit-in-kind subsidies is an arbitrary decision; these programs could not be categorized as transfer payments (reproduced from the Committee for Economic Development, *Redefining Government's Role in the Market System,* p. 49).

gories, the most noticeable being in the areas of health and education. Because of incomplete data, it is not possible to find out the magnitudes of subsidies in several important areas for 1978 but, judging from the growth rates between 1970 and 1975, they are expected to have been quite sizable.

Table 4.3 gives some estimates of federal loans and loan guarantees for the years 1977 to 1979. As can be seen from the table each of the categories listed therein showed substantial year-to-year increases. In sheer dollar amount, these loans and guarantees amounted to about $100 billion in 1979.

Regardless of the form of the subsidy, the important question is: Why are such subsidies given? The advocates of subsidies contend that because of one or more market failures discussed in Chapter 2 the prices, output, and product mixes that result from the operation of the marketplace are not socially optimal. Therefore, subsidies in these situations will lead to optimal results. Recall the spillin-type externality considered in Chapter 2, say, as represented by Figure 2.4(b). In this case because the social costs are less than the private costs (at all levels of output), the private market produces only q_1 units of output whereas from society's viewpoint the optimal output should have been q_2. Therefore, in this case a corrective subsidy equal to the difference between P_1 and P_2 per unit output will bring forth the socially desirable additional output of q_1q_2. More often than not, however, this advocacy is superficial; the real reason for the subsidies is income redistribution, not to remedy any market failure. The real purpose of the farm price-support program,, for example, is simply to guarantee the farmers a certain level of income.

Another question that may be raised is: Are subsidies a viable (i.e., less costly) alternative to direct regulation? For example, the Civil Aeronautics Board (CAB) has for many years permitted the practice of *cross-subsidization* in the airline industry, whereby fares on long-distance travel are deliberately kept above their incremental or marginal cost and those on short-distance travel are deliberately kept below their marginal cost. In effect, the long-distance travelers are

TABLE 4.3
NEW FEDERAL CREDIT EXTENDED, FISCAL YEARS 1977–1979
(Millions)

Type of credit assistance	1977	1978*	1979*
Direct loans, on budget	$21,854	$29,361	$26,575
Direct loans, off budget	13,558	16,871	17,575
Guaranteed loans†	40,794	44,669	53,354
Total	76,206	90,901	97,504

*Estimates.
†Primary guarantees, adjusted.
Source: Office of Management and Budget, Executive Office of the President, *Special Analyses: Budget of the United States Government, Fiscal Year 1979,* Special Analysis F, pp. 127, 128, 140 (reproduced from The Committee for Economic Development, *Redefining Government's Role in the Market System,* New York, 1979, p. 51).

subsidizing the short-distance travelers. Economists generally agree that in this case direct subsidies may be preferable to direct regulation via cross-subsidies. This is because if each type of air travel were to be priced according to its marginal cost, there would be optimal production of total travel (see also Section 12-4). But cross-subsidies discourage long-distance travel and encourage short-distance travel, thus artificially changing the output mix. Similarly, serious economists argue that instead of controlling the price of gasoline (because of the monopoly power of OPEC), it is better for the market to determine the price of gasoline and for the government to directly subsidize poor consumers who are severely affected by the higher market-determined price of gasoline. (The topic of cross-subsidization is discussed in greater detail in Chapter 11, Section 7.)

Although used extensively, the method of subsidy can be criticized on the ground that it leads to serious misallocation of resources. The farm price-support program, cross-subsidization of air travel, and controlling the price of gasoline are but a few examples of misallocation of economic resources. A few more examples will illustrate the point further. As is well known, the interstate price of natural gas is controlled by the Department of Energy, but not the price of intrastate gas; until the recent deregulatory moves by Congress, the former was much lower than the latter. As a result, gas-producing states were not willing to ship much gas out of their states. This is the root cause of the so-called natural gas shortage. (See Chapter 13 for further discussion of natural gas pricing.)

The subsidies given by the federal government to the U.S. maritime industry is another illustration of misallocation of resources. By the Merchant Marine Act of 1936, the Federal Maritime Commission (FMC) pays ``construction differential subsidies'' for new vessels built in American shipyards. The maximum amount of the subsidy can equal the difference between United States and estimated foreign ship construction costs, up to the maximum of 50 percent of the cost. During 1971 to 1975 such subsidies amounted to $811 million. There is no question that such subsidies lead to misallocation of resources, and more so because of the cost-plus nature of U.S. shipping construction costs, whereby the shipbuilders receive some markup (profit) over their costs. Naturally, there is little incentive to cut construction costs, at least up to the limit of the subsidy (50 percent of the cost). Nonetheless, such subsidies are given in the name of national defense and national security.

Indirect or "Invisible" Subsidies

Sometimes subsidies, instead of being given overtly in cash or cash-equivalent benefits, are given in kind. Some examples are: land grants made to railroads or to some state universities, known as land-grant universities;[6] payment of above

---

[6]A land-grant university is a state educational institution on land given by the federal government under provision of the Morill Act of 1862, on the condition that it offer courses in agriculture and the mechanical arts.

competitive prices for the purpose of government stockpiling of some goods (e.g., military stockpiling); the usage by water carriers of government-improved and -financed rights-of-way without paying toll for their use; use by air carriers of air traffic control systems without paying the full cost of the system; reservation of the market for domestic shipping companies, as in the case of restriction of all military cargo movement and half of government shipments to the American flag fleet, or the cabotage or "coasting laws," which reserve commerce along and between Atlantic and Pacific coasts to domestically built U.S. flag ships.

Although all these subsidies are "invisible" in the sense that they do not appear explicitly in the government budget, they are quite sizable. For example, it has been estimated that during busy hours the subsidized air traffic control system of Chicago's O'Hare Airport costs the government about $1000 per general aviation flight. As another example, it has been estimated that between 1952 and 1972 the Military Sealift Command paid indirectly up to $3.8 billion because it chartered the U.S. flag vessels, whose charter rates were twice the foreign rates.

What justification can be offered for all these subsidies? Recalling our discussion about the theories of regulation in Chapter 2, we cannot offer much economic justification for all these "invisible" subsidies from the viewpoint of allocative efficiency. Such subsidies increase the cost of business, especially for the government, which means ultimately the taxpayers are footing the bill. There is little doubt that the cargo preference and cabotage laws are sheerly for the benefit of the American merchant shipping industry, although the industry would argue that such subsidies are justified in the name of national security. Can they be justified from the distributive equity viewpoint? It is difficult to say whether subsidies, direct or "invisible," can be so justified because they involve the very difficult task of comparing losses and gains of those who are adversely affected and those who are favorably affected by them.[7]

Tax Preferences

Sometimes subsidies are disguised in the form of preferential tax treatment for certain groups, the avowed objective being either to encourage an activity if it is beneficial or to discourage it if it is harmful to society. But very often these benefits are a ruse for transferring income from one group to another. Like subsidies, these preferential tax benefits can take several forms.

Tax Preference for Extractive Industries   Mineral industries, such as oil, copper, etc., are allowed by law a percentage depletion allowance whereby they can deduct a certain percentage of their gross sales revenue as a tax-deductible item in determining profits. Such depletion allowance is, in effect, accelerated

---

[7]On this difficult question of comparing interpersonal gains and losses, see Edward N. Gramlich, *Benefit-Cost Analysis of Government Programs,* Prentice-Hall, Englewood Cliffs, N.J., 1981, ch. 7.

depreciation which allows these industries to write off their investment costs faster than would be the case otherwise. The proponents of depletion allowance argue that extracting, say, oil is a risky business — eight out of ten wells dug turn out to be dry or without oil. Without such a rapid tax write-off the oil industry would find it difficult to attract venture or risk capital into the industry.

Selected Regulatory Tax Preferences Depletion allowance is but one form of tax preference. Others involve special tax treatment for specific industries or for specific purposes. Thus, Congress has allowed for rapid amortization (write-off) for pollution control equipment installed before 1976 in order to ease the financial burden of compliance with the air pollution control laws. Similary, to stimulate U.S. shipping, Congress allows U.S. vessel operators to defer payment of taxes on earnings if such earnings are deposited in a Capital Construction Fund (CCF). Such deposits as well as any income earned from them by way of interest or dividend are tax-deferred. Not only that, but if funds are drawn from the CCF to buy a US–built vessel, those funds (recall that they are deferred earnings) are completely tax-exempt.

Energy-Related Tax Preferences To conserve energy usage, the National Energy Act, passed during the Carter administration, allows owners of residences who install energy-conserving equipment (insulation, etc.) to claim tax credit up to 15 percent of the first $2000 spent on such equipment, but subject to the maximum amount of $300.

The magnitude of all these tax preferences for the years 1970, 1975, and 1978 can be seen from Table 4.4, the 1978 estimates being tentative. What is

TABLE 4.4
DIFFERENTIAL LOWER TAX TREATMENT
(Billions)

	1970	1975	1978
Agriculture	$0.9	$1.1	$1.1
Health	3.2	5.8	9.8
Manpower	0.6	0.7	4.3
Education	0.8	1.0	1.7
International	0.3	1.5	2.1
Housing	8.7	12.9	16.0
Natural resources and energy	2.0	4.1	3.1
Transportation	—	0.1	0.9
Commerce and industry	14.1	19.3	33.8
Other	9.4	13.1	22.6

Source: Joint Economic Committee, U.S. Congress, *Federal Subsidy Programs* (Washington, D.C., U.S. Government Printing Office, October 1974), p. 5; and Office of Management and Budget, Executive Office of the President, *Special Analyses: Budget of the United States Government, Fiscal Year 1979*, pp. 148–174 (reproduced from the Committee for Economic Development, *Redefining Government's Role in the Market System*, New York, 1979, p. 47).

revealing here is the steady increase in such tax benefits over the years, especially in the areas of housing and commerce and industry.

From the preceding discussion it is apparent that these tax preferences are essentially regulatory in character, for they are intended to achieve one or more goals of regulation, be it the development of natural resources, encouragement of domestic production of goods and services, or the reduction of dependence on foreign oil. A pertinent question is: Do these schemes have any side effects; that is, in conferring preferential tax benefits to some groups, do they distort the allocation of scarce economic resources?

There is little doubt that the aforementioned proposals have undesirable side effects or negative externalities. For example, the oil depletion allowance may lead to more rapid and uneconomic exploitation of economic resources: without such allowance, oil producers will extract depletable natural resources only when the present value of those resources exceeds their present cost of exploitation, given the expected rate of return on investment. Besides rapid exploitation of natural resources, there is the question of environmental degradation. (But more on this in Chapter 17.) Similarly, the rapid amortization of pollution control equipment may in fact lead producers to install expensive and more capital-intensive equipment — a kind of Averch-Johnson effect.[8] Likewise, would not homeowners insulate their homes to save fuel cost even if no rebate were given for such insulation?

Effluent Taxes or Fees

In situations where there is divergence between private and social costs because of externalities (see Chapter 2), the method of taxes or fees or user charges may be used to bring about equality between them. In other words, taxes and fees can be used to "internalize" the spillout effects.

To see how taxes can be used for this purpose, consider the case of air pollution. The advantages of clean air are obvious, but pollutant-free air is not a free good. Its acquisition requires some costs, costs involved in installing air pollution control equipment. For the sake of simplicity, assume that the benefits and costs of clean air are represented by their respective curves, as shown in Figure 4.2.

As Figure 4.2 shows, the incremental or marginal cost of obtaining clean air increases with the degree of cleanliness (why?). On the other hand, the incremental or marginal benefit of clean air decreases as the purity of air increases (recall the law of diminishing utility). We can interpret the marginal benefit (*MB*) curve as the demand curve and the marginal cost (*MC*) curve as the supply curve of clean air. Then, from elementary supply and demand analysis it follows

---

[8]In their article, "Behavior of the Firm under Regulatory Constraints," *American Economic Review,* vol. 52, December 1962, authors Harvey Averch and Leland L. Johnson have demonstrated why regulation of public utility rates might lead to overinvestment in capital, that is, investment in excess of what is socially desirable.

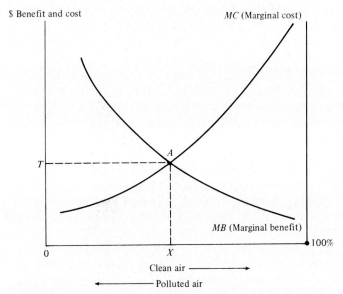

FIGURE 4.2
Optimum amount of clean air and optimum amount of air pollution tax.

that the equilibrium or optimum quantity of clean air is *OX* and the equilibrium price is *OT*. Therefore, if the government imposes an air pollution tax (or an effluent tax in case of water pollution) equal to *OT*, there will be every incentive to air polluters to install pollution control equipment up to *OX* level of cleanliness, for up to this level the *MC* is less than the *MB* and it is also less than the tax *OT*. Beyond *OX*, however, the polluters will simply pay the amount of the tax *OT*, for beyond *OX* the *MC* is greater than the *MB* but is less than *OT*. We can call *OT* the optimum level of the pollution tax.

The preceding discussion points out one important fact of (economic) life, namely, that the goal of 100 percent clean air, however desirable, is not economically viable, for the cost of accomplishing this far exceeds the benefits, as the Figure 4.2 shows vividly.

Economists generally favor effluent-type taxes to direct control of pollution (air, water, noise, etc.) by establishing mandatory standards, because the former approach is more economical and comparatively easy to monitor: Once the level of clean air and the corresponding level of effluent tax are fixed, the government's job is to see that a given plant or factory sticks to the standard or pay the fine. Moreover, this approach does not tell the factory owner how to go about achieving the prescribed standard; the owner is free to use whatever technology deemed appropriate. Note that such effluent taxes have been used successfully in West Germany's Ruhr valley, a highly industrialized area with limited water supply, and they have helped to maintain the water quality of local rivers in the valley. (In Chapter 17 we will go more deeply into the economics of such taxes versus the standards approach and consider their relative merits and demerits).

Marketable Pollution Rights or Emission Permits

A novel alternative to effluent charges for pollution problems is marketable or saleable pollution rights, or emission permits. Although not yet implemented by any environmental regulatory agency, the idea behind this approach can be explained with the aid of Figure 4.3.

As noted elsewhere, according to the Council on Environmental Quality, an average car emits about 87 grams of carbon monoxide per mile of driving. Under the Clean Air Act the maximum amount of carbon monoxide that will be ultimately allowed will be about 3.4 grams per mile. Suppose the EPA determines that in a given town no more than 34,000 grams of carbon monoxide can be emitted during a day by car drivers. To ensure this, suppose the EPA decides to auction off competitively 10,000 permits, each permit entitling the buyer to emit no more than 3.4 grams of carbon monoxide per mile of driving. The resulting supply of emission permits is fixed and therefore the supply curve of these permits is vertical (or perfectly inelastic), as shown in Figure 4.3. The demand curve for pollution rights, like the demand curve for any commodity, is downward-

FIGURE 4.3
Hypothetical demand and supply curves for pollution permits.

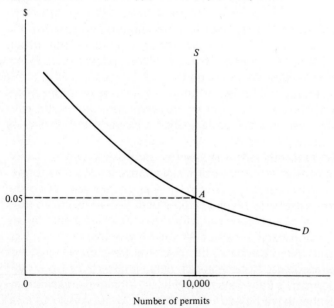

sloping: The lower the price of emission rights, the higher the quantity demanded, assuming all other things remain the same. Now at *A*, the demand curve intersects the fixed supply curve resulting in 5 cents as the equilibrium price per permit. Thus, if I want to drive 10 miles a day and my car emits 17 grams of carbon monoxide per mile, I will need 50 emission permits at a cost of $2.50 ($10 \times 17 \div 3.4 = 50$ permits).

As the hypothetical example above shows, the emission permit essentially acts like a tax, albeit a novel one. But it has advantages over direct taxation. First, because the maximum quantity of pollution is determined in advance, there is no uncertainty about the level of pollutants tolerated in the air. Second, an ordinary tax fixed in a dollar amount becomes less burdensome during inflationary periods because of the loss in the purchasing power of the dollar. Therefore, polluters may simply pay the (emission) tax and not worry about the quality of the air. But this is not possible with emission rights, for it specifies the maximum amount of pollution tolerated, which is independent of any monetary value. Of course, there are some disadvantages to this approach. The very idea of selling permits to pollute air, even in small amounts, is not politically appealing. Then there is the big question about deciding the maximum allowable quantity of pollutants, which, by the way, exists for other methods of pollution control. The bureaucrats may impose unrealistic standards, which may have the side effect of slowing down economic growth. (For additional discussion, see Chapter 17.)

4.5 UNITIZATION

In Chapter 2 we discussed that in the ''common pool'' resources situations without clearly defined property rights (e.g., fishing in the nation's waterways) the government has a definite role to play to stave off inefficient exploitation of such resources. But, as noted there, even where the property rights are well-defined, the common pool problem may be so serious as to demand government's attention. The case in point is two oil wells owned by two owners, A and B, located in proximity of each other and drawing oil from the common subterranean oil field. Now when A draws oil he affects B's output by drawing away the fugitive oil and by reducing gas pressure. Under private ownership, therefore, there is every temptation for A to pump oil faster to capture oil from B's land. Of course, B is not going to sit idly by. Similarly, both A and B will be tempted to drill as many oil wells as possible to get as much oil out as possible. The end result would be inefficient oil pumping and oil drilling.

One solution to the problem is ''unitization'', that is merger of the two owners for the purpose of producing oil under the unified control of, say, a jointly appointed manager and dividing the production pro rata. This would avoid the temptation of inefficient oil production as before, because now whatever output is produced will be shared proportionately and it does not matter from whose oil field the oil is produced.

4.6   RATE OF RETURN REGULATION OF NATURAL MONOPOLIES

As we saw in Chapter 2, in cases of natural monopolies (declining average cost over a wide range of output) it is preferable to have a single firm (i.e., monopoly) providing a particular good or service than several competing ones (see Figure 2.3). That is why there is a single company providing gas, electricity, or phone service in a town or similar political division. Now, as we shall show in Chapter 6, such monopolies may not be allowed to pursue the price-output mix they choose because such a mix may not be in the best interest of their consumers. Typically, such monopolies are allowed to charge prices which guarantee them a reasonable rate of return on their invested capital. State or local public utility commissions are generally entrusted with the job of determining this rate of return, which may range between 10 and 14 percent on the invested capital. (Some additional details of how the utility commissions determine fair rates of return are given in Chapter 6.)

4.7   PUBLIC ENTERPRISES[9]

Public enterprises represent the extreme form of government regulation. Local, state, or the federal government may decide to provide a good or service either directly or by heavy public subsidies via a public enterprise which may be totally or partially controlled by the government.

Table 4.5 gives a list of some of the public enterprises in the United States by the degree of control as well as by the amount of subsidies given. As this table shows, there are a variety of public enterprises in the United States, notwithstanding the popular impression that the country is dominated by private enterprises. The question that arises immediately is: Why public enterprises? The reasons are many.

First, many developing countries leaning toward socialism (broadly defined as an economic system in which the means of production such as capital equipment, buildings, and land are owned by the state) go in for public enterprises, especially in the key sectors of the economy. In India, for example, industries such as airlines, steel, coal, railroads, telephone, telegraph, and many others are publicly owned; the first prime minister of India, Jawaharlal Nehru, believed that a resource-poor country like India could ill afford to trust these enterprises to the private sector. The subsequent events have proved him to be wrong, but that is another story.

Second, as we noted in Chapter 2, the private sector is generally not interested in the provision of pure public goods. Therefore, both in the advanced and developing countries provision of such goods has become a government monopoly.

Third, sometimes semipublic goods (e.g., education) are provided by public

---

[9]For an extended discussion, see William G. Shepherd and Claire Wilcox, *Public Policies Toward Business,* 6th ed., Richard D. Irwin, Homewood, Ill., 1977, Part IV.

TABLE 4.5
SELECTED PUBLIC ENTERPRISES IN THE UNITED STATES BY DEGREE OF CONTROL AND PUBLIC SUBSIDY

Full subsidy	Weapons purchasing and management	Census bureau	
	Veterans Administration hospitals	Corps of Engineers	Primary education
	Military R&D contracting	Prisons	Child-care programs
Degree of public subsidy	SST programs	Mental hospitals	Public law
	Public universities	Federal maritime programs	Federal courts
	Medicaid		Municipal transit
	Medicare	Local courts	Social Security
	Public housing	State courts	U.S. Government Printing Office
	Performing arts centers	Airports	AEC enrichment plants
	Tennessee Valley Authority	FAA programs	Municipal utilities (water, sewage)
	FHA housing program	Amtrak	
	Federal research board	National land management	
	Port of New York Authority	State liquor stores	
No subsidy	**Slight control**	**Partial control**	**Full control**

Deree of effective control

Source: William G. Shepherd and Claire Wilcox, *Public Policies Toward Business,* 6th ed., Irwin, Homewood, Ill., 1979, table 16-1, p. 407 (adapted).

authorities in the belief that the private sector may not provide them in the quantity desired by the public.

Fourth, public enterprises are often a means of taking over sick or declining industries. The railroad industry in the United States has been in decline for many years now, and the government has been forced to subsidize some railroads heavily or absorb some of the bankrupt ones, the most famous bankruptcy being that of the *Penn Central.* Although we will discuss this question further in Chapter 11, note here that a public takeover in this situation may be justifiable not only from the viewpoint of saving thousands of jobs, but also to provide a ready means of transportation in cases of national emergencies, not to mention the need to do so in view of soaring oil prices, which may make public transportation, because of scale economies, cheaper than private motor transportation.

Regardless of the reasons for public ownership, public enterprises face the same optimal pricing-output-investment decisions that private enterprises do.

But unlike private enterprises, public enterprises, especially the ones in developing countries, do not follow the criterion of profit maximization. As a result, many such enterprises run into losses year after year because of lack of efficiency, which is often the result of the top-heavy bureaucracy often created to run such enterprises. But there is no reason why efficient allocation of scarce economic resources is any less of a criterion simply because an enterprise is run by the government.

4.8 SUMMARY AND CONCLUSIONS

Having explored the regulatory structure in the previous chapter, we examined in this chapter the various methods that have been or can be used by regulatory authorities to achieve the goals or regulation. Broadly speaking, there are six methods of regulation, namely, informal methods, the standards approach, licensing, economic incentives or disincentives, rate of return, and public enterprises.

The informal approach is typified by the technique of "jawboning," or moral suasion, by which the government or a regulatory body tries to bring moral pressure to accomplish one or more objectives, such as wage, price, interest, or dividend control during inflationary times. Although the method of jawboning is toothless in the sense that it has no legal compliance power, used judiciously it can be effective, at least in the short run. It is not a long-run or permanent solution because it may not necessarily answer the root cause of the problem.

The standards approach, performance or specification, may be necessary in situations where potential risks are great and consequences severe. If a choice is possible, it is preferable to use performance standards rather than specification standards because the former are more flexible than the latter — performance standards specify only the maximum or minimum level of a given activity whereas specification standards tell how an activity must or should be done. Perhaps in the area of nuclear power strict specification standards may be called for, especially in view of the scare generated by the near mishap at Three Mile Island plant.

Licensing, a variant of the standards approach, is often used as a regulatory device in certain occupations or professions. Registration and certification, milder forms of regulation, can be defended on several grounds. Licensing proper is justifiable in circumstances where there is lack of information or where questions of health and safety are involved. However, it is often used (or misused) by regulatory bodies, such as the American Medical Association or the American Bar Association, as an entry-controlling device to restrict membership so as to guarantee some minimum level of income for members — a classical trade union tactic.

Economic incentives via subsidies, or disincentives via taxation, constitute another approach to regulation. The idea behind this approach is to devise subsidy and tax policies in such a manner that a desirable activity will be rewarded and an undesirable one will be discouraged, if not totally nullified. We considered several forms of such subsidies and taxation and showed the areas where they have been used. We also considered the relative merits and demerits of these forms. As we saw, the incentives approach is quite powerful in accomplishing the goals of regulation, but very often these incentives are used for the wrong reason. They do not remove some of the impediments to efficient allocation of economic resources; they are used to redistribute income in favor of certain groups, groups which are economically or politically powerful. A case in point is the government's farm price-support program.

In situations of natural monopoly, because of declining average cost of production over a wide range, a more direct method of government intervention may be necessary to bring about optimal price-output mix. In practice, such intervention has taken the form of the government (usually a public commission) determining a reasonable rate of return on the invested capital.

Instead of resorting to any of the previous methods of regulation, the government (local, state, or federal) may decide to get into the production of goods and services itself. In situations where the private market is not willing to provide a good or service because it falls into the category of a pure public good, a strong case can be made for a public enterprise. But very often, especially in developing countries of the third world, public enterprises become a vehicle of national or social preference. It is believed that in such countries key sectors of the economy may not be left in private hands for fear of some kind of exploitation. But whether an enterprise is owned privately or publicly, the critical problems of determining the optimal pricing-output-investment decisions must still be resolved. Very often in public enterprises these decisions are made inefficiently because of the absence of the profit motive, which is the guiding force in allocating resources in the private sector.

The regulatory methods discussed in this chapter provide a general background against which one may examine specific regulatory activities. Therefore, we will refer to this chapter when discussing concrete regulatory experiences in Parts Three and Four of this text.

QUESTIONS

4-1 Trace the history of wage-price controls during the Nixon administration and find out the consequences of those controls. Why did Nixon resort to such controls instead of relying on "jawboning"?

4-2 What criteria would you use in granting subsidies to individuals or groups of individuals or business?

4-3 Discuss the merits of "negative" income tax as proposed by Milton Friedman. In What ways is it preferable to, say, the federal AFDC program?

4-4 Would you consider granting depletion allowance to coal producers? Why or why not?

4-5 Are indirect subsidies really indirect? What economic justification can you offer for such subsidies?

4-6 The Federal Insurance Administration, under the *National Flood Insurance Program,* provides federally *subsidized* flood insurance to property owners in flood-prone areas. Why is such a subsidy necessary? What would happen to property values without such insurance?

4-7 The Federal Insurance Administration also administers the *Riot Reinsurance Program* in areas subject to possible civil disorder. What is the rationale behind such a program?

4-8 The Overseas Private Insurance Corporation (OPIC), an executive branch agency, was established in 1969 to offer U.S. investors assistance in finding investment opportunities, insurance to protect their investments, and loans and loan guarantees to help finance projects. Are there any subsidies involved in the operations of the OPIC? If so, how would you justify them? What would happen to U.S. foreign trade if the OPIC did not offer any subsidies?

4-9 Why is interest income from state and local government bonds exempt from federal income tax? Is this a subsidy to the holders of these bonds? If so, what justifies such a subsidy?

4-10 Suppose that the National Highway Traffic Safety Administration (NHTSA) wants to establish standards for auto breaking distance, which is a function of the design of the brakes, tires, or suspension systems, or a mix of all three. Assuming the need for a standards approach, would you recommend a performance standard or a specification standard specifying the exact design of the brakes, tires, and suspension systems? Justify your choice.

4-11 Comment: ``Effective sanction and enforcement mechanisms are critically important to a standards approach.''

4-12 Suppose the brewery grain is below the rodent or insect contamination standard, but the cooking, filtering, and chemical action of the brewing process guarantees a safe beer. Should the FDA seize and destroy the brewery grain? If it does, who benefits and who loses?

4-13 In July 1971 New York City imposed a nicotine and tar tax on cigarettes at the following rate (This tax is in addition to the standard 2 cents tax per pack of ten cigarettes): 1.2 cents for every ten cigarettes in which either the tar content exceeds 17 millgrams per cigarette or the nicotine content exceeds 1.1 milligrams per cigarette (note that this is an example of a performance standard).

What is the logic of or justification for the tar and nicotine tax? Should the government be concerned with the welfare of smokers? Why? What happens, say, if New Jersey, an adjoining state, does not impose a similar tax?

4-14 From newspaper and other sources find out what, precisely, happened at the Three Mile Island plant. What lessons does it have for the regulation of nuclear power in this country?

4-15 Consider the hypothetical supply and demand curves for interstate natural gas shown in Figure 4.4 at the top of the facing page. Assume that the controlled price of interstate gas is fixed at P_1 by the Department of Energy. What is the extent of gas shortage at this price? What price would make the shortage disappear?

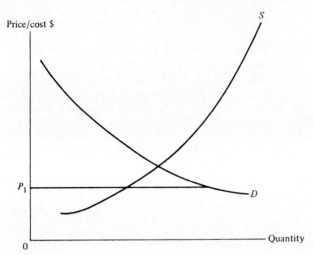

FIGURE 4.4
Hypothetical demand and supply curves for interstate natural gas.

4-16 Refer to Figure 4.2 in the text. What would happen if the pollution tax rate were more than *OT?* If the *MC* curve shown there were to shift upward to the left, what would be the consequences of such a shift? If, instead of the *MC* curve shifting, the MB curve were to shift upward to the right, what would be the corresponding consequences?

4-17 Suppose it is socially desirable to give farmers some minimum level of income. Could you suggest an alternative to the present farm-price support program which is less costly to the government?

4-18 What would be the consequences of letting private business provide postal service?

4-19 Can licensure and certification be justified on the basis of failure of the market to obtain adequate information? Justify your reasoning.

CHAPTER 5

THE ECONOMIC IMPACT OF REGULATION: THE BENEFITS AND COSTS OF REGULATION

The primary purpose of this chapter is to discuss the economic impact of regulation, this impact being measured by the benefits and costs of regulation. Our emphasis throughout will be on the conceptual basis of cost-benefit analysis and some of the problems involved in such an analysis.

5.1 ON THE MEASUREMENT OF BENEFITS AND COSTS OF REGULATION

In this chapter we make an attempt to answer two important questions: (1) what are the costs of government regulation of business? and (2) what are the resulting benefits? These are very important questions because, given scarce economic resources, society cannot afford to regulate an activity, however desirable, beyond the point where the incremental or marginal cost of regulation exceeds the incremental or marginal benefit of regulation. This is the gist of the celebrated economic principle of *cost-benefit (C-B) analysis.*[1]

Although the principle of C-B analysis is very sound, its actual implementation, especially in the area of public regulation, is beset by many difficulties. On the benefit side, very often we have a vague idea about the benefits of regulation although it is not very easy to measure those benefits. Thus, we can all feel the effects of clean air or clean water, but it is not easy to quantify them. Moreover, it is not always possible to identify who the beneficiaries are. On the cost side,

---

[1]For technical details of cost-benefit analysis, see Ezra J. Mishan, *Cost-Benefit Analysis: An Introduction,* Prager, New York, 1977; and A. R. Prest and R. Turvey, "Cost Benefit Analysis: A Survey," *The Economic Journal,* December 1965.

it is not a simple matter to identify all the costs, direct as well as indirect, let alone measure them. For example, by requiring that the Food and Drug Administration (FDA) scrutinize all new drugs thoroughly before allowing their marketing, it is possible that some drugs, although proven effective in other countries, may not be adopted in the United States, which might lead to some deaths whose cost is hard to compute.

Therefore, in the area of public regulation one may be forced to replace C-B analysis by *cost-effectiveness (C-E) analysis.* In C-E analysis, one assumes that a certain activity is to be regulated and tries to find out the best method of achieving it. Thus, if the objective of autoemission regulation is to reduce the level of nitrogen oxide from 4.0 grams per mile to 0.4 gram per mile, C-E analysis will take this objective as a given and would seek for the least expensive method of accomplishing this objective. By contrast, C-B analysis consists of evaluating the incremental cost associated with the incremental benefit of, say, reducing the level of nitrogen oxide from 4 grams per mile to 3 grams per mile. As long as the incremental cost is less than, or at most equal to, the associated incremental benefit, such a reduction may be undertaken. Of course, the crux of the problem is how to measure the benefits of a gram's (per mile) worth of reduction of nitrogen oxide; this problem is avoided in C-E analysis, for the goal is prespecified. But notice that, in both C-B and C-E analyses, one still has to measure the costs of regulation, which is by no means an easy task.

From the preceding discussion it is clear that the whole area of C-B and C-E analysis of government regulation is difficult to handle at the theoretical level and much more so at the empirical level, that is, in terms of providing numerical estimates of the costs as well as the benefits of regulation. (For some finer points of theory, see the appendix to this chapter.) What we intend to do in this chapter is to look conceptually at the various aspects of costs and benefits of regulation and, wherever possible, to provide some estimates of them. But the reader is forewarned that the cost-benefit estimates provided in this chapter are at best educated guesses in most instances and therefore should be taken with a grain of salt. It is no exaggeration to say that the cost-benefit or cost-effectiveness analysis of public regulation is still in its infancy and a great deal of research remains to be done.

5.2 TYPES OF REGULATORY COSTS

Figure 5.1 shows in capsule form the types of costs that might result from regulation. Let us examine each category in some depth.

Direct Costs of Regulation

The most visible are the direct costs of regulation, that is, costs involved in administering the relevant regulation and in complying with the mandates of that regulation. These costs are borne by the government as well as by the industry regulated.

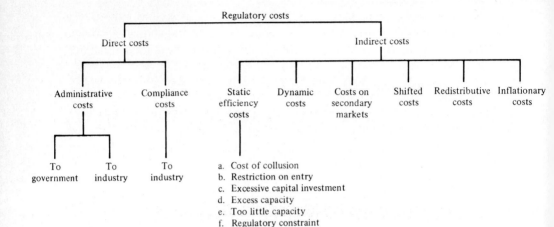

FIGURE 5.1
Types of regulatory costs.

Administrative Costs to the Government   These costs refer to the administrative costs of the various regulatory agencies and are the most visible and highly publicized costs of government regulation. We have already seen in Chapter 1 (see Table 1.2) that these costs have increased tremendously over the past few years. As shown there, in the 5 years between 1974 and 1979 these costs increased by 115 percent, the largest increase of 222 percent being recorded by agencies in the areas of environment and energy, followed by 105 percent increase for consumer safety and health, 102 percent for job safety and working conditions, and so on. Compared to a major economic indicator such as the rate of growth of the federal budget or the rate of growth of GNP or the rate of growth of per capita income, the growth rates in regulatory expenditures just mentioned are truly astounding.

Administrative Costs to Private Business   In complying with the various rules and regulations, the private sector is required to file some 44,000 different forms with federal regulatory agencies.[2] To give some idea about the paperwork burden, consider Table 5.1, which gives, for 1976, the number of worker-hours the private sector had spent just in the reporting requirements of major government agencies.

As the table shows, in 1976, some 75 million worker-hours were spent doing paperwork. Assuming an average yearly compensation of $15,000 and an average work year of 2000 hours, the General Accounting Office (GAO) and the Office of Management and Budget (OMB) estimated that in 1976 the cost of worker-hours shown in Table 5.1 exceeded $565 million. Note that these costs

---

[2]The Standard Oil Company of Indiana, for example, is required to file about 1000 reports annually with some thirty-five federal agencies.

do not reflect all the administrative costs incurred by business; the cost of time spent in telephone conversations with regulatory authorities or personal visits to Washington about regulatory matters are additional costs that should be reckoned with.

Compliance Costs to Private Business   The costs incurred by the private sector in complying with the provisions of regulation are undoubtedly the largest element of total regulatory costs. Unfortunately, reliable estimates of these

TABLE 5.1
ESTIMATED WORKER-HOURS REQUIRED BY REPORTING REQUIREMENTS OF REGULATORY AGENCIES FOR YEAR ENDING JUNE 1976*

	Estimated worker-hours, fiscal 1976
Independent regulatory agencies:	
Civil Aeronautic Board	283,780
Commodity Futures Trading Commission	32,990
Consumer Product Safety Commission	40,710
Federal Communications Commission	48,076,930
Federal Maritime Commission	69,500
Federal Power Commission	1,987,800
Federal Trade Commission	742,050
Interstate Commerce Commission	2,670,790
Nuclear Regulatory Commission	4,918,480
Securities and Exchange Commission	45,120
Administrations, departments, and agencies:	
Department of Transportation:	
Federal Aviation Administration	3,065,138
Federal Railroad Administration	238,609
National Highway Traffic Safety Administration	204,911
Department of Agriculture:	
Animal and Plant Health Inspection Service	1,468,565
Packers and Stockyards Administration	25,863
Department of Commerce: Maritime Administration	146,692
Department of Interior: Mining Enforcement Administration	192,460
Department of Labor:	
Employment Standards Administration	1,658,491
Occupational Safety and Health Administration	192,460
Department of Health, Education, and Welfare: Food and Drug Administration	861,015
Environmental Protection Agency	596,839
Federal Energy Administration	7,845,900
Total	75,395,093

*Special tabulation by the General Accounting Office for the Independent Regulatory Agencies and the Federal Energy Administration (FEA) and special tabulation by the OMB for administrative departments and agencies except the FEA.
Source: Senate Study on Federal Regulation, vol. VI, p. 37.

TABLE 5.2
ANNUAL COST OF FEDERAL REGULATION, BY AREA, 1976
(Millions of Dollars)

Area	Administrative cost	Compliance cost	Total
Consumer safety and health	1,516	5,094	6,610
Job safety and working conditions	483	4,015	4,498
Energy and the environment	612	7,760	8,372
Financial regulation	104	1,118	1,222
Industry specific	474	26,322	26,796
Paperwork	(*)	18,000	18,000
Total	3,189	62,309	65,498

*Included in other categories.
Source: The Cost of Government Regulation of Business, a study prepared for the use of the Joint Economic Committee, Subcommittee on Economic Growth and Stabilization, U.S. Congress, April 1978, p. 26 (Murray L. Weidenbaum is the author of the study).

costs are not available. What we have are specific instances and some broad estimates by some researchers.

The Weidenbaum Estimates   One of the boldest, if somewhat controversial, attempts to measure the economywide private compliance as well as administrative costs has been made by Dr. Murray L. Weidenbaum and his associates at the Center for the Study of American Business at Washington University in St. Louis.[3] Table 5.2 gives these estimates by major regulatory areas.

The table shows that for 1976 the estimated total private direct costs amounted to about $65.5 billion of which $62.3 billion or about 95 percent was for compliance purposes (installing safety equipment, air pollution control equipment, etc.). These estimates were later updated in $71.1 billion for 1977 and $102 billion for 1979.

The Weidenbaum estimates have been criticized by several people as being overly optimistic, but Weidenbaum himself has maintained that if these estimates err at all, they err on the low side.

The OMB Estimates   Another attempt to assess the economywide impact of government regulation has been made by the OMB. These estimates along with a critique of them by the General Accounting Office, the congressional watchdog agency, are given in Table 5.3.

As the table reveals, the OMB has not been able to provide cost estimates for several important categories, possibly because of the difficulties involved in making such estimates. As a result, the OMB estimates are of little help in either substantiating or refuting the Weidenbaum estimates. Moreover, the objections

[3]For their methodology of estimating costs, see Robert DeFina, ''Estimating Expenditures for Regulation,'' *Proceedings, Business and Economic Section,* American Statistical Association, 1979, pp. 365–370.

TABLE 5.3

OMB ESTIMATES OF THE COST OF REGULATION AND GAO COMMENTS
(Dollar Amounts in Billions)

Item	Estimated cost		GAO comment	Implied GAO estimate		Our comment
	Gross	Net		Gross	Net	
Economic regulation						
Trade restrictions						
Foreign:		$15.0	This includes oil import quotas (1,500,000,000) and assumes excess capacity in agriculture due to foreign barriers to trade (3,000,000,000 to 5,000,000,000); neither applies today		$3.0–$5.0	OMB acknowledged GAO's points; none of these are included in cost of regulation in this paper, which deals only with domestic regulation
Domestic:						
Fair trade laws		2.0	This is an income transfer, not a welfare loss to society			No longer relevant since fair trade laws are unenforceable under new legislation
Robinson-Patman Act		(*)				OMB said at least as costly as fair trade but no estimate available
Regulated industries						
Transportation:						
Surface		4.0–9.0	The lower estimate seems reasonable		4.0	This is based on T. R. Moore's estimate; almost certainly exaggerated; see J. R. Nelson, pp. 79–92
Air		2.0–4.0	Based on a simple extrapolation of San Francisco–Los Angeles fares; (*) not necessarily correct for the country as a whole		(*)	
Maritime:						
Rate structure	(*)					
Cargo preference	(*)					
Jones Act						

TABLE 5.3 (*Continued*)
OMB ESTIMATES OF THE COST OF REGULATION AND GAO COMMENTS
(Dollar Amounts in Billions)

Item	Estimated cost		GAO comment	Implied GAO estimate		Our comment
	Gross	Net		Gross	Net	
Communications: Television-	$8.0		Based on Noll, Pack, and McGowan's estimate of what 7 channels of TV would be worth to consumers; not the cost of regulation but of localism in TV	$2.4		Based on what San Diego cable subscribers are willing to pay for 4 more channels
Energy (gas, electric, nuclear):		(°)				
Financial institutions:						
Banking, savings and loans		(°)				
Secondary security markets		(°)				
Agricultural marketing orders:		(°)				
Labor:						
Minimum wage		$7.0–9.0	Just a transfer payment; the amount by which wages were increased by the 1973 act; not the amount of output reduced			
Divs.-Bacon Act		$1.0	No comment	$1.0		
State and local regulation						
Insurance:		(°)				
Banking:		(°)				
Transportation:		(°)				
Price fixing (milk, real estate settlement fees):		(°)				
Professional and occupational licensure		(°)				
Building codes and zoning requirements:		$2.0–4.0	No comment	$2.0–$4.0		

Environmental health and safety, quality standards				
Environment:	$40.0–60.0	$10,400,000,000 per 3d annual report of Council on Environmental Quality, gross rather than net cost	$10.4	By 1975 it was $14,400,000,000 per 7th annual report, p. 145
Except clean air, auto emissions	$6–0	The source cited by OMB concluded that auto emissions controls were worth the costs or would be with revisions in the nitrogen oxide standards	0	These costs are included in the environmental controls figures given above
Safety:				
Automobile	$0.5	(*) No comment	$0.5	GAO gives $2.9 for the model year; see page 133 of this paper
OSHA	$3.5	(*)	$3.5	
Quality standards:				
Food and drugs	$0.3–0.4	Based on estimates of costs of 1962 amendments— should be $0.25 to $0.30 and this is just the net cost of the requirement that drugs be effective; GAO feels that the safety standards of FDA have a net positive effect	0	
Direct cost				
Public sector:				
Federal	$2.0	No comment	2.0	
State and local	(*)	(*)		
Private sector:				
Paperwork	1.0†	No comment	1.0	
Other (Washington lawyers, etc.)	$4.0–5.0‡	(*) (*)	4.0–5.0	

*Not available.
†More than.
‡Probably at least.
Source: *Senate Study on Federal Regulation,* vol. VI, pp. 64–65.

TABLE 5.4
ESTIMATES OF INCREASED PRODUCTION COSTS FROM
OSHA STANDARDS

Standard	5-year capital expenditures (millions)	Annual operating expenditures (millions)
Noise (90 decibels)	$10,500*	na
Coke-oven emission	$450–$860	$170–$1150
Inorganic arsenic	na	$110
Benzene	$267*	$74

*See Ch. 16 for a revision of these figures.
Source: Committee for Economic Development, *Redefining Government's Role in the Market System,* New York, July 1979, p. 63. (The original source is Albert Nichols and Richard Zeckhauser, "Government Comes to the Workplace: An Assessment of OSHA," *The Public Interest,* 49, Fall 1977, pp. 39–69).

raised by the GAO to some of the OMB estimates raise serious questions about the reliability of these estimates.

The Business Roundtable Study At the behest of Business Roundtable, a nonprofit organization representing private business, Arthur Anderson and Company made a study of the annual incremental costs of complying with the regulations of six federal agencies.[4] The incremental costs refer to the additional costs over and above those that would have been incurred in the absence of any new federal regulations. For the forty-eight companies who participated in the study, it was found that for 1977 the estimated incremental cost was about $2.6 billion, of which $2 billion or about 77 percent was for the Environmental Protection Agency (EPA) regulations alone. The remaining 23 percent was distributed among the following categories: 8 percent for equal employment opportunity, 7 percent for occupational safety and health, 5 percent for energy, 2 percent for employee retirement security, and 1 percent for the Federal Trade Commission.

Estimates of Increased Production Costs from OSHA Standards The Occupational Safety and Health Administration (OSHA) commissioned a series of studies of the 5-year capital and operating costs incurred by business in compliance of the OSHA standards. These estimates are supplied in Table 5.4.

As can be seen from the Table, the noise-abatement standards, the most stringent of their kind, alone will cost about $10.5 billion in capital expenditure over a 5-year period. The estimates of the accompanying annual operating costs are not known. But they can be substantial, as the estimates of costs for coke-oven emission standards given in the table so clearly show. (See Chapter 16 for further studies on OSHA standards and their costs.)

Regulatory Cost Increases in the Automobile Industry Perhaps one of the most detailed studies of the cost of government regulation has been made for

[4]Arthur Anderson and Company, *Cost of Government Regulation Study for the Business Roundtable,* March 1977.

the auto industry. Table 5.5 lists the incremental as well as the cumulative cost of the various auto safety equipment and emission standards that have been made mandatory by the government since 1968. To allow for inflation, the annual totals are also expressed in 1977 dollars. Because of regulation, the average price of a car increased by about $520 (current dollars) or by about $666 (1977 dollars).

Depending on the price-elasticity of demand, some or most of these cost increases will be borne by the consumer. According to the U.S. Office of Science and Technology, if all the recommended safety and emission features that were required of the 1976 model year were implemented, the average price of a car would have increased by approximately $873. The domestic output of cars in 1976 was 7,838,000; this would have cost the consumers in aggregate an additional $6.8 billion for that year alone, by no means an insignificant amount.

Table 5.5 also points out an interesting fact, namely, the ever increasing amount of safety and other equipment imposed on the industry and the consumer. Whether all these safety features have had any substantial impact on the health and safety of the auto drivers and passengers is another matter. (More will be said about this later; see Section 5.4.)

Other Individual Cost Estimates In July 1978, the Caterpillar Tractor Company disclosed that it had spent over $67 million in regulatory compliance costs in a single year, 90 percent of which was due to EPA and OSHA regulations alone. Notice that the EPA and OSHA did not exist prior to 1970!

TABLE 5.5
INCREASE IN RETAIL PRICE OF AUTOMOBILES DUE TO FEDERAL REQUIREMENTS, 1968–1978

Model year	Improvements made	Initial retail price	Year total	Total adjusted for inflation*
1968	Seat and shoulder belt installations	$11.51		
	HEW standards for exhaust emission	16.00	$27.51	$47.84
1968–1969	Windshield defrosting and defogging systems	.70		
	Windshield wiping and washing systems	1.25		
	Door latches and hinge systems	.55		
	Lamps, reflective devices, and associated equipment	6.30	8.80	14.53
1969	Head restraints	16.65	16.65	27.48
1970	Lamps, reflective devices, and associated equipment	4.00		
	Standards for exhaust emission systems	5.50	9.50	14.77
1968–1970	Theft protection (steering, transmission, and ignition locking and buzzing system)	7.85		
	Occupant protection in interior impact (glove box door remains closed on impact)	.35	8.20	12.75

TABLE 5.5 (*Continued*)
INCREASE IN RETAIL PRICE OF AUTOMOBILES DUE TO FEDERAL REQUIREMENTS, 1968–1978

Model year	Improvements made	Initial retail price	Year total	Total adjusted for inflation*
1971	Fuel evaporative systems	19.00	19.00	28.33
1972	Exhaust emission standards required by Clean Air Act	6.00		
	Warranty changes resulting from federal requirement that all exhaust emission systems be warranted for 5 years or 50,000 miles	1.00		
1972	Safety features voluntarily added in anticipation of future safety requirements	2.00		
	Seat belt warning system and locking device on retractors	20.25	29.25	42.37
1972–1973	Exterior protection (standard #215)	69.90	69.90	95.29
1973	Location, identification, and illumination of controls	.60		
	Reduced flammability of interior materials	5.80	6.40	8.72
1969–1973	Side door strength	15.30	15.30	20.85
1974	Interlock system and other changes to meet federal safety requirements	107.60		
	Exhaust emission systems to comply with federal Clean Air Act	1.40	109.00	133.50
1975	Additional safety features associated with federal motor vehicle safety standards #105, #208, and #216	10.70		
	Installation of catalytic converter	119.20	129.90	146.66
1975–1976	Removal of interlock system (quality decrease) and add'l installation of catalytic converters *net* effects (Oct. 1976)	18.00		
1976	FMVSS #105 hydraulic brake system	6.50		
	FMVSS #215 improved bumpers	4.80		
	FMVSS #301 leak-resistant fuel system	2.10		
	Improved emissions control system	7.60	39.00	41.54
1977	FMVSS #215 improved bumpers	1.30		
	FMVSS #219 structural changes	.95		
	FMVSS #301 leak-resistant fuel system	4.70		
	Improved emission control system	14.30	21.25	21.25
1978	Redesign of emission control systems to meet HEW air quality standards	9.99	9.99	9.99
	TOTAL	$519.65	$519.65	$665.87

*Yearly totals are expressed in 1977 dollars by use of the consumer price index.
Source: Compiled from data supplied by the U.S. Department of Labor, Bureau of Labor Statistics, by Dr. Murray L. Weidenbaum for *The Cost of Government Regulation of Business,* op. cit., pp. 20–22.

In April 1976, while testifying before a subcommittee of the Joint Economic Committee of Congress, executives of the Dow Chemical Company stated that on an extremely conservative basis its compliance costs amounted to $147 million in 1975 and $186 million for 1976, an increase of some 27 percent in just 1 year. In their view, about one-third of this increase was unnecessary.

The highly regarded annual McGraw-Hill survey of business expenditures estimated that in 1976 the private sector had spent about $3.2 billion just to comply with the rules and regulations of a single federal agency, OSHA.

Indirect Costs of Regulation

The indirect costs of regulation, though less visible than direct costs, can be as, or even more, important. Unfortunately, given the current state of knowledge, we have very little information about the quantitative magnitudes of the indirect costs of regulation. Nonetheless, it is important to spell out the nature of these costs.

Static Efficiency Costs   These costs result when government regulation leads the private sector to utilize economic resources in inefficient ways, that is, in ways which do not produce a given output at the least possible cost or which, for a given cost, do not produce the maximum possible output (recall the discussion of efficiency and Pareto optimality from Chapter 2). A few examples will illustrate the point.

Cost of Collusion   By exempting trucking and maritime shipping companies from antitrust regulation, agencies such as the Interstate Commerce Commission (ICC) and the Federal Maritime Commission (FMC) have in effect permitted collusion among these companies by allowing them to determine their own rate structures (tariffs) collectively (details are given in Chapter 11). These collectively determined rates are invariably higher than if competition were to prevail. That this is the case is dramatically demonstrated by the airline industry. Before the Airline Deregulation Act of 1978, the Civil Aeronautics Board (CAB) determined the fares airlines could charge for various types of travel. But since the 1978 act, there has been a gradual deregulation of the authority of the CAB to determine these fares. As a result, the airfares have declined dramatically despite the soaring cost of the fuel oil. In Chapter 6 we will show how the monopoly-type prices resulting from collusive practices harm the consumer.

Restriction on Entry   Regulatory agencies such as the CAB and ICC have rigidly regulated entry of firms into the aviation and trucking industries. As noted elsewhere, in years the CAB has not allowed a new commercial trunk airline (this situation is expected to change; the CAB is expected to go out of business by 1985). Apart from restricting output, such entry restrictions often lead to inefficient production because without competition, inefficient firms may not be weeded out of the industry. In addition, there may be excess profits (i.e., profits above competitive levels) to the firms already in the industry. (Recall from Chapter 2 Posner's theory of regulation.)

Excessive Capital Investment It was pointed out in Chapter 2 that natural monopolies, such as electric, gas, and telephone utilities, are usually regulated by state or local authorities which determine the rate of return these monopolies can earn on their capital stock, the so-called rate base. The rate of return regulation generally operates by setting prices that generate sufficient revenues for a regulated firm to pay all its costs and earn a normal rate of return (anywhere from 9 to 14 percent) on its capital stock. Now one way a utility can increase its total profits is to increase the amount of its capital stock or the rate base and earn the allowed profit rate on a larger rate base. This tendency will be more pronounced if the allowed rate of return far exceeds the (marginal) cost of capital, that is, the incremental cost at which the firm can borrow funds in the capital markets. This, the so-called Averch-Johnson effect alluded to in Chapter 4, is thus likely to induce public utilities "(1) to adopt an excessively capital-intensive technology and (2) to take on additional business, if necessary, at unnumerative rates."[5]

Excess Capacity Another consequence of regulation can be excess standby (production) capacity, that is, capacity in excess of normal or peak demand. Such excess capacity results when prices are set above long-run minimum average cost or when the allowed rate of return exceeds the cost of capital, which leads to excessive capital investment (as mentioned previously). Obviously, when excess capacity is not expected to be matched by additional demand, a sheer waste of economic resources results.

Besides the public utilities, there are other instances of excess capacity. The civil aviation industry before the Airline Deregulation Act of 1978 provides a good example. Until then the industry was rigidly controlled by the CAB, which decided which airline could fly where as well as what it could charge. Because of the lack of price competition and the fact that the CAB-determined prices were above competitive levels (as proven by the change in airfares since the 1978 deregulation act), very often the airlines were flying half empty. Between cities such as New York and Chicago airlines were "competing" for customers by engaging in what is known as nonprice competition. Thus, one airline would say, "We depart every hour on the hour," while another would advertise, "We depart every hour on the half hour." Needless to say, flying half empty, the airlines wasted a lot of fuel, not to mention the resulting congestion at the nation's major airports. It is also debatable whether the advertising expenditure on the so-called nonprice competition was a productive investment. (More details can be found in Chapter 12.)

Too Little Capacity This is the opposite of excess capacity, and it too can be the outcome of regulation; the best example is the natural gas industry. As we have already seen, the Department of Energy (DEO; formerly the Federal Power Commission) regulates the price of natural gas entering into the interstate market, although the gas sold in intrastate markets is not regulated. By keeping the well-head price of interstate gas below the market-clearing price of that fuel,

---

[5]Alfred E. Kahn, *The Economics of Regulation,* Wiley, New York, 1971, vol. II, p. 49.

the DEO has unduly encouraged its consumption. This in turn has discouraged gas producers from putting new resources into exploration and development of new gas fields. Moreover, as already noted, gas producing states are trying to sell as much of their gas as possible in the unregulated intrastate market. The net result has been a shortage of capacity relative to demand, and this shortage has become all the more noticeable because of the recent sharp increases in the prices of other fuels, noticeably oil (more on this in Chapter 13).

   Regulatory Constraint and Peak-Load Pricing   The demand for gas, electricity, and telephone services is characterized by fluctuations so that during certain hours (the peak hours) the demand is up to full productive capacity whereas during other hours (the off-peak hours) the demand is much below capacity. This raises the question of how to price the peak and off-peak demands so that production capacity is efficiently utilized. Now if costs are divided into variable costs (fuel, labor, raw material) and fixed or overhead costs, the peak demand should be so priced that the unit price, on the average, covers both variable and fixed costs. This is because productive capacity is usually designed to accommodate the peak demand and hence the peak demanders must bear the fixed costs of capacity on top of the variable costs. During off-peak hours, however, the price should be proportional to variable costs only because the fixed costs will have to be incurred anyhow. An electric utility, for example, must stand ready to supply electricity on a 24-hour basis and will have to incur the overhead of running the plant no matter what the level of demand. Such a dual pricing policy, known as peak-load pricing, will keep the capacity as fully utilized as possible: There will be some customers who will shift their demand from peak to off-peak hours to take advantage of the lower off-peak rates, say, by doing their laundry at night instead of during the day.

   The foregoing ideas can be illustrated graphically, as in Figure 5.2: D_1 and D_2 represent the peak and off-peak demand curves for electricity and MR_1 and MR_2 the associated marginal revenue curves. Given the capacity level (measured in kilowatt, kw), the line labeled a represents the marginal (operating) cost of providing electricity (measured in kilowatthours, kwh), which for simplicity is assumed constant. The line labeled $a + b$ represents the sum of the marginal (operating) cost a and of the marginal cost b of increasing productive capacity just enough to produce an additional kilowatthour. Again for simplicity, b, like a, is assumed constant. Since capacity is chosen to accommodate the peak demand, the marginal cost of providing an additional kilowatthour to demanders during the peak hours is $a + b$, whereas it is only a to demanders in the off-peak hours because the capacity is already there.

   Now, following the usual MC = MR rule of profit maximization, the firm will charge the demanders during peak hours the price of P_1 per kilowatthour while the off-peak demanders will pay the price of P_2 per kilowatthour, the peak and off-peak outputs being Q_1 and Q_0, respectively. Such a dual pricing policy will not only maximize the firm's profits but will also keep the productive capacity (determined by the optimal level of peak output of Q_1 units) best utilized.

   But this sensible pricing policy is not uniformly followed by the regulating

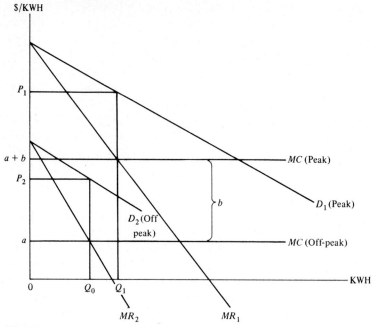

FIGURE 5.2
Peak-load pricing.

bodies. Take, for instance, the demand for telephone services, which exhibits the peak–off-peak phenomenon, the peak hours being generally from 8 a.m. to 5 p.m. followed by a slackening of demand between 5 p.m. to 11 p.m. and then followed by a period of very low demand (relative to peak capacity) between 11 p.m. and 8 a.m. Recognizing this, most states allow the local telephone utilities to charge different rates (per minute or per 3 minutes) for the different time periods.

In contrast to this policy, consider the Federal Energy Regulating Commission's (formerly the FPC) formula for natural gas pipeline rates as pronounced in its famous Atlantic Seaboard decision of 1952.[6] With occasional departures, this decision stated that half of (capital) capacity costs would be distributed on a 50-50 basis between peak and off-peak costs and the remaining half would be assigned according to their peak period demands. As a result, the off-peak customers were required to bear a large proportion of capacity costs. This had the undesirable effect of encouraging consumption during the peak period since the peak-period price was below the true marginal cost of production; that is, the full amount $a + b$ in Figure 5.2 was not included in the price.

---

[6]In the matter of *Atlantic Seaboard Corporation v. Virginia Gas Transmission Corporation,* Opinion No. 225, 11 FPC 43 (1952).

Dynamic Costs Technological change and entrepreneurial creativity have been the hallmark of American business. But it has been observed that regulation tends to slow down expenditures on research and development (R&D), which is an essential ingredient of technological change and innovation.[7] Several examples can be cited.

The ICC has been slow to allow innovative technology in the railroad and trucking businesses. Consider the case of the unit train. An entire train can be used to haul coal from a single mine to a single power plant. This reduces switching costs, and a large part of terminal and clerical costs, and ultimately the total cost of shipment. But as early as 1897 the ICC declared cost savings resulting from the unit train illegal. It was not until 1962 that some railroads were allowed to shift to the unit train.

The ICC, by its rate policies, also discouraged another major rail innovation, namely, "piggybacking," where truck trailers are carried on flatcars. Piggybacking takes several forms:[8] (1) a single trailer on a short flatcar, (2) two trailers on a long one, (3) complete trailers, or (4) merely the container without the wheels. The lowest-cost form is one container on a short flatcar because the container is easy to secure to the flatcar and offers less wind resistance. Additionally, the shorter flatcar is more stable on a curving roadbed, can negotiate sharper turns, is easier to switch, and avoids excess capacity when only one container is shipped. However, the ICC rail form A specified a minimum revenue for a fully loaded flatcar, which meant the price charged per container for a single-container flatcar had to be twice that of a two-container car, despite the lower cost of the single-container car. Obviously, there was little incentive to use the new technology.

Another example of how regulation can inhibit innovation is from the telecommunications field. Although satellite technology is much cheaper than ocean cables, the Federal Communications Commission (FCC) restricted the Communications Satellite Corporation's (COMSAT) operations in order to protect the interests of the five ocean cables, the last being approved by the FCC in 1968 although satellite technology was well developed by then. The comptroller general of the United States has reported that the Bell System was a strong advocate of the fifth ocean cable because it would increase the system's rate base and allowable profits (Averch-Johnson once again!).[9] Use of satellites in place of the cable would have required the Bell System to lease channels from COMSAT, for which it would be reimbursed only on a dollar-for-dollar basis. (Further details are given in Chapter 15.)

Another glaring example of how regulation can interfere with R&D is the drug industry. Since the 1962 Kefauver-Harris Amendments to the Food, Drug and Cosmetics Act, the control of the FDA over new drugs has become much more

---

[7]See William Capron, ed., *Technological Change in Regulated Industries*, Brookings, Washington, D.C., 1971.

[8]The following discussion is based on the *Senate Study on Federal Regulation*, vol. VI, p. 47.

[9]See *Government Regulatory Activity: Justifications, Processes, Impacts, and Alternatives.* Report to the Congress by the Comptroller General of the United States, June 3, 1977, p. 35.

rigid. The FDA now requires approval prior to human testing and proof of effectiveness as well as safety prior to marketing. As a result, the average clearance time — the *regulatory lag* — for new chemical products has increased from an average of 2½ years in 1962 to about 7½ years in 1972. Also, the average cost of development of new chemical products has increased from $1.2 million in 1962 to $11.5 million in 1972, a good proportion of the increase being due to the stringent regulations.

All these developments have retarded the entry of new drugs into the U.S. market as well as increased the prices of pharmaceutical products.[10] Because of the more onerous drug regulations, the United States was the thirtieth country to approve the antiasthma drug metaproterenol, the thirty-second country to approve the anticancer drug adriamycin, the fifty-first country to approve the antituberculosis drug rifampin, the sixty-fourth country to approve the antiallergenic drug cromolyn, and the one hundred and sixth country to approve the antibacterial drug co-trimaxzole. All told, it has been estimated that between 1950 and 1961, on the average, fifty new drugs were introduced every year into the U.S. market, whereas between 1963 and 1975 this number was only seventeen per year, a decline largely ascribable to the 1962 amendments. An unintended consequence of these amendments has been to shift initiative in drug development to other countries where rules and regulations on drug development and testing are less demanding; the United States is no longer the dominant country it once was in this area. Of course, one could argue that the country is willing to pay this price in order to ensure that when a new drug reaches the market, it is safe beyond a reasonable doubt.

Costs on Secondary Markets   The industries that use the products or services produced by regulated industries are also affected by regulation, although they are not a direct party to it. For example, the ICC tariff for shipping iron ore is lower than that for shipping scrap iron and steel. Naturally, since these products are competing or substitute products for one another, this pricing policy of the ICC alters their relative prices; because of differential tariffs in favor of raw iron ore, relatively speaking it is cheaper than scrap iron. This has the untoward consequence of increasing the mining of iron ore to greater levels than would otherwise be desirable as well as affecting the location of iron and steel plants, which may not necessarily be best from the resource allocation viewpoint. (For additional details from an environmental viewpoint, see Chapter 17.)

Shifted Costs   Regulation often shifts cost of production from one party to another. For example, many OSHA regulations shift the cost of production from the worker (the expected loss of income from injury or illness) to the firm (the cost of removing the hazard). Similarly, compliance with the EPA environmental

---

[10]For details, see Sam Peltzman, "An Evaluation of Consumer Protection Legislation: The 1976 Drug Amendments," *Journal of Political Economy,* September–October 1973.

standards shifts costs of production from society (the loss due to environmental degradation) to the firm (the cost of pollution control equipment).

Now to the extent that such costs internalize externalities (see Chapter 2) by bringing into equality private and social costs of production, such shifts are obviously welcome. But one must be careful to note that such shifts do impose undue costs on one party, which might ultimately stagnate economic growth. Unfortunately, at present there is not much information about the magnitude of the shifted costs.

Redistributive Costs As pointed out in Chapter 2, allocative efficiency (efficient allocation of scarce economic resources) and distributive equity (equity or fairness of income distribution) are two major problems of economics. Most of the effects of regulation discussed thus far pertain by and large to allocative efficiency. But regulation can and does alter the distribution of income among economic participants. For instance, if a regulation grants an individual or a group of individuals or an industry excess profits or excessive rate of return (in excess of what would prevail under competitive conditions), this in effect transfers income to these entities from those which are not so fortunate. If the truckers earn excess profits because of ICC regulation of rates, then, in effect, income is transferred from consumers to truckers. Likewise, the farm price-support program is a means of transferring income from consumers to the farmers. The reader will see shortly that such transfer costs can be sizable (see the federal milk order case study discussed in Section 5.4).

The Inflationary Costs Any regulatory activity which increases the cost of production is likely to lead to higher prices, especially if the government's monetary policy is accommodative (i.e., the Fed does not reduce the rate of growth of money supply to offset any inflationary tendencies). But this by itself does not constitute inflation, for against the increased costs one must offset the benefits that might accrue from regulation. It is only when the net cost (net of benefits) is positive that it might lead to inflation, especially if regulation is quite widespread.

If the net cost of regulation is positive, it amounts to a "hidden" tax on the consumer, hidden in the sense that it has not been expressly authorized by any governmental body. Such a hidden tax is essentially a sales tax, and it is well known that sales tax is generally regressive, that is, it falls more heavily on lower- than higher-income groups.

As is the case with most of the indirect costs of regulation considered above, there is little quantitative knowledge about the inflationary impact of regulation in the economy as a whole, although there are several economists who argue that the high rates of inflation observed in 1979 and 1980 [the consumer price index (CPI) recording an increase of 18 percent at the annual rate in early 1980] were to a great extent due to regulation, especially regulation in the areas of the environment and health and safety. In a study done for the EPA, Chase Econometrics has forecast that because of EPA regulations alone, by 1983 the CPI will increase by 0.3 to 0.4 percent per year (this topic is discussed further in Chapter 18).

5.3 THE BENEFITS OF REGULATION

Although we have devoted considerable space to the discussion of the various costs of regulation, we are left with the uneasy feeling that we have very few hard estimates. The situation is even worse when it comes to the measurement of the benefits of regulation, although it is not difficult to perceive them. No one can deny the benefits of clean air, clean water, or clean rivers (see Chapter 17 for details). Nor can one deny that one can regulate a natural monopoly and still reap the benefits of the economies of scale (see Chapter 6 for some theoretical considerations of this topic). What is difficult is to know the precise quantitative magnitudes of such benefits. And without such knowledge, a cost-benefit analysis or a cost-effectiveness analysis is difficult to perform. Lacking comprehensive knowledge about the costs and benefits of regulation as a whole, the best one can do is to approach the subject on a case-by-case basis. What we will do in the remainder of the chapter (and in the chapters to follow) is to examine a few case studies that give us some idea of the costs as well as the benefits and also give us insight into some of the measurement problems. As knowledge of various forms of regulation grows, maybe in the future, economists will have a better understanding of the economic impact of regulation on the economy as a whole.

5.4 CASE STUDIES OF BENEFITS AND COSTS OF REGULATION

The ICC Study of Benefits and Costs of Freight Regulation[11]

Among one of the very few studies of C-B analysis of regulation is the ICC study of freight regulation. The ICC has divided benefits into two categories — quantifiable and nonquantifiable. These categories are given in Table 5.6.

As the table shows, among the quantifiable benefits, the largest amount pertains to the benefits resulting from regulation of trucking freight rates. It was the contention of the ICC that between 1969 and 1975 the truck freight rates rose by 41 percent, whereas during the same period the wholesale price index (WPI) rose by about 64 percent. The "savings" of $3.7 billion shown in Table 5.6 is due to this differential. In other words, the ICC is contending that if the freight rates had increased by 64 percent instead of 41 percent, it would have cost the consumers $3.7 billion additionally. But one should be very wary of computing benefits in this manner, for it does not tell one very much about productivity growth in the industry and the rate of growth of wage and nonwage costs.

---

[11]The Interstate Commerce Commission, Bureau of Economics, *A Cost and Benefit Evaluation of Surface Transport Regulation* (Statement No. 76-1, undated). For additional studies, see Ch. 11.

TABLE 5.6
PURPORTED BENEFITS OF ICC REGULATIONS

Benefits capable of quantification	Amount (billions)	Benefits incapable of quantification
Rate level:		Adequate rate and service levels to rural areas
Motor	$3.740	and small businesses without the need for
Rail	(.500)	direct subsidies
Abandonment proceedings	.300	
Railcar utilization	.149	Stability of rate and service levels
Carrier financing	.035	Enhanced market competition
Inventory reduction	0.59	Consumer and shipper assistance
Loss and damage impact	.613	A more adequate and balanced car supply
Total	4.496	Effects on national defense
		Effects on capacity
		Incentives for technological changes
		Environment and conservation

Source: ICC, Bureau of Economics, "A Cost and Benefit Evaluation of Surface Transportation Regulation," Statement No. 76-1, undated, p. 28.

If the rate of growth of productivity exceeds the rate of growth of costs (wage and nonwage) in the trucking industry vis-à-vis the rest of the economy, the unit cost of production and therefore the freight rates are likely to rise at a slower rate in that industry than in the rest of the economy. Now unless it can be shown that the regulatory policies of the ICC have directly contributed to such an outcome, it is very hard to accept the commission's contention that it has saved consumers $3.7 billion. All that one can say is that if the ICC method of setting rates were the same in 1969 as in 1975, then the change in rate levels reflects only changes in industry average costs.

The next-largest item of benefit is $0.613 billion, which is the amount of loss the shippers suffered and which was ordered paid by the ICC. But this benefit too cannot be ascribed to ICC regulation, for without the ICC the insurance companies of the railroad and trucking companies would have paid similar benefits. The next sizable benefit of $0.3 billion is due to the insistence of the ICC that the railroads not abandon some railroad services. But the nature of this benefit is not clear. By forcing the railroads to continue operating in economically unprofitable areas, the ICC is in fact misallocating economic resources (see Chapter 11 for details). If somehow the extent of this misallocation can be quantified, it might very well be the case that the costs of misallocation exceed the alleged benefit of $300 million. (More on this in Chapter 11, where we discuss the economics of railroad service abandonment.)

Although the nonquantifiable benefits sound impressive on first reading, they may be more apparent than real. The category "enhanced market competition" deserves a word or two. Given the fact that the freight rates in the trucking industry are monopoly or cartel rates and that entry into this industry is severely restricted by the ICC, it is hard to imagine that there is enhanced competition in the trucking industry. As a matter of fact, the Motor Carrier Act of 1980 was passed by Congress because it realized that regulation of the trucking industry by the ICC had led to uncompetitive rate structures and monopoly profits (a topic we discuss further in Chapter 11).

Against the aforementioned benefits, however dubious, one must consider the costs of regulation. According to the ICC, these costs amount to about $1.7 billion; about $60 million of this is clearly identifiable as the commission's annual budget, and the rest represents the increase in trucking rates due to regulation.[12] But these cost estimates reflect only the direct costs of regulation due to agency action and do not include direct compliance costs as well as various types of indirect costs discussed previously. For example, there is no estimate of the costs of empty "back hauls" of trucks, that is, the costs of trucks returning empty to the point of origin, because under the rules prevailing before 1980 the truckers could not by law carry any goods on their return trip. Thus, an agricultural trucker who carries fresh tomatoes from the fields to the plants could not carry, say, a load of tomato soup on his return trip! If all such costs are reckoned with, the costs of regulation will far exceed the reported amount of $1.7 billion, perhaps far in excess of the benefit of $4.5 billion reported in Table 5.6, a figure which is suspect to begin with.

Cost-Benefit Analysis of Federal Milk Marketing Orders[13]

Believe it or not, the price you pay for milk is regulated by the federal government since the great depression via the so-called federal milk marketing orders. Each milk order defines the geographical area within which the U.S. Department of Agriculture (USDA) determines the prices of grade A and Grade B milk. At the end of 1975 there were fifty-six milk marketing orders under which more than 69 billion pounds of producer milk, representing about 80 percent of all fluid grade milk produced, were marketed.

Various researchers have attempted to compute the social costs as well as benefits of the milk orders. Table 5.7 lists some of the cost estimates. As the table shows, three types of costs are estimated by the researchers mentioned therein. The first is the increase in the price of milk at the retail level. Although the data bases are not exactly comparable, it seems that milk prices per gallon increased at the retail level by 7 percent according to the Ippolito and Masson estimates but by more than 20 percent by the estimates obtained by Kwoka

---

[12]Since the trucking deregulation in Great Britain, the freight rates there decreased by 10 percent. The ICC therefore believes that because of regulation the truck freight rates are higher by 10 percent in the United States. It is this figure which it uses in computing its cost of regulation, a procedure which is questionable, to say the least (why?).

[13]For details, see Paul W. MacAvoy, ed., *Federal Milk Marketing Orders and Price Supports,* American Enterprise Institute, Washington, D.C., 1977. (This study is one of the several studies in what is known as the *Ford Administration Papers on Regulatory Reform.)*

TABLE 5.7
SUMMARY OF SOCIAL COSTS OF MILK REGULATION AS ESTIMATED BY VARIOUS RESEARCHERS

Researcher and category of cost	Cost
Ippolito and Masson (1973 data)[a]	
Fluid milk price increase at retail[b]	7% (4.5 cents/gallon)
Deadweight social loss from:	
Pricing mechanism of federal orders[c]	$50 million/year
Cooperative monopolization and state regulation[d]	$70 million/year
Prohibitions on reconstitution[d]	$125 million/year[e]
Total deadweight loss	$125–$245 million/year[e]
Transfer payments from:	
Pricing mechanism of federal orders[c]	$50– $100 million/year
Cooperative monopolization[f]	$150–$200 million/year
State regulation and prohibition on reconstitution[f]	$200–$300 million/year[e]
Total transfer payments	$250–$500 million/year[e]
Kwoka (1970 data)	
Fluid milk price increase at retail[g]	22% (20.8 cents/gallon)
Total deadweight loss of regulation[h]	$202 million/year
Gross transfer payments from fluid sales[i]	$805 million/year
Roberts (1974 data)	
Potential price decrease from allowing unrestricted reconstitution of milk	33 cents/gallon

[a]The October 1976 draft by Ippolito and Masson states a conservative figure for the cost of state plus federal regulation at about $10 million less than the January 1976 draft.
[b]Ippolito and Masson, "The Social Costs of Federal Regulation of Milk," p. 16.
[c]Ibid., p. 15.
[d]Ibid., n. 17.
[e]With what information was available, the figures on reconstituted milk are highly speculative and may represent a "best guess" of maximum possible effect.
[f]Ippolito and Masson, "The Social Costs of Federal Regulation of Milk," p. 18.
[g]John E. Kwoka, "Pricing under Federal Milk Market Regulation: Theory, Objectives, and Impact," unpublished paper, 1975, p. 25.
[h]Tanya Roberts, "Review of Recent Studies," Public Interest Economics Center, 1975, p. 42; summarizes Kwoka's findings.
[i]Ibid., p. 27.
[j]Ibid., p. 33.
Source: Paul W. MacAvoy, ed., *Federal Milk Marketing Orders and Price Supports*, American Enterprise Institute, Washington, D.C., 1977, p. 111.

and Roberts. The next category is the deadweight loss. A deadweight loss (as we will explain more fully in Chapter 6) is the net value of goods and services not produced because of departure from competitive conditions. It represents a sheer loss of productive assets or goods to society. In the present context it means the net value of milk not produced because of various regulatory features of the milk orders. As the data of Table 5.7 show, the deadweight losses can be sizable. The Ippolito and Masson as well as the Kwoka estimates put this loss in the range of $125 to $245 million. The third category is the costs of transfer payments to milk producers from various sources. These transfer payments too can be sizable, in the range of $250 to $500 million (Ippolito and Masson) or $805 million (Kwoka).

Note that the cost estimates just mentioned do not reflect costs due to the federal milk price-support program, which is independent of the milk order scheme. The price-support program primarily supports the price of grade B milk; that is, the government subsidizes the producers of grade B milk if the market price is below the support price. By one estimate, the deadweight loss due to the price support ranges between $15 to $95 million.[14]

To understand the benefits of the milk order, one has to consider the goals behind the order, which were stated in the Agricultural Adjustment Act of 1933, the act that authorized the milk orders. These goals were: (1) to raise the income of dairy farmers, (2) to maintain "orderly marketing conditions" such that there is an orderly flow of milk to market throughout its normal marketing season to avoid unnecessary fluctuations in supply and price, (3) to assure an adequate and dependable supply of fluid grade milk, and (4) to prevent price levels that are either in excess of those necessary to achieve the goals of the act or those in the public interest.

It is not easy to express these goals in quantitative terms. To the author's knowledge, no explicit quantitative estimates of the benefits of the milk orders have been made. But there is some qualitative information given in the Ford administration study on federal milk orders (see footnote 13). This study points out that " . . . it is not likely that the federal order system has greatly enhanced the income of dairy farmers above the general level of income in other types of farming in light of the relatively minor entry barriers to dairying."[15] If we take price stability as an indicator of "orderly marketing conditions," then the Ford administration study concludes that prices received by milk handlers (dealers), on the average, fluctuated less than those received by the dairy farmers themselves, which would seem at odds with the original intent of Congress to provide price stability for farmers. The same study concludes that price levels in many markets were excessive because there was chronic excess supply of grade A milk in these markets. This would not have happened if the government-determined prices were not excessive (in relation to cost of production).

Although there are some cost estimates of the federal milk order system, a cost-benefit analysis cannot be conducted because there is a lack of numerical estimates of the benefits of the federal orders. As such, it is hard to say whether on balance the benefits outweigh the costs. But judging by the chronic excess supply of grade A milk, it would seem that perhaps on balance the costs of the program exceed the claimed benefits. A detailed examination of the Ford administration study on this subject would tend to confirm this conclusion. As a matter of fact, this study recommends a phased deregulation of milk marketing in the country.

[14]Ibid., p. 109.
[15]Ibid., pp. 115–116.

Benefits and Costs of Auto Safety Regulation

The GAO has attempted to evaluate the benefits of auto safety regulation. Comparing the car accidental death rate per model year, it concluded that the required safety devices through 1970 had saved about 28,000 driver and passenger lives through 1974. Similarly, a National Highway Traffic and Safety Administration (NHTSA) study reports that since 1966 (when most safety devices were instituted) the fatality rate has been reduced from 5.7 to 3.3 deaths per 100 million miles of travel, a reduction of some 40 percent.[16] Had the fatality rate remained at the 1966 level, nearly 200,000 more persons would have been killed since that year and an additional 35,000 would have died in 1977 alone. These estimates have been challenged by some researchers.[17]

As we noted earlier, by 1978 the average price of a car had increased by about $666 (in 1977 dollars) on account of the government-mandated safety and emission standards, the aggregate cost being around $7 billion. Whether this cost increase is more than offset by the reduction in travel fatalities cited above is a difficult question, for it requires putting a dollar value on human life. One can make some rough calculations about the value of human life by taking into account a person's expected lifelong earnings potential and using some reasonable rate of return to compute the present value of such earnings. This value times the number of lives saved would provide an estimate of the aggregate benefit of auto safety regulation. Needless to say, these computations are fraught with several difficulties, such as accurate estimates of the earning profile, age-sex-occupational differences, the appropriate rate of return to compute the present value, etc. As a result, any estimates of the benefits that one obtains are likely to be highly conjectural. Hence, any evaluation of the costs and benefits of auto safety regulation is bound to remain uncertain.[18]

Benefits and Costs of Pollution Control

The Council on Environmental Quality (CEQ) makes annual estimates of pollution control expenditures on an incremental basis, that is, the expenditures made necessary by the EPA-mandated pollution control programs. For 1975, its estimates of these costs were: $9 billion for air pollution, $4.7 billion for water

[16]National Highway Traffic Safety Administration, "The Benefits of Automobile Regulations," June 1978.

[17]See Sam Peltzman, *Regulation of Automobile Safety*, American Enterprise Institute, Washington, D.C., 1975.

[18]For an excellent discussion on the problems involved in evaluating the value of human life, see E. J. Mishan, "Evaluation of Life and Limb: A Theoretical Approach," *Economic Efficiency and Social Welfare*, G. Allen, London, 1981, pp. 89–99. Some of us may be shocked at the notion that a dollar value can be placed on a human life. Isn't the value of a human life infinite? But wouldn't such a view lead to some extreme resource allocation problems? Even when the probability of loss of life were small, with an infinite value, we would devote *all* our resources to saving lives. How much would it cost to produce a car in which it would be impossible for a passenger to be killed in a collision? Put this way, it may not be too difficult to see why in practice some finite value on a human life may have to be placed.

TABLE 5.8
COMPARISON OF NATIONAL POLLUTION DAMAGE ESTIMATES

Media: study	Basic year	Range (in billions of dollars)	Estimates, in 1975 dollars
Air: Ridker (1966)	1970	7.3 to 8.9	10.1 to 12.3
Air: Gerhardt (1969)	1968	6 to 15.2 (best 8.1)	9.2 to 23.3 (best 12.4)
Air: Barrett & Waddell (1973)	1968	16.1	24.6
Air: Babcock & Nagda (1973)	1968	20.2	30.9
Air: Justice, Williams & Clement (1973)	1970	2 to 8.7	2.8 to 12
Air: Waddell (1974)	1970	6.1 to 18.5 (best 12.3)	8.4 to 25.6 (best 17)
Air: National Academy of Sciences (1974)	1973	15 to 30 (best 20)	17.9 to 35.8 (best 23.9)
Air: Heintz and Hershaft (1975)	1973	9.5 to 35.4 (best 20.2)	11.3 to 42.2 (best 24)
Water: Abel, Tihansky, & Walsh (1975)	1970	5.5 to 15.5 (best 10.6)	7.6 to 21.4 (best 14.7)
Water: Horak and Heintz (1975)	1973	4.5 to 18.6 (best 10.1)	5.4 to 22.2 (best 12)

Source: R. G. Ridker, "The Problem of Estimating Total Cost of Air Pollution: A Discussion and an Illustration," *Report to the U.S. Public Health Service,* Washington, D.C., July 1966; P. H. Gerhardt, "An Approach to Estimation of Economic Losses Due to Air Pollution," National Air Pollution Control Administration (mimeo, June 1969); L. B. Barett and T. E. Waddell "The Cost of Air Pollution Damages: A Status Report," AP-85 (Environmental Protection Agency, February 1973); L. R. Babcock, Jr., and N. L. Nagda "Cost Effectiveness of Emission Control," Journal of the Air Pollution Control Association (March 1973), pp. 173–79; C. G. Justice, J. R. Williams, and J. D. Clement, "Economic Costs of Air Pollution Damage," STAR CR-103, prepared by Science, Technology and Research, Inc. (for Southern Services, Inc., Birmingham, Ala., May 1973); T. E. Weddell, "The Economic Damages of Air Pollution" EPA-600/5-74-012 (Washington, D.C., Government Printing Office, 1974); National Academy of Sciences, National Academy of Engineering, "Air Quality and Automobile Emission Control," vol. I, *Summary Report Prepared for the Committee on Public Works,* U.S. Senate, 93d Cong., 2d Sess., ser. no. 93-24 (Washington, D.C., Government Printing Office, September 1974), p. 121; Fred H. Abel, Dennis P. Tihansky, and Richard G. Waish, "National Benefits of Water Pollution Control" (Washington, D.C., Environmental Protection Agency, 1975); H. T. Heintz, Jr., and A. Hershaft, "National Benefits of Controlling Water Pollution," prepared for the Environmental Protection Agency by Enviro Control, Inc., under contract No. 68-01-2821, 1975. All cited in *Environmental Quality, the Sixth Annual Report of the Council on Environmental Quality,* 1975, p. 517; *Senate Study on Federal Regulation,* vol. VI, p. ₁0.

pollution, and $0.7 billion for solid waste. These expenditures, respectively, are estimated to increase to $18.6 billion, $19.5 billion, and $1.36 billion by 1984. (For other cost estimates, see Chapter 17.)

The benefits from pollution control are many but are not easy to quantify. Nonetheless, a few researchers have attempted to measure them. Their estimates are given in Table 5.8. (Benefits are to be understood in terms of damages saved.) The estimates given in Table 5.8 are based on several assumptions. But the striking feature of these estimates is their diversity. Take for instance the estimates of benefits resulting from air pollution control. In terms of 1975 dollars, they range from $2.8 billion to $42.2 billion. If one takes the higher figure, the estimated benefits definitely exceed the estimated costs of air pollution cited by the CEQ. On the other hand, if one takes the lower estimate, the estimated costs of air pollution control exceed the estimated benefits. The same conclusion holds true regarding the estimates of costs and benefits of water pollution control. Once again, one is in the unenviable position of having to draw uncertain conclusions about the net benefits (net of cost) of pollution control. Unfortunately, that is the state of the art at the moment! (For more discussion, see Chapter 17.)

5.5 SUMMARY AND CONCLUSIONS

To judge the success of any regulation, one needs to know how much it costs and what the ensuing benefits are. At the margin, if the benefits exceed the costs, one may pursue that regulatory activity. This is the gist of the common-sensical principle of cost-benefit analysis or the notion of efficiency. Of course, to conduct a cost-benefit analysis of any regulatory measure, one needs to have reliable estimates of both its costs and benefits. Unfortunately, in the area of public regulation at present there are no reliable estimates of such costs and benefits. Nonetheless, it is essential to know what the nature of these costs and benefits is; without this knowledge any exercise in the measurement of costs and benefits of public regulation would be meaningless.

Regulatory costs can be divided into two categories, direct and indirect. The direct costs are the administrative costs incurred by the government and by business, as well as costs of business compliance with the requirements of regulation. Of these, the compliance costs are the more sizable, although their precise estimates are generally not available. But from some individual as well as government research efforts it would seem that these costs can be substantial, especially those relating to entities such as the EPA and OSHA.

Less visible, but perhaps more important than compliance costs, are the indirect costs of regulation. These can assume several forms, such as static efficiency costs, dynamic costs, costs on secondary markets, transfer costs, redistributive costs, and inflationary costs. Unfortunately, quantification of these costs is usually a very difficult task, making cost-benefit analysis of public regulation all the more difficult.

The other side of the cost coin is regulatory benefits. There is no gainsaying the benefits of clean air, clean water, clean rivers, or a safe product. Unfortunately, one cannot readily quantify these benefits, although several attempts have been made. And where such attempts have been made, the estimates differ so vastly that it is difficult to know what the true benefits are.

Lacking estimates of the overall costs and benefits of regulation, the best we can do in the current state of knowledge is to present and examine the several case studies of cost-benefit analysis. These case studies concern the ICC's freight regulation, federal milk marketing orders, auto safety regulation, and pollution control; they provide some concrete numerical estimates of costs and benefits, and they point out some of the problems involved in obtaining these estimates. As our experience with regulation grows, especially in the area of social regulation, may be in the future we will be able to conduct a more effective cost-benefit analysis of public regulation.

QUESTIONS

5-1 The 1962 amendments to the Food, Drug and Cosmetic Act of 1938 required that the FDA not allow the marketing of a new drug unless it is safe (as required under the 1938 act) as well as effective in its intended use. This has slowed down the entry of new drugs in the U.S. market. What would happen if the requirement that "the drug be safe in its intended use" is relaxed?

5-2 Suppose a tragedy such as the thalidomide episode of 1961–1962 takes place. How would the marketplace handle such a tragedy without government intervention? (It was found in Europe that some mothers who took thalidomide during pregnancy gave birth to deformed babies. This drug was not used in the United States except on an experimental basis by some physicians.)

5-3 Under the federal milk marketing order program processors and distributors of milk who want to sell reconstituted milk (i.e., milk produced from powdered milk) in the market order areas are required to pay into a fund, called the producers' settlement fund. They pay into the fund the difference between the price of powdered milk they use and the price of class I milk (grade A and Grade B milk), which is higher than the former. What are the consequences of this policy on (1) the sales of powdered milk in the market order areas and in areas where such orders do not exist, (2) the prices of liquid as well as powdered milk, and (3) resource allocation in general?

5-4 Figure 5.3 shows annual per capita consumption of fluid milk and cream and the weighted-average class I price per hundred-weight in federal milk order markets

FIGURE 5.3
Annual per capita consumption of fluid milk and cream and weighted-average class I prices per hundredweight in federal milk order markets, 1965–1974.

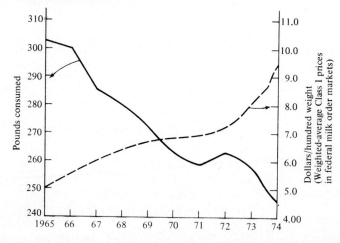

for the period 1965-1974. Is the observed decline in per capita consumption solely due to the increase in the weighted price of fluid milk and cream? If so, what can you say about the economic effect(s) of the milk orders? What other factors might account for the decline in per capita consumption of fluid milk and cream?

5-5 Given a guranteed rate of return on their capital, is there any incentive for public utilities to resort to peak-load pricing? Why or why not?

5-6 If utilities are allowed differential prices to take into account the peak-load phenomenon, would there be excess production capacity? Explain with reason. (You may use Figure 5.2 to answer the question.)

5-7 What steps would you recommend to encourage pharmaceutical research and innovation in the United States?

5-8 In a move to promote competition in international communication, the FCC on April 22, 1980, announced that it would allow COMSAT to offer international voice and data transmission to the public in competition with such established leaders as RCA Global Communication, ITT, and Western Union International. If Congress goes along with the FCC, what would be the consequences of such a move? Who would benefit from such a move and who would lose?

5-9 To understand the economics of a natural gas "shortage," consider Figure 5.4, in which S is the supply curve of gas producers. The demand curve is divided into two parts: D_1 represents demand by those customers who are assured gas supplies at the government-controlled price of P_1. The difference between D_2 and D_1 represents the demand by those gas customers who are willing to pay a higher price but cannot get it because of the gas shortage created by fixing the price at P_1. If there were no government regulation of the well-head price of natural gas, what would have been the price of gas and the quantity supplied? Would you recommend such a policy even if it "hurts" the consumers who can get gas at the price P_1? Explain carefully.

FIGURE 5.4
Hypothetical supply and demand curves for regulated and nonregulated natural gas markets.

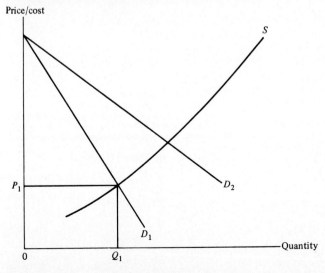

5-10 How would you conduct a cost-benefit study of the ban proposed by the FDA on saccharin, a suspected cancer-causing artificial sweetener?

5-11 Until very recently the City University of New York (CUNY) was known as "free tuition" university; qualified high school graduates living in the city could join any of the City University's several colleges without paying any tuition. How would you evaluate the social benefits and costs of the free tuition program? Would you advocate that other universities in the country follow the CUNY example? Why or why not?

5-12 How would you assess the economic costs and benefits of the suggestion that the Social Security System be abolished?

5-13 To assess the impact of pollution load, Paul W. MacAvoy obtained the statistical results shown in Table 5.9. What general conclusions can you draw from these results?

TABLE 5.9
REGULATORY EFFECTS ON POLLUTION

Sector	Trend effects on pollution volume*	Cycle effects on pollution volume*	Regulatory effects on pollution volume*	Percentage of the variation in pollution explained by these factors (R^2)
Minerals production	Positive	Positive	Negative	.61
Automobile utilization	Positive	na	*Negative*	.98
Chemical production	Negative	Negative	Positive	.62
Primary metals	*Negative*	Negative	Positive	.76
Electric utilities	Negative	Positive	*Negative*	.98
Petro refining	*Negative*	Positive	Negative	.79
All industries†	*Negative*	Positive	Positive	.19

*Those coefficients statistically significant from zero are italicized where significance is according to Students' t at probability of 0.05.

†Includes industrial, residential, commercial, and institutional fuel combustion, and oil and gas production and marketing, in addition to sectors listed.

Source: Regression analysis by the author. The general form of the equations was as follows:

Emissions/output = $a_0 + a_1$ trend + a_2 cycle + a_3 regulation + (a_iP_i),

where emissions = tons of pollutant i (EPA, unpublished data)
output   = index of production for industry (Federal Reserve Board), except demand for gasoline (Department of Commerce)
trend   = time trend, 1968 = 1
cycle   = index of capacity utilization for industry (Federal Reserve Fund Board)
regulation = variable equals 1 for the presence of regulation of pollutant i, and zero otherwise
P_1 = dummy variable for pollutant i for four of the five major pollutants: particulates, sulfur oxides, carbon monoxide, hydrocarbons, and nitrogen oxides. For the all-industries equation, additional dummy variables were added for each industry after the first. Estimation was two-stage least squares, correcting at the first stage for serial correlation

Paul W. MacAvoy, *The Regulated Industries and the Economy*, Norton, New York, 1979, p. 103.

5-14 To assess highway safety of automobile driving, suppose you are given the following statistical model:

$$Y = a_0 + a_1X_1 + a_2X_2 + a_3X_3 + a_4X_4 + a_5X_5 + a_6X_6 + e$$

where Y = accidents per vehicle-mile
X_1 = the cost of accident insurance
X_2 = personal income level
X_3 = driving speed
X_4 = driver's age
X_5 = alcoholic intoxication
X_6 = secular time trend
e = all other factors

A priori, what would be the relationship of each X variable to the dependent variable Y (state whether positive, negative, or no relationship)? How would you use the above model to assess auto safety during the pre- and postregulation periods (approximately since 1966). (See if your answers agree with those of Sam Peltzman in his *Regulation of Automobile Safety*).

APPENDIX: The Economics of Social Cost-Benefit Analysis

It was noted in the chapter that a cost-benefit analysis of an activity (be it production of a good or a service or regulation) undertaken by government is not an easy task. This is because such an activity generally raises some thorny problems of welfare economics,[19] especially problems relating to measurement as well as comparison of satisfactions of different members of society. To fix the ideas, consider two individuals A and B and a proposed government activity, say, construction of a highway. Now consider Figure 5.5.

In all the figures we represent A's and B's satisfaction (or welfare, loosely speaking) measured in some units on the two axes, and their respective positions before the proposed highway (marked by *X*) and after it (marked by *Y*).

Now if the situation is as shown in Figure 5.5, left diagram, clearly the change from *X* to *Y* has benefited both since each person's satisfaction has increased after the change. Loosely speaking, one can say that social welfare (the aggregate satisfaction of the two) has increased by the change. If the situation is as shown in Figure 5.5, middle diagram, where A's satisfaction remains the same while that of B goes up after the change, one can still say that social welfare has increased. Both these situations, as discussed in Chap-

---

[19]Welfare economics is that branch of economics which evaluates the social desirability of alternative economic states or systems.

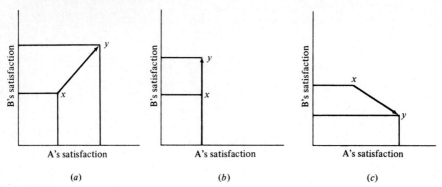

FIGURE 5.5
Social welfare before and after a proposed change.

ter 2, are Pareto-optimal. But the situation in Fig. 5.5, right diagram, is radically different. For now while A gains from the change, B loses (most government regulatory activities usually fall in this category). Now what can be said about social welfare in this situation? Has it increased or decreased? This is one of the hardest questions to answer in (welfare) economics. Nicholas Kaldor of England would argue that social welfare in such a situation can be said to have increased if the gainer A can somehow compensate the loser B and still come out ahead, that is, after the compensation A still gains. Whether in practice one can devise such compensating schemes or even talk about the concept of social welfare in situations such as that in Figure 5.5, right diagram, is extremely controversial and is beyond the scope of this book.[20] Suffice it to note here that the entire area of social cost-benefit analysis is beset with all kinds of controversies and that is why one can never be sure whether a proposed government activity is or is not socially beneficial.

[20]For a clear and readable exposition, see P. R. G. Layard and A. A. Walters, *Microeconomic Theory*, McGraw-Hill, New York, 1978, pp. 29–44.

GENERAL PURPOSE REGULATION: THE U.S. ANTITRUST LAWS AND HOW THEY WORK

As noted in Chapter 1, broadly speaking there are two types of regulation: general purpose and industry, consumer or product-specific. In Part Two, we consider general purpose regulation as exemplified by the U.S. antitrust laws. The overall goal of these laws, at least on paper, is to preserve and encourage competition in the economy as a whole by discouraging monopolies or tendencies toward monopolies by concentrating economic power in the hands of a few sellers or oligopolists.

Since the general thrust of the antitrust laws is against monopoly, Chapter 6, entitled ``Monopoly: The basis of the U.S. Antitrust Laws,'' discusses the meaning and types of monopoly, sources of monopoly power, measurement of this power by concentration ratios, and, more importantly, the economic effects of monopoly. It will be seen that with some qualifications, and compared to perfect competition, monopoly leads to a higher price and reduction in the output of the monopolized product. This has the effect of reducing economic efficiency and therefore consumer welfare. Considered also in this chapter are the sociopolitical objections to monopoly as well as the methods of regulating monopoly. We also discuss the special problems facing natural monopolies and how such monopolies may be regulated.

After outlining an approach to the study of the U.S. antitrust policies, we discuss in Chapter 7 the U.S. antitrust laws and the provisions of the major antitrust laws, namely, the Sherman Act of 1890, the Clayton Act of 1914, as amended by the Robinson-Patman Act of 1936 (the antiprice discrimination law), the Celler-Kefauver Anti-Merger Act of 1950, and the Federal Trade Commission Act of 1914. We also consider very briefly the administrative structure that has been created to enforce these laws.

Chapter 8, ``The Sherman Act in the Courts,'' discusses ten landmark antitrust cases tried under the Sherman Act. In each case we follow a standard format, namely, a brief introduction, facts of the case, legal decision in the case, and a critical evaluation of the decision.

Chapters 9 and 10 are devoted to the working of the Clayton Act. In Chapter 9 we consider two of the Clayton Act's four major provisions, namely, price discrimination and tying contracts. We first consider the economics of (monopolistic) price discrimination and point out the conditions under which a monopolist may engage in price discrimination and also when such price discrimination may benefit not only the monopolist but also the society at large. We then consider two leading cases that shed light on the legal thinking on price discrimination. It will be seen that economists and the courts do not look at price discrimination in the same light. We then discuss the tying contracts and their effect on competition with the aid of two landmark cases. Here too, the legal outcome is at odds with the economic view of tying.

In Chapter 10 we discuss the remaining two provisions of the Clayton Act, namely, mergers and acquisitions and interlocking directorates, with major emphasis on the former because of their controversial nature. After distinguishing among horizontal, vertical, and conglomerate mergers, we then examine the antimerger provisions contained in Sec. 7 of the act and their fate in the hands of the courts as evidenced in four landmark decisions. Once again we will see that what is justifiable from an economic viewpoint is not necessarily so from the point of view of the courts. This chapter also presents a somewhat extended discussion of the Justice Department's *Merger Guidelines* issued in 1968, and revised in 1982, which discuss the circumstances in which the Justice Department may initiate antimerger proceedings. This chapter concludes with a brief discussion of the relatively unused Sec. 8 of the act, which deals with interlocking directorates.

The topic discussed in the preceding chapters may prompt the reader to raise these questions: (1) Who makes the antitrust laws? (2) Has the American economy become more or less competitive as a result of these laws? and (3) What is the future of these laws?

Although the antitrust laws are passed by the Congress, these laws are often stated in such vague and open-ended words that it is ultimately the Supreme Court's responsibility to pass judgment, on a case-by-case basis, on what Congress had meant when it passed a particular antitrust law. This has, willy-nilly, conferred a tremendous power on the judges in interpreting the various statutes, a power that may not have been used consistently for the benefit of consumers, the group that was supposed to be the prime beneficiary of the antitrust laws.

Although it is hard to be categorical about the effects of the antitrust laws on the American economy, one thing that stands out very clearly from the various case studies is that in the eyes of the courts protection of competition has meant protection of the competitors. Case after case the courts seem to be moved by the "small business per se" philosophy, with the result that the final outcome may not be necessarily desirable from the view of economic efficiency, a point of view strongly espoused by several economists. The courts have been entrusted, either by design or by default, with the twin job of balancing efficiency versus equity, a job very difficult to do under the best of circumstances. But in the pro-small business view expressed in many a Supreme Court decision, it seems, the Court has weighed the equity aspect more heavily.

What is the future of the U.S. antitrust laws? Notice that, with the exceptions of the 1936 and 1950 amendments, these laws predate 1915. Since then the economy of the country has undergone several important structural changes. Therefore, what was good at the turn of the nineteenth century and early twentieth century, is not necessarily so now, especially when one considers the fact that the world economy has become much more interdependent and that other countries do not have the kinds of antitrust laws that prevail here. Therefore, the major U.S. antitrust laws need to be changed to fit the changing U.S. and world economic conditions. The direction of the change that may be effected will be outlined in the last part of this text, which deals with regulatory reforms in general (see Chapter 18).

CHAPTER 6

MONOPOLY: THE BASIS OF THE U.S. ANTITRUST POLICIES

The primary goal of the U.S. antitrust policies is to promote competition and discourage monopoly. We have already seen in Chapter 2 that under some highly restrictive assumptions the theorem of the invisible hand provides theoretical justification for competition. With the assumed conditions it was seen that, among other things, competition leads to economic efficiency, that is, efficient allocation of scarce economic resources. An implication then is that in cases of imperfect competition, such as monopoly, resources will not be allocated efficiently.[1] In this chapter we show to what extent this is true and whether monopoly is necessarily an evil under all circumstances. We also raise the question of the extent to which the economic theory of monopoly provides a basis for the U.S. antitrust laws.

6.1 DEFINITION AND TYPES OF MONOPOLY

To facilitate our discussion, let us at the outset define monopoly and distinguish various types of monopoly.

---

[1]Besides monopoly, other forms of imperfect competition discussed in the literature are: duopoly (two sellers), oligopoly (a few sellers with interdependent behavior and reaction), and monopolistic competition (several sellers selling differentiated products which may be imperfect substitutes for one another). Our discussion of the economic effects of monopoly, with some modifications, can be extended to the other forms of imperfect competition just listed. We take monopoly as the antithesis of competition or the extreme form of imperfect competition.

Definition of Monopoly

"A monopolist is a seller (or group of sellers acting like a single seller) who can change the price at which his product will sell in the market by changing the quantity that he sells."[2] This definition brings out several important points.

First, although in some cases a monopolist can be both a single producer and a single seller of a product, this need not be the case. A group of producers of a product can get together and form a cartel (a collusive agreement) and let it decide the price at which the members of the cartel will sell the product (such collusive agreements are illegal in the United States, as we will see later). Thus, effectively there is a single seller, although several producers. The most celebrated example is the Organization of Petroleum Exporting Countries (OPEC) cartel, which is an association of some eleven major producers of oil in the world who collectively determine the price they will charge for their oil.

Second, the essence of monopoly is power or control over price. This power is due to the ability of the monopolist to regulate the rate of his or her output (or outputs of the members of a cartel, if there is a cartel, which is done via some quota system). This would tend to imply that, to be successful, a monopolist must control 100 percent of the output or sale of the product sold. In reality, however, such a complete control over output or sale is rarely accomplished, save in the case of the public utilities, which are controlled by state or local governmental authorities. In practice, therefore, very often "monopoly" is construed to mean a substantial control over the output or sale of a product, this control being measured by a suitable statistical measure, such as the Herfindahl index or the *concentration ratio,* which is explained in Section 7. This has created several problems for both the courts and the antitrust division of the Department of Justice, when it comes to determining whether monopoly exists in a given situation. We will examine these problems later on.

Third, to have effective control over price means that the monopolized product has no close substitutes. If that is not the case, consumers will switch to competing products if the monopolist decides to increase his or her price by curtailing output.[3] This is not to say that in the long-run competing or substitutable products will not develop. If that happens, obviously, monopoly power will decline.

Types of Monopolies

Figure 6.1 gives the types of monopolies that one may encounter. Broadly speaking there are two types of monopolies, natural and "pure."

As noted in Chapter 2, a natural monopoly (e.g., a gas pipeline company or

---

[2]Richard A. Posner, *Antitrust Law: An Economic Perspective,* The University of Chicago Press, Chicago, 1976, p. 8.

[3]This is likely to be the case in monopolistic competition. Sellers of different brands of cigarettes have a limited monopoly of their brand. But if one seller decides to increase price substantially, consumers might very well switch to another brand. That is why one does not find a substantial variation in the prices of various brands of cigarettes.

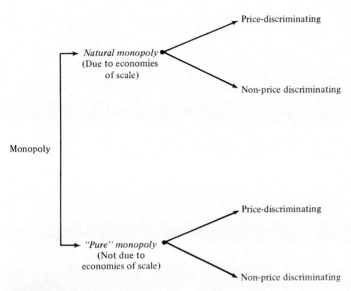

FIGURE 6.1
Types of monopolies.

a telephone, gas, or electric utility) occurs when the average cost of production of a single firm in the industry falls over such a large range of output that the single firm can produce the total quantity sold at a lower average cost than can two or more smaller firms. When this happens, the said firm has (internal) *economies of scale*:[4] the larger the output, the lower the average cost of production. In Figure 2.1, we showed why in the case of economies of scale it is better to have a single firm than, say, ten or more firms. Here monopoly has advantage over competition; it is not necessarily an evil.

A "pure" monopoly, on the other hand, need not exhibit economies of scale; that is, after a certain range of output, its average cost of production instead of decreasing actually increases (see Figure 6.3, later in this chapter). If that happens, there are diseconomies of scale. Of course, in some cases the average cost curve can be horizontal over a certain range of output, which means that there are neither economies or diseconomies of scale. What explains the emergence of monopolies in cases where there are no economies of scale? The answer is provided in the next section.

Now a monopoly, natural or "pure," can be of the price-discriminating or non-price-discriminating type. By price discrimination we mean that different buyers (or groups of buyers) are charged different prices for the same good or

[4]For the sources of internal economies of scale, see Section 6.2. It should be noted that economies of scale can be external, that is, external to the firm. They may arise because of, say, some technological innovation which benefits all the firms in the industry.

service, the difference not related to differences in the costs of sale. As is well known, public utilities such as electric and telephone companies charge different prices to residential, commercial, and industrial customers, although the product they sell as well as the cost of sale is the same. As we will show in Chapter 9, such price discrimination can be economically justifiable.

6.2   SOURCES OF MONOPOLY POWER

Before we examine the economic consequences of monopoly, it is instructive to find out how monopolies arise. There are several sources of monopoly, some of which are as follows.

Economies of Scale

As noted previously, if the average cost of production declines over a fairly large range of output (i.e., economies of scale), a single firm can produce an industry's output more cheaply than several small firms can (see Figure 2.3). This is often the genesis of natural monopolies, such as gas pipeline companies and public utilities. As pointed out in Chapter 2, the total gas pipeline construction costs are proportional to the circumference of the pipeline and therefore to its radius. Since the square of the radius increases more rapidly than the radius, it follows that cost per unit decreases continuously as the pipeline's capacity increases.

Such (internal) economies of scale may be due to specialized or superior production technology, managerial ability, marketing, or capital raising ability of the management or a combination of one or more of these factors: The use of such specialized inputs often requires the firm to produce a large enough volume of output so as to keep them fully utilized. Regardless of the source, the net effect of such economies of scale is that the average cost of production declines over an extended range of output, and in this case, as noted previously, it is better to have a single firm than a large number of competitors. Recognizing this fact, state and local authorities generally permit only one electric, telephone, or cable TV company in any given geographical area.

Ownership of Scarce Economic Resources

Very often a firm, although not a monopoly initially, succeeds in achieving monopoly power because it has acquired control over some scarce resource(s) and has been successful in preventing other firms from owning it. The classic example is that of the Aluminum Company of America (Alcoa), which until World War II controlled the production of all aluminum by effectively owning bauxite, the essential ingredient in the production of aluminum. It did this by signing long-term contracts with the companies producing bauxite, with the stipulation that they not sell it to any other company (we will see the legality of this practice in a later chapter). Another example is the DeBeers Company, which controls the world's diamond market. DeBeers is actually a selling agent for a group of diamond manufacturers from South Africa who control about 75 percent of the world's diamond production.

Patents

A patent is the exclusive right granted by the government to an inventor to manufacture, use, or sell an invention for a certain number of years (17 years in the United States). Thus a patent grants monopoly by law. There are literally thousands of patents granted by the government. The Patent and Trademark Office of the United States issues more than 70,000 patents annually, which range from highly complex and sophisticated machinery to a simple plastic safety razor. The idea behind granting patents is not only to preserve the property rights of the patentees but also to give incentive to invent, to invest in research and development (R&D), to commercialize new technology, and to make inventions public that would otherwise be kept secret.

Trademarks and Copyrights

A trademark or a brand name is made of any distinctive word, name, symbol, or device used by a manufacturer, merchant, or businessperson to identify his or her goods or services and to distinguish them from those sold by others. Take, for instance, the name "Sanka," which is a brand of decaffeinated coffee. Until other competing brands of decaffeinated coffee came along, the name Sanka was synonymous with decaffeinated coffee; even today people who drink decaffeinated coffee often ask for Sanka although they may be served some other brand of decaffeinated coffee. Thus the trademark or brand name Sanka has conferred some monopoly on the producers of this coffee. Another well-known case is the name Xerox, which has become synonymous with instant photocopying of printed material.

A copyright is the exclusive right granted by law to its owner to reproduce the copyrighted work in copies or phonorecords and distribute them to the public by sale, rental, lease, or lending. For example, the McGraw-Hill Book Company has the exclusive copyright to the author's book *Basic Econometrics*. So long as McGraw-Hill owns the rights, no other publisher (not even the author) can reproduce the book. In short, McGraw-Hill has monopoly in *Basic Econometrics*; it is the sole seller of the book. This, of course, does not mean that it has a monopoly on textbooks in econometrics in general.

Licensing and Exclusive Franchises

Licensing is another source of monopoly power. For example, in New York City (and most other cities) one cannot drive a taxicab without a license, known as a "medallion." Until 1937, anyone would get a medallion by paying a nominal fee to the city. But since then the city has put a limit on the number of medallions issued, which effectively fixed the total supply of the medallions. The effect was that the owners of the medallions acquired a valuable property right which they could sell in the open market if they so wished. As a result, over the years the price of the medallion in the open market increased substantially; at present a medallion sells for about $45,000, an astronomical increase over the initial license fee of about $5 even when allowance is made for inflation. (Recall Chapter 4 for the reasons behind licensing.)

An exclusive franchise, which grants a certain privilege to an individual or a business entity, is yet another source of monopoly power. For example, local authorities grant exclusive privileges to cable TV companies to serve some well-defined geographical areas; in any given area only one cable TV company is authorized to serve the residents of that area (Why?). Similarly, the Interstate Commerce Commission (ICC) has granted exclusive trucking routes to trucking companies with well-defined geographical bounds. Likewise, the Civil Aeronautics Board (CAB) defines which airline will serve which areas. In all these cases, the franchisee does not have to worry about competition, for there is no free entry allowed.

All the above sources of monopoly may be called *barriers to new entry.* Recall that one of the characteristics of a competitive industry is free entry and free exit. But for monopoly to succeed it must somehow prevent new entry, whether the prevention is due to economies of scale, ownership of a scarce resource, patent laws, trademarks and copyrights, or licensing and exclusive franchises.

6.3 ECONOMIC EFFECTS OF MONOPOLY

To understand the antimonopoly and pro-competition bias of the U.S. antitrust laws to be discussed in the next chapter, it is important to know the economic consequences of monopoly vis-à-vis competition. The most straightforward way of doing this is to compare how price and output decisions are made under monopoly with those made under competition (we have already discussed the latter in Chapter 2).

To fix the ideas, consider the long-run supply (S) and demand (D) curves in a competitive industry, as shown in Figure 6.2. For expositional purposes the industry demand curve is assumed linear. The industry supply curve is simply the sum of the marginal cost curves of the individual firms in the industry (see any elementary textbook in microeconomics for an explanation). The competitive equilibrium price and equilibrium output are determined at the point at which the demand curve intersects the supply curve, that is, at point f, giving P_c (or point d), say, $1, and Q_c 2000 as the equilibrium price and quantity.

Now suppose that all the firms in the industry decide to form a cartel and let it decide on the price and output decisions. In effect, therefore, we now have a monopoly. The change from competition to monopoly necessitates some changes in the geometry of Figure 6.2. First, we must introduce the marginal revenue curve MR: Given the downward-sloping demand (or average revenue,

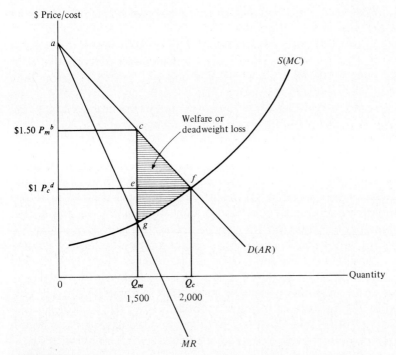

FIGURE 6.2
Competitive and monopoly price-output decisions and the welfare loss due to monopoly.

AR) curve, the only way a pure monopolist can increase the quantity sold is by reducing the price. Therefore, unlike the case of a purely competitive firm facing a horizontal demand curve and therefore a horizontal marginal revenue curve which is identical with the demand curve, the marginal revenue and the demand curves of the monopolist will be different; the MR curve will lie below the AR curve as shown in Figure 6.2.[5] Second, the supply curve S of the competitive industry now becomes the marginal cost (MC) curve of the monopolist; unlike a competitive firm the monopolist is a price setter and does not have a supply curve in the competitive sense. (This is because a monopolist can either set a price and see what the market will demand at that price or decide to fix the quantity and see what price will be forthcoming in the market. Hence he does

---

[5]To see why this must be so, consider a monopolist selling 100 units of output at $10 per unit, obtaining a total revenue of $1000. Because of the downward-sloping AR curve, she can sell 101 units only, say, at a price of $9.95 a piece, generating the total revenue of $1004.95. Therefore, although the 101st unit sells for $9.95, its contribution to total revenue (i.e., marginal revenue) is only $4.95 because to sell 101 units she is charging 5 cents per unit less; this costs her $5 in lost revenue on the 100 units, which she could have sold at $10 apiece. She cannot do so now, however, because she has to charge the same uniform price of $9.95 for all 101 units.

not have a supply curve in the sense of showing the maximum amount that he will produce per unit time at different prices.)

The monopoly equilibrium price and equilibrium quantity are at the point at which the marginal revenue curve intersects the marginal cost curve, that is, at point g in Figure 6.2. This, say, gives P_m $1.50 and Q_m 1500 as the monopoly equilibrium price and equilibrium output.

In short, the competitive solution (P_cQ_c) is changed to the monopoly solution (P_mQ_m). But this change has the following consequences:

1 There is an increase in the unit price from P_c to P_m or from $1 to $1.50.

2 The quantity sold has decreased from Q_c to Q_m or, from 2000 to 1500.

3 There is a transfer of income from consumers to the monopolist of the magnitude given by the area *bced*. This transfer results from the fact that before monopolization the consumers could have bought the quantity *de* (or OQ_m) at the competitive price P_c but for the same amount they are now paying P_m. Hence $(P_m - P_c)$. *de* or the rectangle *bced* represents the amount of income transfer from consumers to the monopolist (in the diagram it is $0.50 \times 1500 = $750). But note carefully that this transfer of income does not involve any efficiency loss, that is, loss due to inefficient allocation of resources; there is only redistribution of income in favor of the monopolist.[6]

4 The efficiency loss is given by the sum of the two triangular areas, *cfe* and *efg*. This sum is called the welfare or *deadweight loss,* which, as noted in Chapter 5, is the net value of goods and services not produced because of departure from competitive conditions. The area *cfe* is the deadweight loss to the consumers (more technically, the deadweight loss in the consumer's surplus): at the competitive price P_c they would have bought the amount *ef,* which they did not want to buy at the higher monopoly price P_m. The area *efg* is the deadweight loss to the producer, that is, the monopolist (more technically, the deadweight loss in the producer's surplus). This is because the units *ef,* whose cost of production (given by the *MC* curve) is less than the competitive price P_c are not now produced; the monopolist chose to cut his output, which raises the price. In short, the total area *cfg* represents the efficiency or deadweight loss to society, the consumers' share of the deadweight loss being $250 (50 cents times 500 units not purchased) or the area *cfe*.

The economic case against monopoly thus rests on two grounds. First, there is a transfer of income from consumers to the monopolist. In terms of Figure 6.2, the monopolist's gain is equal to the area *bced* minus the area *efg*. The consumers lose the area *bced*. Now if before monopolization the distribution of income was what Paul Samuelson calls "ethically" correct, then such a transfer of income would obviously hurt the consumers. Second, and important from the economist's viewpoint, there is the welfare or efficiency loss to the tune of the area *cfg*. In other words, resources under monopoly tend to be misallocated. The reason is: the consumers would in fact prefer the additional quantity

---

[6]As shown immediately below, however, the monopolist's net gain is the area *bced* minus the area *efg*.

ef but cannot get it at price P_c. The monopolist, on the other hand, by not producing the same quantity, is releasing resources that would have gone into its production. If the rest of the economy is in competitive equilibrium, these released resources would disturb that equilibrium; resources are diverted to other industries where they are not needed and where their value (i.e., opportunity cost) is less.

6.4 SOCIOPOLITICAL OBJECTIONS TO MONOPOLY

Besides the economic case against monopoly, there are some sociopolitical objections to monopoly which will be briefly noted. These are very well spelled out by Posner as follows:[7]

1 " . . . monopoly transfers wealth from consumers to stock-holders of monopolistic firms, a redistribution that goes from less to more wealthy."

2 ". . . monopoly, or more broadly any condition (such as concentration) that fosters cooperation among competing firms, will facilitate an industry's manipulation of the political process to obtain protective legislation aimed at increasing the industry's profits."

3 By limiting monopoly, a small business per se policy will promote economic efficiency.

Insofar as point 1 above is concerned, we have already shown how monopoly can lead to redistribution of income. Now whether such a redistribution is good or bad is often an ethical question and the economist qua economist does not have much to say about it. That is why, in discussing the virtues of free competition in Chapter 2, it was assumed that the income distribution is ethically correct but whose *ethics* are another question.

In regard to point 2 above, this is nothing but the capture theory of regulation discussed in Chapter 2. Whether a monopolized industry is in a better position to obtain special privileges (restriction of entry, a higher price, or a higher rate of return) than a competitive one is a moot question. Moreover, considering the fact that industries such as agriculture, trucking, local broadcasting, banking, medicine, etc., which are not intrinsically monopolistic, have also obtained protective legislation (recall the federal milk price-support program), it is not clear whether monopoly per se has more political clout.

With reference to point 3 above, Posner argues that promotion of small business as an antimonopoly policy is ill-conceived. In his words:

> The best overall antitrust policy from the standpoint of small business is no antitrust policy, since monopoly, by driving a wedge between the prices and the costs of the larger firms in the market (it is presumably they who take the lead in forming cartels), enables the smaller firms in the market to survive even if their costs are higher than those of the large firms.[8]

[7]Posner, op. cit., pp. 18–19.
[8]Posner, op. cit., p. 19.

What Posner is saying can be seen from Figure 6.2. In this figure the monopoly price P_m far exceeds the marginal cost of production of the monopoly output, which is given by point g in the figure. Therefore, even if a small firm's marginal cost of production is greater than g, it can survive as long as its marginal cost is smaller than the monopoly price P_m.

For these reasons it is doubtful whether a strong case against monopoly can be made on purely sociopolitical grounds. If one places a strong emphasis on efficiency, as economists do for reasons already explained, then that should form the basis of the antitrust laws. But as we will show in the ensuing chapters, the courts have not adopted an exclusively economic view. As a matter of fact, on innumerable occasions the courts have adopted a small business per se policy, that is, without regard to whether such businesses are efficient or not. Whether this is desirable is a moot question; we will have more to say about it in the following chapters.

6.5   REGULATION OF MONOPOLY[9]

Granted that monopoly involves some social welfare loss (as measured by the deadweight loss), what can be done about it? One may adopt two broad approaches: (1) price regulation and (2) taxation.

Price Regulation

To see how price regulation works, consider Figure 6.3. Without any regulation, the monopolist of Figure 6.3 will set price at P_m and produce Q_m units of output (the $MC = MR$ rule). The monopoly profits are equal to the rectangle $bckj$, which is the difference between total revenue and total cost. Now from Figure 6.2 we know that the competitive solution would be price P_c and output Q_c. Therefore, the government or a similar regulatory authority could establish P_c as the price the monopolist should charge. This would result in a lower price per unit (P_c versus P_m) and higher output (Q_c versus Q_m). Although monopoly profits still exist (given by the rectangle $fl \times OQ_c$ or the difference between total revenue and total cost), consumer welfare has increased. Those who bought Q_m units before at P_m price can still buy the same amount but at a lower price P_c and also some new consumers can buy the additional amount Q_mQ_c at the lower price. In other words, the deadweight losses of Figure 6.2 disappear.

The regulatory authorities can go overboard, however. In their zeal to wipe out monopoly profits they may set the price where $AR = AC$, that is, where the average revenue or price is equal to the average cost of production (at point i in Figure 6.3).[10]

---

[9]The following discussion is based on Richard H. Leftwich, *The Price System and Resource Allocation*, 7th ed., The Dryden Press, Inc., Hinsdale, Ill., 1979, pp. 280–283.

[10]Economists define the long-run average cost to include the opportunity cost of all inputs employed, including the capital supplied by the owner. The opportunity cost of this capital is measured by what it would have earned by way of rate of return in the best alternative use. Therefore, pricing where $AR = AC$ will wipe out only the profits over and above this opportunity rate of return. Such excess profits are called "pure" or "monopoly" profits.

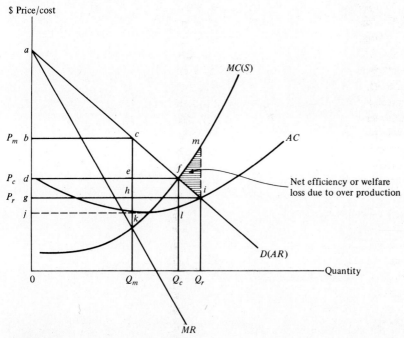

FIGURE 6.3
Regulation of monopoly by price control.

On the surface it sounds like the ideal policy, for now the regulated price P_r is even lower than the competitive price P_c and the output is greater than even the output under competition, Q_r versus Q_c. But economically this is a bad policy, for as Figure 6.3 shows, at the output level Q_r the marginal cost m is greater than even the average revenue or price P_r the consumer is willing to pay. The shaded area *fmi* in Figure 6.3 shows the net welfare loss from overproduction. This inefficiency loss is as bad as the one resulting from the monopoly solution, although the magnitude of the two losses may be different.

Taxation

Instead of price regulation, one may use taxation to curb monopoly power. To see how this can be accomplished, consider Figure 6.4. As before, the unregulated monopoly equilibrium price and quantity are P_m and Q_m and the monopoly profits are given by the rectangle *abfe*. Suppose the government puts a lump-sum (i.e., some fixed dollar amount) tax on the monopolist which shifts the average cost curve from AC to AC_t. Since it is a lump-sum tax, it does not affect the marginal cost curve. Therefore, the monopoly price and output decisions remain as before, namely, P_m and Q_m. The effect of the tax is to reduce the monopolist's profits from the rectangle *abfe* to the rectangle *abdc*. The government could, if it wishes, refund the total tax collected (equal to the rectangle

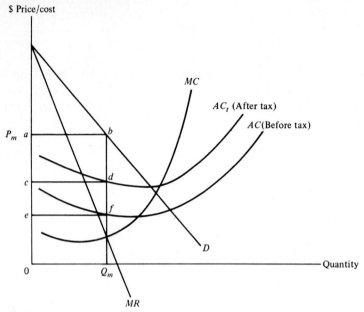

FIGURE 6.4
Regulation of monopoly by a lump sum tax.

cdfe) to consumers by way of rebates. Note that the effect of this lump-sum tax is felt by the monopolist alone. (Also note that there is no change in deadweight loss from monopoly. Why?) Things can be different if instead of a lump-sum tax the government imposes a specific or variable tax per unit of output. In this situation the tax burden may be borne by consumers as well as the monopolist (see question 6-14).

6.6 REGULATION OF NATURAL MONOPOLIES

In Sections 6.3 and 6.5 we examined the reasons behind regulating monopolies as well as the methods that may be used to regulate them. The natural monopolies, because of the falling average cost curve over a substantial range of output, pose some additional problems for regulation, which we now discuss in this section.

To fix the ideas, consider Figure 6.5, which is a reproduction of Figure 6.3 except that the AC curve now declines over a fairly long range of output. Since the AC curve is falling, the MC curve lies below it for much the same reason that the MR lies below the AR curve when the latter is downward-sloping. As in Figure 6.3, $(P_m\ Q_m)$, $(P_c\ Q_c)$ and $(P_r\ Q_r)$ represent, respectively, the monopoly competitive, and regulatory solutions. Clearly, the monopoly solution is not in the best interest of the public because the monopoly price far exceeds the marginal cost of production: As a matter of fact, between Q_m and Q_c consumers, as shown by the demand curve, are willing to pay a price greater than the marginal cost of production but cannot get the product if the monopolist sticks to Q_m.

The choice, therefore, lies between the regulatory and competitive solutions. With the regulatory solution, price equals average cost and hence such a solution might sound optimal; the monopolist is not making any profits over and above what may be allowed by way of some rate of return on her capital, which is included in the AC curve. But this is not an optimal solution. The optimal solution is the competitive solution (P_c Q_c) because it avoids the deadweight loss shown by the triangle *fhi:* Between P_r and P_c, the price (as read from the demand curve AR) exceeds the marginal cost of production. Therefore, if the price was fixed at P_r, it would mean that consumers are denied the additional output Q_rQ_c although until the output level Q_c they are willing to pay a price greater than the marginal cost. In short, it is with the competitive solution that the resources are allocated more efficiently.

The competitive solution, however, creates a problem because at the competitive price P_c the average cost exceeds the price, meaning that if the monopolist were forced to charge the price P_c there would be (financial) losses for her, the total magnitude of the loss being Q_c times ($P_c - AC$ given by point *j*). But

FIGURE 6.5
Pricing under natural monopoly.

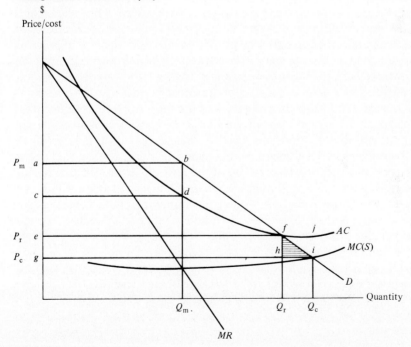

this loss is not efficiency loss; it is simply a transfer of income from the monopolist to the consumers. (Note that at the monopoly price P_m compared to either the regulatory or competitive price, there is a transfer of income from consumers to the monopolist.)

Now one way to avoid the transfer loss just noted is to price the product at the competitive price P_c but then subsidize the monopolist to the tune of the transfer loss. Maybe besides paying the competitive price P_c consumers will be asked to pay a surcharge in such a way that the total surcharge will equal the magnitude of the transfer loss. This solution has the virtue that it will lead to maximum possible output.

An alternative solution is to allow the monopolist to charge different prices, that is, to price-discriminate.[11] Thus, in Figure 6.5 the monopolist, say, an electric utility, can charge the price P_r for the first Q_r units consumed and P_c for any subsequent units. This implies that the first Q_r units will cover both the variable and fixed or overhead costs while the additional units beyond Q_r will cover only their marginal cost. Most electric utilities charge such discriminating prices, also known as part or block pricing — one price for residential consumers, one for commercial consumers, and one for industrial consumers.

In practice, however, most state public utility commissions, which approve the prices (tariff or rate structure) that the utilities can charge, do not exactly follow the scheme just suggested. Instead they will allow the utilities to cover their variable costs of production plus a ''fair'' rate of return on the invested capital, which is called the rate base. The fair rate of return, which is supposed to reflect the cost of capital (i.e., the rate or price at which capital can be borrowed from various sources), generally ranges between 10 to 14 percent. Now given the fair rate of return on the rate base, it is up to the individual utilities to devise the actual rate structure that takes into account the demand elasticities of the relevant groups of customers. Thus, the unit price per kwh is likely to be higher for residential than industrial consumers, for the latter can resort to competitive fuels for their needs while an average consumer cannot do so readily.

We will not go into the actual mechanics of the rate structure determination of the public utilities[12] except to point out that if the fair return allowed by the regulatory commissions exceeds the cost of raising capital, utilities will have incentive to overinvest. They might increase the rate base, for it will increase the net revenue of the utility owners, net of the cost of capital. Thus, if the fair rate of return is determined at 16 percent whereas the cost at which funds can be obtained in the financial markets is only 12 percent, the owners can increase their revenue by 4 percent. This effect, known in the literature as the Averch-Johnson effect and to which a reference has been made previously, generally

---

[11]The topic of price discrimination in general will be discussed in greater detail in Chapter 9. Suffice it to note here that economists define price discrimination as the practice of selling the same product or service to different customers at different prices, the differences not related to cost differences in providing that good or service.

[12]For a thorough discussion, see Alfred E. Kahn, *The Economics of Regulation*, vols. I and II, Wiley, New York, 1970.

encourages utilities to carry more reserve capacity than is really needed or to invest in more highly capital intensive production processes than is necessary (e.g., nuclear power plants in preference to fossil fuel plants). Therefore, there may be very little incentive for such utilities to reduce their costs of operation.

6.7 THE MEASUREMENT OF MONOPOLY POWER: THE CONCENTRATION RATIOS

Although the economic meaning of the term *monopoly* is well-defined, in practice the term is used loosely to mean some degree of monopoly power. But how does one measure this power? Now theoretically we know from Figure 6.2 that in the case of monopoly there is a divergence between price and marginal cost, with price exceeding the marginal cost. Therefore, one can measure the strength of monopoly by considering the difference between the monopoly price and the marginal cost. One such measure is Abba Lerner's index of monopoly power, which is defined as

$$\text{Lerner index of monopoly power} = \frac{(\text{price} - \text{marginal cost})}{\text{price}}$$

In terms of Figure 6.2 this index is measured by the distance cg divided by the distance cQ_m. Thus if the unit price is $1.50 and the marginal cost is 50 cents, the Lerner index is $1.00/$1.50 or 0.67 or 67 percent. Of course, the higher the value of this index, the greater the monopoly power. (Note: The extreme value of the index will be 1 when the marginal cost of production is zero, an unrealistic prospect.)

Although appealing, the Lerner index is not easy to compute in practice because information on marginal cost is not easy to come by (why would a monopolist disclose his marginal cost anyway?). Clearly, we need viable alternatives. But here we face a major difficulty, namely, how to identify whether monopoly exists in any given industry. Except in the field of public utilities, it is very difficult to find a single seller dominating any industry. Very often what we have are a few companies in an industry who account for a sizable proportion of the industry's size variable (output, sales, employment, profits, assets, expenditure on R&D, etc.) and several others who account for a small proportion of the size variable. Therefore, instead of talking about a single seller, in practice, we construe the term *monopoly* to mean the proportion of an industry's size variable accounted for by, say, two or four or at most the eight largest firms in the industry. If this number of firms accounts for a sizable proportion of the industry's size variable, we say that that industry is comparatively more monopolized than an industry in which the chosen number of leading firms account for a smaller proportion of the industry's size variable. This is essentially the idea behind the frequently used proxy of monopoly power, namely, the *concentration ratio*. Graphically the concentration ratio can be depicted in Figure 6.6.

As the point *A* on the concentration curve shows, in the hypothetical case

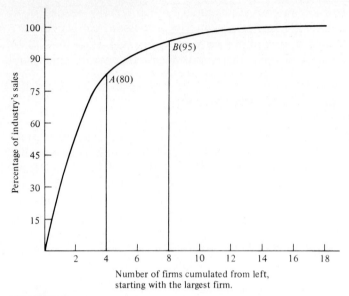

FIGURE 6.6
The concentration curve and concentration ratios.

the top four firms in the industry account for 80 percent of that industry's sale, hence the (four-firm) concentration ratio is 0.80 or 80 percent. Similarly, the top eight firms in the industry account for 95 percent of the industry's sales, hence the eight-firm concentration ratio is 0.95 or 95 percent (point *B*). The remaining ten firms in the industry account for only 5 percent of the industry's sale.

The concentration ratio presented above is known as the absolute concentration ratio. But one can also derive a relative concentration ratio, that is, the percentage of an industry's size variable accounted for by a given percentage of the firms in that industry. The details of this relative concentration measure can be found in question 6-6.

The Bureau of the Census of the U.S. Department of Commerce computes concentration ratios for most industries in the United States every few years. A sample of such ratios is given in Table 6.1. As the table shows, the degree of concentration varies from industry to industry. Compared to the women's and Misses' suits and coats industry, for example, the electric lamps industry is highly concentrated. Similarly, the cigarette industry is much more concentrated than the cement industry.

Uses and Limitations of Concentration Ratios

As the preceding discussion shows, the concentration ratios give us some idea about the distribution of firms in an industry according to some size variable, such as sales, output, employment, profit, asset size, R&D expenditure, etc. But

TABLE 6.1
1972 CONCENTRATION RATIOS FOR REPRESENTATIVE INDUSTRIES

Industry	4-firm ratio, %	Number of firms
Motor vehicles and car bodies	93	165
Electric lamps	90	103
Chewing gum	87	15
Cigarettes	84	13
Household laundry equipment	83	20
Primary aluminum	79	12
Aircraft engines and engine parts	77	189
Photographic equipment and supplies	74	555
Tires and inner tubes	73	136
Calculating and accounting machines	73	74
Primary copper	72	11
Aircraft	66	141
Metal cans	66	134
Motorcycles, bicycles, and parts	65	219
Soaps and other detergents	62	577
Environmental controls	57	117
Railroad equipment and locomotives	56	128
Watches and clocks	55	183
Radio and TV receiving sets	49	343
Farm machinery and equipment	47	1465
Motors and generators	47	325
Blast furnaces and steel mills	45	241
Toilet preparations	38	593
Flour and other grain mill products	33	340
Petroleum refining	31	152
Footwear, except rubber	30	153
Bread, cake, and related products	29	2800
Pharmaceutical preparations	26	680
Cement	26	75
Meat packing	22	2293
Paints and allied products	22	1318
Men's and boys' suits and coats	19	721
Fluid milk	18	2024
Newspapers	17	7461
Bottled and canned soft drinks	14	2271
Wood household furniture (not upholstered)	14	2160
Women's and Misses' suits and coats	9	5254
Signs and advertising displays	6	3221

Source: "Concentration Ratios in Manufacturing," Bureau of the Census MC72(SR)-2, issued October 1975, Table 5 items. Reproduced from: William J. Baumol and Alan S. Blinder, *Economics: Principles and Policies,* Harcourt, Brace, New York, 1979, p. 480.

what use can be made of these ratios? Obviously, such ratios will be meaningful if they tell us something about the behavior of the firms in any given industry, behavior being measured by some criterion, such as price or profit or advertising expenditure, etc. For example, if in a highly concentrated industry (say, the four-firm concentration ratio in excess of 90 percent), profits are higher than in an industry not so highly concentrated (say, the four-firm concentration ratio less than 15 percent), assuming all other factors remain the same, one may say that the highly concentrated or monopolized industry earns higher profits than a competitive one. In short, then, if meaningful relationships can be established between concentration ratios and some economic variables of interest, one may find the concentration ratios a useful statistical device to learn something about the characteristic of an industry.

In practice, however, the concentration ratios as measures of monopoly power face several problems. First, there is no unanimity about the choice of the variable with respect to which one may compute the concentration ratios. Whether one should measure the concentration ratio in terms of sales, output, employment size, or advertising expenditure is not clear a priori. Second, suppose one computes the four-firm concentration ratio using, alternatively, asset size and sales measures. Suppose on the basis of the former, the four-firm (asset size) concentration ratio is 80 percent, but on the basis of sales, this ratio is 40 percent. Could one say that this industry is highly concentrated or comparatively competitive?[13] Third, even if one decides on a single size variable for concentration, say, output, one must still relate this ratio to some characteristic of monopoly.

As we saw, the essence of monopoly is the monopolist's control over price (or output) and the extent of this control can be measured by the discrepancy between price and marginal cost (or the Lerner index). But since information on marginal cost is rarely available, one must look for other indicators of monopoly behavior. For example, are profits likely to be greater in a monopolized industry than in a competitive one? From monopoly pricing it can be shown that monopoly or pure profits may persist under monopoly even in the long run, whereas under competition there are no pure profits in the long run. (In Figure 6.4 monopoly or pure profits are represented by the area *abfe* before taxation or *abdc* after taxation). Similarly, do monopolies spend more on innovations than competitive industries? If so, are there differences in the R&D expenditures between monopolized and competitive firms? Do monopolies spend relatively more on advertising expenditure than their competitive counterparts? One can look at several such variables and try to relate them to the concentration ratios to learn something about the nature of monopoly.

Several empirical studies have attempted to do just that.[14] Unfortunately, the

---

[13]There is empirical evidence, however, to suggest that the correlation between concentration ratios measured on alternative variables is generally above 0.9.

[14]For an overview, see Douglas Needham, *The Economics of Industrial Structure, Conduct and Performance,* St. Martin's, New York, 1978.

statistical results are not unequivocal. Some studies have found a high correlation between profits and concentration ratios, others have found weak or no relationship at all. Similarly, some authors argue that there are likely to be more innovations under competition than under monopoly, whereas others argue to the contrary. Very often the results depend on the kind of data available and on the type of statistical model used.

Given the uncertain nature of the statistical findings and noting that the concentration ratios are not unique, it is no wonder that these ratios have not provided any definite guidelines in the implementation and enforcement of the U.S. antitrust laws.

The Herfindahl Index

In June 1982 the Antitrust Division of the Justice Department announced that in the division's future antitrust cases it will use the Herfindahl index to measure concentration of market power instead of the hitherto used four- or eight-firm concentrations ratios. One reason for the change is that the concentration ratios do not take into account all the firms in the industry beyond the first four or the first eight-largest firms. Thus, if two industries have identical four-firm concentration ratios of 70 percent (say, measured by sales) and the remaining 30 percent is shared by two firms in the first industry but by thirty in the second industry, it is hard to maintain that the two industries are really equally highly concentrated. The other problem with the concentration ratios is that they weigh each firm included in the ratios equally regardless of their relative market shares. Consider, for example, two industries A and B where the market shares in the sales of the four top firms are as follows: industry A: 40 percent, 20 percent, 10 percent, and 6 percent; industry B: 19 percent, 19 percent, 19 percent, and 19 percent. In both the cases the aggregate four-firm concentration ratio is 76 percent. Intuitively, there is something wrong with such a measure of market power, for the first firm in industry A gets the same weight in the aggregate concentration ratio as the second firm although it is twice as large as the second and six times as large as the fourth firm.

Both these problems can be avoided by the Herfindahl index, named after the late economist Orris C. Herfindahl. The Herfindahl index (HI) is defined as follows:[15]

$$HI = \sum_{i=1}^{N} s_i^2$$

where N = number of firms in the industry and s_i = the market share of the ith firm ($i = 1, 2, \ldots, N$).

---

[15]Although popularly known as the Herfindahl index, it is known in the literature as Hirschman-Herfindahl index for the codiscoverer A. O. Hirschman.

In words, the Herfindahl index is calculated by summing the square of each firm's market share in sales, profits, assets, or a similar-size variable. The calculations and the logic behind this measure of market power can best be illustrated by the following example. For simplicity assume that there are three industries, each consisting of five firms.

Industry	Firm no.	Market share (s_i)	Squared market share (s_i^2)	HI
A	1	0.20	0.04	
	2	0.20	0.04	
	3	0.20	0.04	
	4	0.20	0.04	
	5	0.20	0.04	
		1.00	0.20	0.20
B	1	0.350	0.1225	
	2	0.200	0.0400	
	3	0.170	0.0289	
	4	0.155	0.0240*	
	5	0.125	0.0156*	
		1.000	0.2310	0.2310
C	1	0.500	0.2500	
	2	0.125	0.0156*	
	3	0.125	0.0156*	
	4	0.125	0.0156*	
	5	0.125	0.0156*	
		1.000	0.3124	0.3124

*To four decimal places.

Notice these features of the HI. First, its maximum value is unity (which occurs when there is one firm in the industry) and the minimum value is $(1/N)$ (which occurs when all the N firms in an industry are of equal size, as in the case of industry A). If the market shares are expressed in percentages, the maximum value is 10,000 (the square of 100) and the minimum value is $(10,000/N)$. On this basis, the HI for the three industries listed above is 2000, 2310, and 3124, respectively. Second, the HI assigns weights of unity to each firm's market share but because of the squaring of the firm shares the larger firm contributes more than proportionately and the smaller firm less than proportionately to the overall value of the index. Thus, in industry B the first firm's market share is only 35 percent but it contributes more than 50 percent to the overall index (0.1225 out of 0.2310). On the other hand, the fifth firm, although its market share is 12.5 percent, contributes only about 7 percent to the aggregate index (0.0156 out of 0.2310). Finally, on the basis of the four-firm concentration ratio, industries B and C are equally concentrated, the concentration ratio being 0.875 or 87.5

percent. But on the basis of the HI index, we see that industry C is more concentrated than industry B (0.3124 v. 0.2310 or 3124 v. 2310). Why?

In Chapter 10 we will see how the Antitrust Division plans to use the Herfindahl index in its antitrust investigations.

6.8 SUMMARY AND CONCLUSIONS

Before we embark on a study of the U.S. antitrust laws and how they work, it is important to examine at the outset the rationale behind the pro-competition and antimonopoly thrust of these laws. For this purpose we first defined monopoly and distinguished various types of monopolies and also considered the various sources of monopoly, such as the economies of scale, ownership of scare economic resources, patents, trademarks, and copyright laws, licensing, exclusive franchises.

We then examined the economic consequences of monopoly in comparison with competition. It was shown that compared to competition, monopoly leads to a higher price and a reduction in the output. This has two major effects: (1) a transfer of income from consumers to the monopolist, which results from the higher monopoly price, and (2) a welfare or deadweight loss, which results from the reduction in output as a result of the higher monopoly price. This is an efficiency loss, for it curtails the employment of economic resources in the monopolized industry and frees them for use in other industries where they may not be needed (in which case they remain idle) or where their value (as measured by their marginal productivity) is less. It is this misallocation of economic resources that could provide a powerful rationale to the antimonopoly or antitrust laws. It is in this sense that monopoly is an evil.

This is not to suggest that in actuality the U.S. antitrust laws are based on this purely economic objection to monopoly. As we have remarked earlier, and as we will see in the ensuing chapters, some noneconomic considerations, such as preserving small business for its own sake, have been as or more important than the purely economic considerations of allocative efficiency.

There are some authors who go so far as to argue that monopoly is not necessarily an evil if the objective is *productive efficiency,* that is, effective coordination of economic resources or inputs to produce the greatest possible output. Very often an indication of productive efficiency is the economies of scale experienced by a large firm in an industry. As we saw in the case of natural monopolies, in this situation it may be better to have a single seller than a host of smaller firms. That is, in such cases, small may not be necessarily beautiful. We will see in the case studies in the ensuing chapters the extent to which productive efficiency has governed some of the antitrust decisions.

To minimize the ill effects of monopoly, we considered price regulation and taxation as the remedies. By forcing the monopolist to charge a lower price, the regulatory authorities can increase social welfare. The extent of this increase depends on where the regulated price is in relation to the monopoly price.

Sometimes, overregulation can in fact lead to an efficiency loss. A lump-sum tax has the effect of reducing monopoly profits without affecting the level of monopoly output or price. But if the tax is specific or variable, its burden may fall on consumers as well as the monopolist.

Turning from theory to practice, we saw that the term *monopoly* is often used loosely to mean concentration of monopoly power in the hands of a few sellers in the industry. This concentration is measured by the Herfindahl index or concentration ratios, which measure the size of an economic variable (sales, output, profits, employment, etc.) accounted for by four or eight leading firms in the industry. We observed that the statistical studies which relate the concentration ratios to variables such as profits, advertising expenditure, and expenditure on research and development are flawed and that the positive relationship between these variables and the concentration ratios expected a priori is weak at best.

In the ensuing chapters we will refer to the various aspects of the economics of monopoly discussed in this chapter and elaborate upon some other aspects (e.g., price discrimination, etc.) as the occasion arises.

QUESTIONS

6-1 Table 6.2 provides data on the estimated costs of providing a particular facility for transmitting various types of messages via microwave radio with varying alternative capacities. The figure of $368,000 represents the starting-up costs — the costs of land, tower, building and access roads, etc., and must be incurred whether the capacity is 600 circuits or 6000 circuits.

Compute the average and marginal costs from the data in the table and sketch the corresponding curves roughly. What can you say about the economies of scale in this particular instance?

6-2 Continue with the data of question 6-1. Suppose that the anticipated demand for circuit capacity is 6000 channels. Suppose there are ten applicants who are willing to supply the total capacity at 600 channels apiece. Given the cost data, would you advise that there be ten companies providing the service? Why or why not? If your answer is negative, would you recommend that these ten companies merge and form a monopoly? If you do, would it not lead to efficiency or welfare loss? Explain your logic fully.

TABLE 6.2
ILLUSTRATIVE COSTS FOR TD2 RADIO RELAY SYSTEMS PER
REPEATER STATION

Voice grade circuit capacity	Total costs
600	$368,000
3,600	492,000
6,000	574,000

Source: Alfred E. Kahn, *The Economics of Regulation,* vol. I, p. 125. (The original source is the testimony of Albert M. Groggat, FCC Docket No. 16258, Bell Exhibit 24, May 31, 1966, table I).

6-3 Refer to Figure 6.2 in the text. Suppose that the competitive price (P_c) and the competitive output (Q_c) are $1 and 1000 units, respectively. After monopolization of the industry, the monopoly price (P_m) and the monopoly output (Q_m) are $1.50 and 700 units, respectively. What is the deadweight loss to the consumer as a result of the monopolization of the industry? What is the amount of the income transfer from consumers to the monopolist? Is this transfer good or bad?

6-4 Comment: "Monopoly is a bad thing for consumers, but a good thing for producers. So, on balance, we can't be sure that monopoly is responsible for any loss in economic efficiency." (The quote is from Jack Hirshleifer, *Price Theory and Applications,* Prentice-Hall, Englewood Cliffs, N.J., 1976, p. 301).

6-5 As noted in the text, besides the efficiency loss, monopoly involves a transfer of income from consumers to the monopolist. Should the courts and the antitrust laws be concerned with the question of income redistribution? Would it not be better if they confine their attention to the efficiency loss only? Answer carefully.

6-6 *Relative Concentration ratios:* Consider the following figure, which relates the cumulative percentage of an industry's size variable accounted for by a stated percentage of the firms in the industry. The resulting curve is known as the Lorenz curve, shown in Figure 6.7.

Also shown in the figure is the *line of absolute equality* (25 percent of the firms accounting for 25 percent of the industry's size variable, 50 percent of the firms accounting for 50 percent of the industry's share, and so on). How can you use the Lorenz curve to find out whether an industry is highly concentrated or not? Which concentration measure would you choose: the absolute concentration ratio or the relative concentration ratio given by the Lorenz curve? Why?

FIGURE 6.7
Percentage of firms cumulated, starting with the smallest size.

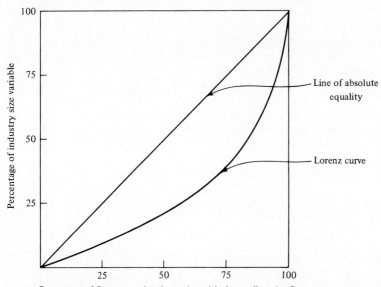

Percentage of firms, cumulated, starting with the smallest size firm

6-7 Refer to Figure 6-6 in the text. Define the *marginal concentration ratio* as the change in the value of the (absolute) concentration ratio as a result of adding a firm in the measurement of the concentration ratio. What is the marginal coentration ratio in Figure 6.6 as a result of using the eight-firm rather than the four-firm concentration ratio? Is the notion of the marginal concentration ratio of any use? How can the regulatory authority use such a measure?

6-8 Would you expect a positive relationship between concentration and expenditure on advertising? Why?

6-9 Would you expect more innovations under monopoly than under competition? Why?

6-10 As Table 6.1 in the text shows, there is a great deal of variation in the concentration ratios in U.S. industries. What factors determine whether an industry will be highly concentrated or will be relatively competitive?

6-11 If an industry is highly concentrated, does it necessarily mean that it will behave like a monopoly? Why or why not?

6-12 Would you recommend that big corporations such as IBM and GM be split into smaller companies? What factors will govern your decision?

6-13 Why would anyone pay $45,000 for a medallion to drive a taxicab in New York City if the original price of the medallion was but $5? What would be the consequences of issuing medallions freely at the prie of $5 each?

6-14 Instead of imposing a lump-sum tax on the monopolist (see Figure 6.4 in the text), suppose the government decides to impose a specific or per unit tax on the product of the monopolist. As a result, the marginal as well as the average cost curves of the monopolist shift, as shown in Figure 6.8. In comparison with Figure 6.4 of the text, what are the consequences of the per unit tax? Would you recommend a lump-sum tax or a specific tax? Make your reasons explicit.

6-15 Although the OPEC cartel establishes a common price for its members it does not restrict their output. Now it is quite possible for a member firm whose cost of production is lower than the average for the group to cheat a little by accepting a lower price and thus increase its share of the oil market. Until recently this has not happened to a great extent. Why? Why has OPEC been successful in maintaining an artificially high price (in relation to the average cost of production) for such a long period although it is historically the case that most cartels do not last long? Do you think OPEC will eventually break up? Why?

6-16 Trade unions are exempted by law from the antitrust laws. What is the rationale behind this exemption even though the unions are essentially monopolies?

6-17 Should trade associations such as the American Bar Association or the American Medical Association be regarded as monopolies? If so, would you recommend that they be brought under the antitrust laws? Give your reasoning.

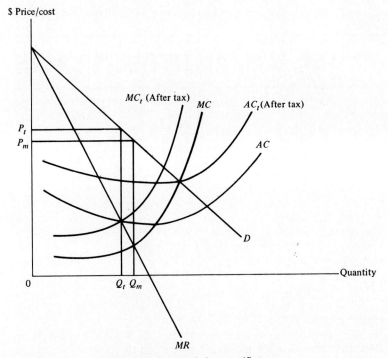

Regulation of monopoly by a specific tax

FIGURE 6.8
Regulation of monopoly by a specific tax.

CHAPTER 7

THE U.S. ANTITRUST LAWS

The primary purpose of this chapter is threefold: first, to develop a framework to study the vast and complex field of antitrust regulation; second, to consider the main features of the important antitrust laws; and third, to discuss the administrative machinery that has been created to enforce the various antitrust statutes. Against this backdrop, we will study in the succeeding chapters the actual working of the antitrust laws and some of the administrative and legal problems they face.

7.1 AN APPROACH TO THE STUDY OF THE U.S. ANTITRUST POLICIES

In a nonspecialized book of this type probably the best strategy one could adopt to study the complex and continually evolving field of antitrust regulation is as follows.

Historical Origin

Any piece of legislation, whether in the field of antitrust or any other field, has some history behind it; laws simply do not get enacted without their being some demand for them. (Recall, for example, the economic theory of regulation.) Therefore, we should first trace the historical origin of the present-day antitrust laws. In tracing this development, it is essential to sketch the important happenings of the time that prompted Congress to pass certain laws and what the congressional intent was behind those laws.

Major Provisions of the Antitrust Laws

Having considered the history behind them, it is essential to know exactly what the provisions of the various antitrust laws are. In particular, we will discuss the Sherman Antitrust Act of 1890, as amended by the Miller-Tydings Act of 1937; the Clayton Act of 1914, as amended by the Robinson-Patman Act of 1936 and the Celler-Kefauver Act of 1950; and the Federal Trade Commission Act of 1914, as amended by the Wheeler-Lea Act of 1914 and the McGuire Act of 1952. We will also comment briefly on some of the recent developments since the above three laws were passed.

As we will see, the provisions of the various laws are often stated in such broad terms that there is considerable leeway in interpreting what exactly the Congress meant in a given instance. For example, the terms "restraint of trade" and "monopolize" used in the Sherman Act are nowhere defined in the act itself. One can argue that the vagueness in the language of the various statutes has been deliberate because Congress did not want to be pinned down by the rigidity and inflexibility of language in its pursuit of a competitive business economy. But the generality of the statutes forces the administrative agencies and the courts to shoulder the responsibility of interpreting and applying the various laws on a case-by-case basis.

Administrative Enforcement of the Laws

The Antitrust Division of the Department of Justice and the Federal Trade Commission (FTC) are the principal agencies, aided by private or public complaints, who initiate the antitrust proceedings against an offending party. As we will see, the antitrust proceedings can be very expensive and time-consuming. Therefore, the above agencies have to be careful in choosing which cases they will prosecute, a choice that may not always be easy to make.

The Power of the Courts

In the ultimate analysis, it is the responsibility of the courts to provide definitive interpretation of the antitrust laws and their applicability in specific instances. As one scholar of antitrust puts it: "Antitrust is, first and most obviously law, and law made primarily by judges."[1] Therefore, anyone wishing to study the field of antitrust has to examine some leading cases to find out what the court's thinking was (usually the Supreme Court's) in any given instance. It is no exaggeration to say that the field of antitrust cannot be studied without examining some important cases, cases that have attempted to throw light on the interpretation of the various antitrust statutes.

What we intend to do in the rest of this chapter is to, first, study the historical foundation of the U.S. antitrust laws, then list the provisions of the laws previ-

[1]Robert H. Bork, *The Antitrust Paradox: A Policy at War with Itself,* Basic Books, New York, 1978, p. 10.

ously cited, and finally consider the administrative structure that has been created to enforce the laws. In subsequent chapters, we will consider the actual working of these laws, their enforcement by the administrative agencies, and their fate in the hands of the courts.

7.2   A HISTORICAL PERSPECTIVE

The passage of the Sherman Antitrust Act in 1890 heralded the beginning of a congressional attack on private monopolies in this country. Until then, the English common law, with its long-time prohibition against conspiracies, governed the behavior of private business in the United States.[2] But common law proved very inadequate to handle the great eighteenth- and nineteenth-century economic and social changes that were taking place in the country, especially changes since the Civil War.

As is well-documented, since the end of the Civil War in 1865, America experienced truly phenomenal economic growth: 14 million immigrants entered the country between 1865 and 1900, leading to the growth of new settlements, which was made possible by a rapidly growing network of railroads and an emerging national banking system. Along came a new form of business organization, the "trusts." A trust, or a holding company, was an "arrangement whereby the owners of stock in two or more companies transferred their securities to a set of trustees, receiving in return certificates which entitled them to share in the pooled earnings of the jointly managed companies."[3] The name *trust,* however, soon became identified with suspect or shady business conspiracies or monopolies, which explains the origin of the term *antitrust.*

Just to give the flavor of the power of the trusts, consider the case of the Standard Oil Company of Ohio.[4] In 1862 John D. Rockfeller advanced $4000 to Samuel Andrews to finance the improvements of an oil refinery. After the oil refinery proved successful, in 1870 John D. Rockfeller, William Rockfeller, Henry M. Flagler, and several others formed the Standard Oil Company of Ohio. Within the next 2 years, the company acquired most of Cleveland's oil refineries (about forty in number). By 1880, it further acquired a large number of oil refineries in New York, Pennsylvania, and other parts of Ohio. To consolidate their position, the founders of the company extracted preferential freight rates from the railroads to force competitors to leave or join them. By these means, between 1882 and 1899, besides the Ohio, the Rockfeller group acquired forty corporations. All these were later reorganized into the Standard Oil Trust, whose stock was subsequently transferred to the Standard Oil Company of

---

[2]The English common law, dating back to medieval England, is an unwritten law based on custom or court decisions and stands in strong contrast to the statutory Roman law, which relies on deliberate lawmaking by legislative and judicial bodies. For obvious reasons, the United States followed the common-law tradition.

[3]Donald Dewey, *Monopoly in Economics and Law,* Rand McNally, Chicago, 1959, p. 140.

[4]The description is based on Eugene M. Singer, *Antitrust Economics, Selected Legal Cases and Economic Models,* Prentice-Hall, Englewood Cliffs, N.J. 1968, pp. 27–28.

New Jersey, a holding company. In 1911 a suit was brought against this company under the Sherman Act; we will study the details of this case in the next chapter.

While trusts were being formed in other lines of business, there was a fervent battle raging between some powerful businesspeople to acquire control of the vital railroads. The parties involved in this ugly battle were Daniel Drew, Jay Gould, and Jim Fisk on the one hand and Commodore Cornelius Vanderbilt (and later J. Pierpont Morgan) on the other. Vanderbilt had control of the New York Central Railroad and had wanted to acquire a potential competitor, the Erie Railroad, which was controlled by Daniel Drew and his associates. To acquire control of the Erie, Vanderbilt began purchasing stock of that company on the open market. But the more stocks he bought the more of them became available in the market because Drew had issued countless unauthorized stocks of Erie. To stop this, Vanderbilt purportedly bribed a New York City judge to issue injunctions against his rivals. Not to be outdone, Jay Gould went to Albany and reportedly paid $1 million in bribe to state legislatures to seek legislation favorable to his stock manipulations and to retain control of the Erie Railroad. The Vanderbilt-Drew battle is but one episode in the struggle to gain control of the railroads. There were others in the west as well as in the east, although perhaps not as dramatic as the above episode.

The Standard Oil case, the Vanderbilt-Drew battle, and the growth of the trust movement in general led to many demands in Congress for some kind of legislative action. The need for such action grew intense when the growth in the factory system of work, a concomitant of industrial growth, brought forth many abuses of the factory system. These abuses included long work hours, child labor, unsafe and unsanitary working conditions, etc. At the same time, the farmers were also very unhappy; they complained of declining farm prices and higher discriminatory freight rates charged by the railroads as well as higher interest demanded by the banks for farm loans. To complicate life, there was a wave of business mergers which led to the manipulation of stock prices by shrewd businesspeople.

All these developments led to such strong antimonopoly feeling that politically active groups such as the Grangers, Populists, and others actually ran an antimonopoly candidate for U.S. President and succeeded in electing to Congress and to state legislatures several candidates who were opposed to monopoly. Several states passed antimonopoly laws, called "baby Sherman Acts" — there were about eighteen such acts by 1881.

In the 1888 presidential election, the Democrats as well as the Republicans pledged to act against monopolies. That election was won by the Republican candidate Benjamin Harrison, who had promised to act against the trusts during his campaign. After assuming the presidency, he encouraged antimonopoly bills in the Congress, although the election fervor against monopoly was lost. Several bills were introduced in Congress in 1889, including the one by Senator Sherman. After very little debate, a bill was produced by the Senate Judiciary Committee which had some elements of the Sherman bill. The Judiciary Committee's bill was passed in the Senate by a vote of 52 to 1 and was given the name of

Sherman purely out of courtesy to the senator, although the bill that finally emerged had little to do with the original Sherman bill. President Harrison signed the bill into law on July 2, 1890, which became known as the Sherman Antitrust Act, the first and most basic of the U.S. antitrust laws.

Against this backdrop, let us now examine the provisions of the Sherman Act and the other antitrust laws that followed it.

7.3   THE SHERMAN ANTITRUST ACT OF 1890

As just noted, the Sherman Antitrust Act of 1890 was the first important response of Congress to the antimonopoly feeling then prevailing. The main provisions of this landmark legislation are contained in Sec. 1 and 2 of the act, which are as follows:

Section 1

Every contract, combination in the form of trust or otherwise, or conspiracy, in restraint of trade or commerce among the several States, or with foreign nations, is declared to be illegal. . . . Every person who shall make any contract or engage in any combination or conspiracy declared by sections 1 to 7 of this title to be illegal shall be deemed guilty of a felony, and, on conviction thereof, shall be punished by fine not exceeding one million dollars if a corporation or, if any other person, one hundred thousand dollars or by imprisonment not exceeding three years, or by both said punishments, in the discretion of the court. [ch. 647, § 1, 26 Stat. 209 (1890) (as amended at 15 U.S.C. § 1 & Supp. I 1975)]

Section 2

Every person who shall monopolize, or attempt to monopolize, or combine or conspire with any other person or persons, to monopolize any part of the trade or commerce among the several States, or with foreign nations, shall be deemed guilty of a felony, and, on conviction thereof, shall be punishable by fine not exceeding one million dollars if a corporation or, if any other person, one hundred thousand dollars or by imprisonment not exceeding three years, or by both said punishments, in the discretion of the Court. [July 2, 1890, ch. 647, § 2, 26 Stat. 209 (1890) (as amended at 15 U.S.C. § 2 & Supp. I 1975)][5]

While the text of Sec. 1 makes ''illegal per se'' (that is, once the existence of something prohibited is proved, its illegality is established without regard to its economic effect in the particular case) any ''contract,'' ''combination in the form of trust,'' Sec. 2 makes illegal the end result of ''restraint of trade,'' namely, monopolization by an individual or a group of individuals or even the attempt to monopolize by an individual or a combination of individuals. In short, the two sections of the Sherman Act were clearly intended against cartels and other forms of combinations.

---

[5]Before the 1975 amendments, the activities proscribed by the act were a misdemeanor rather than a felony, the maximum fine levied against an individual was $5000, the maximum punishment was 1 year, and there was no mention of punishment or fine for corporation.

Since there was very little debate preceding the passage of the act, it is hard to know what the true intentions of Congress were when it passed the act. A superficial reading of the text of the act would tend to imply that the act was merely concerned with the *form* (or structure), namely, cartel per se, rather than the *substance* (or conduct), that is, the effects of monopoly on output, prices, deadweight loss, and so on (discussed in Chapter 6). In other words, if there were a cartel without monopoly behavior (restriction of output, for example), would it be declared illegal per se? Since there is little discussion about it in the act or the congressional deliberations before the passage of the act, it was up to the courts to decide what the intentions of Congress really were when it enacted the Sherman antitrust measure. In the next chapter we will see how the courts have interpreted the act.

There are a few features of the act that should be noted at the outset. First, the act is applicable only to interstate or foreign commerce; the intrastate activities were left to the state and local governments and, as noted previously, several states have passed their own antimonopoly laws. Of course, whether a particular activity is interstate or intrastate is open to question and once again the courts have to step in to decide each case on its merits.

Second, the act provides for both civil and criminal penalties. Although the size of these penalties has been increased substantially by the 1975 amendments to the act, it is a matter for empirical verification whether the increased penalties have discouraged persons or corporations from engaging into the proscribed activities. (We will refer to this topic in a later chapter.)

Third, the act, in one of its other sections, provides for private parties to bring civil suits against one another and for the successful party to receive *treble damages,* that is, three times the value of the damage suffered by the injured party. The Antitrust Improvement Act of 1976 (the Hart-Scott-Rodino Antitrust Improvement Act) further expanded the incentive to prosecute the offending party by allowing state attorneys general to sue on behalf of the residents and to collect treble damages for the state in successful cases. Finally, the Miller-Tydings Act passed in 1937 amended Sec. 1 of the act by providing exemption for resale price agreements (minimum price below which a product may not be sold) between manufacturers of products identified by a brand name or a trademark and suppliers in states which have their own "fair trade" laws which explicitly sanction resale price agreements. The Miller-Tydings Act has since been repealed; Congress abolished fair trade laws in 1975, and the Supreme Court has upheld this decision.

Although the first landmark antimonopoly law, the Sherman Act was ineffective in preventing the formation of new trusts and combinations. There are several reasons for this.[6] First, the attitude of the President and his political philosophy were important. There were only eight antitrust suits instituted during the administrations of Harrison and Cleveland (the latter during his second term in

---

[6]The following discussion draws on, Roger Sherman, *Antitrust Policies and Issues,* Addison-Wesley, Reading, Mass. 1978, pp. 35–37.

office) and three by President McKinley. Richard Olney, the first attorney general under President Cleveland was not very sympathetic to the act.

Second, the politicians were busy grappling with some important socioeconomic problems of the closing years of the nineteenth century, such as the war with Spain, the development of a new navy, a new tariff policy (the existing one favored big business at the cost of consumers), deforestation of national forests, the western states' demand for the coining of silver, and rampant corruption in government.

Third, to stave off its financial difficulties, the state of New Jersey repealed its own antitrust law and instituted an extremely liberal business incorporation law which permitted one company to own another, thus making holding companies legal and granting unlimited size and life to corporations. Since companies incorporated in New Jersey could operate in other states, there was an influx of new companies to New Jersey. And although trusts were illegal under the Sherman Act, they were in effect legal in New Jersey.

Finally, although the Republican administrations of Teddy Roosevelt and William Howard Taft succeeded in preventing J. P. Morgan and E. H. Harriman from bringing about a merger between their Northern Pacific and Hill's Great Northern railroads and although the Supreme Court in 1911 ordered that the American Tobacco Company and the Standard Oil Company each be broken into a number of smaller companies, the Supreme Court injected the "rule of reason" doctrine in deciding antitrust cases under the act: The rule of reason doctrine in antitrust law means that an action is illegal only if it has the demonstrable effect of impairing competition; thus it stands in strong contrast to the doctrine of per se illegality. As a result, an agreement, combination, or conspiracy was not deemed to be illegal unless it used visible coercion or other tactics to achieve its monopoly power. In other words, the substance (i.e., conduct) and not merely the form (combination, for example) became the important determinant of action under the Sherman Act. By this logic, companies such as Kodak and International Harvester, although monopolies by any reasonable standard in their heydays, were acquitted because they did not visibly use coercive power to acquire their monopoly status. The rule of reason reached its zenith in the 1920 U.S. Steel case: Although U.S. Steel was formed by J. P. Morgan by merger, and although it accounted for 60 percent of the steel market, the Supreme Court held that size per se was not illegal. We will examine the details of this case in the next chapter, but it is important to note here that the rule of reason, by declaring that monopoly per se is not illegal or bad, just about pulled the teeth out of the act.

7.4 THE CLAYTON ACT OF 1914

The rule of reason enunciated by the Supreme Court in the U.S. Steel case of 1920 left many members of Congress unhappy, for it was apparently against the intent of Congress as reflected in the Sherman Act. The wording of that act was clearly against monopoly and it did not make any distinction between "reasonable" and "unreasonable" monopolies; the Supreme Court's verdict in the U.S.

Steel case meant that only "unreasonable" (i.e., coercive) monopolies would be barred by the Sherman Act. The congressional unhappiness reached its expression in the passage of the Clayton Act in 1914, an act passed during the Woodrow Wilson administration. The avowed purpose of the Clayton Act was:

> . . . to prohibit certain trade practices which . . . singly and in themselves are not covered by the [Sherman Act] . . . and thus to arrest the creation of trusts, conspiracies and monopolies in their incipiency and before consummation.

In other words, the Clayton Act was designed to clarify what acts would be unreasonable and thus illegal. In particular, it outlawed four specific types of conduct: (1) price discrimination, Sec. 2, as amended by the Robinson-Patman Act; (2) tying arrangements and exclusive dealings, Sec. 3; (3) corporate acquisitions and mergers, Sec. 7, as amended by the Cellar-Kefauver Act of 1950; and (4) interlocking directorates, Sec. 8.

Section 2: Price Discrimination The original Sec. 2 of the act was replaced by Sec. 1 of the Robinson-Patman Act passed in 1936 in response to the complaints of independent dealers and wholesalers that chain stores (a new development then) were obtaining from their suppliers unwarranted advantages in the form of lower prices, greater advertising allowances, etc., advantages which threatened to destroy the traditional producer-wholesaler-retailer arrangement of marketing goods. The amended Sec. 2 (or Sec. 1 of the Robinson-Patman Act) has six clauses and reads as follows:

Section 2(a) It generally denounces price discrimination by providing in part that:

> It shall be unlawful for any person engaged in commerce, in the course of such commerce, either directly or indirectly, to discriminate in price between different purchasers of commodities of like grade and quality, . . . and where the effect of such discrimination may be substantially to lessen competition or tend to create a monopoly in any line of commerce, or to injure, destroy, or prevent competition with any person who either grants or knowingly receives the benefit of such discrimination, or with customers of either of them. . . .

This section allows for discrimination based on *cost differential* by providing that

> . . . nothing herein contained shall prevent differentials which make only due allowance for differences in the cost of manufacture, sale or delivery resulting from the differing methods or quantitites in which such commodities are to such purchasers sold or delivered. . . .

Section 2(b) Another exception to the price discrimination charge is contained in Sec. 2(b) which permits such discrimination if it is done in good faith solely to "meet competition." This section reads, in part:

> . . . that nothing herein contained shall prevent a seller rebutting the prima facie case thus made by showing that his lower price or the furnishing of services or facilities to any purchaser or purchasers was made in good faith to meet an equally low price of a competitor, or the services or facilities furnished by a competitor.

Section 2(c)   To prevent arrangements whereby buyers exact price discrimination disguised as brokerage commissions, allowances, discounts, etc., this section provides, in part:

> That it shall be unlawful for any person engaged in commerce, in the course of such commerce, to pay or grant, or receive or accept, anything of value as a commission, brokerage, or other compensation, or any allowance or discount in lieu thereof, except for services rendered in connection with the sale or purchase of goods, wares, or merchandise, either to the other party to such transaction or to an agent, representative, or other intermediary therein where such intermediary is acting in fact for or in behalf, or is subject to the direct or indirect control of any party to such transaction other than the person by whom such compensation is so granted or paid.

Section 2(d)   Another form by which a manufacturer may disguise price discrimination is by offering promotional allowances and services whose end result is effectively a reduction in price. To prevent this practice, this section provides:

> That it shall be unlawful for any person engaged in commerce, in the course of such commerce, to pay or grant, or receive or accept, anything of value as a commission, brokerage, or other compensation, or any allowance or discount in lieu thereof, except for services rendered in connection with the sale or purchase of goods, wares, or merchandise, either to the other party to such transaction or to an agent, representative, or other intermediary therein where such intermediary is acting in fact for or in behalf, or is subject to the direct or indirect control of any party to such transaction other than the person by whom such compensation is so granted or paid.

Section 2(e)   Section 2(d) applies where the supplier gives money or similar benefit to the buyer for him to perform the services mentioned in that section. But what about the seller herself providing such services? Section 2(e) proscribes that too by stating:

> That it shall be unlawful for any person to discriminate in favor of one purchaser against another purchaser or purchasers of a commodity bought for resale, with or without processing, by contracting to furnish or funishing, or by contributing to the furnishing of, any services or facilities connected with the processing, handling, sale, or offering for sale of such commodity so purchased upon terms not accorded to all purchasers on proportionally equal terms.

Section 2(f)   To prevent large buyers from extracting favorable terms from the seller, this section provides:

> That it shall be unlawful for any person engaged in commerce, in the course of such commerce, knowingly to induce or receive a discrimination in price which is prohibited by this section.

In short then, the amended Sec. 2 of the Clayton Act prohibits overt or covert price discrimination. We will see in Chapter 9 whether this prohibition against price discrimination, overt or covert, is economically justifiable and what has been its fate in the courts.

Section 3: Tying Arrangements, Exclusive Dealing, and Requirement Contract   A tying agreement is one where the purchase of one good is made conditional upon the purchase of another good, as in the case of the *International Salt Co. v. United States,* in which the company was charged under the act for leasing its patented self-dispensing salt machine on the condition that the lessee purchase all its salt requirement from the company. *Exclusive dealing* is an arrangement whereby the purchaser cannot handle competing lines, as would be the case if, for example, a Mobil gas station would agree to sell Exxon's gas. *A requirement contract* is one where the purchaser is forced to buy all or most of its needs from a single supplier, which would be the case if, say, a restaurateur is required to buy all the products she sells from a single dealer. All these arrangements are illegal under Sec. 3 of the act, which provides in part that:

> It shall be unlawful for any person engaged in the course of such commerce, to lease or make a sale or contract for sale of goods, wares, merchandise, machinery, supplies, or other commodities . . . on the condition, agreement, or understanding that the lessee or purchaser thereof shall not use or deal in the goods, wares, merchandise, machinery, supplies, or other commodities of a competitor or competitors of the lessor or seller, where the effect of such lease, sale, or contract for sale or such condition, agreement, or understanding may be to substantially lessen competition or tend to create a monopoly in any line of commerce.

Section 7: Corporate Acquisitions and Mergers   Section 7 of the act, as amended by the 1950 Celler-Kefauver Anti-Merger Act, prohibits mergers between competing firms either by acquisition of stock or by acquisition of assets.[7] In part, the section reads:

> No corporation engaged in commerce shall acquire, directly or indirectly, the whole or any part of the stock or other share capital and no corporation subject to the jurisdiction of the Federal Trade Commission shall acquire the whole or any part of the assets of another corporation engaged also in commerce, where in any line of commerce in any section of the country, the effect may be substantially to lessen competition, or tend to create monopoly.

Section 8: Interlocking Directorates   Interlocking directorate is a practice whereby a director serves on the board of directors of more than one company, including companies which may be competitive. This section prohibits such interlocking of directorates between corporations engaged in commerce where one of them has a capital and surplus of more than $1 million and where "the elimination of competition . . . between them would constitute a violation of any of the provisions of the antitrust laws."

In addition to Sec. 2, 3, 7, and 8, there is an important section, Sec. 4, which

---

[7]Before the Celler-Kefauver Amendment, only mergers by stock acquisition were considered illegal; some of the Supreme Court decisions allowed mergers by acquisition of assets, hence the amendment.

gives any private party the right to sue for treble damages for an injury to his property or business as a result of violations of the antitrust laws by an individual or a corporation. Section 4 specifically states:

> That any person who shall be injured in his business or property by reason of anything forbidden in the antitrust laws may sue therefor in any district court of the United States in the district in which the defendant resides or is found or has an agent, without respect to the amount in controversy, and shall recover threefold the damages by him sustained, and the cost of suit, including a reasonable attorney's fee.

To sum up, the Clayton Act tried to clarify the Sherman Act by explicitly listing the practices that were considered injurious to competition. And by allowing private suits and treble damages, it tried to discourage the mentioned anticompetitive practices. But in most of its sections, it inserted the key phrase, '' . . . where the effect may be substantially to lessen competition.'' This meant that it was ultimately up to the courts to determine whether a particular activity did in fact substantially lessen competition.'' Needless to say, such phraseology was an open invitation to lengthy and costly litigations. But more on this in succeeding chapters.

7.5 THE FEDERAL TRADE COMMISSION ACT OF 1914

Like the Clayton Act, the Federal Trade Commission (FTC) Act was also passed in 1914. Compared to the specific activities proscribed by the Clayton Act, the FTC Act is very broad and is directed against *unfair methods of competition and unfair or deceptive acts and practices.* The key provision of the act, as amended by the Wheeler-Lea Act of 1938, is contained in Sec. 5, which reads in part:[8]

> Unfair methods of competition in commerce, and unfair or deceptive acts or practices in commerce, are hereby declared illegal.

This is indeed a sweeping statement, for it goes beyond the monopoly problem. No doubt, the clause "unfair methods of competition in commerce" would include unreasonable restraint of interstate and foreign commerce. As such, it certainly overlaps the provisions of the Sherman and Clayton acts against monopoly. But the phrase "unfair or deceptive practices in commerce" would imply injury not to a competitor per se but to the public at large. As a matter of fact, in practice the FTC act is construed to mean the prohibition of acts such as false or misleading advertising, undue claims about the quality or performance of a product, etc.

To carry out the mandate of Sec. 5, the act created the FTC, an independent regulatory commission consisting of five members each appointed by the President for a 7-year term. It authorized the FTC to hold courtlike hearings and obtain "cease-and-desist" orders against offenders by applying to the circuit

---

[8]The phrase "unfair or deceptive acts or practices" was inserted by the 1938 Wheeler-Lea Amendment.

court of appeals. In 1975, the Magnuson-Moss FTC Improvement Act expanded the powers of the FTC by amending Sec. 5 as follows:

> Unfair methods of competition *in or affecting commerce,* and unfair or deceptive acts or practices in or *affecting commerce,* are declared unlawful. [Emphasis added]

The 1975 act further tried to strengthen the powers of the FTC by allowing it to seek remedies stronger than the mere cease-and-desist orders and by permitting it to promulgate rules for regulating trade. In 1980, fearful of the growing power of the FTC, Congress tried to curb some of the investigative and rule-making powers of the FTC by means of the legislative veto, as noted previously. But because of the recent (June 1983) Supreme Court decision declaring such vetos to be unconstitutional, it remains to be seen what the Congress does.

7.6   SUMMARY OF THE MAIN PROVISIONS OF THE U.S. ANTITRUST LAWS

For easy reference, Table 7.1 gives in capsule the main provisions of the major U.S. antitrust laws.

It should be noted that the provisions of some of the laws are overlapping, and a particular case may be tried under one or more of these laws. Thus, a

TABLE 7.1
MAIN PROVISIONS OF THE U.S. ANTITRUST LAWS

I. It is illegal
   (i) to form a trust or to enter into a contract or conspiracy whose objective is restraint of trade (Sherman Act, Sec. 1)
   (ii) to monopolize, to attempt to monopolize, or to combine or conspire to monopolize trade (Sherman Act, Sec. 2)

II. If an activity threatens to substantially lessen competition or tend to create monopoly, it is illegal
   (i) to discriminate in price between different purchasers of commodities of like grade and quality unless such discrimination is due to differences in the cost of manufacture or is done solely to meet competition in good faith (Clayton Act, Sect. 2(a) and 2(b), as amended by the Robinson-Patman Act of 1936)
   (ii) to hide price discrimination in the guise of (a) brokerage commission, allowances, discounts, etc., (b) to give promotional allowances and services to the buyer, (c) for the seller herself to perform promotional services, or to give promotional allowances, and (d) to give favorable treatment to large buyers (Clayton Act, Sec. 2(c) to 2(f), as amended by the Robinson-Patman Act)
   (iii) to enter into tying agreements, exclusive dealings, and requirement contracts (Clayton Act, Sec. 3)
   (iv) to effect mergers either by acquisition of stock or assets (Clayton Act, Sec. 7, as amended by the Celler-Kefauver Act of 1950)
   (v) to serve on the board of directors of competing companies (Clayton Act, Sec. 8)

III. It is illegal
   (i) to use unfair methods of competition (Federal Trade Commission Act, Sec. 5)
   (ii) to use unfair or deceptive acts or practices (Federal Trade Commission Act, Sec. 5, as amended by the Wheeler-Lea Act of 1938)

case apparently under the jurisdiction of the Sherman Act may also be tried under the FTC act, since the provision that it is illegal to "use unfair methods of competition" would certainly include monopoly or monopolization. In practice, the decision about which law has jurisdiction over a case depends on the nature of the administrative structure that has been created to enforce the antitrust laws, a topic discussed in Section 7.8.

7.7 EXEMPTIONS FROM THE ANTITRUST LAWS

Although the scope of the antitrust laws is quite broad, there are several categories that are expressly exempted from their application. Some of the exemptions are as follows:

1 Trade unions. Although technically monopolies in their spheres of operation, they are excluded because labor is not a commodity. But the real reason was the vehement opposition by labor and the initial fear that no antitrust law will be enacted that included labor unions as a possible target of antimonopoly action by the government.

2 Since 1922, professional baseball, because it is sport and not commerce. Curiously, however, professional football, hockey, etc., are not so exempt.

3 Public utilities, because they are controlled by state and local governments.

4 Much of the banking and insurance industries, because they are also controlled by state and local governments.

5 Milk and other selected farm products. Milk, as noted elsewhere, is regulated by the federal milk marketing orders.

6 Industries such as the railroads, trucking, airlines, shipping, and stock exchanges because they are regulated by regulatory commissions such as the ICC, CAB, FMC (Federal Maritime Commission), and SEC (Securities and Exchange Commission).

It is a paradox of the U.S. antitrust policies that on the one hand they are designed to promote competition but on the other hand to stifle it. Thus, the ICC approves cartel-determined (or monopoly) freight rates in the trucking industry, which by all accounts are higher than what they would have been had competition prevailed in the trucking industry. The antitrust laws cannot do much about them, however, because of the explicit exemption in the law (more on this subject in Chapter 11). The same is true of the milk industry. Although basically a competitive industry, milk prices are determined by the federal marketing orders, which, as noted in Chapter 5, have substantially raised the price of milk. Yet, the antitrust laws are powerless because of the protection afforded by law to the milk industry. These examples show clearly how some powerful interests can obviate the mandates of the antitrust laws and how the government can be a party against its expressed preference for a competitive economy.

7.8   ENFORCEMENT OF THE ANTITRUST LAWS: THE ADMINISTRATIVE STRUCTURE[9]

The antitrust laws can be enforced by the Antitrust Division of the Department of Justice, by the FTC, and by private parties either on their own or sometimes cooperatively.

The Antitrust Division

The Antitrust Division of the Department of Justice, with a budget of about $30 million and made up of some 460 lawyers and about 60 economists (1978 figures), is the principal executive branch agency charged with the responsibility of enforcing the nation's antitrust laws, specifically the Sherman and the Clayton acts. Its primary role is that of a public prosecutor, although from time to time it will render advisory opinions on prospective or impending mergers which may be against the Celler-Kefauver Amendment to the Clayton Act antimerger provisions.

To enforce the laws, the division is organized into a number of sections, such as the economic section, the foreign commerce section, etc. The organizational structure of the division is as shown in Table 7.2.

The actual working of the system may be briefly described as follows:[10] The work of the division begins when there is a complaint against some party that it has violated one or more provisions of the antitrust laws. Such a complaint may originate within the division (because of an internal staff study) or without, say, from citizens, consumers, businesspeople complaining about their competitors, Congressmembers trying to help a constituent or some other government agency. Very often the outside complaints are frivolous and have nothing to do with the antitrust laws. Therefore, the division has to decide which complaints are worth pursuing.

Once it decides to investigage a complaint, it may proceed gradually; initially it may resort to some informal methods of gathering information about the nature of the complaint but, as the investigation proceeds, it may resort to increasingly harsher methods of investigations including FBI investigations and the convening of a grand jury in case criminal action is contemplated.

After the initial stage of the enquiry is over, the division may either decide that the facts of the case do not warrant any more investigation and hence the case should be dropped or it may decide that the complaint is well-founded in which case it may want to bring a civil suit or a criminal suit or both against the offending party. The purpose of the civil action is to proscribe future violations

---

[9]The following discussion leans heavily on Jerrold C. Van Cise's *The Federal Antitrust Laws,* 3d ed., American Enterprise Institute for Public Policy Research, Washington D.C., 1975, ch. 5.

[10]For an interesting account of the working of the Antitrust Division, see Suzanne Weaver, "Antitrust Division of the Department of Justice," in James Q. Wilson, ed., *The Politics of Regulation,* Basic Books, New York, 1980.

TABLE 7.2
THE U.S. ANTITRUST DIVISION

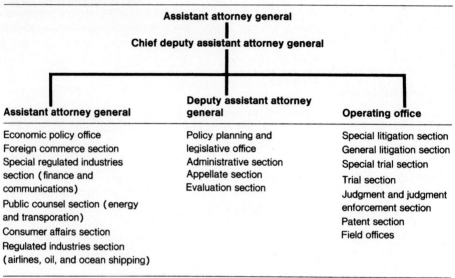

Assistant attorney general	Deputy assistant attorney general	Operating office
Economic policy office	Policy planning and legislative office	Special litigation section
Foreign commerce section	Administrative section	General litigation section
Special regulated industries section (finance and communications)	Appellate section	Special trial section
	Evaluation section	Trial section
Public counsel section (energy and transporation)		Judgment and judgment enforcement section
Consumer affairs section		Patent section
Regulated industries section (airlines, oil, and ocean shipping)		Field offices

of the law, whereas the purpose of the criminal suit is to punish by fine or imprisonment or both for violating the antitrust laws, as happened in the celebrated electrical conspiracy case,[11] in which the guilty corporate executives were fined a total of $1,787,000 and seven defendants were each sentenced to spend 30 days in jail. It should be added that the division may institute a civil suit even if the criminal suit against the same violation has been unsuccessful. A successful civil suit may direct the offending party

> . . . to deal where he does not want to deal, license where he does not wish to license, surrender contractual and other rights, and be subjected in perpetuity to government visitations. The court injunction, moreover, may order the divestiture of stock, or of assets, and even the outright dissolution of offending organizations.[12]

The Federal Trade Commission

The Federal Trade Commission, an independent regulatory commission established by the Federal Trade Commission Act of 1914, is empowered to bring antitrust action against businesses using unfair methods of competition. Unlike the Antitrust Division, with its primarily prosecutorial nature, the FTC has

---

[11]During the 1950s, the leading manufacturers of electrical equipment in the United States conspired to set prices and divide the market from the very small items to huge turbine generators.
[12]Van Cise, op. cit., p. 45.

encouraged voluntary compliance with the FTC and other antitrust laws, although it has not hesitated to force compliance with its mandates in the courts. As noted previously, the activities of the FTC are much broader in scope in that it is also supposed to protect the consumer against unfair or deceptive practices.

Private Actions

Besides the Antitrust Division and the FTC, a private person can institute proceedings under the antitrust laws (1) to recover triple damages she has suffered at the hands of an antitrust violator, (2) to seek injunctive relief against that violator, and/or (3) to counterclaim antitrust violations against a plaintiff who is suing her in another action related or unrelated to the antitrust laws. Lately, however, the Supreme Court has been discouraging such claims on the grounds that a person should not escape his or her own private (contractual) obligations by merely saying that the plaintiff has violated the antitrust laws.

Some of the private suits have been quite successful and in some cases the courts have awarded punitive damages against the violators. Not only that, but the law now allows a private person to use the judgment entered into between the Antitrust Division and the violator to seek his own damages even though he himself cannot adduce independent evidence against the violator. The objective here seems to discourage violations of the antitrust laws by penalizing the offending party as much as possible.

In short, then, the public (Antitrust Division and the FTC) and private (private suits) remedies can be used to seek redress in cases of harm done to an affected party by violators of the antitrust laws.

7.9 SOME RECENT DEVELOPMENTS

As noted earlier, antitrust is an evolving field where either new acts or amendments to existing ones or both are made from time to time with the objective of making the economy more competitive, or sometimes make it less competitive, by making the antitrust laws inapplicable to certain activities or industries (e.g., the McCarran-Ferguson Act of 1945 has exempted the casualty insurance industry from the antitrust laws). Such new laws, or amendments to the existing ones, usually reflect the economic and political trends at the time.

Currently, some members of Congress have turned their attention to big conglomerate mergers, that is, mergers between companies engaged in dissimilar activities or businesses. To understand the wrath against the conglomerate mergers, one has to look to the phenomenal growth of such mergers during the 1960s when companies like the Litton Industries, IT&T, and Gulf and Western grew impressively by acquiring firms in unrelated businesses. Thus, Gulf and Western acquired companies producing such diverse products as auto parts, sugar, paper, metal, movies, etc. But in the 1970s the conglomerate merger bubble burst when the big conglomerates experienced reduced earnings and some of them nearly went broke. The case in point is Ling-Temco-Vought (LTV), a company that started from obscure beginnings in the early 1960s but by 1970 became the fifteenth-largest industrial firm in the country. Soon thereafter, however, declining military contracts (a major source of LTV's business) and threats of antitrust actions nearly made the company bankrupt. Needless to say, any such major development in the industrial world is bound to attract the attention of trustbusters and others interested in antitrust.

Taking note of the conglomerate merger phenomenon, the Hart-Scott-Rodino Antitrust Improvements Act of 1976 now requires large companies (those with assets of about $100 million or more) to notify the Justice Department in advance of any contemplated merger and to wait for a specified period of time before consummating the merger.

But to some members of Congress this is not enough. They believe that "bigness per se is bad" and, even if such mergers do not necessarily lessen competition, it leads to serious social problems. A leading proponent of the "bigness per se is bad" philosophy is Senator Edward Kennedy, chairperson of the powerful Senate Judiciary Committee during the Carter administration. He, along with Senator Howard Metzenbaum of Ohio, introduced a bill in the Senate whose objective was to stop or control big conglomerate mergers. This bill provides that: (1) companies with $2.5 billion of sales or $2 billion of assets would be prohibited from merging with one another, (2) companies with $350 million of sales or $200 million of assets would have to prove that a merger would be procompetition or yield economies of scale or other efficiencies, and (3) the restrictions in item 2 above would also apply to mergers between companies with more than $100 million of assets if their combined assets amounted to more than $1 billion.

Although Sec. 7 of the Clayton Act (as amended by the Celler-Kefauver Act of 1950) prohibits mergers which "substantially lessen competition" or "tend to create monopoly," this section was written before the time of the big conglomerate mergers. Therefore, as we will show later, the status of conglomerate mergers before the Clayton Act may not be quite clear. This is why the proposed Kennedy bill was specifically designed to deal with conglomerate mergers. But with the election of Ronald Reagan as President it is debatable whether such a bill would be passed, especially because Kennedy is no longer chairperson of the Senate Judiciary Committee and because the Democrats lost their majority in the Senate in the 1980 presidential elections.

Although we will consider the problem of mergers — horizontal, vertical, and conglomerate — later, it may be noted that there are economists, notably from the University of Chicago and the University of California at Los Angeles, who have compiled empirical evidence which suggests that big companies can be vigorous competitors and do play an important role in the growth of the economy by innovative expenditures on R & D. Therefore, in their view, the "bigness per se is bad philosophy" may be ill-conceived. (We will have more to say about this later; see also Chapter 6 for the discussion on productive efficiency as defense of monopoly.)

7.10 SUMMARY AND CONCLUSIONS

After outlining an approach to the study of the antitrust laws, we discussed the following topics in this chapter: (1) the provisions of the major U.S. antitrust laws, namely, the Sherman Act of 1890, the Clayton Act of 1914 as amended by the Robinson-Patman Act of 1936 and the Celler-Kefauver Act of 1950, and the Federal Trade Commission Act of 1914; (2) the exemptions from these laws conferred on some individuals or some activities; (3) the enforcement mechanism to seek the observance of the laws; and (4) some recent developments, particularly the proposed Kennedy-Metzenbaum bill against big conglomerate mergers; the bill's objective is to either stop such mergers completely or put severe limitations on them.

The general thrust of the Sherman Act is against monopoly and monopolization. The amended Clayton Act is directed against four specific activities if they tend to lessen competition substantially or tend to create monopolies. These activities are: (1) price discrimination; (2) tying, exclusive dealing, and requirement contract arrangements; (3) corporate acquisitions and mergers; and (4) interlocking directorates. The FTC Act of 1914 prohibits unfair methods of competition in commerce as well as unfair or deceptive acts in commerce. The scope of this act is much broader than merely preventing monopoly or monopolization; it is designed to protect the consumer from shady business practices, such as false or misleading advertising, unsafe products, and so on.

Thus, by passing these laws,

. . . Congress has placed in the custody of the courts what amounts to a three-headed Cerberus to guard our competitive economy from the encroachment of undesirable private restraints. Its "Sherman" head is instructed to watch for present dangers to this economy; its "Clayton" (including Robinson-Patman) head is directed to look for probable threats; and its "commission" [the FTC] head has a roving mission to detect unfair hazards. The courts, however, with the advice and consent of public and private plaintiffs, are given final authority to determine when, where, and how this antitrust guardian is to be unleashed against any such intruding restraints which endanger that free economy.[13]

In what follows, we will examine, with the aid of several legal cases, the extent to which the "three-headed Cerberus" and the courts have managed to keep the American economy free and competitive.

QUESTIONS

7-1 Judging from the texts of the Sherman, Clayton, and FTC acts, what do you think is the overall goal of the U.S. antitrust laws?

7-2 Comment: "The only legitimate goal of American antitrust law is the maximization of consumer welfare." (Bork, *The Antitrust Paradox*, p. 51.)

7-3 Considering the economics of monopoly discussed in Chapter 6, do you think that

---

[13]Van Cise, op. cit., p. 14. Cerberus, in Greek and Roman mythology, was a three-headed dog guarding the entrance of Hades.

the basic antimonopoly thrust of the Sherman Act is justifiable from an economic viewpoint?

7-4 Are you in favor of the treble-damage provision of the Sherman Act? Present arguments pro and con.

7-5 Comment:

The modern corporation is a good pooler of risks. Other things being equal, the larger the firm, the more it can cancel off one risk against another, the more it can economize on inventory, excess peak-capacity, and taxes, and the more it can spread the indivisible costs of the best-grade research among its many units. Larger size tends to help, and if it emulates the example of General Motors and other efficient decentralizers of decision making, there are almost no penalties from larger size. I conclude that trying to prevent monopolies is a fight against nature. (Paul A. Samuelson, *Economics,* 10th ed., McGraw-Hill, New York, 1976, p. 534).

7-6 What is the logic behind the per se illegality rule? Do you approve of it? Why or why not?

7-7 How would you justify the "rule of reason"? Do you think it hinders or help antitrust prosecution?

7-8 What weight would you accord to "structure" versus "conduct" or "form" versus "substance" in deciding antitrust suits under the Sherman Act?

7-9 The phrase in the Clayton Act " . . . may be substantially to lessen competition or tend to create a monopoly" has introduced a doctrine in the antitrust law, namely, the *doctrine of incipiency*. By this doctrine, a court or an administrative agency (e.g., the Antitrust Division) may bring an antitrust suit against a party if there is potential (but not necessarily actual) damage to competition. Do you think this is a sound doctrine? Why or why not?

7-10 Why is only baseball among the professional sports excluded from the antitrust laws? Is it not a business and is it not engaged in interstate commerce?

7-11 Section 2 of the Webb-Pomerene Export Trade Association Act exempts from the Sherman Act those acts or agreements made in the course of export trade by an association of producers formed solely for the purpose of engaging in export trade. What is the logic of this provision? Does it not mean that monopoly is harmful domestically but not in international trade?

7-12 Section 6 of the Clayton Act exempts agricultural organizations from the Sherman Act. It states in part:

Nothing contained in the antitrust laws shall be construed to forbid the existence and operation of . . . agricultural, or horticultural organizations, instituted for purposes of mutual help and not having capital stock or conducted for profit, or to forbid or restrain individual members of such organizations from lawfully carrying out the legitimate objects thereof; nor shall such organizations or the members thereof be held or construed to be illegal combinations or conspiracies in restraint of trade under the antitrust laws.

(The Capper-Volstead Act extends this exemption to capital stock agricultural cooperatives also.) What is the rationale behind this antitrust exemption? What are the likely economic consequences of this exemption? Discuss fully.

7-13 If a business is purely intrastate, would the Sherman Act apply to it if it is found that it violates the actions prohibited by the act?

7-14 Suppose wholesale liquor dealers in a state decide to divide the state market among themselves by standardizing liquor prices, the effect of which is to essentially forestall competition. Although this is purely an intrastate arrangement, would this come under the purview of the Sherman Act?

7-15 Suppose the local office of a national car rental agency enters into a price-fixing agreement with three local competitors. To evoke the Sherman Act, must it be shown that such price-fixing affects interstate commerce or is it sufficient to show that being a national company it automatically comes under the interstate commerce clause of the act and hence is liable for prosecution under the act? What if the company contends that the said practice is confined to only one branch which does its business purely intrastate?

7-16 Do you think there is any merit in the proposed Kennedy-Metzenbaum bill against big conglomerate mergers? What would be the economic consequences of the bill if it were to become law?

7-17 *Right of contribution among antitrust defendants:* In what is known as the corrugated container antitrust case, thirty-seven manufacturers were accused of participating in an 18-year nationwide conspiracy to fix the prices of corrugated containers and sheets, with ultimate liability estimated as high as $5.9 billion. Most of the defendants settled out of court, agreeing to pay the plaintiffs (purchasers of the containers and sheets) more than $300 million. But three defendants, Westvaco, the Packaging Corporation of America, and the Georgia-Pacific Corporation, refused to settle. The trial is now taking place in federal court in Houston.

The three companies asked the trial court to let them file cross-claims against the companies that had settled, seeking through the so-called right of contribution to ensure that if they are found guilty, they will not have to pay for the entire industrywide liability.

The trial court, affirmed by the federal court of appeals, refused to allow the cross-suits on the grounds that such a right would lessen antitrust deterrence by decreasing the potential liability of each individual violator. Thereupon, the three companies asked for Supreme Court review on the ground that without a right of contribution, "the right to trial may be rendered meaningless by a system which forces defendants to settle cases at exorbitant levels without regard to the merits."

On June 16, 1980, the Supreme Court agreed to review the case (*Westvaco Corporation v. Adam Extract Co.,* No. 79-972).

Were the trial and the federal courts of appeals right in rejecting the claim of the three companies? Should the Supreme Court have agreed to hear the case? If you were a justice of the Supreme Court, how would you decide the case? Reason carefully.

CHAPTER 8

THE SHERMAN ACT
IN THE COURTS

A textual reading of Secs. 1 and 2 of the Sherman Act raises several questions to which answers are not readily apparent from the wording of the act. Some of these questions are as follows:

1 What is the meaning of the term *restraint of trade?*

2 Is there always a presumption of restraint of trade when two or more parties enter into a contract?

3 What is the meaning of the word *monopolize?*

4 What is the distinction between *to monopolize* and *attempt to monopolize?*

5 Are monopolies to be always condemned even if some of them may be economically beneficial?

6 Are there "good" trusts (combinations) and "bad" trusts?

7 Is there any distinction under the law between horizontal mergers and vertical mergers?

8 Is price-fixing, vertical as well as horizontal, necessarily illegal?

9 When is the *per se* rule and when is the *rule of reason* appropriate?

10 Is it the purpose of the act to support small business even if it is economically inefficient?

One could go on and on, but the above list gives some idea about the kinds of questions that one may want to examine when studying the Sherman Act (and other U.S. antitrust laws). But as noted in the previous chapter, the wording of the act is so general and omnibus that of necessity one has to resort to legal cases to shed light on what the law had in mind in specific instances. It is well to recall Robert Bork's remark that, ''antitrust is, first and most obviously, law, and law made primarily by judges.''

What we intend to do in this chapter is to discuss very briefly some of the leading antitrust cases under the Sherman Act. After an introductory word or two, in each case we present the bare-bone facts of the case, the legal decision(s) in the case, and some of the highlights of the case. After these case studies, we comment generally on the nature and goals of the act as perceived by the judges.

8.1 SOME TERMINOLOGY

To facilitate understanding of the case studies, we discuss below the meaning of several terms that will crop up now and then in the various legal decisions.

Market An area or institution in which sales and purchases are made.

Market Structure A market may be characterized by the number of sellers, the number of buyers, the nature of the product (standardized or differentiated), the ease of entry into and exit from the industry. Traditionally, one can distinguish four broad market structures: monopoly, oligopoly, monopolistic competition, and perfect competition (see footnote 1, Chapter 6 for brief descriptions of these various market structures).

Market Behavior or Conduct This refers to the way a firm or an industry acts and is often related to the market structure in which it operates.

Market Performance The end result of market behavior as measured by price, output, profit, technical progress, and other similar criteria.

Monopoly Power The ability of a single seller to affect the market price or output.

Merger or Integration The fusion of two or more separate firms into one.

Horizontal Merger or Horizontal Integration When two or more firms in the same business merge, it is called a horizontal or lateral merger or integration. (e.g., two banks merging into one).

Vertical Merger or Vertical Integration When two or more firms that are suppliers or customers of one another merge, it is called vertical merger or integration (e.g., a steel producer acquiring a coal mine).

Horizontal Price-Fixing Competing sellers in the same business agreeing upon a common price (e.g., OPEC cartel's price-fixing).

Vertical Price-Fixing A manufacturer fixing the price at which a wholesaler or retailer or both can sell his or her product. Sometimes called the resale price maintenance (RPM) agreement.

Restraint of Trade Under the common law, this phrase meant all arrangements whereby two or more parties agree to limit competition among themselves in some specified market. Whether the Sherman Act had such an omnibus purpose in mind is not clear. Some people believe that the Sherman Act was mainly concerned with the price and output consequences of monopoly.

With these concepts, let us now study some important antitrust cases under the act.

THE TRANS-MISSOURI CASE*

The *Trans-Missouri* case, decided in 1897, was one of the early cases to be tried under Sec. 1 of the act. The main issue involved was the legality of a price-fixing agreement among a number of railroad companies.

FACTS

Eighteen railroads, operating west of the Mississippi River, formed an association to set "reasonable" rates and regulations for all the railroads. Invoking Sec. 1 of the act, the government contended that such rate-fixing was "restraint of trade" as understood by common law and therefore asked for dissolution of the association. But the defendant, the Trans-Missouri Freight Association, countered by saying that Sec. 1 proscribes only those acts which were expressly illegal at common law. (The common law upheld most of the restrictive combinations whose participants could establish that they had some common economic interest and that this common interest was not motivated by sheer enmity toward third parties.)

JUDGMENT

The trial court, following the common law, decided the case in favor of the defendant because the government had failed to show that the rates fixed by the association were unreasonable. In the circuit court of appeals the trial court's decision was upheld. However, when the case reached the Supreme Court, by a majority of 5 to 3, it reversed lower courts' decisions and upheld the government.

Justice Peckham, writing for the majority, stated that Sec. 1 of the Sherman Act condemned every restraint of trade with-

United States v. Trans-Missouri Freight Association, 166 U.S. 290, 1897.

out exception and hence it was unnecessary to apply common-law practices to determine whether the said activity was reasonable or unreasonable and hence legal or illegal. Thus, Peckham introduced the per se illegality rule for cartel price-fixing; the association was nothing but a cartel established for the purpose of rate-fixing. This rule, as noted in Chapter 7, means that once the existence of something prohibited is proved, its illegality is established without regard to its economic effect in the particular case. But this rule, we will explain, has caused lots of problems.

Justice White dissented from the majority on the ground that the courts did not have jurisdiction over the case as the activities of the railroads were expressly controlled by the ICC. But more importantly, he argued that the Sherman Act prohibited only unreasonable agreements, thus introducing what later became known as the rule of reason (see the *Standard Oil* case on p. 181). As noted in Chapter 7, the rule of reason in antitrust means that an action is illegal only if it has the demonstrable effect of impairing competition; it is the antithesis of the rule of per se illegality.

COMMENT

Since the Sherman Act was passed in 1890, the *Trans-Missouri* case was one of the first cases that attempted to shed some light on the meaning of Sec. 1, and especially its relationship with the common-law concept of "restraint of trade," which determined the legality of some trade practices before the passage of the act. From the opinion of Justice Peckham, it is clear that he interpreted Sec. 1 very literally. But he did more than that.† First, he established the per se illegality of combinations in restraint of trade, although a

†The following discussion is based on Robert H. Bork, *The Antitrust Paradox: A Policy at War with Itself,* Basic Books, New York, 1978.

careful reading of his decision would reveal that he did not declare all cartel agreements illegal per se when the objective was the creation of economic efficiency and increase in consumer welfare. Second, by sticking closely to the wording of Sec. 1, he stated that the Sherman Act was different from the common law, which is often a body of unclear and confusing precedents. Third, by refusing to make a distinction between "reasonable" and "unreasonable" restraint of trade, and thereby declining to accept the rule of reason, he left little discretion to the administrative agencies to prosecute under Sec. 1. By these actions, " . . . he helped shape a law that became, and for a long time remained, the politically potent symbol of the virtues of free and unregulated markets."‡

‡Bork, op. cit., p. 26.

THE ADDYSTON PIPE CASE*

United States v. Addyston Pipe and Steel Co. is one of the landmark antitrust cases which tried to clarify the goals of the Sherman Act and provided a method for judging when an agreement is in restraint of trade.

FACTS

Six manufacturers of cast-iron pipe entered into an agreement to fix price and divide territory in southern and western states, about three-fourths of the United States. These manufacturers accounted for about 65 percent of cast-iron producing capacity in these states. It was charged that the price fixed was such as to keep eastern manufacturers out of the territory but somewhat higher than that which would have prevailed had the local producers competed vigorously. The defendants argued that the prices fixed were reasonable and hence protected by the common-law test of "a reasonable price."

JUDGMENT

Instead of following Justice Peckham's *Trans-Missouri* decision, Circuit Judge Taft

*United States v. Addyston Pipe and Steel Co., 85 F. 271 (6th Cir. 1898), affirmed, 175 U.S. 211 (1899).

chose to show that the defendants' argument to fix prices was illegal even under the common law, let alone under the Sherman Act. In reaching this conclusion, he accepted neither Justice White's rule of reason construction of a reasonable price standard (for that would open up a "sea of doubt") nor Justice Peckham's strict rule of per se illegality. Rather, he made a distinction between *primary or naked restraint* and *ancillary or partial restraint* and declared that only naked restraints were illegal per se, but not the ancillary ones; the latter might in fact be socially desirable. What, however, is an "ancillary restraint"?

> To be ancillary, and hence lawful, an agreement eliminating competition must be subordinate and collateral to a separate legitimate transaction. The ancillary restraint is subordinate and collateral in the sense that it makes the main transaction more effective in accomplishing legitimate purposes.†

According to Taft, the following agreements are essentially ancillary and hence lawful. Agreement (1) by the seller of property or business not to compete with the buyer in such a way as to derogate

†Bork, op. cit., p. 27

from the value of the property sold; (2) by a retiring partner not to compete with the firm; (3) by a partner pending the partnership not to do anything to interfere, by competition or otherwise, with the business of the firm; (4) by the buyer of the property not to use the same in competition with the business retained by the seller; and (5) by an assistant, servant, or agent not to compete with the master or employer after the expiration of his or her time of service. These categories, however, are the very ones held valid at common law. What Taft did was to state that such agreements, although valid, must be "merely ancillary to the main purpose of a lawful contract, and necessary to protect the covenantee [i.e., the promisee] in the enjoyment of the legitimate fruits of the contract, or to protect him from the dangers of an unjust use of those fruits by the other party." Also, he warned that the ancillary contract must not be couched in such terms as to suggest that it is part of a plan to gain monopoly control of a market. In the case under consideration Taft found the agreement among the six manufacturers to be primary restraint and thus illegal.

COMMENT

The importance of *Addyston Pipe* lies in Taft's commonsensical approach to the legality of an agreement. As Bork put it:

> [Taft's] doctrine of naked and ancillary restraints offered the Sherman Act a sophisticated rule of reason, a method of preserving socially valuable transactions by defining the scope of an exception for efficiency-creating agreements within an otherwise inflexible per se rule. . . . [T]he *Addyston* opinion may well have been the high-water mark of rational antitrust doctrine.‡

‡Bork, op cit., p. 30.

THE NORTHERN SECURITIES COMPANY CASE*

The issue raised in this case is whether a horizontal merger constitutes restraint of trade and is hence illegal under Sec. 1 of the Sherman Act.

FACTS

J. P. Morgan and James Hill, participants in many battles involving railroad mergers, used the Northern Securities Company of New Jersey, a holding company, to acquire working control over the Northern Pacific and Great Northern railroads. These two railroads, parallel and competing lines, served most of the northern tier of the

*Northern Securities Company v. United States, 193 U.S. (1904).

western United States. The government charged the company with violation of Sec. 1 of the Sherman Act.

JUDGMENT

When the case reached the Supreme Court, by a majority of 5 to 4, the Court held that the combining of two parallel and competing lines was clearly restraint of trade and hence violation of Sec. 1. Justice Harlan, acting for the majority, ordered the holding company to be dissolved and ownership returned to the two units.

In reaching this conclusion, the majority did not consider the extent to which the two railroads competed, whether other competing railroads existed (in fact, they did), or the impact of the merger. It seems that the majority adhered to Justice Peckham's per se illegality rule. Justice Harlan wrote:

> The mere existence of such a combination and the power acquired by the holding company as its trustee constituted a menace to, and a restraint upon, that freedom of commerce which Congress intended to recognize and protect, and which the public is entitled to have protected.

Justice Holmes, speaking for the minority, stated that the Sherman Act said "nothing about competition" and that the act was not intended to maintain every form of competition. To him the critical test was whether the said combination prevented a third party from competing. Moreover, in the case at hand the coming together of the two railroads was nothing but a fusion or horizontal merger and not a restraint of trade. Hence it is nonsensical to apply the per se illegality rule to it. Holmes was careful to distinguish such a merger from a cartel; in the latter there is intent to suppress competition and hence it is illegal per se. Justice Harlan thought otherwise. To him, it was not a merger but merely a profit-pooling arrangement.

COMMENT

The critical question raised by this case is whether a horizontal merger as opposed to a cartel (which is illegal per se) is in violation of the Sherman Act. Although Justice Harlan did not address this question squarely, the judgment rendered implies an affirmative answer. Justice Holmes, on the other hand, did not agree with this judgment. According to him, there is no difference between a single corporation building two railroad lines and the same corporation acquiring the two railroads after they are built. If such an acquisition is illegal, then growth by merger is ruled out. (We will refer to this topic in Chapter 9 when we discuss the Clayton Act's provision for mergers).

THE DR. MILES MEDICAL COMPANY CASE*

This case involves the legality of vertical price-fixing agreements between the manufacturer of a product and the dealers who handle the product.

*Dr. Miles Medical Company v. John D. Park & Sons Company, 220 U.S. 373 (1911). Note here that the Miller-Tydings Act passed in 1937 legalized retail or resale price-maintenance agreements; the act was repealed in 1975, however, because the growth of discount stores in 1950s and 1960s made such agreements practically useless. As a result, whereas by 1952 forty-five states had such "fair trade" laws, by 1975 only twenty-one had retained them.

FACTS

Dr. Miles Medical Company, a manufacturer of proprietary (i.e., patented) medicine developed a price-maintenance system whereby it fixed the prices at which some 400 wholesalers and about 25,000 retailers could sell its products. The purpose of this scheme, known as vertical price-fixing (becuase it is imposed by the manufacturer downward), was to establish minimum prices at which sales would be made by the vendees and by all subsequent purchasers who trafficked in the products of the manufacturer.

John D. Park & Sons, the defendant, was a noncontracting wholesaler but acquired the Miles products by inducing contracting wholesalers to sell the products to it in violation of their contracts with Miles and to sell the products at "cut prices." Dr. Miles Company thereupon sued John D. Park & Sons by invoking the established doctrine that "an actionable wrong is committed by one who maliciously interferes with a contract between two parties and induces one of them to break that contract to the injury of the other" and sought relief.

JUDGMENT

The trial court dismissed the complaint, the court of appeals affirmed the trial court's verdict, and the Supreme Court reaffirmed it. The *Miles* case was based on the grounds that (1) its practice of (vertical) retail price maintenance (RPM) was valid because it related to medicine manufactured under a patented (and secret) formula and that (2) apart from this, a manufacturer is entitled to control the prices on the sale of its own product. Moreover, it was not a horizontal or cartel price-fixing (which is illegal per per se) but a vertical one.

Rejecting both the arguments, Justice Hughes, for the majority, stated:

> . . . where commodities have passed into the channels of trade and are owned by dealers, the validity of agreements to prevent competition and to maintain prices is not to be determined by the circumstance whether they were produced by several manufacturers or by one, or whether they were previously owned by one or by many. The complainant having sold its product at prices satisfactory to itself, the public is entitled to whatever advantage may be derived from competition in the subsequent traffic. . . .

In short, Justice Hughes said that RPM agreements, whether entered into by competing manufacturers (i.e., horizontal restraint) or by a single manufacturer (i.e., vertical restraint), are illegal.

Dissenting from the majority, Justice Holmes remarked:

> I think we greatly exaggerate the value and importance to the public of competition in the production or distribution of an article (here it is only distribution) as fixing a fair price. . . . The Dr. Miles Medical Company knows better than we do what will enable it to do the best business. . . . I cannot believe that in the long run the public will profit by this court permitting knaves to cut reasonable prices for some ulterior purpose of their own and thus to impair, if not to destroy, the production and sale of articles which it is assumed to be desirable that the public should be able to get. . . .

COMMENT

By equating vertical price-fixing with horizontal price-fixing, Justice Hughes is in fact saying that if a manufacturer imposes vertical price restraint on retailers, it has the same motives and experiences the same consequences as if the retailers were themselves to form a cartel and fix prices (i.e., horizontal price-fixing). This is a questionable view, for the manufacturer obviously has nothing to gain from a horizontal price-fixing by retailers, whereas vertical price-fixing is for its own benefit. The two cannot have the same motives or experience the same consequences.†

†For a detailed discussion of the economics of the resale price maintenance laws, see Lester G. Telser, "Why Should Manufacturers Want Fair Trade?" *Journal of Law and Economics,* vol. 3, 1960, pp. 86–105, and Richard A. Posner, *Antitrust Law: An Economic Perspective,* The University of Chicago Press, Chicago, 1976, ch. 7.

THE STANDARD OIL CASE*

This is a landmark case not because of the issues involved but because of Chief Justice White's elaboration of his now famous rule of reason.

FACTS

The history behind the Standard Oil Company was briefly sketched in Chapter 7. The principal charges against the company were as follows: (1) conspiracy to monopolize and restraint of trade in crude oil, refined oil, and other petroleum products; (2) large preferential rates and rebates over competing oil companies which forced small companies to join Standard Oil or to go out of business; (3) power over the pipeline companies from the eastern oil fields to the midwestern oil refineries; (4) creation of bogus companies as "fighting companies" to show that there was competition; and (5) local oil price-cutting.

JUDGMENT

Although the facts of monopolization and restraint of trade were clear enough to indict the company under Sec. 1 and 2 of the Sherman Act, Chief Justice White used this case to shed light on the meaning of these sections and in the process expounded his rule of reason; he was waiting for his opportunity because in earlier cases (e.g., the *Trans-Missouri* case) he had tried to invoke this rule without much success. He wrote:

> . . . having by the 1st section forbidden all means of monopolizing trade, that is, unduly restraining it by means of every contract, combination, etc., the 2nd section seeks, if possible, to make the prohibitions of the act all the more

*Standard Oil Company v. United States, 221 U.S. 1 (1911).

complete and perfect by embracing all attempts to reach the end prohibited by the 1st section, that is, restraints of trade, by any attempt to monopolize, or monopolization thereof, even although the acts by which such results are attempted to be brought about or are brought about be not embraced within the general enumeration of the 1st section. And, of course, when the 2nd section is thus harmonized with and made as it was intended to be the complement of the 1st, it becomes obvious that the criteria to be resorted to in any given case for the purpose of ascertaining whether violations of the section have been committed is the *rule of reason* guided by the established law and by the plain duty to enforce the prohibitions of the act, and thus the public policy which its restrictions were obviously enacted to subserve. . . . [Emphasis added]

Applying this interpretation to *Standard Oil,* White concluded:

> Defendant's many acquisitions and mergers give rise in the absence of countervailing circumstances, . . . to the prima facie presumption of intent and purpose to maintain the dominancy over the oil industry, not as a result of *normal methods of industrial development,* but by new means of combination . . . with the purpose of excluding others from the trade and thus centralizing in the combination a perpetual control of the movements of petroleum and its products in the channels of interstate commerce. . . .
>
> This prima facie presumption of intent to restrain trade, to monopolize and to bring about monopolization . . . is made conclusive by considering, 1, the conduct of the persons or corporations who were mainly instrumental in bringing about the extension of power

in the New Jersey Corporation before the consummation of that result and prior to the formation of the trust agreements of 1879 and 1882; 2 by considering the proof as to what was done under those agreements and the acts which immediately preceded the vesting of power in the New Jersey Corporation as well as by weighing the modes in which the power vested in that corporation has been exerted and the results which have arisen from it. [Emphasis added]

COMMENT

From the preceding quote it is clear that to Justice White the mere possession of monopoly power (i.e., Sec. 1) is not enough to convict a defendant. What is required is also the purpose underlying the acquisition of monopoly power and, more to the point, its intended use. If the intent and purpose of the defendant was to exclude competitors and secure dominant market power, it would constitute offense under the Sherman Act. And in this situation it does not matter whether this dominance was achieved by a single seller or a group of sellers by forming a combination. *In short, to fall under the act, the monopolist (either singly or in combination) must have both the power to monopolize and the intent to monopolize.*

Thus White enshrined the rule of reason in the annals of the U.S. antitrust laws. According to Bork, the rule of reason is a three-part test. The first part is the "inherent nature" or the "per se" test. This would cover pure cartel-type agreements whose avowed purpose is to stave off competition by controlling price or output. The second part is the "inherent effect" or "market power" test, that is, how effective is the monopoly. Finally there is the "evident purpose" or "specific intent" test, that is, whether a monopoly is acquired by means other than pure economic efficiency (e.g., due to economies of scale) such as, for example, predatory pricing, that is, the practice of charging price below (marginal) cost so as to drive competitors out of market and then charging a monopoly price. The *Standard Oil* case, although it could have been decided by the per se illegality test, was ultimately decided by the "evident purpose" test; there was plenty of evidence of abuses, predatory practices, coercion, and other methods used by Standard Oil in acquiring its market power.†

†One scholar of this case, John S. McGee, argues that whatever the factors behind Standard's monopoly, predatory price discrimination was not one of them. See his well-known article, "Predatory Price Cutting: The Standard Oil (N.J.) Case," *Journal of Law and Economics,* October 1958.

THE CHICAGO BOARD OF TRADE CASE*

This case provides an example of the application of Justice White's rule of reason and points out the situations where "partial" restraint of trade may be justifiable or even necessary.

*Chicago Board of Trade v. United States, 246 U.S. 231 (1918).

FACTS

In 1918 the Department of Justice sued the Board of Trade of Chicago, the leading grain market in the world, on the ground that its trading rules amounted to price-fixing. The board handles three types of trade: (1) spot sales, that is, sales of grain already in Chicago in railroad cars or in elevators and ready for immediate delivery; (2) future sales, that is, agreements for delivery later in the current or in some future month; and (3) sales "to arrive," that is, agreements to deliver on arrival grain which is already in transit to Chicago or is to be shipped there at a specific time. Spot and future sales are made at the regular sessions of the Board from 9.30 a.m. to 1.15 p.m., whereas the "to arrive" sales are made at special sessions, termed *call,* which are held immediately after the close of the regular session. At these call sessions (usually lasting for about 30 minutes although no fixed time was prescribed) transactions were permitted only among the members of the board either for themselves or acting as agents for others. In 1906 the board adopted the so-called call rule, which prohibited members from purchasing or offering to purchase during the period between the close of the call and the opening of the session on the next business day any grain "to arrive" at a price other than the closing bid on the call. Thus, between 2 p.m. Monday and 9.30 a.m. Tuesday, bids could be made only at the closing call bid as at 2 p.m. Monday; before the adoption of this rule members of the board could bid at any price they saw fit. The Department of Justice argued that this was price-fixing pure and simple.

JUDGMENT

The district court voted in favor of the government, although the defendant, the Chicago Board of Trade, argued that the call rule was in no way intended to prevent competition or control prices but was simply for the convenience of the trade. As a matter of fact, the board argued, the rule was meant to increase competition by breaking the monopoly of four or five warehouseowners in Chicago who controlled the "to arrive" sale.

On appeal to the Supreme Court, the district court's ruling was overturned and the Court upheld the board's call rule.

Writing for the majority, Justice Brandeis said:

> The case was rested on the bald proposition, that a rule or agreement, by which men occupying positions of strength in any branch of trade fixed prices at which they would buy or sell during an important part of the business day, is an illegal restraint of trade under the Antitrust Law. But the legality of an agreement or regulation cannot be determined by so simple a test as whether it restrains competition. Every agreement concerning trade, every regulation of trade restrains. To bind, to restrain, is of their very essence. The true test of legality is whether the restraint imposed is such as merely regulates and perhaps thereby promotes competition or whether it is such as may supress or even destroy competition. To determine that question the Court must ordinarily consider the facts peculiar to the business to which the restraint is applied; its condition before and after the restraint was imposed; the nature of the restraint and its effect, actual or probable.

Considering the nature of the call rule, Justice Brandeis found it to be reasonable. As regards the scope of the rule, he found that the rule applied only to a small segment of the board's trade, namely, the "to arrive" sale, and it applied only during a small part of the business day. Regarding the effect of the rule, he found no appreciable effect on general market prices because the "to arrive" sale was quantitatively small compared to the overall trading volume of the board. Justice Brandeis also found that the rule had improved market conditions by creating a market in the "to arrive" grain, that is, by bringing buyers and sellers into more direct contact; each buyer and seller knew at which price the "to arrive" grain could be bought or sold after the end of the trading session.

COMMENT

The *Board of Trade* case thus brings out the essence of the rule of reason. Judged by the "inherent intent" criterion, the call rule was not meant to restrain competition but to provide a systematic means of trading when the market was officially closed.

THE UNITED STATES STEEL COMPANY CASE*

This is another case which brings out the essential characteristic of the rule of reason, namely, that the mere possession of market or monopoly power unaccompanied by any intent to misuse it is not an offense under the Sherman Act.

FACTS

The United States Steel Company (USS) was formed in 1901 as a holding company by bringing under a unified control some 180 independent companies accounting for some 50 percent of the iron and steel output. The government charged the company with monopolization and engaging in price-fixing schemes such as the "Pittsburgh Plus," a type of basing-point price system,† and asked for the divestiture and dissolution of the holding company.

JUDGMENT

The case went through various legal battles. The district court decided that there was no need for dissolution or divestiture

United States v. United States Steel Corporation, 251 U.S. 417 (1920).

†The basing-point price system works as follows. Some number of plants in an industry are designated "bases," and a base price is set, which is price at the factory gate (ex-factory). A standard system of freight charges is then laid down, which is based on the distance from the "base." All base prices and the standard fright charges are known to all sellers. The buyer has no option but to buy at the base price plus the prescribed freight. In the *Steel* case, Pittsburgh was chosen as the "base."

of the company because the company did not dominate the market nor could it do so alone. Moreover, the court accepted USS's argument that the mergers were solely for the purpose of taking advantage of the economies of scale offered by vertical integration and specilization (one plant making one product rather than twenty or forty). The government appealed to the Supreme Court.

Justice McKenna, writing for the majority, ruled against the government. In his decision he relied on the rule of reason and stated that the mere possession of monopoly power is not unlawful; it is the unreasonable use of the power which is illegal. In his words:

> The Corporation is undoubtedly of impressive size, and it takes an effort of resolution not to be affected by it or to exaggerate its influence. But we must adhere to the law, and the *law does not make mere size an offense or the existence of unexerted power an offense.* It, we repeat, requires overt acts and trusts to its prohibition of them and its power to repress or punish them. It does not compel competition nor require all that is possible. [Emphasis added]

Justice McKenna found that the corporation had not engaged in activities such as: (1) securing favorable freight rebates, (2) increasing profits by reducing employees' wages, (3) increasing profits by·lowering the quality of its products or creating artificial scarcity in them, (4) oppressing or coercing its competitors, or (5) engaging in resale price maintenance agreements.

In short, Justice McKenna developed the ''abuse theory'' or ''good trust theory,'' which states that, as long as there are no abusive market practices, the mere size or the mere possession of market power is no offense under the law.

COMMENT

The government botched the case. It first tried to show that smaller steel companies were forced to follow USS's prices for fear of retaliation by the company. But when evidence was not forthcoming, it switched its strategy by stating that ''the Corporation by its size restrains competition by its necessary effect and therefore is unlawful regardless of purpose.'' The majority did not buy this argument.

Justice Day, however, dissented vigorously from the majority and remarked:

> From the earliest decisions of this court it has been declared that it was the effective power of such organizations to control and restrain competition and the freedom of trade that Congress intended to limit and control. That the exercise of the power may be withheld or exerted with forebearing benevolence does not place such combinations beyond the authority of the statute which was intended to prohibit their formation, and when formed to deprive them of the power unlawfully attained.
>
> It is said that a complete monopolization of the steel business was never attained by the offending combinations. To insist upon such result would be beyond the requirements of the statute and in most cases practicably impossible. . . .

In short, Justice Day seems to be adhering to the ''per se illegality'' rule.

THE ALCOA CASE*

After a lull of more than two decades during which Justice White's rule of reason more or less governed antitrust litigation, the first important case to appear in the post–World War II era was that of the Aluminum Company of America (Alcoa). This is a landmark case because it raised the important question of what is the relevant market for assessing monopoly power and also because it dealt a blow to the ''good trust theory'' of the *Steel* case and deemphasized the rule of reason.

FACTS

Alcoa was formed in 1888. In 1889 it acquired the patent on the Hall process of

producing aluminum, and in 1903 it acquired the patent on the Bradley method of smelting aluminum without the use of external heat. By 1909 both these patents had expired, but in the intervening period Alcoa had entered into contracts with several electric utilities to buy power from them on the condition that they not sell their power to any other producer of aluminum. It also entered into agreements with foreign producers to limit the import of aluminum into the United States. By 1912, by a consent decree with the United States government, the company agreed to stop these practices.

The government charged Alcoa for monopolizing the following markets: bauxite, water power, alumina, virgin aluminum (pig and ingot), castings, cooking utensils, pistons, extrusions and structural shapes, foil, and shaft cables.

*United States v. Aluminum Company of America, 148 F.2d 416 (2d Cir. 1945).

JUDGMENT

In the district court Judge Caffey found Alcoa not guilty of monopolizing any of the above products. The case then went to the Supreme Court, but for lack of a quorum the case was sent to the Second Circuit Court of Appeals. There the majority found Alcoa guilty of monopolizing the aluminum market. The majority opinion was written by Judge Learned Hand.

The first question raised in the case was: Did Alcoa in fact have monopoly power? Judge Hand believed so, for Alcoa controlled about 90 percent of the virgin ingot aluminum used in the United States just before World War II. But a question arose as to whether one should include only virgin aluminum or also consider secondary aluminum (i.e., metal reclaimed from scrap); if the latter were included, Alcoa's share of the combined virgin and secondary markets would have been about 64 percent. The company argued that the secondary market should be included because it provided a product that was substitutable with virgin aluminum. But Judge Hand contended that even then the company had substantial market power. Moreover, he argued, the amount of secondary aluminum available is itself a function of the company's own previous production of virgin aluminum and its current production and price policies would take that fact into account.

The company then presented several defenses. First, even assuming that it had monopoly in the aluminum market, it did not abuse it by hurting either consumers or other producers. Hence, following the *Steel* case (the good trust theory), it did not violate the Sherman Act. Second, the availability of imported and secondary aluminum put a limit on what price the company could charge; its monopoly power, if it existed, was thus limited. Third, it did not achieve exhorbitant profits; its net return on capital invested had been around 10 percent, not an unreasonable rate of return.

But the majority did not accept any of these defenses. To the company's defense that the secondary and imported markets put a limit on its prices, Judge Hand said that this is not the same thing as not having power in the market: "A six foot man in an eight-foot room is subject to a ceiling, but he can still reach higher than a dwarf." To the defense that its profits were not excessive, Judge Hand replied, "the mere fact that a producer, having command of the domestic market, has not been able to make more than a "fair" profit, is no evidence that a "fair" profit could not have been made at lower prices...." To Alcoa's defense that it did not misuse its market power and that following the *Steel* case it should be absolved of the charge of monopolization (the good trust theory), Judge Hand retorted:

But the whole issue is irrelevant anyway, for it is no excuse for "monopolizing" a market that the monopoly has not been used to extract from the consumer more than a "fair" profit. The Act has wider purposes. Indeed, even though we disregarded all but economic considerations, it would by no means follow that such concentration of producing power is to be desired, when it has not been used extortionately. *Many people believe that possession of unchallenged economic power deadens initiative, discourages thrift, and depresses energy; that immunity from competition is narcotic, and rivalry is a stimulant to industrial progress; that the spur of constant stress is necessary to counteract an inevitable disposition to let well enough alone.*

Moreover, Congress did not condone "good trusts" and condemn "bad" ones; it forbade all. Moreover, in so doing it was not necessarily actuated by economic motives alone. It is possible, because of its social or moral effect, to prefer a system of small producers, each dependent for his success upon his own skill and character; to one in which the great mass of those engaged must accept the direction of a few.... *Throughout the history of these statutes it has been constantly assumed that one of their purposes was to perpetuate and preserve, for its own sake and in spite of possible cost, an organization of industry in small units which can effectively compete with each other.* We hold that Alcoa's monopoly of ingot was of the kind covered by [Sec.] 2.

In order to fall within [Sec.] 2, the monopolist must have both the power to monopolize and the intent to monopolize. To read the passage as demanding any "specific" intent makes nonsense of it, for no monopolist monopolizes unconscious of what he is doing. So here, Alcoa meant to keep, and did keep, that complete and exclusive hold upon the ingot market with which it started. That was to monopolize that market, however innocently it otherwise proceeded. [Emphasis added]

COMMENT

The Alcoa case raises several questions.

1 Did Alcoa really have monopoly of the aluminum market? Justice Hands' statement, "That percentage [90 percent according to him] is enough to constitute a monopoly; it is doubtful whether 60 or 64 percent would be enough; certainly 33 percent is not," an oft-quoted statement, would have absolved Alcoa of the monopolization charge if Judge Hand included the secondary market in his definition of the relevant market. With the secondary market included, as noted previously, Alcoa's market share would have been 64 percent and therefore according to Hands own criterion Alcoa's monopoly would have been doubtful. It was not until the *Cellophane* case (see p. 190) that the proper definition of what is the

relevant market was squarely faced by the courts.

2 Did the Alcoa ruling bring back Justice Peckham's rule of per se illegality? Is monopoly illegal per se? Not necessarily so. What Judge Hand is implying is that monopoly power means power to fix price and therefore it cannot be saved by saying that it has been used reasonably (see point 6 below).

3 What then is the difference between the *Standard Oil* and *Alcoa* cases? In both cases, the existence of market power was established. Also, in both cases an enquiry was made into the "intent" or "purpose" behind the power. In *Standard Oil*, to Justice White monopolization meant "a departure from normal methods of industrial development," whereas in Alcoa Judge Hand found that, "given an intent to retain power, it is irrelevant whether its actual use is reasonable or not."

4 Is small necessarily "beautiful"? Judge Hand's decision seems to imply that Congress desired a small business per se philosophy, although such businesses may not be efficient.

5 Is "market structure" more important than "market behavior"? By refusing to subscribe to the abuse theory or good trust theory, Judge Hand is saying that market structue per se is more important than market behavior.

6 When may a monopoly be acceptable? According to Judge Hand, monopoly may be acceptable where there is no "positive drive" on the part of the monopolist to acquire monopoly power. He explained:

Persons may unwittingly find themselves in possession of a monopoly, automatically so to say; that is, without having intended either to put an end to existing competition, or to prevent competition from arising when none had existed; they may become monopolists by force of accident ... A market may, for example, be so limited that it is impossible to produce at all and meet the cost of production except by a plant large enough to supply the whole demand [e.g., a natural monopoly such as an electric utility company]. Or there may be changes in taste or in cost which drive out all but one purveyor. *A single producer may be the survivor* out of a group of active competitors, *merely by virtue of his superior skill, foresight and industry.* [Emphasis added]

Thus, Judge Hand would accept a monopoly based on "superior skill, foresight and industry." But how is one to know that Alcoa did not fall into this category? As a matter of fact, some scholars believe that Alcoa acquired monopoly power by the very acts Judge Hand mentioned in the preceding quote, although he maintained that Alcoa's initial behavior of exclusive long-term contracts with electric utilities exhibited an element of "positive drive" to acquire monopoly power. But Judge Hand did not consider the fact that Alcoa had stopped such activities before 1912, and he did not find out whether between 1912 and 1945 the company exhibited any elements of "positive drive" or whether during this period its power was on account of superior skill, etc. In any event, the *Alcoa* decision dealt a severe blow to the rule of reason that had governed antitrust litigation until then.

THE UNITED SHOE MACHINERY CASE*

This is a post-Hand *Alcoa* case and the ruling followed a similar decision.

FACTS

The United Shoe Machinery Corporation (USM) of New Jersey was formed in 1899 through a merger of seven manufacturers of shoe-making equipment. Subsequently, it acquired fifty companies which held complementary shoe machinery patents. In 1918 the government brought a suit against USM charging that (1) its sole objective was to dominate the shoe-making machinery market and that (2) its selling practice was such that it only leased its machines without giving the lessee the option to buy them and that its lease clauses were such as to make it impossible for the lessee to deal with other manufacturers; USM machinery could not be used with the machines produced by other manufacturers. But the company won this first suit on the ground that its acquisition of fifty companies made it possible to reap the benefits of vertical integration because the patents were complementary. In 1922, however, the company, by a consent decree, modified its leasing method by removing the "tying clause" which had forced the lessee to buy supplies from USM when it leased USM's machinery.

In 1953 another antitrust suit was brought against the company under Sec. 2. It was tried in the District Court of Massachusetts by Judge Wyzanski. The facts in this new trial were essentially unchanged from the first trial and were as follows: (1) the company supplied between 75 to 85 percent of the machinery used in the boot and shoe industry; (2) the company followed its traditional practice of leasing and not selling — the leases were usually for 10 years; (3) the company had an excellent service record and there was no dissatisfaction on the part of its customers. One new feature was that in the new "cement" process of manufacturing, a competitor, Compo, successfully competed with USM.

*United States v. United Shoe Machinery Corporation, 110 F. Supp. 295 (D. Mass 1953), *affirmed per curiam*, 437 U.S. 521 (1954).

As a result, in this particular market the company adjusted its lease charges which were lower than in other markets where there was no substantial competition.

JUDGEMENT

Judge Wyzanski noted three sources of USM's market power. (1) The original formation of the company by merger and acquisition. But because of the 1918 decision, this charge of monopolization could not be levied against the company. (2) The acquisition of market power because of the superiority of USM's product and services. But because of Hand's *Alcoa* decision, which would permit monopoly because of superior skill, etc., the company could not be charged with monopolization on account of "positive drive" to monopolize. (3) The company's leasing practices and its effect on the company's rivals. Judge Wyzanski found the company's leasing policies unacceptable and therefore found the company guilty of monopolization under Sec. 2. He wrote:

> . . . they [the leasing practices] are not practices which can be properly described as the inevitable consequences of ability, natural forces, or law. . . . They are contracts, arrangements and policies which, instead of encouraging competition based on pure merit, further the dominance of a particular firm. In this sense they are *unnatural barriers* [to entry]: they unnecessarily exclude actual and potential competition: they restrict a free market. While the law allows many enterprises to use such practices, the Sherman Act is now construed by superior courts to forbid the continuance of effective market control based in part upon such practices.

Judge Wyzanski, while finding the company guilty of monopolization, refused to break up the company. Instead, he ordered it to purge its leases of their restrictive features and also to shorten the life of the lease and give the lessee the option to buy the patented machines by paying appropriate royalties. The government was not happy with these remedial measures and ten years later appealed to the Supreme Court for further remedy. The Supreme Court ruled that divestiture of the shoe machinery assets would be an appropriate remedy, but later the company, by a consent decree, agreed to divest enough of its assets to reduce its market share to about 33 percent. This share, according to Judge Hand's *Alcoa* dictum, would "certainly" not constitute a monopoly!

COMMENT

According to Bork, Judge Wyzanski made a serious economic error in not recognizing that the net effect of the USM leasing system was (economic) efficiency creation; even the customers of USM thought so. Incidentally, Wyzanski introduced the notion of barriers to entry but did not expound upon what barriers were proper and what were improper. This is an important question, for all businesses create some barriers to new entry. Such barriers can be justified only if they are efficiency-oriented and confer benefits on society. But the judge did not address this question at all. According to Bork: "The real, the only, issue in the case – was United trying to be efficient or predatory? – was never even discussed."†

Of course, one may not agree with Bork's purely economic approach to the problem. From an equity viewpoint one may accept Judge Hand's view in *Alcoa* that unless a monopoly is due to superior skill, foresight, and industry (which, according to Judge Wyzanski, was not the case in *United Shoe*) one may accept "an organization of industry in small units which can effectively compete with each other" in spite of possible cost.

†Bork, *op. cit.,* p. 139.

THE CELLOPHANE (DU PONT) CASE*

This case sheds light on what constitutes the appropriate market for the purpose of measuring monopoly power. The decision in this case stands in strong contrast to that of *Alcoa*, considered earlier.

FACTS

The federal government brought a civil action against du Pont under Sec. 2 of the Sherman Act. It charged the company with monopolizing, attempting to monopolize, and conspiracy to monopolize the inter-state market in cellophane and cellulosic caps and bands.

JUDGMENT

In the district court the company was absolved of the charges leveled against it. The government appealed the decision to the Supreme Court, but only that part of the decision which found the company not guilty of monopolizing the cellophane market.

The main question facing the Supreme Court was therefore to decide whether du Pont had monopolized the cellophane market and hence was in violation of Sec. 2. It was established that the company produced about 75 percent of the cellophane sold in the United Stated, but considering the sales of all flexible packaging materials (e.g., aluminum, cellulose acetate, chlorides, wood pulp, rubber hydrochloride, ethylene gas, etc.) du Pont's share was less than 20 percent. Judge Leahy of the district court had held that the relevant market was not just cellophane but all flexible packaging materials. Justice Reed, writing for the majority, concurred with this view and stated in part:

The government asserts that cellophane and other wrapping materials are neither substantially fungible nor like

*United States v. E. I. du Pont de Nemours & Company, 351 U.S. 377 (1956).

priced. For these reasons, it argues that the market for other wrappings is distinct from the market for cellophane and that the competition afforded cellophane by other wrappings is not strong enough to be considered in determining whether du Pont has monopoly power. . . . The ultimate consideration in such a determination is whether the defendants control the price and competition in the market for such part of trade or commerce as they are charged with monopolizing. *Every manufacturer is the sole producer of the particular commodity it makes but its control in the above sense of the relevant market depends upon the availability of alternative commodities for buyers: i.e., whether there is a cross-elasticity of demand between cellophane and the other wrappings.* The interchangeability is largely gauged by the purchase of competing products for similar uses considering the price, characteristics and adaptability of the competing commodities.

Commenting on the "market" for the purpose of defining monopoly power, Justice Read stated:

The "market" which one must study to determine when a producer has monopoly power will vary with the part of commerce under consideration. The tests are constant. That market is composed of products that have *reasonable interchangeability* for the purposes for which they are produced — price, use and qualities considered.

Chief Justice Warren dissented, stating that cellophane was not a close substitute to the aforementioned products and it therefore constituted a separate market. As proof, Warren noted that between 1923 and 1947 the sale of cellophane grew phenomenally: In 1923 its production was about 361,000 pounds and its total revenue about $1.3 million, whereas in 1947 its production was 133,503,000 pounds, with a total revenue of $55.39 million. Considering the fact that the average price of cellophane was higher than that of competing products, such a phenomenal growth can be attributed only to the uniqueness of cellophane; it is distinct from other packaging material. And since du Pont controlled 75 percent of this market, it certainly monopolized the market. Moreover, its net return of 15.9 percent (between 1937 and 1947) was also excessive.†

†Not only Justice Warren but also some economists thought that du Pont's behavior was monopolistic. See George W. Stocking and Willard F. Mueller, "The Cellophane Case and the New Competition," *American Economic Review,* vol. 45, no. 1, March 1955. But some believe that government action itself increased competition. See Don E. Waldman, "The DuPont Cellophane Case Revisited: An Analysis of the Indirect Effects on Antitrust Policy on Market Structure and Performance," *Antitrust Bulletin,* vol. 25, no. 4, Winter 1980, pp. 805–830.

COMMENT

The uniqueness of the *Cellophane* case lies in the discussion about what constitutes the relevant market for assessing competition or lack of it. Justice Read's criterion of the *cross-elasticity* of demand (the percentage change in the quantity of a commodity A demanded in relation to a small percentage in the price of another commodity, say, B) in assessing the extent of competition between two products is economically very sound. If the cross-elasticity of demand between two products is positive and reasonably high, the two products are competing or substitutable.

The real question then in this case was the extent of the cross-elasticity between cellophane and the other products. Justice Reed believed it to be positive and high, whereas Chief Justice Warren believed it to be low. Unfortunately, no numerical estimates of cross-elasticity were presented in the case.

8.2 THE SHERMAN ACT: SOME GENERAL COMMENTS

We have considered some ten leading cases that were tried under the Sherman Act. They by no means exhaust the whole list, but they give us some idea about the courts' thinking over the years and are thus helpful in answering some of the questions mentioned in the introduction of this chapter.

Although each case brings out a new point or two, it is perhaps safe to say that by and large, from the courts' perspective, the overall goal of the Sherman Act is the maintenance of competition by preventing monopoly and its associated evils such as price or output control. The question then seems to be one of determining whether monopoly exists in the case at hand.

But here the court decisions are not unequivocal. How does one judge the presence of monopoly — by structure or by conduct? In the *Alcoa* case Judge Hand adhered to a strictly structural approach. By his calculations, Alcoa controlled 90 percent of the virgin aluminum market and was therefore guilty of monopolization (notwithstanding the company's defense of "good" behavior), whereas in the earlier *Steel* case Justice McKenna developed the conduct theory of good trust and bad trust.

Even if one believes in the purely structural approach, a blind adherence to it can be dangerous if one is not careful in defining the relevant market to measure the monopoly power. In the *Cellophane* case the majority argued that because of the high cross-elasticity of demand between cellophane and other flexible packaging material, the relevant market was not just cellophane but all flexible packaging products; it thus absolved du Pont of the monopoly charge. But in the *Alcoa* case Judge Hand paid lip service to this point. Had he not done so, then by his own standards Alcoa's market share of about 64 percent would not have constituted monopolization.

How does one resolve the conflict between the structural versus conduct theories? Here is where Justice White's rule of reason becomes very important. He would consider both structure and conduct or power and intent in deciding cases under the Sherman Act. According to him, the defendant must *have both the power as well as the will to exclude competitors*. Of course, how much weight to give to each of these elements will depend on the nature of the case. In the *Trans-Missouri* and *Standard Oil* cases there was no difficulty in convicting the defendants because both the power and intent to exclude competitors was very clear. But such clear-cut cases are rare these days. Most cases fall in the category where there is some power, not an overwhelming amount, and some action, not overly aggressive. It is these cases which require a careful attention of the courts. And this is where the distinction between primary and ancillary restraints introduced by Justice Taft in *Addyston Pipe* becomes an important factor; its correct application was visible in the *Chicago Board of Trade* case.

Recall that in Chapter 6 we discussed the economic theory of monopoly and stated the economist's case against monopoly vis-à-vis competition. As stated there, monopoly, under certain conditions, leads to efficiency or welfare (deadweight) loss. The reader may very well ask: Was the Supreme Court's decision, say, in *Alcoa*, meant to eliminate a deadweight loss due to the fact that the price was above marginal cost? Was the consumer's welfare increased by, say, the *Northern Securities* decision? In short, how do we judge the cases we have discussed in view of the economic theory of monopoly discussed in Chapter 6?

After reading the cases carefully, it is very difficult to maintain that the criterion of economic efficiency was the basis of most of the decisions. Even in cases such as *Trans-Missouri* and *Northern Securities*, where the charge of monopolization was sustained, there was no significant evidence to suggest that there were efficiency losses. On the contrary, in *United Shoe Machinery Corporation* the charge of monopolization was upheld despite the finding that the company's leasing practice was a reflection of economic efficiency and not of any predatory intent.

Of course, one could raise a legitimate question: Should the economic criterion of efficiency be the sole criterion to decide antitrust cases under the Sherman and the other antitrust acts? What about perpetuating and preserving, ''for its own sake and in spite of possible cost, an organization of industry in small units which can effectively compete with each other,'' as Judge Hand opined in *Alcoa*? As a matter of fact in so many other antitrust cases (see Chapters 9 and 10) the pro-small business philosophy of the courts comes through so clearly and loudly that it seems that the equity aspect and not the efficiency aspect is of primary importance to the courts. The implication is that the distribution of income would be more equitable (equal) if size were limited. This surely is an unsubstantiated claim and the courts rarely have adduced any proof to that effect. Are the courts saying that the distribution of income is less equitable when competition forces the less efficient firms out of business? The question of equity is so thorny that it is debatable whether the courts are the right forum to resolve it.

What is the future of the Sherman Act? Our case studies reveal that this anti-trust law has been evolutionary, reflecting the socioeconomic and sociopolitical winds prevailing at the time each case was resolved. The best one can say is that "periods of advance and periods of consolidation in antitrust may continue to succeed each other as the industrial development of the United States changes in response to economic needs."[1] (For some suggested reform of the act, see Chapter 18).

8.3   SUMMARY AND CONCLUSIONS

In this chapter we considered several leading antitrust cases to find out the goals of the Sherman Act as seen by the judges. Although these cases do not exhaust the list of cases tried under the act, they are sufficient to prove that the courts have a lot to say in the antitrust matters.

We first considered the *Trans-Missouri* case, which declared once and for all that cartel-type or horizontal price-fixing is illegal per se. Then we considered the *Addyston Pipe* case, which established the principle that not all restraint of trade is illegal; only the primary or naked restraints are illegal but not the secondary or ancillary ones. The *Northern Securities* case dealt with the legality of horizontal mergers; they were judged illegal in this particular case. However, Justice Holmes's dissent in the case raised the possibility that horizontal mergers are not necessarily illegal. Horizontal price-fixing was declared illegal in *Trans-Missouri*. But what about vertical price-fixing, price-fixing of the resale price maintenance type? In the *Miles* case, Justice Hughes held that such price-fixing was illegal too.

The *Standard Oil* case, although a clear-cut case of monopolization which could have been decided by the per se illegality rule, gave Justice White the long-awaited opportunity to expound his rule of reason regarding the legality of monopoly. According to White, the mere possession of monopoly power is not enough to convict under the Sherman Act. What is required also is the intention behind such power. If the intent is bad (e.g., to exclude competitors), then monopoly power is illegal. Otherwise, it is not necessarily illegal. In short, monopoly power and intent must be looked at in totality to convict under the act. The *Chicago Board of Trade* case provided an example of the application of the rule of reason; it declared that the board's call rule was not restraint of trade but was merely for the convenience of the trade. The *U.S. Steel* case provides another example of the use of the rule of reason. Although a sizable

[1]A. D. Neale, *The Antitrust Laws of the U.S.A.,* 2d ed., Cambridge University Press, 1970, p. 18.

market force, USS was absolved of the charge of monopolization because of its good behavior; it was a "good trust."

The 1945 *Alcoa* decision dealt a serious blow to the rule of reason. In this case Judge Hand ruled that mere possession of market power can be illegal under the act, and there is no need to show malintent on the part of the defendant. This view was reinforced in the *United Shoe Machinery* case; Judge Wyzanski found the company guilty of monopolization by virtue of the company's leasing practices, although there was no question about the superior performance of the company. The 1956 *Cellophane* case, although it did not have much to say about the rule of reason, raised the important question of what constitutes the appropriate market for a product. By invoking the economic notion of cross-elasticity of demand, this case established the point that where the cross-elasticity between two (or more) products is positive and high, they together constitute the market. Thus, considering the market for all flexible packaging material, Justice Reed found that cellophane was only a small part of such market and therefore du Pont did not have monopoly of the market thus defined.

In the cases discussed in the chapter, the courts seemed to be caught in the dilemma of weighing between efficiency and equity, if equity is construed to mean "the preservation of small business for its own sake." Whether the courts should get involved with the thorny question of equity is a debatable issue. That is why economists have been emphasizing the efficiency aspect. Their general case against monopoly is on the grounds that it leads to welfare loss.

QUESTIONS

8-1 "There is no absolute monopoly power in the real world, short of monopoly of everything." (A. D. Neale, *The Antitrust Laws of the U.S.A.*, Cambridge University Press, 1979, p. 120.) Comment.

8-2 "Economic theory as well as law is made by antitrust litigation." (Donald Dewey, *Monopoly in Economics and Law*, Rand McNally, Chicago, 1959, p. 235.) Do you agree? Why or why not?

8-3 What is the rationale, if any, behind the per se illegality rule? Do you agree with Justice Perkham's per se illegality verdict in the *Trans-Missouri case*? Explain.

8-4 In what ways is the *Addyston Pipe* case "the high-water mark of rational antitrust doctrine?"

8-5 Are the following restraints primary or ancillary? Explain your reasoning.
  a A contract between a publisher and an author by which the publisher binds the author to publish all his books with her and not with any other publisher.
  b A contract between a publisher and the author of the book *Government and Business* that the latter will not publish a book on this topic with another publisher.

8-6 Dissenting from the majority in the *Northern Securities* case, Justice Holmes said that "the [Sherman] Act said nothing about competition." What did he have in mind when he made that statement?

8-7 Do you think that the majority, represented by Justice Hughes, erred in its *Miles* decision, which in effect declared that vertical price-fixing is illegal? Reason carefully.

8-8 In the *Standard Oil* case Justice White tried to distinguish between Sec. 1 and 2 of the Sherman Act. What precisely is the distinction between the two sections?

8-9 What did Justice White mean by the phrase ''normal methods of industrial development'' in assessing the intent of monopoly power?

8-10 In his *Steel* decision Justice McKenna stated that '' . . . the law does not make mere size an offense or the existence of unexerted power an offense.'' Do you think he was interpreting the Sherman Act correctly? Justify your answer.

8-11 What criteria would you use in distinguishing between ''good trusts'' and ''bad trusts''?

8-12 Do you think that the *Alcoa* decision makes a bad law? Following this verdict, would you have convicted the U.S. Steel Company? Why?

8-13 Critically evaluate the *Standard Oil* and *Alcoa* decisions, pointing out the similarities and dissimilarities between them and then comment on the appropriateness of the decision rendered in each case.

8-14 The rule of reason takes into account both the market power and market behavior of the defendant. How would you decide how much weight you want to assign to these two factors in deciding an antitrust case?

8-15 How have the courts measured market or monopoly power? Can you lay down some general criteria based on the court decisions?

8-16 Compare the *Alcoa* and *du Pont* decisions and decide which makes better economic sense and why.

8-17 How would you defend the pro-small business bias seen in several Supreme Court decisions?

CHAPTER 9

THE WORKING OF THE CLAYTON ACT—I: PRICE DISCRIMINATION AND TYING CONTRACTS

As noted in Chapter 7, Congress was very unhappy about the way the courts interpreted the Sherman Act, especially their adoption of the rule of reason in deciding whether a monopoly was reasonable or unreasonable. To strengthen the Sherman Act and to minimize judicial discretion, Congress passed the Clayton Act in 1914, which specifically proscribed four activities, namely, (1) price discrimination, (2) tying contracts and exclusive dealings, (3) corporate acquisitions and mergers, and (4) interlocking directorates. The Robinson-Patman Act of 1936 and the Celler-Kefauver Act of 1950 amended, respectively, the price-discrimination and merger provisions of the Clayton Act by plugging some loopholes.

In this chapter we look at the economic and legal aspects of price discrimination and tying contracts and defer to the next chapter the remaining provisions of the Clayton Act.

9.1 THE ECONOMIC MEANING OF PRICE DISCRIMINATION

Section 2 of the Clayton Act, as amended by Sec. 1 of the Robinson-Patman Act of 1936 (the anti-price-discrimination law), prohibits overt price discrimination that cannot be justified on account of cost differences (Sec. 2(a)) or which is not due to "meeting competition in good faith" (Sec. 2(b)).[1] It also prohibits covert or disguised price discrimination, that is, price discrimination disguised in the form of brokerage commissions, allowances and discounts (Sec. 2(c)), or pro-

---

[1]Hereafter, we will use the term *amended* Sec. 2 of the Clayton Act to indicate the changes introduced by the Robinson-Patman Act.

motional allowances for the promotional activities performed by the buyer (Sec. 2(d)) or the seller himself providing promotional services without cost to the buyer (Sec. 2(e)), or the quantity discounts given to large buyers (Sec. 2(f)). Incidentally, note that the cost-justification defense of Sec. 2(a) is not applicable to the acts mentioned in Sec. 2(c) to 2(f).

Whether it is overt or covert, the term *price discrimination* as understood by the courts is not the same as that used by the economist, and it is essential at the outset to notice the difference. The "legal" meaning of price discrimination is simply a price difference. Thus, in *FTC v. Anheuser-Busch, Inc.,* a case decided in 1960, the Supreme Court held that "a price discrimination within the meaning of that provision [i.e., Sec. 2 of the amended Clayton Act] is merely a price difference."

To the economist, price discrimination means something else. It means the "practice of selling the same product to different customers at different prices."[2] More technically, it means "selling at a price or prices such that the ratio of price to marginal cost is different in different sales."[3] Thus, if P_A and P_B are the prices charged for the same commodity to two buyers A and B (or two markets A and B) and if MC_A and MC_B are the corresponding marginal costs, then if $P_A/MC_A = P_B/MC_B$, there is no economic price discrimination. On the other hand, if $P_A/MC_A \neq P_B/MC_B$, there is economic price discrimination. Figure 9.1 shows this graphically. (For simplicity it is assumed that the marginal cost in both markets is both equal and constant.) By this definition, if P_A and P_B are identical but MC_A and MC_B are different, there is price discrimination; that is, charging identical prices when marginal costs differ is economic price discrimination. Unfortunately, the courts do not consider this price discrimination under the Robinson-Patman Act: To the courts, there must be price difference to establish price discrimination!

Since the general thrust of the Robinson-Patman Act is against price discrimination, although the term is not synonymous with the economist's usage of it, the question that naturally arises is: Is price discrimination necessarily bad? To answer this question, we need to examine the economic consequences of price discrimination. But before we undertake that task, we must answer another question: Why would a seller engage in price discrimination to begin with? The answer is obvious: A seller will engage in price discrimination if by charging different prices to different sets of consumers or different markets the overall profits would be greater than if she were to charge a single price to all her customers. The question then is: What are the conditions under which a seller can successfully price-discriminate between customers or between markets?

Economic theory tells us that for price discrimination to succeed the following conditions must be satisfied. First, the seller must have a substantial market or monopoly power so that he can control price (or output). Second, the seller

---

[2] Richard A. Posner, *Antitrust Law: An Economic Perspective,* The University of Chicago Press, Chicago, 1976, p. 62.
[3] Ibid., p. 62.

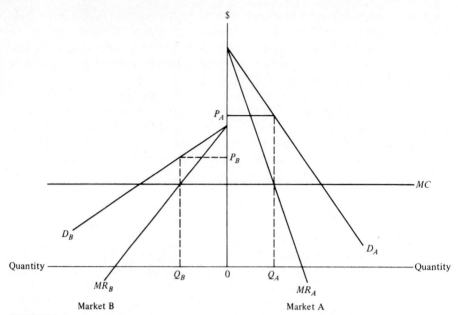

FIGURE 9.1
Price discrimination assuming constant marginal cost.

must be able to keep his markets or groups of buyers distinct, that is, he must so segment his markets that a buyer from one market where the price is higher cannot take advantage of the lower price charged in another market. The degree of market segmentation, that is, the extent to which the monopolist can succeed in preventing market crossovers, will be greater as the cost of transportation between markets is greater. Thus, a monopolist may charge a higher price in the domestic market and a lower one in the foreign market without fear of the domestic buyer buying the product in the foreign market and bringing it home because of the costs involved in such a transaction; such costs (transportation, currency fluctuations, import duties) may wipe out any price difference that exists between the two markets. Finally, and more importantly, the price-elasticity of demand in different markets must be different, enabling the monopolist to charge a higher price in the comparatively price-inelastic market (as in market A of Figure 9.1) and a lower price in the comparatively price-elastic market (as in Market B of Figure 9.1). This explains why a local electric utility, a natural monopoly, often charges a comparatively higher unit price for residential customers than for industrial customers; the latter can take advantage of alternative sources of fuels if there are effective differences in their prices, but to an average residential customer there is very little choice.

Assume that the above conditions are met so that it is profitable for the monopolist to engage in price discrimination. What are the economic consequences of such a practice? It was pointed out in Chapter 6 that under pure or

non-price-discriminating monopoly, economic resources in general are not allocated as efficiently as under competition and therefore economic welfare is not
as great as it is under competition. The question now is: Can economic welfare
be increased with price discrimination, although it may not be as great as under
competition?

The answer to the preceding question is not clear-cut. Richard A. Posner, for
example, contends that "a price difference not justified by a difference in cost
may distort competitive relationships and impair efficiency at the customer
level."[4] What he means is as follows: Suppose a monopolist has two customers,
A and B, A being located 50 miles from her and B about 100 miles. Suppose the
monopolist charges a price of $1 per unit of, say, widgets, to both customers.
(This is an example of the basing point pricing system explained in the *Steel* case
in Chapter 8) Here economic price discrimination is involved, for although the
unit price charged A and B is the same, the cost of transportation is not the
same. If the (long-run) marginal cost of the widget is, say, 90 cents, and the true
unit costs of transportation to A and B are 5 cents and 15 cents, respectively,
then, the prices charged A and B should be 95 cents and $1.05, respectively.
But by charging the uniform price of $1 per unit, the monopolist is hurting A; A
probably located its plant near the monopolist to take advantage of the lower
transportation cost, but with the above pricing policy that advantage is lost. Of
course, B has benefitted at the cost of A.

There are economists who take a different view. Joan Robinson, a noted British economist, has argued that under some situations production will be greater
with than without price discrimination.[5] If this is the case, economic welfare
might in fact increase with price discrimination; some consumers who cannot
buy the product at the (higher) uniform price can do so in those markets where
prices are reduced because of price discrimination. Economic theory also shows
that in the case of a *perfectly discriminating monopoly*, that is, where the
monopolist can charge each consumer or each market a price based on the
price-elasticity of demand of that market, the output produced will be the same
as that produced under perfect competition. Hence there will not be any deadweight losses.[6]

The point to note is that price discrimination is not necessarily an evil; as a
matter of fact, in some situations it may be socially desirable. Consider the case
of a small town which cannot afford the services of a medical specialist if he
were to charge a uniform price to all his customers. But if he is allowed to price-
discriminate by charging a higher price to wealthier members of the town and
a lower price to those who are not so fortunate, it is possible to retain the services of the specialist. In this case, where the choice is between some service

---

[4]Richard A. Posner, *The Robinson-Patman Act,* American Enterprise Institute for Public Policy
Research, Washington, D.C., 1976, p. 3.

[5]Joan Robinson, *The Economics of Imperfect Competition,* MacMillan, New York, 1933, pp.
188–95.

[6]For proof and details, see Jack Hirshleifer, *Price Theory and Applications,* 2d ed., Prentice-Hall,
Englewood Cliffs, N.J., 1980, ch. 11, sec. 11. E. 3.

(or output) with price discrimination or no service at all at a uniform price, society will opt for price discrimination, and rightly so.

In sum, then, it is quite possible, although not absolutely certain, that economic resources may be allocated more efficiently with than without price discrimination. From this perspective, it would seem that the anti-price-discrimination emphasis of the Robinson-Patman Act may be misplaced. As a matter of fact, there is general consensus among respected economists and legal scholars that the Robinson-Patman Act, strange as it might seem, is anticompetition and anticonsumer and that it should be repealed. Although some efforts are being made in Congress to dilute the provisions of the Robinson-Patman Act, it does not seem likely that the law will be repealed.[7] Be that as it may, let us turn to the act as it exists and look at some of its provisions more carefully.

9.2 PRICE DISCRIMINATION UNDER THE ROBINSON-PATMAN ACT

Purposes of the Act

The Robinson-Patman Act, as perceived by the courts, is meant to prevent *primary-line injury to competition* (i.e., injury at the sellers' level) as well as *secondary-line injury to competition* (i.e., injury to the buyers of a seller) due to price differences which cannot be cost-justified or which are not due to "meeting competition in good faith."

To illustrate the meaning of primary-line injury to competition, consider the case of two sellers S_1 and S_2 who sell competitively a product in, say, New York City. Seller S_1 also sells the product in nearby Jersey City, but S_2 does not sell in that market. If S_1 reduces her price below (the long-run) marginal cost in the New York City market with the sole purpose of driving S_2 out of that market (i.e., predatory pricing) and succeeds in doing so, this would constitute primary-line injury to competition; in the Jersey City market S_1 may not reduce his price, and if conditions permit, he may in fact increase it there to recoup his losses in the New York City market.[8] Incidentally, note that the inury in the above example must be "substantial" within the meaning of Sec. 2(a) of the act.

To illustrate the meaning of secondary-line injury to competition, suppose there are two buyers B_1 and B_2 of seller Z. Suppose Z decides to give a bulk or quantity discount to B_1 because of her higher trade volume. The net effect is a lower unit price to B_1 as compared to B_2. If this puts B_2 at a "substantial" disadvantage so that he cannot compete with B_1 successfully, it would constitute secondary-line injury to competition.

---

[7]Some of the reforms are considered in the White House Task Force on Antitrust Policy (Neal Task Force). For details, see Posner, *op. cit.,* pp. 50–53.

[8]As noted in Ch. 8, the Standard Oil case, the company was charged with predatory pricing. But as noted previously, J. S. McGee in his article, "Predatory Pricing: The Standard Oil (N.J.) Case," *Journal of Law and Economics,* October 1958, argues that this is a myth, for Standard Oil did not really resort to price wars to acquire its monopoly. Rather it bought out competitors on comparatively handsome terms in the hope of earning higher monopoly profits from the diminished competition.

The original 1914 Clayton Act prohibited primary-line injury only. As a result, there was a loophole in the act which permitted big buyers to extract discounts from sellers. This was best exemplified in the growth of chain stores in the late 1920s and early 1930s. The chain stores, because of their centralized buying and distribution, were able to win substantial discounts from producers. This, it was alleged, put the local grocer and small retailer at a competitive disadvantage. It was their cry in the post–great depression era that ultimately led to the passage of the Robinson-Patman Act in 1936, which declared that secondary-line injury to competition on account of price differences is as pernicious as primary-line injury.

What rationale can be provided for the Robinson-Patman Act prohibition of price discrimination which results in primary-line or secondary-line injury to competition? Consider first primary-line injury to competition. Here we should make a distinction between whether there are several sellers in the market or just one (i.e., monopoly). If there are several sellers in a market and there are price differences, that does not mean there is price discrimination or injury to competition; such price differences are a normal way by which imbalances in supply and demand are reflected and eventually adjusted. But persistent price differences between markets or consumers where there is only a single seller is another story. Here it is possible that the monopolist may engage in deliberate predatory pricing tactics, charging a lower price (i.e., lower than the long-run marginal cost) in the market where there may be substitutes for her product but not charging a similar lower price in the market where there is no competition. In this case the act duplicates the Sherman Act, for Sec. 2 of the latter outlaws such predatory pricing.

What about secondary-line injury to competition? Here the law has the potential of being misapplied. For instance, quantity discounts, which are generally prohibited by the act, can be economically justifiable; costs of production or purchase are often inversely related to the volume of production or purchase. Therefore, by outlawing such discounts (Sec. 2(c)), and the fact that the Federal Trade Commission (FTC) generally does not look favorably on them, the act is likely to deny consumers lower prices resulting from such quantity discounts given the big buyers. As Robert Bork puts it:

> The result of the law's inability and, in part, refusal to recognize cost differences is the destruction of efficiency and wealth. When sellers are not permitted to recognize cost differences in price differences, purchasers lose an incentive to take over distributive functions they can perform more efficiently.[9]

9.3 SOME PROBLEMS IN THE APPLICATION OF THE ROBINSON-PATMAN ACT

Aside from the points just raised, there are several other aspects of the Robinson-Patman Act that may be noted.

[9]Robert H. Bork, *The Antitrust Paradox: A Policy at War with Itself,* Basic Books, New York, 1978, p. 393.

Scope of the Act

The scope of the act is narrow. First, it applies to commodities and not to services. Therefore, price discrimination in commodities is illegal but is perfectly all right in services. Thus, if a leading stockbroker were to charge a lower brokerage commission to a large buyer and a higher one to a small buyer, he would be immune from the act. Second, it applies when the commodities are sold, not leased. Therefore, by leasing her product rather than selling it, a seller can avoid all the strictures of the law. The computer industry, for example, where leasing is more prevalent than outright selling, can therefore get by the act and engage in price discrimination very successfully. Finally, the act applies only when there are price differences but not when prices are identical, as in the basing-point price schemes where the customers pay the same unit price regardless of their location. But we have seen already that charging identical prices when marginal costs are different is every bit as discriminating as charging different prices when marginal costs are identical.

Incipiency Nature of the Act

The key phrase that runs through most of the act is: "where the effect. . . *may* be substantially to lessen competition." This phrase makes the law an "incipiency statute." That is, "a court or the Federal Trade Commission need not believe it sees any actual injury to competition before applying the law, but must strike down price differences it thinks may inflict such injury."[10] As a result, there is the possibility that the law will be invoked the moment the FTC sees any price difference. And since the burden of proof does not rest with the FTC, a seller without adequate legal expenses may be an unwitting victim of this incipiency statute. Even a giant seller can fall prey to this incipiency doctrine, as our discussion of the *Morton Salt* case will shortly reveal.

The Cost-Difference Justification: Sec. 2(a)

Section 2(a) of the amended Clayton Act allows for price differences which are solely due to cost differences. But this cost-difference justification is not as easy as it sounds. First, the burden of proof that cost differences justify price differences lies entirely with the defendant. And this is a heavy burden, for it is not always easy to apportion fixed or overhead costs over several buyers or markets. Moreover, the FTC considers only historical or accounting cost data, whereas from the economic viewpoint the correct measure is the *opportunity cost* — the cost of a resource in use, say, A is its value in its best alternative use. For example, if I invest some capital in my own business, its interest cost is what I could have earned if I had loaned the same amount to someone else. Thus, for comparable risk, if my capital could earn 15 percent return elsewhere, I must

---

[10]Ibid., p. 390.

regard the cost of capital to me of at least 15 percent. Because of the fundamental difference between the economic and accounting notions of cost, a real or opportunity cost differential may not be perceived by the FTC and therefore it may turn down the cost-difference justification of a defendant if it only considers accounting costs.

Second, and more important, the FTC is very reluctant to accept the opportunity cost or historical cost difference. As M. Adleman puts it:

> The burden of proof of a cost differential is on the seller. Any cost differential is presumed to be "unjustified" unless and until the Commission finds to the contrary. The procedural requirements are such that a cost differential must be disregarded unless it is certain and precise. But, since cost differentials are inherently uncertain and imprecise, most of them cannot exist in the contemplation of law.[11]

The "Good Faith Meeting of Competition" Defense: Sec. 2(b)

Another exception to price differentials is provided in the "good faith competition" defense contained in Sec. 2(b) of the amended Clayton Act. This section allows a seller to lower his price "to meet an equally low price of a competitor." This is a rather strange provision because if seller A lowers his price because B has done so and B has done so because C has done so and so on, how can the vicious circle be broken and the ultimate culprit pinned down? Be that as it may.

The real problem with Sec. 2(b) is that it is in contradiction with the Sherman Act prohibition of price-fixing. This is so because "to meet competition in good faith" the competitors are forced to know each other's prices, which is ultimately bound to lead to price-fixing. Recently a group of wallboard suppliers was absolved of the price-fixing charge when they argued that they "verified" each other's prices to satisfy the "good faith competition" defense under Sec. 2(b) of the Robinson-Patman Act!

Prohibition Against Brokerage Commission: Sec. 2(c)

The primary purpose of Sec. 2(c) is to prevent price discrimination being disguised in the form of brokerage commission, discount, and the like. For example, a large buyer, B, instead of getting a price reduction from the seller, S, may ask S to pay Z (B's agent) a "brokerage fee," which in turn will be handed over by Z to B. This is prohibited by Sec. 2(c), as no real brokerage service is rendered. But suppose the buyer performs some service in connection with the transaction which has some economic value. Should the buyer be reimbursed for this service? By and large, the FTC has looked down upon such services and has disallowed brokerage commissions thereon. For example, suppose B ordinarily deals with S through Z, but now decides to dispense with Z's services and deal directly with S. Should B get that amount that was paid Z for her services?

---

[11]M. Adleman, *A&P: A Study in Price-Cost Behavior and Public Policy*, Harvard, Cambridge, Mass., 1959, pp. 164–165.

No, this is not allowed by the law. The upshot of all this is that Sec. 2(c) virtually does not recognize any real brokerage function by the buyer. Although this view may be mistaken, it seems it is there for practical reasons, namely, that the FTC does not have the resources to probe into each case to find out whether the observed differences are genuine or disguised. Thus the FTC is playing it safe.

Prohibition Against Promotional Allowances and Services: Sec. 2(d) and 2(e)

Section 2(d) prohibits promotional allowances and discounts unless they are "available on proportionally equal terms to all other customers competing in the distribution of such products or commodities." This may be a questionable provision, however. According to Posner:

> The requirement of proportional equality, as interpreted, does not adequately recognize the differences in advertising value among different types of retail outlet, or the costs of giving small allowances to small outlets when that is the price of being permitted to grant large allowances to large outlets.[12]

The preceding comment applies with equal force to Sec. 2(e), which prohibits the seller himself from performing promotional services on behalf of his customers.

Prohibition Against Discounts to Large Buyers: Sec. 2(f)

The logic behind Sec. 2(f) is that a large buyer, by extracting heavy discounts from the producer or seller, may injure competition by putting small buyers at a competitive disadvantage. But this may not be necessarily so. First of all, if there are several sellers in a market, there is little chance that a single large buyer will extract "undue" discounts from a competitive seller. Second, if a single seller has monopoly of the market and a large buyer tries to win a large discount from such a monopolist, so much the better. This will dampen the monopoly power and the consumer will ultimately benefit from reduced prices on account of the discount.

To summarize, our discussion shows that the provisions of the Robinson-Patman Act are not all devoid of controversies. Some of the provisions may not be justifiable from a strictly economic viewpoint, especially the overall philosophy of the act: injury to competitors means injury to competition. But in a competitive setup where there are several sellers and where price differences perist, very often in matching supply with demand some sellers may have to go out of business. But that is not ruining the competition.

---

[12]Richard A. Posner, *The Robinson-Patman Act,* American Enterprise Institute for Public Policy Research, Washington, D.C., 1976, p. 47.

9.4   SOME LEGAL CASES UNDER THE ROBINSON-PATMAN ACT

PRIMARY-LINE INQUIRY TO COMPETITION: UTAH PIE CO. CASE*

This case is an illustration of primary-line injury to competition.

FACTS

Until 1957, frozen dessert pies in the Salt Lake City area were largely supplied by three national companies, namely, Pet Milk, Carnation Milk, and Continental Baking. In 1957, the Utah Pie Company, a local producer of pies for well over 30 years, decided to enter the frozen pie market very aggressively by undercutting the prices charged by the three rivals. Because of this price-cutting and its locational advantage, Utah Pie's entry into the frozen pie market proved to be highly successful. In 1958, just 1 year after its entry, the company captured about 67 percent of the frozen pie market, with Pet, Carnation, and Continental accounting for, respectively, 16 percent, 10 percent, and 1 percent of that market, the remaining 6 percent going to several sundry producers.

Recognizing the competition, the three producers reduced their prices in the Salt Lake City market without making such reductions in other markets where Utah Pie was not competing. Thus, in 1958 Utah Pie charged $4.15 per dozen frozen pies, whereas the prices charged by the three competitors were $4.92 (Pet), $4.82 (Carnation), and $5 (Continental). By 1961 the prices charged by these three companies were $2.75, $3.30 to $3.40, and $2.85, respectively. To meet these lower prices, Utah Pie reduced its price to $2.75 per dozen. As a result of these price cuts, the market shares of the four companies at the end of 1961 were: Utah 45 percent, Pet 29 percent, Carnation 9 percent, Continental

8 percent, the remainder going to other small producers.

In 1961, Utah Pie sued the three rivals under Sec. 1 and 2 of the Sherman Act (the conspiracy charge) and also sued each competitor individually for violation of the Robinson-Patman Act; each of these competitors had lowered its price in the Salt Lake City market without effecting similar reductions in other markets where they sold frozen pies—a case of price discrimination.

JUDGMENT

The local jury, while absolving the three defendants of the conspiracy charge under the Sherman Act, found each of them guilty of the price-discrimination charge under the Robinson-Patman Act. But the court of appeals exonerated them from this charge too on the ground that there was not sufficient evidence of "probable injury to competition" within the meaning of Sec. 2(a) of the Robinson-Patman Act. The case then went to the Supreme Court, where in 1967, Justice White, acting for the majority, reversed the court of appeals and found the defendants guilty of violation of Sec. 2(a). In reaching this decision, Justice White noted that there was intent of predation (i.e., to drive the Utah Pie frozen pie business from the Salt Lake City market) on the part of the three defendants because they had priced their pies below cost in the Salt Lake area without making such reductions in other parts of the country. Justice White did not give much weight to the fact that despite the price reduction, Utah Pie had increased its sales volume and continued to make a profit.

COMMENT

Justice Stewart, with Justice Harlan concurring, dissented from the majority. He

*Utah Pie Co. v. Continental Baking Company, 386 U.S. 685 (1967).

raised an important question: Did the defendants' action have the anticompetitive effect required by the Clayton Act as a cause for action? In his view, the answer was no. He said that, despite a decline in its market share from 67 percent in 1958 to 45 percent in 1961, Utah Pie was still the dominant company in Salt Lake City. What the three competitors did was to make the market more competitive, which benefitted the consumer in terms of higher volume and reduced prices. In Justice Stewart's view, the majority's thinking that "injury to competitors means injury to competition" was erroneous. It is true that the three rivals had hurt Utah Pie by taking a share of its market away, but they in no way hurt competition. If anything, their action increased competition. After all, "lower prices are the hallmark of intensified competition. . . . "

Several scholars also have criticised the

Utah Pie decision. In Bork's view, the decision was anticompetition and anticonsumer. According to him, "the defendants were convicted not of injuring competition but, quite simply, of competing."† An anomaly of the decision was that it held that a price differential is illegal even if it is directed against a dominant company; usually the situation is the other way around, where a dominant firm price-discriminates against a smaller competitor. Posner argues that Justice White, when he said that the three defendants had sold their pies below cost, was probably referring to the average cost of production and not the economically correct notion of long-run marginal cost. If that is in fact the case, the defendants may not be guilty of price discrimination in the economic sense of the term.

†Bork, op. cit., p. 387.

SECONDARY-LINE INJURY TO COMPETITION: MORTON SALT CASE*

This case represents secondary-line or buyer-level injury to competition, in which small buyers who cannot take advantage of the quantity discounts offered by the seller are, according to the FTC, discriminated against in favor of large buyers.

FACTS

Morton Salt, a leading manufacturer of branded table salt, sold several different brands, including the famous Blue Label, partly through wholesalers or jobbers (who in turn sold it to retailers) and partly through large retail chain stores. It sold the Blue Label salt on a standard discount sys-

Federal Trade Commission v. Morton Salt Company, 334 U.S. 37 (1948).

	Price per case
Less-than-carload (LTC) purchases	$1.60
Carload purchases	1.50
5000-case purchase in any consecutive 12 months	1.40
50,000-case purchase in any consecutive 12 months	1.35

Only five companies, mostly the large chain stores, ever bought enough Blue Label salt to obtain the price of $1.35 per case, a discount of 25 cents per case from the base price of $1.60 per case. The FTC found the above price schedule a violation of the Robinson-Patman Act and issued a cease and desist order.

JUDGMENT

The circuit court of appeals reversed the FTC, stating that the commission had failed to adduce evidence to support its claim that the discount schedule had violated the Robinson-Patman Act. The FTC appealed to the Supreme Court, which reversed the appellate court and ruled in favor of the FTC.

Justice Black, speaking for the majority, argued as follows. First, although the price discounts were available to all in theory, in practice they were available only to a few buyers: The record showed that no single independent retailer or grocery store or even a wholesaler bought as much as 50,000 cases of salt in a year. Not only that, very few small retailers ever bought a carload purchase of Blue Label salt to quality for the 10 cents discount per case. Moreover, "the legislative history of the Robinson-Patman Act makes it abundantly clear that Congress considered it to be an evil that a large buyer secure a competitive advantage over a small buyer solely because of the large buyer's quantity purchasing ability."

Second, the defendant's argument that there was no evidence that its discount policy had injured competition is beside the point, for the Robinson-Patman Act "requires no more than that the effect of the prohibited price discriminations may be substantially to lessen competition. . . or to injure, destroy or prevent competition."

Third, the defendant's claim that the FTC itself had not produced concrete evidence of injury to competition is also beside the point because "the Commission is authorized by the Act to bar discriminatory prices upon the 'reasonable possibility' that different prices for like goods to competing purchasers may have the defined effect on competition."

COMMENT

According to one scholar, "the *Morton Salt* case established that in cases involving secondary-line injury, in sharp contrast to seller-line injury proceedings where a demonstration of a substantial adverse impact is required absent proof of predatory intent, the courts may rely on broad inferences of adverse competitive effects based on the mere existence of substantial price differentials among competing customers."† Moreover, by not putting the onus of proof on the FTC, the Supreme Court, according to the dissenting Justice Jackson, has said that "no quantity discount is valid if the Commission chooses to say it is not."

†Earl W. Kintner, *A Robinson-Patman Primer,* Macmillan, New York, 1970, p. 131.

In this section we have presented but two cases tried under the Robinson-Patman Act. Although space limitation prevents us from citing many more such cases, the general tenor of these cases is well-exemplified by the two preceding cases. In primary-line or seller-level injury cases the general philosophy seems to be that "injury to competitors means injury to competition," and in buyer-level injury it seems that discounts and allowances have either no or a minimum economic role to play. From the economist's viewpoint, both these views are open to serious question.

9.5   THE ECONOMICS OF TYING CONTRACTS[13]

Section 3 of the Clayton Act, among other things, prohibits tying contracts. In this section we examine such contracts with a view to finding whether there is any rationale to the law's ban on them, and if not, what may be done about it.

Definition

A tying contract is one in which the seller of a product X (the tying product) requires her purchaser to buy yet another product Y (the tied product) from her. For example, if IBM were to require the buyers of its computers (the tying product) to also buy punch cards (the tied product) from the company, it would constitute a tying contract. As a matter of fact, in *IBM Corporation v. USA* (293 U.S. 131), decided in 1936, IBM was found guilty of doing precisely that and was ordered to cease that practice.

Types of Tying Contracts

The tying and tied products may be related in several ways. As in the case of nuts and bolts, they may be used in fixed proportion; as in the case of the computer and the punch card, they may be used in a complementary way; or as in the case of seed and fertilizer, they may be used together or separately.

But regardless of the type, the law generally disapproves of such contracts where the tying and the tied products are sold by the same seller. Why? To answer this question, it behooves us to find out why such arrangements exist to begin with.

Reasons for Tying Arrangements[14]

There are several reasons why tying contracts are entered into.

Dual Monopoly   A seller having monopoly of the tying product may want to extend it to the tied product. This is the so-called transfer of monopoly power, or leverage, theory — a monopolist in one product leveraging (using) his way into a position of monopoly in another product. And as we will see, this "theory" still governs most cases tried in this area.

Although appealing, the "transfer of monopoly power" theory is very soft. Consider the case where the monopolist in the tying product sets the price of the tied product above what other competitors of the tied product are charging; there may be one giant producer of computers but there may be several companies producing punch cards. In this case the combined unit cost of the tied and tying products would be higher than would be the case if the tied prod-

---

[13]The following discussion applies with equal force to *reciprocal contracts* in which firm A agrees to buy from firm B on the condition that B buys another product from A.

[14]The following discussion draws on Phillip Areeda, *Antitrust Analysis, Problems, Text, Cases,* Little, Brown, Boston, 1974, pp. 568–573.

uct were sold competitively. This may ultimately reduce the sale of both the tying and the tied product by encouraging eventual competition via new products. A rational or profit-maximizing monopolist would not pursue such a policy.

Now consider the case where the tied product is sold below its long-run marginal cost. Would the seller acquire monopoly of the tied product? If the intent here is predatory pricing, then it is possible that such a monopoly would result. But in this case we do not need Sec. 3 of the Clayton Act, for the Sherman Act can take care of such a situation. Absent predatory intent, it is hard to see how a profit-maximizing monopolist would sell a product at a price that does not recoup its long-run marginal cost. Therefore, the "leverage" theory seems suspect.[15]

In reality, most cases of tying are such that a monopolist of the tying product (say, acquired through patents) also produces products which are complementary and for which there may not be competing products. For example, IBM produces a self-correcting Selectric II typewriter for which it has a patent. It also produces typing ribbon specially designed for use with this typewriter. Other producers of ribbons have not yet shown any great interest in producing a ribbon for the Selectric II typewriter. As yet, we have little knowledge about how IBM goes about pricing its ribbons for the Selectric II typewriter. When other competitors start producing typewriters with a self-correcting mechanism, it will be interesting to see how IBM reacts in terms of the price of both the typewriter and the ribbon.[16]

Price Discrimination   Tying contracts are a sophisticated means of price discrimination. To see how this is done, consider the case of *Heaton Peninsular Button-Fastener Co. v. Eureka Specialty Co.*, 77 F. 288, (6th Cir. 1896). Although the case predates the Clayton Act and the issue involved was one of patent misuse, it does show the subtle form in which price discrimination can be effected. Heaton acquired a patent for inventing a machine to staple buttons to high-button shoes, an operation previously done manually at a higher cost. Since buyers of the machine could use it with varying intensity, Heaton would have liked to charge a price in proportion to the intensity of its use. But this would have been difficult to monitor. Therefore, instead of charging different prices for the machine, the company sold the machine practically at cost to any buyer with the proviso that he or she would buy all the buttons required from Heaton only. The buttons were priced at a price higher than the marginal cost of production. And since the company knew how many buttons each buyer bought, the more intensive users of the machines paid higher amounts as compared to less intensive users. This meant that Heaton earned a higher rate of return from

[15]For a theoretical discussion, see M. L. Burstein, "The Economics of Tie-in Sales," *Review of Economics and Statistics,* vol. 42, February 1960.

[16]Smith Corona and a few other typewriter producers have started producing typewriters with self-correcting mechanisms. Reacting to the potential competition, IBM now offers, from time to time, discounts on both the typing and correcting ribbons. But with the rapid growth of electronic word processors the traditional typewriter (electric, manual, self-correcting, and what not) is facing increasingly stiff competition and one can expect a substantial reduction in its price.

the intensive users, for all the users paid the same price for the machine. In effect, therefore, there was price discrimination.

Since under the Robinson-Patman Act price discrimination is generally illegal, the courts could have condemned tying contracts as a form of discrimination. But they have rarely considered these contracts as a form of price discrimination. Hence, the preceding discussion is somewhat academic.

Economies of Scale Very often there are economies of scale when the tying and tied products are sold together, especially if they are of complementary nature. Such economies of scale may be due to production, distribution, centralized buying, or centralized financing. That is why one often finds the producers of patented machines also selling the servicing of such machines. For example, the producer of a photocopying machine also provides the photocopying paper as well as servicing of the machine in case it breaks down. One could buy these products or services separately, but the costs of such separate sales often exceed the cost of the whole package.

Protection of Goodwill Although the courts do not so perceive, tying arrangements are a means of protecting the good name of the seller. Manufacturers of products such as refrigerators, air conditioners, dishwashers, etc., usually like to service their own products because of their specialized knowledge of those products. If someone else is allowed to service their products, there is every possibility that the product may be damaged for lack of specialized know-how. A disgruntled customer may in this case blame the manufacturer of the product despite her warning that she may not be responsible for the product if it is serviced by an unauthorized dealer.

As the preceding discussion shows, tying contracts can be justified because of economies of scale or protection of the goodwill of the seller. But by and large, the courts have deemed them to be illegal per se because they have adhered to the leverage theory without questioning it critically. This attitude is reflected in Justice Frankfurter's statement in *Standard Stations v. United States,* 377 U.S. 293 (1949) that "Tying agreements serve hardly any purpose beyond the suppression of competition." This attitude is further reflected in the case studies that follow.

9.6 LEGAL CASES INVOLVING TYING CONTRACTS

THE INTERNATIONAL SALT CASE*

In this case it was held that tying contracts are illegal because of their "obvious tendency" toward monopoly.

International Salt Co. v. United States, 332 U.S. 392 (1947).

FACTS

The International Salt Company, the largest producer of salt for industrial use, had patents on two machines, known as Lixator and Saltomat. The Lixator dissolves rock salt into a brine used in various industrial processes and the Saltomat injects salt, in tablet form, into canned products during the canning process. Both these machines are leased under the condition that the lessee buy from International Salt all salt and salt tablets, although these products are not patented. In other words, the lease amounted to a tie-in agreement.

The government brought civil suit against the company to enjoin it from carrying the provisions of the lease because they violated Sec. 1 of the Sherman Act as well as Sec. 3 of the Clayton Act. Upon the company's answer and admission of fact, the government moved for a summary judgment under Rule 56 of the Rules of Civil Procedure on the ground that no issue as to a material fact was presented, and that, on the admissions, judgment followed as a matter of law. Judgment was granted, but it was immediately appealed to the Supreme Court.

JUDGMENT

Justice Jackson, speaking for the majority, affirmed the judgment won by the government. In part, he stated:

The Appellant's [i.e., the defendant, International Salt] patents confer a limited monopoly of the invention they reward. From them appellant derives a right to restrain others from making, vending or using the patented machines. But the patents confer no right to restrain use of, or trade in, unpatented salt. By contracting to close this market for salt against competition, International has engaged in a restraint of trade [which is a violation of Section 1 of the Sherman Act] for which its patents afford no immunity from the antitrust laws. . . .

To the defendant's claim that the lower court, in issuing a summary judgment against it, had not bothered to find out whether the said restraint was reasonable under the Sherman Act or whether it substantially lessened competition or tended to create monopoly under the Clayton Act, Justice Jackson simply replied " . . . the tendency of the arrangement [i.e., the tying contract] to accomplishment of monopoly seems obvious. Under the law, agreements are forbidden which 'tend to create a monopoly'. . . ."

COMMENT

In his verdict, Justice Jackson did not give any reason why he thought that the tying contracts of the type entered into by International Salt had the "obvious" tendency toward monopoly. As Bork correctly questions: "The tie-in tended to the accomplishment of *what* monopoly?"† Monopoly in the machines or monopoly in the salt? How could the purchase of salt lead to a monopoly in the machines? It would in fact have the opposite effect, for the buyer could simply refuse to lease the machines if he were forced to buy the salt too. Similarly, how could the company hope to achieve monopoly in a product such as salt; these machines used only a small percentage of total salt produced in the country.

As remarked earlier, the *International Salt* case exemplifies the questionable leverage theory of monopoly. Because the company had monopoly in the machines by virtue of the patents, the courts thought, it was out to acquire monopoly in the tied product, salt.

†Bork, op. cit., p. 367.

THE LOEW'S CASE*

This case involves the legality of the practice of block-booking films. In block booking, the buyer (e.g., a TV station) is required to buy a group of films together, some of which are box-office hits and some duds. For example, in this case, one of the TV stations which wanted to show *The Man Who Came to Dinner* was also required to show *Gorilla Man* and *Tugboat Annie Sails Again,* as well as other films. Thus, block-booking involves tie-in; the good films are the tying product and the inferior ones are the tied product.

FACTS

The U.S. government brought separate civil antitrust suits in the southern district of New York in 1957 against six major distributors of pre-1948 copyrighted motion picture feature films for television, alleging that each defendant had engaged in block booking in violation of Sec. 1 of the Sherman Act. The main point involved was the manner in which each defendant had marketed the product.

JUDGMENT

The district court enjoined (among other things) the six distributors from engaging in the tie-in agreements implicit in block-booking. That is, the distributors could not force the buyers to buy inferior films along with the good ones if they did not want the former.

The defendants appealed to the Supreme Court. The highest court not only upheld the district court but further modified the lower court's decree by requiring the distributors to list the price of each block-booked or packaged film separately if the buyer so wishes. Justice Goldberg, speaking for the majority, wrote the decision.

*United States v. Loew's Inc., 371 U.S. 38 (1962).

The first question that the Supreme Court considered was the applicability of Sec. 1 of the Sherman Act in cases of tie-in contracts. Citing Justice Frankfurter's precedent-setting statement in the *Standard Stations* case that "tying agreements serve hardly any purpose beyond the suppression of competition," Justice Goldberg stated that such agreements are an object of antitrust concern for two reasons: "They may force buyers into giving up the purchase of substitutes for the tied product ... and they may destroy the free access of competing suppliers of the tied product to the consuming market." Justice Goldberg went on to say:

A tie-in contract may have one or both of these undesirable effects when the seller, by virtue of his position in the market for the tying product, has economic leverage sufficient to induce his customers to take the tied product along with the tying item. The standard of illegality is that the seller must have "sufficient economic power with respect to the tying product to appreciably restrain free competition in the market for the tied products. . . .

The requisite economic power is presumed when the tying product is patented or copyrighted. . . . This principle grew out of a long line of patent cases which had eventuated in the doctrine that a patentee who utilized tying arrangements would be denied all relief against infringements of his patent. . . .

Since one of the objectives of the patent laws is to reward uniqueness, the principle of these cases was carried over into antitrust on the theory that the existence of a valid patent on the tying product, without more, establishes a distinctiveness sufficient to conclude that any tying arrangement involving the patented product would have anticompetitive consequences. . . .

Justice Goldberg further alluded to the Supreme Court's decision in *United States v. Paramount Pictures, Inc.,* 334 U.S. 131 (1948), a case also involving block-booking, which stated that "Where a high quality film greatly desired is licensed only if an inferior one is taken, the latter borrows quality from the former and strengthens its monopoly by drawing on the other."

COMMENT

Once again what we see is an application of the leverage theory of monopoly developed in the *Standards Station* case and applied to many other cases. But as noted, the economics of this theory is very spongy, and especially so in this case. This has been succinctly put by George Stigler in his comment on the *Lowe's* decision as follows:

Consider the following simple example. One film, Justice Goldberg cited 'Gone With the Wind', is worth $10,000 to the buyer, while a second film, the Justice cited "Getting Gertie's Garter', is worthless to him. The seller could sell the one for $10,000 and throw away the second, for no matter what its cost, bygones are forever bygones. Instead the seller compels the buyer to take both. But surely he can obtain no more than $10,000, since by hypothesis this is the value of both films to the buyer. Why not, in short, use his monopoly power directly on the desirable film? It seems no more sensible, on this logic, to blockbook the two films than it would be to compel the exhibitor to buy 'Gone with the Wind' and seven Ouija boards, again for $10,000.†

†George Stigler, "United States v. Loew's, Inc.: A Note on Block Booking," *Supreme Court Review,* 1963, pp. 152–153. Reproduced from Bork, op. cit., p. 374.

Although the two preceding cases do not exhaust the list, they reflect the general attitude of the courts toward tie-in contracts, almost a per se ban against such contracts, based on the controvertible leverage theory of monopoly. If a case is to be made against tying contracts, it could be made on the basis that such contracts involve price-discrimination, which in some situations may be undesirable (see Posner's view discussed earlier). But the courts have not followed this line of reasoning.

We have also seen that tie-ins could be defended on the grounds of economies of scale and protection of the goodwill of the producer of the tying product. If the courts would accept these grounds, the blanket condemnation of tie-in agreements exemplified by our case studies may be undesirable from the consumer's viewpoint. Whether that will happen generally remains to be seen.[17]

[17]In *United States v. Jerrold Electronics Corporation* (Eastern District Court of Pennsylvania, 1960, later affirmed by the Supreme Court) both the lower court and the Supreme Court accepted the "protection of goodwill" defense of the defendant Jerrold Electronics. In the early 1950s Jerrold was a pioneer in the development and provision of community television antennae systems, installing more than 75 percent of the systems in operation in the country. Because of the highly sensitive and yet not fully proven nature of the system, Jerrold was afraid that servicing of the systems by outsiders might damage them and thereby hurt the reputation of the company. Therefore, the corporation required the purchaser of its system also to purchase maintenance services from the company, a tie-in arrangement. Although the Court accepted this arrangement in the beginning to protect the goodwill of the new venture, it warned that such a tie-in sale would not be reasonable once the technical requirements of the system were more widely understood so that it could be easily serviced by outsiders (see also question 9-14).

9.7 SUMMARY AND CONCLUSIONS

In this chapter we considered the economic and legal aspects of two of the four main provisions of the Clayton Act, namely, price discrimination and tying contracts.

Sec. 2 of the Clayton Act, as amended by Sec. 1 of the Robinson-Patman Act, generally prohibits price discrimination, be it overt or covert. The only exceptions provided are when such discrimination is due to cost differences or due to "meeting competition in good faith." The objective of the amended Sec. 2 is to prevent primary-line (i.e., at the sellers' level) as well as secondary-line injury (i.e., at the buyers' level) to competition.

Although the act talks about price discrimination, the meaning of the term as understood by economists is very much different from that adopted by the courts. To the economist, price discrimination means selling the same product or service at prices such that the ratio of price to marginal cost is different in different sales. But the courts view price discrimination simply as a price difference. This means if a seller charges identical prices in two markets, although the marginal costs of production are different, the courts will presume that there is no price discrimination. But to the economist, selling at the same price when marginal costs differ is as much price discrimination as selling at different prices when marginal costs are identical.

Aside from the fundamental difference in the notion of the term *price discrimination* used by the economist and by the law, the Robinson-Patman Act as it stands has several questionable features. First, the cost-difference justification [Sec. 2(a)] that may be invoked to justify price differences is generally not encouraged by the FTC, which is principally responsible for monitoring the Clayton and FTC acts of 1914. This is partly because of the difficulty in apportioning fixed or overhead cost among products and partly because the FTC recognizes only historical or accounting cost, whereas the more meaningful concept is that of the opportunity cost. Second, the "good faith meeting of competition" defense of Sec. 2 (b) seems to be ill-conceived, for it is in direct contradiction of the Sherman Act prohibition of price-fixing: "To meet competition in good faith", competitors are forced to know each other's prices, which is likely to result in price-fixing.

The other provisions of the Robinson-Patman Act contained in Sec. 2(c) to 2(f) are also debatable. They are tantamount to saying that discounts, brokerage allowances, and promotional allowances have very little economic role to play, which flies in the face of reality: Because of economies of scale in production, distribution, and marketing, the incremental cost of doing business decreases with the volume of trade, which can justify discounts and similar allowances. If such allowances are banned, consumers may be deprived of the resulting lower prices; the *FTC v. Morton Salt* decision reflects this very well.

Respected economic and legal scholars have dubbed the Robinson-Patman Act as anticompetition and anticonsumer. The *Utah Pie* decision is the case in point. In this decision, you will recall, the defendants were found guilty of competing and bringing down the prices of frozen pies.

Sec. 3 of the Clayton Act prohibits tie-in contracts, contracts in which to buy a product A from a seller the buyer has to buy product B also. This prohibition is based on the leverage theory of monopoly — monopoly in the tying product means monopoly in the tied product. But it was seen that the economics of this theory is very shaky. A rational (or profit-maximizing) monopolist having monopoly in the tying product has no inherent need of acquiring monopoly in the tied product.

The law's primary reliance on the leverage theory of monopoly in condemning the tie-ins, as noted in the *International Salt* and *Lowe's* decisions, has resulted in the neglect of the useful role the tie-in arrangements can play in practice. Very often tie-ins are resorted to when there are economies of scale in the sale or lease of the tying and tied products. Such contracts are also a means of protecting the goodwill of the producer of the tying product. Producers of computers, photocopying machines, and similar products often insist on servicing their own products for fear that servicing by competitors without the know-how of the particular product may impair the functioning of that product. After all, the seller of the patented product is in the best position to know the inner working of that product. Unfortunately, the courts have inadequately recognized the importance of economies of scale and the protection of goodwill as elements in the tie-in contracts. If these factors are taken into account, the legal sanctions against the tie-ins will be less stringent.

The preceding views are from the point of view of economists, who are generally concerned with efficient allocation of scarce resources and, to a lesser extent, with the question of equitable income distribution for reasons discussed in Chapter 2. But it seems that the judges are more concerned with equity. They would like to see small businesses survive regardless of the efficiency aspect. Maybe they honestly believe that that was the congressional intent behind all the antitrust laws. Of course, one could debate about whether efficiency should have priority over equity or vice versa. The reasons why economists emphasize the efficiency criterion are already spelled out in Chapter 2.

QUESTIONS

9-1 Suppose a gasoline supplier S sells gasoline to B_1, a retailer, as well as to an independent wholesaler W, who in turn sells it to B_2, another retailer who is in competition with B_1. Suppose further that S sells the gasoline to W at a lower price than that charged B_1, which ultimately results in a lower price to B_2 which enables her to underprice B_1. Can B_1 claim competitive injury under the Robinson-Patman Act and why? (Such an injury, if it exists, is called *third-line* injury to competition.)

9-2 In *Perkins v. Standard Oil of California*, Perkins, an independent integrated wholesaler-retailer, complained that another retailer, Regal, who was also selling Standard Oil, sold it below the price charged by Perkins. Regal could do so because it had purchased the oil from the Western Highway Oil Company, which in turn had purchased it from the Signal Company, which itself had purchased it from Standard Oil at a price lower than that charged Perkins. Schematically, the distributional pattern was:

Standard Oil ⟶ Perkins
   ↳ Signal ⟶ Western Highway ⟶ Regal

In short, because of the lower price paid by Signal, Regal could ultimately underprice Perkins. Could Perkins sue Standard Oil under the Robinson-Patman Act? Give your reasoning. (If there is a competitive injury in this case, it is called *fourth-level* injury to competition.)

9-3 From the discussion in the text and given **9-1** and **9-2** above, how would you distinguish among primary-level, secondary-level, third-level, and fourth-level injury to competition?

9-4 What may be the rationale behind not allowing the cost-difference justification of Sec. 2(a) to the items covered by Sec. 2(c) to 2(f) of the amended Clayton Act?

9-5 Why do you think the Robinson-Patman Act was not made applicable to services?

9-6 Since the basing-point pricing system involves price discrimination, should it be illegal under the Robinson-Patman Act? Why?
Do you believe in the "incipiency doctrine"? Justify your answer.

9-8 If you do not believe in the incipiency doctrine, how would you rationalize the *Morton Salt* decision?

9-9 Primary-line or seller-level injury must be "substantial" before Sec. 2 of the Clayton Act may be invoked. But this is not necessary to establish secondary-line or buyer-level injury. What is the reason, if any, for this asymmetry?

9-10 When will injury to competitors constitute injury to competition?

9-11 Does the possession of a patent necessarily confer monopoly on the possessor of that patent? Why or why not?

9-12 Comment: "If there is one purpose a tie-in does not serve it is the suppression of competition." (Bork. op. cit., p. 367.)

9-13 Comment: "The entire theory of tying arrangements as menaces to competition is completely irrational in any case." (Bork, op. cit., p. 368.)

9-14 If a tied product is so closely integrated with the tying product so that the two together constitute a package, should the courts recognize the legality of such tie-ins? [See *United States v. Jerrold Electronics Corporation,* 187 F. Supp. 545, *affirmed per curiam* 365 U.S. 567 (1961).]

9-15 Suppose an "irrational" (i.e., non-profit-maximizing) seller having monopoly in the tying product wants to extend it to a complementary (i.e., tied) product for its own sake. Should such behavior form the basis of public policy banning tie-in contracts? Reason cogently.

9-16 Carl Kaysen and Donald Turner are in favor of a per se ban on tie-ins. Their reasoning is as follows:
A tie-in always operates to raise the barriers to entry in the market of the tied good to the level of those in the market for the tying good: The seller who would supply the one can do so only if he can also supply the other, since he must be able to displace the whole package which the tying seller offers. Developing a substitute for the tying product may be very difficult, if not impossible. Thus tying tends to spread market power into markets where it would not otherwise exist. For

example, few firms are prepared to supply machines such as those of IBM, whereas many may be prepared to supply punch cards. (Carl Kaysen and Donald Turner, *Antitrust Policy,* Harvard, Cambridge, Mass., 1959, p. 157.) Critically evaluate the above quote, stating whether you agree or disagree with it.

9-17 *Samuel H. Moss, Inc. v. FTC,* 148 F.2d 378 (2d Cir.) *cert. denied,* 326 U.S. 734 (1945). Moss, a supplier of rubber stamps, sold stamps of the same size at different prices to different customers in eight specified instances. As a result, the FTC charged, trade was diverted to Moss from his competitors. It was the position of the FTC that it was up to Moss to prove, following Sec. 2(b) of the Clayton Act, that the price differences were due to "meeting competition in good faith," or "to meet an equally lower price of a competitor." The FTC went on to say that the defendant could not do so because "it did not know its competitors' prices." In its view, the defendant simply "bid low enough to get the business." The FTC won the case in the lower court, and the victory was further confirmed by the Supreme Court when it refused to review the lower court's decision.

Do you agree with the court decision? Can a defendant ever successfully invoke Sec. 2(b)? If he or she did, would she not be charged with price conspiracy? Should the burden of proof under Sec. 2(b) rest entirely with the defendant?

9-18 *Times-Picayune Publishing Co. v. United States,* 345 U.S. 594, (1953). Times-Picayune, the defendant, published New Orleans' only morning paper, the *Times-Picayune,* hence acquiring a monopoly of that market. It also published an afternoon paper, the *States,* in competition with another such paper, the *Item.* Under the company's "unit plan" advertisers were not permitted to buy space in either of its newspapers separately, but had to insert identical copies in both or none. As a result of this policy, the *States* enjoyed a substantial increase in classified and general advertising space in comparison with the competitor, the *Item.* The district court held the company's unit plan to be a tie-in, with the *Times-Picayune* (the morning paper) as the tying product and the *States* as the tied product. Since the company used its monopoly of the morning newspaper to extend it to the afternoon paper, argued the court, it violated Sec. 3 of the Clayton Act as well as the Sherman Act, for the unit plan was anticompetitive.

On appeal to the Supreme Court the defendant won the case against the government. By a majority of 5 to 4, the Supreme Court argued that considering all advertising space that appeared in all three newspapers, the *Times-Picayune's* share was only 40 percent, which in its view was not a dominant position. Therefore, it could not be said that the company was trying to "leverage" its monopoly in the morning newspaper to acquire monopoly in the afternoon market.

Do you agree with the district court's decision against the defendant? Do you think that the Supreme Court was right in reversing the lower court? If you were the presiding judge, how would you have decided the case? Make your argument explicit.

9-19 In Robert Bork's view the Robinson-Patman Act is "the misshapen progeny of intolerable draftsmanship coupled to wholly mistaken economic theory." (Bork. op. cit., p. 382.) Do you think Bork is taking an extreme view of the act? Justify your answer.

9-20 Based on our discussion of tying contracts, discuss the economics of the reciprocal contracts. For a legal status of such contracts, consult A. D. Neale, *The Antitrust Laws of the U.S.A.,* Cambridge University Press, New York, 1977.

CHAPTER 10

THE WORKING OF THE CLAYTON ACT—II: MERGERS AND INTERLOCKING DIRECTORATES

In this chapter we discuss the economic and legal aspects of Sec. 7 and 8 of the Clayton Act which deal, respectively, with corporate mergers and acquisitions and interlocking directorates.

As noted in Chapter 7, Sec. 7 of the Clayton Act, as amended by the 1950 Celler-Kefauver Anti-Merger Act, prohibits mergers between firms either by acquisition of stock or by acquisition of assets, where the effect of such acquisition "may be substantially to lessen competition or tend to create a monopoly." Sec. 8, a section of rather minor importance, prohibits a person from serving on the boards of directors of competing firms where the effect may be to eliminate or substantially reduce competition between such firms.

Because of the controversial nature of the merger topic, the bulk of this chapter is devoted to it. Throughout, our objective will be to find out the rationale, if any, behind the law's restrictions on merger activities.

10.1 TYPES OF MERGERS

Although Sec. 7 does not say so explicitly, the Supreme Court, especially since the 1950 amendment, has stated that it covers all types of mergers or integrations, namely, horizontal, vertical, and conglomerate.[1] Therefore, it behooves us at the outset to describe the three types carefully. The term *merger* itself may be defined as the fusion of two or more separate firms into one. Oftentimes, such a fusion is brought about by a larger firm (in terms of sales volume or assets) acquiring a smaller firm, in which case it is called an *acquisition*. The

---

[1]The terms *merger* and *integration* will be used interchangeably in this text.

larger firm is called the *acquiring firm* and the smaller one is called the *acquired firm.* The acquisition may be effected by cash payment or by the exchange of stock (usually common stock) of the acquiring firm for that of the acquired firm.

Horizontal Mergers

When two firms in the same line of business (i.e., competitors) merge, this is known as a *horizontal* or *lateral merger.* Thus, if two commercial banks in a given town join hands and become one entity, there is a horizontal merger.

Vertical Mergers

Where two firms that are suppliers or buyers (customers) of one another decide to merge, this is known as *vertical merger* or *integration.* Thus, if a coal company (the coal supplier) and a steel company (the coal buyer) were to unite, it would constitute a vertical merger. If it is the coal company that is looking forward to the merger with the steel company, it is called *forward integration,* whereas if the steel company is interested in pursuing the coal company, it is called *backward integration.* Whether it is a forward or backward integration depends on the sequence in which productive activity takes place; in the present example coal is used as the fuel to produce steel, hence it takes precedence in the chain of production.

Conglomerate Mergers

A merger that is neither horizontal nor vertical may be called a *conglomerate merger.* In such a merger, a firm (usually a holding company) engaged in one line of business may acquire a firm in a wholly dissimilar line of business. Thus, when CBS acquired the New York Yankees (which it later sold), it was a conglomerate merger.

The preceding distinctions often are not watertight. As our discussion of the *Brown Shoe* case will show later, a merger can be both horizontal and vertical. In that case, Brown Shoe, primarily a manufacturer of shoes with a few retail outlets, acquired Kinney Shoe, primarily a retail chain although it also manufactured shoes on a small scale. Here, Brown's acquisition of Kinney's retail outlets assumed the character of a vertical merger, and the acquisition of its manufacturing plants amounted to a horizontal merger at the production level. Also, since before the merger Brown and Kinney were competitors in the retail market, the acquisition meant that there was a horizontal merger at the retailing level too.

10.2   REASONS FOR MERGERS

Whether it is horizontal, vertical, conglomerate, or a mixture thereof, why do mergers take place? Several reasons can be cited:

Economies of Scale

One important reason for mergers is economies of scale. One can distinguish several scale economies, namely, production economies (decrease in the average cost of production as output increases), distributional economies (e.g., Brown's acquisition of Kinney's retail outlets thereby eliminating the commission paid the wholesalers), financial economies (obtaining funds in the capital markets on favorable terms) and advertising and promotional economies (large companies can advertise more cheaply per unit of output than smaller companies).

Note that scale economies of the types described above may be obtained by a single firm by internal growth, that is, starting from a small beginning and growing into a large company. But very often it is less costly, in terms of money and time, to achieve such economies by acquisitions and mergers. This point is very important, for we will see that the courts have looked upon expansion by internal growth more favorably than expansion by the merger route for fear that the latter might lead to concentration of economic power in the hands of a few companies.

Weeding Out Inefficient Management

Quite often mergers, especially conglomerate ones, are a way of revitalizing sluggish companies by improvement of managerial efficiency. Such efficiency can be improved, "either through the replacement of mediocre executives or the reinforcement of good ones with aids such as superior data retrieval or more effective financial control systems."[2]

Improving the Efficiency of Capital Markets

As happens not too infrequently, a company owned by a single or a few owners, and starting from a very small beginning, reaches a point in its growth where its owners need large amounts of capital to proceed to the next scale of operation. In such situations, the owners may either actively seek suitors with substantial financial backing or may simply sell out the business. In either case, the merger route may make the transition smooth as well as increase the market value of small businesses.

Failing Companies

Companies which for a variety of reasons are not anymore viable operations on their own or are in imminent danger of bankruptcy are called *failing companies*. More often than not, the root cause of the failure is poor management. For such companies, mergers are a way out; although failing, the prospective

[2]Robert H. Bork, *The Antitrust Paradox: A Policy at War with Itself,* Basic Books, New York, 1978, p. 249.

buyers may want to buy such companies because they may possess some valuable patent rights. The courts, under the "failing company doctrine," have recognized the utility of mergers in these situations and have allowed such mergers, mergers which might otherwise violate Sec. 7.

In short, mergers can and do perform valuable economic and social functions. But this does not mean that all mergers are necessarily socially beneficial. As noted in Chapter 7, during the late nineteenth century and through the early 1920s a lot of mergers took place with the sole objective of acquiring monopoly power so as to restrict output and increase prices, the most outstanding example being the *Standard Oil* case discussed in that chapter. Whether on balance a merger is socially desirable can be answered only in broad terms, as follows:

> Some mergers seem to serve only the parties' interests. Others serve society as well. Perhaps all can be said to reflect the social interest in a free market in stocks, assets, and whole companies. The market is the means by which economic units transfer resources from less to more efficient hands and for their mutual benefit. This is not to say that every exchange necessarily benefits society at large. But it is to say that the process of free exchange can facilitate entry via merger, can effect graceful exit and thereby make original entry somewhat more likely, and can generally contribute to more efficient production and distribution.
>
> The important point to realize is that neither social harm nor social benefit will be precisely identifiable or quantifiable in every case. Yet, the lawmaker or interpreter must take care to remember the general benefits of a free market in capital assets. It would be wrong to suppose that nothing would be lost to society by, for example, presumptively condemning all mergers. Nor can one evade the problem by saving only those mergers with provable effects of social benefit.[3]

10.3   THE PHILOSOPHY BEHIND SEC. 7 OF THE CLAYTON ACT

From the text of the amended Sec. 7 one can surmise that the overall goal of the antimerger provision of the Clayton Act is to preserve and promote competition by preventing collusive activities that might ultimately lead to monopoly. To what extent this is the case can be learned from the interpretation of this section by the courts, especially the Supreme Court. A careful reading of the Supreme Court decisions in merger law, some of which will be considered in some detail shortly, reveal the following to be the goals of Sec. 7 as seen by the judges.

Prevention of Economic Concentration

Since the primary thrust of the Clayton Act is on the preservation of competition by discouraging monopoly or heavy concentration of economic power in the

---

[3]Phillip Areeda, *Antitrust Analysis, Problems, Text and Cases*, Little, Brown, Boston, 1974, p. 690.

hands of a few sellers (i.e., oligopolies), one could presumably agree with the Supreme Court that Congress wants to prevent market concentration. Unfortunately, however, Congress has not provided any quantitative guidelines as to when market concentration (say, as measured by the concentration ratios or the Herfindahl index) can be regarded as intolerably high. Unfortunately also, economics, both at the theoretical and empirical levels, has no definitive guidelines to offer about the relationship between economic concentration and variables such as prices, profits, rate of return, or rate of innovation, except possibly in the polar case of monopoly. As a result, we cannot say categorically that, for example, an industry where there are 100 firms each controlling 1 percent of the total sales becomes less competitive if after a merger activity there are now 25 firms each controlling 4 percent of the market sales: Competition does not necessarily mean a large number of firms, although that is one of the attributes of the perfectly competitive market model.

Failing to get a clear signal from the Congress or from the economic profession, the Supreme Court has used variable standards in deciding merger cases.[4] In the famous *Brown Shoe* case the Court turned down the merger between Brown and Kinney although the postmerger market share of the two companies in terms of production was less than 5 percent. Similarly, in the *Von's Grocery* case the merger between Von and Shopping Bag controlled only 7.5 percent of the grocery sales in the Los Angeles area, but the Supreme Court disallowed the merger. On the other hand, in the *Philadelphia Bank* case the Court adopted a benchmark of a ''30–33'' percent market share to decide the legality of mergers.

Preservation of Small Business: The Social Theory of Concentration

In the congressional debates preceding the passage of the Celler-Kefauver Amendment to Sec. 7 there were references to the ''rising tide of economic concentration'' in the American economy. The Supreme Court (see the *Brown* and *Von's Grocery* cases below) construed this to mean that Congress wanted to preserve small businesses per se.

If one subscribes to the social (i.e., small business) theory of concentration, one has to face up to the question of the trade-off between economic efficiency and smallness per se. That is, to what extent is society willing to sacrifice economic efficiency just to preserve small but economically inefficient business units. As we noted in Chapters 8 and 9, this is a difficult policy question, and it is debatable whether the Supreme Court is the right body to handle it. It is probably better to leave it to the Congress. Let Congress declare once and for all that small businesses are to be preserved regardless of the social costs involved.

---

[4]In 1968 and 1982, however, the Department of Justice issued its own guidelines as to when it might initiate antimerger proceedings. The guidelines are discussed briefly in Section 10.5.

From strictly an equity viewpoint, who is to say that that cannot be the goal of social policy?

Encouragement of Potential Competition

The clause in Sec. 7, "may be substantially to lessen competition," has been construed by the Supreme Court to mean that mergers may have the effect of thwarting "potential competition." This, the "potential competition doctrine," being essentially an incipiency doctrine, is rather difficult to apply in practice. For, to assess the potentiality of "potential competition" requires considerable knowledge about market price elasticities of demand and costs and benefits of market collusion, a knowledge hard to come by even for a trained economist. As a result, an indiscriminate application of this doctrine is likely to cause some problems, as can be seen from the case of *United States v. Penn-Olin Company,* 370 U.S. 158 (1964).

Pennsalt Chemicals Corporation and Olin Mathieson Chemical Corporation undertook a joint venture to build a sodium chlorate plant to serve the southern United States. There were already two other producers in the area. The government objected to the proposed joint venture on the ground that in the absence of the joint venture the two companies would have built separate plants to produce sodium chlorate. In that case there would have been four producers of the product instead of three (if the joint venture were allowed). Hence competition would have been "substantially" reduced by the intended joint undertaking.

Although the lower court agreed, and the Supreme Court concurred, that the two companies probably would not have built separate plants, the Supreme Court nonetheless returned the case to the lower court to find out (1) what would have happened if the joint venture were blocked and one of the companies built a plant while the other remained a "potential competitor," and (2) what would have been the effect of the block on the pricing of sodium chlorate. Needless to say, this was a difficult task. Nonetheless, on remand, the trial court said the joint venture was legal and that there was little chance that either of the two companies would have entered the market alone. The same doctrine was later applied in the *Clorox Case,* where the final outcome requiring Procter & Gamble to divest itself of Clorox was not necessarily a triumph for Sec. 7.

From the preceding discussion it seems that in the eyes of the Supreme Court the merger law is governed largely by the social philosophy of preserving small businesses per se. Whether that really was the congressional intent is not entirely clear.

10.4   KEY FEATURES OF SEC. 7

There are three key phrases in Sec. 7 that need some discussion since they have a great bearing on the outcome of any merger case under the law. These phrases are: "line of commerce," "section of the country," and "may be substantially to lessen competition."

"Line of Commerce"

"Line of commerce" simply means the relevant product market. Since the framers of the amended Sec. 7 were concerned with market concentration and its effect on variables such as prices, output, and profits, it is extremely important to define the scope of the market in relation to which market concentration is to be measured; by defining a product market narrowly or broadly, one can artificially increase or decrease the numerical value of a concentration ratio, however measured. Recall that in the *Cellophane* case discussed in Chapter 8 the Supreme Court held that although du Pont produced about 75 percent of the cellophane sold in the United States the relevant line of commerce or the product market was all flexible packaging materials and du Pont had less than 20 percent of this (broadly defined) market. Thus the narrow market definition would have put du Pont's market share at 75 percent, which would have found the company in violation of the Sherman Act, but the broader definition, under which du Pont did not have high market concentration, absolved the company of the monopolization charge. A problem is that the Supreme Court has not been consistent in its definition of "relevant market," as the subsequent discussion will reveal.

Economically speaking, it can be said that products A and B, although apparently different, belong to the same product market if the *cross-price elasticity* of demand between them is positive and fairly high, say, in excess 0.8.[5] By this definition, products such as butter and margarine may belong to the same product market or several brands of coffee may also belong to the same product market. By the same token, if the cross-price elasticity between two products is fairly low, they may belong to different markets. In short, one can say that two or more products belong to the same line of business if they are close substitutes in consumption (or production).

Deciding whether two products are close substitutes or competing products is often not easy. In *United States v. Continental Can Co.*, 378 U.S. 441 (1964) the Supreme Court held that glass and metal containers constituted the same "line of commerce" and hence disallowed Continental Can's acquisition of the Hazel Atlas Company because of the fear of increasing market concentration: Continental and Hazel had, respectively, 22 percent and 3 percent share of the

---

[5]Let A = butter, B = margarine, P_A = price of butter and P_B = price of margarine, Q_A = quantity of butter, and Q_B = quantity of margarine.

Then the cross-price elasticity between butter and margarine is defined as the percentage change in the quantity of butter (margarine) demanded for a small percentage change in the price of margarine (butter). Symbolically,

$$\text{Cross-price elasticity} = \frac{\%\ \text{change in } Q_A \text{ (or } Q_B)}{\%\ \text{change in } P_B \text{ (or } P_A)}$$

market thus defined. Now it is arguable whether can and glass containers are closely interchangeable substitutes. In some uses, such as beer and soft drinks, they may be, but in some others they may not be. Also, why exclude plastic and paper containers from the market? If these products were included, Continental and Hazel companies' market shares would have been still smaller. Would the Supreme Court have allowed the merger in this case? It is anybody's guess.

"Section of Country"

This phrase simply means the relevant geographic market, that is, "the area where the effect of the merger on competition will be immediate and direct." (This was how it was defined in the *Philadelphia Bank* case discussed below). Here again it is not easy to delineate what constitutes the appropriate geographic market to measure the concentration of economic power. In the *Brown Shoe* case the Supreme Court decided that the entire nation was the relevant market but in *United States v. Pabst Brewing Company,* 384 U.S. 546 (1966) the Court defined it much more narrowly. This case involved a merger between Pabst and Blatz Brewing companies. After the merger Pabst became the fifth-largest brewer in the country, with 4.49 percent of the national market (before the merger, Pabst and Blatz were, respectively, the tenth- and eighteenth-largest companies in the nation). But in the tri-state area of Wisconsin-Michigan-Illinois the postmerger share of Pabst was about 11.32 percent. The Supreme Court held that the relevant market was the tri-state area where it felt the proposed merger posed a serious threat to competition. It is interesting to point out that Justice White, who voted with the majority, said that the merger lessened competition in the entire nation, whereas Justices Harlan and Stewart, who also concurred with the majority, felt that the merger lessened competition in the tri-state area or in Wisconsin only.

May Be Substantially to Lessen Competition

This key phrase, which runs through most of the Clayton Act, is essentially an incipiency doctrine: Congress meant Sec. 7 to be not only *corrective,* that is, to redress the anticompetitive effects of an already consummated merger, but also *preventive,* that is, to stop mergers which may be potentially harmful to competition (potentiality measured in terms of reasonable probabilities and not just possibilities). But since Congress did not specify any quantitiative measures as to when potential competition is harmed or when it is substantially lessened, it was left to the courts to decide each case on its merits. And although deciding each case on its merits has the virtue of flexibility, it also gives much discretion to the judges to interject their own personal views as to what constitutes harm to potential competition. That the final outcome may be questionable has already been noted in the *Penn-Olin* case and can be seen more clearly in the case studies that follow.

SOME LEGAL CONSIDERATIONS UNDER SEC. 7

BROWN SHOE CASE*

This landmark case provided the first Supreme Court interpretation of the amended Sec. 7 of the Clayton Act. Some of the views expressed in this case have become precedents for later cases.

FACTS

In 1955, the U.S. government brought a civil suit in the U.S. District Court for the District of Missouri alleging that the merger between the Brown Shoe Company and the G. R. Kinney Company was in violation of Sec. 7 of the Clayton Act. It asked for dissolution of the merger.

Brown, primarily a shoe manufacturer, produced about 4 percent of the nation's total footwear production in 1955 and was the nation's fourth-largest manufacturer of shoes. Although in the past it had its own retail outlets, by 1945 there were none. But beginning in 1951, Brown again began acquiring retail outlets for its shoes and by 1956 it had about 846 such outlets and was looking for more. Hence the interest in Kinney, which was primarily a family-style retailer with 400 retail outlets in about 270 cities. In 1955 Kinney was responsible for about 1.6 percent of the nation's retail shoe sales. It also owned and operated four manufacturing plants producing men's, women's, and children's shoes. The combined output of these three categories was about 0.5 percent of the nation's production of shoes, making Kinney the twelfth-largest shoe manufacturer in the country. At the time of the merger, Kinney sold 20 percent of its shoes from its own production, the rest were from different manufacturers, but none were from Brown. But by 1957, Brown supplied about 7.9 percent of all Kinney's needs.

The merger between Brown and Kin-

*Brown Shoe v. United States, 370 U.S. 294 (1962).

ney was thus both horizontal and vertical. It was horizontal at the manufacturing level (because both companies produced shoes) as well at the retail level because before the merger they sold shoes competitively. It was also vertical because after the merger Brown and Kinney were essentially in the supplier-customer relationship.

JUDGMENT

The district court held that the merger of the manufacturing activities was not substantial enough to violate Sec. 7. At the retail level, however, the court deemed the merger in violation of Sec. 7. The district court found that there was a "definite trend" toward vertical integration, that is, the manufacturer acquiring retail outlets to sell its shoes. Besides Brown's pre-1956 acquisitions, the court noted that between 1950 and 1956 nine independent shoe chain stores with 1114 retail outlets were acquired by the largest shoe manufacturers in the country, which included companies such as International, Endicott Johnson, and General Shoe. This had the effect of foreclosing manufacturer-owned retail outlets to other independent manufacturers who did not have their own retail outlets. The district court found that this had the effect of substantially lessening competition, hence they ruled against the Brown-Kinney merger.

The defendants appealed the case to the Supreme Court. But the highest court upheld the district court's ruling and supported the government. In the process the Court enunciated its views on the interpretation of Sec. 7. The majority opinion was written by Chief Justice Warren.

Chief Justice Warren first defined the "line of commerce" and "section of country" in the present case. Men's, women's, and children's shoes constituted the lines of commerce, each with its own distinctive feature. The relevant geographic market was the entire nation or an appropriate section of it. Since the act is applicable only when the effect of the merger "may be substantially to lessen competition or tend to create monopoly," the Chief Justice said that since Congress had not defined either quantitatively or qualitatively the preceding phrase, each merger had to be judged on its own merits, considering factors such as the following:† (1) whether the merger is to take place in an industry not yet concentrated, (2) whether there was any noticeable trend in the domination of the industry by a few leaders, (3) whether substantial business was foreclosed to competition, and (4) whether new entry into the industry was readily possible.

The Court readily accepted the district court's finding that there was an "increasing tendency toward concentration" in the shoe industry. Although the Court recognized the percentage of the market foreclosed by the merger as an indication of concentration or market power, this index itself was not a determining factor, save in the polar cases of very high concentration (i.e., monopoly) or very low concentration (de minimis). But in between, one has to consider various economic and historical factors pertaining to that industry as well as, or perhaps more importantly, congressional intent. Citing the Federal Trade Commission's 1948 report on the merger movement in the country, which stated in part, "where several large enterprises are extending their power by successive small acquisitions, the cumulative effect of their purchases may be to convert an industry from one of intense competition among many enterprises to one in which three or four large concerns produce the entire supply," the Chief Justice concluded, "The shoe industry is being subjected to just such a cumulative series of vertical merg-

ers which, if left unchecked, will be likely 'substantially to lessen competition.'"

But it was ultimately congressional intent that was the determining factor for Chief Justice Warren. He wrote:

> Of course, some of the results of large integrated or chain operations are beneficial to consumer. Their expansion is not rendered unlawful by the mere fact that small independent stores may be adversely affected. It is competition, not competitors, which the Act protects. But we cannot fail to recognize Congress's desire to promote competition through the protection of viable, small, locally owned businesses. Congress appreciated that occasional higher costs and prices might result from the maintenance of fragmented industries and markets. It resolved these competing considerations in favor of decentralization. We must give effect to that decision.

In the course of his decision, the Chief Justice had something to say about vertical as well as horizontal mergers in general and with reference to *Brown* in particular. About vertical merger he opined: "The primary vice of a vertical merger or other arrangement tying a customer to a supplier is that, by foreclosing the competitors of either party from a segment of the market otherwise open to them, the arrangement may act as a 'clog on competition!'" The Chief Justice also regarded vertical mergers as similar to tying contracts, for both have the effect of shutting off a segment of the market to competition. And since tying contracts are "inherently anticompetitive," by implication, vertical mergers are also anticompetitive.

Speaking about horizontal mergers, the Chief Justice said that they may be allowed if there are "mitigating factors" such as the failing company doctrine or if two smaller companies merge to compete effectively

---

†See A. D. Neale, *The Antitrust Laws of the U.S.A.*, Cambridge, New York, 1970, p. 184.

with a powerful company in the market. But since Brown and Kinney were "large" companies, letting them merge would reduce competition in the shoe industry by making the industry oligopolistic, that is, controlled by a few large sellers. He also stated that although the market for shoes is the whole nation, a particular section of the country (town, city, etc.) also can be treated as the relevant market, and in many cities the combined market share of Brown and Kinney exceeded 20 percent.

COMMENT

The *Brown Shoe* decision was indeed sweeping. There are several points worth noting about the decision. First, by invoking the "exclusionary theory" or "foreclosure theory," and putting them on par with tying contracts, the Court in effect said that vertical mergers may not be tolerated; this notwithstanding the many advantages that vertical mergers confer. The extracted Warren quote cited previously implies that protection of small business is more important than any benefits the consumers may derive from vertical integration. In this sense the *Brown Shoe* decision may be anticonsumer.

Second, the Court seems to have been harsh on horizontal mergers. The Court feared that if mergers are allowed in an industry, then eventually the industry may become oligopolistic. But this view is dubious because, as noted elsewhere, an industry consisting of 100 firms each controlling 1 percent of the market does not become suddenly anticompetitive if there are now 25 firms each controlling 4 percent of the market. The Court also failed to recognize that at the time there were no great economies of scale in the shoe industry that would have posed any barriers to entry into the industry.

Third, the Court indicated that it might allow mergers in cases of failing companies. But one does not know whether Congress meant to save all failing companies. What if a small firm fails because of managerial inefficiency? Should such a firm be saved just because it is small?

Fourth, the Court took a purely structuralist approach in making the decision. That is, it concentrated primarily on the market shares of the two companies in the nation as a whole and some of its segments without considering any behavioral aspects of the companies, such as prices, profits, rate of return, and the like. There was no discussion about what would happen to these variables before and after the merger.

Fifth, if Congress really wanted to preserve small businesses for their own sake, then, as noted before, it should have said so in the act. Some of the "small business philosophy" propounded by the Chief Justice may be entirely his own and may not reflect the true congressional intent in the passage of Sec. 7 in 1914 and its subsequent amendment in 1950.

Finally, neither Congress nor the courts enunciated any criteria about when competition may be lessened. According to Neal, the *Brown Shoe* decision meant that the principal criterion in assessing the effects of a merger was to be its "qualitative substantiality," that is, its overall impact on the competitive process in the given industry, rather than merely its "quantitative substantiality," that is, the size and the market share of the companies involved.† In the *Philadelphia Bank* case the Court tried to devise a measure of quantitative substantiality, but it was quickly dropped in the *Von's Grocery* case, which was decided soon after *Philadelphia Bank*.

---

†Neale, op. cit., p. 185.

PHILADELPHIA BANK CASE*

This case, involving horizontal merger and decided only a year after *Brown Shoe,* reversed the *Brown Shoe* approach of deciding each case on its own merit and laid down some explicit quantitative rules about market concentration in deciding the legality of a merger.

FACTS

The proposed merger involved the Philadelphia National Bank (PNB) and Girard Trust Corn Exchange Bank (Girard), respectively the second and third largest of the forty-two commercial banks in the Philadelphia metropolitan area, which consists of the city itself and its three contiguous counties in Pennsylvania. As of 1959, PNB, a national bank, had assets over $1 billion, making it the twenty-first–largest bank in the country, and Girard, a state bank, had assets of about $0.75 billion.

With the merger, the two banks would have been the largest single bank in the four-county area, with about 36 percent of the area banks' total assets, 36 percent of total deposits, and 34 percent of total net loans. The merged banks together with the second-largest bank, First Pennsylvania Bank and Trust Company (the largest bank before the proposed merger) would have controlled about 59 per cent of the total assets, 58 percent of deposits, and 58 percent of the net loans. Considering the 4 largest bank concentration ratio, these figures would have been 78, 77, and 78 percent, respectively. Incidentally, it may be noted that PNB and Girard themselves grew out of previous mergers; between 1950 and 1959 PNB had acquired nine formerly independent banks and Girard, six.

Citing increasing concentration in the banking industry (i.e., tendency toward

*Philadelphia National Bank v. United States, 374 U.S. 321 (1963).

monopolization via oligopolies, also known as *shared monopoly*), the government brought a suit against the two banks, charging them with violation of Sec. 1 of the Sherman Act as well as Sec. 7 of the Clayton Act.

JUDGMENT

The district court ruled in favor of the two defendant banks. This decision was based on several considerations: First, the district court, after defining the banking business (the product market), stated that the relevant geographic market (section of the country) was where the parties to the merger actually did business, that is, where they and their branches were located. On this consideration, the court found the banking industry to be quite competitive. The court also accepted the defendants' contention that since there were forty other banks in the area competition would remain vigorous even after the proposed merger. Second, the defendants argued that the banking industry was so heavily regulated by such government agencies as the Federal Reserve System and the Federal Deposit Insurance Corporation (FDIC) that there was no fear of anticompetitive behavior on account of concentration in the industry. Finally, the court accepted the defendants' contention that the merger was justified because (1) it would offer the banks the opportunity to follow customers to their suburbs and retain their business; (2) the increased financial strength after merger would enable them to compete vigorously with the large out-of-state banks, particularly banks from New York City, for very large loans; and (3) it would help the economic growth of the Philadelphia metropolitan area by attracting new business to the region.

The government appealed the decision to the Supreme Court, which, with Justice Brennan speaking for the majority, overruled the district court and enjoined the merger. Justice Brennan gave several reasons for the reversal. First, the appropriate "section of the country" in this case was not just where the offices of the banks were located; because of branch-banking the area affected was the four-county Philadelphia metropolitan area. Therefore, this was the relevant geographic market within which to assess the effects of the proposed merger on competition.

Second, responding to the argument that because banking business is so heavily regulated one need not fear anticompetitive effects of concentration in the banking industry, Justice Brennan remarked:

> There is no reason to think that concentration is less inimical to the free play of competition in banking than in other service industries. On the contrary, it is in all probability more inimical. . . . Small businessmen especially are, as a practical matter, confined to their locality for the satisfaction of their credit needs. If the number of banks in the locality is reduced, the vigor of competition for filling the marginal small business borrower's needs is likely to diminish. At the same time, his concomitantly greater difficulty in obtaining credit is likely to put him at a disadvantage vis-a-vis larger businesses with which he competes. *In this fashion, concentration in banking accelerates concentration generally.* [Emphasis added]

Third, to assess whether the effect of the intended merger "may be substantially to lessen competition," Justice Brennan, like Chief Justice Warren in *Brown Shoe*, noted Congress's concern with the "rising tide of economic concentration" when it amended Sec. 7 and stated that:

> . . . [this concern] warrants dispensing, in certain cases, with elaborate proof of market structure, market behavior, or probable anticompetitive effects. Specifically, we think that a merger which

produces a firm controlling an undue percentage share of the relevant market, and results in a significant increase in the concentration of firms in that market is so inherently likely to lessen competition substantially that it must be enjoined in the absence of evidence clearly showing that the merger is not likely to have such anticompetitive effects.

Without attempting to specify the smallest market share (degree of concentration) that would pose a threat to competition, and also noting that Sec. 7 or its legislative history did not specify a minimum, Justice Brennan stated that:

> . . . we are clear that 30 percent presents that threat. Further, whereas presently the two largest banks in the area (First Pennsylvania and PNB) control between them approximately 44 percent of the area's commercial banking business, the two largest after the merger (PNB-Girard and First Pennsylvania) will control 59 percent. Plainly, we think, *this increase of more than 33 percent in concentration must be regarded as significant.* [Emphasis added]

Finally, Justice Brennan rejected the defendants' claims (1), (2), and (3) cited earlier. To the defense that the merger would enable the two banks to develop the suburban banking business, he said that this could be accomplished by opening new branches since branch banking was allowed in Pennsylvania. To the claim that the merger would enable the defendants to compete vigorously with large New York City banks, he said that, "[even] if all the commercial banks in the Philadelphia area merged into one, it would be smaller than the largest bank in New York City." Justice Brennan turned a deaf ear to the claim that the merger would be beneficial to the economic development of the Philadelphia region. Saying that it is beyond the court's ordinary limit of judicial competence to decide broad social goals, Justice Brennan reiterated the intent of Congress in amending Sec. 7, namely, to preserve our "traditionally competitive economy." "It therefore proscribed anticompetitive mergers, the benign and the malignant alike, fully aware, we must assume, that some price might have to be paid."

COMMENT

The significance of *Philadelphia Bank* lies in the "30–33 percent" rule, which provided a quantitative test of the legality of an intended merger. In effect the rule stated that if a firm already controls about 30 percent of a market and if the proposed merger is likely to increase that share by 33 percent or more, that merger will be ruled out because it is anticompetitive.

Whether good or bad, the 30–33 percent rule has the virtue of explicitness, and if applied consistently one would not have to worry about the legality or otherwise of a merger. But as we will see shortly, the rule was abandoned in the *Von's Grocery* case, decided in 1966, in which a merger involving less than 5 percent of the market share was ruled illegal.

From a strictly economic viewpoint the rule may not be very sound, for economic theory provides no definite guidelines specifying what level of concentration injures competition, save the extreme case of monopoly. According to Harold Demsetz "[we] *have no theory that allows us to deduce from the observable degree of concentration in a particular market whether or not price and output are competitive.* [Emphasis Demsetz's]"†

Therefore, a blind adherence to the 30–33 percent rule, by preventing mergers that would exploit economies of scale or lead to more efficient allocation of economic resources, might be more anticonsumer than pro-competition.

†Harold Demsetz, "Why Regulate Utilities," *Journal of Law and Economics,* 1968, p. 59.

VON'S GROCERY CASE*

This case involving horizontal merger was decided just 3 years after *Philadelphia Bank,* but the decision rendered rejected the 30–33 percent rule enunciated in that case.

FACTS

On March 25, 1960, the U.S. government brought a suit under Sec. 7 of the Clayton Act to prevent the proposed merger between Von's Grocery Company and Shopping Bag Food Stores, two of the Los Angeles area's large retail grocery compa-

United States v. Von's Grocery Company, 384 U.S. 270 (1966).

nies. Based on the value of retail sales, in 1958 Von's and Shopping Bag were the third- and sixth-largest companies in the Los Angeles metropolitan area; the intended merger would have made them the second-largest company after the leader Safeway. In 1960, the two parties to the merger controlled 1.4 percent of the grocery stores and 7.5 percent of the grocery sales in the Los Angeles area.

Although the above market shares are far below the 30–33 percent norm of *Philadelphia Bank,* the government contended that there was a rising trend toward concentration in the grocery business in the Los Angeles area (the so-called supermarket revolution) and, that this trend should be checked. To substantiate its claim, the government presented the following statistics: In 1950 there were 5365 owner-operated grocery stores but by 1961 this number was down to 3818, a decline of some 29 percent. At the same time, between 1953 and 1962 the number of chain companies with 2 or more grocery stores increased from 96 to 150. Moreover, between 1949 and 1958 nine of the top 20 chain grocery companies acquired 126 stores from smaller independent companies.

JUDGMENT

In the district court the government lost the case because Von's contended that the grocery industry was highly competitive and would remain so even after the merger. The government appealed the case to the Supreme Court and sought to nullify the merger. The Supreme Court overruled the district court and supported the government. The majority opinion was written by Justice Black.

Justice Black accepted the government's statistics about the growing trend of concentration in the grocery industry and stated that "these facts alone are enough to cause us to conclude contrary to the District Court that the Von's-Shopping Bag merger did violate Section 7." In readily accepting the government's statistics, Justice Black considered the congressional intent behind the amended Sec. 7. He wrote:

By using these terms [where the effect may be to substantially lessen competition] in Section 7 which look not merely to the actual present effect of a merger but instead to its effect upon future competition, Congress sought to preserve competition among many small businesses by arresting a trend toward concentration in its incipiency before that trend developed to the point that a market was left in the grip of a few big companies. Thus, where concentration is gaining momentum in a

market, we must be alert to carry out Congress's intent to protect competition against ever increasing concentration through mergers.

The facts of this case present exactly the threatening trend toward concentration which Congress wanted to halt.

COMMENT

Justice White, while concurring with the majority, did not want to declare a merger involving 7.5 percent or less of the market share (as in the present case) illegal per se because of an increasing tendency toward concentration. Rather, he proposed a criterion similar to the *Philadelphia Bank* 30–33 percent rule: If the eight leading companies in an industry control more than 40 percent of the market, mergers between such companies should be discouraged unless there are some compelling reasons for the merger, such as bankruptcy of one of the companies.

The majority decision was severely criticized by Justice Stewart, with Justice Harlan joining him. He remarked: "I believe that even the most superficial analysis of the record makes plain the fallacy of the Court's syllogism that competition is necessarily reduced when the bare number of competitors have declined"; recall that the government made much of the fact that there was a decline of 29 percent in the number of grocery stores between 1950 and 1961. He went on to say:

Sec. 7 was never intended by Congress for use by the Court as a charter to roll back the supermarket revolution. Yet the Court's opinion is hardly more than a requiem for the so-called "Mom and Pop" grocery stores . . . that are now economically and technologically obsolete in many parts of the country.

Justice Stewart further argued that the Court did not weigh all the facts carefully.

According to him, competition in the grocery industry in the Los Angeles area was "vigorous to a fault." As indications of this, he cited several facts. First, because of the continuing population explosion (including migration) the market itself was expanding. Second, there were three large cooperative buying organizations to which small grocers could belong without any restriction and thereby reap the benefits of large-scale centralized buying. Third, there were no significant barriers to entry into the industry, which can be seen from the fact that between 1953 and 1962 173 new chain stores were opened and 119 went out of business, a net addition of 54. Fourth, the price wars in which the stores engaged themselves from time to time were a clear indication that competition in the industry was "pugnacious." Finally, although the combined market share of the top twenty firms increased from 47 to 57 percent between 1948 and 1958, the share of the top five fell; seven of the top twenty companies in 1958 were not even in existence in 1948. In the same time span, the market share of the leader in the industry, Safeway, declined from 14 to 8 percent.

Justice Stewart, noting that the majority was consistent in deciding merger cases based on the congressional intent of preserving small business, retorted, "the sole consistency that I can find is that under Sec. 7 the government always wins." He went on to warn that the majority *Von's* view might in the long run harm competition by discouraging new entrants into the grocery industry if they believe that at a future date they won't be able to sell their business to a competitor because of Sec. 7. Clearly, this is not what Sec. 7 had intended; it was interested in preserving competition, not merely the competitors.

CLOROX CASE*

This case involving a conglomerate merger was enjoined by the Supreme Court on the grounds of harm to potential competition.

FACTS

The Federal Trade Commission (FTC) found that the 1957 acquisition by Procter & Gamble of the assets of the Clorox Chemical Company, the leading manufacturer of household liquid bleach, violated Sec. 7 of the Clayton Act; it therefore sought dissolution of the merger. At the time of the merger, Clorox controlled 48.8 percent of household liquid bleach sales and had 13 manufacturing plants scattered

Federal Trade Commission v. Procter & Gamble Company [Clorox case], 386 U.S. 568 (1967).

around the country. Its nearest competitor, Purex, accounted for 15.7 percent of the market. The industry was highly concentrated: Clorox and Purex together accounted for 64.5 of the national sales, and they with the next 2 leading firms accounted for 80 percent of the market. The remaining 20 percent was shared by 200 small, mostly local or regional, producers.

Procter & Gamble, a large diversified manufacturer of soaps, detergents, and cleansers, with sales of about $1.1 billion and assets of about $500 million in 1957, did not produce any liquid household bleach. The soap-detergent-cleanser industry was itself highly concentrated, with Procter & Gamble, Colgate-Palmolive, and Lever Brothers accounting for about 80 percent of the market. To retain its market position, Procter & Gamble engaged in a heavy advertising and promotional campaign: In 1957, it spent some $80 million on advertising and $47 million on promotional expenses. Because of its dominant market position, it was alleged, Procter & Gamble was able to secure huge discounts from the advertising media.

The FTC objected to the merger mainly because the acquisition lessened competition in the household bleach industry. If there were no merger, there was every possibility that Procter & Gamble would have entered the industry with its own brand of bleach since it would have nicely complemented its soap-detergent-cleanser line of business. Hence the merger reduced potential competition, a violation of Sec. 7.

JUDGMENT

The U.S. Court of Appeals for the Sixth Circuit reversed the FTC decision. But on appeal from government, the Supreme Court reversed the lower court's decision and supported the FTC. The majority opinion was written by Justice Douglas.

In its decision the majority of justices were swayed by some of the FTC arguments. The commission argued that if the merger were allowed, retailers would be induced to give Clorox preferential shelf space because of Procter & Gamble's dominance in the soap-detergent-cleanser products. Moreover, there was the possibility that Procter & Gamble might use its dominant position to underprice Clorox bleach, thereby driving competition out of business (it could subsidize the loss from its dominant position in the soap and related product lines). Furthermore, because of its massive advertising budget and the discounts it got from the advertising media, Clorox would be able to advertise its bleach products more heavily, which would increase the barriers to new entry into the market. Absent the merger, Procter & Gamble would have entered the household bleach market on its own and checked Clorox's monopoly position of that market. Hence the merger would have the effect of reducing potential competition.

COMMENT

While concurring with the majority, Justice Harlan did not agree with some of its thinking. First, although the household bleach industry was oligopolistic because of a few dominant sellers, there was no reason to believe that the oligopoly would become much "more rigid" with Procter & Gamble's acquisition of Clorox. Second, the majority's emphasis on vast economies of scale in advertising, and hence the fear of barriers to new entry, was exaggerated. Even with massive advertising it is not easy to introduce a new brand of liquid bleach, a product with high transportation cost and low sales value. Finally, the FTC stated that there was merely a possibility that Procter & Gamble might enter the bleach industry (i.e., potential competition), but it refused to establish any reasonable probability of its doing so. But this "threat to potential competition" doctrine is a fragile reed on which to decide mergers. He writes:

> It must be noted, however, that economic theory teaches that potential competition will have no effect on the market behavior of existing firms unless present market power is sufficient to drive the market price to the point where entry would become a real possibility. So long as existing competition is sufficient to keep the market price below that point, potential competition is of marginal significance as a market regulator.

Despite the preceding arguments, Harlan joined the majority in condemning the merger. One reason for his action was that

Procter & Gamble had not presented its case strongly. In his view, the company, instead of stating that there were a lot of small competitors in the industry (about 200), should have shown that the prices of unadvertised bleaches, which were cost-determined, set an effective ceiling on market price through the mechanism of an acceptable differential and therefore despite its size Procter & Gamble could not have controlled the market. Despite Justice Harlan's elaboration, the final decision is still open to some questions. First, the Court is saying implicitly that that growth by internal expansion is all right, but growth by acquisition or merger, is not all right. That is, if Procter & Gamble were to manufacture its own brand of liquid bleach and then acquire a sizable market position, that is fine; it cannot do so, however, by acquiring an established company. Why this preference for internal growth as opposed to growth by merger? The "answer" was given in the *Brown Shoe* case, discussed earlier, which set a precedent for this case. In *Brown Shoe* it was stated:

> Internal expansion is more likely to be the result of increased demand for the company's products and is more likely to provide increased investment in plants, more jobs and greater output. Conversely, expansion through merger is more likely to reduce available consumer choice while providing no increase in industry capacity, jobs or output.†

The preceding logic cannot be supported either by theoretical or empirical economics. If carried to extreme, it would mean all mergers are illegal. As Robert Bork puts it, "Growth is preferable to merger only in one type of case: where merger would create a market share so

large that the result would be restriction of output. There is no other general reason to prefer internal expansion to merger."‡

Second, the objection to the merger in the Clorox case is largely based on Clorox's alleged domination of the market. But as Justice Harlan states, "Domination is an elusive term, for dominance in terms of percentage of sales is not the equivalent of dominance in terms of control over price or other aspects of market behavior. . . ." In other words, the majority simply looked at the structure of the bleach industry in terms of the concentration ratios without taking into account any behavioral aspects.

Third, the FTC contended that although economies of scale gained by merger may in fact increase the vigor of competition, this may not be true of economies of scale due to advertising. In the commission's view, advertising economies "only . . . increase the barriers to new entry" and are "offensive to at least the spirit, if not the letter, of the antitrust laws." This view was rebutted by Justice Harlan as follows:

> This process [i.e., advertising] contributes to consumer demand being developed to the point at which economies of scale can be realized in production. The advertiser's brand name may also be an assurance of quality, and the value of this benefit is demonstrated by the general willingness of consumers to pay a premium for the advertised brands. Undeniably advertising may sometimes be used to create irrational brand preferences and mislead consumers as to the actual differences between products, but it is very difficult to discover at what point advertising ceases to be an aspect of healthy competition. . . . It is not the commission's function to decide which lawful elements of the "product" offered the

†Bork, op. cit., p. 206.

‡ibid., p. 206.

consumer should be considered useful and which should be considered the symptom of industrial "sickness". It is the consumer who must make that election through the exercise of his purchasing power.

Fourth, the commission based its case on the premise that, absent the merger, Procter & Gamble would have entered the bleach market on its own. What was the probability of this happening? There was not much discussion about it in the commission's brief, although Procter & Gamble in its brief had stated that it had no intention of entering the household bleach market. Richard Posner argues that if Procter & Gamble had been serious about entering the market, it would not have offered the very high price it paid to acquire Clorox; it paid $30 million in its own stock in exchange for Clorox stock. If Procter & Gamble had been serious about entering the market and competing successfully with Clorox, the latter's market value would have tumbled in anticipation of such an eventuality.

Considering all the factors, it seems once again that the Clorox case was ultimately decided by the pro-small business philosophy that the Court had espoused for quite some time.

A SUMMARY OF SUPREME COURT'S VIEWS OF MERGERS

Although we have considered but four merger cases, they shed considerable light on the thinking of the Supreme Court concerning the nature and scope of the amended Sec. 7 of the Clayton Act. The Court's views may be summarized as follows:*

1 Because of the rising tide of concentration in American industries, mergers should be looked upon with great suspicion (*Brown Shoe*).
2 Congress is interested in retaining "local" control of business (*Brown Shoe*).
3 Congress is interested in protecting small businesses (*Brown* and *Von's Grocery*).
4 A merger cannot be necessarily defended because it leads to efficiency due to economies of scale (*Procter & Gamble*).

*This summary is due to Bork, op. cit., pp. 202-210.

5 What is called efficiency is really a "competitive advantage" or "barriers to entry" and hence is anticompetitive (*Procter & Gamble*).
6 Even if it does not confer any "competitive advantage" or create "barriers to entry," efficiency is bad anyway because Congress intended to protect small companies from increased efficiency of rivals (Chief Justice Warren's statement in *Brown Shoe*).
7 Concentration should be nipped in the bud in its incipiency. Otherwise, step by step an industry will be highly concentrated (*Von's Grocery*).
8 Internal growth is to be preferred to growth by merger (*Brown* and *Procter & Gamble*).

We have commented on most of the above views at various places. Needless to say, all the preceding statements are highly controvertible.

A NOTE ON BARRIERS TO ENTRY

Since the theme of "barriers to entry" runs through many an antitrust case, it is important to know what exactly is the nature of such barriers. The term *entry barrier* itself may be defined as any obstacle that may prevent or make it very difficult for new producers to enter the industry. Such barriers may arise on account of product differentiation (brand name), economies of scale, or advertising. An established producer with a famous brand name may have developed such an image for its product that a newcomer may find it very difficult to make any headway without substantial selling expenditures. Or, the optimum scale of production plant may be so large that a small producer will not be able to take advantage of the cost savings associated with large-scale production. Or, the established producers may be spending such large sums of money on advertising that a newcomer cannot hope to match them.

Whatever the source of the barriers, why do the FTC and the courts look down upon the barriers themselves? It may be because they have in mind the model of perfect competition. As we discussed in Chapter 2, under the assumptions of perfect competition, especially the assumption of free entry, in the long run the price for a competitive firm equals the (long-run) average cost. But if there are barriers to entry, price can exceed average cost, the difference between the two reflecting the "height" of the barriers. But in that case the competitive model shows that the economy's resources will not be allocated efficiently.

In practice, however, the competitive norm may not be directly applicable. Recall that in developing the competitive model we assumed constant returns to scale. But

if there are economies of scale, economic theory shows that in some cases it is actually better to have a single firm than a host of others. The courts seem to have recognized this fact in some of its decisions in the area of antitrust. But if such economies of scale can be recognized in production, why can they not be recognized in, say, advertising? If advertising informs consumers, and information is a valuable part of the product, then advertising economies are just as important as production economies and should not be singled out as "undesirable" barriers to entry.

In short, one needs to look at the barriers to entry carefully and not simply extrapolate the competitive model based on specialized assumptions. In this connection it may be well to remember the following remarks:

> First, whether entry into an industry will occur depends upon the *post-entry* behavior of established firms anticipated by potential entrants. This anticipated behavior can take various alternative forms, each of which implies a different level of profits accruing to the entrant, and need not necessarily correspond to the pre-entry behavior of established firms. Second, the effect of entry on industry price and output depends upon the actual post-entry behavior of firms in the industry including any new entrants, and varies with the exact nature of firms' assumptions regarding rivals' reactions after entry has occurred.[†]

†Douglas Needham, *The Economics of Industrial Structure Conduct and Performance*, St. Martin's, New York, 1978, p. 169.

10.5 THE DEPARTMENT OF JUSTICE'S MERGER GUIDELINES, 1968 AND 1982

In 1968, for the first time, the Department of Justice (DOJ) issued Merger Guidelines, whose objective was to acquaint the business community, the legal profession, and other interest groups and individuals with the standards applied by the department in determining whether to challenge corporate acquisitions and mergers under Sec. 7 of the Clayton Act. In June 1982 the department revised these guidelines, the revisions reflecting the changes in economic and legal thinking on the antitrust laws in general and the merger aspect in particular as well as the antimerger-enforcement experience since 1968. We first discuss the 1968 guidelines and then consider the 1982 revisions of these guidelines.

The 1968 Merger Guidelines

General Enforcement Policy   The primary role of Sec. 7 enforcement is to preserve and promote market structure conducive to competition. The emphasis on market structure is because market conduct or behavior is dependent on market structure and because enforcement policy emphasizing a limited number of structural factors also facilitates both enforcement decision making and business planning which involves anticipation of the DOJ enforcement itself. Hence attention is focused primarily toward the identification and prevention of those mergers which alter market structure in ways likely now or eventually to encourage or permit noncompetitive conduct. But in suitable circumstances the DOJ may not rely on these guidelines alone, especially in industries where basic technological changes are taking place.

After defining product and geographical markets, the DOJ then listed its policies toward horizontal, vertical, and conglomerate mergers, which are as follows:

Horizontal Mergers   As a matter of general policy, the DOJ will not accept the economies of scale defense to merger primarily because there are several difficulties in accurately estimating the existence and magnitude of such economies. Moreover,

1 *In highly concentrated markets* (four-firm concentration ratio equal to or exceeding 75 percent or more), the department will generally challenge mergers between fims accounting for the following percentages of the market:

Acquiring firm	Acquired firm
4%	4% or more
10%	2% or more
15% or more	1% or more

2 *Markets less highly concentrated* (four-firm concentration ratio less than 75 percent). The department will ordinarily challenge mergers between firms accounting for approximately the following market shares:

Acquiring firm	Acquired firm
5%	5% or more
10%	4% or more
15%	3% or more
20%	2% or more
25%	1% or more

3 *Markets with trend toward concentration.* In a nonconcentrated industry, a trend toward concentration is considered present when the aggregate market share of any grouping of the largest firms in the market from the two largest to the eight largest has increased by approximately 7 percent or more of the market over a period of time extending from any base year 5 to 10 years prior to the merger.

4 Regardless of the provisions in items 1, 2, and 3 above, a merger will be challenged if the acquisition of a competitor is particularly "disturbing" or "disruptive."

5 A merger will usually not be challenged if it is done with good intention to rescue a company from business failure; a failing company must be one which has no prospect of being viable without outside help.

Vertical Mergers   As in the case of horizontal mergers, as a matter of general policy, vertical mergers may not be allowed merely on the grounds of economies of scale, for such economies can also be obtained by other means, such as internal expansion. Also, as a general policy, mergers that foreclose competition and raise significant barriers to entry will be challenged. In particular, the following types of mergers will be challenged:

1 A merger where the supplying firm accounts for 10 percent or more of the sales in its market and the purchasing firm accounts for about 6 percent or more of the total purchase of that market, unless it can be shown that there are no significant barriers to entry in the business of the purchasing firm(s).

2 A merger where the purchasing firm accounts for 10 percent of its market and the supplying firm accounts for 20 percent of the sales in its market.

3 A merger in an industry where there is a significant trend toward concentration by vertical merger which would increase the barriers to entry into the industry or if there are no clear economies of production or distribution not related to advertising or other promotional economies.

4 A merger where the acquired firm is a viable business entity and is not genuinely in danger of bankruptcy.

Conglomerate Mergers   The policy toward conglomerate mergers, although still in the formative stages, is as follows:

1 *Mergers involving potential entrants.* The DOJ will generally challenge any merger between one of the most likely entrants into the market and (1) any firm with 25 percent or more of the market, (2) one of the two largest firms in a market in which the shares of the two largest firms amount to approximately 50 percent or more, (3) one of the four largest firms in a market in which the shares of the eight largest firms amount to approximately 75 percent or more, provided the merging firm's share of the market amounts to about 10 percent or more.

2 *Mergers creating danger of reciprocal buying will be challenged.* A significant danger of reciprocal buying (i.e., favoring one's customer when making purchases of a product which is sold by the customer) is present whenever approxately 15 percent or more of the total purchases in a market in which one of the merging firms (the selling firm) sells are accounted for by firms which also make substantial sales in markets where the other merging firm (the buying firm) is both a substantial buyer and a more substantial buyer than all or most of the competitors of the selling firm.

3 *Mergers with entrenched market power and other conglomerate mergers will be challenged.* Where an acquisition of a leading firm in a relatively concentrated or rapidly concentrating market may serve to entrench or increase the market power of that firm or raise barriers to entry in the market, such a merger will be challenged. For example, in the case of a merger which produces a very large disparity in absolute size between the merged firm and the largest remaining firm in the relevant markets or a merger which may enhance the ability of the merged firm to increase product differentiation in the relevant markets, such a merger may not be allowed.

4 The provisions regarding failing companies that apply to horizontal and vertical mergers also apply to conglomerate mergers; that is, in cases of genuinely failing companies conglomerate mergers may be permitted.

The 1982 Merger Guidelines

The Merger Guidelines issued by the Justice Department in June 1982 are generally lenient insofar as vertical and conglomerate mergers are concerned. As a matter of fact, the new guidelines now distinguish only between horizontal and nonhorizontal mergers; all mergers that are not between companies on the same level of the distribution chain are now declared nonhorizontal, be they of the vertical or conglomerate type. Unlike the quantitative norm (in terms of concentration ratios) laid down under the 1968 guidelines, the new guidelines merely state that nonhorizontal mergers will be challenged when they are likely to have considerable anticompetitive horizontal effects, such as elimination of a potential competitor, creation of barriers to entry, or collusion between buyers and sellers. But since it is difficult to determine these effects, some scholars believe that nonhorizontal mergers "have been virtually immunized against challenge."[6]

Insofar as horizontal mergers are concerned, the new guidelines, at least on

[6]Joe Sims and William Blumenthal, "The New Era in Antitrust," *Regulation*, July–August 1982, p. 25.

paper, are not much different from the old ones. But there are significant procedural changes. Under the new guidelines, the first thing to be determined in such merger cases is: What is the relevant market in which competitive harm might occur? As the *Alcoa, Cellophane,* and other cases discussed in Chapter 8 reveal, this is the most critical question in most antitrust cases. To determine the relevant market, the new guidelines now incorporate many tests based on the economic concepts of price and cross-price elasticities; in the past these concepts were considered only in passing. After defining the relevant market, the next step is to determine the market power or the degree of concentration. Under the 1982 guidelines this power is measured by the Herfindahl index and not by the concentration ratios, as under the old guidelines (see Chapter 6 for a discussion of the Herfindahl index vis-à-vis the concentration ratios). In highly concentrated markets, defined as having a Herfindahl index of 1800 or more, a merger may not be challenged if it is not likely to increase the index by more than 50 points. But if the merger increases the index by 50 to 100 points, it will be challenged ''more likely than not''; it will ''likely'' be challenged if the index increases by more than 100 points. Moreover, if the leading firm in an industry has a market share of 35 percent or more and is at least twice as big as the second-largest firm, a challenge to merger is ''likely'' if the leading firm acquires another firm which has at least 1 percent of the market share. Besides market power as determined by the index, factors such as product homogeneity, transaction size and frequency of transaction, and the pricing structure will also be considered in the department's challenge to a merger.

According to Sims and Blumenthal, in the new guidelines ''economic considerations have now achieved primacy over social and political considerations as the basis for merger policy, whereas these three considerations used to receive more or less equal billing.''[7] The old guidelines reflected social concerns such as ''the desirability of retaining 'local control' over industry and the protection of small businesses'' (the Supreme Court in *Brown Shoe,* 1962) and the perpetuation and preservation of, ''for its own sake and in spite of possible cost, an organization of industry in small units which can effectively compete with each other'' (Judge Learned Hand in *Alcoa*). Why this preference for economic considerations? According to Sims and Blumenthal, advances in economic understanding on two fronts have been the main reason:

First, it is now recognized that the relationship between concentration and noncompetitive performance is not so well defined as had been previously supposed. Some economists, such as Harold Demsetz, have shown, and most economists would agree that the 1968 guidelines were too stringent and failed to take proper account of the fact that numerous economic characteristics other than concentration influence a market's competitive state. Second, it is now recognized that mergers may yield efficiencies for many more reasons and to a far greater degree than had been previously supposed. Under the older view, the principal efficiencies realized through merger were attributable to economies of scale. The newer view goes further and recognizes

[7]Ibid.

additional efficiencies attributable to reduction in the cost of information and creation of intrafirm "markets" for capital, labor and other resources."[8]

Only future antitrust cases will tell us to what extent the Department of Justice has abided by the new guidelines and with what effect.

Ironically, on the day the Justice Department announced its new guidelines (June 14), the FTC (which has joint responsibility in this area), for the first time, announced its own guidelines concerning horizontal mergers. Although the two sets of guidelines are similar in many ways, they differ in two important respects. Unlike the department's guidelines, those by the FTC avoid specific quantification of the points (the Herfindahl index) at which a merger might be regarded as anticompetitive, and it will still consider the social and political objections to merger in addition to the economic ones. Since the FTC reviews about twice as many mergers as the Justice Department, it is interesting to see which view ultimately prevails and with what consequences. Needless to say, the courts are not bound by either the FTC guidelines or the Justice Department guidelines.

10.6 SECTION 8 OF THE CLAYTON ACT: INTERLOCKING DIRECTORATES

To round up the discussion of the Clayton Act, we discuss very briefly the interlocking directorate provision of Sec. 8. As noted before, in interlocking directorates a person may be on the board of directors of more than one company. In this situation there is every possibility that competition among such companies may be reduced or eliminated. In other words, the method of interlocking directorates may be a way of accomplishing a covert merger. It was to stop such an eventuality that Sec. 8 was directed. For practical considerations, however, the section was made applicable if only one of the corporations involved had "capital surplus and undivided profits aggregating more than $1 million."

Sec. 8 has been difficult to enforce for several reasons. First, a defendant threatened with suit under Sec. 8 may simply resign one of the directorships and perhaps assume it later on. Second, it is not clear whether the act covers all types of mergers, namely, horizontal, vertical, and conglomerate. In the 1966 *Paramount Pictures v. Baldwin Montrose Chemical Company* case, Judge Palmer held that Sec. 8 applies only to horizontal relationships, that is, those involving two companies selling similar goods or services. Third, the act does not cover the case of, say, the treasurer of company X, who is not a member of the board of directors of that company, from being a director of a competing company Y so that in effect the same goals would be achieved if he or she were a director of X as well. Finally, one important reason for the relative neglect of Sec. 8 is what Philip Areeda calls the "unenthusiastic enforcement" policy of the Department of Justice.

[8]Ibid, p. 26. See also, Yale Brozen, *Mergers and Concentration: The Empirical Evidence,* American Enterprise Institute for Public Policy Research, Washington, D.C., 1982.

It is for the above reasons that one can say that Sec. 8 is probably the least used section of the Clayton Act. It is probably for these reasons that the Reagan administration is considering relaxing the ban on interlocking directorates.

10.7 SUMMARY AND CONCLUSIONS

In this chapter we considered in some depth the antimerger provisions of Sec. 7 of the Clayton Act as amended by the 1950 Celler-Kefauver Act.

Sec. 7, as perceived by the courts, covers all types of mergers, namely, horizontal, vertical, and conglomerate. A horizontal merger is a fusion of two or more companies engaged in the same line of business. A vertical merger involves fusion of companies which stand in supplier-customer relationship. A merger that is neither horizontal nor vertical is called a conglomerate merger; in such a merger a company engaged in one line of business may acquire a company engaged in a wholly dissimilar line of business.

We discussed briefly the reasons why mergers take place. Some of the reasons are: economies of scale, weeding out inefficient management, improving the efficiency of capital markets, and salvaging a failing but potentially viable company.

Despite their beneficial effects, mergers are controlled by Sec. 7 of the Clayton Act. As interpreted by the courts, the primary goal of this section is to prevent the concentration of economic power in the hands of a few sellers by encouraging potential competition and by preserving small businesses. Perhaps the courts are echoing the congressional sentiment to that effect, although such a sentiment is not expressly stated in Sec. 7.

Turning to the working of Sec. 7, we first discussed the key phrases of the section, namely, "line of commerce," "section of country," and "may be substantially to lessen competition." It was argued that the Supreme Court's interpretation of these terms has not been always consistent.

We then considered four landmark cases: *Brown Shoe, Philadelphia National Bank, Von's Grocery,* and *Procter & Gamble* (Clorox). Although the facts of each case vary, the final outcomes were the same, namely, in each case the merger was deemed a violation of Sec. 7. All these cases were decided largely by the pro-small business goal attributed to Sec. 7 and the fear of a "rising trend of concentration" in the American economy. The outcome has been severely criticized by legal scholars. Bork calls Sec. 7 a "virulently anticompetitive regulation." But this may be a polar view.

We also considered in this chapter Sec. 8 of the Clayton Act which puts limitations on interlocking directorates. The main concern of this section is that if the same person is allowed to be on the boards of directors of two or more competing companies, competition is likely to be stifled between or among them. In practice, however, Sec. 8 has been used infrequently for several reasons, not the least of which is the government's "unenthusiastic enforcement" policy.

QUESTIONS

10-1 Critically evaluate: "Mergers are an important mechanism in the creation of social wealth." (Bork, op. cit., p. 226.)

10-2 Can you make a strong case why small businesses need the kind of protection attributed to the amended Sec. 7 of the Clayton Act?

10-3 State with reasons whether you agree with the statement: "Antitrust's concern with vertical mergers is mistaken. Vertical mergers are means of creating efficiency, not of injuring competition." (Bork, op. cit., p. 226.)

10-4 It seems that the law makes a distinction between vertical mergers and vertical growth (i.e., a firm undertaking backward or forward integration by self-expansion) in that it looks at the former with great suspicion whereas the latter seems somehow commendable. Is there any real difference between vertical mergers and vertical growth? Is the law's bias against growth by vertical merger justified? What factors may a firm take into account in deciding on growth by vertical merger versus vertical growth?

10-5 In the *Von's Grocery* case the majority adopted the view that competition is necessarily reduced when the number of competing sellers has declined. Is this really so? Was this true of the grocery industry in the Los Angeles area in which Von operated?

10-6 Comment critically: "The doctrine of potential competition was introduced into antitrust law by the Supreme Court, and the Court can abandon it – and it should do so." (Richard A. Posner, *Antitrust Law, An Economic Perspective,* The University of Chicago Press, Chicago, 1976, p. 123.)

10-7 Do you agree with the following statement? Why or why not?
" . . . collusion is more likely the less elastic is the demand for the output of the potentially colluding firms at the competitive price and the lower are the costs of collusion." (Posner, op. cit., p. 114.)

10-8 What lesson(s) can you draw from the following episode. In October 1957, Purex, Clorox's nearest competitor, decided to enter the previously unexplored market of Erie, Pennsylvania, where the leaders in the (bleach) market were Clorox, with 52 percent of the market, and Gardner Manufacturing Company (with its "101" brand), with a market share of 29 percent. Purex launched a vigorous advertising and promotional campaign to test one of its new brands in Erie. Within 5 months it captured 33 percent of the market. As a result, the market shares of Clorox and "101" dwindled to 33 and 17 percent, respectively. Clorox countered the Purex entry into Erie by reducing the price of its bleach in that market and by offering a $1 value ironing board cover for 50 cents with every purchase of Clorox bleach. Simultaneously, it stepped up its advertising on local TV. As a result, Clorox not only gained its original market share but increased it slightly, while Purex's market share toppled to 7 percent. (Scenario from Phillip Areeda, op. cit., p. 791, fn. 3)

10-9 In what way(s) can you say that the *Brown Shoe* decision was anticonsumer?

10-10 What are the similarities and dissimilarities between the cases of *Brown Shoe* and *Von's Grocery*? What was the overriding concern of the Supreme Court in both these cases?

10-11 Do you agree with Bork when he states that, "*Brown Shoe* was a disaster for rational, consumer-oriented merger policy." (Bork op. cit., p. 216.)

10-12 Recall the Clorox case. Do you think that Procter & Gamble would have entered the household bleach market if it were not to acquire Clorox? What factors would

Procter & Gamble take into account if it were to enter that market on its own? Based on these factors, do you think the Procter & Gamble acquisition of Clorox was economically justifiable?

10-13 Should there be a law (e.g., Sec. 7) that applies more strict standards to size by merger than to size by internal growth? Why or why not?

10-14 From the material presented in the text what do you think has been the attitude of the courts toward horizontal, vertical, and conglomerate mergers?

10-15 Is there any merit to the statement: "If a society were to intervene in every activity which might possibly lead to a reduction of competition, regulation would be ubiquitous and the whole purpose of a public policy of competition would be frustrated." (George Stigler, "Mergers and Preventive Antitrust Policy," *University of Pennsylvania Law Review,* vol. 104, pp. 176–177).

10-16 Critically evaluate the Department of Justice's Merger Guidelines, pointing out their strengths and their weaknesses.

10-17 *Federal Trade Commission v. Consolidated Foods Corporation,* 380 U.S. 592 (1965): Consolidated Foods Corporation, a large food processor and distributor, acquired Gentry, Inc., a manufacturer of dehydrated onion and garlic. The FTC held that the acquisition violated Sec. 7 of the Clayton Act because it created the danger of "reciprocal buying" whereby Consolidated, being a large buyer, would force its suppliers to buy onion and garlic from Gentry, products which are used by the suppliers. The FTC alleged that this would lessen competition substantially because other producers of dehydrated onion and garlic would find a part of their market foreclosed.

The U.S. Court for the Seventh Circuit reversed the FTC finding largely on the ground that the 10-year postacquisition history showed that while Gentry's share of the dehydrated onion market had increased by 7 percent, its share of the garlic market had declined by 20 percent, this, according to the court, shows the ineffectiveness of reciprocity. On appeal to the Supreme Court, however, the finding of the FTC was sustained. Justice Douglas, speaking for the majority, accepted the argument by the FTC that "if reciprocal buying creates for Gentry a protected market, which others cannot penetrate despite superiority of price, quality or service, competition is lessened whether or not Gentry can expand its market share."

Do you agree with the Supreme Court's decision? Does the verdict imply that reciprocity-creating mergers are invalid per se? If you were told that in 1950, immediately prior to the merger, Gentry had 32 percent of the market share in the two products and its principal competitor, Basic Vegetable Products, Inc., had 58 of the market share (the two thus accounting for 90 percent of the market), and that 8 years after the merger the shares of the two rivals were 35 and 55 percent, respectively, would this knowledge change your opinion about the decision? Why or why not?

10-18 *Ford Motor Company v. United States,* 405 U.S. 562, (1972): The Ford Motor Company's acquisition of the assets of the Electric Autolite Company (Autolite) in 1961 was deemed by the government a violation of Sec. 7 of the Clayton Act. The assets included the Autolite trade name, Autolite's only spark plug plant in the country, a battery plant, and extensive rights to its nationwide distributional organization. The case involved only the Autolite name and the spark plug plant.

In the spark plug industry there were three major competitors: Autolite, Champion plugs, and General Motor's AC brand, with market shares of 15, 50, and 30 percent, respectively, in 1960. Ford considered entering into the spark plug business itself but decided agains that course of action because it would have taken the company about 5 to 8 years to penetrate the market and that it would have been costlier than the acquisition.

The district court held that the acquisition had the effect of substantially lessening competition for these reasons: First, Ford remained a potential entrant in the spark plug business and second, the acquisition marked "the foreclosure of Ford as a purchaser of about 10 percent of total industry output."

In the decree ordering the divestiture of the acquisition these conditions, among others, were laid down: (1) Ford is prohibited from producing spark plugs on its own for 10 years; (2) Ford is to purchase for 5 years one-half of its total spark plug requirements from the divested plant under the Autolite name; (3) also for a period of 5 years, Ford cannot use its own name on spark plugs; and (4) Ford is to require the purchaser of the divested plant to assume the existing wage and pension obligations of the employees of the Autolite plant at New Fostoria and to offer employment to any employee displaced by a transfer of nonplug operations from the divested plant.

The majority of the Supreme Court justices concurred with the decision of the district court.

Do you think it was a fair decision? Even if the decision was fair, do you think the decree was severe? If General Motors could produce its own spark plugs, why could Ford not do so immediately after the divestiture, that is, why the 10-year waiting period? What is the logic behind requiring Ford to purchase half its spark plug requirements for 5 years from the divested Autolite plant? In what way does this provision increase competition?

PART THREE

ECONOMIC REGULATION

From the general purpose regulation we now turn our attention to industry or product-specific economic regulation. As noted in Chapter 1, economic regulation is largely concerned with the determination of prices, rate of return on capital, output level, and entry into and exit from industry. We specifically consider five areas of economic regulation: railroad and trucking (Chapter 11), civil aviation (Chapter 12), energy (Chapter 13), securities markets (Chapter 14), and broadcasting and telecommunications (Chapter 15).

In each case we follow more or less a common format: the history of regulation, the administrative structure created to administer the regulation, its working, a critical evaluation of what has been accomplished vis-à-vis the goals of the enabling statutes, and some of the recent deregulatory initiatives. Wherever possible, we consider pertinent empirical evidence bearing on one or more aspects of the regulation so that the reader will have a better appreciation of some of the complexities as well as some of the controversies surrounding many economic regulations.

Although each episode is somewhat unique, there are some common themes that consistently emerge from these five regulatory experiences: (1) Regulation is initially justified to remedy one or more market failures discussed in Chapter 2 but lingers on even if the original justification no longer exists. (2) This is because in due course the regulators become captive of the regulated, who tend to manipulate the regulators to seek regulation beneficial to themselves. (3) The regulated protect their self-interest by obtaining entry restrictions, dividing markets among themselves, padding the rate base to obtain higher rates of return, charging one group of consumers more than some others (the charges not reflecting any cost differences), using the method of cross-subsidization to justify certain pricing practices, and the like. (4) All these practices, in varying degrees, lead to economic inefficiencies or deadweight losses, but they are often continued in the name of equity or public interest. (5) These practices ultimately reach a point where they cannot be justified any longer and some move toward deregulating one or more of these practices is made. In all the industries studied in this part, in every one of them the trend toward deregulation is quite visible, although it is not as dramatic as in the case of airline deregulation.

These five regulatory experiences do not exhaust the entire field of economic regulation. They are intended to provide a frame of reference against which the reader can examine other economic regulations to see (1) whether the features of economic regulation mentioned above are present in those experiences also, and if so (2) whether (and why) they too follow the trend toward deregulation that we have seen in these five examples.

CHAPTER 11

THE ICC AND THE REGULATION OF THE RAILROAD AND TRUCKING INDUSTRIES

Economic regulation in the United States can be said to have begun with the establishment of the Interstate Commerce Commission (ICC) following the Interstate Commerce Act of 1887. Although the commission was originally created to regulate the railroad industry, over the years its mandate has been extended to regulate all means of surface transportation, such as trucking companies, bus lines, freight forwarders, water carriers, oil pipelines, transportation brokerage companies, and express agencies. After discussing the history, goals, organizational structure, and functions of the ICC, we will devote the bulk of this chapter to a critical evaluation of the commission's role in the regulation of the railroad and trucking industries (historically and quantitatively, the two industries most affected by ICC regulatory activity). We will also discuss in some detail the recent trend toward deregulation of these industries and the controversies it has generated.

11.1 THE ORIGIN AND OBJECTIVES OF THE ICC[1]

Section 8 of Article 1 of the Constitution authorizes Congress the right to "regulate commerce with foreign nations, and among several states . . . [and also] to make all laws which shall be necessary and proper for carrying into execution the foregoing powers. . . ." This presumably meant that Congress could regulate interstate rail commerce.

---

[1]The following discussion draws on: "Federal Regulation and Regulatory Reform," *Report by the Subcommittee on Oversight and Investigations of the Committee on Interstate and Foreign Commerce,* House of Representatives, 94th Cong., 2d Sess., October 1976, ch. 9 (hereafter, referred to as the House *Study on Federal Regulation*).

However, up until 1887, Congress chose not to do so. Before then it was believed that the railroads were so highly essential to national commerce that their growth should be encouraged as much as possible. Toward that end, the federal and state governments granted the railroad companies loans, land grants, and charters with few restrictions. As a result, there was rapid growth of the industry, from 3 miles of track in 1828 to 125,000 miles in 1885. But this growth was not unblemished. Liberal loan and charter policies created powerful railroad oligopolies, a few companies dominating the industry (recall the battles between Drew-Gould-Fisk and Vanderbilt to acquire railroad monopoly). There were also too many crisscrossing railroad lines and not enough traffic to support them. This led to fierce competition among the railroads for available traffic, which resulted in certain questionable practices, such as charging more for the short haul (i.e., short distance) than the long haul,[2] not basing price discrimination on cost differences, granting rebates to large shippers to the discomfort of small farmers, and controlling the economies of large areas by monopolizing nontransportation industries in those areas and thereby making them a captive clientele for the railroad services. The Grange movement alluded to previously was the farmers' response to these questionable practices. Despite these practices, the financial plight of the railroads was quite precarious: In 1885, their combined indebtedness was four times the size of the federal debt!

Recognizing the danger of the growing power of the railroads, several states decided to regulate them on their own. In this they were aided by the Supreme Court's *Munn v. Illinois,* 94 U.S. 113 (1877) decision, which upheld the right of the state of Illinois to regulate grain elevators even though these elevators were involved in interstate commerce, an area presumably of federal concern. By 1887, there were about twenty-five states with railroad regulatory agencies. But in most cases these agencies were weak and were certainly no match for the powerful railroad oligopolies. Moreover, whatever limited regulatory power they had was dealt a severe blow by the 1886 Supreme Court decision in *Wabash, St. Louis and R.R. v. Illinois,* 118 U.S. 557 (1886). This decision effectively stated that the states could regulate only intrastate railroad operations, particularly the railroad rates; interstate railroad operations were deemed the responsibility of the Congress.

The *Wabash* decision practically emasculated any regulatory authority the states had. But it was this decision that ultimately promoted Congress to pass the Interstate Commerce Commission Act of 1887 to regulate the nation's railroads. The act created the ICC, the first independent regulatory commission (it actually became independent in 1889), with the objective of promoting safe, adequate, and economical service in surface transportation. The commission was further entrusted with the responsibility of fostering a healthy economic

---

[2]This is cross-subsidization as discussed in Ch. 2. There we discussed why such cross-subsidization may not be conducive to efficient allocation of economic resources. For a technical discussion on cross-subsidization, see Section 11.7 as well as Section 2.6 and Ch. 4.

environment for carrier operations while encouraging the creation of reasonable charges for transportation services without unjust discrimination, undue
preferences or advantages, or unfair or destructive competitive practices.[3]

Despite the preceding mandate, the commission's ability to regulate the railroads up until 1897 may be characterized as nominal, for its decisions were still
dependent on voluntary compliance by the railroads. But more importantly, the
ICC Act did not spell out clearly what the functions of the commission were to
be. As a consequence, some of its early decisions were turned over by the
Supreme Court, as we will see shortly.

11.2   THE EVOLUTION OF U.S. TRANSPORTATION POLICIES
AND THE EXPANSION OF THE MANDATE OF THE ICC

The first challenge to the regulatory authority of the ICC came in *Interstate
Commerce Commission v. Alabama Midland Railroad Company,* 168 U.S. 144
(1897). In that case the Supreme Court held that there were circumstances
under which more could be charged for the short than the long haul and that
the commission did not have the power to forbid short haul–long haul price
differentials pending a full review of the facts; the commission had interpreted
its mandate about nondiscriminatory pricing to mean the prohibition of such
short haul–long haul price differences. In *Maximum Freight Rate,* 167 U.S. 479
(1897) the Supreme Court declared that the commission did not have the power
to set new rates to correct the existing rates, that power being legislative and
not judicial, executive, or administrative. In other words, in the Court's view the
commission is partly a judicial and partly an executive-administrative body but
not a legislative one. The Court's decisions in the cases of *United States v. Trans-
Missouri Freight Association,* 166 U.S. 290 (1897) and *Joint Traffic Association,*
171 U.S. 505 (1898) prohibited the ICC from approving the rates set by railroad
traffic associations (the rate bureaus) because they violated the Sherman Antitrust Act of 1890. As we will discuss later, the ICC favored such collective rate
making and the Congress went along with this decision by amending the ICC
Act in 1948 (see the Reed-Bulwinkle Act of 1948, below).

The upshot of all these adverse decisions was to render the commission practically a toothless regulatory agency. They had one salutary effect on the Congress, however: That august body was forced to define more clearly the commission's regulatory mission. And Congress took that challenge up by passing a
series of laws which not only ''clarified'' the mission of the ICC but increasingly

---

[3]It may be noted that the terms *unjust discrimination, undue preferences,* and *destructive competition* used by the framers of the act are not necessarily in conformity with the economist's definition of them. Thus, as noted in Ch. 6, in terms of the antitrust laws, ''price discrimination'' simply
means a price difference; to the economist it means charging different prices to different customers
for the same good or service, the differences not related to the differences in their marginal cost
of production. ''Destructive competition'' probably refers to the practice of ''predatory'' price-
cutting mentioned in the chapters on antitrust laws (see the *Utah Pie* decision).

burdened the agency with additional responsibilities (a development that may be the root cause of some of the regulatory problems of the agency, a topic that will be explored fully later).

The various laws that were enacted by Congress are as follows.

The Elkins Antirebating Act of 1903

To prevent secret rebates and other rate-cutting devices, Congress passed this act, which outlawed rates other than those filed with the ICC. In effect, price competition was ruled out.

The Hepburn Act of 1906

Pushed by the ICC (because of the *Maximum Freight Rate* case) and supported by President Theodore Roosevelt, Congress strengthened the commission's regulatory power by enacting the Hepburn Act in 1906. This act declared that the commission did indeed have important "quasi-legislative" as well as "quasi-judicial" and administrative responsibilities. Under the act:

1 The commission could prescribe maximum rates for the future.

2 The commission's rate-regulatory orders were to be effective immediately after announcement and to remain so unless set aside by the courts.

3 The scope of the ICC Act of 1887 was extended to include express companies, sleeping car companies, and pipeline companies transporting oil.

4 The Commodity Clause was established. It prohibited the railroads from transporting commodities (other than timber) which they themselves produced or owned. This was done to prevent the railroads from monopolizing nontransportation industries in the areas of their operation and causing those industries to become a captive market for the railroad services.

5 The size of the commission was increased from five to seven members (increased to nine in 1917 and further increased to eleven subsequently), the term of office was increased from six to seven years, and the salaries of the commissioners as well as their power to obtain information was also increased.

The net effect of the Hepburn Act was to make the commission an effective regulatory agency, and the commission has since been able to regulate the railroad industry more directly.

The Mann-Elkins Act of 1910

This act increased the powers of the ICC further. In particular, the act

1 Empowered the commission to suspend any rate changes effected by the railroads on their own and put the burden of proving the necessity of the changes on them

2 Authorized the commission to put restrictions on the short-haul–long-haul rate differentials

3 Established a commerce court to review ICC decisions. (This court was abolished by Congress later when it was found that the court had turned over a number of ICC decisions)

4 Gave the commission new power over telegraph, telephone, and cable lines

The Transportation Act of 1920

Since the Hepburn Act of 1906, the perception of Congress toward the railroad problem had changed. Prior to 1920, the primary emphasis of the legislation was on preventing the railroads from establishing abusive monopolistic practices (cited earlier in this chapter); the ICC Act of 1887, the Sherman Antitrust Act of 1890, and the FTC Act of 1914 were all concerned with such practices. But since 1920 the objective of the Congress was to help the railroads provide reliable service by achieving financial stability (competition from the trucking industry was looming on the horizon although it was not yet intense). This changed philosophy of regulation meant that the commission and the railroads became partners rather than antagonists (the capture theory of regulation?). Under the act the commission was given the power to do the following:

1 Fix a fair rate of return for the railroads at 6 percent
2 Set minimum rates; it already had the power to set maximum rates
3 Specify the types of services the carriers could provide
4 Control entry into and exit from the industry
5 Approve or disapprove consolidations and mergers of the railroads

Commenting on the significance of the 1920 act, Roger Noll wrote:

The Transportation Act of 1920 was the first of a series of laws passed over the course of two decades that embodied an entirely new type of mandate. First, the laws were often distinctly anti-competitive rather than antimonopoly. The power to set minimum rates and the duty to oversee the orderly development of an industry — the principal additions of the 1920 act to the ICC's responsibilities — have a distinctly different philosophy than did the maximum-rate regulation and the clear prohibition against the short-haul, long-haul rate differentials which were established in 1887. Second, the delegation of responsibility to the regulatory agency ceased being specific. No longer was the mandate simply to present certain reasonable well understood (if not well defined) practices. Agencies were now given very general, unspecified authority to manage an industry in the ''public interest''. The thrust of these two additions to the responsibilities of regulation was to make regulatory agencies a form of legal cartel for regulated firms. Activities that would be clear violations of antitrust statutes if practiced by trade associations or informal meetings of industry executives were permitted and even condoned if overseen by regulators.[4]

In short, the regulated captured the regulators!

---

[4]Roger G. Noll, *Reforming Regulation,* Brookings, Washington, D.C., 1971, pp. 37–38.

The Motor Carrier Act of 1935

Although the truckers had begun competing with the railroads for business, this competition did not pose a serious threat to the railroads until the onset of the great depression. During the depression, an increasing number of shippers, especially the farmers, turned their business away from the railroads to the truckers largely because of the inflexibility of the cartel- (i.e., rate bureau-) determined railway rates.

The shippers switched also because the railroads refused to change their "value-of-service" rate structure, a type of price discrimination whereby rates were based on the commodities transported rather than on the cost of transporting them. Thus, they charged higher rates per ton-mile for watches than for furniture, and higher rates for furniture than for coal. The theory presumably was that the demand for transportation by the more valuable commodities was price-inelastic while that by the lower-value commodities was price-elastic. Therefore, the theory goes, if the railroads charge a uniform per ton-mile price across all commodities, they will lose the lower-value traffic; railroad capacity would hence remain underutilized. So long as the rates charged on the lower-value traffic are greater than the incremental or marginal cost of carrying such traffic, the value of service price-discrimination (actually cross-subsidization) practiced by the railroads not only will utilize their capacity more fully but also the added traffic will contribute something to the common (i.e., overhead) costs. (See our discussion of price discrimination by a monopolist in Chs. 6 and 9.)

As Alfred Kahn argues, such a theory "may well have been appropriate when railroads had a virtual monopoly. It became irrelevant once trucks were available to compete for that business. The common carrier truckers, in general, merely matched the rail rates; and because of the superiority of their service (greater speed and door-to-door delivery, without need for intermediate loading and unloading) they were able in this way to take away the bulk of this more valuable business."[5] (Recall from Chapter 2 that a natural monopoly (e.g., a railroad) is only "natural" in a given technological or economic environment.)

Alarmed by the inroads made by the truckers, the railroads clamored for regulation of the trucking industry. Some of the truckers themselves wanted to be regulated because of rate-juggling and the "cut-throat" competition in which some truckers were engaged during the depths of the depression. Some of the shippers, too, favored regulation to ensure stable rates and scheduled services. From all these demands emerged the Motor Carrier Act of 1935. The only group which opposed regulation were the farmers, who obviously relished the lower rates they got from the truckers.

The main objectives of the act were:

1 To increase financial stability in the trucking industry

2 To balance the interests of the railroads as well as the truckers to "equalize" competitive conditions

3 To provide the shippers a broader range of surface transportation

[5]Alfred E. Kahn, *The Economics of Regulation: Principles and Institutions,* vol. II, Wiley, New York, 1971, p. 14.

The act divided the interstate trucking industry into three classes:

Common Carriers These are carriers available to the public to carry all persons or goods. The act required the ICC to regulate these carriers by "requiring them to obtain certificates of convenience and necessity which specify the services to be rendered and the routes over which the carrier is authorized to operate" and further "requiring that all rates must be reasonable and non-discriminatory." The commission was also authorized to prescribe the maximum, minimum, and actual rates for these carriers and was allowed to suspend rates up to a period of 7 months.

Contract Carriers These are carriers which offer specialized services for particular shippers and deal with only a few shippers. Under the act, these carriers "must obtain a permit, providing that they are fit, willing and able to perform the contract service consistent with public interest and the national transportation policy."

Exempt Carriers These are carriers which haul their owner's goods (private carriers); motor vehicles owned by railroads, water carriers, or freight forwarders incidental to their business; local carriage; vehicles carrying fish, livestock, or agricultural commodities; trucks exclusively carrying newspapers; and trucks owned and operated by agricultural cooperatives.

After the passage of the 1935 act, the ICC set truck rates for common carriers on levels comparable to those charged by the railroads and brought the previously competitive truck rates in "alignment" with the rail rates. This was obviously done to protect the interests of the railroads, which had a "moral" claim on the commission, being the first to be regulated (the first-regulated, first-served capture theory?). Needless to say, the anticompetitive spirit ushered in by the Transportation Act of 1920 was carried to the trucking industry, all in the name of a balanced transportation policy!

The Transportation Act of 1940

Despite the 1920 and 1935 acts, the railroad industry continued to be sick. By 1938, the financial plight of the railroads worsened so much that President Franklin D. Roosevelt appointed two committees to undertake a comprehensive study of the industry. The recommendations of these committees ultimately led to the passage of the Transportation Act of 1940. This act tried to spell out anew the mandate of the ICC, a mandate which had by then become very broad and confusing. The preamble to this act states, in part, that the national transportation policy of the Congress is:

1 To provide for fair and impartial regulation of all modes of transportation so administered as to recognize and preserve the inherent advantage of each.
2 To promote safe, adequate, economical and efficient service and foster sound economic conditions in transportation and among the several carriers.

3 To encourage the establishment and maintenance of reasonable charges for transportation services without unjust discriminations, undue preferences or advantages, or unfair or destructive competitive practices.

" . . . all the above to the end of developing, co-ordinating, and preserving a national transportation system by water, highway, and rail, as well as other means, adequate to meet the needs of the commerce of the United States, of the Postal Service, and of the national defense."

One of the significant provisions of the 1940 act was to extend the commission's authority to the regulation of water carriers. Although few water carriers were actually affected because of the other provisions of the ICC Act, the change was effected to improve the competitive position of the railroad. Like the truckers, the water carriers now became a threat to the survival of the rail-road industry.

The Reed-Bulwinkle Act of 1948

This act, amending the ICC Act of 1887, recognized the legality of the rates determined by industry associations or the rate bureaus and brought them under the commission's regulation. This was done to protect the cartel-determined rates from antitrust suits. The philosophy of this act is thus contrary to the goals of the Sherman Antitrust Act, but this was all done in the name of industry survival and stability — objectives which are hard to defend on grounds of allocative efficiency.

The Transportation Act of 1958

All the previous efforts to rescue the ailing railroads proved fruitless; the financial plight of the railroads continued to worsen due, in large measure, to the diversion of traffic to the trucking industry. This act provided, for the first time, guaranteed loans to the financially troubled railroad companies to stave off bankruptcies.

The 1970 Passenger Service Act

Notwithstanding the 1958 act, the financial health of the railroads, especially in the northeast corridor (Boston–New York–Washington, D.C., New Haven–Springfield, Harrisburg–Philadelphia), continued to decline so much so that railroads, such as Boston and Maine, Central of New Jersey, Erie-Lackawana, Lehigh Valley, Penn Central, and Reading went into bankruptcies. The most startling bankruptcy was that of the Penn Central, which earned about 38 percent of the eastern district's total revenue; in 1971 its revenue was $1.8 billion and it operated 19,864 miles of rail lines. Even those railroads which were solvent earned a distressingly low rate of return on equity; in 1970 and 1971 the industry as a whole earned almost zero rate of return on the stockholders' equity.

The bankruptcies and the precarious financial health of the survivors posed the threat of loss of several intercity passenger train services. To avoid this, Congress passed the Passenger Service Act of 1970 and created Amtrak (National Railroad Passenger Corporation), a fully independent but for-profit quasi-government company, to take over bankrupt rail passenger transportation lines. The ICC was given the added responsibility of establishing and enforcing standards of adequate service by the railroads operating intercity passenger trains.

The Regional Rail Recovery Act of 1973

This act was yet another congressional attempt to rescue the declining railroad industry. Its objectives were: "to restore, support and maintain modern, efficient rail service in the Northeast region of the U.S.; to designate a system of essential rail lines in the Northeast region, and to provide financial assistance to certain carriers."

The act created the United States Railway Association (USRA) with the mandate of developing a "final" plan to reorganize the railroads of the northeastern and midwestern regions. It also directed the ICC to establish a Rail Service Planning Office to evaluate and assist in the preparation of the final plan. The act further established another quasi-government corporation, Consolidated Rail Corporation (Conrail), to take over selected northeastern and midwestern railroads upon the completion of the final system plan.

The Railroad Revitalization and Regulation Act of 1976 (The 4R Act):

Realizing for the first time that all the previous efforts to save the railroads were at best of marginal significance and that they addressed only the symptoms and not the root cause of the railroad problem, Congress passed the Railroad Revitalization and Regulation Act, the 4R Act, in 1976. The act calls for the "elimination of needless or harmful regulatory constraints on railroads, and prescribe[s] ratemaking practices which will encourage effective competition and protect consumers."

The preamble to the act explains that it is the policy of the Congress to:

1 Balance the needs of carriers, shippers, and the public

2 Foster competition among all carriers by railroad and other modes of transportation, to promote more adequate and efficient transportation services, and to increase the attractiveness of investing in railroads and rail-service-related enterprises

3 Permit railroads greater freedom to raise or lower rates for rail services in competitive markets

4 Promote the establishment of railroad rate structures which are more sensitive to changes in the level of seasonal, regional, and shipper demand

5 Promote separate pricing of distinct rail and rail-related services

6 Formulate standards and guidelines for determining adequate revenue levels for railroads

7 Modernize and clarify the functions of railroad rate bureaus

Title III of the act contains provisions to reform and improve the commission's regulation of the railroads. Among other things, it requires the commission to cut delay in the issuance of its orders, to establish a permanent Office of Rail Public Counsel, to prohibit discriminatory tax treatment of transportation property, to develop a uniform cost and revenue accounting system, to make the Rail Services Planning Office permanent, and to conduct a modernization and revision of the ICC Act.

The 4R Act represents a radical departure in congressional thinking about the railroad problem; the emphasis has now shifted from protection to competition, at least in some aspects such as price flexibility, seasonal pricing, etc. We will examine this act and the regulatory activity of the ICC more thoroughly in Sections 11.5 and 11.7.

The Staggers Rail Act of 1980

This act legislates one of the objectives of the 1976 4R Act, namely, to permit the railroads greater freedom to raise or lower rates for rail services in competitive markets. It allows the railroads more flexibility in setting rates and more authority to enter into long-term contracts with freight shippers. More importantly, it permits the railroads to drop uneconomical rail routes more easily; in the past the commission required the railroads to operate economically unprofitable routes pending the commission's hearings, which were often protracted.

The Motor Carrier Act of 1980

Just as the 4R Act marked a significant change in congressional attitude toward the railroads, the Motor Carrier Act of 1980 represents a substantial modification in congressional views about the trucking industry. As with the railroads, Congress realized that the trucking industry had become highly regulated, leading to monopoly profits and generally higher rate structures not justified by the economics of trucking transportation. We will examine this act in some depth in Section 11.9.

11.3 A SUMMARY OF U.S. SURFACE TRANSPORTATION POLICY

From the preceding discussion, we can distinguish four periods in the development of U.S. transportation policy, namely, prior to 1920, 1920 to 1957, 1958 to 1975, and 1976 to date. In the period prior to 1920, the ICC was responsible for regulating the railroad industry only. The primary thrust of regulation was against monopolistic practices of the railroads. But the effectiveness of the commission's regulatory activity was hampered by a lack of clarity about the precise functions of the commission. As a result, there were successful challenges in the courts against several of the commission's decisions, especially those relating to rate determination and rate structure.

Because of the Transportation Act of 1920, the Motor Carrier Act of 1935, and the Transportation Act of 1940, the period 1920 to 1957 saw a tremendous growth in the mandate and power of the commission. But unlike that of the previous period, the commission's attitude toward regulation was pro-industry rather than pro-competition. It was felt that the declining railroad industry and the growing trucking industry both needed rate and entry protection to secure financial stability. But there was a definite bias in favor of the railroad industry, perhaps because it was the first to be regulated but largely because it was continually in financial trouble.

The period 1958 to 1975 may be characterized as the period in which Congress passed haphazard and piecemeal measures to help the financially dying railroad industry, but to no avail.

The period since 1976 represents the general "deregulation mood" prevailing in the Congress; it was heralded by the passage of the Airline Deregulation Act of 1978 (see Chapter 12 for details). The 4R Act of 1976 and the Staggers Rail Act of 1980 are an explicit admission that the root cause of the railroad problem was past regulation itself (or the way it was implemented, e.g., in pursuit of the goal of price stability, the ICC encouraged the rate bureaus to determine the rates, which in fact led to rate rigidity and monopolistic rate structures). Likewise, the Motor Carrier Act of 1980 recognized that the lack of competitive rate structure in the trucking industry was also due to regulation or the way it was carried out.

The U.S. transportation policy, which was pro-competition before 1920, pro-industry between 1920 to 1957, and in a state of limbo between 1958 to 1975, is again pro-competition as of 1976. Although it is too early to tell the ultimate effect of the changed mood, whatever fragmentary evidence is available seems to be beneficial to the consumer (but more on this later)

11.4 IMPLEMENTATION OF THE MANDATE: THE SCOPE, ORGANIZATIONAL STRUCTURE, AND COMPLIANCE PROCEDURES OF THE ICC

The ICC Act of 1887 established the Interstate Commerce Commission as the agency to carry out the mandate of the original act which, as pointed out in the previous section, has been extended substantially over the years. In this section we discuss briefly the scope of ICC activities, its organizational structure, and its compliance procedure.

The Scope of ICC Regulatory Power

By the original ICC Act and its subsequent modifications, the ICC now regulates all forms of surface transportation, namely, railroads, trucks, barges, oil pipelines, freight forwarders, transportation brokers, and express agencies, but not with equal intensity. For example, it regulates 100 percent of the railroads but 50 to 60 percent of the motor carriers and only 10 percent of the water carriers.

For the regulated carriers, the commission's regulatory mission falls into three broad categories: transportation economics, transportation services, and consumer protection.[6]

Transportation Economics   In this area, the commission

1 Approves or disapproves maximum, minimum, or exact rates. (This authority is now modified by the Motor Carrier Act of 1980 and the Staggers Rail Act of 1980, which have made rate flexibility and rate competitiveness the important goals of deregulation)

2 Settles controversies over rates and charges among competing and like modes of transportation, shippers and receivers of freight, passengers, and others

3 Rules upon application for mergers, consolidations, acquisitions of control, and the sale of carriers and issuance of their securities

4 Prescribes accounting rules, awards reparations, and administers laws relating to bankruptcy

5 Acts to prevent unlawful discrimination, destructive competition, and rebating

6 Has jurisdiction over the use, control, supply, movement, distribution, exchange, interchange, and return of railroad equipment

7 Is authorized, under certain circumstances, to direct the handling and movement of traffic over a railroad and its distribution over other lines of railroads

Transportation Service   In this area, the commission

1 Grants the right to operate to trucking companies, bus lines, freight forwarders, water carriers, and transportation brokers

2 Approves applications to construct or abandon lines of railroads

3 Rules upon the discontinuance of passenger train service

Consumer Protection   In the realm of consumer protection, the commission assures that the public obtains full measure of all transportation service to which entitlement is guaranteed by the various acts. The Rail Service Planning Office, established by the Rail Reorganization Act of 1973 and made permanent by the 1976 4R Act, is entrusted to assure that public interest is represented in the restructuring and revitalization of railroads, especially the railroads in the northeast and midwestern regions.

The Organizational Structure of the ICC

To carry out its huge mandate, the ICC is constituted as shown in Figure 11.1. The commission consists of eleven members or commissioners who are

[6]The following discussion is drawn from the *United States Government Manual, 1978–1979,* Office of the Federal Register, National Archives and Record Service in the General Services Administration (hereafter referred to as *Government Manual*).

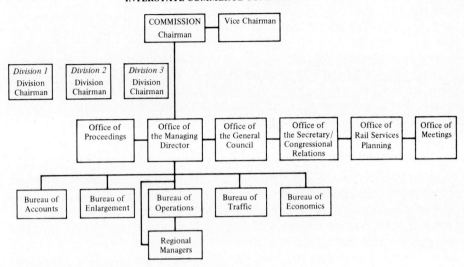

INTERSTATE COMMERCE COMMISSION

Bureau of Enforcement   The agency's prosecutor, charged with enforcing civil and penal provisions of the act and related statutes. The bureau also takes part in specific ICC proceedings to assist in developing facts and issues in the public interest.

Bureau of Operations   Maintains close liaison with the activities of railroads, motor, carriers, water carriers, freight forwarders, and rate bureaus to ensure that these industries operate in compliance with ICC policies.

Bureau of Traffic   Is concerned with the publication, filing and interpretation of tariffs, and their suspension before they become effective if they appear unreasonable or unlawful.

Bureau of Accounts   Is concerned with the accounting phases of effective economic regulation—prescribing uniform accounting rules, auditing carriers' books and reviewing financial reports.

Bureau of Economics   Performs transportation research and conducts economic and statistical analysis relating to regulation and to specific proceedings before the agency.

Office of Proceedings   Processes formal cases pertaining to operating rights, financial matters, rates and competitive practices.

Office of the General Counsel   Defends commission orders if challenged in court. As "house counsel" the general counsel also renders legal opinions to the commission.

Office of the Secretary/Congressional Relations   The issuance and documentation center of the ICC. The secretary is custodian of the commission's seal and records and is responsible for issuing ICC decisions and orders.

Office of Hearings   Staff of administrative law judges responsible for conducting commission hearings.

Office of the Managing Director   Directs commission activities in respect to money, manpower, materials and methods.

Rail Services Planning Office   Was created to assure that the public interest was represented in the restructuring of railroads in the northeast. It now provides long-range planning support for the commission.

FIGURE 11.1
Organizational chart of ICC.

appointed by the President and confirmed by the Senate, the chairperson of the commission serving at the pleasure of the President. These commissioners serve staggered 7-year terms. Each commissioner, save the chairperson, is assigned to one of the commission's three working divisions, namely, Division 1 (Operating Rights), Division II (Rates and Practices), and Division III (Finance and Service). Each commissioner has his or her own personal staff.

As Figure 11.1 shows, the commission staff is organized into five major bureaus: Accounts, Enforcement, Operations, Traffic, and Economics, all under the general supervision of the managing director. The functions of each of these bureaus are listed in Figure 11.1. The rest of the commission's Washington staff is divided among the offices of General Counsel, Secretary of Congressional Relations, Office of Railway Services Planning, and Office of Hearings. Then there are several regional offices. In each regional office, a regional auditor reports to the Bureau of Accounts, a regional counsel reports to the Bureau of Enforcement, and a regional manager reports to the managing director.

The Compliance Procedures of the ICC

To discharge its law enforcement responsibilities, the commission employes both formal and informal methods, such as rule making, review of fitness, review of applications, review of investigations, etc. If one or more provisions of the ICC and related acts are violated, the commission may issue cease and desist orders proscribing certain practices. In case a criminal proceeding is called for, the commission refers the matter to the Department of Justice. Civil claim settlements, a responsibility of the Bureau of Enforcement, are generally handled within the framework of the Federal Claims Collection Act of 1906.

11.5   THE ICC AND RAILROAD REGULATION: A CRITICAL EVALUATION[7]

There is no question that the railroads have played a crucial role in the economic development of this country. Even today, they carry about 38 percent of all ton-miles of freight compared to 23 percent and 16 percent, respectively, by motor and inland water carriers, 70 percent of the automobile production in the country, 66 percent of the food, 78 percent of the lumber and wood, 60 percent of the chemicals, 60 percent of the primary metal products, and 70 percent of the pulp and paper. Even so, one can characterize the industry as a declining one, marred by extremely low rate of return on equity (less than 2 percent in recent years) and beset by bankruptcies, including the mammoth bankruptcy of the Penn Central. All the congressional attempts to resuscitate the industry between 1958 and 1976 failed. The big question is why? There are several factors responsible for the railroad decline; they can be grouped into two broad classes, external and internal.

External Factors in the Railroad Decline

Some of the external factors are as follows:

Trends in Intermodal Competition   An important factor in the decline has been the growth of alternative means of transportation, which can be seen from

[7]The following discussion has benefitted greatly from Paul W. MacAvoy and John W. Snow (eds.), *Railroad Revitalization and Regulatory Reform,* Ford Administration Papers on Regulatory Reform, American Enterprise Institute for Public Policy Research, Washington, D.C., 1977, ch. 1.

Tables 11.1 and 11.2. As this table shows, both in freight and intercity passenger traffic, the railroad's share between 1950 and 1976 declined from 57 percent to 36 percent for freight traffic and from 7 percent to 0.76 percent for passenger traffic, the slack being taken up by the other means of transportation. Although part of the decline is undoubtedly due to people's change in taste for transportation services, a large part is due to ICC regulation, as shown later.

Financial Vulnerability Due to Low Profits   Historically, the railroad industry has recorded relatively low profit rates because the industry is supposed to be a low-risk industry. But since 1967 the industry has experienced such low rates of return on equity (1.8 percent in 1967 to almost zero in 1970) that the industry has not been able to attract new capital to modernize many outdated rail lines. This has been one of the critical factors in the bankruptcies of several railroads. These bankruptcies have negative spillover or spillout effects on the surviving companies in the industry because the railroads are a national system and must rely on their interconnections to transact their freight business. Therefore, bankruptcies of one or more railroads are bound to affect the others. Because they cannot borrow easily to finance capital expansion, many railroads are forced to resort to lease capital, which is often expensive, thereby further aggravating the industry's financial problems.

Shifts in National Transportation Demand   The structural changes in the economy are another contributory factor. In recent years, the economy has shown relatively more growth in the service industries, such as finance, trade, and government (local as well as federal). But these industries have little demand for railroad services. On the other hand, the traditional demanders of the railroad services, such as agriculture, forestry, and mining have not prospered that much, thus affecting the railroads adversely.

Shifts in Government's Transportation Policies   Although the 1940 and 1976 transportation acts speak of a balanced transportation policy, in reality the government's policy is contrary to this goal. After supporting the railroad industry for a long time, the government's transportation policy, especially since World War II, has favored the trucking, inland waterways, and airline industries. As indications of this change, notice the massive infusion of federal funds in the development of interstate highway systems, in the improvement of inland waterways, in the construction of the Saint Lawrence Seaway, and in the financing of a network of airports and airways.

ICC Regulatory Policies   By far the most critical factor in the decline of the railroads seems to be the government's regulatory policies as carried out by the ICC. Some of these policies are as follows:

Rigid Price Structure   By prescribing minimum and maximum rates (and actual rates in some cases), and by not allowing the railroads to adjust the rate structure to changing economic conditions, the commission has established such rigidity in the railroad rates that the railroads cannot compete successfully with

TABLE 11.1

INTERCITY TRAFFIC

VOLUME OF DOMESTIC INTERCITY FREIGHT TRAFFIC, BY TYPE OF TRANSPORT: 1950–1976

(In billions of ton-miles, except percent. Prior to 1960, excludes Alaska and Hawaii, except as noted. A ton-mile is the movement of 1 ton (2000 pounds) of freight for the distance of 1 mile. Comprises public and private traffic, both revenue and nonrevenue. See also *Historical Statistics, Colonial Times to 1970,* ser. Q 12–22)

Year	Total traffic volume	Railroads* Volume	Railroads* Percent of total	Motor vehicles Volume	Motor vehicles Percent of total	Inland waterways† Volume	Inland waterways† Percent of total	Oil pipelines Volume	Oil pipelines Percent of total	Domestic airways‡ Volume	Domestic airways‡ Percent of total
1950	1,094	628	57.44	173	15.80	163	14.93	129	11.81	.3	.029
1955	1,298	655	50.43	223	17.20	217	16.68	203	15.66	.6	.037
1960	1,330	595	44.73	285	21.46	220	16.56	229	17.19	.8	.058
1961	1,326	586	44.17	296	22.36	210	15.82	233	17.59	.9	.068
1962	1,387	616	44.38	309	22.30	223	16.08	238	17.14	1.3	.093
1963	1,469	644	43.82	336	22.89	234	15.94	253	17.26	1.3	.088
1964	1,556	679	43.65	356	22.90	250	16.08	269	17.27	1.5	.096
1965	1,651	721	43.67	359	21.76	262	15.89	306	18.56	1.9	.116
1966	1,759	762	43.33	381	21.66	281	15.95	333	18.93	2.3	.128
1967	1,776	742	41.79	389	21.88	281	15.85	361	20.33	2.6	.145
1968	1,839	757	41.16	396	21.55	291	15.85	391	21.28	2.9	.157
1969	1,895	774	40.84	404	21.32	303	15.98	411	21.69	3.2	.168
1970	1,936	771	39.83	412	21.28	319	16.46	431	22.26	3.3	.170
1971	1,953	746	38.19	445	22.78	315	16.13	444	22.73	3.5	.170
1972	2,071	783	37.80	470	22.70	339	16.35	476	22.98	3.7	.179
1973	2,232	858	38.51	505	22.66	358	16.08	507	22.75	3.9	.175
1974	2,212	852	38.52	495	22.38	355	16.05	506	22.87	3.9	.180
1975	2,066	759	36.74	454	21.97	342	16.55	507	24.54	3.7	.193
1976	2,188	799	36.52	510	23.31	352	16.09	523	23.90	3.9	.182

*Includes electric railways. Beginning 1970, excludes mail and express.

†Includes Great Lakes and Alaska for all years, and Hawaii beginning 1966.

‡Revenue service only for scheduled and supplemental carriers. Includes express, mail, and excess baggage.

Source: U.S. Interstate Commerce Commission, Annual Report; "Intercity Ton-Miles, 1939–1959" (Statement No. 6103), and *Transport Economics.*

TABLE 11.2

VOLUME OF DOMESTIC INTERCITY PASSENGER TRAFFICE, BY TYPE OF TRANSPORT: 1950–1976

(In billions of passenger-miles, except percent. Prior to 1960, excludes Alaska and Hawaii. A passenger-mile is the movement of 1 passenger for the distance of 1 mile. Comprises public and private traffic, both revenue and nonrevenue. See also *Historical Statistics, Colonial Times to 1970*, ser. Q 1–11)

Year	Total traffic volume	Private automobiles		Domestic airways*		Bus (excludes school bus)		Railroads†		Inland waterways‡	
		Volume	Percent of total	Volume	Percent of total	Volume	Percent of total	Volume	Percent of total	Volume	Percent of total
1950	508	438	86.20	10	1.98	26	5.20	32	6.39	1.2	.23
1955	716	637	89.01	23	3.18	25	3.56	29	4.01	1.7	.24
1960	784	706	90.10	34	4.33	19	2.47	22	2.75	2.7	.34
1961	791	714	90.18	35	4.37	20	2.56	21	2.59	2.3	.30
1962	818	736	89.95	37	4.58	22	2.66	20	2.47	2.7	.33
1963	853	766	89.83	43	5.02	23	2.64	19	2.19	2.8	.32
1964	896	802	89.53	49	5.49	23	2.61	18	2.05	2.8	.32
1965	920	818	88.86	58	6.31	24	2.58	18	1.91	3.1	.34
1966	971	856	88.19	69	7.14	25	2.53	17	1.78	3.4	.33
1967	1,021	890	87.18	87	8.55	25	2.44	15	1.50	3.4	.33
1968	1,079	936	86.80	101	9.38	25	2.27	13	1.23	3.4	.32
1969	1,138	977	85.86	120	10.54	25	2.19	12	1.08	3.8	.33
1970	1,185	1,026	86.60	119	10.01	25	2.14	11	.92	4.0	.34
1971	1,230	1,071	87.11	120	9.76	26	2.07	9	.73	4.1	.33
1972	1,300	1,129	86.82	133	10.24	26	1.97	9	.66	4.0	.31
1973	1,356	1,174	86.58	143	10.55	26	1.92	9	.67	4.0	.29
1974	1,331	1,143	85.88	146	10.97	28	2.10	10	.75	4.1	.30
1975	1,352	1,164	86.09	148	10.95	26	1.92	10	.74	4.0	.30
1976	1,441	1,236	85.77	165	11.45	25	1.73	11	.76	4.0	.28

*Covers scheduled and supplemental commercial revenue service, and private pleasure and business flying.
†Includes electric railways.
‡Includes Great Lakes.
Source: *U.S. Interstate Commerce Commission, Annual Report; Transport Economics;* and *Statistical Abstract of the United States*, 1978, p. 639.

other means of transportation. It is only since 1976 that the Congress and the commission have realized the shortsightedness of this pricing policy.

Discriminatory Pricing Policies   Despite the proclaimed policy of non-price discrimination, the railroad rate structure is often price-discriminatory. For example, perishable goods are charged lower rates than nonperishables, and the differences are not justified by cost differences. In effect, the nonperishables are subsidizing the transportation costs of the perishables. This is nothing but *cross-subsidization,* that is, charging one product less in relation to its marginal cost and recouping the difference by charging another commodity a higher price in relation to its marginal cost. As noted in Chapter 4, very often such a policy is not in the public interest, for it can lead to misallocation of economic resources as well as distortions in the income distribution.[8] In Section 11.7 we show how these inequities can come about.

Railway Abandonment Policy and the Problem of Excess Capacity   Because of structural changes in the economy, over the years, several rail routes have become economically unprofitable; in some cases there is simply not enough traffic even to cover the out-of-pocket expenses. Despite this, the commission forces the railroads to operate such routes pending its review of each case. But the review process is usually very protracted, which means that the railroads are forced to carry excess capacity until the abandonment decisions are made by the commission; running freight cars empty is a common indicator of excess capacity. This excess-capacity problem has been instrumental in the bankruptcies of several railroads: If timely rail route abandonment decisions had been made by the commission, it would have lessened the already severe financial burden of such railroads.

Rate Bureau Activities   As noted previously, the 1948 Reed-Bulwinkle Act gave the industry rate bureaus immunity from antitrust proceedings. Up until the 1980 legislative changes, these rate bureaus determined the rates that can be charged a class of goods. Being cartel-determined, the rates had very little relationship to the cost of transporting goods. The rate bureaus justified such pricing policy in the name of industry price stability. Yes, it did achieve price stability, but at the cost of price inflexibility; this accelerated the growth of other means of transportation, including private carriers.

Lengthy Merger Proceedings   Mergers are often a way out for financially troubled railroads to become economically viable; even the antitrust laws allow mergers in such cases, as we saw in Part 2. But since mergers between railroads need to be approved by the commission, and since the commission is not known for making decisions promptly (in one case it took more than 12 years), in practice it is very difficult to consummate mergers quickly to stave off bankruptcies. These delays further aggravate the plight of the financially troubled railroads. What is worse is that ''a rational and coherent federal policy toward

---

[8]If cross-subsidization is deemed necessary, it can be accomplished by alternative means (see Ch. 4 for further discussion).

rail mergers has never been developed and implemented by the ICC and the Executive Branch."[9]

Lack of Joint Usage   Although the railroad network is national in character, the commission's rules and regulations are such that oftentimes joint usage and joint control of common rail trackage are prohibited, which leads to inefficient service and expensive operating practices.

Tax Burden   Unlike the trucking industry, the railroads own their rail track-age, which, being a capital asset, is subject to state and local taxes. Some states tax such assets at higher rates than other assets. On the other hand, the truckers use national highways paid for in large measure by consumer taxes. Such a tax burden does not help the already financially poor health of most railroads.

Regulatory Lag   Regulatory lag may be defined simply as the time it takes a regulatory agency to make its decision on a given subject. A long regulatory lag very often leads to misallocation of economic resources and retardation of tech-nological progress. A case in point is the celebrated "Big John" case. In 1961, the Southern Railroad company published rates, effective August 10, 1961, to ship a minimum of 450 tons of cargo in 100-ton "Big John" cars (aluminum hopper cars). But before the rates could go into effect, the commission suspended them for a period of 7 months.

After a series of maneuvers, in May 1963 the commission prescribed new rates for "Big John," which were 16 percent higher than those proposed by the company. Thereupon, the company challenged the commission's decision in the District Court of Cincinnati. In May 1964 the court reversed the commission's decision and approved the original lower rates proposed by the company. Whereupon, the commission appealed to the Supreme Court. In January 1965 the highest court upheld the lower court and thereby the company. Finally, in September 1965 the commission approved the company's original rates.

Thus it took the commission 4 years to make up its mind, and at what cost: One can only imagine the deadweight loss from not shipping goods at the lower rate for a period of 4 years, the cost to the taxpayer to carry all the legal expenses, and the indirect costs involved in postponing new technology for years. What was the reason for the commission's refusal to accede to the company's original request? It was done to protect other "competitive" interests, meaning simply to discourage competitive rates!

Internal Factors in the Railroad Decline

The following internal causes, coupled with the external ones just discussed, have made the railroad industry all the more sick.

Sluggish Management   Despite serious competition from other means of transportation, the railroad management has been very slow to adopt changes

[9]U.S. Department of Transportation, *Western Railroad Mergers,* a Staff Study by the Office of the Assistant Secretary for Policy Development and the Federal Railroad Administration, Washington, D.C., January 1961, p. 1.

and technical innovations. Partly this is the result of regulation itself, as well-illustrated by the "Big John" case, and partly due to the thinking that somehow the government will step in and bail out the industry.

Labor   The railroad industry is well known for archaic work rules and for featherbedding practices. Since the railroads are a declining industry, the trade unions are obviously interested in protecting jobs even if the jobs are technologically obsolete. The current work rules regarding the size of the crews that run the trains and crew payment practices are such that they have adverse impact on labor productivity and consequently on labor costs, which are more than half the industry's total expenses.

Rail Network   The rail network that connects the various railroads was put into place some 50 to 60 years ago. But because of mergers and bankruptcies, the interconnecting terminals have become obsolete and inefficient. Moreover, despite intense competition from other means of transportation, there has been no joint control or even cooperation with competing modes, such as intermodal piggyback, rail truck, and containerized systems to serve branch-line territories.

Special Problems of the Northeastern Railroads   The railroads in the east, historically the oldest system, have faced some special problems not shared by other railroads. For one thing, the northeastern region of the United States has experienced a dramatic change in its economic growth — away from bulk commodities and toward service industries which do not require the same freight movement. Also, because of environmental regulations, there has been a serious cut in the demand for high-sulphur coal in this area, which was a major source of revenue for the area's railroads. The problem is further aggravated by regulatory restraints on rate flexibility and railroad abandonments, an important factor in some of the bankruptcies in this area.

11.6   SOME ESTIMATES OF COSTS AND BENEFITS OF RAILROAD REGULATION

From the preceding discussion, it is clear that regulation in one form or another has caused the present doldrums in which the railroads find themselves; apparently there seem to be many costs of regulation, and very few benefits. In Chapter 5 we discussed in general the problem of defining and measuring the costs and benefits of regulation. We now consider this topic in relation to the railroads.

Costs of Regulation

In Chapter 5 we distinguished various costs of regulation, such as (1) costs from inefficient provision of services, (2) opportunity costs of the loss from the shifting of traffic from low-cost to high-cost modes of transportation, (3) static welfare loss, (4) distortion in other sectors of the economy arising out of distortional locational decisions, and (5) dynamic costs caused by a reduction in the incentive to innovate, a la "Big John."

We also pointed in Chapter 5 that it may be conceptually easy to identify these costs, but to measure them is another matter. Nonetheless, some attempts to measure these costs of regulation, total as well as item-specific, have been made by a few investigators. We present them here not because they are the last word on the subject but because they give us some idea about the magnitudes involved. The reader is forewarned that these estimates are based on several assumptions and that the amount of the true costs involved is still a matter for debate. With this caveat, let us present some of these estimates.

Ann F. Friedlander has estimated that for 1969 the losses due to excess capacity caused by regulation were about $2.4 billion.[10] Using a somewhat different methodology, Theodore Keeler estimated this cost at $3.5 billion.[11] Also Friedlander has estimated, for the 1960s, the deadweight loss of regulation (i.e., the loss due to some commodities not being shipped because of the higher rates) as between $300 and $400 million annually. The annual regulatory costs due to transfer of business between railroads and trucks have been estimated at $125 million by Kenneth Boyer (for sixteen manufacturing commodities),[12] at $17 million by Richard Levin and Merton Peck (for forty-five commodities),[13] $500 million by Theodore Keeler, but practically zero by Joseph Altonji.[14]

Benefits of Regulation

Measuring the costs of regulation is difficult enough, but measuring the benefits is much more so for the the reasons discussed in Chapter 5. In the area of surface transportation, the only study that is readily available is the one made by the ICC and reported in Table 5.6 (Chapter 5). We have already commented on the findings of this study, especially its extremely dubious estimate of the benefit of $3.4 billion due to regulation; among other things, the methodology of the study is faulty in not considering productivity and technological changes in computing the benefits.[15] Moreover, since there are not other independent studies of the benefits of rail and trucking regulation that the author is aware of, one

[10]Ann F. Friedlander, *The Dilemma of Freight Transportation,* Brookings, Washington, D.C., 1969.

[11]Theodore Keeler, "On the Economic Impact of Railroad Freight Regulation," Working Paper No. SL-7601, Department of Economics, University of California, Berkeley, September 1976.

[12]Kenneth Boyer, "The Price Sensitivity of Shippers: Mode of Transport Selection and Intermodal Allocation of Freight Traffic," Ph.D. dissertation, University of Michigan, 1975.

[13]Richard Levin and Merton Peck, "Allocation in Surface Freight Transportation: Does Rate Regulation Matter?" Department of Economics Discussion Paper No. 31, Yale University, August 1976.

[14]Joseph Altonji, "Estimating Misallocation of Traffic between Rail and Truck Transport," *Proceedings, Seventh Annual Meeting, Transportation Research Forum,* Oxford, Ind., Richard B. Cross Co., 1976.

[15]For a critical review of the ICC study, see W. Bruce Allen and Edward B. Hymson, "The Costs and Benefits of Surface Transport Regulation: Another View," in the *Ford Administration Papers on Regulatory Reform,* op. cit.

should not put too much faith in the commission's findings about the benefits of regulation.

Realizing the problems involved in measuring the costs and benefits of regulation in this area, the best guess that one can make is that the costs probably exceed the benefits. This seems to be the implicit assumption in the 1976 and 1980 deregulatory moves initiated by Congress. It therefore behooves us to look into the question of deregulation in some detail. We first consider the pros and cons of deregulating the railroad industry and then consider the same aspects with respect to the trucking industry.

11.7 DEREGULATING THE RAILROADS: PROS AND CONS

The 1976 4R Act has ushered in an era of (partial) deregulation in the railroad industry. Some of the major provisions of this act are as follows:

1 The railroads can freely raise those rates which are below the variable or out-of-pocket costs, thus providing for upward rate flexibility.
2 They can also reduce rates down to variable costs, thereby providing for downward rate flexibility.
3 The commission may not engage in ''umbrella'' (i.e., broad commodity group) rate-making.
4 The rate bureaus must allow for rate flexibility in the area of single-line and joint-line rates.
5 Discriminatory state taxation of rail and other carriers is illegal.
6 Merger decisions are to be determined expeditiously.
7 The commission is to act promptly on railroad abandonment applications.

Apart from the preceding specific provisions, however, the general thrust of the 4R Act, as noted in its preamble, is to foster competition among all modes of surface transportation and provide greater freedom and flexibility in the railroad rate structure. This policy was given further impetus in the Staggers Rail Act of 1980, which, as noted, now allows the railroads such rate flexibility as well as more authority to enter into long-term contracts with freight shippers.

Before the passage of this act in October 1980, the commission took a historic step in August 1980 when by a majority of 5 to 2 it struck down the power of the industry rate bureaus to determine rates collectively; in effect the Reed-Bulwinkle Act of 1948, granting the railroads antitrust immunity, was abolished. In reaching this decision, the commission stated:

> Collective rate making tends to inflate rate levels through setting of uniform rates acceptable to a majority of carriers, including the less efficient. . . . It creates an atmosphere of consensus that discourages the establishment of innovative price and service options by individual carriers.[16]

---

[16] *The New York Times,* Aug. 14, 1980, p. A-1.

Any reform bill, especially one dealing with such a tightly regulated industry as the railroads, is bound to lead to controversies. Those who are for deregulation will praise the benefits, intended or actual, of the move, whereas the opponents will argue to the contrary. Let us first consider the arguments against deregulation.

Arguments Against Deregulation[17]

The opponents of deregulation, which include the trade unions, some railroad companies, and some politicians, contend that deregulation will lead to: (1) predatory pricing — that is, some powerful railroads may deliberately reduce rates below cost to drive competing truckers or railroads out of business and acquire monopoly to certain routes; (2) increased price discrimination in regard to commodities, shippers, or geographical location; (3) increased concentration of economic power because the railroads will try to acquire other means of surface transportation, such as trucks; (4) industry instability due to price flexibility; and (5) increasing abandonment of economically unprofitable lines so that some areas will be without railroad services.

Let us consider each of these arguments carefully. Consider the issue of predatory pricing against competing means of transportation, say, the truckers. Absent regulation, there are no serious barriers to entry into the trucking industry because the available empirical evidence shows that there are no noticeable economies of scale in the industry; anyone with a license, a truck, and a driver can enter the industry. Therefore, if the railroads cut their rates below marginal costs to drive the truckers out of business, they will simply lose money, and if the truckers have the staying power, they will lose business too. What about predatory pricing against competing railroads? Although this is possible, how is it to benefit the predator in view of the generally declining demand for railroad services and growing competition from other means of transportation?

What about the argument of price discrimination? We have stated elsewhere that for this to be possible three conditions must be fulfilled, namely, the seller must have a monopoly power, the price elasticity of demand must differ between markets, and the cost of market segmentation must be such that it is not possible for the demander in the low-elasticity–high-price market to transfer his or her demand to the high-elasticity–low-price market. Do the railroads have a monopoly? They certainly do not have it in the short-haul market because of competition from the truckers. In the long-haul market, too, they do not seem to have the monopoly because, using Thomas Moore's words, ``goods shipped from one region must compete with goods shipped from elsewhere.'' Therefore, the fear of price discrimination is just that.

Will deregulation lead to increased concentration of economic power in the

---

[17]The following discussion draws on Thomas Gale Moore, ``Deregulating Surface Freight Transportation,'' in Almarin Phillips (ed.), *Promoting Competition in the Regulated Markets*, Brookings, 1975, ch. 3.

hands of the railroads? This also seems unlikely in view of the Canadian experience. In Canada, where railroads are allowed to own other modes of transportation, two major railroads, Canadian Pacific and Canadian National, each operate a large trucking firm, an internal airline, and a major steamship line. But neither company has monopolized the market. As a matter of fact, railroads in Canada do not own more than 10 percent of the entire trucking industry.

The argument that there will be less stability in the industry because of pricing competition is putting the cart before the horse, for it was the price rigidity due to regulation that led to many bankruptcies in the railroad industry. Moreover, in a competitive price system price fluctuations are the mechanism which adjusts any imbalance between supply and demand. As such, price fluctuations therefore are not an indication of lack of stability in the industry.

Would deregulation of the railroad industry lead to increasing abandonment of economically unprofitable lines (e.g., rail services to rural areas or passenger train service, which for several years has become unremunerative; if it were not for the cross-subsidization provided by freight service, the passenger train service would have long been abandoned)? There is no question that this will happen. The current stringent rules about the abandonment of light-density economically unprofitable lines have lead to significant excess capacity in the industry. For example, in 1971, the industry was operating about 205,000 route miles of lines out of which 21,000 miles were light-density lines for which the carriers incurred losses; these 21,000 miles of line carried less than 1 percent of total rail freight. The Federal Railroad Administration has estimated that by discontinuing these lines, the railroads could save up to $57 million annually. The problem is more severe in the northeast. The trustees of the bankrupt Penn Central Railroad estimated that in 1972 80% of Penn Central's freight revenues were attributed to 11,000 miles of its 20,000-mile lines, that is, 9000 miles of line were excess capacity.

By forcing the railroads to operate unprofitable lines, the commission is contributing to misallocation of scarce transportation resources. Before we show this graphically, one may raise the following argument: Granted the allocative inefficiency involved in cross-subsidization, would it be desirable from an equity viewpoint to abandon rail services to rural areas and small communities simply because they are not profitable? Can one simply ignore the total social and economic needs of the people living in such communities in the name of allocative efficiency alone? Did not the Supreme Court declare in *Alabama Public Service et al. v. Southern Railroad Company,* 341 U.S. 341, 353 (1951) that the public service obligations of the railroads "cannot be avoided merely because it will be attended by some pecuniary loss"? If it is the objective of public policy to provide rail services to certain areas regardless of their profitability, there is not much economists can say about it. All they can do is to point out the efficiency and equity aspects of such a policy and let the politicians ponder them.

To show the welfare consequences of the cross-subsidization policy we can use Figure 11.2, developed by Alfred Kahn.[18] Figure 11.2 depicts hypothetical

[18]See Alfred Kahn, op. cit., pp. 190–191.

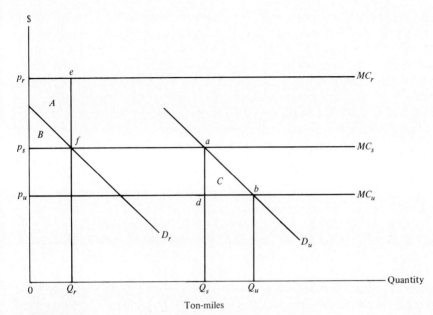

FIGURE 11.2
The economics of cross-subsidy.

demand and marginal cost curves for rail transportation for rural and urban customers. (D_r = rural demand, D_u = urban demand, MC_r = rural marginal cost, MC_u = urban marginal cost, MC_s = uniform marginal cost curve for rural and urban customers under cross-subsidization.) For simplicity, the marginal cost curves are assumed constant, hence the supply curves are also constant.

From the given demand and cost curves, it is obvious that without government (i.e., ICC) intervention, the rural demand for rail transportation will be zero (because D_r lies below MC_r) but the urban demand will be Q_u. Now suppose that because of the cross-subsidization policy, the marginal cost of supplying transportation to both rural and urban customers is fixed at MC_s (somewhere between MC_r and MC_u). As a result, the rural demand is now Q_r while the urban demand has declined to Q_s as a result of the higher MC_s. What are the ensuing consequences?

First, there is loss of economic efficiency given by the sum of the areas C and A. C represents the deadweight loss (see Chapter 6) because at the higher price urban consumers do not demand the quantity Q_sQ_u. Now the total cost of producing the quantity Q_r is given by the rectangle OP_reQ_r, but the corresponding total revenue is only OP_sQ_r that is, there is a loss of P_sP_ref or the area $A + B$. But of this the efficiency loss is only A because B represents consumer surplus of the rural customers — they will be willing to give this amount to acquire Q_r units (consumer surplus is the area under the demand curve D_r but above the price line P_s). Hence, as stated, the aggregate efficiency loss is $C + A$ — the deadweight loss plus the loss ($= A$) that could be avoided if Q_r is not produced.

But let us say that society is willing to pay this cost simply to provide rail services to the rural customers on equity grounds alone. So let us neglect the areas A and C. Now because of cross-subsidization, the rural customers gain by the magnitude of the area of the consumer surplus B. But what about the urban customers? They lose the area $P_s a d P_u$ because for the quantity Q_s they paid P_u per unit before cross-subsidization, but for the same quantity they have to pay the higher price P_s. One can legitimately ask the question: To transfer income of the area B to rural customers do the urban customers have to forego a much larger area $P_s a d P_u$? Will the resulting income distribution be any better than before? Alternatively, is this the most efficient way of transferring income to the rural customers?

As the preceding discussion reveals, both from the point of efficiency and equity, cross- or internal subsidization may be what Alfred Kahn calls "a very crude device of promoting egalitarian objectives."[19] It may be better for the railroads to drop the economically unprofitable lines and let the truckers move in, for most of the light-density rail lines handle short-haul traffic, which is better suited to the trucking industry. This will help the railroads not only financially, but it will also enable them to concentrate on the long-haul traffic for which they have a comparative advantage over the truckers. This will lead to a better allocation of the nation's transportation resources. If this sensible course is not taken, there will be more railroad bankruptcies. Whether the commission abides by the 1976 4R Act mandate about expeditious abandonment of economically unprofitable lines remains to be seen.

In sum, then, the arguments contrary to deregulation are not weighty enough to outweigh the benefits that might accrue from it. But what are these benefits? The U.S. Department of Transportation has estimated that if the 1976 act's provisions are implemented, the railroad industry will save annually the sums shown in Table 11.3.

Whether the benefits cited in Table 11.3 will materialize or not, only time will tell. But considering the plight in which the railroads find themselves, and further considering the fact that regulation itself has been a major contributory factor in this plight, one can argue that the recent deregulatory moves are a step in the right direction.

11.8 A CRITICAL EVALUATION OF ICC REGULATION OF THE TRUCKING INDUSTRY[20]

With the 1935 Motor Carrier Act, the ICC assumed the responsibility of regulating the trucking industry, a large and complex industry with some 100,000 firms which account for about 23 percent of all intercity ton-miles of freight traffic. As noted, the commission regulates the intercity common and contract

---

[19]Alfred Kahn, op. cit., p. 191.
[20]The following discussion draws heavily on Paul MacAvoy and John W. Snow (eds.), *Regulation of Entry and Pricing in Truck Transportation,* the Ford Administration Papers on Regulatory Reform, American Enterprise Institute for Public Policy Research, Washington, D.C., 1977.

TABLE 11.3
ANNUAL SAVINGS TO THE RAILROAD INDUSTRY RESULTING FROM THE 1976 4R ACT

Type of Benefit	Amount ($ million)
From increasing all rates to variable costs	150
From permitting the ICC to raise intrastate rail rates to interstate levels	50
From rate flexibility within the range of 7% the first year, 12% the second year, and 15% the third year	250
From reduction in costs because of regulatory lag	250
From downward price flexibility	50
From reduction in discriminatory state taxation	55
From interest rate guarantees (to finance investment in rights-of-way, etc.)	50
From railroad restructuring (the lower estimate if 1% reduction in railroad costs, the higher estimate if 10% reduction in these costs)	130 to 1,300

Source: Paul W. MacAvoy and John P. Snow (eds.), Papers on *Railroad Revitalization and Regulatory Reform*, Ford Administration Regulatory Reform, American Enterprise Institute for Public Policy Research, Washington, D.C., 1977, table 6-1, pp. 87–88.

carriers but not the private and exempt carriers. The commission's regulation of these carriers is of two types, rate and entry. We will consider each separately and then consider the important changes in them brought about by the Motor Carrier Act of 1980.

Rate Regulation

There are two types of rates, one for less-than-truckload (LTL) cargo and another for truckload (TL) cargo. For TL traffic, the rates are essentially competitive, determined by negotiation between the carrier and the shipper, and these rates often reflect the actual cost of moving the traffic. The LTL rates, however, are determined by the industry rate bureaus and are approved by the ICC. These rates are class rates — commodities are divided into twenty-three broad commodity classes, each class with its own rate. Very often, the assignment of a commodity to a class is arbitrary. The rate bureau or industry cartel-determined rates are very rigid in that they do not change with the season, there is no peak off-peak variation, and the rates for front-haul (or primary) and back-haul (return trip) traffic are the same, although the latter is generally light (due to commodity regulation discussed below) and there is excess capacity.

Whether the rates are for LTL or TL traffic, the commission uses two modes of regulation. It decides what commodity or commodities a regulated carrier can carry but gives the carriers the flexibility of choosing their routes, or it fixes the routes over which the carriers may operate but not the goods they carry. The first type of regulation may be called "commodity-but-not-route" and the second the "route-but-not-commodity" rate regulation. It should be noted that no carrier is allowed to carry the cargo over the entire length of the journey; cargo must be changed at designated points. The route regulation is complex and involves lot of route circuity – traffic from point A to point B must go via point C although the distance thus involved is much greater than the distance between A and B directly. In the case of commodity-but-not route regulation, there are further restrictions on the goods a carrier can haul on its back-haul traffic; very often a carrier is practically running empty on its back-haul movement because it cannot carry goods other than those allowed by the commission, and very often there is no demand for those goods allowed on the return trip.

The Economic Effects of Rate Regulation The commission's trucking rate regulation policies have been criticized by several people, including academicians, politicians, and government officials. Some of the criticisms are as follows:

The Rates Are Too High Because of the complex and rigid rate structure and because of circuitous routes and empty backhauls, trucking rates are unduly high, that is, high in relation to what they would have been if they were determined competitively. Dramatic evidence of this was provided in the mid-1950s when fresh and frozen fruits and vegetables were changed from the regulated to the exempt category. Acording to the U.S. Department of Agriculture (USDA) studies it was found that following the change, rates dropped by 33 percent on poultry and 19 percent on fruits and vegetables. It was also found that the quality of the service improved substantially and the use of private carriers by the shippers dropped considerably; the shippers had resorted to private carriers because of the higher rates charged by the regulated carriers.

An indication that the regulated rates are high and profitable can be seen in the market value of the operating rights or licenses. Since it is almost impossible to get an operating license from the ICC, the only way a trucker can enter the industry is by buying the operating rights in the open market. These operating rights fetch some very high premiums. For example, in 1964 Eazer Express, Inc., acquired certain operating rights from Fleet Highway Freight Lines, Inc., for $200,000. In 1973 these same rights were purchased by Yellow Freight System, Inc., for $800,000, an increase of some 300 percent in 9 years (about 16.6 percent annual compound rate). Obviously, such high prices (in relation to the interest rates then prevailing) for the right to operate trucks represent the value of the monopoly power conferred upon the certificate-holder by the present regulatory system: Operators are willing to pay such huge premiums because regulation has made it possible for them to earn monopoly profits.

One can use the geometry of monopoly pricing introduced in Chapter 6 to explain the emergence of such huge premiums. Figure 11.3 shows the hypothetical demand, marginal revenue, long-run marginal cost, and long-run average cost curves of a trucker who has ICC-conferred monopoly rights over a certain route. Following Chapter 6, the monopoly solution, equating $MR = MC$, gives P_m and Q_m as the profit-maximizing monopoly price and monopoly output, respectively. Since the long-run average cost curve includes a reasonable rate of return on the owner-supplied capital, the shaded rectangle in the figure represents long-run monopoly or pure profits. Assuming that the demand and cost curves remain the same, a prospective entrant into the industry will have to

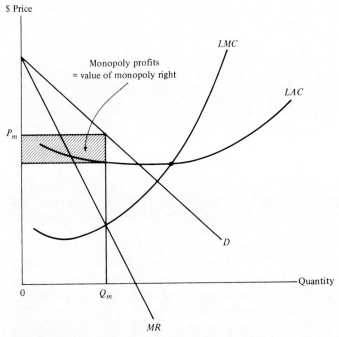

FIGURE 11.3
Monopoly pricing, profits, and value of monopoly rights.

offer the existing monopolist a premium equal to the shaded area to obtain the operating rights. The numbers $200,000 or $800,000 quoted in the preceding paragraph are simply a quantification of such shaded area; technically they are the present value of the shaded area; discounted over the length of time monopoly profit is expected to prevail.

Rates and Services Are not Flexible   Since for the LTL traffic the rates are fixed by the industry rate bureaus, trucking service is less flexible and the quality of service is constrained. That is why some shippers use private carriers, a business they would rather entrust to the truckers if the trucking industry were competitive. The Ford Administration Papers on trucking regulation report the case of a small manufacturer (less than $5 million annual sales) of industrial glass who ships 85 percent of his output by private carriers because of lower costs, even though 38 percent of the carrying capacity on the back-haul traffic is empty because of ICC regulations. The cost savings are made possible by accumulating orders up to a week until a full truckload (twelve to fifteen separate orders) is obtained.

Many Rates Are Irrational   Being tied to the class rate, many rates do not reflect the actual costs of carrying the relevant commodities. Also, rates (i.e., price per mile) are often higher for short distances than they are for long distances for the same commodity traveling on the same route and in the same direction; this despite the fact that there are no noticeable economies of scale in the trucking industry.[21] To cite but one example from the Ford Administration Papers, the cost of shipping goods from Trinidad (Colorado) to Allenmine (Colorado) is more than 20 percent higher if the trip originally starts in Dallas than if it originally starts in Los Angeles, although the physical distance from Trinidad to Allenmine is the same in both cases!

Rates Are Discriminatory The commission mandates (via the rate bureaus) the same rate to all shippers moving similar traffic between specific points, although in many cases the costs are not the same. Charging the same rates despite cost differences is every bit as discriminatory as charging different prices when (marginal) costs are the same. Consider, for example, prime-haul and back-haul traffics. Since prime-haul load is usually greater than back-haul load (because of commodity and route regulation), the prime-haul rates should be greater than the back-haul ones since the costs of the latter are lower due to available excess capacity (see our discussion on peak-load pricing in Chapter 5). But the commission does not permit such price differentials for fear of "opening up" competition. This policy has an adverse effect on the shippers' locational decisions because it discourages shippers from locating in areas where they would add to back-haul traffic. This further stimulates front-haul traffic and discourages back-haul traffic, thereby exacerbating the excess-capacity problem.

Another element of price discrimination consists in not distinguishing between peak and off-peak traffic (see again our discussion on peak-load pricing in Chapter 5). By charging the same rates to shippers with seasonal demand and to those with stable demand, the commission's regulatory policies lead to chronic shortages during peak season (e.g., right after the harvesting season). If peak seasonal demand were charged a higher rate, it would be possible to avoid such shortages by investing in additional car capacity. In this respect, the commission could learn from the telephone, electric, and gas utilities where peak–off-peak pricing policies are now routinely followed.

Yet another element of price discrimination can be found in the practice of the value-of-service pricing policy. Like the railroads, the trucking industry is allowed to charge higher rates for high-valued goods compared to low-valued goods, although the cost of transportation is the same in both cases, save the difference due to higher insurance cost for high-valued goods. For example, rates on nylon hosiery are twice as much for shipment out of the Carolinas as the rates on cotton hosiery, although the shipping characteristics of the two products are the same. The effect of this pricing policy has been to divert the

[21]As noted in Ch. 6, if the average cost of production declines over a wide range of output (i.e., economies of scale), price discrimination may be restored to in order to cover the average cost of production while making as full a use of existing capacity as possible. In the absence of economies of scale, the practice of charging higher rates for short as compared to long distances is nothing but cross-subsidization by the former to the latter. We have already discussed the economics of cross-subsidization (see Fig. 11.2).

high-valued goods traffic to the airlines. (See also the discussion on value-of-service pricing in Section 11.2.)

Needless Complexity of Rates If the trucking rates were determined competitively, they would be based on factors such as distance, weight or volume, special handling characteristics of the product, insurance cost, and so forth. But the present rate system is based on artificial commodity classifications which, because of route and back-haul restrictions, is enormously complex; one must wade through hundreds of pages of the tariff book to find out the relevant rate.

Entry Regulation

The negative effects of rate regulation have become all the more severe because of the commission's restrictions on entry into the trucking industry. Until the passage of the 1980 act, there were only two ways to secure entry into the industry: (1) under the "Grandfather Clause," which granted operating rights to those carriers who were in business in 1935 when the industry was first regulated, and (2) by establishing the test of "public convenience and necessity." But this has been a difficult test to pass, for the commission, to protect the interests of existing carriers, requires the newcomer to prove that the applied-for route/commodity entry cannot be satisfied by existing operators. If an existing carrier tells the commission that it can satisfy the need without the new entry, the burden of proof to the contrary lies with the new applicant (capture theory again!). The net effect has been to severely curtail entry into the industry, which has had the following undesirable effects.

Market Concentration and Monopoly Power Because of route and commodity restrictions, only a few carriers are available to carry any given shipment on many routes, especially those in rural areas. This has fostered concentration of economic power in the hands of a few firms. In 1972, the top four firms in the industry (the four-firm concentration ratio) accounted for 17 percent of the industry's operating revenues, the corresponding figure being 23 percent for eight firms. There is also substantial variation in the concentration ratios across regions. In terms of operating revenues, in 1972, the four-firm concentration ratios were 32 percent, 27 percent, and 17 percent in the eastern, southern, and western regions of the country; the corresponding eight-firm ratios were 41 percent, 40 percent, and 26 percent, respectively. Of course, concentration is much higher on individual routes. (See Chapter 6 for a discussion of concentration ratios and their usefulness.)

Operating Inefficiencies As explained earlier, the commission has two types of operating regulations, commodity-restricted and route-restricted, each having its own set of undesirable consequences.

Commodity-Restricted Regulation This, the most prevalent form, limits the type of cargo that a carrier can haul. In 30 percent of the cases, this type of regulation allows the carriers to carry certain goods only in one direction and requires them to travel empty on their return trip; this is an enormous waste of economic resources, including the waste of gasoline consumed on such return trips. In a 1972 survey it was found that about 28 percent of the ICC-regulated carriers stopped for the survey were running empty solely because of this type of regulation.

Route-Restricted Regulation This type of regulation specifies the exact route over which carriers must travel; deviations from the prescribed routes are rarely permitted. Moreover, as noted, the routes are often circuitous, which increases the time of the journey between the point of origin and the final destination. The absurdity of such route-restriction regulation can be noted from the fact that in 1974, the height of the energy crisis, the commission denied Consolidated Freightway its request to reduce route circuitry by 37 percent on movement between Minneapolis-St. Paul and Dallas because the ``mileage savings would reduce transit time and thus adversely affect competing carriers in the market''! Since no carrier is allowed to carry its cargo over its entire length of destination, there are frequent changes of the cargo at designated points, which unnecessarily increases the handling costs as well as the time of the journey.

Service to Rural Areas Under the current regulatory practices, the trucking industry (like the railroads) is required to charge lower rates (in relation to marginal cost) on traffic to rural areas as compared to traffic to urban areas. In other words, the higher urban rates are subsidizing the lower rural rates; there is thus *cross-subsidization*. The commission defends this practice on the grounds that without the cross-subsidy truckers would not serve the rural areas. This argument implies that rural traffic is inherently unprofitable without the subsidy. But this argument can be challenged. First, if the rate regulation were abolished and the rates were determined competitively, there would still be carriers who would serve the rural areas, as we will point out later. The private carriers are a case in point. As stated earlier, before frozen and fresh fruits and vegetables were removed from the regulated category, many shippers used private carriers because they charged lower rates. But since the transportation of these products was freed from regulation many shippers have given up the private carrier business and returned to the exempt public carriers.

Second, even if one accepts the commisison's argument about cross-subsidy, the important question is whether there are alternatives which can accomplish the objective of serving rural areas at least possible cost. One could think of giving some tax benefits directly to the rural shippers but let them pay the true cost of transportation. This would at least reduce or minimize the loss due to misallocation of scarce transportation resources resulting from the current regulatory practices. If one still insists on continuing the practice of cross-subsidization, then the consequences we discussed in Section 11.7 about cross-subsidizing rural rail transportation applies with equal force here too.

11.9 DEREGULATING THE TRUCKING INDUSTRY: THE MOTOR CARRIER ACT OF 1980

From the preceding discussion it is clear that the ICC rate and entry regulations of the trucking industry have had serious negative economic effects. These effects, in brief, are: higher rates than could be justified on cost basis, misallocation of transportation resources by distorting shippers' choice of the mode of transportation, and concentration of economic power and monopoly profits reflected in the premiums paid for operating rights.

Despite these evils, for a long time the industry resisted any attempt at deregulation. The entrenched interests, the truckers and the Teamster's Union, put forward the kinds of arguments that were advanced by the opponents of railroad deregulation, namely, that deregulation of the trucking industry will lead to market chaos, monopolization of the industry by a few operators, predatory pricing, price discrimination, lack of service to rural areas, more road accidents resulting from highway congestion due to free entry into the industry, and the likelihood of the depression of the 1930s. There is no need to answer these arguments, for they were given when we discussed the railroad deregulation problem; the statements made there apply with equal force to the deregulation of the trucking industry.

The real reason for the status quo is simple: Those who have acquired valuable operating rights do not want to give up the monopoly profits that go with them. Of course, the question of deregulating the trucking industry is now somewhat academic, for on July 1, 1980, President Carter signed into law the Motor Carrier Act of 1980; after some 45 years of rigid regulation, this act has ushered in an era of deregulation comparable in spirit to the deregulation of the airline industry. This act is far-reaching in consequence, as can be seen from its provisions, which are as follows. The act

1 Directs the ICC to issue operating permits to any individual who is able to provide service that will serve a useful public purpose

2 Shifts the burden of proof from the applicant and eliminates entry tests to show why current service is inadequate

3 Directs the ICC within 180 days of enactment to eliminate rules that require carriers to stop at specific intermediate points or take circuitous routes

4 Directs the ICC to consider removing restrictions on categories of commodities that may be hauled and intermediate stops that a carrier may make and to eliminate unreasonable limitations that may waste fuel

5 Relaxes food and some agricultural requirements for carriers if the truck owner is the driver and the amount is no more than half the annual tonnage hauled

6 Exempts from ICC regulation transportation of goods diverted from aircraft to trucks because of adverse weather or other conditions

7 Exempts from ICC regulation agricultural feeds, plants, and seeds if they are going directly to an agricultural production site or an agricultural market

8 Removes some restrictions on financial and contractual arrangements between parent trucking companies and their subsidiaries

9 Promotes competitive trucking service by establishing zones in which a carrier may raise rates by 10 percent 1 year before the effective date of the proposed change and may lower rates by 10 percent below the charge in effect July 1, 1980, or 1 year prior to change

10 Ends collective rate-making and antitrust immunity for single-line rates as of January 1, 1984, with a possible 6-month extension

11 Appropriates $3 million for a study of collective rate-making and antitrust immunity

12 Establishes civil and criminal penalties for coercing a driver to pay for unnecessary loading and mandates that the shipper or receiver requiring unnecessary loading pay the expenses

13 Requires the ICC to improve procedures, study services to communities, establish through routes between truck and water carriers if necessary, and to make recommendations to the President and to Congress

14 Requires carriers to have at least $5 million insurance for vehicles carrying hazardous material and $750,000 insurance for those hauling other goods

15 Directs the Labor Department to maintain lists of employment available in the trucking industry and to help out-of-work trucking employees find jobs

16 Directs congressional committees to conduct periodic oversight hearings on the effects of this legislation, with annual hearings for the first 5 years after enactment

These provisions of the 1980 act tell in a nutshell what has been wrong with trucking regulation in the past. The most significant provisions pertain to the easing of entry into the industry, the removal of antitrust immunity to the rate bureaus, and some rate flexibility. Although it is too soon to judge the effects of the act, there are indications that it has begun to achieve some of its intended results. On December 10, 1980, the commission reported that the truckers had nearly doubled their requests for new operating rights; in one region the applications for new individual freight rates had nearly quadrupled. Furthermore, some truckers have reduced the LTL rates by resorting to discounting and other pricing strategies. As expected, some long-haulers have begun dropping small communities from their routes. But the Texas Railroad Commission, which governs commerce in that state, reports that local or regional carriers are moving in to fill the gap, which is also according to a priori expectations.

11.10 SUMMARY AND CONCLUSIONS

The primary goal of this chapter was to describe and evaluate ICC regulation of the railroad and trucking industries, two of the nation's prime means of surface transport. Up until the 1974 4R Act, the commission's regulatory power was omnipotent. It covered every aspect of these industries, namely, rates, rate of return, routes, types of commodities to be transported, the distances over which they can be transported without interchanging, entry into and exit from the industry, accounting and financial practices, service to rural areas, abandonment of routes, and a host of others.

The ICC Act of 1887, which established the commission, was designed to prevent some of the abusive monopoly practices engaged in by the then existing railroads. Over the years, however, the primary concern of regulation has been to protect established industry interests in the name of industry stability and financial solvency. In pursuit of this policy, the actions of the commission became more anticompetition than antimonopoly. As a result, the commission's regulatory policies have had undesirable economic effects.

Insofar as the railroads were concerned, the cartel-determined rigidity of the rate structure fixing the minimum as well as maximum rates, the discriminatory pricing policies reflected in cross-subsidization and the value-of-service principle, excess capacity due to the delay in deciding the fate of the uneconomically unprofitable lines, the procrastinations about merger decisions, and the failure to coordinate joint usage of facilities among competing modes of transportation have all contributed to the ill health of the railroad industry.

With regard to the trucking industry, the commission's regulatory activities have been anticompetition. Its rate regulation has resulted in rates which are (1) high in relation to cost, (2) highly inflexible, (3) discriminatory in that they do not recognize the seasonal, peak–off-peak characteristics of the traffic, and (4) unduly complex on account of route circuitry and restrictions on back-haul trips. Its entry regulation until the 1980 act was such that it was well-nigh impossible for a new applicant to get a foothold in the industry. As a result, there have been monopoly profits in the industry as reflected in some very high premiums paid to acquire operating rights. Its commodity/route regulations have led to excess capacity evidenced by empty back-haul trips and they have distorted the shipper's choice about industrial location.

The 1976 4R Act, for the first time, recognized that regulation was responsible for most of the ills of the railroad industry. This act together with the Staggers Rail Act has introduced some price flexibility in the rate structure and has made it easier to quicken the commission's railroad abandonment and merger decisions. Although these moves are a far cry from complete deregulation, they represent a step in that direction.

The Motor Carrier Act of 1980 correctly recognized the anticompetition nature of the commission's rate and entry regulations of the intercity freight trucking industry. When all the provisions of the act are implemented, it is expected that the trucking industry will become much more competitive, with a salutary effect on the consumer. Already, the act has had a beneficial impact on some segments of the country.

There is general consensus among scholars that the recent deregulatory initiatives in the Congress should continue. Some of the specific suggestions for further deregulation are considered in the final chapter of this text.

QUESTIONS

11-1 Which theory or theories of regulation discussed in Chapter 2 best explain the regulation of surface transport in the United States?

11-2 Considering the various transportation acts discussed in the text, what do you think have been the overall goals of U.S. transportation policy? Has the ICC succeeded in achieving these goals? Why or why not?

11-3 Evaluate: "Congress in the Transportation Act of 1940 created as many contradictions as were dissipated." (Theodore J. Lowi, the House *Study on Federal Regulation,* p. 339)

11-4 If the method of cross-subsidization were abolished, "transportation rates would rise substantially and retail prices in rural areas would rise astronomically." Do you agree with statement? Why or why not?

*11-5 Based on the data for the eighteen largest railroads in 1968 (excluding the Penn Central), Thomas Moore obtained the production function for the railroads (see fn. 17, p. 271).

$$\text{Log } F = \text{constant} + 0.936 \log K_f + 0.082 \log L_f$$
$$\qquad\qquad\qquad (0.050) \qquad\quad (0.008) \qquad\qquad R_2 = 0.961$$

where

$$F = \text{ton-miles of freight shipped}$$
$$K_f = \text{freight-specific capital}$$
$$L_f = \text{freight-specific labor}$$

the figures in parentheses = the estimated standard errors

The sum of the coefficients of log K_f and log L_f gives estimates of returns to scale. Assuming the validity of these results, what can you say about the nature of returns to scale in the railroad industry? Do the results imply that the railroad industry is a natural monopoly?

11-6 Under the current practice, on class rates, the ICC requires the same rates be charged on prime-haul as well as back-haul trips. Consider a route with only two shippers: Shipper A has balanced traffic whereas shipper B's traffic is uneven, as shown below.

	Shipper A	Shipper B	Total
Prime-haul trips	5	15	20
Back-haul trips	5	5	10
Total	10	20	30

The total traffic on the routes requires twenty round trips. If rates were cost-based, shipper A would pay for five round trips or five-twentieths of the total cost, and shipper B would pay for fifteen round trips or fifteen-twentieths of the total cost. But under the present system, shipper A pays for ten-thirtieths of the total cost (which is greater than five-twentieths) and shipper B pays twenty-thirtieths of

*Optional. See Thomas Gale Moore, op. cit., p. 96.

the total, (which is less than fifteen-twentieths). Why? What are the effects of the current pricing policies? (Example taken from: *Regulation of Entry and Pricing in Truck Transportation,* Ford Administration Papers, p. 16).

11-7 State with reasons whether you agree or disagree with the statement of Mr. Bent C. Whitlock, president of the American Trucking Association, that "collective rate making is the best way to make rates." (Quoted from *Fortune,* June 18, 1979, p. 144.)

11-8 Evaluate: " . . . Deregulation is an experiment the cost of which we who work in the industry cannot afford." (Frank E. Fitzsimmons, general president, International Brotherhood of Teamsters, testifying before Congress, June 26, 1979.)

11-9 If the railroads were allowed to abandon economically unprofitable lines, what would be the consequences for the manufacturing, agriculture, retailing and wholesaling, mining, and logging industries? See if your reasoning agrees with that of the U.S. Department of Transportation as given in "Rail Abandonments and Their Impacts," in *Railroad Revitalization and Regulatory Reform,* Ford Administration Papers, op. cit., ch. 1).

11-10 What would be the consequences of deregulating the interstate bus industry? Do you think companies such as Greyhound would object to such a move? Why? (The industry is now deregulated. See Chapter 18. See if your answer changes.)

11-11 In view of the energy crisis facing the country from time to time, would you advocate that the government subsidize mass transportation systems such as the railroads, innercity rail transportation, intercity bus companies, and the like? If you do, how would you raise the subsidy revenues? For example, would you recommend that the federal tax on gasoline be raised by, say, 5 cents a gallon, as was done recently? Why or why not?

CHAPTER 12

THE CIVIL AERONAUTICS BOARD AND THE AIRLINE INDUSTRY

After nearly 40 years of economic regulation, the domestic airline industry was substantially deregulated when President Carter signed into law the Air Deregulation Act of 1978 on October 24, 1978. A remarkable provision of this act is that on January 1, 1985, the Civil Aeronautics Board (CAB), the independent regulatory commission which has controlled the industry so thoroughly all these years, is itself supposed to close shop. This is an unusual development, for very few, if any, regulatory agencies once established go out of business; bureaucracies seem to have perpetual lives.

How did this happen? In this chapter an attempt has been made to provide an answer to this question. In particular, we proceed as follows. After discussing the history, origin, and mandate of the CAB, we consider the regulatory policies of the board in some detail and then critically evaluate the economic effects of these policies. This is then followed by the move toward deregulation beginning around 1976 and its culmination in the passage of the 1978 act. We then discuss the effects of the act, intended and actual, and find out what they portend for deregulatory initiatives in other areas. We have already seen that the 1978 act has had considerable influence in the deregulation of the railroad and trucking industries.

12.1 THE HISTORY, ORIGIN, AND MANDATE OF THE CAB[1]

The history of aviation can be said to have begun in December 1903 when the Wright Brothers flew the first airplane in existence over the sand dunes of Kitty

---

[1]The following discussion draws heavily on Bradley Behrman, "Civil Aeronautics Board," in James Q. Wilson (ed.), *The Politics of Regulation,* Basic Books, New York, 1980; and Mary Bennett Peterson, *The Regulated Consumer,* Nash Publishing, Los Angeles, 1971.

Hawk on the coast of North Carolina. Initially only the army took note of this invention, which was later to open up an entirely new vista in transportation: The army's interest was largely for defense purposes. However, between 1903 and 1917 only 200 planes, military and nonmilitary, were produced, but they became obsolete very soon.

The U.S. entry into World War I led to a frantic demand for airplanes. Within a year of the entry, orders were placed for some 30,000 planes, but because of the technology then prevailing, the production rate was very slow. After the armistice, the war surplus planes, although few in number, were sold almost for a song and most of the aircraft production facilities were disbanded. For almost a decade the airline industry, such as it was, stayed dormant; commercial aviation as such was virtually nonexistent.

The impetus to commercial aviation came after the passage of the Air Mail Act of 1925 (called the Kelly Act), which instituted a subsidy program for private carriers to transmit U.S. mail along with passengers; until then the airmail was carried by army planes. By paying more than the actual cost of carrying airmail, the subsidy program was designed to get the commercial aviation industry off the ground. It was also a means of regulating the industry, for without the mail contract it was unprofitable for any airline, especially the small ones, to fly; until the mid-1930s, passenger traffic was very light, accounting for less than 10 percent of total revenue. (It was not until 1938 that the passenger revenue exceeded the mail revenue.) As yet, there was no entry or rate regulation of the industry. The Air Commerce Act of 1926 regulated only safety standards.

Between 1929 and 1933, the great depression era, there was some abuse of the subsidy program in that Postmaster General Walter Brown, disregarding legal provisions about competitive bidding, awarded airmail contracts to a few large carriers and that, too, at a higher level of subsidy than before. As a result, the Air Mail Act of 1934 was passed, which both tightened the competitive-bidding procedure of awarding mail contracts and divided jurisdiction over such contracts between the U.S. Postal Service and the ICC; the U.S. Postal Service was to be responsible for the award of the contracts as well as for determining routes and schedules, and the ICC was to determine the appropriateness of pay rates to each contractor. In addition, the act created a Federal Aviation Commission to study aviation and advise the President about new legislation.

In January 1935, the Federal Aviation Commission submitted a report to President Franklin Roosevelt urging him to create an independent agency to regulate entry, pricing, and other aspects of the aviation industry. While recognizing the "need" for regulation, the President did not think that a new regulatory agency was called for since the ICC could do that job along with its duties in the other areas of transportation.

Between 1935 and 1938 the industry grew rapidly, but the growth was accompanied by severe financial losses, which the airlines attributed to both the competitive bidding system for airmail contracts and the free entry into the industry. Therefore, the airlines argued that it was in the public interest to regulate the industry. Since the country was still recovering from the great depression, there was great ambivalence toward the working of the free market system. As a result, Congress was favorably disposed to the idea of some economic regulation of the industry to stave off future financial crises.

The only serious opposition to regulation came from the U.S. Postal Service and the Department of Commerce (which looked after air safety); they argued that regulation would retard efficiency and innovation in the industry. But the pro-regulation people dismissed this opposition as jealousy since these two departments would lose their regulatory powers over the industry. As this discussion shows, the economic theory of regulation seems to be at work here for the big air carriers had found that the mail contracts awarded without competitive bidding was a valuable economic good which offered a substantial economic benefit to them.

Although there was considerable debate in the Congress about regulation of the industry, there was no consensus about who should administer the regulation, the ICC or another agency. After considerable procrastination, Congress passed the Civil Aeronautics Act of 1938 in June of that year; President Roosevelt signed it into law in August 1938. The act called for the formation of the Civil Aeronautics Authority, and by the reorganization plans III and IV of 1940 it was renamed the Civil Aeronautics Board (CAB). The act entrusted the CAB with the task of economic as well as safety regulation.[2]

The Civil Aeronautics Act of 1938

The goals of this act were:

1 To foster sound economic conditions in air transportation

2 To promote adequate, economical, and efficient service

3 To promote competition to the extent necessary to assure the sound development of an air transport system properly adopted to the needs of the foreign and domestic commerce of the United States, of the U.S. Postal Service, and the national defense

Some of the specific provisions of the act were as follows:

1 It abolished the competitive bidding system and replaced it by a subsidy scheme.

2 The CAB was authorized to set mail rates, taking into account the need of each carrier for compensation.

3 It established the "Grandfather Clause," whereby those carriers which were providing regular service 4 months prior to the passage of the act were granted route certificates with perpetual eligibility for mail pay (and subsidy).

4 The CAB was empowered to set minimum rates as well as limitations on new entry. An entry certificate (non-grandfather type) will be granted only if the board finds that the applicant is "fit, willing and able" to perform the proposed

---

[2]Safety regulation was actually the responsibility of the Air Safety Board, established by the act. But the 1940 reorganization plan abolished the board and transferred its functions to the CAB.

service and that such service is required by the "public convenience and necessity." Otherwise, such application will be denied.[3]

The Federal Aviation Act of 1958

Following several midair collisions of aircraft that occurred in the mid- and late 1950s, President Eisenhower asked the Congress for legislation to establish systematic air traffic management to prevent, within the limits of human ingenuity, a recurrence of such accidents.

Congress responded by passing the Federal Aviation Act of 1958, which was signed into law by President Eisenhower on August 23, 1958. The act superseded the 1938 act. It removed the air safety aspect of regulation from the CAB and lodged it with a new agency, the Federal Aviation Agency (FAA); the CAB was now responsible solely for economic regulation. This act spelled out anew the overall objectives of aviation regulation, which were:

1 The encouragement and development of an air transport system properly adapted to the present and future needs of the foreign and domestic commerce of the United States, of the U.S. Postal Service, and of the national defense

2 The regulation of air transportation in such a manner as to recognize and to preserve the inherent advantages of, assure the highest degree of safety in, and foster sound economic conditions in, such transportation, and to improve the relations between, and coordinate transportation by, air carriers

3 The promotion of adequate, economical, and efficient service by carriers at reasonable charges, without unjust discriminations, undue preferences or advantages, or unfair or destructive competitive practices

4 Competition to the extent necessary to assure the sound development of an air transport system properly adapted to the needs of the foreign and domestic commerce of the United States, of the U.S. Postal Service, and of the national defense

5 The promotion of safety in air commerce

6 The promotion, encouragement, and development of civil aeronautics

The act left pretty much intact the economic functions of the board as defined under the 1938 act.

Until the passage of the 1978 act, the above objectives were supposed to govern the policies of the CAB. Has the board fulfilled its mandate? Has it, for example, developed an airline industry which is economical and competitive? Or, has the industry been more stable under the CAB? Questions such as these obviously call for answers. We will try to do that in Section 12.5.

12.2   THE ADMINISTRATIVE STRUCTURE OF THE CAB

As noted, the 1938 act created the CAB, an independent regulatory commission consisting of a chairperson and four other members all appointed by the Presi-

---

[3]Notice the similarity with the early trucking regulation discussed in Ch. 11.

dent for a period of 6 years and confirmed by the Senate. To carry out its regulatory mission, the board is organized as shown in Figure 12.1. As the figure shows, the board's activities are divided into six major categories, each headed by a bureau chief. In the following section we examine the overall functions of the board, which are distributed among the six bureaus.

12.3   THE FUNCTIONS OF THE CAB

The 1978 act has drastically altered the regulatory authority of the board. But in this section we will consider the functions of the board under the 1958 act and take up the changes in them in Section 12.8. To understand why the 1978 act came about, it is essential to examine the board's activities prior to it. Apart from providing a historical perspective, this examination will show what went wrong with the regulation prior to 1978.

Functions of the Board under the 1958 Act[4]

The functions of the board under the 1938 act, as modified by the 1958 act, were as follows:

Certification   Section 401 of the 1958 act

1 Prohibited an air carrier from engaging in any air transportation without prior board authorization
2 Outlined the standards and procedures relating to the issuance of certificates of public convenience and necessity
3 Set forth the various duties of certified carriers
4 Prescribed the contents of certificates, their method of alteration, suspension, revocation, etc.

The board may issue a certificate only if it finds that the "public convenience and necessity" require a particular service and that the applicant is "fit, willing and able to perform" such service and willing to abide by the requirements of the act. Although fitness tests are not specifically defined by the law, the board requires showing of ability to finance, inaugurate, and operate a given service.

A certificate, if and when issued, specifies the terminal points and the intermediate points, if any, between which the transportation is authorized and the service is to be rendered. The board may impose certain restrictions on some carriers, e.g., nonstop service, "close door" service, or long-haul restrictions.

The board may alter, amend, modify, or suspend a certificate in whole or in part if it finds that the public convenience and necessity so require. Certificates may not be transferred without the board's prior approval nor do they confer any proprietary or exclusive rights in airspace or air navigational facilities. Abandonment of service on one or more routes also requires the permission of the board.

[4]The following discussion draws on "Existing Economic Regulatory Provision," *Congressional Digest,* Washington, D.C., June–July 1978, pp. 168–169, 192.

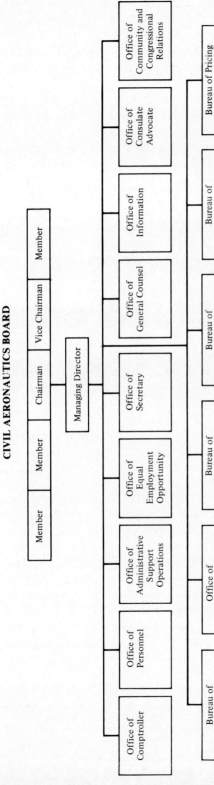

CIVIL AERONAUTICS BOARD

FIGURE 12.1
Civil Aeronautics Board.

Once certified, however, an airline can change the frequency of flights or change schedules or add new planes or other equipment without seeking sanction from the board.

Rate-Making   Section 403 of the act requires every air carrier to file its tariffs with the CAB. Tariffs may be changed only on 30 days' notice, and only if the changes are not detrimental to competitors or discriminatory to the consumer. Later we will consider the various formulas the board has used in making rate decisions.

Transportation of Mail   Section 405 of the act specifies the various powers and duties of the postmaster general and the responsibilities of carriers with respect to the transportation of mail. The board is empowered to fix maximum loads and the carriers are required to transport the mail tendered.

Section 406 gives the CAB the authority to fix mail rates. These rates are based on a two-tier formula: (1) a so-called service rate designed to provide a fair return on investment attributable to the mail service and (2) a subsidy or need rate which is greater than just compensation and which is designed to sustain the carriers' operations, usually fixed on a plane-mile basis without regard to mail actually transported.

Prior to 1953, all mail rates (service as well as subsidy) were paid by the postmaster general. But since then the board disburses the "subsidy" portion of the mail pay, and the postmaster general pays the service rate.

Intercarrier Relations   It is the board's duty to approve or disapprove all proposed mergers, acquisitions of control, interlocking relationships, and agreements between air carriers, considering the interests of travelers, shippers, and other air carriers who may be adversely affected.

As a watchdog agency, the board is authorized to look into whether the carriers and travel agents engage in unfair methods of competition and deceptive practices in the sale or conduct of air transportation services.

International Aviation   In international aviation, the International Air Transport Association (IATA), backed by the participating governments, has the authority to fix airfares. (It is generally conceded that the IATA has used this authority to fix high and noncompetitive rates on international traffic.[5]) The CAB helps the State Department to negotiate with the IATA bilateral or multilateral route and rate agreements. The CAB also participates in international aviation conferences to represent U.S. interests.

---

[5]See Mahlon R. Straszheim, *The International Airline Industry,* Brookings, Washington, D.C., 1969, pp. 131–149, 170–172, 194–196. Apart from regulating the fares, the IATA, from time to time, has imposed restrictions on such matters as maximum allowable knee room, types of lunches to be served, and the charges on in-flight motion pictures and other entertainment. It was not until the appearance of Freddi Laker with his discount fares to London that there was some competition in the international markets.

Carrier Accounting and Reporting   For the sake of uniformity and comparability, the board is authorized to establish a uniform system of accounts and reports and to see that the carriers conform with prescribed accounting and reporting regulations.

Statistical and Analytical Activities   The board collects financial, traffic, and operational data from regulated carriers and publishes the information in a unified form for its own benefit and for the benefit of the public. This information is published annually in the *Handbook of Airline Statistics.*

12.4   POLICIES OF THE CAB[6]

It is one thing to describe the statutory functions of a regulatory agency, and quite another to know how the agency actually conducts it business in practice. In what follows, an attempt is made to provide a broad view of the board's policies and practices since its creation.

One can distinguish three overlapping periods in the life of the board: 1938–1976, 1976–1978, and 1978 to date. The first period may be characterized as the period during which the industry was highly "cartelized," with the board determining who was allowed to enter the industry and on what routes and at what prices. The second period represents a relaxation of the iron-fisted policies of the first period, thanks in large measure to the personalities of John Robson and Alfred Kahn, the regulatory initiatives taken by Senators Edward Kennedy and Howard Cannon, and the sympathetic attitudes of Presidents Ford and Carter. The period since 1978 represents a substantial deregulation of the industry on all scores. In what follows we will discuss in some detail the board's policies in the first two periods, deferring the last period to Sections 12.8 and 12.9.

Board Policies during 1938–1976

To appreciate the policies of the board during this period, let us first consider the structure of the industry that had evolved during that period. There were about six types of air carriers, which are as follows:

Trunk Carriers   Carriers such as American, Delta, Continental, Northwest, Eastern, TWA, and United, all certified under the "Grandfather Clause," are known as trunk airlines and are allowed to provide scheduled air service between major city pairs. Quantitatively, this is the most important category; traditionally they have accounted for 90 percent of the industry's revenue passenger miles (one fare-paying passenger carried 1 mile).

Local Service Carriers   Carriers such as Allegheny (now U.S. Airways), Frontier, Ozark, and Piedmont, which were certified during the 1940s and 1950s, are allowed to provide scheduled service between points not served

---

[6]This discussion is influenced by Bradley Behrman, op. cit.

by the trunk carriers. They are essentially regional carriers, often providing service to lightly traveled areas in which the major airlines were not interested or had abandoned them as unprofitable.

Nonscheduled Carriers These carriers, known as "nonskeds" (or irregulars), are carriers which fly on a contract or nonscheduled basis using mostly small aircrafts. They also include air taxis and commuter airlines. A few of these airlines (about twenty-three) were later made "supplementals" and were permitted to provide charter service to areas not served by the trunk or local carriers.

Air Cargo Carriers As the name suggests, they carry primarily air cargo.

Alaskan and Hawaiian Airlines These are the airlines specially certified to serve Alaska and Hawaii because of their special locational features.

Intrastate Airlines Airlines such as Pacific Southwest, Air California, Southwest Airline of Texas fly strictly within state boundaries.

Insofar as the trunk airlines were concerned, the board's general policy during this period was to control their rates, routes, and entry so rigidly that there was practically no price competition allowed. A reason for this highly protectionistic policy can be found in the board's concern for the financial soundness of the carriers. Recall that before the 1938 act, because of the competitive bidding system for airmail contracts coupled with the great depression, the airlines had suffered heavy financial losses. It was believed that the only way to avoid the recurrence of such losses was to control the industry totally in terms of price, entry, and route regulations. And the board did precisely that: Between 1950 and 1974 it turned down ninety-four applications for new trunk line routes.

With regard to the local carriers the general attitude was a bit less restrictive since they did not directly compete with the trunk lines, the prima donnas of the industry.

The nonskeds were generally exempt from any route or rate regulations because they were run mostly by small operators who did not receive any subsidy from the board. Moreover, air taxis and similar nonskeds were essentially providing feeder services, bring passengers to the scheduled carriers. However, after World War II the picture began to change. Many ex-World War II pilots bought war surplus small planes at nominal prices and set themselves up in the nonsked business. By 1951 the nonskeds accounted for 7 percent of the nation's airline traffic. Sensing potential trouble for the scheduled airlines plus knowing the strong lobbying efforts of these airlines, the CAB began to restrict the activities of the nonskeds not in terms of route or prices but in terms of how many flights they could fly (capture theory again?). Thus, they could not fly more than three flights a month on the eleven most heavily traveled routes and not more than eight flights a month on others. Also, the board declined ninety-seven applications for new nonsked operations. In 1959, twenty-three of the large nonskeds were granted the status of "supplementals," airlines which essentially provide charter-type services at lower rates. But the board refused to certify them as scheduled carriers.

The intrastate airlines were totally exempt from CAB regulation, although they were subject to state regulations, which were generally very nominal. As we will see later, this lack of federal control created a situation whereby the intrastate airlines, which operated in states such as Texas and California, could and did underprice the CAB-controlled interstate airlines.

In sum, then, the period 1938–1976 was one of great protectionism of the industry. This was due to the board's belief, appropriately nurtured by the vested interests in and out of the industry, that, being an infant industry, it could not be left to the free play of the marketplace and needed the kind of rate, route, and entry protection that the CAB actually offered.

Although in the initial years of 1938–1976 one could have accepted the "infant-industry-therefore-protection" argument, the board's anticompetition practices continued even when the industry became an "adult" during the 1960s and early 1970s. As a matter of fact, in the period 1969–1974 the board adopted such exceptionally strong anticompetition practices that they may have ultimately triggered the passage of the 1978 act. Some of these practices were: a total moratorium on new route applications; encouragement to the carriers to enter into intercarrier capacity limiting agreements which reduced flight frequency on many routes; a revised rate formula which allowed the carrier a reasonable rate of return based on the assumption that the load factor (the percentage of seats actually occupied) was 55 percent; and alteration of the rate structure by allowing the airlines to charge fares proportional to flight mileage, regardless of the actual cost of transportation or the density of the traffic.

It is worth considering this last point about charging a uniform rate per mile regardless of the length of the trip, for it leads to cross-subsidization of short-distance travelers by long-distance travelers, a practice we found questionable from both efficiency and equity viewpoints in Chapter 11. To see how the cross-subsidization comes about, remember that the costs at airport terminals (such as ticket sales, baggage check-in, loading and unloading, landing and takeoff) are practically fixed regardless of the length of the trip.[7] Hence the average fixed cost of travel (AFC) declines continuously over the length of the travel (measured by miles). The cost of the flight itself will of course vary with the length of the journey. Assume, for simplicity, that it is proportional to the distance of the trip, which is to say that the average variable cost (AVC) is constant. When the declining AFC is added to the constant AVC, the resulting average cost (AC) will taper off until it almost (but not quite) approaches the AVC, as shown in Figure 12.2.

Consider two trips, one involving a distance of 200 miles and another a distance of 1000 miles. From the geometry of Figure 12.2, the average cost of the short-distance trip is $\$C_s$ per mile, while it is $\$C_l$ for the long-distance trip. Enter the CAB with its uniform charge of $\$C_r$ per mile. This price is obviously beneficial to the short-distance traveler, who will save ($\$C_s - \$C_r$) per mile, but harmful to the long-distance traveler, who in effect will pay a tax of ($\$C_r - \$C_l$) per mile. In sum, then, the long-distance traveler is subsidizing the short-distance

_____
[7]See Alfred Kahn, _The Economics of Regulation,_ vol. I, Wiley, New York, 1970, p. 153.

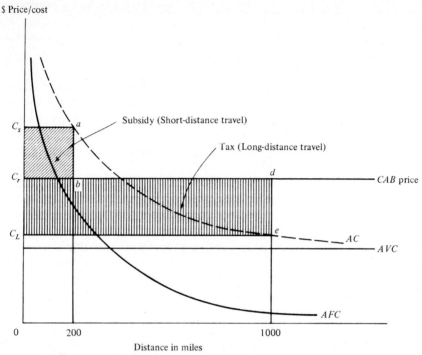

FIGURE 12.2
The economics of short/long distance pricing under regulation.

eler – a cross-subsidy pure and simple. Such an internal subsidy redistributes income in favor of the short-distance traveler. Can one truly say that such a redistribution of income is desirable from an equity viewpoint when to transfer income in the magnitude of the area of the rectangle $C_s abC_r$ one has to give up income represented by the much larger rectangle $C_r deC_L$?

The reasons for these anticompetitive practices were many. During the great economic expansion of 1963–1968, domestic air traffic grew at annual rates exceeding 20 percent, rates of return on investment averaged more than 8 percent (thanks to discount airfares of all sorts), and there was a reduction in the costs of air transportation due to conversion from turbo airplanes to jets. Buoyed by this growth, the industry ordered several wide-bodied Boeing 747s and DC-10s. But by the time their delivery came, the 1969 economic recession had set in, upsetting the industry's economic calculus. The simultaneous existence of recession and inflation reduced industry traffic and therefore profit margins. The industry's fortunes were always tied to the business cycle – good profits during business expansions and losses during business downturns – and the 1969 recession was felt to be severe. As often happens, when times are bad, the regulated often turn to the regulators for relief (another indication of the capture hypothesis). And the relief came in the form of the various anticom-petition practices listed previously.

Board Policies during 1976–1978

The foregoing policies as well as the diminishing recession helped the industry to regain its profitability. But, as so often happens with regulation, there was no letting up of the anticompetition practices. On the contrary, they were rein-forced when Robert Timm because chairperson of the CAB in March 1973. It was his philosophy that travelers' interests lay in the profitability of the industry. The unyielding attitude of Timm aroused congressional suspicion in 1974. Sen-ator Edward Kennedy, then chairperson of the Senate Subcommittee on Admin-istrative Practices and Procedures, decided to hold hearings on the competition-restricting practices of the board. The actual hearings began in February 1975. (Prior to this action, in June 1974 the so-called Timm scandal triggered further interest in the board's highly protectionistic policies. It seems that Timm had gone on a trip to Bermuda which was paid for by some airlines and an aircraft manufacturer.)

The Kennedy hearings in 1975 prompted the Ford administration to introduce an airline reform bill in the Congress primarily as one of the weapon's in the administration's fight against inflation, which was running at the annual rate of 12 percent in 1974. In March 1975 President Ford appointed John Robson as chairperson of the CAB. Unlike his predecessor Timm, Robson was favorably disposed to competition and promised to reassess the board's past regulatory practices.

Soon after taking office, Robson appointed a task force (the Pulsifer task force headed by Roy Pulsifer, a CAB lawyer) to look into the board's regulatory poli-cies. The task force submitted its report in July 1975. In part the report stated:

> The general conclusion of the Special Staff on Regulatory Reform is that protective entry control, exit control, and public utility-type price regulation under the Federal Aviation Act [of 1958] are not justified by the underlying cost and demand character-istics of commercial air transportation. . . .
>
> The present system of regulation causes higher than necessary costs and prices (which in turn suppress demand), weakens the ability of carriers to respond to market demand and other constantly changing conditions, narrows the range of price/quality choice to the user, and thus produces a misallocation of the nation's economic resources. . . .
>
> Accordingly, the Special Staff recommends that protective entry, exit, and public utility-type price control in air transportation be eliminated within three to five years by statutory amendment to the Federal Aviation Act.[8]

Chairperson Robson agreed with the general conclusion of the Pulsifer Report and, without waiting for congressional action, took several administra-tive actions to ease the anticompetition practices of the Timm administration.

[8]"Executive Summary," *Report of the CAB Special Staff on Regulatory Reform,* pp. 1–2.

Specifically, the board under his guidance instituted these reforms: (1) end of route moratorium; (2) a significant relaxation of restrictions on the activities of the supplemental airlines, giving them more freedom to compete with the scheduled airlines; (4) approval of Texas International's "peanut fare," a 50 percent discount on selected flights over five medium-length routes in the southwest; (5) approval of American and two other airlines' "super saver" discount fair between New York and California — a 50 percent discount for passengers booking their travel 30 days in advance and staying for a minimum of 7 days or a maximum of 45 days; and (6) approval of Freddie Laker's Skytrain flights between London and New York at a one-way fare of $135, which was some 45 percent below the lowest fare charged by the other transatlantic airlines.

In the 1976 presidential elections, Jimmy Carter had made airline deregulation an important goal of his administration if he were elected. And he did fulfill that promise, for within 2 months of his taking office, on January 20, 1977, he chose Alfred Kahn to head the CAB, an appointment that was to affect profoundly the course of the airline industry. President Carter also appointed Elizabeth Bailey to the membership of the board. Both Kahn, an experienced hand in regulatory matters and a firm believer in the marketplace, and Bailey, a serious academic scholar, were staunchly for competition in the industry.[9] And although the other members of the board were for some change but not for total deregulation, Kahn and his staff ultimately succeeded in selling them the virtues of the marketplace.

Although there were several bills in the Congress to deregulate the airline industry in various ways, Kahn did not wait for their outcome. After he became chairperson of the board in June 1977, he moved vigorously to continue Robson's pro-competition policies by readily approving new discount fares and by deciding route applications in favor of those applicants who offered low fares.

The policies propounded and pursued by Robson and Kahn proved to be enormously popular as well as successful. Discount fares multiplied rapidly, Super Saver fares were extended to other markets, and Freddi Laker–type airfares were granted other airlines.

Since nothing succeeds like success, Kahn, obviously encouraged by his success so far, pressed his pro-competition policies with added vigor. He molded the board's route-award policies to encourage price competition and gave blanket permission to airlines to reduce rates by as much as 50 percent below the board-determined rates. In April 1978, he introduced the "multiple permissive entry," a policy that would grant route authority to all airlines which were "fit, willing and able" to perform the proposed service, this criterion being interpreted deliberately loosely. All these policies virtually amounted to de facto deregulation of the industry.

It is of interest that in taking all these steps, Kahn gave free reign to his upbringing as an economist, paying little heed to the purely technical or legal

---

[9]Before his appointment to the CAB, Kahn was chairperson of the New York State Public Utility Commission and before that professor of economics at Cornell (to which he has now returned).

aspects of deregulation. Based on sound economic theory and common sense interpretation of it, he was able to convince his colleagues that the industry was ripe for deregulation; the CAB special staff study mentioned earlier had already provided the necessary theoretical and empirical support for deregulation.

Noting the success of the defacto deregulation by the CAB, the Congress ultimately realized the benefits of deregulation and passed the Airline Deregulation Act of 1978. This act is of profound importance not only to the airline industry, but to others as well as a prototype to follow: The deregulation of the railroad and trucking industries, discussed in the previous chapter, was in no small way influenced by this act. We will discuss the details of this act in Section 12.8, but before that we turn to a critical evaluation of board policies between 1938–1976 to provide a historical perspective as well to show why the 1978 act was almost inevitable.

12.5 A CRITICAL EVALUATION OF CAB POLICIES PRIOR TO 1976[10]

The dynamic personality and the dry wit of Kahn were no doubt instrumental in hastening the move toward the 1978 act. And it might seem that the deregulation mood in the country was sudden, what with the Super Saver fares and Freddie Laker. This is not the case, however, for economists had for a long time made a case for deregulation based on theory as well as practical experience of the competitive intrastate air carriers in California and Texas. In particular, they had argued that the board's regulatory practices in the areas of pricing, market entry, intercarrier agreements, and route abandonment were not in the best interest of the consumer or even the airlines themselves. It is worth looking into the economists' case for deregulation.

Pricing

The 1938 act, as amended by the 1958 act, gave the CAB absolute authority to set maximum as well as minimum rates. Moreover, it had the power to suspend any rates which it deemed "unjust, unreasonable, unjustly discriminating, unduly preferential or unduly prejudicial." In case of suspension, the affected party could ask for a hearing, but because of the regulatory lag, such hearings were often delayed.

In determining airfares, the board established certain policies. In the 1950s and 1960s, airfares were based on average industry cost, with allowance being made for long-haul and short-haul traffic; the long-haul rates were such that they yielded a profit margin which was one-quarter greater than that of the short-haul traffic. In other words, the long-haul rates were relatively higher than the

---

[10]This section draws heavily on Paul W. MacAvoy and John W. Snow (eds.), *Regulation of Passenger Fares and Competition among the Airlines,* the Ford Administration Papers on Regulatory Reform, American Enterprise Institute for Public Policy Research, Washington, D.C., 1977 (hereafter referred to as the Ford Administration Papers on Civil Aviation).

short-haul rates and were in effect (cross-) subsidizing the latter (see our discussion in the previous section). This cross-subsidization was justified by the thinking (unverified) that short-haul traffic is more price-elastic than long-haul traffic, hence necessitating a relatively lower price.[11] Recall that the railroad rate structure also had a long-haul–short-haul rate differential, except in that case the short-haul rates were relatively higher than the long haul; hence the cross-subsidization was the other way around.

During the Timm administration the rate formula was modified. Fares were now based on four factors: a 55 percent load factor, a standard plane-seating configuration, a reduced per mile charge for long distances, and the average cost of operating an aircraft.

The preceding pricing policies are open to several objections. First, economically speaking, prices (fares) should be equal to the marginal cost in the short run or to the average total cost in the long run. The board followed neither of these principles, however. It simply based prices on the short-run average cost, and not even the average cost of each carrier but of the industry as a whole, with the result that "the average carrier made zero excess profits, . . . that each airline not the same as the average would do better or worse."[12]

Second, apart from the possibility that the short-haul market is not necessarily price-elastic or that the long-haul market is not necessarily price-inelastic, the long-haul–short-haul price differential did not allow for traffic densities, that is, how heavy the traffic is. Generally, prices should be lower in markets with higher traffic volume, for the increased load factor reduces the average cost of transportation; a plane with a 100-seat capacity generally incurs the same total cost of flying between two points whether it carries 40 passengers (load factor of 40 percent) or 60 passengers (load factor of 60 percent), yet the average cost of flying is much lower in the latter case.[13]

Third, and as we said in the previous chapter, if one wants to subsidize air traffic to smaller communities, one can better accomplish this via some direct tax relief rather than through distortion in the rate structure. As a matter of fact, it will be shown later that following the 1978 act many smaller communities are now served by commuter airlines, which operate small propeller planes quite economically.

Fourth, once the CAB determined the rates, however structured, the airlines could not compete in prices anymore. This then leads to so-called nonprice or service competition, such as greater frequency of flights (whether the planes are full or not), adopting more modern equipment, attractive flight attendants,

---

[11]The real reason for the subsidy was to provide services to small communities which, it was alleged, would not receive them without cross-subsidization. As we have noted in the previous section and in Ch. 11, this is not necessarily the best way of giving the subsidy.

[12]Paul W. MacAvoy, *The Regulated Industries and the Economy*, Norton, New York, 1979, p. 40.

[13]The key element in the profit margin is the load factor. Other things remaining the same, the higher the load factor, the lower the cost of operation. During the period of tight regulation of the industry, the load factors generally hovered around 50; on the average, planes were flying half-empty (or half-full).

free lunches, free drinks, in-flight entertainment, more leg room, free tooth-brushes, etc. As Alfred Kahn puts it:

> When limitations are put on price competition, but market conditions are such as to make continued interfirm rivalry likely, the consequences will be an accentuation of service competition.[14]

An important consequence of service competition is that it increases the oper-ating costs of the airlines, thus affecting their profit margin. Or, to quote Kahn again:

> Mark the general principle: . . . If price is prevented from falling to marginal cost in the short run or to average total cost in the long run, then, to the extent that com-petition prevails, it will tend to raise *cost* [because of service competition] to the level of *price* [determined by the CAB].[15]

What Kahn is saying can be visualized graphically, in Figure 12.3. In this graph we show the long-run marginal and average cost curves of a hypothetical airline. If price competition were allowed, and assuming no entry barriers, the com-petitive price P_C will be where $P_C = LMC = LAC$. But since price competition is not allowed, and assuming the CAB-regulated price P_r as shown in the figure, the hypothetical airline will engage in nonprice competition (better seating arrangement, more soothing interior decor, high-quality meals, etc.) to attract a larger share of the market to such an extent that eventually its cost curves will be pushed upward to the point where $P_r = MC_r = AC_r$ (where MC_r and AC_r are the marginal and average cost curves that include expenditures on nonprice competition). Hence this type of regulation forces costs to match the regulated price. In Figure 12.3 it is seen that the hypothetical firm has been able to increase its market share. But if all the airlines follow nonprice competition, it is quite likely that the respective market shares may remain as they were before except that the average cost will be pushed upward toward the regulated price.

Does it mean that if there were no price regulation, nonprice competition would not take place? Far from it. What it means is that in that case the airlines would be able to offer a variety of price-service packages and let consumers choose the one that fits their purse. If I am willing to fly without any frills, I will be glad to have a lower fare. Those who desire frills should be able to pay for them.[16] Obviously, Freddi Laker knew what he was doing; he tried to give the passenger the option of flying to London or New York with the least frills. Until 1974, the board did not give the consumer that option; it was an all or nothing proposition.

In sum, these board policies regarding pricing resulted in generally higher than necessary cost of travel and reduced industry profits. It is ironic that the industry,

---

[14]Alfred Kahn, op. cit., p. 209.
[15]Ibid.
[16]If the airlines were to price their frill services separate from their cost of flying, would one not expect some passengers to opt out of such frills?

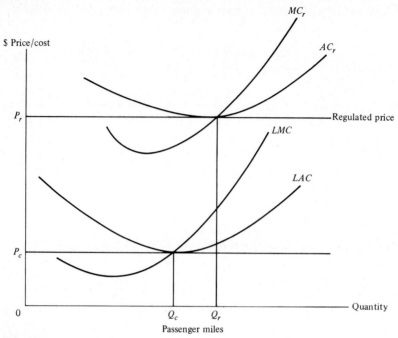

FIGURE 12.3
Equilibrium output and price under price and non-price competition.

although based on monopoly pricing, did not achieve monopoly profits. Between 1947 and 1976, the rate of return on investment of the CAB-controlled airlines exceeded 10 percent only in 6 years; for the remaining years it remained between 5 to 10 percent, not a spectacular performance by any stretch of the imagination.

How can we be sure that had the CAB not intervened, fares would have been lower and profits generally higher? Is it not merely the dream of an ivory-tower economist? Fortunately, we have almost a "controlled" experiment in public policy in the experience of the CAB-free intrastate airlines in California and Texas, an experience worth looking into.

Intrastate Airline Price Competition in California and Texas   Pacific Southwest Airlines (PSA) and Air California are intrastate airlines operating within the state limits of California. The PSA, operating since 1949, is the largest of the two, serving a total of twelve points within the state. Air California, in existence since 1967, has ten points. Both these airlines are controlled by state regulatory authorities, but the control is minimal and does not cover rate regulation. As a result, within the state, these airlines have been able to engage in price competition, offering price-quality combinations. Of course, the CAB-controlled scheduled airlines also operate in California. Therefore, here one has a controlled experiment in that the state of California is served by the regulated as well as nonregulated airlines. What has been the result? The data in Table 12.1 tell the story.

The statistics of Table 12.1 are quite startling: In the medium-haul traffic, the CAB-determined rates in 1972 were some 93 percent higher than the free market rates. No wonder, between 1965 and 1971, traffic on the California intrastate carriers increased by some 250 percent or at an annual average of about 23 percent. Compare this with the average annual growth in all domestic short-haul (less than 500 miles) traffic of only 4.7 percent during the same period. This traffic growth has resulted in higher load factors of the California airlines; in 1974 it was about 70 percent for these airlines compared to 55 percent for the CAB-controlled airlines. Predictably, this has resulted in respectable profits for these airlines. In each of the years 1972, 1973, and 1974 the California airlines earned a return of more than 24 percent on operating investments. And all this was accompanied by an excellent safety record; safety was not sacrificed for price reduction.

The same story is told in Texas. Southwest Airlines, the largest Texas state carrier operating since 1971, charged in 1975 the fares shown in Table 12.2. These fares were considerably lower than those charged by the CAB-certified carriers.

To sum up, the California and Texas experiences poignantly show that given freedom of pricing, airlines can come up with price-service combinations which not only benefit the traveler but also increase the load factors and thereby the profitability of the carriers.

Can we translate the California and Texas experiences to the nation as a whole? Well, the deregulatory initiatives taken since 1976 and the experience since the 1978 act would show that the California and Texas experiences need not be unique. We will discuss this more fully in Section 12.9.

Entry Regulations

What makes the board's price regulation tenable is that it is accompanied by severe restriction on entry into and exit from the industry. As noted, Sec. 401 of the 1958 Act gave the board the authority to determine which carriers oper-

TABLE 12.1
DIFFERENTIAL BETWEEN INTERSTATE AND INTRASTATE FARES IN CALIFORNIA, 1972

Length of haul	Intrastate fares per mile, ¢	Interstate fares per mile, ¢	Interstate fares/ intrastate fares
Very short haul (65 miles)	16.923	23.585	1.394
Short haul (109 miles)	9 .363	16.858	1.800
Short–medium haul (338–373 miles)	5 .021	9 .685	1.929

Source: Paul W. MacAvoy and John W. Snow (eds.), *Regulation of Passenger Fares and Competition among the Airlines,* the Ford Administration Papers on Civil Aviation, American Enterprise Institute for Public Policy Research, Washington, D.C., 1977, table 2-1, p. 42.

TABLE 12.2
COMPARISON OF INTERSTATE AND INTRASTATE LEVELS IN SELECTED TEXAS MARKETS, DEC. 1, 1975

Fare type	Dallas–Houston	Dallas–Harligen*	Dallas–San Antonio	Houston–Harligen*
CAB interstate				
First class	$48		$51	
Coach†	35	$57	37	$42
Economy	32	51	33	38
Southwest intrastate				
"Executive class"	25	40	25	25
"Pleasure class"	15	25	15	15

*Also applicable for interstate carriers to Brownsville and McAllen.
†Jet coach or jet custom class service.
Note: All fares include tax.
Source: Paul W. MacAvoy and John W. Snow (eds.), *Regulation of Passenger Fares and Competition among the Airlines,* the Ford Administration Papers on Civil Aviation, American Enterprise Institute for Public Policy Research, Washington, D.C., 1977, table 2-3, p. 45.

ate and on what routes. Moreover, by rigidly interpreting the tests of "fit, willing and able to perform" and the "public convenience and necessity," the CAB virtually ruled out new entry. Recall that between 1959 and 1974 not a single new trunk line route was allowed. Also, many carriers were denied the status of the supplemental or charter airlines.

Thus, with entry virtually controlled, the only way the carriers could compete was in prices. But, alas, that was out of the question. No wonder, the only means of competition left for them was service and nonprice competition. We have already seen that this has had the effect of increasing the airlines' operating costs and reducing their profit margins. The net effect of entry and exit restrictions has been well summed up by Richard Caves as follows:

> The control of entry and exit, both in the national market and in city-pair markets, has raised the cost of air transportation through protecting inefficient firms and through maintaining seasonally imbalanced route structures that require firms to own many types of aircraft.[17]

Anticompetition Agreements

Despite the price and entry regulations, the airline industry continued to exhibit high unit costs and low profits, the profits exhibiting a strong cyclical behavior — up with business expansions and down with business recessions. During the period 1950–1970, the aftertax profit rate averaged only 6.4 percent. Therefore, from time to time the air carriers were allowed to enter into capacity-

[17]Richard E. Caves, "Performance, Structure, and the Goals of Civil Aeronautics Board Regulation," in Paul W. MacAvoy (ed.), *The Crisis of the Regulatory Commissions,* Norton, New York, 1970, p. 134.

limiting agreements (reduced flight frequency or stopovers, etc.) and in some cases to merge with other airlines, the merger activity being exempt from the purview of the antitrust laws.

The capacity-restricting agreements do increase industry load factors and hence profitability, but at the cost of consumer welfare. Had price and entry regulations not been imposed, the resulting competition too would have increased load factors and reduced industry costs — while charging lower fares. As the California and Texas episodes tell, this would have benefitted one and all.

Route Abandonment

The CAB regulations until 1976 were such that not only was entry into the industry not generally permitted but also it was not easy to exit from the industry by abandoning one or more routes on the carrier's route authority. Moreover, the rate and route regulations were such that frequently it was not possible for a scheduled airline to fly to lightly traveled communities without some subsidy. This subsidy came in the form of cross-subsidy (charging higher rates on the long-haul traffic and lower rates on the short-haul traffic) or direct cash allowance (see the discussion on cross-subsidization given earlier and in Chapter 11). If that subsidy was not feasible, or even when feasible but not profitable from the overall-system viewpoint, the only recourse left for the affected airline was to abandon the unprofitable routes. But that was not easy under the CAB rules. Before a route could be discontinued, there were extensive hearings while attempts were being made to provide some service on such routes by local carriers or the nonskeds. But all this took considerable time (the usual regulatory lag), putting severe pressure on the profitability of the airlines.

Commenting on the board's route abandonment policies, the Ford Administration Papers on Civil Aviation state:

> Carriers should not be forced to serve unprofitable markets. A party forced to provide service will seek to minimize the amount of service it provides, and losses in one community will have to be made up in excess profits in other communities.[18]

To sum up: CAB regulatory policies until 1976 were such that there was virtually no price competition and that entry, with a few exceptions, was well-nigh impossible. As a result, the scheduled carriers were forced to engage in non-price competition, capacity-limiting agreements, and abandonment of unprofitable routes, the latter effected with considerable regulatory lag. All these practices denied consumers the freedom of price-quality combinations deemed best for them, and they distorted consumers' choice between air and nonair modes of transportation, clearly leading to misallocation of the nation's economic resources. The California and Texas interstate airline experiences show how real

---

[18]John W. Snow, *The Problems of Airline Regulation and the Ford Administration Proposal for Reform*, the Ford Administration Papers on Civil Aviation, p. 13.

these consequences can be. The following section gives some idea of the cost of such misallocation.

12.6 ESTIMATES OF COSTS AND BENEFITS OF CAB REGULATION

Costs of Regulation

Bearing in mind the usual caveat about cost estimates (See Chapter 5), we provide some cost figures that have been obtained by various researchers. In Chapter 5 we cited the Office of Management and Budget (OMB) estimate of the cost of regulation as $2 to $4 billion. In 1977 the General Accounting Office (GAO) estimated that airline deregulation would save consumers between $1.4 and $1.8 billion annually.[19] For 1969, George Douglas and James Miller estimated that the average airfare was high by about 4 to 6 percent as a result of the rate regulation.[20] For 1974, Theodore Keeler's estimates show that the airfares were higher by some 30 to 50 percent as a result of the regulation.[21]

Perhaps these aggregate estimates do not reveal the gravity of the problem. We consider two areas where regulation has had an adverse effect, namely, on innovation and on airport congestion.

Effect on Innovation   Elsewhere we have talked about the A-J effect, the tendency to overinvest (i.e., more than socially desirable) in capital equipment due to guaranteed rate of return or price. This effect often attributed to public utilities can be observed in the airline industry, too. As a result of rate regulation, airlines were encouraged to introduce technological innovations even when the social costs of such innovations exceeded the social benefits.

The case in point is the introduction of the DC-7 airplane. This propeller plane, introduced in the 1950s, was designed to make nonstop, coast-to-coast flights at costs somewhat lower than the alternative DC-6B, which required a refueling stop. It was known at that time, however, that the DC-7 would soon be replaced by the jet plane. Nonetheless, the airlines rushed to introduce it. Why? There are two reasons. First, since the rate policy then prevailing permitted charging relatively higher rates on the long-haul traffic compared to the short-haul traffic, there was every incentive to go for the DC-7s. Second, because the airlines could not compete in price, introduction of this plane was a means of nonservice competition, for passengers flying coast-to-coast would

---

[19]U.S. Comptroller General, "Lower Airline Costs Per Passenger Are Possible in the United and Could Result in Lower Fares," CED-77-34, February 1977.

[20]George Douglas and James C. Miller, *Economic Regulation of Domestic Air Transport,* Brookings, Washington, D.C., 1974.

[21]Theodore E. Keeler, "Domestic Trunk Airline Regulation: An Economic Evaluation," part of *A Framework for Regulation,* U.S. Senate Government Operations Committee, U.S. Government Printing Office, Washington, D.C., 1978.

rather do so nonstop. But of course if one airline did so, others, following the principle of the ''prisoner's dilemma,'' would follow suit.[22]

Now if the CAB had allowed price competition, the DC-6B would have offered the DC-7 competition in price; consumers would have been given the choice between lower price but longer journey time (the DC-6B) and higher price but shorter travel time (the DC-7). This would have slowed the introduction of the DC-7, which was to become obsolete anyhow. But that was not to be the case due to the rate regulation.

Effect on Airport Congestion   An element of regulatory cost that is hidden is the cost of airport congestion, especially during peak hours. As noted, because of lack of price competition until 1976, airlines engaged in nonprice competition such as increased frequency of flights even though the load factors were generally low (around 50 percent). During peak hours, in the nation's busy airports such as O'Hare and Kennedy this nonprice competition resulted in considerable delays in landing and takeoff, not to mention the opportunity cost of passengers' wasted time and of air pollution.

Although no estimates of congestion costs are directly available, what with all the measurement problems, one can gauge them indirectly. For example, in 1968 the New York airports increased the landing fee for small planes during the peak hours, from $5 to $25. Although this seems a slight change, the traffic of small planes during the peak hours declined by some 40 percent. If price competition had been allowed, and if a peak–off-peak rate differential had been introduced, there would have emerged a landing and takeoff pattern that would have reduced airport congestion: Those who wanted to fly during peak hours would have paid higher fares compared to those who chose to fly during off-peak hours. This is not farfetched, for utilities such as telephone companies have differentiated rate schedules that take into account traffic (call) densities – the rates during business hours are much higher than those during the evening and night hours (see the discussion on peak-load pricing in Chapter 5). Perhaps a far better landing pattern would emerge if the landing rights during peak hours were auctioned off like the marketable pollution rights discussed in Chapter 4.

Benefits of Regulation

What can we say about the benefit side of the ledger? We do not have any concrete estimates.[23] What we have are qualitative statements of those who

---

[22] The prisoner's dilemma: Two suspects, A and B, are caught together for an alleged crime and are put in different cells and interrogated separately. If A confesses to the crime while B does not, A goes free and B gets 10 years and vice versa. If both confess, they each get 3 years, but if both remain silent they each get 1 year. Assuming ''no honor among thieves,'' what would be the best strategy for each suspect so as to maximize his or her self-interest? By analogy what would happen if one airline introduced DC-7 and another one did not?

[23] We do not consider the benefits due to air safety regulation, which is the responsibility of the FAA and will continue to be so in the future.

are opposed to deregulation. In the view of the pro-regulators or status quo believers: The CAB regulations have provided job security for airline managers; job security as well as higher wages and fringe benefits for airline workers, including the pilots (they retain their seniority in cases of mergers); security to stockholders (no airline has gone into bankruptcy because of merger provisions); and security to lenders, who know that in case of financial trouble the board would bail out the ailing company. But all these benefits are essentially private and not public.

We leave it to the reader to decide whether these benefits, if they exist as described, outweigh the costs of regulation; keep in mind the critical evaluation of the board's policies made in Section 12.5.

12.7 THE PROS AND CONS OF DEREGULATION[24]

As we have seen, beginning around 1976 the CAB began introducing some price and entry flexibility which ultimately culminated in the passage of the Airline Deregulation Act of 1978. But when the winds of deregulation were gathering momentum, there was considerable opposition to it from within and without the industry. And this opposition, although abated considerably, has persisted even after the 1978 act became reality. It is therefore worthwhile to spend some time looking into the cons of deregulation and evaluate them critically.

Service to Small Communities Will Suffer

This familiar argument runs as follows: Since the CAB-determined rate structure (at least until 1976) was such that the long-haul rates subsidized the short-haul rates, it was possible for the airlines to provide service to small communities. Introduce price competition, it is alleged, and this will disappear, prompting the carriers to abandon services to such communities.

But before accepting this argument against deregulation, consider the true situation. When an airline gets the certificate of public convenience and necessity, there is often the requirement that some service be provided to small communities (population less than 100,000). But the certificate does not require that such service be provided on a systematic basis (e.g., every day). Hence carriers are allowed considerable discretion; they may fly once or twice a week or make one flight a day or some similar arrangement. In passing, it may be noted that historically airlines have used less than 20 percent of their route authority, with the result that many small communities are not served by scheduled airlines at all. Why? One reason is that even with the cross-subsidy (about which we have written at length) it was not profitable to fly to lightly-traveled areas because of lack of volume. Moreover, the development of highways in the 1950s and 1960s made it possible for the traveler to use the automobile to go to the

---

[24]The following discussion leans heavily on the *Ford Administration Papers on Civil Aviation* (see the paper by John W. Snow, op. cit.)

regional airports where they could catch the scheduled flights. Also, because of nonprice competition the carriers preferred the jet planes to the smaller propeller planes, making travel to smaller communities less attractive.

But what was woe to the big airlines was weal to the local carriers and the nonskeds; many local carriers and nonskeds have entered into the markets abandoned by the major airlines. And as we will see in Section 12.9, following the 1978 act, many airlines are now serving smaller communities which never had air service before. Therefore, the fear that without regulation the smaller communities will be left out in the cold has proved to be just that — a fear.

There Will Be Market Chaos

According to the opponents, deregulation of the industry will lead to "market chaos," an expression with several meanings. It is alleged that: deregulation will lead to increased managerial discretion about where, when, and at what price to fly; there will be concentration of market power in the hands of a few powerful airlines; airlines will not honor each other's reservation or transfer baggage from one to another; and so on. The opponents to deregulation do not offer cogent reasons why the consequences they fear will materialize. What is so special about the airline industry that it needs continued protection?

In any case, the proof of the pudding lies in the eating. Examine the experience of the intrastate airlines in California and Texas. They have provided scheduled service, fares are not changed daily, baggage is not lost in transit, and the airlines themselves have prospered although their fares are much lower than the CAB-regulated rates. The same is true of some of the newer commuter lines in existence since the 1978 act. New York Air, a commuter airline in operation since December 19, 1980, shuttles between New York and Washington at a one-way fare of $49 during the working week and at $29 during weekends and off-peak hours, compared to the established giant, Eastern, whose regular one-way fare is $59. Predictably, within 3 weeks Eastern was forced to reduce its fare to the level of New York Air. But no "market chaos" has yet resulted.

Emergence of Predatory Pricing and Cut-Throat Competition

To acquire monopoly of a route, the argument runs, a predator may cut price below marginal cost (or below average variable cost) so as to drive competitors out and then charge a monopoly price to recoup the losses. But as we have commented often, predation can succeed only if the predator has superior resources to withstand short-term losses, and, more important, if there are such barriers to entry, say, on account of economies of scale, that it is not easy to enter the industry. All the available empirical evidence shows that there are no noticeable economies of scale in the industry and the real barrier to entry is the CAB itself, with its severe restriction of entry into the industry (at least until 1976).[25]

---

[25]On economies of scale, see the Ford Administration Papers on Civil Aviation

Once again it is worth considering the California and Texas experiences. These intrastate airlines, much smaller than the CAB-certified trunk lines, are successfully competing with the latter, proof positive that economies of scale are not the restraining factor. In any case, if an airline, in pursuit of monopoly power, charges prices less than (long-run) average cost, one can resort to the Sherman or Clayton Acts to curb that airline. There is no need for the CAB to do that job.

The Role of Antitrust Enforcement in Deregulated Markets[26]   As we have seen, under the various regulatory laws some of the practices followed or approved by the regulatory agencies are exempt from the antitrust laws. For example, until the recent deregulatory moves in the railroad and trucking industries, the rates fixed by the industry rate bureaus (which were esentially monopoly rates) were exempt from the scope of the antitrust laws, thanks to the Reed Bulwinkle Act of 1948. But under the Motor Carrier Act of 1980, for example, this antitrust immunity will end by January 1, 1984. When this happens, the Antitrust Division of the Justice Department as well as the public will have to be more vigilant about the rate-making practices in the trucking industry. The same is true of the railroad industry.

In general, there is no doubt that antitrust enforcement will have an increasingly important role to play as deregulation spreads to other sectors of the economy. Thus, when the CAB goes out of business in 1985 there will be no regulatory agency to look into the public's complaint about rate-making in the airline industry. Ultimately the courts, with the aid of the antitrust laws, will be increasingly called upon to check into any alleged monopoly practices in the deregulated industries. But that should not be an argument against deregulation in the airlines or any other industry.

Airlines Are Public Utilities

The CAB rate policies give the impression that the airlines are like public utilities or natural monopolies, hence they need to be regulated. This argument is foggy. Recall that a natural monopoly is characterized by declining average cost (economies of scale); there is no evidence that there are such economies of scale in the industry.[27] "Granted," the opponents might counter, "but aren't the airlines, like the public utilities, obliged to provide service on demand? Shouldn't they therefore be regulated?" There is some twisted logic here, for

> [public] utilities are not regulated because they are required to serve; they are regulated and required to serve because they are monopolies. That is not the airline situation because airlines are not natural monopolies.[28]

---

[26]For further discussion, see the Senate *Study on Federal Regulation,* vol. VI, pp. 92–93.
[27]Notice that a larger plane may have lower unit cost of operation than a smaller one. But as long as small and large airlines can buy such large planes, there are no scale barriers.
[28]Ford Administration Papers on Civil Aviation, p. 29.

Airlines Are Unique

Another argument states that the industry is unique because of the complexity of route scheduling, interlining (connections with other airlines), baggage transference, common airport facilities, and because of the industry's inability to inventory its product – once a plane has departed, all the empty seat capacity is gone.

Why, then, is the hotel industry not unique? It, too, cannot inventory its product; on a given day all unoccupied rooms simply represent idle space. But that industry is not regulated. As a matter of fact, it is highly competitive. What makes the airline industry unique is that, unlike the hotel industry, it is highly regulated!

Question of Air Safety

Wouldn't free entry into the industry lead to more airplane crashes because of congestion of the airspace, poor inspection, etc.? There is a real possibility of this. Although the freer intrastate California and Texas airlines have had excellent safety records, the new entry since 1976 has been accompanied by many fatal accidents per 100,000 flights. But because of an FAA crackdown, there has been substantial improvement: The accident rate per 100,000 flights decreased by 23 percent between 1979 and 1980. It is important to bear in mind that no deregulator has ever advocated sacrificing air safety. The FAA is fully authorized to regulate air safety to the fullest possible extent.

In passing it may be noted that whether the airlines are regulated or not by the FAA, one can never expect 100 percent safe air travel. As we will show in Chapter 16, on occupational health and safety, one can talk about the optimal level of safety – that occurs where the incremental amount spent on safety measures is equal to the incremental benefit resulting from such measures. (For further details, see Chapter 16.)

To summarize: On closer scrutiny, the arguments against deregulation are not convincing enough to outweigh the undesirable economic consequences of CAB regulation prior to 1976. Moreover, as we will see shortly, the experience of deregulation since 1976 has been on the whole beneficial to the consumer and the industry alike. It is against this backdrop that we examine the provisions of the 1978 act.

12.8   THE AIRLINE DEREGULATION ACT OF 1978

The deregulation act that finally emerged from the Congress, the Airline Deregulation Act of 1978, was signed into law by President Carter on October 24, 1978. In broad terms, the provisions of the act are as follows:[29]

---

[29]Based on the summary in *Federal Regulatory Directory,* Congressional Quarterly, Inc., Washington, D.C., 1979–1980, pp. 84–86.

1 Ensuring safety of travel, the CAB was instructed to place "maximum reliance" on competition.

2 Cities now listed on airlines' certification, especially the small communities, are to be guaranteed essential air service for 10 years and the board is to pick up the tab for a carrier's losses if it is to continue to serve and no replacement can be found.

3 Interstate airlines are exempt from state regulation of their rates and routes.

4 On routes where one airline is operating, although several others are authorized but not functioning, the board is to allow operating rights to any applicant fit to serve.

5 If a route is served by two or more lines, the CAB may grant that route to another airline if such is "consistent with the public convenience and necessity."

6 To ease entry restrictions, during the period 1979–1981, an operating airline was allowed to add one additional route each year without waiting for CAB's formal approval. Each carrier was also permitted to protect one of its existing routes each year by designating it as ineligible for automatic entry by another carrier.

7 The board is to be notified when an airline wishes to suspend or discontinue a service.

8 After January 1, 1983, the amount of subsidy paid to a carrier for carrying U.S. mail must take into consideration the company's total revenue, not merely the revenue on the subsidized routes.

9 As before, the CAB is required to approve airline consolidations, mergers, purchases, leases, operating contracts, and acquisitions. The burden of proving the anticompetition effects of such actions is placed on the party challenging an intended merger.

10 All intercompany agreements affecting air transportation are subject to the board's approval. No competition-restricting agreement is to be allowed unless it is to serve a "serious transportation need" or to provide an "important public benefit."

11 Carriers can lower rates as much as 50 percent or raise them up to 5 percent above the "standard industry fare" without seeking the board's prior approval, the standard industry fare being that which was in existence on July 1, 1977 (which is subject to semiannual review).

12 The board can suspend a rate if deemed predatory, meaning usually a price which is below marginal cost or average variable cost.

13 The life of the Board itself is to be phased out as follows: Authority over domestic routes to end by December 31, 1981, authority over domestic rates and fares, mergers, and acquisitions to expire on January 1, 1983, and the board itself to go out of existence by January 1, 1985.

14 After the board goes out of business, the local subsidy program will be transferred to the Department of Transportation. The foreign air transportation authority will be handled by the Justice and Transportation departments. The mail subsidy program will go back to the U.S. Postal Service.

As a first step, in March 1979 the board relinquished its control over domestic cargo carriers and freight forwarders. These modes of transportation are no longer required to file tariffs or obtain certification.

Considering the 1938 and 1958 acts and the way in which the industry had been regulated in the past, the 1978 act is truly an astonishing achievement: The provision for the abolition of the board's domestic route authority, abolition of its authority over domestic rates and fares, etc., and its own demise are almost unheard of for any regulatory authority created by the Congress. There is no question that both the proponents and opponents of deregulation are and will be watching the fortunes of the industry as it plunges into the turbulent waters of the marketplace. Among those watching will be those in the other regulated sectors of the economy.

12.9 THE AIRLINE INDUSTRY SINCE THE 1978 ACT

What has the 1978 act accomplished? Has the industry become more competitive or has there been an increase in economic concentration? Has the industry experienced healthy profits? What about service to small communities? What aobut air safety? Has the consumer been given price and quality choices of service?

Two to 3 years of deregulation is not an adequate time period to answer all these questions. Moreover, until all the regulatory authorities of the board are abolished, we will not be able to provide categorical answers. Nonetheless, some general observations may be made about the experience thus far.

So far as industry profitability is concerned, in 1978 airline operating profits of $1.4 billion were the highest ever. They dipped to $215 million in 1979. 1980 was the worst year, with operating losses in excess of $200 million, which was largely due to the 1979–1980 economic recession as well as to skyrocketing fuel prices. Despite this, intrastate airlines such as Southwest recorded spectacular growth. In the first 9 months of 1980 Southwest's operating revenue was a record high of $155 million, up 62 percent from the previous year, and the net income of $20.5 million was about 67 percent higher than in the previous year. The same gains were true for many commuter airlines. What this means is that the smaller airlines have managed to do well.

In the case of the small airlines, the 1978 act has been a real bonanza to them. Airlines such as Golden Gate, Air Wisconsin, and Big Sky, using mostly small cost-effective planes, are flying over routes abandoned by the major carriers. Newcomers such as Midway Airline, New York Air, and People Express are flying side by side with the major trunk carriers. As noted, the commuter liner New York Air is giving keen competition to Eastern. The commuter airlines together carried 11 percent more passengers in 1980 over 1979, whereas the trunk airlines actually suffered a dip. An important reason for this is that during the years of regulation the major carriers went in for modern heavy gas-using planes, expensive labor contracts, and all kinds of frills, with the end result that when competition came along they could not get away from the rigidity of their cost structure.[30] Also, airlines such as Midway, a Chicago-based carrier, and People Express, a Newark, New Jersey, carrier are using formerly abandoned or lightly used airports such as Midway in Chicago and Newark in New Jersey; they are avoiding the crowded airports of O'Hare and Kennedy, with beneficial impact on their profitability. Thus, it seems that the greatest beneficiaries of the 1978 act are the commuter airlines; the established carriers may not have fared so well. But who ever said that deregulation will necessarily benefit each competitor in the marketplace?

It is interesting to observe that the fear of loss of service to several communities has proven to be exaggerated. Although the major carriers have abandoned some of their unprofitable routes, the newer carrier have taken up the slack and have expanded their services to many new areas. They have also provided greater convenience to travelers who live in the suburbs of some cities, in downtown areas of some others, and in some smaller cities. Air Florida, for instance, has a service between White Plains in the Westchester County of New York and Chicago. People living in this county can thus avoid the hassle of going to Kennedy or Laguardia airports, a hassel that only those who have gone to these airports can appreciate. Similarly, Texas International has service between Bradley Field, in Windsor Locks, Connecticut, and the Baltimore-Washington Airport with some fares cheaper than Eastern's New York–Washington shuttle.

From the preceding discussion, it would seem that deregulation has proven to be successful thus far. But there may be some minuses. Because of the bargain fares on several routes, airplanes on these routes are often very crowded. In some cases the ticketing procedure has become complex. There is more pressure on the traveler to shop around to find out which airline gives the best deal. All these consequences are to be expected, however.

In sum, then, it would seem that the greatest beneficiaries of deregulation are the consumers. They are now given a variety of price-service packages, and overall competition has brought down the average level of fares, a tribute to the marketplace in spite of the burgeoning fuel prices and the higher levels of inflation. In the words of Marvin S. Cohen, the former chairperson of the CAB:

> The simple premise of deregulation is that a naturally competitive industry will perform at least as well — and probably much better without Government intervention.
>
> In theory, competition forces the individual firm to be innovative and efficient; benefits are then passed on to the public in the form of more efficient use of resources, lower fares or more service or both.

---

[30]Some of these factors may explain the collapse of Braniff International Airlines in 1982. Saddled with a debt of $732 million, it filed for protection under the Federal Bankruptcy Act. The severe 1981–1982 economic recession was also a contributory factor.

Competition has forced the airlines to become more efficient and to pass these cost savings on to consumers in lower fares. Fares are today much lower than they would have been under regulation. [And] while some cities have lost some of their service, ... many cities, such as Boise, Idaho; Albany, N.Y.; Amarillo, Tex.; Billings, Mont.; and Eugene, Ore., have gained additional service as the airlines have shifted supply to meet demand. . . .

From 1970 to 1976, years of tight airline regulation, load factors averaged 52.8 percent. In 1978, the first year of real pricing freedom, load factors jumped to 61.7 percent. In the first nine months of this year [1979], the domestic trunk load factor was 65.1 percent.[31]

12.10 SUMMARY AND CONCLUSIONS

After nearly four decades of regulation, the airline industry is now substantially deregulated and by 1984 it will be totally deregulated, except for safety regulation. In this chapter we discussed how the rise and fall of regulation in this industry came about. This is a unique episode in the annals of U.S. economic regulation, for regulation and regulatory agencies once established rarely go out of business.

Because of the great depression and the resulting losses in the 1930s, which the industry attributed to lack of price and entry regulations, the Congress first attempted to control the civil aviation industry when it passed the Civil Aeronautics Act of 1938. This act instituted rate, route, and entry regulations and created the Civil Aeronautics Board to enforce them. The act was strengthened when Congress passed the Federal Aviation Act of 1958.

Since its inception in 1938 until 1976, the CAB controlled the airline industry so stringently that price competition and entry into the industry was virtually impossible. Exit from the industry by abandoning one or more routes was also highly regulated.

All these restrictions have had adverse impact on the consumer and the industry itself. The consumer was denied price competition or new suppliers (new airlines or routes). And since the CAB rates were determined by unsound economic principles (e.g., pricing at short-run average cost), these rates were unduly high. Because of this rate regulation, says the General Accounting Office, the consumers in the aggregate were charged extra to the tune of $1.4 to $1.8 billion annually. The industry, too, has suffered. Prohibited from competing in prices, the airlines were forced to engage in nonprice competition, which had the effect of inflating the industry's cost structure and hence adversely affecting its profitability. The net effect has been misallocation of the nation's transportation resources.

Beginning in 1976 things began to change. Chagrined by the board's refusal

---

[31]Marvin S. Cohen, "Airline Deregulation Is Working," *The New York Times*, Dec. 22, 1979, p. 23.

to relax its regulatory policies, some House members and Senators took initiatives to decontrol the industry's regulations. Sensing the uneasiness in the Congress, CAB Chairperson Robson in 1976 and Chairperson Kahn in 1977 began to loosen the board's uncompetitive rules about pricing and entry. The results were immediately favorable to both the consumer and the industry; the former got several bargain fares and the latter started earning good profits. Buoyed by this outcome, the initiatives of Senators Kennedy and Cannon, and the backing of Presidents Ford and Carter, the Congress ultimately passed the Airline Deregulation Act of 1978, an act of profound importance to the fortunes of this industry as well as to the fortunes of other industries which are highly regulated and where deregulatory moves are in the offing. By 1985, the 1978 act will put the industry totally back into the marketplace; all pricing, entry, and route regulations of the domestic airline industry will cease completely.

Despite opposition to deregulation from several quarters, the results of deregulation so far are encouraging. The consumer now has a choice between various packages of rates and quality of service, a choice mostly denied under old regulation. Another beneficiary of the deregulation has been the small commuter operator. Many small operators have come into being since the deregulation and are serving the needs of travelers at competitive rates. Moreover, they have started services to areas abandoned by the major carriers or areas which had no service at all. The major airlines have not fared so well in comparison largely due to previous regulation which had forced them into expensive labor contracts, excessive frills, and gas-guzzling, huge airplanes. Of course, as time passes, these carriers will adjust to the thrust of the marketplaces. But nobody ever guaranteed that deregulation would benefit all participants equally.

Has the airline deregulation experience thus far any lessons for other regulated industries? As we saw in the previous chapter, deregulation of the railroad and trucking industries was prompted by the 1978 act. The experience in those industries, although quite limited, shows that the kind of competition that has been unleashed by the airline deregulation will eventually emerge in those industries. And the consequences to the consumer and small operators will be as beneficial in those industries as they seem to have been in the airline industry. If this happens, the winds of deregulation in other regulated sectors will gather additional momentum.

QUESTIONS

12-1 Which theory or theories of regulation discussed in Chapter 2 best explain the emergence of the CAB?

12-2 Is the airline industry a natural monopoly? Why or why not? If it is a natural monopoly, would this justify its regulation? .

12-3 The load factor, the percentage of passenger seats actually occupied, has been greater for the intrastate airlines of California and Texas than for the CAB-regulated airlines. What factors might account for this difference? Put otherwise, what are the determinants of the load factor?

12-4 Did the CAB fulfill the goals of the Federal Aviation Act of 1958? In particular, did it promote "adequate, economical and efficient service by carriers at reasonable charges without unjust discriminations, undue preferences or advantages or unfair or destructive competitive practices"?

12-5 Recall the days of the youth fare, when passengers between the ages of 12 and 22 could travel at greatly reduced fares. Is this discriminatory pricing? How would you justify such rates economically?

12-6 Many airlines offer fares which are lower for night travel than for day travel? How would you defend this practice economically?

12-7 "This kind of [nonservice] competition, like persuasive advertising, is in considerable measure self-defeating." (Alfred Kahn, *The Economics of Regulation,* vol. II, p. 242.) In what sense is this so?

12-8 In the practice known as "cream-skimming," it is alleged that without entry restriction, competitors will naturally serve only the lucrative markets (say, between New York and Florida) and neglect other markets (say, the rural markets or other lightly traveled areas). Assuming the existence of such a practice, do you think that entry regulation is the only answer to stop it? What alternatives can you suggest?

12-9 What do you think of the idea of selling landing rights during peak hours by competitive bidding? Would this alleviate airport congestion? What would be its effect on the demand for air travel?

12-10 What would be the consequences of relaxing controls over price and product competition but retaining the entry control?

12-11 Comment: " ... Increased pricing flexibility and liberalized entry go hand-in-hand." (The Ford Administration Papers on Civil Aviation, p. 7).

12-12 Until the passage of the Airline Deregulation Act of 1978, New York, unlike California and Texas, could not develop a commuter airline because the landing and takeoff patterns in New York City had to cross New Jersey and Connecticut airspace; hence interstate commerce, which brings the CAB regulation. But since the deregulation, New York Air, a commuter airline operating between New York and Washington, is operating very successfully and giving Eastern a run for its money. What does this tell about the CAB regulatory policies of the past? Who is the beneficiary of the new competition?

12-13 One of the arguments against decontrol is that it would lead to concentration of economic power in the hands of a few large companies. But this has not happened so far? Why? Do you think it will happen in the future? And why?

12-14 Why do you think that so many new commuter airlines have come into being since the deregulation of the industry?

12-15 Do you personally believe that the 1978 act has been beneficial to you? In what ways?

12-16 Suppose that after the CAB goes out of business the industry runs into financial trouble. Would you then recommend that the CAB be put back into business and bring back the old regulatory apparatus? Why or why not?

12-17 In the days of service or nonprice competition suppose that two airlines, A and B, had the following course of action and the corresponding payoff in terms of profits or losses:

Airline B

		Buy Boeing 747	Do not buy Boeing 747
		I	II
Airline A	Buy Boeing 747	3%, 3%	8%, −2%
		III	IV
	Do not buy Boeing 747	−2%, 8%	0%, 0%

The above box, known as a payoff matrix, gives the outcome of the two actions, to buy or not to buy Boeing 747. Thus if A buys it but B does not, A's profits go up by 8 percent, whereas B's profits go down by 2 percent (box II). All other figures are to be interpreted similarly. Assuming that A and B act independently, do you have any idea how the two airlines will make their decisions? What additional information would you need? (This is a version of the prisoner's dilemma mentioned earlier in this chapter.)

CHAPTER 13

THE DEPARTMENT OF ENERGY AND ENERGY REGULATION

From the transportation sector we now turn to the energy sector, especially to the two major components of it, oil and natural gas. The importance of energy to our economic well-being can hardly be exaggerated in view of the "energy crisis" facing the nation since the October 1973 Yom Kippur War between Israel, on the one hand, and Syria and Egypt on the other. In the wake of the war, the Arab members of the Organization of Petroleum Exporting Countries (OPEC) put an embargo on the export of oil (crude oil and petroleum products) to the United States and at the same time quadrupled the price of a barrel of oil (42 gallons) from under $3 to about $11.[1]

At the time of the embargo, the United States was importing about 13 percent of its domestic oil consumption from the OPEC countries. But this cutoff was big enough to cause long lines at the gasoline stations because domestic production, although sizable, and imports from the non-Arab members of OPEC could not supply consumers with all that they wanted at the prices then prevailing. These prices had been controlled by the federal government in a complicated manner since 1971 (see Sections 13.2 and 13.4). Hence the emergence of the "energy crisis"; at the prevailing prices for various grades of oil the quantity demanded exceeded the quantity supplied, thus creating oil shortages.[2]

---

[1]OPEC consists of eleven major oil-producing countries, some Arab and some non-Arab. The Arab members constituting the OPEC include Saudi Arabia, Kuwait, Iraq, United Arab Emirates, Libya, Algeria, and Quatar; the non-Arab members are Iran, Venezuela, Nigeria, and Indonesia.

[2]The economist's notion of a shortage is quite different from that used in popular parlance. To the economist, a shortage arises if the price of a product is kept artificially below its market-clearing price, that is, at the level where supply is equal to demand.

But the "energy crisis" is not confined to oil alone. It extends to natural gas, which is second only to oil as a source of energy; oil and gas together account for well over 70 percent of our energy needs. Beginning about 1972, there were spot shortages of natural gas which became very serious in the harsh winter of 1976–1977, when industrial customers (especially in the midwest) who had firm commitments of gas supplies from gas pipeline and local utilities found their supplies seriously interrupted. This disruption caused work stoppages, leading to unemployment and loss of income. As we will see in Section 13.11, like oil, prices of natural gas are determined by the federal government, and the prices are well below their market-clearing levels.

The primary goal of this chapter is to find out how we got in this situation of oil and natural gas shortages. Toward that end, we examine in detail the government's regulatory policies concerning these fuels over the past several decades. It will be shown that our "energy crisis" is really not due to OPEC or some greedy oil companies but is largely due to the myopic regulatory policies of the government. Also discussed in this chapter are the new legislative initiatives taken under the Carter administration to deregulate the oil and natural gas industries and some of their consequences. We then discuss the question of energy independence from the politically volatile OPEC members and explore the ways of finding alternatives to oil and gas. We first consider the oil industry and then take up the natural gas industry.

13.1 THE OIL INDUSTRY: STRUCTURE, PRODUCTION, CONSUMPTION, AND IMPORTS

As a backdrop, we discuss in this section the salient features of the oil industry and provide some facts about domestic production, domestic consumption, and imports of crude oil and oil products from OPEC and non-OPEC members.[3]

Structure of the Oil Industry

There are five segments of the industry: exploration and production, gathering and crude purchasing, transportation of oil by pipelines, refining, and marketing. All told there are about 30,000 firms in the industry operating in one or more of these segments. But only a handful of them (about twenty-five), called integrated companies or majors, operate in all the five segments; most firms concentrate on only one chain in the exploration to marketing cycle. Some of the big majors are Exxon, Mobil, SoCal, Standard Oil of Indiana, Texaco Gulf, Shell, and ARCO.

Most economists who have studied the domestic oil industry conclude that,

---

[3]The non-OPEC members are: Mexico, Canada, Virgin Islands, Netherlands Antilles, Trinidad and Tobago, Bahamas, and Puerto Rico.

on the basis of concentration ratios, rate of profit, and barriers to entry into the industry, the industry is workably competitive except in the pipeline segment, which has elements of natural monopoly and is therefore controlled by the Federal Energy Regulatory Commission, an independent commission within the Department of Energy.[4]

Table 13.1 gives the four- and eight-firm concentration ratios for U.S. crude oil reserves, crude oil production, oil refining capacity, oil refining runs, and gasoline sales for selected years. For comparison, similar data are provided for the natural gas, coal, and uranium industries. As these data show, the four-firm concentration ratios do not give the impression that the industry is monopolistic or highly oligopolistic (or shared monopoly) in nature, notwithstanding such impression given by the news media.

What about entry into the industry? Here it may be noted that in 1977, the independents, that is, firms not associated with the majors, drilled 81 percent of new oil and natural gas wells and discovered 88 percent of new fields, indicating that entry barriers in the exploratory stage of the industry do not seem to be constraining.[5] In the refining segment, despite high costs of initial capital investment, forty-three new firms entered the industry between 1950 and 1972 and thirteen more between 1972 and 1975.[6] In the marketing end of the industry, because of comparatively small capital investment requirements, the field is open to newcomers.

What about the profit rate? Table 13.2 sheds some light on it. As the table shows, the composite profit rate (profit as a percentage of invested capital) for the industry as a whole averaged about 10.8 percent between 1967 and 1972, which compares with the same figure for the manufacturing sector for 1967 to 1971. This profit rate does not seem to be excessive by any reasonable standard. Even individual companies such as Exxon and Mobil do not seem to be out of line with the industry average. The higher profit rate obtained in 1973 is partly a reflection of the Arab oil embargo and partly some policy changes of the government. But even then it is doubtful whether the observed aggregate profit rate of 15.1 percent is excessive enough to label the industry oligopolistic (more recent data do not show any dramatic changes). Incidentally, between 1973 and 1975, the oil industry invested about $112 billion in plant and equipment in the exploration and production of energy, which amounts to about 35 percent of all such expenditures in the U.S. economy. Previously, the industry's share in the total investment was between 25 and 30 percent, suggesting that a large part of the higher postembargo profits has gone into capital investments.

With all these pieces of evidence combined, the conclusion stated at the outset that the oil industry is "workably" competitive may not be far off the mark.

[4]For a contrary and critical view, see John M. Blair, *The Control of Oil,* Vintage Books, New York, 1978.
[5]*Wall Street Journal,* April 7, 1978, p. 1.
[6]Edward J. Mitchell, ed., *Vertical Integration in the Oil Industry,* American Enterprise Institute for Public Policy Research, Washington, D.C., 1976, p. 45.

TABLE 13.1
CONCENTRATION RATIOS—SEGMENTS OF THE U.S. ENERGY INDUSTRY

	1954	1955	1960	1965	1970	1975	1976
Proven crude oil reserves *							
Big 4						36.2	38.7
Big 8						55.5	57.3
Proven natural gas reserves*							
Big 4						26.9	26.2
Big 8						39.7	38.6
U.S. crude oil production*							
Big 4		18.1	20.8	23.9	26.3	26.0	25.5
Big 8		30.3	33.5	38.5	41.7	41.2	40.5
U.S. natural gas production*							
Big 4		21.7	16.8	20.8	25.2	24.2	23.5
Big 8		33.1	28.4	33.6	30.1	36.8	35.6
U.S. oil refinery capacity†							
Big 4			32.0	30.4	32.5	29.9	29.7
Big 8			55.0	54.3	57.5	43.5	51.8
U.S. oil refinery runs†							
Big 4		33.1	33.2	31.0	34.2	32.9	32.7
Big 8		57.7	56.8	55.3	61.0	57.7	56.9
U.S. gasoline sales†							
Big 4	31.2				30.7	29.5	29.3
Big 8	54.0				54.6	50.3	49.9
Bituminous coal production (U.S.) *							
Big 4		17.8	21.4	26.6	30.7	26.4	25.1
Big 8		25.5	30.5	36.3	41.2	36.2	34.3
U.S. uranium oxide concentrate production*							
Big 4		79.9	51.4	55.4	55.3	58.7	57.7
Big 8		99.1	72.4	79.3	80.8	82.2	71.3
U.S. energy (BTU basis) production‡							
Big 4		12.3	12.3	15.2	18.1	18.3	17.3
Big 8		20.6	21.8	25.1	29.6	29.7	28.0

*American Petroleum Institute, "Concentration Levels in the Production and Reserve Holdings of Crude Oil, Natural Gas, Coal and Uranium in the U.S., 1955–1976," Discussion Paper No. 4R, September 1977.

†Americal Petroleum Institute, "U.S. Petroleum Market Shares: 1950–1976 Individual Company Data," Discussion Paper No. 3R, September 1977.

‡American Petroleum Institute, "Concentration in Energy Production, 1955–1976," Discussion Paper No. 7R, September 1977.

Source: Walter J. Mead, *Energy and the Environment: Conflict in Public Policy,* American Enterprise Institute for Public Policy Research, Washington, D.C., 1978, p. 11.

TABLE 13.2
PROFITS AS A PERCENTAGE OF INVESTED CAPITAL FOR THE TWENTY LARGEST U.S.
PETROLEUM FIRMS

Firm (ranked according to 1971 sales)	Average profit rate (1967–72)	Profit rate (1973)
Exxon	12.3	19.4
Mobil Oil	10.7	16.0
Texaco	13.8	17.6
Gulf Oil	10.4	14.8
Standard Oil of California (Chevron)	10.4	15.7
Standard Oil of Indiana (Amoco)	9.7	13.1
Shell Oil	10.6	11.1
Atlantic Richfield	8.4	7.8
Continental Oil	10.1	14.5
Tenneco*	11.2	NA
Occidental Petroleum	14.2	7.2
Phillips Petroleum	8.4	12.4
Union Oil of California	9.2	10.1
Sun Oil	9.5	10.8
Ashland Oil	11.6	18.2
Standard Oil of Ohio (Sohio)	8.2	6.8
Getty Oil	8.5	9.1
Marathon Oil	11.4	15.9
Clark Oil	15.2	33.4
Commonwealth Oil Refining	11.5	20.5
Oil Industry Composite	10.8	15.1
Average for all manufacturing (1967–1971)	10.8	

NA: Not available.
*Tenneco is a conglomerate with only about 15 percent of revenues derived from oil operations.
Source: Ford Foundation Energy Policy Project, *A Time to Choose: America's Energy Future,* Cambridge, Mass.: Ballinger, 1974, p. 237.

Production, Consumption, and Imports

To provide a perspective on the "energy crisis," it is instructive to examine the data on production, consumption, and imports of oil and oil products. The relevant statistics for the period 1960–1977 are given in Table 13.3.

It should be pointed out that up until 1946 the United States was a net exporter of crude oil. But beginning in 1947 it became a net importer, the imports in that year constituting some 8 percent of our aggregate domestic consumption. Since then imports as a percent of our consumption have significantly trended upward. What is important to note is that after staying within the range of 15 to 20 percent until 1969, the imports began to take off. Ironically, despite the sharp price increase following the 1973 embargo, the imports zoomed to such high levels that in 1977 about 46 percent of domestic oil consumption needs had to be imported. (For reasons behind the sharp increase in oil imports, see the discussion on the oil entitlements program in Section 13.5.) While imports were increasing, domestic production of crude more or less stagnated.

What explains the fact that over the period shown in Table 13.3 domestic consumption increased at a faster rate then domestic production, necessitating ever-increasing amounts of imports? One reason is that that oil is very convenient and easy to transport — a barrel of oil packs the same wallop as 5700 cubic feet of natural gas or about one-fourth ton of coal. But the true reason lies in the real price of oil, that is, price adjusted for inflation. Table 13.4 provides some revealing figures.

As can be seen from Table 13.4, from 1950 to 1970 (and continuing up to the 1973 oil embargo) the real price of oil declined continuously: In 1967 dollars, the price of a barrel of oil declined from $3.07 to $2.88 and that of a gallon of gasoline from 27.9 cents to 21.2 cents. A decline in the real price of a commodity makes it cheaper in relation to other commodities, making it a relatively desirable commodity. This is precisely what happened to oil. It is true that since the 1973 embargo the real price of oil has gone up astronomically, but even then consumers did not reduce their consumption immediately, largely out of inertia (change takes time and is generally painful) but more importantly because the government did not allow the domestic price of oil to go up as high as that charged by OPEC. Thus, the per barrel price of domestic crude was $7.85,

TABLE 13.3
CRUDE PETROLEUM, PETROLEUM PRODUCTS, AND LIQUEFIED NATURAL GAS
(Millions of barrels)

Year	Consumption	Domestic production	Imports	Exports	Net imports* as a percent of consumption
1960	3586	2916	644	74	16
1961	3641	2983	700	64	17
1962	3796	3049	760	61	18
1963	3921	3154	775	76	18
1964	4034	3209	827	74	19
1965	4202	3290	901	68	20
1966	4411	3496	939	72	20
1967	4584	3730	926	112	18
1968	4902	3883	1039	84	19
1969	5160	3956	1155	85	21
1970	5364	4129	1248	94	22
1971	5553	4078	1433	82	24
1972	5990	4103	1735	81	28
1973	6317	4006	2283	84	35
1974	6078	3832	2231	80	35
1975	5958	3667	2210	76	36
1976	6391	3577	2676	82	41
1977†	6712	3636	3169	83	46

*Net imports are imports minus exports.
†Preliminary.
Source: *Minerals and Materials*, U.S. Department of the Interior, Bureau of Mines, February 1978, p. 19.

TABLE 13.4
ENERGY PRICES, ACTUAL AND ADJUSTED FOR INFLATION

	Actual prices			
	Gasoline retail, regular grade excluding excise tax*	Natural gas & electricity consumer price under 1967 = 100*	Crude oil per barrel	Bituminous coal, f.o.b. mine, per short ton†
1950	$.201	81.2	$ 2.51‡	$ 4.84
1960	.210	98.6	2.88‡	4.69
1970	.246	107.3	3.18‡	6.26
1975	.455	169.6	13.93§	19.23
1977	.518 (Oct.)	21.3 (Oct.)	14.53§ (July)	21.97 (June)

	Adjusted prices			
	Deflated by consumer price index		Deflated by wholesale price index	
	1967 dollars	Index 1967 = 100	1967 dollars	1967 dollars
1950	$.279	112.6	$ 3.07	$ 5.92
1960	.237	111.2	3.03	4.94
1970	.212	92 .3	2.88	5.67
1975	.282	105.2	7.96	10.99
1977	.281 (Oct.)	118.9 (Oct.)	7.46	11.30

*U.S. Department of Commerce, *Survey of Current Business.*
†1950–1975 "representative price" as estimated by U.S. Bureau of Mines, June 1977, estimated on basis of Bureau of Mines f.o.b. utilities price.
‡Average wellhead price U.S. domestic crude oil, U.S. Bureau of Mines.
§Imported price (refiner acquisition cost). *Monthly Energy Review,* Federal Energy Administration, October 1977, p. 75.
Source: Walter J. Mead, *Energy and the Environment: Conflict in Public Policy,* American Enterprise Institute for Public Policy Research, Washington, D.C., 1978, p. 2.

$8.02, and $8.18 for 1974, 1975, and 1976, respectively, whereas for the same years the price of the Saudi Arabian crude was $12.31, $11.21, and $11.51, respectively. Had the government allowed the domestic prices to rise to the Saudi Arabian prices, there would have been a significant decrease in domestic consumption and therefore in the imports. But why did the government not follow such a policy? The answer is provided in the sections that follow.

13.2   REGULATION OF THE OIL INDUSTRY BEFORE 1971[7]

Although the genesis of the "energy crisis" can be traced to President Nixon's Economic Stabilization Program, instituted in August 1971, for a historical per-

[7]This and the following two sections draw heavily on Paul W. MacAvoy (ed.), *Federal Energy Administration Regulation. Report of the Presidential Task Force,* the Ford Administration Papers on Regulatory Reform, American Enterprise Institute for Public Policy Research, Washington, D.C., 1977. (Hereafter referred to as the Ford Administration Papers on Energy Regulation.)

spective it pays us to look at the overall regulatory policies of the government which date back to the 1930s. In the early 1930s large oil fields were discovered in Texas and Oklahoma, which led to overproduction (in relation to demand) to such an extent that the price of a barrel of crude oil dropped to as low as 10 cents compared to the price of $1.45 in 1929. To stop the overproduction, the governors of these states declared martial law and closed down several oil fields. But this was only a temporary solution to the glut.

In 1935 the major oil-producing states signed the Interstate Oil Compact to conserve oil and natural gas, the objective being to enhance long-run production and stabilize prices. Toward that end, they introduced or encouraged the following regulatory mechanisms.

Prorationing

Under this scheme, members of the Oil Compact determined the maximum amount of crude oil to be produced in any given time and the allocation of this amount among the participants. Stated differently, the Oil Compact was essentially a producers' cartel and prorationing was the monopolistic device they used to curtail total production and allocate it among its members.

The effect of prorationing was what one would expect a priori. It stabilized the market price of crude oil since there was no need to compete because each producer could sell his or her quota at the market price. Of course, the market price that resulted was higher than the one prevailing before the compact, which too is to be expected since aggregate production was not allowed to exceed the anticipated demand. The market price stabilized around $3 a barrel.

Mandatory Oil Import Program (MOIP)

The prorationing scheme kept the domestic crude prices above the world market price. But in the 1950s, because of the huge oil discoveries in the Middle East, foreign crude oil became much cheaper. As a result, there was an increasing amount of foreign oil entering the country. Obviously, this disturbed the domestic producers, who clamored for import restrictions. It was alleged that unrestricted imports of cheap foreign oil would dampen capital investments in the oil industry and that this would make us increasingly dependent on foreign oil, which would threaten our national security. President Eisenhower succumbed to this fear and in 1959, by executive proclamation, established the Mandatory Oil Import Program (MOIP). The MOIP set volumetric limits (i.e., quotas) on the amount of crude oil and its products that could be imported from abroad; the quota was set at some percentage of domestic production.

The Ford Administration Papers on Energy Regulation describe the consequences of the MOIP as follows:

> The effect of the MOIP was to insulate the price of American crude oil from lower
> world prices. Since there was a relatively fixed ceiling on imports of crude oil, the

marginal barrel of oil needed to supply domestic demand would have to come from domestic sources. Thus, the price of domestically produced petroleum set the price charged domestic consumers.[8]

In terms of dollars, the price of a barrel of domestic crude in 1960 was about $5.55, whereas the Saudi crude was priced at $2.95; that is, the former was higher by about 88 percent.

Besides keeping the domestic crude prices relatively high, the MOIP created the problem of allocating import licenses, an inevitable consequence of the quota system. The government devised a complicated allocation program, giving the small oil refiners a disproportionately large share. Thus, in 1969, a 10,000 barrel-a-day oil refiner got a license to import 1950 barrels of cheap foreign oil, or about 20 percent of her daily output, wheras a 500,000 barrel-a-day refiner could import only 21,050 barrels of foreign crude, or about 4.2 percent of his daily output.[9]

Now each import license was a valuable property, the value being equal to the difference between the higher domestic price and the lower foreign price. In 1969, the import license was worth $1.25 a barrel, which meant the MOIP gave a subsidy of about 24.4 cents a barrel to the small refiner (1950 $\times$ 1.25/ 10,000) but only 5.3 cents to the large refiner (21,050 $\times$ 1.25/500,000). That is, the smaller refiner benefitted more from the MOIP even though she may not have been as efficient as the large one. This is an instance of the so-called tyranny of the few.

In 1973 the MOIP was abolished since the price of foreign crude (before the oil embargo) was comparable to the domestic price because of increases in freight and insurance charges. In its place, President Nixon instituted a scheme of license fees (or tariffs) at 21 cents a barrel for crude and 63 cents a barrel for petroleum products, but there was no restriction on the amount of imports.

From the preceding discussion it is clear that the prorationing and the MOIP were clearly designed to protect the interests of domestic producers. But the resulting higher prices have had the effect of transferring wealth from consumers to producers. One scholar has estimated the magnitude of this transfer at $6.6 billion for 1969.[10] In other words, in that year consumers in the aggregate paid $6.6 billion more for oil than they would have had there been no restrictions on the import of the cheaper foreign crude.

13.3 REGULATION OF THE OIL INDUSTRY FROM 1971
UNTIL THE 1973 OIL EMBARGO

To deal with the problem of "stagflation" (stagnation in the growth of real output and employment coupled with inflation), President Nixon, atypical for a

---

[8]Ibid., p. 5.
[9]These figures are taken from Edward J. Mitchell, *U.S. Energy Policy: A Primer,* American Enterprise Institute for Public Policy Research, Washington, D.C., 1974, pp. 37–38.
[10]Ibid., p. 50.

Republican president, imposed a 90-day wage and price freeze on August 15, 1971. Except prices of first sale of agricultural products and imported products, all prices (including those of oil and natural gas) were frozen (at the August 15 level) until November 13, 1971. This was phase 1 of his Economic Stabilization Program, which was administered by the Cost of Living Council (CLC).[11] Then came phase 2, which lasted until the end of 1972. During this phase, average prices were not to increase by more than 3 percent per year. But this change offered little incentive to the oil industry to increase domestic production. The net result was spot shortages of crude oil and its products. Phase 2 was followed on January 11, 1973, by phase 3, which lasted until June 13, 1973. During this phase, the price regulations introduced in phase 1 and modified by phase 2 were to be continued voluntarily.

But because of the pent-up demand for oil, especially for heating oil in the New England area, as well as decreased production of domestic crude and a worldwide shortage of crude oil, there was a sharp increase in the price of oil. To deal with the price increase, the CLC imposed a mandatory price control on twenty-four major oil companies but exempted all other producers from it with the result that the latter could raise their prices sharply. The irony of this regulation was that the twenty-four majors were required to sell crude oil to the independents at the regulated price and the independents could sell the refined products at unregulated prices!

Between the end of phase 3 on June 13, 1973, and the beginning of phase 4 in August 1973, there was a 60-day freeze. During this time the CLC was thinking of ways to solve the oil problem, namely, how to deal with the gap in the foreign and domestic prices of crude oil as well as how to ensure oil supplies to meet the ever-increasing domestic demand. The CLC developed a comprehensive set of regulations regarding the prices of crude oil and refined products to each of the the five segments of the industry.

The CLC established a two-tier pricing system, one for "old" or lower-tier oil and another for "new" or upper-tier oil. "Old" oil was that which was produced from oil wells in operation in 1972 or before. "New" oil was that which was produced from wells in operation after 1972 as well as oil from "old" wells in excess of their 1972 level of production. All new crude oil was to be free from price controls, but the price of old oil was fixed at the level prevailing on May 15, 1973, plus 35 cents a barrel. This came to about $5.64 a barrel. At that time a barrel of Saudi Arabian crude cost about $3.95.

The shortage of crude oil continued, however. Small refiners and independents could not get all the crude they wanted, which was not too surprising in view of the price controls on old oil. This prompted congressional action. The Congress gave the President the authority to allocate crude oil and petroleum products — any commodity whose price is regulated below its equilibrium level

---

[11]Later replaced by the Council on Wage and Price Stability, which has since been abolished by President Reagan.

is bound to create allocational problems. Pursuant to the congressional mandate, President Nixon, on June 29, 1973, established the Energy Policy Office (EPO) to do the job of allocation. The EPO was the first of many such agencies to be established in short order.

13.4 REGULATION OF THE OIL INDUSTRY DURING THE OIL EMBARGO OF 1973–1974

The Arab oil embargo created aggravating problems for the Nixon administration; only recently it had established the EPO to allocate crude oil, which was becoming inadequate to meet domestic demand. In the aftermath of the embargo, oil imports decreased from the level of 6.6 million barrels a day in November 1973 to about 5.1 million barrels a day in January 1974. To deal with this new situation, the President, on November 1, 1973, established in the Department of the Interior the Office of Petroleum Allocation to administer a voluntary allocation program for crude oil as well as a compulsory allocation system for propane and middle distillate oil (used in home heating).

But fearing that the voluntary allocation program would not work, Congress passed on November 27, 1973, the Emergency Petroleum Allocation Act of 1973 (EPAA), which required the President to institute mandatory controls for the allocation of crude oil and petroleum products and to regulate all prices. The critical problem hinged around the allocation of old oil, whose price had been pegged at $5.65 a barrel, although the world price of crude had increased very sharply, about $11 to $12 a barrel. The problem was temporarily "solved" by requiring that those refiners who were purchasing old oil on November 1, 1973, were given the right to purchase it at the controlled price.

On December 4, 1973, President Nixon, by executive order, created the Federal Energy Office (FEO) to decide on the allocational rules on a permanent basis. These rules, discussed below, were promulgated on January 15, 1974, and the FEO was made responsible for administering them.

Freezing of Supplier-Purchaser Relationship

Under this rule a supplier of crude oil or petroleum products was required to supply, although the purchaser was not obliged to buy, the amount the latter bought from the former at a certain base period, which was set at 1972. Thus, if a refiner bought 10,000 barrels a day from a crude producer in 1972, the latter was required to supply that much quantity, although the former could buy less. Similarly, in the case of a wholesaler of gasoline who in 1972 supplied, say, 1000 gallons of gasoline a day to a retailer, the latter was entitled to that much purchase although he could choose to buy less. In short, any transaction between parties who stood in supplier-buyer relationship in the chain of distribution was essentially pegged at the level of their 1972 dealings with each other.

Priority Demands

The rule just described was not applicable to the Defense Department, to certain agricultural uses, and to medical space-heating.

Buy and Sell Program

"Under this program, refiners having a higher percentage of crude supplies available, in relation to their refining capacity, than the national average were required to resell their crude to refiners with below normal crude availability."[12] The objective of this program was to "equalize" the quantity of crude oil available to each refiner.

It is important to point out, however, that during the embargo period the price regulations instituted during phases 1 and 2 were substantially unchanged—except that in November 1973 the price of old oil was raised by $1 a barrel due to the growing difference in the prices of old and new oils. Also, oil produced from "stripper wells," that is, wells producing ten or less barrels a day, was totally price-exempt.[13]

13.5 POSTEMBARGO REGULATION OF THE OIL INDUSTRY

The oil embargo ended in the middle of 1974 and OPEC oil once again became available but at a cost of about $12 a barrel compared to the average price of domestic crude of $8 a barrel (it is the average of the prices of old, new, and stripper oil). This posed a policy dilemma for the government. On the one hand, there were those (including most economists) who wanted to abolish all controls so as to make domestic and foreign crude prices the same, save the differences in transportation and insurance costs. But there were those, including politicians, who wanted to keep the regulatory structure but modify it to meet the dynamics of the world oil situation. It seems the latter group won out, for on May 27, 1974, Congress passed the Federal Energy Administration Act of 1974 (FEAA) and created the Federal Energy Administration (FEA) to carry out the following goals:

1 To keep the high OPEC-set price of crude from determining the price of domestic crude oil and petroleum products when supplies of petroleum are adequate

2 To prevent the establishment of unreasonably high prices for petroleum products in the event of an embargo or other temporary supply interruptions

3 To allocate scarce petroleum products on an equitable basis during a shortage

4 To prevent a temporary supply shortage from acting to decrease the extent of competition existing in the petroleum industry

---

[12]The Ford Administration Papers on Energy Regulation, op. cit., p. 10.
[13]Physically, the stipper oil wells could produce more than ten barrels a day, but because of the freedom from price regulation, the producers chose to produce ten or less barrels a day (why not?)

We will comment on these goals in Section 13.8 where we discuss the economics of the government's regulatory policies as a whole. For now, it may be noted that after its establishment the FEA made only a few changes in regulatory policies. Two changes that deserve some attention are as follows.

The Entitlements Program

The price regulation of old oil and the crude allocation scheme devised under the EPAA of 1973 created a serious problem of equity among oil refiners. For instance, refiners who got most of their crude from old oil wells had a definite cost advantage over those whose access to old oil was limited; therefore the latter had to depend on the higher-priced stripper or imported oil. In order to approximately equalize the cost of the crude to refiners, the FEA devised the Entitlements Program, which is simply a scheme to ration old oil. Under the program "for every barrel of crude oil refined, a refinery receives a fraction of an entitlement to purchase old oil, the fraction being equal to the national total domestic refinery purchases of old oil divided by the national total quantity of oil domestically refined."[14] Refiners who exceeded that fraction, that is, had more old oil than they were entitled to, could sell their entitlements to refiners whose fraction fell below the prescribed norm. The FEA was to act as a clearing house and to determine the price of an entitlement. The FEA set the price of an entitlement equal to the difference between the price of uncontrolled oil and the price of old oil. The actual mechanics can be illustrated by the following example.[15]

Suppose that the price of old oil is $5.60 a barrel and that of new oil or imported oil is $14. Further suppose that 25 percent of the oil consumed is old and 75 percent is new or imported. Thus the average price of oil is $11.90 (.25 × $5.60 + .75 × $14). Under the Entitlements Program, for every barrel of oil refined, the refiner gets a 25 percent entitlement for old oil. The value of the entitlement is $8.40 ($14 − $5.60). Now consider refiners A and B. A uses only imported oil. Therefore, for every four barrels that she refines, she is entitled to one barrel of old oil, whose worth is $8.40 or $2.10 per barrel of oil refined. Thus, the net per barrel cost of the imported oil is $11.90 ($14 − $2.10), the same as the average price of oil noted above. B uses old oil exclusively, but he too is limited by the 25 percent entitlements rule. This means that to refine four barrels of oil he will have to buy three barrels from someone else at a cost of $6.30 ($11.90 − $5.60) or $2.10 per barrel. Thus in either case, the refiners face the same effective domestic price of $11.90; both involve a subsidy of $2.10 a barrel from the world price of $14 a barrel.

The apparent objective of the Entitlements Program was to prevent the domestic producers from reaping huge windfall profits had the controlled

[14]James L. Sweeney, "Making the Problem Worse through Regulation," in *Options for U.S. Energy Policy,* Institute for Contemporary Studies, San Francisco, Calif., 1977, p. 186.
[15]Ibid.

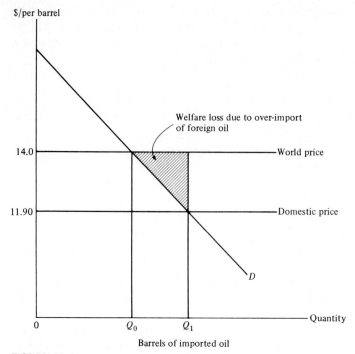

FIGURE 13.1
The effects of the Entitlements Program.

domestic price of $5.60 a barrel been permitted to match the world price of $14 a barrel.[16] It was felt by the policymakers that such profits would be "inequitable." Whether this equity argument is cogent or not, such a policy was not rational from an efficiency viewpoint for, oddly enough, it encouraged importation of the costly foreign oil. This is because each imported barrel of oil entitled the domestic refiner to a certain amount of the cheaper domestic oil, at $5.60 a barrel. As noted, the ultimate effect of the program was a subsidy of $2.10 a barrel to the domestic producer (average domestic price of $11.90 a barrel versus $14 a barrel of imported oil).

Figure 13.1 shows the welfare loss (see Chapter 6) due to overimport of the foreign oil under the Entitlements Program.

Since the average domestic price of crude oil was deliberately kept low, it meant the price charged the final consumer (residential, commercial, or industrial) was also kept low in comparison to what it would have been had the crude oil price been $14 a barrel. Hence, like the crude imports, domestic oil con-

---

[16]Notice that the opportunity cost of a barrel of domestic oil is not $5.60 but $14, its cost in the world market.

sumption, too, was encouraged (albeit unwittingly) whereas the policy goal should have been the opposite.[17] (For more on this, see Section 13.8.)

To further beef up the FEAA of 1974, Congress passed the Energy Policy and Conservation Act of 1975 (EPCA). Among other things, the objectives of the act were:

1 To phase out the price regulations of crude oil over 40 months[18]

2 To establish a fixed national average price for all crude, which will be allowed to increase gradually over time to reflect inflation and other factors

3 To have the FEA establish ceilings on the various types of oil, in order to arrive at the national average price

4 To phase out the price regulations of refined products

13.6   PRESIDENT CARTER'S NATIONAL ENERGY PLAN

In his 1976 presidential campaign candidate Jimmy Carter gave top priority to solving the "energy crisis," calling it the "moral equivalent of war." Soon after taking office in January 1977, he proposed a comprehensive National Energy Plan (NEP), which was made public on April 10, 1977. The NEP is based on ten fundamental principles, which are as follows:

1 Government has responsibility for implementing a national energy policy — informed citizenry must be willing to make sacrifices.

2 Healthy economic growth must continue. Through conservation, our standard of living can be maintained.

3 Environment must be protected through conservation of resources.

4 Vulnerability to potentially devasting embargoes must be eliminated by reducing demand for oil, making the most of our abundant resources such as coal, and developing a strategic petroleum reserve.

5 Sacrifices should be made by consumers and producers of energy alike, thus assuring a fair distribution of responsibility among people from all walks of American life.

6 The cornerstone of the policy is to reduce demand through conservation.

7 Price should generally reflect the true replacement cost of energy.

8 Government policies must be predictable and certain.

9 Shifting from oil and natural gas consumption to coal is necessary, taking care to protect the environment.

10 New sources of energy must be developed now.

---

[17]It is true that the higher price of oil postembargo did discourage the rate of growth of oil consumption. But this rate would have been still lower had the true marginal cost of oil been charged the consumer.

[18]Although we talked mostly about crude price regulation, such regulation also extended to the prices charged by the various intermediaries in the chain from production to retail sales. Thus, retail gasoline stations could not charge more than a certain "margin" or markup on the cost of their wholesale price and other business expenses. These margins ranged between 14 cents and 18 cents a gallon, depending on the grade of gasoline.

These principles bring out five main features of the Carter NEP: Crude oil prices to reflect the true replacement cost of energy (i.e., the market-clearing price); more use of domestic sources of energy and conservation; discovery and development of new sources of energy; preparation for an energy emergency, such as embargo, by creating a strategic petroleum reserve; and fairness or equity.

In pursuit of these objectives, the major goals of the NEP were outlined in terms of three time spans: short-term (now until 1985), medium-term (1985–2000), and long-term (from 2000 on).

In the short term the emphasis will be on conservation as a means of lessening our dependence on foreign oil. Toward that end there will be: (1) a reduction in imports from a potential level of 16 million barrels a day to less than 6 million barrels: (2) a 10 percent reduction in gasoline consumption; (3) insulation of 90 percent of all residences and other buildings; (4) increased coal production of at least 400 million tons a year; and (5) use of solar energy in more than 2.5 million homes.

The medium-term objective is to weather the eventual decline in the availability of world oil supplies (because of their nonrenewable nature) by maximizing the conversion of industries and utilities from natural gas and oil to coal.

The long-run objective is to develop renewable and essentially inexhaustible sources of energy for sustained economic growth by implementing a rigorous research and development program to meet U.S. energy needs in the next century.

Toward achieving these goals, the NEP proposed a number of policies:

1 In pursuit of fundamental principle no. 7, the imposition of a crude oil equalization tax (also called "windfall profit tax") on domestic oil to bring its price on par with the world price. For oil discovered before April 20, 1977, the tax will be equal to the world price of oil minus the price of domestic oil ($5.65 for old and $11.28 for new oil), all prices to be adjusted for inflation. For oil discovered after April 20, 1977, the tax rate will be equal to the difference between the world price of oil and the average domestic price of $13.70 a barrel, again adjusted for inflation. The idea behind the windfall tax is to prevent the producers from reaping the benefits of the higher world price. The tax proceeds were to be used partly to subsidize poor families hurt by increased prices and partly for government research and development expenditures to develop new sources of energy.

2 Elimination of the costly entitlements and allocation programs.

3 Establishment of strategic petroleum reserves (SPR) at various locations in the country.

4 A tax on automobiles with low fuel efficiency, a rebate for those with high fuel efficiency, and tax subsidies for insulation.

5 Reform of local utility rate structures by encouraging peak–off-peak and time-of-day rate structures.

We will comment on the NEP shortly.

13.7 THE CREATION OF THE DEPARTMENT OF ENERGY (DOE)

To carry out the goals of the NEP, Congress, at the urging of the President, passed the Department of Energy Act of 1977 and created the Department of Energy (DOE), a cabinet-level office headed by the secretary of energy. The 1977 act consolidated under the DOE various energy-related agencies, such as, the Energy Research and Development Administration, the Federal Power Commission (FPC), and the Alaska, Bonnville, Southeastern, and Southwestern Power administrations. The administrative chart of the DOE is shown in Figure 13.2.

Overall Functions of the DOE

The DOE is responsible for (1) research, development, and demonstration of energy technology, (2) marketing of federal power, (3) energy conservation, (4) the nuclear weapons program, (5) regulation of energy procurement and use, (6) pricing and allocation of energy, and (7) central energy data collection and analysis.

The department's regulatory activities are handled by two agencies, the Economic Regulatory Administration (ERA) and the Federal Energy Regulatory Commission (FERC).

The ERA handles the regulatory programs other than those assigned to the FERC, that is, the pricing of crude oil, its allocation among refiners, and the management of the import program, all with the objective of ensuring stable and equitable supplies of crude oil, petroleum products, and natural gas liquids among a wide range of domestic users.

The FERC, an independent five-member commission with the DOE, has retained many of the powers of the erstwhile FPC, such as the setting of rates and charges for the transmission and sale of natural gas, the transmission and sale of electricity, the licensing of hydroelectric power projects, and the establishment of rates or charges for the transportation of oil by pipelines as well as the valuation of such pipelines (a job once done by the Interstate Commerce Commission).

13.8 AN EVALUATION OF GOVERNMENT REGULATION OF THE OIL INDUSTRY

Before assessing the economics of oil regulation, some general observations are in order. First, the oil industry is one of the highly regulated industries, and the regulations cover all segments of the industry — from exploration to retailing: (1) The 1930s prorationing laws determine how much a producing state may produce; (2) the various price controls since 1971 determine the prices at which various crudes can be sold to refiners; (3) the ICC, then the FCC, and latterly the FERC decides the rate structure for the pipeline companies; (4) the entitlements and allocation programs control the flow of old oil to refiners, and (5) the gov-

DEPARTMENT OF ENERGY

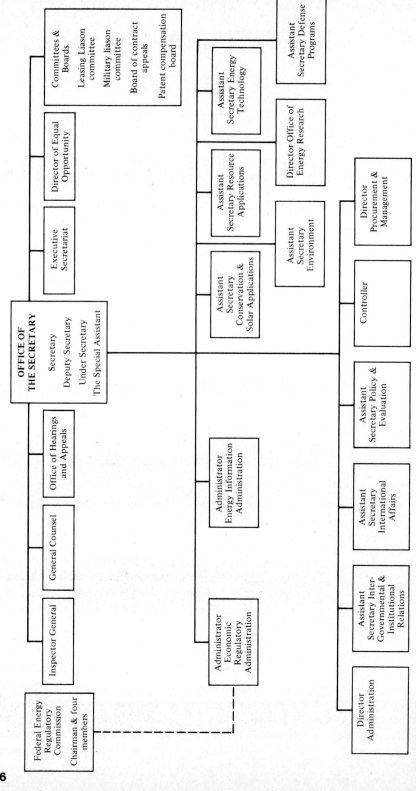

FIGURE 13.2
The Department of Energy.

ernment also determines how much profit margin the retailers can have on the petroleum products they sell.

Second, by and large, the mechanisms of control have been price and quantity regulations – although under the NEP, control by performance standard (emission control, appliance efficiency, etc.) was added.

Third, there is a distinct difference between the regulations prior to 1971 and those since 1971. Before President Nixon's Economic Stabilization Program was put in place in August 1971, the prorationing and the MOIP were designed to insulate domestic producers from foreign competition. Therefore, one could say that the regulation in this period was pro-producer or anticonsumer because the higher prices charged by the domestic producers transferred wealth from consumers to themselves. A consequence of this was that there was generally excess production capacity (in relation to demand) and the problem of shortages did not arise.

Since August 1971, public policy has made a 180° turnabout. The various price and allocation controls were designed to keep the domestic crude price below the world price, which, by subsidizing the consumer, had the effect of transferring wealth from producer to consumer. Unfortunately, the net result of this policy was excess demand and shortages, which were aggravated by the OPEC and Iranian oil embargoes of 1973 and 1979, respectively. Finally, the regulatory mechanism has become so complex since 1971, what with the passages of so many laws and so many regulatory agencies, that it is impossible for the bureaucrats to make quick decisions about allocating crude oil in times of emergencies, such as the cold winters in the northeast. Even after the 1973 OPEC embargo, agency bureaucrats were not prepared to handle the Iranian oil embargo of the spring and summer of 1979, which once again created huge lines at the gasoline stations, necessitating rules such as odd-even days of rationing, minimum $5 purchase of gasoline for four-cylinder cars, and so on. This was all the more inexcusable since we imported a very small percentage of oil from Iran.

What is the economics of all this regulation? What explains the excess demand and shortages observed since 1971? To answer this, consider the crude oil price controls put in place since August 1971 and continued until January 28, 1981, when President Reagan lifted them completely; under the Carter NEP they were scheduled to expire at the end of October 1981. During this period of about 10 years, the average price of domestic crude was kept deliberately below the world price, which for all practical purposes was the OPEC price. The consequence of this policy can be explained by the elementary geometry of supply and demand, which is shown in Figure 13.3.

In Figure 13.3 S and D are the supply and demand curves for crude oil. In the absence of any price (and quantity) controls, the equilibrium or market-clearing price and quantity would have been P_0 and Q_0, respectively, and there would have been no problem of excess demand or shortages. But by regulating the price of crude at P_1, the quantity demanded Q_2 exceeds the quantity supplied Q_1, creating the "gap" or excess demand of Q_1Q_2. This gap could be fulfilled

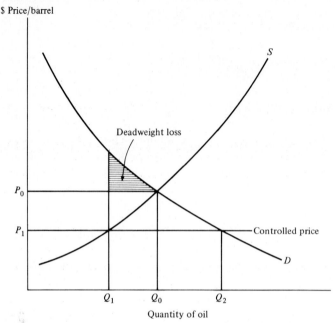

FIGURE 13.3
The economics of oil shortage.

only by importing Q_1Q_2 at the higher world price. In short, by keeping the regulated price below the market price, the government created the shortages; the shortages were thus policy-induced.

That is not the end of the story. By artificially keeping the price at P_1, consumers who were willing to pay the higher market price of P_0 to obtain the quantity Q_1Q_0 were denied that freedom. Hence there is a deadweight loss in the consumer surplus, whose magnitude is shown by the shaded triangle (see Chapter 6); it is the value of oil to consumers who are unable to get it even at the higher price. Thus, price regulation has led to misallocation of scarce economic resources.

There is yet another consequence of price controls, which can be explained by Figure 13.4. As in Figure 13.3, P_0 and Q_0 represent the equilibrium price and the equilibrium quantity, respectively, and P_1 the regulated price, leading to excess demand of Q_1Q_2. Since the regulated price is lower than the market price, there is less incentive for domestic producers to sink new oil wells and produce more crude or add to oil inventories. On the contrary, they are likely to produce less from the existing wells in the hope that one day the regulated price may be lifted. If this does happen, and it has happened especially in the production of natural gas, the domestic supply curve will shift to the left to position S_1 shown in the figure. As a result, other things remaining the same, the quantity of excess demand will increase from Q_1Q_2 to Q_3Q_2, that is, by the amount Q_3Q_1. This would mean still additional imports at the higher world price.

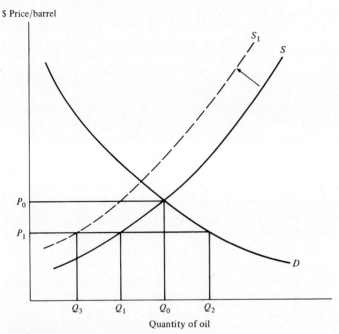

FIGURE 13.4
The effects of price control on production.

13.9 ARGUMENTS AGAINST DECONTROL OF THE OIL INDUSTRY

The fundamental question that arises is: Despite the elementary economics of Figures 13.3 and 13.4, why did the government adhere to price controls for almost a decade? In what follows, an attempt is made to shed light on the answer to this question.

Recall that in Chapter 2 we discussed the public interest (PI) theory of regulation. In nutshell, the PI theory holds that in cases of market failures, such as inadequate supplies of public goods, natural monopolies, externalities, lack of perfect information, and inadequate conservation of natural resources, the government may intervene in the marketplace to remedy one or more of these failures so that economic efficiency can be improved. Otherwise, this job can better be left to the market.

There are some who believe that there are market imperfections in the oil industry which call for government intervention. In particular, they contend that the industry, if not monopolistic, is highly oligopolistic and that the industry has not paid adequate attention to the environment or to the preservation of exhaustible natural resources. Let us examine these arguments briefly.

Is the industry highly oligopolistic? In Section 13.2 we considered the structures of the industry and on the basis of concentration ratios, entry barriers, and the profit rate concluded that the industry is workably competitive. Therefore, the charge of oligopoly per se is not a cause for government intervention. As a matter of fact, whatever element of monopoly power the industry may have acquired can be attributed to past regulatory policies. For example, before 1971, the state prorationing laws and the MOIP shielded domestic producers from foreign competition, and consumers were denied the benefits of the lower price of foreign crude and petroleum products.

What about the environment? The DOE act of 1977 required the Department of Energy "to assure the incorporation of national environmental protection goals in the formulation and implementation of energy programs, and to advance the goals of restoring, protecting, and enhancing environmental quality, and assuring public health and safety."

There is no question that the synthetic fuels on which the Carter NEP put greater reliance as well as nuclear energy pose hazards to the environment and public health and safety. But the critical question is how the price and quantity controls adopted by the government in the past are going to solve the environmental problems associated with the oil and other energy industries (strip mining, for instance, obviously despoils the environment). As noted in Chapter 4, a system of properly devised effluent taxes or marketable pollution rights is more appropriate in these situations than the aforementioned controls. But as yet there is no move in this direction.

What about the depletion of natural resources? It is alleged that without government intervention, the industry will rapidly exploit the supplies of exhaustible fossil fuel resources such as oil and natural gas so that very little will be left for future generations. Although the concern is well taken, ironically the government's regulatory policies in the past may have contributed to this problem. In 1926 the government instituted the system of percentage depletion allowance whereby oil and natural gas producers and royalty owners could deduct a certain percentage (initially set at 27.5 percent) of their gross or before-tax wellhead revenues for tax purposes; that is, the first 27.5 percent of their gross revenue was tax-free. This percentage was later reduced to 22 in 1969, and presently only small oil and gas producers are entitled to it.

Now because the percentage depletion allowance provided tax-free income, there was every incentive for producers and tax-shelter–seeking investors to invest capital in oil and gas exploration. As Walter Mead says:

> . . . the tax subsidies for oil and gas have led to resource misallocation. Development of oil and gas was stimulated at the expense of alternative energy sources. . . . The subsidies led to resources misallocation not only among energy sources, but also over time. By making exploration and production more profitable than they would have been in the absence of such subsidies, the capital flow into oil and gas, as well as some other energy resources, led to their early exploitation, at the expense of future generations. The decline in oil and gas reserves and production that is now part of the energy crisis resulted in part from these tax subsidies.[19]

[19]Walter J. Mead, *Energy and the Environment: Conflict in Public Policy,* American Enterprise Institute for Public Policy Research, Washington, D.C., 1978, p. 18.

Similarly, if the MOIP had not been introduced in 1959 and if the cheaper foreign crude oil had not been allowed to be freely imported, domestic prices of crude would have come down, which would have reduced domestic production and excess capacity. Likewise, after the 1973 oil embargo and the resultant quandrupling of OPEC prices, if the government had lifted all price controls on domestic crude, it would have reduced both consumption and imports while stimulating domestic production to meet the widening excess demand. In short, if the market had been allowed to function freely, it would have resolved the problems of surpluses and scarcities and thereby the appropriate (optimal) rate of exploitation of natural resources. As William Baumol and Alan Blinder state:

> As a natural resource becomes more and more scarce, the operation of markets will give it a higher and higher price unless governments intervene to keep this from happening. And it is precisely this higher price that will keep us from suddenly running out of the scarce resources.[20]

There is one serious argument against decontrol that needs to be answered. This involves not allocative efficiency, but distributive efficiency or equity, namely, the effect of higher prices of oil and gas on the poor if all price controls are suddenly abolished. There is no doubt that the precipitous increase in the price of oil since the Iranian oil embargo of 1979 has had serious adverse effect on some of the neediest poor and on retired people with fixed incomes.[21] But the important question here is whether price controls are the answer to the problem. Most economists argue that they are not. Instead, they advocate that the hard-hit poor be given tax rebates, supplemental social security income, or similar public assistance incomes. Such a policy would not lead to misallocation of economic resources, which is what the price and quantity controls do and have done so far. The Carter NEP has recognized this point and has provided for tax relief for the poor. Unfortunately, this tax relief is to come out of the proceedings of the windfall profit tax, which may give little incentive to the producers to produce more oil.

There are two other arguments against the decontrol of oil prices, namely that, it would lead to (1) higher inflation and (2) windfall profits for the oil producers. Let us consider them briefly.

Before President Carter established the windfall profit tax in 1979 to bring domestic crude prices on par with the world oil prices in a phased manner, it was argued that lifting of the price controls on domestic crude would boost the cost of living. This in turn would lead to demands for higher pay and thus fuel the inflation rate which had been trending upward for quite some time. This argument against decontrol, according to Herbert Stein, is "reminiscent of the youth who, having been convicted of killing his parents, appealed for clemency

---

[20]William J. Baumol and Alan S. Biinder, *Economics: Principles and Policy*, Harcourt, Brace, 1979, p. 841.

[21]Although the OPEC price quadrupled in 1973 to about $12 a barrel, between 1974 and 1978 the price increased only by $2, but since 1979 it has jumped to more than $30 a barrel.

on the ground that he was an orphan."[22] The youth in this analogy is the government, which instituted the price controls to begin with and now does not want to lift them for fear that they will lead to inflation. As a matter of fact, by keeping the domestic price controlled and thereby encouraging imports (see Figure 13.1), the government is telling OPEC that, "No matter what price you charge we will not follow suit." Hence, it is an open invitation for OPEC to increase its prices.

Incidentally, it may be noted that energy accounts for about 8 percent of the consumer price index (CPI). Therefore, the effect of oil price decontrol would not be as grave as it would if it were to account for, say, 25 percent of the CPI. In any case, in the long run there is no question that letting the prices float will have a positive impact on domestic production and a negative impact on consumption and imports. In fact, since the phased NEP came into being, these effects have become plain already — imports have dropped by about 1.5 million barrels a day since 1979 while domestic production has increased by 600,000 barrels a day. This means we are paying OPEC $50 million a day less at 1981 prices of OPEC crude. There is no question that this has had some chilling effect on the OPEC policymakers. Saudi Arabia, the largest producer and the most powerful member of OPEC, is trying to persuade other members of the organization to cut their prices.[23]

Let us turn to the argument of windfall profits. If price controls were lifted, the immediate beneficiaries would be the oil companies, who would reap huge profits on their oil inventories. This was precisely the fear that led President Carter to institute the windfall profit tax, which equals the difference between the world price of oil and the previously regulated price of domestic oil. Although the windfall profit tax is in place now and has been upheld by the Supreme Court, can it be justified? Stein argues against it on the ground that it is against our tax tradition. As he states, "there is nothing in our tradition or common attitudes which suggest that windfall gains are to be prevented or taxed heavily."[24] Under the current tax system, if a person makes an income of $10,000 a year and it suddenly rises to $20,000, he or she will pay, because of the income-averaging provision of the income tax code, less tax than a person whose income had been $20,000 all along, which would be in accord with common ideas of fairness. "But the theory of windfall profit tax is that people should be taxed more if their incomes rise than if they have been always high."[25]

---

[22]Herbert Stein, "Energy — the Wrong Summit," *The AEI Economist,* American Enterprise Institute for Public Policy Research, July 1979, p. 5.

[23]The world oil market at present (mid-1983) is in turmoil. Because of the steep oil price hikes since the 1979 Iranian war, consumers in the industrial west as well as in developing countries have substantially reduced oil consumption. This plus the deregulatory initiatives in the United States as well as the 1981–1982 worldwide economic recession so affected the OPEC countries that at the official price of $38 a barrel there was a serious glut in the world oil supplies. Several OPEC and non-OPEC countries have started cutting the official price (which is around $30 a barrel now), and Saudi Arabia, the largest producer, has started reducing its daily output. Needless to say, the drop in the oil price has eased the balance of payments burden of several developing countries heavily dependent on OPEC oil. The consumer in general has benefitted too.

[24]Stein, op. cit., p. 6.

[25]Ibid.

To sum up: The arguments against decontrolling crude oil prices (and other petroleum product prices) are not very convincing. They are against our national interest, too, for when we deliberately keep domestic prices down and discourage domestic production, the gap between consumption and production will have to be met by the higher-priced imports. This means that instead of giving the benefit of the higher prices to domestic producers, we are actually subsidizing OPEC producers and helping them sustain their oil monopoly. Stein correctly argues that one sure way to break the OPEC cartel is to make the U.S. energy price higher than the OPEC prices by imposing taxes on petroleum products, domestically produced or imported. This will discourage domestic consumption and eventually force OPEC to hold down its prices. In fact, the high gasoline taxes imposed in Japan and Europe have discouraged imports of oil and have put considerable downward pressure on OPEC price increases. If the United States, the largest importer of OPEC oil, follows suit, there is no doubt that eventually the OPEC monopoly will be reined in (recently the Reagan administration did increase the federal gasoline tax by 5 cents a gallon). Already, the oil glut observed since 1982 is one indication that the OPEC monopoly may not last forever.

13.10 THE NATURAL GAS INDUSTRY

As a source of our energy usage, natural gas is only second to oil. According to DOE estimates, on a daily basis, in 1980 we used 16.9 million barrels of petroleum products and the oil equivalent of 9.7 million barrels of natural gas (or 20 trillion cubic feet, or 20 tcf), 7.3 million barrels of coal, 1.3 million barrels of nuclear energy, and 2.4 million barrels of solar and other renewable energy resources.[26] Thus, oil and natural gas together accounted for about 70 percent of our energy needs that year.

Although the growth of natural gas and the natural gas industry is important now, it is a comparatively recent phenomenon. It dates back to World War II when pipeline technology was developed to the point that it was possible to transmit gas from the producing states (largely Arkansas, Louisiana, Oklahoma, and Texas) to the rest of the country. In 1946 the production of natural gas was only 4.9 tcf, whereas it was about 20 tcf in 1979.

The industry has three major segments: production, transmission, and distribution. Production is largely confined to the states listed above, although gas from the Purdhoe Bay in Alaska is now becoming available. The United States imports very little natural gas from abroad, about 4 to 5 percent of its domestic consumption. The imported gas is in liquefied form and is called LNG. Up until 1960, the wellhead price of natural gas was determined in the marketplace, but since then it has been controlled by the FERC (formerly the FPC). The transmission end of the industry has been regulated since 1938 under the Natural Gas

---

[26]A barrel of oil (42 gallons) = 5.8 million Btu; 1 cubit foot of natural gas = 1031 Btu; 1 ton of coal = 25 million Btu; and 1 kwh of electricity = 3413 Btu. Btu, the British thermal unit, is the amount of heat required to raise the temperature of one pound of water by one degree Fahrenheit.

Act of 1938. The gas that the pipeline companies transmit is sold to local public utilities which in turn sell it to residential, commercial, and industrial customers. The public utilities have been traditionally controlled by state or local public utility commissions which determine the rates the public utilities can charge their customers. The rates, as noted in Chapter 4, are so determined that they give the utility a certain rate of return on its invested capital, which ranges from 12 to 16 percent.

In the residential and commercial markets, natural gas faces competition from heating oil, whereas in the industrial and electrical utility markets it faces competition from heavy fuel oil and coal. Although the price of coal is uncontrolled, and although it is plentiful, many industrial customers are restricted from using coal because of environmental considerations.

13.11   REGULATION OF THE NATURAL GAS INDUSTRY

The transmission segment of the gas industry came under federal regulation when Congress passed the Natural Gas Act of 1938. This regulation can be economically justified because pipeline companies, as noted in Chapter 2, Section 2.2, are natural monopolies. Since the transmitted gas was sold by local public utilities, and since these utilities have traditionally been regulated by state and local authorities because they too are monopolies by virtue of franchise, the only segment of the industry that was not regulated was the production front. But that situation changed by the *Phillips* case in 1954.

In the case of *Phillips Petroleum Co. v. Wisconsin,* 347 U.S. 672 (1954), Phillips, the largest independent producer of gas, had been increasing its wellhead price to the pipeline company serving the Wisconsin area. The pipeline company, in turn, passed the price increases on to consumers as "pass-throughs." The attorney general of Wisconsin argued that such pass-throughs were against the interests of consumers in Wisconsin and asked the FPC to regulate the wellhead price charged by the producers. But the FPC argued that it lacked the power to do so under the 1938 act. The attorney general appealed the case to the Supreme Court. The Court held that Phillips, although engaged solely in the production and gathering of natural gas, was a natural gas company within the meaning of the 1938 act and its sale of its products in interstate markets came under the control of the FPC. Hence the FPC could control the wellhead price of gas that entered the interstate markets, but not the price of gas sold intrastate. Unfortunately, the Supreme Court did not find out whether there was monopoly in the production and sale of gas, nor did it tell the FPC how to regulate the wellhead price of gas entering the interstate markets.

The FPC was not prepared for this added responsibility. Initially it was required to fix the wellhead price of some 4000 independent producers, which it did on a company-by-company basis. In determining the price, it followed the practice of public utility rate regulation, in which the price of a product (or service) is based on the average cost of production plus a reasonable rate of return on the invested capital, the so-called rate base. But this case-by-case rate determination took such a long time that the whole process practically came to a standstill, with the result that until the mid-1960s there was no definite direction to the FPC pricing policy. As a stopgap measure, however, it fixed the price of natural gas at the level prevailing in 1958–1959.

Beginning in the mid-1960s, the FPC began determining the so-called area rates, one common rate for a widely defined geographical area. Initially, it established twenty such areas, mostly around Texas. The first such rate was the 1965 Permian basin area rate, which set the limits for the other areas. For each area, the FPC established two ceiling prices, one for old gas, that is gas produced from the existing wells, and another for new gas, that is gas that will be found in the future. In determining the area rates, the commission was to consider regional production costs, investment costs, and rate of return averages. In actuality, however, the initial price ceilings were set at the 1958–1959 level, notwithstanding the fact that the 1958–1959 price was only a temporary measure.

The 1958–1959 ceiling prices continued for a long time because price increase of such an "essential" product as gas was politically always a controversial topic. The FPC routinely declined requests for price increases simply because they were increases.[27] This no-price-increase policy of the commission received a boost by the 1959 decision in *Atlantic Refining Co. v. Public Service Commission,* 360 U.S. 378. In this case the Supreme Court denied a gas price increase because, "this price is greatly in excess of that which Tennessee pays from any lease in Southern Louisiana."[28] For new customers, the average price of gas was 18.2 cents per 1000 cubic feet (mcf) in 1961 and about 19.2 cents per mcf in 1969. Thus, for almost 8 years the price of gas changed little, although the prices of all other fuels during this period increased by 10 to 25 percent.

In 1971 the FPC revised its pricing policies because it realized that the constant pricing policy of the previous decade had had adverse impact on natural gas exploration and production; production was greater than additions to gas reserves (or inventories) because there was little incentive to invest money in new gas developments. Initially, the FPC granted some general price increases to producers but later established a nationwide price for old and new gas, abrogating the area rate policy. As a result of the policy change, the average price of gas for new customers, which was 19.8 cents per mcf in 1969, increased to 33.6 cents per mcf in 1972 and 36 cents per mcf in 1973. Thus within a span of 4 years the price increased by about 70 percent.

Following the severe winter of 1976–1977, the price of natural gas was increased again to the level of $1.45 per mcf in 1978, but this price was still below the market price because there were still gas shortages in many parts of the country where customers could not get new gas connections. Fortunately, with the passage of the 1978 Natural Gas Policy Act the price of new gas will be deregulated by 1986, but more on this in Section 13.13.

---

[27]For details, see P. W. MacAvoy and R. S. Pindyck, *The Economics of Natural Gas Shortage* (1960–1980), North-Holland, Amsterdam, 1975, ch. 1.

[28]Edmund Kitch, "Regulation of the Field Market for Natural Gas by the Federal Power Commission," *Journal of Law and Economics,* October 1968, p. 261.

13.12. ECONOMIC CONSEQUENCES OF NATURAL GAS PRICE REGULATIONS

The price regulation of the industry until the passage of the 1978 act had the predictable effect of keeping the price of gas below its free market level. Not only that, the regulated price was even below the regulated price of domestic oil, both prices being expressed in Btu equivalent. For example, in 1976 the price of a barrel of domestic crude oil was $8.18, that of the Saudi crude $11.50, and that of natural gas 60 cents per mcf, or about $3.50 per barrel of oil in Btu equivalence. Thus the gas price was some 57 percent below the regulated price of domestic oil and about 70 percent below that of foreign crude.

Now when the price of a product is deliberately kept below its market-clearing level, the inevitable consequences are increases in consumption but decreases in production. This can be seen clearly with the aid of Figures 13.3 and 13.4. Putting the price of gas per mcf on the vertical axis and the quantity of gas on the horizontal axis, we see precisely the same consequences as that for oil under price controls, namely, excess demand at the controlled price and, as in Figure 13.4, a dwindling of gas production and reserves. As a matter of fact, between 1967 and 1976 the U.S. gas reserves declined by one-third, implying a decline in future production.

All told, government regulatory policies relating to the gas industry have created these consequences. First, the spot shortages of gas in 1971 and the serious disruption of gas supplies in the harsh winter of 1976–1977 meant that there was uncertainty about future gas supplies even for customers who had long-term contracts with gas producers and suppliers.

Second, since the price of gas was cheaper than the price of oil (in Btu), and since environmentally gas is a cleaner fuel, there was all the incentive in the world for consumers to increase their demand for gas by switching from oil or coal.

Third, since the intrastate price of gas was not regulated by the FPC, the relatively lower interstate price of gas has had the effect of diminishing the supplies of new gas to the interstate markets, which can be seen clearly from Table 13.5. As the table shows, since the FPC resorted to area rate price controls in 1965, there has been a precipitous decline in the supplies of gas to the interstate markets, a decline largely attributable to the difference between the uncontrolled intrastate and controlled interstate prices of gas. In August 1976, for instance, the regulated price was $1.42 per mcf, whereas the intrastate prices were $2.19 in Louisiana, $1.69 in Oklahoma, and $1.97 in Texas.

Fourth, to assure themselves of gas supplies, some companies, especially petrochemical companies, located their operations in the gas-producing states, although intrastate gas was expensive and although other locational factors may not necessarily have dictated such a move.

Fifth, as a consequence of the preceding, some regional inequities have been created: Employment in the sun belt area has been gaining at the cost of the cities in the northeast, which are far removed from the gas-producing states.

TABLE 13.5
DISTRIBUTION OF NEW CONTRACT
COMMITMENTS BETWEEN INTERSTATE AND INTRASTATE
NATURAL GAS PRODUCERS, PERMIAN BASIN AREA,
1966–1970

| Year | Percentage committed | |
	Interstate	Intrastate
1966	83.7	16.3
1967	78.2	21.8
1968	12.8	87.2
1969	16.7	83.3
1970 (6 months)	9.1	90.9

Source: Robert B. Helms, *Natural Gas Regulation: An Evaluation of FPC Price Controls,* American Enterprise Institute for Public Policy Research, Washington, D.C., 1974, p. 45.

Sixth, although the intrastate prices of gas were higher than the regulated interstate prices, the former may not represent the true equilibrium prices in their respective markets. This is because in the absence of interstate price controls gas would have moved freely into the interstate markets, which would have reduced gas supplies in the intrastate markets and thereby raised gas prices in those markets.

Despite these clear-cut negative consequences of price controls, why did the federal regulations continue? The reasons are similar to those we discussed for oil. Simply put, politically it was unpalatable to remove price controls until gas shortages became highly visible.

13.13   THE NATURAL GAS POLICY ACT OF 1978

Recognizing that the shortages of natural gas seen in the mid- and late 1970s were policy-induced (even the FPC admitted that), President Carter, in his NEP, wanted to bring gas prices on par with the Btu-equivalent price of oil. But the Congress did not go that far. Instead, it passed the Natural Gas Policy Act of 1978 (NGPA), an incredibly complex piece of legislation which established some twenty-three price categories for fuel.

Under the law, all old gas (i.e., gas discovered before April 20, 1977) will reach a projected price of $1.90 per mcf in 1985 to all new customers. New gas (that discovered since April 20, 1977) will reach a projected maximum of $4.54, also by 1985. The transition will be made by increasing the 1977 price by the rate of inflation plus 3.7 percent per annum until 1981 and thereafter by the rate of inflation plus 6 percent per annum. By January 1, 1985, all price controls on new interstate as well as intrastate gas will end, and by 1989 all price controls are to expire. The Reagan administration wants to end all natural gas price controls right away but has not succeeded so far.

To lessen the burden of price increases on residential customers, the NGPA introduces the principle of marginal or incremental pricing for industrial customers. Under phase 1 of the act, beginning in January 1985, industrial users that burn natural gas in their boilers may have to pay a price equal to that of residential fuel oil, or about $3.80 per mcf. In phase 2, companies that use more than 300 mcf of gas per day for feedstock, such as petrochemical producers, or in their processes, such as glass manufacturers, will also have to pay the incremental price. The reason for this differential pricing in favor of residential customers is that the industrial customers have the ability to switch to oil or coal more readily than the former.

Although definitely an improvement over the previous pricing policies, the NGPA is not without faults. First, the act is of no help to producers that had entered into long-term contracts (10 to 30 years) to provide gas at prices as cheaply as 30 cents per mcf. Second, although the United States does not import a large quantity of gas from abroad, whatever gas is imported is at substantially higher prices. For example, Canadian gas costs $4.47 per mcf and Mexican gas costs $4.82 per mcf. Thus the domestic price may not still represent the true market price even after the price increases. Third, when the NGPA was passed in 1978 it was believed that oil prices would not jump abruptly. But, as we noted, these prices increased astronomically after the Iranian revolution, exceeding $30 a barrel. Therefore, the gas price standards set under the act are already obsolete.

Yet, the 1978 act has had the desired effect. Since its passage, there has been a surge of oil and gas explorations and vast new gas fields are reported in the Rocky Mountain region and the Gulf Coast of Louisiana.

13.14 ENERGY INDEPENDENCE

In the wake of the OPEC oil embargo, the United States suddenly discovered its vulnerability to political blackmail by OPEC members. President Nixon immediately launched his Project Independence to make the country independent from such oil interruptions by 1980. Unfortunately, 1980 has come and gone, and there is yet no sign of energy independence.

Following the 1979 Iranian oil embargo, President Carter, too, vowed to reduce this country's dependence on foreign oil chiefly by energy conservation and by developing alternative sources of energy. Let us consider these two aspects briefly.

Energy Conservation

Simply stated, *energy conservation* means making better use of scarce energy resources by utilizing them more efficiently. This may involve investment in the insulation of homes and commercial buildings, devising appliances that will use less energy per unit of output, developing cars that will give more mileage per gallon of gasoline, enforcing a 55-mile speed limit, and so on.[29] The tax incentives in the NEP are meant to achieve these goals.

While these developments are taking place, to stave off sudden energy crises, the Emergency Policy and Conservation Act of 1975 authorized a system of strategic petroleum reserves (SPR) to store up to 1 billion barrels of crude oil and petroleum products. But until 1981, the United States had managed to pump only 121.5 million barrels into the five underground storage sites in Louisiana and Texas, barely enough to replace the country's imports for 3 weeks. The future of the SPR under the Reagan administration is uncertain.

Developing Alternative Sources of Energy

The NEP also puts heavy emphasis on developing alternative sources of generating oil and gas as well as on sources that will replace them. Some of these sources, discussed below, were economically unfeasible so long as oil and gas were comparatively cheap. But when the price of a barrel of oil reached $30, some of these alternatives seemed economically viable.

Coal. Until 1925, the "Old King Coal" supplied 70 percent of our energy needs. But thereafter, the cheaper and easier to transport oil and gas relegated it to third place. Apart from the transportational difficulties, coal poses serious problems for the health and safety of miners, pollutes the air by its sulphur dioxide emission, and despoils the environment, especially if coal is obtained from strip mining.[30]

But if methods can be found to get rid of the sulphur (by devising inexpensive scrubber systems to trap sulphur) or liquefy it, coal can provide a very significant proportion of our energy needs, for we have plenty of it. At the current rate of production (780 million tons in 1979) it is estimated that we have coal reserves that will last us several hundred years.

Geothermal or Earth Heat. One of our plentiful but as yet untapped resources is the natural heat of the earth transferred to the surface in water and steam, as in the hot water springs of Boise, Idaho, which have heated homes there since 1890 or the steam that drives turbines at the geysers in California, which produce electricity equal to half of San Francisco's fuel consumption.[31]

It has been estimated by experts that about 32 million quads [1 quad = one

---

[29]All these measures will of course involve costs. But they may be incurred up to the point where the incremental cost of, say, insulating a house is less than or at most equal to the incremental savings in energy cost ensuing therefrom. Hence we are not talking about absolute insulation but optimum insulation, the optimum occurring, as we have noted several times, where the marginal benefit (of an activity) equals the marginal cost (of undertaking that activity).

[30]Strip mining involves stripping away the earth covering a vein of coal. It leaves huge scars and destroys vegetation, which increases the danger of erosion and eliminates refuge for birds.

[31]Geothermal heat results from the radioactive decay of rocks, which raises the earth's temperature an average of 25 degrees Celsius with each kilometer of depth.

quadrillion ($= 10^{15}$) Btus] of energy are simmering within 10 kilometers of the surface of the earth. But as yet technology is not sufficiently well-developed to make this source of energy economically viable. One problem that needs to be considered is the possible seismic disturbance caused by pumping.

Nuclear Energy.   Although 4 percent of the electricity produced in the United States comes from it, nuclear energy has as yet not become a potent source of our energy needs because of some serious problems. Nuclear energy generated from the present light water reactors, which use uranium as fuel, emits harmful radiation, and the spent fuel can remain radioactive for 1000 years and a small portion of it, plutonium, for 24,000 years. There is also the fear that widespread use of uranium may lead to nuclear weapons proliferation; the plutonium that is recovered from the spent uranium is used to build atom bombs.

There is no question, however, that nuclear energy is an extremely important and relatively inexpensive source of supplying our energy needs. The energy uranium holds is awesome. A pound of enriched uranium contains nearly 3 million times the energy in a pound of coal. Moreover, one pellet of uranium costs about $7, has the energy of three barrels of oil (equal to $84 at 1980 prices) or one ton of coal ($29 at 1980 prices). Furthermore, the United States is the world's largest producer of uranium, accounting for about one-fourth of the world's output.

Solar Energy.   Another relatively plentiful but as yet little explored source of energy is the sun. At present it provides only 6 percent of our energy needs, mostly in the form of hydroelectric power and wood. Unfortunately, the economics of solar energy at present is such that for most conventionally constructed homes, switching to it is more expensive than using conventional methods of heating. Also, the technology to generate electricity directly from solar radiation is still in its infancy, although the development of photovoltaic cells is quite promising.

Hydroelectric Power.   With a present output of 3 quad Btu per year, about 14 percent of the electricity consumed in the United States comes from hydroelectric projects, such as dams which harness the water power of rivers to generate electricity. Although production is expected to reach 10 quad Btu per year, the basic limitation is that there is not a great deal of unexploited capacity left.

Shale Oil.   An unconventional source of energy that awaits tapping is the oil embedded in the bituminous shale (or brown coal) that lies in the 11 million acres of land (three-fourths of which is owned by the federal government) containing shale oil deposits. Estimates of shale oil run as high as 2 trillion barrels. Although shale oil is practically free from sulphur or ash, making it an environmentally desirable fuel, its use so far has been limited because of the high cost of extracting such oil. But with the price of conventional oil hovering around $30 a barrel, shale oil may very well have reached the level of feasible economic exploitation.

Outer Continental Shelf Oil and Gas. A vast source of oil and gas that remains to be fully tapped is the Outer Continental Shelf (OCS), that is, the offshore area beyond the 3-mile limit or the 10-mile limit in Texas and Florida, which is largely owned by the federal government. For political as well as environmental reasons (oil spills, danger to the fishing industry, etc.), the federal government has been very slow in leasing the OCS to the private sector. Whenever it does lease, it imposes a "5-year rule," which requires the lessee to begin production within 5 years or return the lease to the government and forfeit the lease payment. Needless to say, this rule is arbitrary and it has made prospective lessees somewhat reluctant to invest large sums of money in OCS oil and gas exploration.

13.15 SUMMARY AND CONCLUSIONS

When the Arab members of OPEC imposed the 1973 oil embargo, the United States suddenly recognized that the days of cheap foreign oil were over and that the country could not continue to gobble up one-fourth of the world's oil production. The short-run impacts of the 1973 and 1979 oil embargoes on inflation, income distribution, employment, and economic growth have been clearly adverse.

Although the oil embargoes may have triggered our "energy crisis," the root cause of our excessive dependence on oil and gas lies in the government's regulatory policies regarding these fuels. Insofar as oil is concerned, the government's price and quantity controls since President Nixon's Economic Stabilization Program of August 1971 (and continued in subsequent administrations) has had the effect of keeping domestic prices of crude oil and oil products below their world levels. The result was that while domestic exploration and production was discouraged, domestic consumption continued to increase. The gap between domestic consumption and domestic production had to be met by the higher-priced imports. Thus there was a transfer of wealth from domestic producers to the OPEC monopoly. The economics of this myopic policy was ultimately recognized by President Carter, who took the initiative to decontrol crude oil prices through his National Energy Plan. President Reagan hastened the decontrol of crude oil prices by moving the terminal date from October to January of 1981. These policy changes already have had beneficial effects on domestic production, and they have also curtailed domestic consumption and hence the imports. There are indications that these developments have begun to dent the OPEC monopoly.

The shortages of natural gas observed in the 1970s too were due to government regulation. By deliberately keeping the wellhead price of gas below its market level, the regulatory policies have led to serious misallocation of economic resources; consequently producers were depleting their gas reserves without bothering to replace them by new finds. Fortunately, the 1978 Natural Gas Policy Act has recognized the problem and has provided for the elimination of all inter- and intrastate gas price controls by 1989. Already, this act has had beneficial effects on new gas discoveries.

Since gas and oil are exhaustible natural resources, there is now a general recognition that we need to develop alternative sources of energy. Some of the alternatives such as shale oil and geothermal energy, which were deemed uneconomical in the days of cheap oil and gas, are becoming economically viable, although the technology to exploit them is not yet fully developed. A significant and comparatively inexpensive source of energy is nuclear power. But because of the concern with radiation and the problem of waste disposal, nuclear energy remains a controversial subject.

One important lesson that one can learn from our study of the oil and gas industry regulations is that unless there are demonstrable externalities, the government should not intervene in the marketplace to determine prices or quantities, at least from an efficiency viewpoint. If it does, all the consequences discussed in this chapter are the result.

QUESTIONS

13.1 Illustrate the consequences of the MOIP discussed in the text with the aid of supply and demand curves.

13.2 The Interstate Oil Compact made in the 1930s was essentially monopolistic in nature. Should the government have tried it under the one or more antitrust laws discussed in Part 2? Why or why not?

13.3 What is the economics of the "buy and sell" program instituted during the Arab Oil Embargo of 1973–1974?

13.4 What would have happened if the government had not instituted the Entitlements Program?

13.5 Instead of lifting price controls on gasoline, some opponents of the oil price decontrol program advocate gasoline rationing to give each consumer so many coupons a month, each coupon allowing the consumer to buy a gallon of gasoline at the controlled price. What would be the consequences of such a scheme if (a) consumers were allowed to sell the unused coupons in the free market and if (b) they were allowed to sell the unused coupons at a price fixed by the government? In general, would you prefer gasoline rationing to gasoline price deregulation? Justify your answer.

13.6 State with reasons whether the following statement is true or false: "If the price of gasoline ration coupons were controlled along with the price of gasoline, black markets would develop." (Sweeney, op. cit., p. 195.)

13.7 The Energy Policy Conservation Act (EPCA) of 1975, among other provisions, mandated fuel efficiency standards for new cars. By 1985, all cars manufactured must get at least 27.5 miles per gallon. If a manufacturer fails to meet the standard, it is subject to civil fines which are not deductible for tax purposes. Now consider (1) a car which gets only 15 miles per gallon but is used to transport six people, and (2) another car which gets 32 miles per gallon but is generally used to transport one person. Under the proposed standard, the EPCA will penalize the manufacturer of the former car. Is such a penalty economically justifiable? What alternative(s) would you suggest to encourage fuel efficiency for new cars that also takes into account not just the miles per gallon but also the intensity of the car usage.

13.8 The Carter NEP justifies the imposition of the windfall profit tax as follows: "If producers were to receive tomorrow's prices for yesterday's discoveries, there would be an inequitable transfer of income from the American people to the producers, whose profits would be excessive and would bear little relation to actual economic contribution." (U.S. Executive Office of the President, *National Energy Plan,* Washington, D.C., 1977, p. xi.)

Do you agree with the above justification for the imposition of the windfall profit tax? Reason carefully.

13.9 Can you offer economic justification for the establishment of the strategic petroleum reserves?

13.10 Comment: "In a free-market economy, the ultimate test of growing scarcity is the behavior of prices. If the price of an item is not rising, it is safe to guess that it is not scarce relative to the demand for it." (Baumol and Blinder, op. cit., p. 655.)

13.11 State with reasons whether you agree or disagree with the statement: "In a sense, the real cost of OPEC oil to us is more than the OPEC price, because each dollar of OPEC oil cost us not only its price in dollars but also its price in insecurity." (Stein, op. cit. p. 8.)

13.12 From publicly available sources find out what has happened to prices, production, exploration, and imports of oil and natural gas since the passage of the NEP and the NGPA.

CHAPTER 14

THE SEC AND REGULATION OF THE SECURITIES MARKETS

Established in 1934, the Securities and Exchange Commission (SEC) is charged with the responsibility of maintaining fair, efficient, and orderly markets for securities and to regulate their distribution for the protection of investors. In this chapter we consider the circumstances that led to the establishment of the SEC, the evolution of the commission's mandate, the need for the regulation of the securities markets, and an evaluation of the job the SEC has done.[1] This is followed by a discussion of some of the deregulatory initiatives taken by the commission in the recent past and their consequences.

14.1 THE ORIGIN OF THE SEC: THE GREAT CRASH AND THE AFTERMATH[2]

The genesis of the SEC can be traced to the "golden" 1920s when the United States was passing through a period of unsurpassed economic growth. During that decade mass production reached its peak, as indicated by car production — in 1909 Ford built only 10,666 cars, by 1919 there were 6.7 millions cars on the road, and by 1929 there were more than 27 million. This phenomenal growth in the auto industry spurred construction of thousands of miles of roadway and gave impetus to oil, rubber, steel, and other Detroit-related businesses.

Alongside the auto industry came the electric power industry, which in turn

---

[1] The terms *securities markets, stock markets,* and *organized markets* will be used interchangeably. The term *security* is generic and includes stock, bond, and other financial obligations of corporations.

[2] The following discussion draws from, "America in 1929: The Prosperity Illusion," *Business Week,* Sept. 3, 1979, pp. 6–10.

led to the growth of power-driven machinery. This machinery reduced manufacturing costs and helped boost the nation's output significantly, by about 30 percent over the decade. The development of electricity fostered the growth of the radio, whose sales soared from $60 million in 1922 to $843 million in 1929. The dynamism of the radio industry was exemplified by the Radio Corporation of America (RCA), which became a symbol of speculation in the market because its price zoomed from a low of $85 in 1928 to a high of $549 in 1929, an increase of 546 percent in a single year.

Then came the phenomenal growth in industries, such as cigarettes, chemicals (especially cosmetics and rayon), and the movies. The movie industry led to the development of the chain operation and the ensuing merger battles of the 1920s.

The chain method of marketing soon spread to retailing, as evidenced by the five-and-dime stores, cigar chains, drug chains, and grocery chains. The chain concept even extended to banking and public utilities. The combination of the chain and holding company instruments was soon used for playing a financial power game (empire building) which was in no small measure responsible for the speculative boom in the stock market.

The speculative boom was further aided by continuous productivity growth, a growth not matched by similar growth in wages. As a result, the unit cost of production and, therefore, unit prices declined, which inflated business profits. With such prosperity, people had money and were looking for investment outlets, and the stock market seemed to offer just the right opportunity. The flow of money into the stock market made it unbelievably easy to raise venture or equity capital and funds for business expansion. As if this was not enough, the brokerage houses allowed their customers to buy stocks on a margin (down payment) of 10 percent only, loaning them the rest of the amount. Thus, to buy 100 shares of a stock at a price of $10 a share, the customer need put down only $100, borrowing $900 from the broker. Investors did not worry about what interest the broker charged for the loan because they all believed that the growth in stock prices would make them rich quickly. The stock market fever has been described thus:

> The rich man's chauffeur drove with his ears laid back to catch the news of an impending move in Bethlehem Steel: He held 50 shares himself on a 20-point margin. The window cleaner at the broker's office paused to watch the ticker, for he was thinking of converting his laboriously accumulated savings into a few shares of Simmons. [One reporter] told of a broker's valet who made nearly a quarter of a million in the market; of a trained nurse who cleaned up $30,000 following the tips given her by grateful patients; and of a Wyoming cattleman, 30 miles from the nearest railroad, who bought or sold a thousand shares a day.[3]

The stock market reached dizzying heights between March 3, 1928, and September 3, 1929, the day of the peak. The "high flyers" were: American Can

---

[3]*Newsweek,* op. cit., p. 9. (The quote is taken from Frederick L. Allen, *Only Yesterday.* Harper & Row).

from $77 to $182, AT&T from $179 to $335, Anaconda Copper from $55 to $162, and Electric Bond and Share from $90 to $203. Even the seasoned stocks recorded unprecedented values: General Motors from $139 to $182 and Westinghouse from $92 to $313. The New York Times industrial average of stock prices surged from $176 in 1926 to $245 in 1927 and to $331 by 1928. The trading volume on the New York Stock Exchange (NYSE) skyrocketed from 236 million shares in 1923 to more than 1 billion in 1929. To add fuel to the fire, commercial banks followed liberal loan policies to the brokerage houses: By the fall of 1920, brokers owed the banks $7 billion, up from $3.5 billion at the end of 1927.

But the speculative bubble burst on October 24, 1929 (Black Thursday), when stock prices tumbled so drastically that everyone was taken by surprise. Stuck with huge margin accounts, stockbrokers rushed to sell the margined securities to recoup their loans, which put further downward pressure on stock prices. Overnight, billions of dollars were lost in the market. The tumble did not spare even the stalwarts such as the U.S. Steel Company; its stock dropped from a high of $261 in 1929 to a woeful low of $21 in 1932. Several lesser-known stocks were not even worth the paper they were printed on.

As if things were not bad enough, the Federal Reserve System (the Fed), the nation's central banker, started slowing down the growth of the money supply precisely at the time when it should have done the opposite. Then the roof caved in in the form of several bank failures in the midwest and south, which led to a run on the commercial banks to convert deposit money into cash. As Milton Friedman notes, the critical date was December 11, 1930, when the Bank of United States, a private commercial bank despite its pretentious name, was allowed to go bankrupt by the Fed, although technically it was a sound bank. According to Friedman, had the Fed rescued the Bank, there would not have been the failure of 352 other banks in December 1930 alone.[4]

When things go wrong, it seems, they really go wrong. In September 1931 Great Britain went off the gold standard. To stave off the outflow of gold, the Fed increased the interest or discount rate it charged banks, a patently foolhardy thing to do in the face of the serious depression of the previous 2 years. This move was highly deflationary. Matters came to a head in the bank panic of 1933 when several banks went bankrupt. Defeated in the 1932 elections, President Hoover did not want to take actions to stem the crisis without the consent of President-elect Franklin D. Roosevelt. Roosevelt, for political reasons, did not want to do anything until he assumed office, which he did in March 1933. On March 6, 1933, President Roosevelt declared the Banking Holiday to calm down the crisis.

Roosevelt ushered in the era of the New Deal by proposing a series of measures to rescue the economy from the throes of the great depression. One of his early moves was the signing of the Securities Act of 1933, which was fol-

---

[4]Milton and Rose Friedman, *Free to Choose: A Personal Statement,* Harcourt, Brace, New York, 1980, ch. 3.

lowed in short order by the Securities Exchange Act of 1934. These two acts marked the entry of the federal government into the regulation of the securities markets.

14.2   THE MANDATE OF THE SEC[5]

The mandate of the SEC is spelled out by a succession of acts, beginning with the Securities Act of 1933. Until the passage of this act, corporations were not required to register their stocks with any regulatory authority. Therefore, there was no need for any kind of disclosure of their activities by publicly owned corporations. The stock market itself was self-regulated by the NYSE, the oldest and the most powerful of the nation's stock exchanges. But as we will see, besides fixing the brokerage commission rates, the NYSE was not particularly interested in monitoring the activities of the corporations whose stock was listed on the exchange.

The Securities Act of 1933

Heralded as the "Corporate Freedom of Information Act," the 1933 act was the first major piece of federal legislation relating to the private corporate sector. This act requires issuers of securities making public offerings in interstate commerce or through the mails, directly or by others on their behalf, (1) to file a registration statement containing financial and other pertinent data about the issuer and the securities being offered; (2) to adhere to prescribed accounting standards, principles, and practices as well as the form and content of the registration statement and other public filings; and (3) not to make fraudulent or deceptive statements or to engage in fraudulent or deceptive practices in the sale of corporate securities. Failure to abide by one or more of these requirements subjects the guilty party to civil as well as criminal penalties.

The act had two major objectives, namely, to protect investors by providing decision-making information and to serve the broader public interest of improving the economic performance of the securities markets.

The proponents of the act believed that the speculative excesses of the 1920s were due to lack of information about corporations and their activities. Therefore, argued the proponents, the requirements under the act would help investors to better understand the activities of corporations and assess the risk as well as return from a particular investment. Whether this has happened is an empirical question, which is dealt with in Section 14.5.

The securities markets are undoubtedly an important economic institution in that they facilitate savings and investment first through making it possible for

[5]The following discussion is based on "Federal Regulation and Regulatory Reform," *Report by the Subcommittee on Oversight and Investigations of the Committee on Interstate and Foreign Commerce,* House of Representatives, 94th Cong., 2d Sess., October 1976, ch. 2 (hereafter referred to as the House *Study on Federal Regulation*); and *U.S. Government Manual.*

investors to dispose of securities quickly if they wish to do so, and second, by channeling savings into productive investments over time as well as contemporaneously. The framers of the 1933 act believed that the provisions of the act would allow the securities markets to perform these twin functions more efficiently. It remains to be seen whether this has actually happened (see Section 14.6).

The Securities Exchange Act of 1934

No sooner had the 1933 act been passed than it was realized that the act governed only the sale of stocks for the first time (i.e., new issues) but not their subsequent dealings on the organized exchanges. And since on any given day the organized stock exchanges deal mostly in stocks already issued, it was felt that continuous monitoring of such stocks is essential to protect the interests of potential buyers and sellers of such securities. With that in mind, the Securities Exchange Act of 1934 contained the following provisions:

1 All national securities exchange and national securities associations must register with the SEC, an independent regulatory commission created by the act to administer this and the 1933 act (which was until then administered by the Federal Trade Commission), and adopt rules which are designed, among other things, to promote just and equitable principles of trade. The commission has the authority to change these rules if that is deemed desirable in the public interest.

2 Companies which are listed on the organized exchanges as well as companies with assets of $1 million or more and 500 or more shareholders are required to file registration applications and annual and other reports with the exchanges and with the SEC. Such applications and reports must contain financial and other data prescribed by the commission as necessary or appropriate for the protection of investors and assure fair dealing.

3 Proxies must be sought according to the rules and procedures prescribed by the act.

4 Corporate officers and directors must disclose their purchases or sales of the corporation's securities (these are known as insider tradings or dealings).[6]

5 The SEC is authorized to promulgate rules governing the repurchase by a corporation of its own stock (corporations sometimes do that if they have idle funds and if their own corporate securities are underpriced and thus are a good buy).

6 Brokers and dealers who deal in any over-the-counter (OTC) securities are required to register themselves with the SEC.

7 The commission has the broad rule-making power with respect to short sales, the trading of options on the national securities markets, stabilizing trans-

---

[6]As we will see in Section 14.5, the scope of insider trading has been increased considerably over the years.

actions, floor trading, and activities of the specialists and odd-lot dealers (those selling less than 100 shares of a security).

8 The board of governors of the Federal Reserve System is empowered to make rules relating to the extensions of credit by brokers and dealers for securities transactions. Such rules include the establishment of minimum margin requirements with respect to securities traded on the national exchanges and certain securities traded in the OTC market.

The 1933 and 1934 acts constitute the major acts dealing with corporate disclosure and the working of the securities markets. But over the years, the SEC was entrusted with the following additional responsibilities.

The Public Utility Holding Company Act of 1935

This act gave the SEC the authority to regulate the purchase and sale of securities and assets by companies in electric and gas utility holding company systems, their intrasystem transactions, and service and management arrangements. It limits holding companies to a single coordinated utility system and requires simplification of complex corporate capital structures and elimination of unfair distribution of voting power among holders of system securities. The proponents of the act believed that some of the speculative excesses of the 1920s were due to the holding company management system, which made it possible for a parent company to have controlling interests in several subsidiaries and manipulate their capital structure.

The National Bankruptcy Act of 1938

Chapter 10 of this act provides for commission participation as adviser to federal courts in proceedings for the reorganization of insolvent corporations. The commission makes recommendations on the fairness and feasibility of proposed plans of reorganization.

The Trust Indenture Act of 1939

The purpose of this act is to protect the interests of purchasers of publicly offered debt securities issued in accordance with trust indentures (i.e., contracts). The act requires, among other things, that the issuing corporation may not include clauses that will exempt them from certain actions which may not be in the best interest of the debt holders. This act also prescribes the qualifications and relationships of indenture trustees.

The Investment Company Act of 1940

An SEC study of investment trust companies (mutual funds) discovered many abuses, from larceny and embezzlement to misuse of investors' funds and self-dealings by the insiders (e.g., officers of the funds getting interest-free loans, etc.). The 1940 act requires such companies to register with the commission and to follow certain practices. It prohibits certain types of fee arrangements, makes unlawful the practices of investment advisers involving fraud or deceit, and requires, among other things, disclosure of any adverse interest the advisers may have in transactions executed for clients.

The Investment Advisers Act of 1940

A companion legislation of the preceding act, this act provides that persons who, for compensation, engage in the business of advising others with respect to their security transactions must register with the commission. Some of the provisions of the Investment Company Act of 1940 regarding fee arrangements and deceptive practices are also incorporated in this act.

The Securities Investor Protection Act of 1970

In many ways the 1960s were a time filled with the kind of hectic stock market activity that was seen during the 1920s, thanks to the continuous economic expansion of 1963–1968. During that period the trading volume increased so significantly that brokerage houses were caught in a severe ''paper crunch'' — there were considerable delays in recording and transferring securities, delays caused by lag in the introduction of high-speed computers. As a result, some prestigious as well as some lesser-known brokerage firms went bankrupt, inflicting serious financial losses on their customers. To stave off such a possibility in the future, Congress passed the Securities Investor Protection Act of 1970 and created the Securities Investors Protection Corporation (SIPC) in line with the Federal Deposit Insurance Corporation (FDIC) (which insures accounts in commercial banks up to $100,000 per customer). To protect customers' funds and stocks left with the brokerage houses, the SIPC requires the latter to provide insurances against losses by paying prescribed premiums to the SIPC. In cases where the SIPC is unable to protect creditors, the SEC has the right to take legal action on their behalf.

The Securities Act Amendments of 1975 (The 1975 Amendments)

The primary goal of the 1975 amendments, the first major overhaul of the 1934 act, was to develop securities markets which are not only freely competitive but are also orderly, open, and protective of the interests of public investors. To achieve this goal, the SEC was mandated to develop a national securities market whereby various stock exchanges in the country (the NYSE, American, Midwest, Boston, Philadelphia, and Pacific) would be electronically linked so that an investor anywhere could be assured of getting the best price for his or her trading order.

Until the new mandate, the dominant position of the NYSE was taken for granted. The SEC seems to be so awed by the preeminence of the NYSE that up until 1975 it followed a hands-off policy in the internal affairs of that exchange, which was virtually a monopoly. But the 1975 amendments changed that passive role of the commission. In the words of the proponents of the 1975 amendments, "The SEC must participate and indeed lead in the building of a new trading system, national in scope, free and open, and protective of the public interest and public investors."[7] The amendments specifically gave the commission the power to look into the inner working of the NYSE, especially its cartel-like pricing and admissions policies.

From the preceding discussion it may be concluded that the general thrust of SEC regulation has been twofold, namely, (1) to protect investors by providing them information via the various disclosure rules, and (2) to promote competitive securities markets, ultimately linking all of them by a national securities market.

To what extend has the SEC succeeded in achieving these goals, assuming that these are desirable policy goals? This is an empirical question, and we will examine the empirical evidence in Sections 14.5 and 14.6. But in the meantime it is natural to ask: What is the economic rationale, if any, behind the regulation of the securities industry? An answer to this question will provide a backdrop against which we may examine the empirical evidence discussed subsequently. We consider this important question in Section 14.4, after we take a brief look at the administrative structure of the SEC.

14.3   THE ADMINISTRATIVE STRUCTURE OF THE SEC

As noted elsewhere, the SEC is an independent regulatory commission consisting of five members who are nominated by the President and are subject to Senate approval. One member of the commission acts as chairperson at the pleasure of the President. No more than three members can come from the same political party.

The various tasks of the commission are divided into several divisions and field offices, as shown in Figure 14.1. This diagram is self-explanatory.

14.4   WHY REGULATION?

According to Irwin Friend, regulation requiring corporations to disclose their finances and activities may be justified because of the "belief that the provision of information to prospective investors is a necessary condition for efficient markets."[8] The term *efficient* (capital) *market* means that "new information is widely, quickly and cheaply available to investors, that this information includes

---

[7] *House Study on Federal Regulation,* op. cit., p. 23.
[8] Irwin Friend, "The SEC and the Economic Performance of Securities Markets," in Henry G. Manne (ed.), *Economic Policy and the Regulation of Corporate Securities,* American Enterprise Institute for Public Policy Research, Washington, D.C., 1969, p. 187 (a symposium sponsored by the National Law Center, the George Washington University, and the American Enterprise Institute; hereafter, referred to as *Symposium*).

SECURITIES AND EXCHANGE COMMISSION

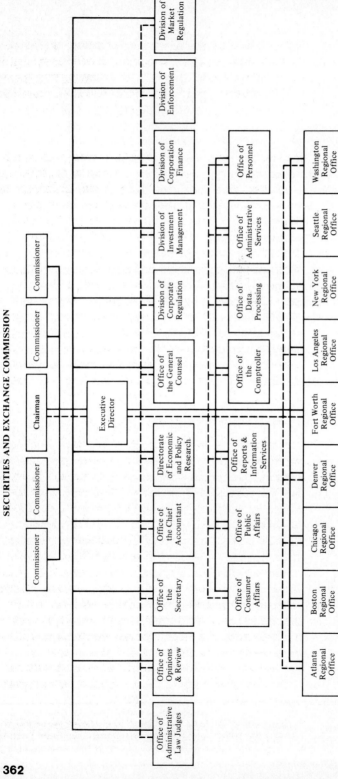

FIGURE 14.1
Securities and Exchange Commission.

what is knowable and relevant for judging securities, and that it is very rapidly reflected in security prices."[9] In Friend's view:

> With full disclosure we would expect less drastic shifts in estimates of expected profitability of a given issue as a result of the greater initial level of economic information (and, presumably, the reduction in the possibility of surprises from this source), a greater scope for scientific investment analysis, a diminished reliance on and use of rumors, and a reduction in the scale of manipulative practices.[10]

As we have noted in Chapter 2, lack of adequate information may be a cause of market failure which may justify government intervention in the marketplace. But before government steps in, it may be emphasized that information is not a free good — its production costs economic resources. Therefore, as Friend himself says, "the provision of new information entails additional costs which may offset some or all of the operational savings referred to."[11] A similar view is expressed by Harold Demsetz as follows:

> . . . If regulation is the instrument by which it is hoped to reduce the effects of imperfections, it is essential that some notion be formed as to the likely costs and benefits of regulation.[12]

He further adds:

> The rate of return to investing in regulation is the present value of the stream of future benefits minus future costs, all divided by the initial investment requirement.[13]

According to Demsetz, the rate of return to investing in regulation depends on the characteristics of the regulatory situation, which involves: "(1) the self-interest of the regulators, (2) the resources that already are devoted to accomplishing the regulatory task, and (3) the prognostic requirements of the task."[14]

If the self-interest of the regulators is at odds with the removal of information imperfections, argues Demsetz, the benefits of regulation will be small or even negative. This is especially so in the case of self-regulation, such as regulation by the NYSE, the American Medical Association, or the National Association of Security Dealers; these agencies obviously are not going to sacrifice their self-interest just to remove market imperfections.

About the scale or scope of regulation, Demsetz writes:

> If the scale of the task is great and, as generally is the case, if taxpayers are unwilling to provide enough funds to have the task performed well, then regulators increasingly will tolerate implicit self-regulation. As the gap increases between the funds required to do the regulatory task well and the funds that are available to do the task, regu-

---

[9]James Lorie and Richard Brealey (eds.), *"Modern Developments in Investment Management: A Book of Readings,"* Preager, New York, 1972, p. 101.

[10]*Symposium,* op. cit., p. 179. (This is a quote by the author from his article, "The SEC through a Glass Darkly," *Journal of Business,* October, 1964.)

[11]Ibid., p. 187.

[12]Harold Demsetz, "Perfect Competition, Regulation and the Stock Market," *Symposium,* op. cit., p. 4.

[13]Ibid.

[14]Ibid.

lators will resort more frequently to stamping an official approval on requests originating from those who are supposed to be the regulated. Regulation gives way to self-regulation and the benefits that can be expected to result from regulation are reduced correspondingly. The histories of railroad and utility rate regulation, two very large-scale regulatory tasks, are replete with examples of this process.[15]

Recall the capture theory of regulation.

Allan Meltzer agrees with Demsetz that some idea about the costs and benefits of regulation is necessary to evaluate any social regulation. Then he goes a step further and questions whether, in situations where the benefits of regulation exceed the costs, the government is the agency best-suited to intervene. As he puts it:

> If society gains from using private and public resources to disclose information and enforce disclosure rules, it may be possible to increase the gain by choosing methods that are more efficient than coercion [say, by government edict].[16]

In short, Meltzer seems to be echoing the Coase theorem (see Chapter 2).

So much for information disclosure. What about the other aspect of regulation — regulation of the securities markets to improve their efficiency? On this Meltzer writes:

> Prices are important pieces of information for decision making. By preventing large, frequent, or sudden changes in the price of outstanding securities, regulation improves the quality of the information provided by stock prices and thus increases the social value provided by the existence of a securities market. I regard this argument, whether true or false, as the main economic argument for regulation of the securities markets.[17]

In short, then, sound arguments can be advanced for the regulation of the securities markets as well as for corporate disclosure of information. The critical question is whether the government is the right agency to do so and, if so, whether it can do the job. In what follows, an attempt has been made to shed some light on this question.

14.5 THE EFFECTS OF REGULATION ON DISCLOSURE OF INFORMATION

The Stigler Study

Since the primary goal of the 1933 act requiring regulation of new issues was that it would help the investor make informed decisions, George Stigler wanted to find out how investors fared "before and after the SEC was given control over the registration of new issues."[18]

---

[15]Ibid., p. 6.
[16]Allan H. Meltzer, "On Efficiency and Regulation of the Securities Industry," *Symposium,* op. cit., p. 221.
[17]Ibid., p. 222.
[18]George Stigler, "Public Regulation of the Securities Market," in *The Citizen and the State: Essays on Regulation,* The University of Chicago Press, Chicago, 1975, p. 82. (Originally published in the *Journal of Business,* October 1964.)

TABLE 14.1
NEW STOCK PRICES RELATIVE TO MARKET AVERAGES (M) OR ISSUE YEAR (I)
Large Stock Issues*
(Issue Year = 100)
Averages and (Standard Deviations)

Period	Year after issue				
	First	Second	Third	Fourth	Fifth
A. Common stocks (M):					
1923–1927	89.9 (38.8)	77.9 (45.6)	72.5 (44.4)	66.2 (56.3)	70.7 (80.6)
1949–1955	87.9 (21.2)	79.1 (25.2)	78.4 (27.7)	77.7 (27.6)	74.9 (36.0)
B. Preferred stocks (M):					
1923–1927	82.3 (15.1)	63.2 (19.9)	56.5 (25.2)	53.5 (40.0)	59.6 (54.5)
1949–1955	91.5 (15.1)	76.9 (14.0)	69.5 (16.7)	62.2 (37.2)	59.1 (49.3)
C. Preferred stock (I):					
1923–1927	100.1 (17.0)	97.6 (30.7)	94.9 (30.7)	85.2 (53.5)	65.4 (55.2)
1949–1955	107.2 (18.5)	99.0 (13.7)	101.9 (20.3)	107.8 (51.9)	114.4 (66.5)

*Issues over $2.5 million 1923–1927, over $5.0 million 1949–1955.
Source: George J. Benston, "The Effectiveness and Effects of the SEC's Accounting Disclosure Requirements," in Henry G. Manne (ed.), *Economic Policy and Regulation of Corporate Securities,* American Enterprise Institute for Public Policy Research, Washington, D.C., 1969, table V, p. 49.

To test this statistically, Stigler considered all the new issues of industrial stocks with a value of $2.5 million in 1923–1928 (the pre-SEC period) and $5 million in 1949–1955 (the post-SEC period). For each issue, he compared its price at the beginning of the period and for each of the subsequent 5 years by computing the price relative P_t/P_0, where P_t equals price at the end of period and P_0 equals price at the beginning of the period; the price relative measures the rate of appreciation of a security's price. To allow for differences in general market conditions, he computed similar price relatives for the market as a whole, M_t/M_0, where M_t = value of the Standard & Poor's (S&P) index at the end of the period and M_0 its price at the beginning of the period. He then divided P_t/P_0 by M_t/M_0, which may be called the market-adjusted price relative; it measures the rate of appreciation of a security's price after taking into account the changes in the market.[19] He then examined the behavior of this price relative for various time spans of the pre- and post-SEC periods, as shown in Table 14.1.[20]

Table 14.1 shows that there is not a great deal of statistical difference in the market-adjusted price relatives in the pre- and post-SEC periods, although their

[19]Thus, if between 1923 and 1928 the price of a stock rose from $20 to $40 and the market from, say, $80 to $130, $P_t/P_0 = 2$ and $M_t/M_0 = 1.625$. Hence $(P_t/P_0)/(M_t/M_0) = 1.23$. That is, although the price of the stock doubled, relative to the market it appreciated only 23 percent.

[20]The results incorporate the correction made by Irwin Friend and Edward S. Herman in the original calculations by George Stigler.

absolute values tend to be generally larger in the latter period. But the most striking feature of these relatives is that their standard deviation is in many cases considerably smaller during the post- than the pre-SEC period, suggesting that although the SEC regulation may not have increased the rate of return (as measured by the price relative) on new issues, it did reduce risks of wide fluctuations in these returns. Perhaps the information disclosure requirement under the law did help investors to make a better decision about their investments. Stigler, however, does not think so. In his view, "A more plausible explanation lies in the fact that many more new companies used the market in the 1920s than in the 1950s — from one viewpoint a major effect of the SEC was to exclude new companies."[21] Stigler seems to be suggesting that the reduction in the standard deviation was obtained at the cost of precluding companies with high risk which might have been successful.

It would be hard to test Stigler's suggestion. But that may be beside the point, for the real question is: How do the benefits of risk reduction reflected in the relatively smaller post-SEC standard deviations compare with the costs of compliance under the 1933 act? That we will never know, because the data for such an enquiry are simply not available.

The Benston Study[22]

The purpose of the 1933 act was "to provide full and fair disclosure of the character of securities" to aid investors to form educated opinions about investment in corporate securities. This act required corporations to file their last 3 years' income and retained earnings statements as well as a summary of earnings of at least 5 years.[23] Benston was interested in finding out how provision of such information affects stock prices.

In Benston's view the value of accounting information depends on how relevant it is for decision making as well as how timely it is. Now accepting the efficient market hypothesis, he argues that only unanticipated (accounting) information has market value, and only if it is used as quickly as possible. As a statistical measure of unanticipated information, he used the difference between the current value of an accounting variable, AR^R, (e.g., net sales, cash flow, or net operating income) and its value in the previous year or its average value over past 3 or 5 years, AR^E, the superscripts R and E indicating the reported and expected information. Now instead of relating the measure thus constructed directly to the price or the rate of return of a security, he proceeds as follows.

---

[21]Stigler, op. cit., p. 85.
[22]George J. Benston, "The Effectiveness and Effects of the SEC's Accounting Disclosure," *Symposium,* op. cit., pp. 23–81.
[23]The 1934 act, as amended in 1964, requires most corporations with 500 or more stockholders and $1 million in assets to file these reports with the SEC: 10K (the annual report) to be filed within 120 days of the close of the fiscal year, 9K (the semiannual report) to be filed within 45 days of the end of the semiyear, and 8K (the current report) to be filed after important happening(s), for example, changes in company's capital stock, election of new officers, etc.

First, he uses the following model, known as the *market model* in the financial literature:

$$R_{jt} = a_j + \beta_j \log M_t + e_{jt} \tag{1}$$

where R_{jt} = rate of return (yield) on the jth security[24]
M_t = rate of return on the market (as represented by the S&P index)
e_{jt} = residual (it is that part of R_{jt} not explained by M_t)
t = time
a_j = intercept
β_j = slope coefficient

In the financial literature, β is known as the *beta coefficient* and is a measure of the systematic risk of a security, that is, how its return is affected by the general market conditions as represented by the market index, either Dow Jones or S&P or a similar broad index. The beta coefficient is also known as the *volatility coefficient* — the higher the value of β, the the greater the market risk

Using the regression methodology,[25] Benston obtains $\hat{a}_j$ and $\hat{\beta}_j$, the estimates of a_j and β_j, and transforms Equation (1) as follows:

$$e_{jt} = R_{jt} - \hat{a}_j - \hat{\beta}_j \log M_t \tag{2}$$

where e_{jt}, as noted, is that part of a security's return that cannot be explained by general movements in the market. Alternatively, it is that return that is specific to a given security (company).

Having obtained e_{jt}, Benston then tries to explain it as:

$$e_{jt} = a + b(AR^R - AR^E) + v_{jt} \tag{3}$$

where v_{jt} is a residual. In words, Equation (3) postulates that if unanticipated information (as measured by the difference between AR^R and AR^E) has any value, it should be related to e_{jt}. Put differently, if past accounting information required by the SEC is of any value to the investor, it should be reflected in the behavior of the residuals e_{jt}.

Once again, Benston uses the regression technique, obtaining the results shown in Table 14.2. As the table shows, Benston chose four pieces of SEC-

---

[24]R_{jt} is computed as: $\left[\dfrac{P_{jt} + D_{jt}}{P_{j,(t-1)}} \right]$

where P_{jt} = price of security J at time t
$P_{j,(t-1)}$ = its price at the end of time $(t-1)$
D_{jt} = cash dividend, if any, declared between time t and $(t-1)$

Benston uses monthly data.
[25]On how to interpret regression results, see Question 2-12. For a comprehensive but elementary treatment of the subject, see the author's *Basic Econometrics*, McGraw-Hill, New York, 1978.

TABLE 14.2
THE RELATIONSHIP BETWEEN REPORTED ACCOUNTING DATA AND STOCK PRICES: SUMMARY OF FINDINGS
Regression Coefficients (b) of Unanticipated Accounting Data ($AR^R - AR^E$)
(Coefficients of Other Independent Variables Not Shown)
Dependent Variables Change in Stock Prices (P^a - e_{jt})
(483 observations, 456 and 455 degrees of freedom)

| | Accounting data constructs | | | | | Clean surplus |
| | Net sales | | Cash flow | Net operating income | | |
Expectation Models	Annual	Annual + 3d quarter	Annual	Annual	Annual + 3d quarter	Annual
No change expectations						
1963	−.016	NA	.006	.009*	NA	.009*
1964	.042	.104†	.014*	.019*	.019*	.010*
Previous year's change expected						
1964	.029	.042	.011*	.007*	.006	.002
Three-year average of past change expected						
1964	.038	NA	.009	.015†	NA	.008
Five-year average of past change expected						
1964	−.004	NA	.008	.012*	NA	.006
Declining weights applied to past changes						
1964	.041	.129†	.012	.019†	.020†	.012*

*Significant at .05 level (one tail $t \geq 1.65$).
†Significant at .01 level (one tail $t \geq 2.34$).
NA = not available.
Source: George J. Benston, "The Effectiveness and Effects of the SEC's Accounting Disclosure Requirements," in Henry G. Manne (ed.), *Economic Policy and Regulation of Corporate Securities,* American Enterprise Institute for Public Policy Research, Washington, D.C., 1969, table I, p. 37.

required accounting data to measure the impact of unanticipated information on the residuals estimated from the regression in Equation (1). Of the four variables considered by Benston, only the net operating income variable had significant positive effect on e_{jt}; the other variables had only a marginal effect.

If Benston's findings are any guide, the benefits of detailed accounting information going as far back as 5 years may be far outweighed by the costs of supplying such information.

One reason why only one accounting variable had a consistently significant effect on the market-adjusted rate of return may be that an average investor has neither the time nor the expertise to digest all the financial data filed by companies. But what about a professional investor, say, the portfolio manager of a mutual fund who has professional staff capable of absorbing such information? Wouldn't such a manager be able to profit from past accounting data on several variables and earn higher than average profit for the fund's investors? But here too Benston's findings are not very encouraging. After examining the empirical studies of F. E. Brown and Douglas Vickers and also of William Sharpe and Michael Jensen,[26] he concluded that "even very sophisticated users of the accounting reports required by the SEC are not able to profit from them."[27]

Regulation of Insider Trading: The Jaffe Study[28]

Section 16(a) of the 1934 act requires corporate insiders, such as directors and officers, to report their personal dealings in the stocks of the corporation they work for to the SEC within 10 days after the end of the month of such dealings; this information is published in the commissions's *Official Summary* approximately 5 weeks after the end of the month.[29] Section 16(b) further requires them to return to their company any short-term profits they may have made, "short-term" being defined as a period of 6 months. The presumed logic behind these provisions is that corporate insiders who are in a position to acquire valuable information about the working of their company should not use it for their personal gain.

The primary objective of the Jaffe study was to find out whether *changes* in insider regulation have had any effect on either the profitability or the volume of trading of the insiders. It is important to note that he is not interested in whether, on average, insiders benefit from such trading. As a matter of fact, using a model similar to Benston's Equation (2), he shows that insiders do earn "abnormal" profits.[30] What he wants to know is whether *changes* in insider regulation affect their behavior.

Although Sec. 16(a) and 16(b) have been in existence since 1934, the SEC did not use its authority under the sections until the 1960s, when the question of insider trading reached the courts in the cases of (1) *Cady, Roberts and Company* (November 8, 1961), (2) *Texas Gulf Sulphur* (April 19, 1965), and (3) *Texas Gulf Sulphur* (August 19, 1966); these cases are described briefly in Questions 14-9 and 14-10. Since these were the first cases to shed light on insider dealings, Jaffe wanted to find out the effects of the decisions in these cases on the volume as well as the profitability of insider trading several months before and after the

---

[26]Irwin Friend, F. E. Brown, Edward S. Herman, and Douglas Vickers (eds.), *A Study of Mutual Funds* (a study prepared for the SEC by Wharton School of Finance and Commerce), University of Pennsylvania, 1962; William F. Sharpe, "Mutual Fund Performance," *Journal of Business*, vol. 39, January 1966; and Michael C. Jensen, "The Performance of Mutual Funds in the Period 1945-1964," *Journal of Finance*, May 1968.

[27]Benston, op. cit., p. 47.

[28]Jeffrey F. Jaffe, "The Effect of Regulatory Changes on Insider Trading," *Bell Journal of Economics and Management Science*, Spring 1974, vol. 5, no. 1, pp. 93-121. See also J. Jaffe and R. Winkler "Optimal Speculation against an Efficient Market," *Journal of Finance*, March 1976.

[29]The *Williams Act of 1980* further expanded the scope of insider trading by prohibiting the trading of stock based on advance knowledge of takeovers or mergers.

[30]Jaffe and Winkler, op. cit..

decisions were made; the dates of the decisions are shown in parentheses above.

For his statistical analysis, Jaffee used the residuals calculated from the market model as shown in Equation (2) and examined the behavior of these residuals, around the time a particular decision was announced, for the 200 largest securities listed on the stock price tape of the Center for Research in Security Prices (CRSP) of the University of Chicago. Without going into the technical details of the study, we will simply report its conclusions.

> . . . for each of the three regulatory events [the three cases] the average profitability of insider trades before an event was not significantly different from the average profitability of insider trades after that event. [Also] . . . the data do not suggest that regulation changes in the 1960s influenced the volume of insider trading.[31]

Overall, Jaffe says that "the null hypothesis that *changes* in regulation had no effect on the trading of insiders cannot be rejected."[32]

Aside from the preceding findings, one may raise a general question: Is regulation of insider trading necessary? To economists such as Friend the answer is yes, but to economists such as Demsetz the answer is no. According to Friend:

> . . . I have never thought that there was any equity or economic justification for revoking that part [of the 1934 act] which deals with disclosure of insider trading. I think corporate stockholders have a perfect right to know what their employees are doing and get rid of them if they don't like what they are doing.[33]

Demsetz, however, takes a different view. To him, inside information, like patent protection, is "an important method of preventing the rapid communalization of rewards." So long as no fraud is involved, he regards insider dealing that might lead to profits for the insiders as a way of compensating corporate managers and directors; it is an incentive method to generate new ideas and new ventures.

Be that as it may. The real problem with insider trading is one of enforcement, for the SEC must prove that the corporate insider not only made unusual profits but that such profits were obtained on the basis of information not available to the general public. And this is not easy to prove. In short, the return from regulating insider trading may not be worth the costs. Such regulation may in fact be socially undesirable if it breeds corporate secrecy by increasing the time between the production of information and its release to the market.

Line of Business Reporting: Analysis of a Disclosure Rule

Since 1971 certain corporations are required to disclose a 5-year breakdown, in dollars or by percentage, of the revenues and profits before tax by material lines

[31]Jaffe, op. cit., p. 114.
[32]Ibid, p. 93.
[33]Friend, op. cit., p. 118.

of business. A line of business is deemed material if during the most recent 2 years it accounted for at least 10 percent or more of revenue or 10 percent of profit or loss before taxes and extraordinary items; for companies with less than $50 million revenue the corresponding percentage is 15. This information is also to be filed with the Federal Trade Commission, which may use it to enforce the antitrust laws. It is believed that such material line of business reporting (LOBUR) (which is provided in the 10K), or segmented profit and revenue information, will enable investors not only to better forecast the overall profitability of the corporation (the sum of the parts may be greater than the whole) but will also improve the overall efficiency of the company.

The financial analysts have supported LOBUR for obvious reasons. But what has been the effect of LOBUR? Bertrand Horowitz and Richard Kolodny set out to test the "accepted hypothesis that the information content of LOBUR resulting from *required* SEC disclosure affected investor's perception of the risk and return characteristics of securities."[34] In their empirical test of the hypothesis the authors wanted (1) to find out "whether or not perceived risk characteristics of firms changed significantly when the previously non-disclosed information became public," and (2) "to determine whether the added disclosure contained other information which led investors to revaluate securities at the time of disclosure."[35]

For these purposes, they obtained two samples consisting of fifty firms each, the first one was comprised of firms required to file LOBUR (the experimental group) and the second of firms not required to do so (the control group). For each firm monthly data for the period 1965–1973 were obtained on the price of the firm's stock and cash dividend, if any. The 9-year period was divided into three subperiods: (1) 1965–1970, the pre-LOBUR period; (2) a 1-year period around 1971 when LOBUR became effective, and (3) a 2-year period, 1972–1973, the post-LOBUR period. For empirical testing they used the market model as shown in Equation (1) and concentrated their attention on β_j, the beta coefficient, a measure of volatility or systematic risk of a security. A priori, if LOBUR has any effect, one would expect the value of the beta coefficient to be smaller in the post-LOBUR than in the pre-LOBUR period. This is apparently in the belief that providing detailed profit information by line of business will reduce the overall risk of securities since investors will have more knowledge of the activities of LOBUR companies. Unfortunately, this expectation was not borne out by the authors' empirical results: They found that the beta coefficients did not differ much in the pre- as well as in the post-LOBUR periods, for both the control and the experimental group. In other words, providing LOBUR information in the 10K did not materially alter the level of market risk perceived by investors.

As a second part of their empirical testing, they used equation (2), which gives

---

[34]Bertrand Horowitz and Richard Kolodny, "Line of Business Reporting and Security Prices: An Analysis of SEC disclosure Rule," *Bell Journal of Economics and Management Science*, vol. no. 1, Spring 1977, p. 236. (Emphasis in the original.)
[35]Ibid., p. 237.

that part of a security's return that is not affected by general market conditions. They studied the behavior of the residuals for the control and experimental groups both before and after LOBUR came into effect. In the authors' view, if LOBUR did affect investors' perception of risk and return, and if the market was efficient, two effects should be observed in the estimated residuals: (1) "the absolute value of the residuals in the months surrounding disclosure should be greater for LOBUR firms than for non-LOBUR firms," and (2) "if the investors' expectations regarding disclosure firms were systematically favorable (unfavorable) this would be evident in greater (smaller) values of $\bar{e}$ [the average value of residuals] for the LOBUR sample relative to the non-LOBUR sample"[36]

Again, the authors found no such differences. Based on these findings, the authors concluded:

> The null hypothesis that the required disclosure had no effect on the risk and return of securities close to the time of its reporting could not be rejected at the 0.05 level in any of the tests. Thus the authors' results provide no evidence in support of the universally accepted contention that the SEC required disclosure furnished investors with valuable information.[37]

They added, therefore:

> In conclusion, because of the rapidly increasing amount of information that corporations are required to file with the SEC, the authors feel that the results of this study on LOBUR suggest that perhaps, hereafter, the SEC should be required to offer stronger evidence that additional required information will be of benefit to investors. To assert that the information is useful because it seems so is no longer adequate when many regulatory laws are now being subject to a cost-benefit analysis.[38]

But the Horowitz-Kolodny statistical sampling and testing procedures were questioned by Simonds and Collins.[39] They also used the market model, but employed some sophisticated statistical techniques and more disaggregated data and showed that the beta coefficient did in fact decline for firms affected by the LOBUR provisions. In their view, the observed decline in market risk (as measured by the beta coefficient) could be attributed to the "improvements in earnings forecastability which results from LOBUR data."

Horowitz and Kolodny were, however, not daunted by these results. In their rejoinder, they criticized Simonds and Collins for "weak and partially incorrect" assumptions and contended that the reported decreases in the beta coefficients were not strong enough. Even if that were not the case, Horowitz and Kolodny state that Simonds and Collins had not conclusively demonstrated that "disaggregated data provide a better forecast than aggregated data."

The reader caught between the cross fire of these conflicting empirical stud-

---

[36]Ibid., p. 241.
[37]Ibid., p. 247.
[38]Ibid., p. 248.
[39]Richard R. Simonds and Daniel W. Collins, "Line of Business Reporting and Securities Prices: An Analysis of an SEC Disclosure Rule: Comment, *Bell Journal of Economics and Management Science,* vol. 9, no. 2, Autumn 1978, pp. 646–658.

ies may wonder what is going on. But, fortunately or unfortunately, that is the nature of empirical analysis. Perhaps these authors have not posed their queries correctly. The important question that should have been asked is: What is the incremental cost of obtaining an additional piece of information and how does that cost compare with the additional benefits ensuing therefrom? If the marginal cost of incremental information exceeded its marginal benefit, the commonsense of cost-benefit analysis would veto such additional information disclosure. Otherwise, such information may be acquired. The stumbling block to such a study seems to be the insurmountable data problems, both conceptual and statistical.

14.6 SEC REGULATION AND THE WORKING OF THE SECURITIES MARKETS

We now turn to the second major mission of the commission, namely, regulation of the securities markets. Up until the 1975 amendments, the SEC played a rather passive role in this regard, entrusting that job to the NYSE. Whatever the NYSE did, the SEC more or less approved it.

What is the NYSE's record of regulation? At the outset it may be noted that since its inception in 1792 the NYSE has been a monopoly, actually a cartel-type monopoly, which determined who would be admitted to the cartel and at what price. And until 1968, the exchange ruled out any overt price competition among members by fixing the minimum rate of brokerage commission. Actually, there were two rate structures, one for the exchange members and another for nonmembers; the rates for the former were considerably lower than those for the latter.

Two questions immediately arise: (1) Is there something intrinsic about the stock market that calls for monopoly-type rate-fixing, and (2) what have been the consequences of such rate-fixing? In what follows, an attempt has been made to answer these questions.

The Economics of Minimum Brokerage Commission Rates

Ever since its organization in 1792 (the Buttonwood Tree Agreement), the NYSE established minimum brokerage rates that the exchange members were required to charge their customers. This was undoubtedly a price-fixing agreement by members of a private cartel and was obviously against the established antitrust laws and practices. But this price-fixing seems to have been endorsed by the 1934 act because in *Gordon v. New York Stock Exchange*, 422 U.S. 659 (1975) the Supreme Court stated that the application of the antitrust laws to commission rates would "unduly interfere . . . with the operations of the Securities Exchange Act." Given the legal protection and the fact that the exchange had control over entry into the cartel, it was no surprise that the exchange could sustain its monopoly power, the longest such monopoly in U.S. history.

The price-fixing system went unchallenged until 1968 when the Department of Justice, increasingly concerned over the rigidity of the commission rate structure and its discrimination against nonmembers, asked the NYSE whether the minimum commission rates were required or were justified by the objectives of the 1934 act.[40] In response, the exchange submitted a lengthy ''economic'' analysis to justify the system.[41] It argued that the structure of the securities market and the structure of the brokerage industry itself call for continuation of the minimum rate structure and that the introduction of a competitive rate scheme would be disastrous for the securities industry. Let us examine briefly how valid these arguments are.

The Structure of the Securities Market   Since the basic function of a stock market is to provide a continuous auction method of marketing, argues the exchange, this continuity will suffer if brokers leave the exchange if the minimum commission rates are abolished and competitive rates set in. In effect, the exchange is saying that the minimum commission rates guarantee its members a reasonable rate of profit and that this will not happen if the rates are determined competitively.

If the preceding argument is valid, what explains the emergence of the regional exchanges, the over-the-counter (OTC) market, the ''third market,'' and the ''fourth market?''[42] The reason is that, unlike the NYSE, rates in most of these markets are negotiable and probably approximate the cost of providing brokerage services. This would suggest that the minimum commission rates of the NYSE seem to be in excess of providing brokerage services. That this is the case is seen from the fact that since 1971 the exchange made the commission rates negotiable for transactions exceeding $300,000. This was done to stem the flow of institutional business (mutual funds, pension funds, and the like) to the other markets. This suggests that if the NYSE rates are determined competitively, not only the trading volume but the auction method of marketing will improve considerably since there will be no need to divert business to the other markets. As we will see, that seems to have happened since 1975 when the fixed commission rates were abolished by the exchange.

The Structure of the Brokerage Industry   The NYSE also argues that abolition of minimum commission rates will lead to the (1) dropping of such brokerage services as research, use of investment advice, use of stock ticker tape, and so on; (2) exit of serveral firms from the industry and predatory pricing among those who stay in the industry; and (3) destructive competition. Let us examine each argument in turn.

[40]Incidentally, in 1968 the NYSE had applied to the SEC for approval to raise its minimum commission schedule.

[41]The analysis is contained in *Economic Effects of Negotiated Rates on the Brokerage Industry, the Market for Corporate Securities and the Investing Public,* a report prepared for the NYSE by a private consulting firm in 1968.

[42]In the ''third market'' a dealer who is not a member of NYSE still trades in the NYSE-listed securities. In the ''fourth market'' buyers and sellers trade with each other directly without the intermediary of a broker. The OTC market generally deals with stocks not listed on the major exchanges.

It is true that traditionally brokers have not only bought and sold securities but have also provided ancillary services, such as sending investment advisory letters, providing price quotations over the phone, etc. Therefore, a brokerage service is often a "tie-in sale," the ancillary services being the tied product and security transaction the tying product. But does this justify fixing the rate schedule? No, if the tying and tied products can be priced separately. And in theory as well as in practice there is no reason why the two products (services) cannot be priced individually. As a matter of fact, since May 1, 1975, when commission rates became fully negotiable, there have emerged several "discount" brokerage houses which execute only buy and sell orders for customers without providing any ancillary services. For financial advice, customers may resort to publications, such as the *Wall Street Journal, Baron's, Forbes,* and scores of others. Even if the tie-in products cannot be priced separately, there is no reason why the joint price of the two products cannot be determined competitively.

The argument that competitive pricing will lead to a shakeout of the industry is plausible. Firms which are inefficient but are shielded by the fixed commission rate structure would probably leave the industry. But this is just as well from an efficiency viewpoint. The proponents of minimum commission rates also argue that those firms which do stay in the industry will resort to predatory pricing, which will ultimately lead to monopoly or highly concentrated oligopoly. But this argument makes sense only if entry into the industry is forestalled. And entry barriers will exist if there are substantial economies of scale in the industry. But as we will show shortly, this does not seem to be the case.

The argument about destructive competition is somewhat substantial and needs a bit more scrutiny. The term *destructive, ruinous,* or *cutthroat* competition is used loosely to refer to unfettered price competition. This type of competition, say, in the brokerage industry, would lead to sustained losses for firms over a long period of time so that in the long run there would be little new investment in the industry. For such cutthroat competition to exist, a few conditions must be satisfied. These conditions are:[43]

1 A high ratio of fixed to variable costs, especially in the short run.

2 A substantial excess capacity much or most of the time; in conjunction with item **1** this means that the short-run marginal cost is below the average total cost, with the result that the average cost of production declines as output increases, at least over a fairly wide range of output. In short, there are economies of scale. If this is the case, it will lead to the monopolization of the industry by a large single firm (see Chapter 6 for the reasons).

3 Fluctuating and inelastic demand, which means that a reduction in price will not necessarily increase demand to reduce the excess capacity.

4 A large number of sellers and low concentration ratios.

If these conditions prevail, then Kahn argues that unrestrained price competition may not be desirable in the brokerage industry, for

---

[43]Alfred E. Kahn, *The Economics of Regulation: Principles and Institutions,* vol. II, Wiley, New York, 1970, pp. 202–203.

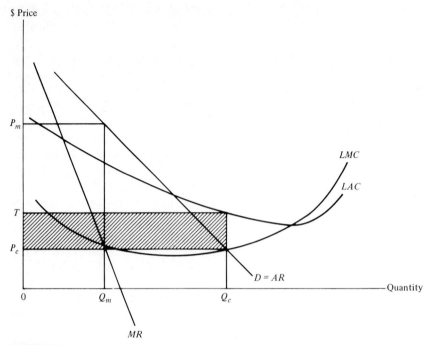

FIGURE 14.2
Pricing under economies of scale.

... extreme fluctuations in commission rates, with periods of deeply depressed earnings during which the industry would be reluctant to provide capacity sufficient for peak demands followed by sharp rate increases, as recovering demand pressed hard on the limits of capacity; and an inability of the industry, in the latter period, to provide the kind of instantaneous execution of orders that the public demands.[44]

The question then is whether the conditions for cutthroat competition listed above prevail in the brokerage industry. Consider first the question of economies of scale. Before we present the empirical evidence, let us examine why competitive pricing may not be appropriate in the presence of economies of scale. To fix the idea, consider Figure 14.2, which shows the cost and demand curves facing a hypothetical brokerage firm (with minor variations, this curve reproduces Figure 6.5).

Figure 14.2 shows that over a fairly large range of output there are economies of scale — the larger the output, the lower the average cost; the cost curves shown in the figure are the long-run cost curves. If the said firm behaves like a monopolist, the equilibrium price and output, following the "marginal cost is equal to marginal revenue" rule, will be P_m and Q_m, respectively, and the monopolist will make a profit since the price exceeds the average cost. Clearly,

[44]Ibid., p. 203.

a competitive solution, which requires that price (given by the demand or average revenue curve AR) be equal to marginal cost, is infeasible in this situation because at the competitive price P_c and the competitive output Q_c, the long-run average cost exceeds the price, leading to the loss shown by the shaded area in the figure. This loss will have to be recouped somhow if the firm is to continue providing the service. One suggested solution is to let the firm charge the competitive price P_c per unit plus a tax equal to TP_c so that together they will cover the long-run average cost.[45] Alternatively, let the firm charge the price $P_c + TP_c$ and let the government subsidize the consumer to the tune of TP_c per unit. Of course such a tax or subsidy involves equity considerations which are apart from efficiency considerations. Some economists suggest that in the case shown in Figure 14.2 the firm should engage in price discrimination, charging prices according to demand elasticities (see Chapter 6, Section 6.6 for further discussion).

The situation depicted in Figure 14.2 is typically associated with natural monopolies (see Chapters 2 and 6) which are regulated by state or local authorities precisely because the usual competitive pricing formula is not applicable. Such regulation generally guarantees monopolists a price (or a set of prices) which will give them a "reasonable" rate of return on the invested capital.[46]

We now turn to the empirical evidence. Does the brokerage industry exhibit economies of scale (or increasing returns to scale) so that some kind of price regulation, be it by the NYSE or by the SEC, is called for? The NYSE contends that that is the case. This claim is based on a statistical analysis a consulting firm did for the NYSE.[47] The statistical or the regression model used was as follows:

$$X_1 = a + bX_2 + cX_2^2 + e \tag{4}$$

where X_1 = total expenses
X_2 = number of transactions
e = error or residual term

Economies of scale will be indicated if the coefficient c in Equation (4) turns out to be negative. The estimated regression was as follows:[48]

$$X_1 = 476,393 + 31.3445X_2 - 1.082 \times 10^{-6}X_2^2 \tag{5}$$

This implies an average cost of:

$$\frac{X_1}{X_2} = \frac{476,393}{X_2} + 31.3445 - 1.082 \times 10^{-6}X_2 \tag{6}$$

---

[45]Such a firm would invariably be a monopoly (why?).

[46]For an excellent discussion of utility rate regulation, see Kahn, op. cit., vol. I, ch. 2.

[47]See fn. 41.

[48]For details, see Richard R. West and Seha M. Tinic, "Minimum Commission Rates on New York Stock Exchange Transactions," *Bell Journal of Economics and Management Science*, vol. 2, no. 2, Autumn 1971, pp. 577–606.

and the marginal cost of:

$$MC = 31.3445 - 2.164 \times 10^{-6}X_2 \tag{7}$$

Plotting Equations (6) and (7), we get Figure 14.3, which gives the impression that there are economies of scale.

But the NYSE statistical study was immediately attacked by economists on theoretical as well as empirical grounds.[49] Michael Mann notes these conceptual problems with the NYSE study. First, the variable X_2 does not accurately measure the actual volume of business done by a brokerage house (a transaction involving a trade of securities worth \$100 is not the same as that involving a trade of \$5000); the NYSE study did not take this into account. Second, the NYSE allocated total costs between fixed and variable components arbitrarily. By shifting costs from the variable to the fixed category, one can show, as Figure 14.3 does, that there are substantial economies of scale. Finally, there was no clear-cut distinction between costs allocated to security commission business and other business.

These problems aside, Mann shows that the NYSE statistical results, reported in Equation (5), are flawed in that they suffer from the econometric problem of heteroscedasticity.[50] Correcting for this, and using the NYSE data, Mann obtains the following regression:

$$X_1 = 342,986 + 25.57X_2 + \text{statistically insignificant coefficient for } X_2^2 \tag{8}$$

Thus there is no longer evidence of economies of scale!

As noted, Mann argues that X_2 is not the appropriate scale variable to measure economies of scale. In his opinion, a more meaningful measure of output (scale) is the number of dollars of commission transacted. Letting X_3 represent total dollar commissions, he obtains the following average cost function from the total cost function: $a + bX_3 + cX_3^2$:

$$\frac{X_1}{X_3} = a\left(\frac{1}{X_3}\right) + b + cX_3$$
$$= 18,319\left(\frac{1}{X_3}\right) + 0.8830 + \text{statistically insignificant } c \tag{9}$$

In this form, the association between output and the average cost per dollar's worth of commission business is very low. But according to West and Tunic, "This result is to be expected, since the size of commissions is highly dependent on the price of an issue, while the costs of providing brokerage services need

---

[49]See H. Michael Mann, "The New York Stock Exchange: A Cartel at the End of Its Reign," in Almarin Phillips (ed.), *Promoting Competition in Regulated Markets*, Brookings, Washington, D.C., 1975, pp. 301–328, and Harold Demsetz in a statement before the SEC, August 1969.
[50]For the nature of heteroscedasticity, see Damodar Gujarati, *Basic Econometrics*, op. cit.

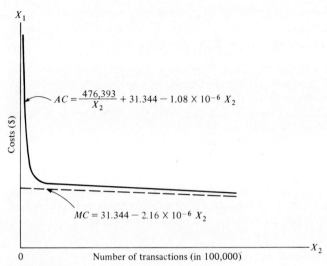

FIGURE 14.3
Economies of scale in the brokerage industry.

not change with the price of issues."[51] On the basis of the preceding results Mann contends that "economies of scale are unimportant in the brokerage industry."[52]

Thus, an important condition of cutthroat competition, namely, the presence of economies of scale, does not seem to prevail in the brokerage industry. What about the other conditions? Take, for instance, wide fluctuations in demand. It is true that the daily volume of trade fluctuates. But is this unique to the brokerage industry? What about excess capacity? If there is excess capacity, it surely can be attributed to the price-fixing by the exchange: If minimum commission rates are guaranteed, what incentive is there for inefficient firms to leave the industry? What about demand elasticity for brokerage services? There must be a great deal of elasticity. Otherwise, what explains the growth of the third and fourth markets? Another indication that the demand elasticity must be substantial can be seen in practices, such as reciprocal agreements and give-ups (rebates or fee-splitting), which were quite widespread in the regime of the fixed commission rates. In give-ups, for example, customer A may tell his broker B to pay part of her commission to another broker C who may have done some favor to A. Thus, a mutual fund manager may ask his broker to share her commission with a nonmember who may have given some research advice to the fund.

[51]West and Tunic, op. cit., p. 595.
[52]This is not to deny that economies of scale may exist with respect to the volume of market transactions in a security. What is stated here is that such scale economies may not exist with respect to the volume of transactions of a particular trader.

To sum up, the NYSE case for retaining the minimum commission rate structure is very weak. On the contrary, as Kahn argues, a strong case can be made for the abolition of such a rate structure:

> The customer who wants to buy execution of orders plus salesmanship, advice, and research pays the same price as the customer that wants only the first of these. The consequence is an inherent tendency to what might be termed service inflation, in which an equilibrium of cost and price is achieved not by reducing price to marginal cost but raising marginal cost to price.[53]

Based on all these considerations, Kahn concludes:

> . . . it is extremely difficult for an economist to accept the alternative system — a system of soft, nonprice, cost-inflation competition, grounded in the desire to protect competitors and having the effect of sustaining the capitalized monopoly profits that are reflected in the price of acquiring membership in a stock exchange.[54]

14.7   PRICE DEREGULATION IN THE BROKERAGE INDUSTRY

When in 1968 the Department of Justice questioned the need for and the legality of the NYSE-determined commission rates, the exchange began to yield to the SEC. In 1968 volume discounts for orders larger than 1000 shares were allowed in the rate schedule; this was a sensible move because the average cost of transacting a trade involving 1000 shares is obviously smaller than that of transacting, say, 100 shares. In 1972 the NYSE introduced another rate schedule which allowed for lower commission rates on multiples of round lot orders (1 lot = 100 shares) and made such rates fully negotiable on transactions exceeding $300,000. For transactions under $300,000, the exchange made the commission rate a function of the number of shares per transaction as well as the price of the share. On May 1, 1975, it eliminated the fixed commission rate structure entirely, thereby ending an era of price-fixing by one of the largest and most enduring price-fixing cartels in the nation's history.[55]

The Effects of Commission Rate Deregulation

What have been the effects of this price deregulation on prices, profitability and brokerage industry structure? We have two empirical studies which shed some light on these aspects.

The Ofer-Melnick Study[56]   To assess the effect of the deregulation on brokerage commission (or price for the brokerage services), Ofer and Melnick ask

---

[53]Kahn, op. cit., p. 207. This point has already been raised in Ch. 13, on airline regulation.
[54]Kahn, op. cit., p. 209.
[55]Note that the 1975 deregulation affected only the commission rates. The securities industry and the NYSE are still heavily regulated in terms of margin requirements, stock registration requirements, and a host of other restrictions.
[56]Aharon R. Ofer and Arie Melnick, "Price Deregulation in the Brokerage Industry: An Empirical Analysis, *Bell Journal of Economics and Management Science*, vol. 9, no. 2, Autumn 1978, pp. 633–641.

the question: What factors would determine brokerage commission in the absence of regulation? Obviously, as in other competitive markets, by the demand for brokers' services and the cost of providing them. Assuming the investors' demand as given, Ofer and Melnik used a relatively simple regression model to explain the cost of providing brokerage services. The model is as follows:

$$C = a + bV + cS + dQ + eAV + fP + gT + u \qquad (10)$$

where C = commission price per share

V = number of shares purchased in the transaction

S = a rank variable based on the broker's total assets, it is equal to 1 for the smallest broker, equal to 2 for the second-smallest broker, etc.

Q = broker quality. $Q = 1$ if the order was executed by a "quality" broker and $Q = 0$ for all other brokers, a quality broker being one who is listed among the top thirty brokers in the Greenwich Associates' survey of brokers

P = the average price of the stock during the month in which the transaction was executed

AV = the average monthly number of shares traded in the stock during the period May 1, 1975, to May 1, 1976

T = a monthly trend variable specified as follows: for May 1975 = 1, for June 1975 = 2, and so on

u = residual or error term

The data for empirical analysis consisted of 3718 purchase orders executed by brokers for the trust departments of ten banks during the period of May 1, 1975, to May 1, 1976. Using these data and Equation (10), Ofer and Melnik obtained the results shown in Table 14.3.

This table reveals some interesting results. First, the coefficient of the transaction variable V is consistently negative and statistically significant, implying that there are economies of scale—other things remaining the same, the higher the number of shares traded, the lower the brokerage commission per share.[57] Second, the positive coefficient of S, the asset size variable, suggests that, on average, the large brokerage firms charge higher per share commission than their smaller counterparts; perhaps customers are willing to pay the higher rates in the belief that the large brokerage firms are somehow qualitatively better. But there seems to be a weak support for this hypothesis, because the quality variable Q is positive and statistically significant in only two cases (Bank nos. 5 and 7). This could very well be due to the way the quality variable was measured. Third, coefficient of AV, the trading activity variable, is generally negative. This indicates that the per share commission is lower if the trading activity is hectic, a plausible result. Fourth, the coefficient of the price variable P is consistently

---

[57]Note that these are economies of scale with respect to the number of shares traded, and they are available whether it is a small trust department or a large one.

TABLE 14.3
REGRESSION RESULTS (EQUATION 10)*

Bank	Intercept	V	S	Q	Coefficient AV	P	T	$\bar{R}^2$	N
1	0.1575	-0.4108×10^{-5}	0.6172×10^{-4}	0.1045×10^{-1}	-0.7126×10^{-5}	0.1911×10^{-2}	-0.4055×10^{-1}	0.5577	481
	(16.85)	(−9.525)	(0.7243)	(1.645)	(−3.127)	(22.64)	(−3.221)		
2	0.1730	-0.5566×10^{-6}	0.1318×10^{-2}	0.2524×10^{-1}	-0.3338×10^{-5}	0.9264×10^{-3}	-0.1622×10^{-1}	03636	227
	(7.502)	(−4.768)	(4.580)	(1.060)	(−0.6052)	(4.942)	(−3.368)		
3	0.2506	-0.1103×10^{-4}	0.8243×10^{-3}	-0.4788×10^{-2}	-0.9813×10^{-5}	0.2832×10^{-2}	-0.1299×10^{-2}	0.1902	654
	(17.38)	(−7.295)	(4.514)	(−0.3600)	(−2.068)	(5.311)	(−7.183)		
4	0.1654	-0.3443×10^{-5}	0.3439×10^{-3}	-0.1050×10^{-1}	-0.2188×10^{-4}	0.2767×10^{-2}	-0.8413×10^{-1}	0.4904	638
	(16.63)	(−10.98)	(3.542)	(−1.562)	(−5.458)	(18.12)	(−7.859)		
5	0.6946	-0.6968×10^{-6}	0.8614×10^{-4}	0.3168×10^{-1}	-0.2561×10^{-5}	0.2243×10^{-2}	-0.1691×10^{-1}	0.4890	301
	(7.683)	(−2.624)	(0.9949)	(4.582)	(−0.7319)	(14.22)	(−1.357)		
6	0.1555	-0.5804×10^{-5}	0.9362×10^{-3}	-0.2984×10^{-1}	-0.2902×10^{-6}	0.1547×10^{-2}	-0.3489×10^{-1}	0.1818	387
	(8.090)	(−3.053)	(4.005)	(−1.641)	(−0.4904)	(7.284)	(−1.507)		
7	0.2323	-0.9108×10^{-5}	0.4297×10^{-3}	0.3473×10^{-1}	0.2018×10^{-2}	0.2149×10^{-2}	-0.1030×10^{-1}	0.3897	329
	(8.935)	(−6.346)	(1.677)	(1.832)	(3.398)	(8.997)	(−2.970)		
8	0.4130	-0.4692×10^{-4}	0.2170×10^{-3}	0.4714×10^{-2}	0.1119×10^{-4}	0.1370×10^{-2}	-0.1115×10^{-1}	0.4623	206
	(9.503)	(−6.463)	(0.7572)	(0.1691)	(1.256)	(8.561)	(−2.117)		
9	0.3109	-0.2340×10^{-4}	0.9833×10^{-4}	0.2427×10^{-1}	0.1528×10^{-4}	0.2077×10^{-2}	-0.5476×10^{-2}	0.6066	293
	(18.10)	(−11.81)	(0.4295)	(1.332)	(2.862)	(13.74)	(−2.243)		
10	0.1945	-0.2248×10^{-4}	0.5729×10^{-3}	-0.2188×10^{-1}	-0.2834×10^{-5}	0.7030×10^{-2}	-0.1110×10^{-1}	0.5611	200
	(5.508)	(−8.524)	(2.767)	(−0.8566)	(−0.3557)	(11.49)	(−2.041)		

*The numbers in parentheses are t values.

Note: As a rule of thumb, for about 30 degrees of freedom (the number of observations minus the number of coefficients estimated), if the absolute value of the t statistic is about 2 or greater, the associated coefficient is statistically significant at the 5 percent level of significance on the basis of the two-tail test. For the one-tail test it is about 1.7.

Source: Aharon R. Ofer and Arie Melnick, "Price Deregulation in the Brokerage Industry: An Empirical Analysis," *Bell Journal of Economics and Management Science*, vol. 9, no. 2, Autumn 1978, table 2, p. 638.

positive and statistically highly significant; other things being the same, the higher the unit price of a share, the higher the commission per share. Such a price policy perhaps indicates that brokers demand a premium on high-priced securities because of the fear of default on the part of their customers. Finally, the consistently negative and mostly significant value of the trend variable T indicates that, after taking into account the influence of all other variables, there was a downward trend in the commission charged per share since May 1, 1975. Commenting on these results, the authors conclude:

> . . . price deregulation in the brokerage industry has led to lower prices and to a pricing structure that more properly reflects the costs of executing different types of transactions than did the fixed commission system.[58]

In view of our examination of deregulation in the airline, trucking, and railroad industries, this outcome should hardly be surprising.

The SEC Study[59]   The commission's study made in 1979 gives some idea about what has happened to prices, profits, and structure of the brokerage industry since the May 1975 deregulation.

Prices   Like Ofer and Melnick, the SEC found that, in contrast to the series of rate increases in the late 1960s and early 1970s (the last one in April 1974), there was a definite downward trend in commissions since deregulation both for individuals and institutional buyers. Figure 14.4 shows this clearly. As the figure reveals, commission rates dropped sharply right after the deregulation for institutional buyers but somewhat moderately for individual buyers. But the downward trend in both cases is clearly visible.

Brokerage House Revenues   The study reports that in the 4 months following deregulation the brokerage firms received $89.6 million less in revenue than they would have had the old fixed-rate schedule prevailed for the volume of trade actually transacted in the 4 months. Put positively, consumers of brokerage services saved nearly $90 million. Between May 1975 and December 1977, according to SEC estimates, consumers saved about $700 million in brokerage commissions.

Profitability   Figure 14.5 shows the pretax return on capital of NYSE firms for the period 1972–1979. *Return on capital* is defined as the ratio of income (after partners' compensation but before taxes) to total capital. *Total capital* is defined as the sum of ownership equity and subordinated borrowings.

Since profitability is a function of the commission rates, volume of stock trad-

---

[58]Ofer and Melnick, op. cit., p. 641.
[59]Securities and Exchange Commission, *Staff Report on the Securities Industry in 1979.* The following discussion is drawn from a review of the *Staff Report* by Jeffrey A. Eisenach and James C. Miller, ''Price Competition on the NYSE,'' *Regulation, American Enterprise Institute Journal on Government and Society,* January–February, 1979, pp. 16–19.

ing, and stock prices, one must consider them in assessing profitability pre- and postderegulation. In the days of the fixed commission rates before 1975, the very poor profit performance of years 1973 and 1974 was clearly due to the economic recession then prevailing; it put downward pressure on both stock volume and stock prices. The 1975 and 1976 comparatively healthy profitability was due to a combination of all the three factors listed above, although it is difficult to isolate their individual contributions. The market conditions worsened in 1977, yet there was, compared to 1974, a reasonably healthy profit, which would tend to suggest that the price competition introduced in 1975 did not necessarily reduce industry profitability. The comparatively good 1978 and 1979 trading volume increased industry profitability considerably, although again it is difficult to pinpoint the contribution of each of the three factors.

Industry Structure.   Since 1975 the brokerage industry has undergone considerable structural changes; for example, consider the growth of discount brokerage houses offering only brokerage service. The SEC *Staff Study* noted,

FIGURE 14.4
Effective commission rates of NYSE firms, April 1975 through 1979.

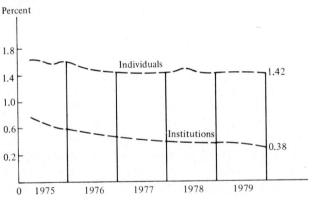

Commission as a percent of principal value, all trades

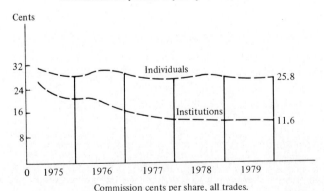

Commission cents per share, all trades.

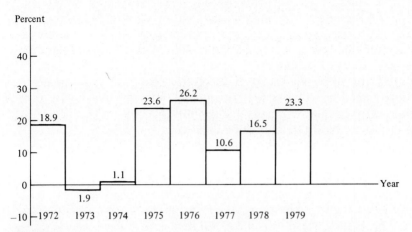

FIGURE 14.5
Pretax return on capital, NYSE firms doing a public business, 1972–1979.

though, that there was an increase in industry concentration — from the first quarter of 1975 until the last quarter of 1978, the percentage of total industry commission accounted for by the top ten firms increased from 38.2 percent to 45.9 percent (concentration measured by equity capital and other variables increased, too).

But the SEC noticed that the trend toward increased concentration started well before May 1975, possibly since some of the partial deregulatory moves made between 1968 and 1975. This development should not be surprising because, anticipating that the days of the fixed commission rates were numbered, some of the firms shielded from price competition found that they would not survive without joining hands with other firms. What is interesting to note is that despite the mergers there was considerable mobility among the top ten firms (measured by commission income, underwriting income, gross revenue, and equity capital) for each of the years between 1972 and 1978. That is to say, some firms which were very low on these concentration measures in 1972 found themselves in the top ten in 1978, while some who were among the leaders in 1972 fell out of the top ten groups in 1978 and in the interim years.

Another interesting feature of the study was that there was no statistically significant correlation between firm profitability and firm size in 1977, 1978, and 1979. This indicated that the increased concentration in the industry observed between 1975 and 1978 was not on account of economies of scale–the larger firms did not necessarily have any cost advantage that was not available to the smaller firms.

The SEC study also found that since the deregulation there was considerable diversification of the industry into areas such as trading, financial planning, and insurance so that the earlier heavy reliance on commission revenues alone has declined substantially. Also, the growth of discount brokerage houses offering no-frill services has offered the consumer the kind of price-quality option that Alfred Kahn talked about while discussing airline deregulation.[60] Consumers can go to such discount houses or to houses which offer "full line" services and pay lower or higher commission rates.

All told, then, the SEC study shows that the price deregulation introduced in 1975 has been beneficial to consumers by offering them generally lower commission rates and price-quality options that did not exist before. The industry as a whole also does not seem to have done badly.

14.8   SUMMARY AND CONCLUSIONS

The primary prupose of this chapter was to investigate the extent to which the Securities and Exchange Commission has fulfilled its twin goals of protecting investors and promoting efficient securities markets.

Insofar as investor protection is concerned, we considered the various information disclosure rules promulgated under the Securities Act of 1933 and the Securities Exchange Act of 1934. The purpose of these rules was to give investors financial and other information that would enable them to make educated decisions about investment in corporate securities. We considered several empirical studies to find out the extent to which the mandated disclosure provisions had helped the investor. According to Stigler, such disclosure had little effect on the rate of return on newly listed securities since the SEC came into being, although it did reduce the variability of return. But this reduction, according to Stigler was probably achieved at the cost of discouraging risky but potentially profitable business ventures. In Benston's view, only unanticipated information has market value and only if it is timely. But his empirical analysis showed that even then it may not have much effect on a security's price. He, therefore, questions the utility of historical accounting data going as far back as 5 years, as required by the SEC. Jaffe was interested in finding out how regulatory changes affect security prices and security returns. He considered the regulatory changes in the insider trading and found that such changes did not have noticeable effect on either the profitability or the volume of insider dealings. Horowitz and Kolodny considered another regulatory change, the one introduced by the SEC in 1970, which required certain corporations to disclose their revenue and profit data by major lines of business. Their statistical study showed that such disclosure did not materially alter investors' perception of risk and return of the securities of the companies affected by the 1970 change. Simonds and Collins, however, challenged this finding, contending that their own study showed that such disclosure did reduce the variability of security returns. Horowitz and Kolodny took issue with the Simonds and Collins study and defended their own conclusion. Examining all the empirical evidence, it seems that the various disclosure

---

[60]According to the SEC, in 1979 there were about ninety-seven discount brokers, accounting for about 8 percent of the total retail market. The SEC found that these discount houses consistently outperformed other NYSE member firms in terms of profitability.

provisions have had some effect on investors' perception of securities' risk and return, but much more empirical work is needed in this area.

Has the SEC succeeded in making the securities markets more efficient? The verdict here, too, is not especially favorable to the SEC, although things are likely to change. So far it has failed to establish a national securities market, linking all the securities markets electronically, as was mandated by the 1975 amendments. Moreover, up until 1975, the SEC played a rather passive role, leaving the task of regulation to the NYSE monopoly. The NYSE used its monopoly power, not surprisingly, to do what a monopolist would do, namely, to fix prices and restrict entry. There was no question that the minimum commission rate schedule established by the NYSE was far above what a freely competitive system would have established — the growth of the "third market" and the "fourth market," and practices such as give-ups and reciprocal arrangements, are clear indications of that. There was no justification for fixing minimum commission rates, for there was no reliable evidence of economies of scale or cutthroat competition, notwithstanding the exchange's claim to the contrary.

Fortunately, the fixed commission system is now gone. Since its abolition in 1975, on average, the commission rates are generally lower as found by the Ofer-Melnick and the SEC staff studies. But more important, investors now have the price-quality options they did not have before: They can now buy only the basic brokerage function of executing their trade or can buy it along with frills, such as investment advice, research facilities, and so on. With the entry of several discount brokerage houses, and the resulting competitive pressures, the price of basic brokerage function is now probably in line with the cost of providing such function. Although the promised national securities market is still not here, it should emerge in the near future, what with the rapid growth and wide availability of high-speed computers.

QUESTIONS

14-1 Consider the following scenario painted by Allan Meltzer:

To a casual observer — an outsider — regulation by independent commission appears to follow a rather regular pattern. In the beginning, the regulator eliminates some of the more vicious, restrictive practices that were used to justify regulation of the industry. Later, new restrictive practices develop after negotiation between the regulators and the regulated. Generally, the new regulations restrict entry, establish standards, and raise the level of education, income, or wealth required for admission to the industry. The restrictions on entry, though different from those prevailing in the earlier, unregulated period, are no less restrictive and perhaps harder to change, since the new restrictions, unlike the old, are sanctioned by law and regulation. Periodically, additional regulations are introduced to eliminate "undesirable" practices that have arisen despite — or perhaps because of — previous regulations. In time, the regulators and the regulated become indistinguishable. The industry helps to draft new regulations. And the trade associations help to convince the more reluctant members to accept most of the new regulations by pointing to the more stringent regulations that might have been imposed. The regulated become the regulators – or the agents of the regulators ("On Efficiency and Regulation of the Securities Industry," *Symposium, op. cit.,* p. 237.)

Discuss the extent to which the above scenario fits the SEC and the securities industry. Which theory or theories of regulation discussed in Chapter 2 explain this scenario well?

14-2 Notwithstanding the Horowitz-Kolodny and Simonds-Collins studies, why may it be difficult to assess the impact of LOBUR statistically? How would you defend the LOBUR provision?

14-3 In early 1969 seats on the NYSE sold for around $500,000. Why would anyone pay such a price to acquire a seat? What does it tell about the fixed minimum rate structure? In a regime of fully competitive rates, what factors would determine the price of an NYSE seat?

14-4 Based on the average size of transactions, Demsetz divided brokerage firms into seven categories and computed the average cost per transaction as shown in the following table (the data were supplied by the NYSE and pertain to the period 1965–1966).

Class no.	Average no. of transactions	Average cost per transaction
I	19,000	$46
II	63,000	43
III	143,000	40
IV	306,000	28
V	735,000	34
VI	1,250,000	28
VII	3,800,000	28

Source: West and Tinic, op. cit., p. 596.

What do these data suggest about economies of scale in the brokerage industry? How do these results differ from those obtained by Mann?

14-5 In their study of the OTC market where there are no fixed minimum commission rates West and Tinic used the following regression model:

$$B = a_0 + a_1P + a_2V + a_3D$$

where B = average brokerage commission incurred by traders in a stock (this figure was multiplied by 200 to make the magnitude of this variable comparable to those of the other variables)

P = the average price of an issue

V = trading activity measured in number of shares

D = number of dealers quoting a price in the stock

A priori, what would be the sign of a_1, a_2, and a_3 (positive or negative) and why? See if your prior expectations are borne out by the authors' results, which were as follows:

$$B = 119.66 + 0.959P - 0.0002V - 1.797D; R^2 = 0.20$$

All the estimated coefficients were statistically significant at the 5 percent level.

14-6 Of the views on insider trading expressed by Friend and Demsetz, which do you find more acceptable and why?

14-7 Why did it take so long for the SEC to force the NYSE to abolish its minimum rate schedule?

14-8 Do you agree with the following viewpoint? Give your reasons.

"Now, in my view, the one thing that is clear about securities regulation is that, whatever the SEC is all about and whatever the regulations are all about, they are not about economic efficiency. It is not that efficiency is irrelevant; but surely lawmaking, the socially legitimatized effort to do something to guide or influence or direct the multiple courses of human behavior is a very much more complex operation than the pursuit of economic efficiency." (Manning, *Symposium,* op. cit., p. 84).

14-9 *The Cady, Roberts and Company case.* On November 6, 1959, the Curtis-Wright Corporation sent invitations to 2000 people to attend a meeting on November 23, 1959, to discover the company's plans for a new engine. Robert Gintel, a broker of Cady, Roberts and Company, was one of the invitees. Between November 6 and the day of the meeting, Mr. Gintel bought about 11,000 shares of Curtis for his clients. Following Curtis' disclosure of its plans, the stock increased in price from $32 to $32.25 on November 24, 1959. From November 24 to 11 a.m. of November 25, Mr. Gintel sold about 6500 shares of the Curtis stock.

On November 25, the directors of the company approved a reduction in dividend for the following quarter. Although the decision was made at 11 a.m. and relayed to Western Union for transmission to the NYSE, the message did not reach the exchange until 12:29 p.m. In the meantime a representative of Cady, Roberts and Company who was present at the directors' meeting immediately conveyed this information to Mr. Gintel. By 11:18 a.m. Gintel had sold another 7000 shares of Curtis. The price of the share fell 4.5 points between 11:18 a.m. and the close of the trading day. (Details taken from Jaffe, op. cit., p. 117.)

The SEC found both Mr. Gintel and his employer in violation of Sec. 10(b), Sec. 17(a) and rule 10(b)-5 of the Securities Exchange Act of 1934. Mr. Gintel was fined $3000 and was suspended from the exchange for 21 days.

Since Gintel and his company were not corporate insiders, do you think the SEC erred in its decision? How would you have decided the case?

14-10 *The Texas Gulf case.* In 1959, Texas Gulf Sulphur began a drilling operation in Ontario which indicated the possibility of huge mineral deposits. Despite this, the company deliberately tried to keep this information secret and even issued on April 12, 1964, a false statement stating that no deposits had been discovered. However, on April 16, 1964, the company reversed itself and stated publicly that such deposits had indeed been discovered.

Since November 1963 some high-level corporate insiders began speculating in the stock of the company and bought a total of 9100 shares between November 1963 and March 1964. They also passed this information to outsiders (known as "tippees") who themselves bought 12,100 shares of the stock. On November 10, 1963, the stock was priced at $17.75. In April 1964 its price increased to $30 and in the following year it reached $71.

On April 19, 1965, the SEC filed a suit against the company and the alleged insiders for violating the insider trading rules. Specifically, the insiders were charged for dealing in the company's stock on the basis of information not publicly available. The commission sought restitution from the violators: it also wanted the company to stop issuing false statements.

On August 19, 1966, a federal court in New York declared that all insider trading prior to April 12 was not unlawful because information about the mineral deposits was not considered to be material at that time. However, trading since April 12 was declared to be in violation of the law. The court did not find anything illegal about the false press release of April 12.

Do you concur with the court's decision? Why or why not? Give your reasons.

CHAPTER 15

THE FEDERAL COMMUNICATIONS COMMISSION

Created in 1934, the Federal Communications Commission (FCC) was entrusted with the task of regulating the technologically complex broadcasting and telecommunications industries. The broadcasting industry is comprised of commercial radio, broadcast television, and cable television, including pay or subscription television. The telecommunications industry consists of telephone companies, companies supplying terminal equipment, telegraph carriers, private microwave carriers, public landmobiles, and satellite carriers.

In this chapter we will examine the forces that led to the establishment of the FCC, the evolution of the commission's regulatory mandate, and the job the commission has done in reconciling the conflicting interests of the various components of the two industries. We also consider some of the recent deregulatory initiatives taken by the commission and the controversies they have generated, including court challenges. Also considered in the chapter is the nascent data communications industry, an admixture of data processing (by computer) and communications, and the problem it has posed for the FCC and the Congress.

15.1 THE ORIGIN AND OBJECTIVES OF THE FCC[1]

The Post Roads Act of 1866, which marked the beginning of federal regulation of interstate electrical communication, authorized the postmaster general to fix

---

[1]The following discussion has been influenced by the *United States Government Manual,* 1978–1979, U.S. Printing Press, Washington, D.C. and *Regulatory Directory,* Congressional Quarterly, Inc., Washington, D.C., 1980.

rates annually for government telegrams. This was followed by the Mann-Elkins Act of 1910, which authorized the ICC to establish uniform systems of accounts for telephone and telegraph carriers. To deal with the growing use of the radio and the resulting pressure on the radio spectrum, Congress passed in 1912 the Radio Act, which was the first attempt to regulate radio communication in general. This act determined the character of emissions, monitored the transmission of distress calls, reserved certain frequencies for government use, and placed licensing of wireless stations and operators under the secretary of commerce and labor. That year also saw the licensing of the first radio stations.

In the wake of World War I, there was increasing demand for commercial radio, but the 1912 act was not designed to handle such broadcasting. Hence problems regarding additional frequencies arose. The first national radio conference, held in 1922, recommended that new broadcasting stations with a minimum power of 500 watts and a maximum power of 1000 watts be set. Following this suggestion, two frequencies were assigned for program transmission.

The growth of radio broadcasting was so rapid, however, that following the recommendations of the second and third national radio conferences, held in 1923 and 1924, respectively, the Department of Commerce allocated the present standard broadcast band and authorized power of up to 5000 watts for experimental use; at that time only AM existed (FM came aboard later). The resulting increase in the number of broadcast stations caused problems of interference so serious that several stations were not clear. The fourth national radio conference, held in 1925, recommended that limits be placed on broadcast time and power. But the secretary of commerce was powerless to deal with the situation, for the courts held that the 1912 act did not give him that authority. As a result, there was further chaos, since many operators jumped their assigned frequency and increased their power and operating time at will.

This situation was remedied when, at the urging of President Calvin Coolidge, Congress passed the Dill-White Radio Act of 1927. This act created a five-member Federal Radio Commission (FRC) to issue station licenses, allocate frequency bands to various services, assign specific frequencies to individual stations, and control their power.

Despite the creation of the FRC, regulation of electronic communication was scattered among several agencies, such as the FRC, the Interstate Commerce Commission (ICC), the postmaster general, and the State Department. Therefore, at the prodding of President Franklin D. Roosevelt, Congress passed the Communications Act of 1934 and created the FCC to consolidate into one agency the regulation of all interstate and foreign communication by wire and radio, including telephone, telegraph, and broadcasting. The 1934 act is the basic law that governs the broadcasting and communications industries to date, even though there have been metamorphic changes in these industries since then.[2] The only other significant law to be passed since 1934 was the Commu-

---

[2]Several attempts have been made in the Congress to rewrite the 1934 act, but as yet they have not succeeded.

nications Satellite Act of 1962, which regulated space communication, about which more will be said later.

The Communications Act of 1934[3]

Section 1 of the act spells out the goals of the act, but it does not specify the means by which to achieve them. It says:

> For the purpose of regulating interstate and foreign commerce in communication by wire and radio so as to make available, so far as possible, to all the people of the United States a rapid, efficient, Nationwide, and worldwide wire and radio communication service with adequate facilities at reasonable charges, for the purpose of national defense, for the purpose of promoting safety of life and property through the use of wire and radio communication, and for the purpose of securing a more effective execution of this policy by centralizing authority heretofore granted by law to several agencies and by granting additional authority with respect to interstate and foreign commerce in wire and radio communication, there is hereby created a commission to be known as the "Federal Communication Commission," which shall be constituted as hereinafter provided, and which shall execute and enforce the provisions of this Act.

To pursue the mandate, the legislation mentioned some nineteen powers of the FCC, but the one referred to most frequently is that the commission "study new uses for radio, provide for experimental uses of frequencies and generally encourage the larger and more effective use of radio in the *public interest*" [Emphasis added]. Whether the FCC has succeeded in achieving this goal will be seen as we go along.

When the 1934 act was passed, the broadcasting and telecommunication industries were still in their infancy. Commercial television was not yet on the horizon, not to mention cable television. Satellite technology was probably not yet dreamed about. Data processing and its interaction with telecommunication was probably in the realm of science fiction.

All these developments have now come to pass. Consequently the FCC, although not expressly authorized by the 1934 act, is increasingly called upon by Congress, the public, business, and the courts to regulate these relative newcomers. This has not only increased the commission's work load, but has also put it in the unenviable position of reconciling the diverse interests of the various segments of the broadcasting and telecommunications industries. For example, when television appeared, the FCC, to protect the interests of the radio industry, was "forced" to allocate limited frequency to it. Similarly, when in the 1960s cable television began challenging broadcast television, the latter pressured the commission to regulate the former in the "public interest." With the

---

[3]The following details are based on "Federal Regulation and Regulatory Reform," *Report by the Subcommittee on Oversight and Investigations of the Committee on Interstate and Foreign Commerce,* House of Representatives, 94th Cong., 2d Sess., October 1976. (Hereafter referred to as the House *Study on Federal Regulation.*)

advent of satellite technology, the FCC was challenged to balance it with the older cable technology. With the rapid growth of computers, the lines between transmission of data by voice and by the computer are so blurred that it is now difficult to tell where communication begins and data processing ends and vice versa.

How has the FCC handled these challenges? As we will show, the commission seems to havé followed the "FIFS" (first-in, first-served) principle as far as possible.[4] For example, to protect the interest of broadcast television, from 1960 to 1980 the FCC followed a highly restrictionist policy toward cable television until it became infeasible to do so, technologically as well as politically. The same is true of the telecommunications industry: For a long time, the commission tried to preserve the monopoly of American Telephone and Telegraph (AT&T) against the competition, although there was no sound economic rationale for such action. We will discuss this more fully in subsequent sections, after we provide some rationale for the regulation of broadcasting and telecommunication in general.

15.2 WHY REGULATION?

Although the 1934 act does not spell out the reasons behind the regulation of the broadcasting and telecommunications industries (except the nebulous doctrine of "the public interest"), one can provide economic rationale for such regulation. This has to do with certain characteristics of the electromagnetic spectrum. First, this spectrum has limits imposed by the paths of radio waves and the technology of radio communication. In this respect, the radio spectrum is a "common pool" of a scarce economic resource, with various claimants on it whose property rights to it are not well defined. As we saw in Chapter 2, in cases of the "common pool" problem, regulation has a legitimate role to play. Second, there is the problem of "spillouts" (negative externality) in terms of the interference in the use of this spectrum — every transmitting device has potential for disturbance. For example, the television set in my apartment becomes fuzzy when someone in the building is using the vacuum cleaner. Third, the spectrum in some sense has the characteristic of a public good. The case in point is television programing: The marginal cost of programing to an additional viewer is zero — if a program is watched by 100 people or 101, its incremental cost to the hundred and first viewer is zero.[5] In Chapter 2 we spelled out the reasons why regulation may be necessary to generate the optimum production or use of public goods. Finally, there is the suitability factor — certain parts of the radio spectrum, better suited to economical use than others, are in great demand. The

---

[4]The FIFS principle seems to be a universal law of regulation. Thus, as we have seen, the impetus behind the ICC regulation of the trucking industry was to protect the interests of the railroad industry, which was the first to be regulated by the commission. The same was true of the Civil Aeronautics Board (CAB) regulation of the regional carriers, the objective being to protect the trunk lines.

[5]This subtle argument has been used by broadcast television against cable television. If the incremental cost of programing to an additional viewer is zero, why should cable television operators charge subscription fees?

case in point is landmobile communication.[6] Because they are free of static land-line connection, landmobiles are in very heavy demand.

As a result of these characteristics, there arises the need for some mechanism to allocate the scarce radio spectrum among competing ends — radios, television, telephone, landmobile, and so on. We have discussed in general in Chapter 2 why, in situations such as this, one may not resort to the private market to provide the optimum amount of the good or service in question and why, therefore, government intervention may be necessary. The question here is only about the form of intervention — direct government regulation versus several methods of government regulation that we discussed in Chapter 4 (the standards approach, subsidies, tax preferences, marketable property rights, and the like). In the present case, the government decided on direct regulation by assigning the scarce electromagnetic spectrum to the competing users and chose the FCC to do this job.

But the FCC, as we will see, did it haphazardly, without developing any rational mechanism: The commission simply gave the scarce spectrum to the various interests free of cost on a first-come, first-served basis, with the result that those who were lucky enough to get part of the spectrum (stations) have acquired very valuable property rights in the spectrum, rights which are routinely renewed by the commission every 3 years or so. And as we will show later, these valuable rights have earned their owners some very handsome monopoly profits.

There are economists who argue that such property rights should not have been given free of charge, for they have opportunity costs — the value of a radio channel assigned to a particular user is measured by its value to the next-excluded potential user.[7] As Ronald H. Coase says:

> I would not argue that there should be no government regulation of the broadcasting industry. But such regulation is not inconsistent with use of the price system. There is no industry which is not in some way regulated. What is extraordinary if we contemplate the allocation of the radio frequency spectrum is that it makes no use at all of the pricing system.[8]

Of course, the real difficulty in the prescription lies in devising a suitable pricing mechanism in frequency allocation. And here the initiative must come from economists, preferably those outside the FCC, for as Coase puts it:

> The FCC is rather like a whale stranded on the seashore, waiting while the local inhabitants, ignorant of whale anatomy, try to show it the direction in which it should swim. If we are to get sensible government policy in this area, it will, I am afraid, have to

---

[6]"Landmobile" is the generic name given to devices, such as rooftop antennas, beepers on doctors and other medical personnel, two-way radio communication used in police cars, delivery vans and taxicabs, wireless telephones, EKG machines in ambulances, and the now ubiquitous citizens band (CB) radio.

[7]For a discussion of the inefficiencies caused by the neglect to take into account such opportunity costs, see Harvey J. Levine, "The Radio Spectrum Resource," *Journal of Law and Economics,* vol. XI, October 1968, pp. 433–501.

[8]Ronald H. Coase, "The Economics of Broadcasting and Public Policy," in Paul W. MacAvoy (ed.), *The Crisis of the Regulatory Commissions,* Norton, New York, 1970, p. 100.

come from the work of economists outside the government service (and, for that matter, outside the industry).[9]

Professional economists have suggested several pricing mechanisms, such as freely transferable rights (the FCC is not required to renew them every 3 years), auctions (selling rights to the frequency spectrum in open market auctions), user charges (charging according to time and intensity of use of the spectrum), and the like.[10] Revenues collected from such schemes could be used for federal research in broadcasting and communications or for other desirable purposes (e.g., public broadcasting or educational television). Unfortunately, the FCC has not yet accepted any of these ideas. The closest it has come to doing so is to approve pay television (a topic which is discussed in some detail later).

15.3   THE ADMINISTRATIVE STRUCTURE AND FUNCTIONS OF THE FCC

Before we take a detailed look at FCC regulatory activities, let us examine the structure and functions of the commission.

As noted, the FCC is an independent regulatory commission consisting of seven commissioners whose tenure is for 7 years. The commissioners are nominated by the President and are approved by the Senate; the chairerson of the commission serves at the pleasure of the President. No more than four members can belong to the same political party.

The present organizational set-up of the commission is as shown in Figure 15.1. This diagram shows that the major functions of the commission are divided into four bureaus, each looking after a major segment of the industry.

The Broadcast Bureau

The Broadcast Bureau looks after the radio and television industries, that is, the transmission of programs by radio and television. Although privately owned, broadcast stations are licensed by the commission for a 3-year period; the license is subject to renewal thereafter for 3 additional years at a time. The commission assigns frequencies and call letters (e.g., WABC, WMBC, WQXR, etc.), sets power limits and operating hours, and licenses technicians who operate broadcast equipment.

Broadcasters are required to ascertain the needs and interests of the community by surveying civic leaders and others and are required to keep logs of programs, commercials, and technical data. The commission also requires television stations to tabulate the amount of merit programing (news and public affairs programs) of all types shown in a randomly selected 1-week period during a year; this information is used to renew the station's license every 3 years. Under the "fairness doctrine," broadcasters are required to broadcast contrast-

---

[9]Ibid.

[10]For details, see Harvey J. Levin, "Spectrum Allocation without Markets," *American Economic Review,* vol. 60, May 1970, pp. 208–218.

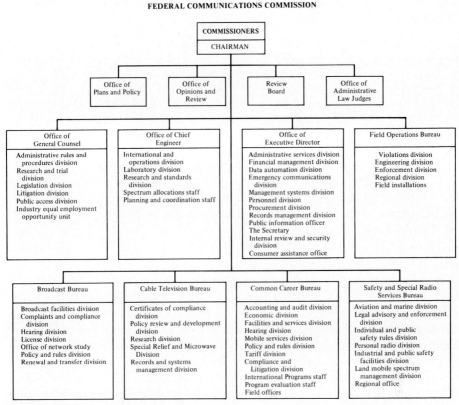

FIGURE 15.1
The Federal Communications Commission.

ing views if they present programs on controversial public issues. Similarly, under the "equal time" provision, all political candidates for an office must be accorded equal time if one candidate is allowed to broadcast politically.

No individual or company is allowed to own more than seven AM, seven FM, and seven television stations (not more than five of which can be VHF). Networks, such as ABC, CBS, and NBC, are not themselves licensed; the stations they own are licensed. However, to further competition in network broadcasting, the commission does not allow the networks to operate dual networks simultaneously or in overlapping territory. Also, television stations in the largest markets are limited in the number of hours of network programing they may carry during prime-time evening hours (6 p.m. to 10 p.m.)

In addition to regulating noncommercial (educational) television stations, the FCC also licenses and regulates the instructional television fixed service (ITFS) for in-school reception: ITFS uses frequencies higher than those used by broadcast television and is not considered a broadcast service.

Since 1968, the FCC has regulated subscription or pay television (STV), a system under which the viewer pays a per program–per month charge (more on this topic later).

The Cable Television Bureau

To operate or to add new signals (stations) to existing operations, a cable system operator or company must obtain a certificate of compliance (COC) from the commission. The COC spells out some of the restrictions that cable systems must observe. For example, up until very recently, there were serious restrictions on the importation of distant (more than 35 or 55 miles) signals to broadcast simultaneously certain programs shown on broadcast television. Also, certain sports events were to be blacked out by cable if they were also blacked out on broadcast television (but more on this later).

The regulation of cable systems is carried out by both federal and local authorities. Local authorities regulate franchising, basic subscription rates, theft of service, taxation, and pole attachments. The FCC regulates signal carriage, pay cable, and technical quality.

The Common Carrier Bureau

Communications common carriers provide telephone, telegraph, facsimile, data, telephoto, audio and video broadcast program transmission, satellite transmission, and other electronic communications services for hire. The FCC sets a reasonable rate of return for the major carriers (AT&T, Western Union, ITT, GTE, etc.). The commission also prescribes accounting rules for telephone and telegraph carriers and prescribes depreciation rates for these carriers. Prior approval of the commission is required for the construction, acquisition, or operation of facilities as well as for discontinuance or curtailment of one or more services. Mergers, consolidations, and acquisitions are subject to the commission's approval.

The commission has a surveillance program under which it evaluates new technologies and utilization of facilities; conducts economic studies and investigations in industry structure and practice; reviews carrier changes, classifications, regulations, and practices, and regulates carrier facility investments and service. The commission also prescribes and enforces equal employment opportunity practices by the carriers.

The Safety and Special Service Bureau

This bureau deals with two-way communication by landmobiles. An FCC license is required to operate any landmobile. The commission regulates the frequency, power limitations, permissible communications, call signals, and related matters. It investigates interference complaints and monitors transmissions for compliance with rules and regulations. Complaints of illegal operations, unlawful interception of calls, and similar activities are investigated by the field force.

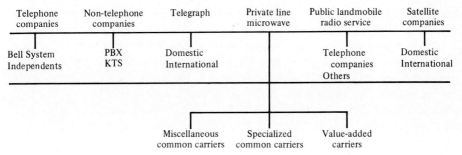

FIGURE 15.2
The structure of the telecommunications industry.

From the preceding discussion it can be seen that the FCC performs three principal functions, namely, adjudication, rule-making, and administration, although the first two functions traditionally belong to the courts and the Congress. But, as we will see shortly, the economics and technology of the broadcasting and telecommunications industries are such that the commission is required to undertake these tasks.

Now that we have examined the overall functions of the FCC, let us look at some of its regulatory activities and achievements somewhat closely. Because of the enormity and complexity of the FCC's regulatory task, what we hope to do is to consider only the most salient aspects of the commission's work relating to the telecommunications and broadcasting industries. We begin with telecommunications.

15.4 THE TELECOMMUNICATIONS INDUSTRY[11]

To understand the complexity of the regulatory task of the FCC in the telecommunications industry, it is essential to examine the structure of the industry first; this is schematized in Figure 15.2

As this figure shows, the industry can be divided into six broad sectors. First, there is the domestic telephone industry, dominated by AT&T (commonly known as the Bell System or Ma Bell). Second, there are the nontelephone companies, which essentially supply terminal equipment. There are two types of producers of this equipment, namely, PBX and KTS. A PBX (private branch exchange) is primarily a switchboard that handles several calls within a building or a hospital or a university. A KTS (key telephone system) does what a PBX does but also allows several outside lines to be connected to internal lines as well as to place calls on hold or to switch them to other lines. Third, there is the telegraph industry, dominated domestically by Western Union and internationally by ITT. This industry is intimately connected with the telephone industry: To send a telegram, one can connect it through the local telephone company.

---

[11]For details, see Bruce M. Owen and Ronald Braeutigam, *The Regulation Game: Stategic Use of the Administrative Process,* Ballinger, Mass. 1978, ch. 7.

Fourth, there are the comparative newcomers, the private-line microwave companies, which use microwave technology — a microwave is an electromagnetic wave of extremely high frequency, usually from 1000 to 30,000 megahertz (hertz, a unit of frequency, equals one cycle per second; a megahertz equals one million cycles per second). This industry is dominated by three types of carriers: common carriers (e.g., AT&T), specialized carriers (e.g., MCI), and value-added carriers. The common carriers transmit television signals to cable firms and certain broadcast stations. The specialized carriers provide point-to-point microwave transmission between certain points (cities); they are in direct competition with AT&T's long-distance service. We will examine shortly the problems this has created for AT&T. The value-added carriers are essentially go-betweens bridging common carriers and some end users. For instance, a computer company may use the local telephone service to transmit data from the computer located in one place to one or more terminals located elsewhere. The fifth sector belongs to landmobile companies, either local telephone companies or independent firms. Finally, there is the comparatively new field of satellite communication, domestic and international; the domestic field is dominated by companies such as AT&T and IBM and the international field is monopolized by COMSAT, a congressionally chartered semiautonomous corporation.

In what follows, we will confine our interest to two major sectors, namely, domestic telephone and international communication.

15.5   THE DOMESTIC TELEPHONE INDUSTRY

The domestic telephone industry is far and away the most significant sector of the communications industry, accounting for well over 95 percent of the industry's gross revenues in 1975. AT&T is the single most dominant entity, accounting for well over 75 percent of the communications industry's operating revenues in 1975. As a matter of fact, the name "AT&T" has become virtually synonymous with the telephone industry.[12] In this section we discuss how AT&T

---

[12]This situation is expected to change considerably now that the 8-year-old antitrust suit against the company has been settled by a mutual agreement between the company and the Justice Department. The January 8, 1982, agreement was finally approved by Judge Greene on August 11, 1982 after major modifications. The suit instituted on November 20, 1974, had alleged that AT&T had abused its monopoly over the telephone industry by consistently taking steps to keep competitors from the markets for equipment and long-distance telephone service. Under the settlement, the company is allowed to retain its lucrative long-distance division and its equipment-manufacturing arm, the Western Electric Company, as well as its research arm, the Bell Labs; it is also permitted to enter competitive, unregulated businesses, including the rapidly growing field of data processing, a field the company could not enter by a 1956 consent decree (as discussed later). But the company is required to divest itself of its twenty-two operating companies, the local telephone companies (see Table 15.1), within 6 months from the data of the consent decree (August 11, 1982) after submitting a plan detailing the divestiture. The actual divesting will take place over a period of 18 months, after each step of the divestiture is approved by the court. The company has now undertaken its divestiture, and beginning in 1984 there will be eight separate corporations — seven regional operating companies to provide local telephone service and a slimmed-down version of the present AT&T which will consist mainly of Western Electric, Bell Labs, the long-distance network, and American Bell; the latter will provide business data communications and other nonregulated computer services. As for the future of AT&T, see the illuminating special report, "Breaking up the Phone Company," *Fortune,* June 27, 1983, pp. 60–92.

has come to acquire such dominance, how the FCC has handled the behemoth, and what are some of the regulatory challenges facing the commission in the face of some recent competition in the industry.

Broadly speaking, the structure of the domestic telephone industry is as illustrated in Table 15.1. As can be seen from this table, production of telephone equipment and the operation of that equipment constitute the two major segments of the telephone industry. The production front is dominated by the major carriers by vertical integration — AT&T owns Western Electric, which manufacturers all of the parent company's telephone equipment needs. GTE, the next dominant carrier, is also vertically integrated. At the operating end, there are the local telephone companies, the long-distance carriers, and the suppliers of terminal equipment. The local utilities, because they are natural monopolies, are regulated by local authorities. These authorities determine their rate of return and approve the rate structure which will guarantee that rate of return. These utilities are either independently owned or are affiliated with AT&T. The affiliates, twenty-two in all, are known as ''Bell operating companies.'' Long-distance transmission has been a virtual monopoly of AT&T all these years, although of late a few competitors (the specialized carriers) have emerged due to new technology. The Long Lines Department of AT&T acts as a conduit, connecting a call originating in city A and ending in City B and vice versa; the calls at both ends are serviced by local utilities there. These local utilities may be independent companies or Bell operating companies. There was a time when AT&T refused to interconnect calls with independent local utilities, but that no longer is the case. ''Terminal equipment'' refers to all the receiving equipment the user has: it could be an ordinary rotary dial telephone or two or the PBX or the KTS.

Table 15.1 also shows that AT&T plays a dominant role in almost all aspects of the industry; for all practical purposes it has a monopoly not only in long-distance calls but also, via Bell operating companies, in major local markets (but this situation will change because of the recent antitrust settlement). As we will see, until the *Carterfone* decision, AT&T had a monopoly in the terminal equipment, too, because the user of AT&T's phone service had to buy the needed phone equipment from the Western Electric Company, an AT&T subsidiary.

TABLE 15.1
THE STRUCTURE OF THE DOMESTIC TELEPHONE INDUSTRY

Production of equipment		Operation of equipment		
Owned by regulated carriers	Independent producers	**Local operations**	**Long-distance operations**	**Terminal equipment**
		Bell operating companies*	AT&T Long Lines Department	AT&T
		Independents	Others	Others

*As noted in fn. 12, these operating companies are expected to become independent of AT&T by the end of 1983 or beginning of 1984.

How did AT&T acquire such a predominant position? A little history is in order.

In 1876 Alexander Graham Bell invented the telephone, for which he secured a patent in 1877. The patent was sold to the American Bell Telephone Company of Massachusetts, which leased it to local telephone companies in selected areas. The AT&T company was organized as a subsidiary of American Bell Telephone to handle long-distance (interstate) transmission. But in a later corporate reorganization, AT&T itself acquired the parent company and began the dominance of the telephone industry that persists even today.

In achieving the monopoly position, the company resorted to several practices. First, it licensed its patents to local telephone companies on the condition that they give AT&T at least a 35 percent interest in their equity capital as well as certain managerial interests in them. Second, after acquiring Western Electric in 1881 to manufacture all its telephone equipment, the company refused to sell Western Electric equipment to independent utilities that refused to give the company the necessary equity interest. Third, it refused to interconnect independent utilities with Bell-affiliated utilities in the long-distance market. All these tactics resulted in the formation of the twenty-two Bell operating companies; they are either fully or substantially owned by Ma Bell and they serve the bulk of the nation's telephone markets. To further its hold, in 1925 AT&T, together with Western Electric, established the Bell Laboratories (twenty in all) to do basic and applied research in telephone technology, including designs for equipment.

Thus what is known today (until the reorganization following the antitrust settlement) as AT&T consists of the Long Lines Department, the twenty-two Bell operating companies, Western Electric, and Bell Laboratories — a mixture of horizontal and vertical integration. Its business is threefold: It manufactures telephone equipment, transmits long-distance calls, and is general in-house consul for the Bell operating companies.

Regulation of the Industry

Until the passage of the 1934 act, there was no serious regulation of the telephone industry, at least in the interstate markets; like local gas and electric utilities, local telephone utilities have generally been regulated by state and local authorities. As noted, the 1934 act for the first time consolidated isolated federal regulations of interstate telephone communication. But even then such regulation was minimal, any serious attempts at regulation being thwarted by the almighty AT&T. The case in point is private-line transmission in the interstate markets.

The 1940s saw the emergence of microwave technology (which meant that large amounts of information could be transmitted by radio beams inexpensively) as well as the birth of television. Because the transmission of television signals requires information capacity many times that carried by telephone channels, the television industry was interested in building microwave systems as an alternative to the use of telephone channels. But Ma Bell successfully convinced the FCC that common carriers such as AT&T were capable of handling the transmission of television signals. Simultaneously, it developed the TD-2 microwave system to provide radio transmission to forestall any competition in this area.

The only other common carrier which could transmit television signals was Western Union. But for Western to provide the service, it was essential that its facilities be interconnected with the Bell System. AT&T vetoed it. It contended that:

> Monopoly was necessary to its effort to provide nationwide service, particularly if the FCC desired to have rates averaged over network links so that routes with heavy traffic would generate revenues sufficiently large to cover some of the transmission costs incurred over the less profitable routes with lighter traffic.[13]

The FCC accepted this argument and did not force the company to interconnect its facilities with Western Union's; consequently, until the end of the 1950s Ma Bell had de facto monopoly of the bulk of the service that needed microwave transmission. This outcome should not be surprising, for we have encountered the cross-subsidization argument previously in the trucking and airlines industries, where the vested interests argued that unless higher rates on the densely traveled routes were granted they would not be able to serve the less profitable, lightly traveled routes. This is an example of how the regulated ultimately capture the regulators!

Toward the end of the 1950s and early 1960s, however, there were many interests clamoring to get into private microwave transmission business. Groups such as the railroads, motor carriers, police authorities, and some utility companies wanted the FCC to grant them frequencies above the 890-megahertz range. The manufacturers of electronic equipment saw a potentially lucrative business in this field if these other interests were granted frequencies. But again Ma Bell opposed. It argued that the scarce radio frequency spectrum better be left in the hands of public common carriers for its efficient utilization and that private entry into microwave transmission would take away the most profitable business from common carriers with the result that the carriers would be forced to increase their rates on other services.

The prospective entrants into the new market argued that they wanted to enter the field because they could provide microwave transmission at much cheaper rates than those charged by AT&T, and at better quality.

In a historical decision, known as the *Above 890* decision (27 FCC 359, 367–379, 386, July 1959), the FCC ultimately agreed with the opposition, stating that:

> In many cases, the operation of private users is such that it is not convenient or practicable for common carriers to provide such service. . . . Even in areas where common carrier facilities and personnel are readily available, there appears to be a need for private systems. . . . Liberalized licensing policies would provide an impetus in the manufacturing of microwave equipment, which, in turn, would result in improvements in the communications art.[14]

---

[13]Owen and Braeutigam, op. cit., pp. 207–208.
[14]*FCC Reports,* 1959 and 1960. Quoted by Owen and Braeutigam, op. cit., pp. 208–209.

The *Above 890* decision marked the first serious crack in the monopoly power of AT&T. But it was just the beginning, as the following case study reveals.

The MCI Case   The *Above 890* decision permitted users to build microwave communication systems for their private use but not to sell microwave service, like the common carriers, to other users. In 1963, however, Microwave Communication, Inc. (MCI), later classified as a specialized carrier, proposed to do just that. Specifically, it sought FCC approval to provide a limited point-to-point microwave transmission between Chicago and St. Louis and nine intermediate points. The service was limited in the sense that it was the subscriber's responsibility to provide the appropriate link between its place of business and MCI's microwave transmission sites. Invariably the transfer link was AT&T's local telephone network.

In proposing the service, MCI claimed these advantages: substantially lower rates than those charged by AT&T for similar service; subscribers with less than full-time communication needs would be able to achieve considerable savings through channel sharing and half-time use provision of its tariff (about 25 percent discount to such customers between 6 a.m. to 6 p.m.) and fewer restrictions on the use of the service than those put by common carriers such as AT&T.

The proposed service was immediately challenged by, among others, AT&T, Western Union, and General Telephone Company of Illinois. AT&T accused the new service as "creamskimming" because it concentrated only on high-density, high-profit markets (such as Chicago and St. Louis), to the neglect of low-density, low-profit markets.[15] Common carriers such as AT&T were required to serve both the high-density, high-profit and low-density, low-profit traffic. They could do so only by rate averaging (actually a form of cross-subsidization), that is, charging the same rate over a given distance regardless of the traffic density of the market. Therefore, argued AT&T, if MCI were allowed to siphon off the high-density lucrative market, the common carriers would not only suffer loss of this market but would have to increase the price in the low-density markets. A further argument was that such siphoning off by the specialized carriers would destroy the scale economies enjoyed by the common carriers and would thus lead to an overall increase in the costs of the services they were providing.

Besides these arguments, all the complainants argued that (1) MCI was not financially qualified to construct and operate the proposed facility, (2) no need was shown for the common carrier service proposed, (3) MCI would not be able to provide a reliable communication service, (4) the proposal represented an inefficient use of the frequency spectrum, and (5) the proposal was not technically feasible.

All these arguments were examined carefully by the hearing examiner at hearings held between February 13, 1967, and April 19, 1967. On balance, he

---

[15]"Creamskimming" simply means entering the most lucrative market.

concluded that the FCC should grant MCI the requested service. The commission concurred with the hearing examiner by a 4 to 3 vote. Agreeing with the majority, Commissioner Nicholas commented, `` . . . I am still looking, at this juncture, for ways to add a little salt and pepper of competition to the rather tasteless stew of regulatory protection that this Commission and Ma Bell have cooked up.''[16]

The MCI decision led to the growth of many specialized carriers, such as CPI Microwave, Inc., Data Transmission Company, and Southern Pacific Communications Company. In 1975, MCI extended its scope of operation by launching Execunet, a microwave transmission service linking twenty-four cities across the country, which uses AT&T's local telephone loops to connect users with the MCI transmission base. The rates charged by Execunet are significantly lower than those charged by AT&T for comparable message toll service. The only bother with Execunet is that one has to dial twenty-two digits instead of ten. But given the tremendous cost savings, this is a minor nuisance. AT&T complained to the FCC about this service and the commission asked MCI to discontinue it. But the commission's order was overturned by an appeals court. The Supreme Court later sustained the lower Court's decision, which led then William McGowan, MCI chairperson at the time, to exult, ``The days of monopoly for monopoly's sake are gone.''[17]

The Carterfone Case[18]   The MCI decision still left unanswered the question of whether a user of a private service can attach equipment to, say, common carrier telephone to get access to specialized carriers. That answer was provided in the now famous *Carterfone* case, decided by the FCC in 1968.

The Carterfone device, invented by Thomas F. Carter, and produced and manufactured since 1959 by the Carter Electronics Corporation, was designed to be connected to a two-way radio at a base station serving a mobile radio system. When callers on the radio and on the telephone are both in contact with the base station operation, the hand set of the operator's telephone is placed on a cradle in the Carterfone device. A voice control circuit in the Carterfone automatically switches on the radio transmitter when the telephone caller is speaking. When he stops speaking, the radio returns to a receiving condition. A separate speaker is attached to the Carterfone to allow the base station operator to monitor the conversation, adjust the volume, and hang up the telephone when the conversation has ended.[19]

The AT&T cited tariff FCC No. 132, filed by the company on April 16, 1957, and approved by the FCC; it informed its customers that use of ``foreign or alien attachments,'' such as the Carterfone, was a violation of that tariff, a violation

---

[16]Quoted by Leonard W. Weiss and Allyn D. Strickland, *Regulation: A Case Approach*, McGraw-Hill, New York, 1976, p. 195. For details of the MCI case, see FCC, *In re Applications of Microwave Communications, Inc., Docket No. 16509.*

[17]Vivienne Killingsworth, ``Corporate Star Wars: AT&T vs. IBM'' *Atlantic*, May 1979, pp. 68–75.

[18]13 FCC 420 (1968).

[19]This is how the Carterfone device was described by the commission.

subject to penalties.[20] The purpose of the tariff was obviously to force customers to use only the equipment manufactured by the company's subsidiary, Western Electric. Although between 1959 and 1966 the Carter Electronics Company sold about 3500 Carterfones, it went out of business because of customers' fear of AT&T's reprisal against them.

Carter Electronics Corporation brought a private antitrust suit against Ma Bell and another company, General Telephone Company of the Southwest. The district court, because of the technical complexity of the problem and because of the doctrine of primary jurisdiction, referred the matter to the FCC but reserved the right to pass final judgment on the antitrust matter. This decision was upheld by the U.S. Court of Appeals for the Fifth Circuit.

On December 21, 1966, Carter Electronics filed a formal complaint with the commission. The issues raised were twofold: (1) whether the regulations and practices in tariff FCC No. 132 of AT&T were properly construed and applied to prohibit any telephone user from attaching the Carterfone device to the facilities of the telephone companies for use in connection with interstate and foreign message toll telephone service, and (2) if so, whether between 1957 and 1966 such regulations and practices were unjust and unreasonable, and therefore unlawful within the meaning of Sec. 201(b) of the Communications Act of 1934 or were unduly discriminatory or preferential in violation of Sec. 202(a) of the act.

On both these counts, the hearing examiner sided with Carter Electronics. He found that there was a need and demand for a device to connect the telephone land-line system with mobile radio systems, which could be met partly by Carterfone. He also found that the device had no material adverse effect on the use of the telephone system. He proclaimed tariff FCC No. 132 to be in violation of the 1934 act because the telephone companies themselves permit the use of their own (e.g., Western Electric–manufactured) interconnecting devices. In his view, the real issue was not about the interconnecting device, but about whose device would be used — Ma Bell's or a private competitor's. The examiner's findings were sustained by the majority of the commissioners, thus in effect striking down tariff No. 132.

In the wake of this landmark decision, many interconnecting devices produced by independent companies are now attached to Bell telephones. The "PhoneMate" and similar phone-answering devices have now become commonplace in many residences and in professional offices.

15.6 NATURAL MONOPOLIES, TECHNOLOGICAL CHANGE, AND REGULATION

When we discussed the topic of natural monopoly in broad terms in Chapter 2, we stated that a natural monopoly is only natural in a given technological con-

---

[20]This tariff provided that no equipment, apparatus, circuit, or device not furnished by the telephone company shall be attached to or connected with the facilities furnished by the telephone company, whether physically, by induction, or otherwise.

text. In the presence of technological changes, as Alfred Kahn puts it, "The natural monopoly of yesterday may be transformed into a natural arena of competition today; and vice versa."[21]

Our discussion of the *Above 890, MCI,* and *Carterfone* cases shows clearly how true this can be. The question that emerges is: How should the FCC regulate a natural monopoly in the face of rapid technological changes? Or one could even raise a more fundamental question about how to define a natural monopoly when technology is changing rapidly.

There is generally no disagreement about the fact that local telephone utilities are natural monopolies and hence need some kind of protection even when technology is changing. But this does not necessarily apply in the case of the Bell System as a whole. Bell itself, however, argues that its entire network is a natural monopoly because[22] (1) there are economies of scale in the provision of a standardized service since the cost per circuit-mile of capacity declines with the number of circuit-miles provided for; (2) aggregate investment costs for installations and capacity expansion are relatively smaller for the system as a whole; and (3) virtually instantaneous connections, automatic switching, and high standards of intelligibility of the signals can be achieved in an integrated manner by the system as a whole to guarantee high level of performance. For all these things to hold true, however, the system must be given a monopoly of lucrative routes as a quid pro quo for serving the nonlucrative markets (hence Bell's opposition to MCI).

One can accept all the preceding arguments for a systemwide natural monopoly status only in a static sense, that is, in the context of a given technology, but not in a dynamic sense, that is, when technology is changing rapidly. If a small company such as MCI can provide a communication service at a lower cost (because of new technology) than can AT&T, one has to reconsider the "naturalness" of Bell's natural monopoly. As Kahn notes:

> The problem is that its [i.e., Bell System's] rates have to carry a very heavy and incompletely depreciated investment in a wide variety or communications technologies, new and old . . . [in short] because traditional depreciation rates have been outrun by technological progress, the average total cost of service, including gross return on historic or book investment, exceeds average total costs under new technology. The emperor [Bell System] has a very heavy and expensive old wardrobe; his challengers [say, MCI] are wearing light new clothing.[23]

The dilemma facing the FCC is how to handle situations such as this. Should it bar the new competitors in order to protect the old monopoly, or what? According to Kahn, "There is no scientific or demonstrably correct answer to these essentially institutional questions."[24] But from his vast experience in regulatory matters, he offers the following personal view:

---

[21]Alfred E. Kahn, *The Economics of Regulation,* vol. II, Wiley, New York, 1971, p. 127.
[22]The following discussion leans heavily on Kahn, ibid., p. 127ff.
[23]Ibid., p. 146.
[24]Ibid., p. 149.

Above all, if this experience [*MCI, Above 890*] demonstrates anything, it demonstrates the virtue of freedom of entry and competition as a device for innovation — for encouraging the development of new and different services and for assuring the optimal development and exploitation of new technology. The single-firm monopolist, even if a highly effective and energetic innovator [as Ma Bell has been in many cases], is unlikely to be able to perceive or vigorously to exploit all the possible unsatisfied kinds of demands or fruitful lines of innovation.[25]

Despite this, Kahn still maintains that the case for natural monopoly at the core of the telephone network cannot be completely eradicated. To him, "The provision of that network and the assumption of centralized responsibility for its planning and for the quality of service it provides is still, it would seem, best left to a chosen instrument [say, AT&T]".[26] However, he hastens to add:

But that a monopoly works best in certain aspects of the operation is not an argument for retaining its exclusive control over those aspects in which it has demonstrably not worked best. The economic ideal would clearly be for the area of natural monopoly to be defined as narrowly as possible, and for the chosen instrument to exercise its responsibility, to the greatest extent possible, by (1) efficient pricing, (2) vigorously anticipating all possible demands on it — thereby subjecting its claim of natural monopoly to the market test — and (3) setting rigorous quality specifications at the critical points — and not before — at which uncontrolled competition demonstrably poses a threat to the quality and efficiency of service.[27]

15.7   REGULATION OF INTERNATIONAL COMMUNICATION[28]

The complex field of international communication is dominated by two types of carriers — *record* carriers and *voice* carriers. The record carriers essentially transfer telegraphic messages (ordinary telegrams; telex service, which is a two-way typewriter service channeled through a public telecommunications system; and private-line service), whereas the voice carriers transmit telephone services (ordinary and private-line). RCA Globcom, Western Union International (WUI), and ITT Worldcom are the only carriers authorized to carry nonvoice services and AT&T is the only carrier authorized to carry voice service. Thus, international communication is dominated by four firms, making it a tightly knit oligopoly.

One must add another company to the field, however. This company is the Communications Satellite Corporation (COMSAT), a congressionally chartered private company authorized by the Communications Satellite Act of 1962. The act granted COMSAT a monopoly to own and operate the nation's internal satellite circuits as well as a global communications network to provide communication to less-developed countries in order to further world peace and under-

---

[25]Ibid.
[26]Ibid., p. 151.
[27]Ibid., pp. 151–152.
[28]The following discussion draws heavily from Owen and Braeutigam, op. cit., ch. 2.

standing via an International Communications Satellite Consortium (INTELSAT). To protect the interests of established voice and record carriers, COMSAT was not allowed to sell satellite circuits directly to final users (but as we will explain, this is soon to change). Rather, the aforementioned carriers were to rent satellite circuits wholesale from COMSAT and then sell them retail to the final user. To further protect the interests of the established carriers, AT&T and other carriers were allowed to own 50 percent of the earth stations used in transmitting signals from one earth station to another earth station via satellite.

The FCC regulatory activities in this oligopolistic industry have been mostly concerned with three aspects of the industry, namely, the market structure, intercarrier competition (except in prices, which are fixed by the commission), and new investments. The regulatory task is complicated by the fact that this industry, as Bruce Owen and Ronald Braeutigam note, is characterized by a high growth rate of demand, rapid rate of technological change, economies of scale, and lumpy investments (necessitated by unpredictable technological breakthroughs).

To illustrate the complexity of regulation, we will consider but one problematical aspect of the industry, namely, the reconciliation of interests among carriers employing competing technology. The case in point is undersea cables versus satellites. Until the advent of commercially feasible satellite technology, the primary means of international communication (short of letters and personal travel) was via undersea cables, which were owned jointly by AT&T and the record carriers at one end and by foreign governments at the other – the unit of ownership is the half circuit, that is, one-half of a circuit from the mainland to the middle of the ocean and back. To accommodate satellite transmission, the FCC developed the "proportional fill" rule, by which total traffic was allocated between satellites and cables so as to keep each mode of transmission utilized to 100 percent of its capacity. This was fine so long as there was no new investment in either mode. But the rule could not prevent, say, the carriers from proposing new capacity investment to meet potential future demand. If this were allowed, obviously, by the proportional fill rule the carriers would be able to increase their market share to the detriment of the satellites; the final user would have little choice as to which method of transmission to use since the "composite" or average price charged for the service would be the same. Therefore, whenever one of the companies in the oligopoly proposed new investments, there was usually controversy about its desirability, as can be seen from the following case.

The TAT-6 Decision

Underseas cables known as TAT-1, TAT-2, TAT-3, and TAT-4 were installed by AT&T in the years 1956, 1959, 1963, and 1965, respectively. Satellites INT-I, INT-II, and INT-III were put into operation in 1965, 1967, and 1968, and INT-IV was authorized in 1971. Although satellite technology was deemed comparatively cheaper than that of cable, the FCC in 1970 granted ATT's request to install TAT-5 but with the promise that it would look into the question of developing appropriate criteria in choosing between the alternative technologies. While its application for TAT-5 was pending before the commission, Ma Bell also sought the commission's permission to install TAT-6 in 1973, using the so-called SF technology, although at that time a more advanced technology known as SG was already available. TAT-6, a 825-circuit cable between the United States and France, costing $86 million and expected to last 24 years, was designed to take advantage of the growing and lucrative North Atlantic market.

The questions facing the FCC were: (1) what rules to use in deciding between competing technologies, and (2) whether to accept ATT's proposal. In its application, the company justified its proposal on the ground that such additional investment was necessary to maintain an "optimal mix" (meaning 50-50) of cable and satellite transmission in the North Atlantic market and also on the ground that cable was economical because COMSAT charged a price of $45,600 a year for one-half circuit whereas the proposed cable would charge only $8600 a year for half a circuit—the COMSAT price was higher because it was based on the average price of serving low- as well as high-density traffic.

AT&T was not the only advocate of the new cable, however. On the grounds of national security and national defense, the Department of Defense supported it. So did the European governments who would have half ownership in the new cable. To pressure the commission, Ma Bell stated that it would withdraw completely from the cable business if its request was not granted; the company had already invested substantial money in the initial spadework, and the commission's denial of its request would have meant that it does not pay to undertake "risky" ventures.

The major opponent of the proposal, besides COMSAT, was the White House Office of Telecommunications Policy (OTP), which found TAT-6 more expensive as well as unnecessary to satisfy toll demand.

The choice between the two technologies revolved around another important factor, namely, reliability of the two modes. Cables were subject to infrequent failures of long duration (e.g., damage by fishing trawlers), whereas satellites were subject to frequent failures of short duration. But in 1971 it was not clear whether, on average, one technology was better than the other on this score.

In any case, the FCC declined the company's request for TAT-6 (SF technology) but, without any formal request from the company, granted it permission to develop the more advanced TAT-6 (SG). In reaching this decision, the commission seems to have played it safe: While giving the appearance that the commission could be tough (in declining TAT-6, SF), it did not want to displease Ma Bell for fear that the company might indeed quit the cable business, deeming it too risky.

Needless to say, the company was pleased, for it got, without asking for it, permission to go ahead with TAT-6 anyhow, albeit with the SG technology. Not only that, the company requested that the capacity of its SG cable be increased from 3500 to 4000 circuits, which was granted. The final license was issued in March 1972. According to Owen and Braeutigam, the TAT-6 decision was a tribute to AT&T's superb strategic tactics of enlisting the support of the Defense Department and the European governments in getting the commission's permission to "creamskim" the lucrative North Atlantic market; recall that the company had decried "creamskimming" in other contexts. Commenting on the whole case, Owen and Braeutigam wrote:

> What generally appears to have been the case is that technological change has resulted in the addition of new firms to previously monopolized industries. The invention of substitutes for the products (or processes) of regulated monopolies could be used, by regulators, as an opportunity for competition and deregulation. Instead, the new technology and the new firms are generally embraced within the preexisting regulatory framework, with the objective, among others, of protecting the interests of the older monopoly or its customers.
>
> Since the object of embracing new firms and technologies within the regulatory fold is precisely to prevent competition, the regulatory agency must take measures to thwart the natural instincts of the members of the industry. In this role, the regulatory agency becomes in effect a "cartel manager." The role of cartel manager has two functions — to maintain industry profits at a satisfactorily high level, and to prevent encroachments by one firm on the market shares of its rivals. . . . Both of these cartel management functions are presumably at variance with the role of the regulator as protector of the consumer. Accordingly, the objective of regulation in such cases is often stated as protection of consumers from "destabilizing competition," and particular emphasis is placed on that group of consumers (usually rural) who would in fact be disadvantaged by the demise of one competitor.[29]

New Initiatives

On April 22, 1980, the FCC announced its intention to deregulate international communication. If Congress goes along, the commission will allow COMSAT to offer international voice and data transmission to the public, in competition with companies, such as Western Union International, RCA Global Communication, and ITT World Communications. COMSAT would offer these services through an arms-length subsidiary to avoid "unfair" competition. The established carriers are obviously opposed to the move; as noted, presently these carriers act as intermediaries between COMSAT and final consumers, buying satellite circuits wholesale and then retailing them. But it is yet too soon to tell whether Congress will go along, notwithstanding the general deregulatory mood prevailing in Washington of late.

15.8 REGULATION OF BROADCASTING: RADIO

Aside from telecommunications, Broadcasting is the other major area where the FCC exercises significant control, although lately there are definite signs that the

---

[29]Ibid., p. 64.

FCC is easing up on some of its regulations. The major components of this industry are commercial radio and television, both over-the-air and cable. In this section we discuss briefly the regulatory activity in the radio industry and take up the other components in the next two sections.

The first AM (amplitude modulation) radio broadcast occurred in 1920 when station KDKA in Pittsburgh, a Westinghouse station, announced the election of Warren G. Harding.[30] But commercial radio broadcast can be said to have truly begun in 1922 when an ATT affiliate, WEAF of New York, began commercial advertising. In 1923 ATT established the first network of radio stations, which, by an agreement, was taken over in 1926 by NBC, a subsidiary of RCA. The CBS network was established in 1927, marking the domination of the industry by the networks, a practice that was later to dominate television. A network either owns several stations in different areas and/or has several stations affiliated to it for the purpose of distributing network-created programs.

In 1940, FM (frequency modulation) broadcasting became commercially available. By the end of 1980, there were about 8900 broadcasting stations, a majority of them being network-affiliated, substantially or partly.

Although the Radio Act of 1912 was passed to regulate radio communication in general, it was not until the Dill-White Radio Act of 1927, which established the Federal Radio Commission (FRC), that a serious attempt was made to license radio stations by allocating definite frequencies. The FRC espoused the network structure, thereby bestowing monopoly on them, although as Ronald Coase has argued, this was not necessary either economically or technologically. The FCC, which superseded the FRC, simply affirmed the latter's policies but added, as usually happens, regulatory constraints on the activities of the stations. These constraints involved: the number of maximum stations that can be owned in a given market, the amount of time the stations can devote to commercials in an hour's broadcasting time, the minimum time the stations must devote to public affairs programming (8 percent for AM and 6 percent for FM), programs for minority interests, and affirmative action programs.

Radio was the most important medium of broadcasting between 1920 and 1950, but with the advent of television its glory began to fade. Because of competition from television, interests within and without the radio industry began to pressure the FCC for relaxation of some of the rules and for making the industry competitive. After a period of procrastination, in the late 1970s the commission proposed some deregulatory moves. In 1979 it announced that it would make these changes: drop the maximum time limits on commercials, relax the minimum time requirements for public affairs programing, drop the ascertainment (survey) under which stations were required to determine community needs, and reduce the "spacing" requirement between AM stations. However, some of the existing rules would continue, such as broadcasters' obligation to

---

[30]For further details, see William G. Shepherd and Clair Wilcox, *Public Policies toward Business*, 6th ed., Irwin, Homewood, Ill., 1979, ch. 13.

serve the public interest, to abide by the fairness doctrine of equal-time standards, to abstain from any discrimination against women or minority interests, and to seek license renewal every 3 years.

The proposed deregulatory initiatives did not sit well with some vested interests.[31] In a *New York Times* article dated June 9, 1979, David King Dunaway, producer at KPFA-FM station in Berkeley, stated that the deregulatory moves would mean that programs of interest to minorities would disappear and that the pressure on affirmative action would decrease. Decrying these moves, he wrote, "Our airwaves are as much a natural resource as the water we drink or the air we breathe; and marketplace competition has improved neither of these. Radio is too valuable a public servant to be dismissed lightly."

The fear behind the preceding view is that under the proposed changes the industry would try to reap as much advertising revenue as possible by curtailing other activities, especially public affairs programs. But the FCC, in a survey of Florida stations, found the radio stations there were already devoting more than the mandated time for public affairs program and less than the maximum allowable time for commercials.

Although it is too soon to tell the impact of the proposed changes, the fears of antideregulators may be ill-founded. Ultimately, it is the consumers who will decide whether a particular radio station is bombarding them with more commercials than they want. If enough consumers feel that way, that radio station will not stay in business for too long.

15.9 REGULATION OF BROADCASTING: BROADCAST TELEVISION[32]

The year 1941 saw the first commercial black and white television; color television was introduced in 1951. Cable television made its debut in 1948 (in Mahanoy City, Pennsylvania), but did not become a serious competitor of broadcast television until the mid-1960s. In what follows, we will first trace the growth of broadcast television and its regulation; in the next section we will discuss cable and pay television and FCC policies toward them vis-à-vis "free" television.

Since the usable radio frequency spectrum is limited, it was inevitable that the FCC would regulate broadcast television. In the late 1940s the commission allocated to broadcast television only the VHF (very high frequency) band of 54 to 216 megacycles per second, which at most could accommodate twelve stations (channels) in any area. In reality, however, very few areas had more than six

---

[31]The Communication Office of the United Church of Christ filed a suit in Federal District Court in Manhattan to enjoin the commission from adopting the new rules.

[32]The terms *broadcast, over-the-air,* and *free* television will be used interchangeably. Free television is free in the sense that the viewer does not pay directly for the cost of programing, which is borne by producers and ultimately supported by commercial sponsors. Of course, viewers pay indirectly on the advertising expenditures included in the price of the product advertised should they buy that product as well as in terms of the opportunity cost in seeing the commercials.

channels. And like in commercial radio, most of these channels were affiliated with the three national networks, ABC, CBS, and NBC — of the 900 stations in existence now about 500 are affiliated with these networks, either fully or partially.

In allocating the channels in the frequency band of 54 to 216 megacycles, the commission made some significant policy decisions in the early 1940s which were to have far-reaching consequences. First, it rejected the idea that television broadcasting should be based on a relatively small number of very powerful regional stations so that some television would be available to virtually every one.[33] Instead, it followed the policy of "localism," whereby there would be a large number of local stations serving the needs of the local community — local television was meant to be like the hometown newspaper, acting as a spokesperson for subjects of local interest. Second, television service was to be "free," supported by advertising revenue. Hence any kind of pay or subscription television was ruled out. It was believed that such a policy would lead to a large number of local stations because advertisers would be eager to take advantage of the new invention. It was visualized that by 1952 there would be some 2000 stations serving about 1300 communities. Third, when it became clear that the commission had seriously underestimated the demand for television, and that twelve VHF channels were not adequate to meet it, the commission in 1952 authorized seventy UFH (ultra-high frequency) channels and allowed both VHF and UHF channels to serve the same market — on your television set, VHF channels run from numbers 2 to 13 and UHF from 14 to 83.

But these policies proved to be extremely short-sighted. First, the policy of "localism" was ill-conceived. As a result of this policy, single coverage areas had to be reduced, with the effect that a large number of U.S. households found themselves without any television service. It was estimated that by 1974 about 6 million U.S. households had to do without any television broadcast; the original dream of 2000 stations was never realized because the commission was far too optimistic about purely advertising-supported television service.[34] Another consequence of localism was that, by limiting coverage, most communities could not support more than one or two stations, for if the audience is limited, advertisers can ill afford to spread their money among many stations.

Second, the 70 UHF channels were useless for all practical purposes — anyone trying to tune in UHF stations will receive at most two or three stations. The problem here is twofold. First, the UHF signals are not easily received and are much more difficult to tune in on the average household set. Second, the commission erred in allowing VHF and UHF stations to coexist in the same market because the UHF, because of their technical inferiority and late start, could not compete successfully with the entrenched VHF stations. This can be seen clearly from the fact that although there are 70 UHF channels they support only 200

[33]For a long time the British Broadcasting Corporation (BBC) in England supplied television broadcasting for the entire nation, a policy opposite to localism.

[34]See Paul W. MacAvoy (ed.), *Deregualtion of Cable Television,* the Ford Administration Papers on Regulatory Reform, American Enterprise Institute for Public Policy Research, Washington, D.C., 1977, p. 4.

stations, whereas the 12 VHF channels support more than 500 stations. Had the commission not intermixed the two systems, that is, had it reserved some markets only for UHF and some only for VHF, the situation just discussed would not have arisen.

Finally, by initially allocating only twelve VHF channels, the commission created deliberate channel scarcity. Moreover, its distribution of these twelve channels conferred substantial monopoly power on the three national networks, a power enhanced by its myopic policy of "localism," which guaranteed that most communities would not get more than three or four stations; at present only 30 percent of all television homes can receive four or more commercial VHF stations and less than 15 percent five or more. Markets such as Boston, Cleveland, Cincinnati, Baltimore, Philadelphia, and Atlanta were given only three VHF stations, mostly affiliated with one of the networks. About the network monopoly power, Peter Steiner notes:

> The networks' dominance, influence and affluence reflect a substantial degree of monopoly power vis-à-vis all other elements in the industry. They are insulated (mainly by past allocation decisions) from new networks or from other challenges to their dominant position. . . . In the main, networks can do what they want.[35]

The network monopoly power, as Stanley Bensen and Thomas Krattenmaker note, has been further enhanced by other actions of the commission; these include, among other things, deliberate slowdown of cable and pay or subscription television (by actions that will be discussed in the next section).[36] The effect of all these policies has been to give the three networks substantial monopoly profits. For 1973, Robert Crandall has estimated that the television broadcasting industry earned a rate of return of 29 percent on capital above and beyond the cost of attracting it — including the cost of capital of 25 percent, the gross rate of return was estimated at 43 percent, a staggering percentage by any reasonable standard.[37]

What is the logic behind restricting VHF channels to twelve and conferring monopoly on the networks? The putative logic, as Crandall notes, was that in return for the monopoly, the network-owned or -affiliated stations would carry public affairs programs (news and other events) and "merit" programs, that is, programs which would not be necessarily as commercially profitable as the entertainment programs. This is a policy of cross-subsidization, which by now should be familiar to us. But is such cross-subsidization necessary? And even if it is, does this justify conferring monopoly power on the networks?

On the first question, Crandall states the FCC insistence on public affairs pro-

---

[35]Peter O. Steiner, "Monopoly and Competition in Television: Some Policy Issues," in *The Crisis of the Regulatory Commission,* op. cit., p. 106.

[36]Stanley M. Bensen and Thomas G. Krattenmaker, "Regulating Network Television: Dubious Premises and Doubtful Solutions," *Regulation,* American Enterprise Institute's Journal on Government and Society, May–June 1981, pp. 27–34.

[37]Robert W. Crandall, "Regulation of Television Broadcasting: How Costly Is the Public Interest?", Brookings General Series, reprint 346, 1978.

grams may justify cross-subsidization if broadcast profits are thereby adversely affected, which could happen "if news and public affairs programs were more expensive to produce per viewer attracted to them than the entertainment programs they displace."[38] But he hastens to add:

> While a higher cost per viewer for news and public affairs is a necessary condition for the existence of cross-subsidy, it is not a sufficient condition. There may in fact be corresponding reduced costs per viewer for the programs the viewers choose to watch instead of the merit programs. Only if all the news and public affairs were offered at times when other types of programs were unavailable could one assert that the higher cost per viewer for such programs would prove cross-subsidization [necessary].[39]

What are some of the facts about programming costs? According to Crandall, in 1973 the three networks combined spent about $9485 per rating point per hour on news and public affairs, or about $66,000 per hour ($9485 times average audience measured by percent of national television homes watching the programs, which averaged about 7 percent), whereas for prime-time entertainment programs the corresponding estimated cost was $170,750 per hour, the actual cost being $180,000 per hour. These figures suggest that the networks probably spend less per viewer for news and public affairs than for entertainment programs shown during prime time. Crandall further suggests that not only are the relative costs of public affairs programs lower, but such programing may in fact be profitable, which can be seen from the desire of the networks to increase the nightly news from a half-hour to an hour; they have not done so mainly because of objections from the affiliated stations. As another indication, consider the intense competition among CBS (*Morning* with Charles Kuralt), NBC *(Today),* and ABC *(Good Morning America)* for the audience for the 7 a.m. programs which are largely news and merit programing. If such programing were not profitable, why the bidding to get the top talent to broadcast such programs?

In short, the available evidence does not justify the cross-subsidization argument for network monopoly. But assume that such cross-subsidization is called for. Does this still justify the network monopoly? The answer is no, for if public affairs programs were not mandated, public demand for news programs would force the networks to show such programs — witness the recent FCC move to drop the minimum-time requirement for public affairs programing by radio stations because it found that they were in fact devoting more time to such programing than was mandated. Moreover, if the commission had not thwarted the growth of UHF stations, such stations would have ventured to show more merit programing, which is precisely what is happening with the recent relaxation of cable and pay-cable television restrictions, as we will see shortly.

In view of the preceding discussion, there really is no justification for the FCC policy of restricting VHF channels to only twelve and for the resultant network

[38]Ibid., p. 34.
[39]Ibid., pp. 34–35.

monopoly. According to Bensen and Krattenmaker, one way to reduce the network monopoly is to ''authorize a number of new VHF stations that would operate at higher power than the new low-power service but at lower power than present VHF stations.''[40] (New low-power service stations were recently authorized by the FCC, mostly in smaller markets.) They also suggest that the FCC not bar direct satellite broadcast service just to protect the broadcasting interest (see Section 15.11 on some recent developments). They further suggest that if the commission does not adopt these suggestions, and if cable is not allowed to grow, the broadcast industry may eventually lose out to the nascent competition from videodiscs and videocassettes, which are outside the control of the FCC.

Some Recent Deregulatory Initiatives by the FCC

On June 29, 1983, by a 5 to 0 vote, the FCC proposed allowing television stations to make their own decisions on how much news and advertising they present, a freedom granted the radio industry in 1981. The deregulation plan, if approved after public comment, would repeal guidelines that (1) specify minimum percentages of air time for news, information, and local programing; (2) limit the number of commercials each hour; (3) require TV station executives to ''ascertain'' the needs and interests of the local audience through interviews; and (4) require strict logging of all programing that is aired. When such guidelines were repealed for the radio industry, there was a suit against the FCC. But in May 1983 the U.S. Court of Appeals for the District of Columbia upheld the commission. It is hoped that the proposed deregulation plan for commercial TV will be upheld too, for as Mark S. Fowler, the current chairperson of the FCC, contends the commission's existing licensing guidelines are a form of ''censorship — pure and simple.'' (The preceding details are based on the article, ''TV Deregulation Plan Proposed by the FCC,'' *The New York Times,* June 30, 1983, p. D2.)

15.10 REGULATION OF BROADCASTING: CABLE TELEVISION OR PAY CABLE TELEVISION

As described by Kenneth Robinson, ''cable television generally refers to the use of coaxial cable to deliver high-clarity television-grade signals directly into subscribers' homes. A super-high antenna typically is erected; over-the-air television signals are received and amplified, and they are then transmitted via coaxial cable or wires to subscribers who pay a monthly charge for the service provided by the community antenna television (CATV) system.''[41] The cable sys-

---

[40]Bensen and Krattenmaker, op. cit., p. 33. The authors were codirectors of the Network Inquiry Special Staff at the FCC from 1978–1980. For details, see FCC, *Final Report, New Television Networks: Entry, Jurisdiction, Ownership, and Regulation.* vol. 1, October, 1980.
[41]See the Ford Administration Papers on Cable Deregulation, op. cit., p. 4.

tems receive their programing via satellite from national cable networks, such as HBO (Home Box Office) and Ted Turner's Cable News Network.[42] The satellites are 22,300 miles above the equator. A satellite receives electromagnetic signals, say, carrying HBO programing, from a dish-shaped antenna on the ground, known as an "earth station." Then the signal is beamed back to an earth station across the country, relayed to cable television transmission centers, and finally carried by wire into subscribers' homes. Another method of transmission is via microwave, by which a signal is sent between antennas and transmitters spaced at up to 50 miles apart.

CATV came into being as a direct response to consumer demand for a clearer television picture and more viewing options, options which were stifled by the 1952 VHF–UHF allocation plan. Initially, cable was confined to areas which were unserved or underserved by broadcast television; these were mostly rural areas. But later it spread even to major markets with several VHF stations (New York, for example) because it afforded the opportunity to present a variety of cultural programs, including nonsponsored programs — a Ralph Nader can be more outspoken on a public issue if he does not have to worry about the sponsor's political views.

The first CATV, as noted, was established in 1948 in Mahanoy City, Pennsylvania. Initially the growth of cable was not spectacular. Up until 1975, there were about 3500 CATV systems in the country, serving about 7700 communities and 11 million homes out of a total of about 90 million homes, a penetration ratio of 12 percent. By contrast, broadcast television's penetration was virtually 100 percent.

But since 1976, the growth of cable has been very rapid. By the end of 1980, there were 4360 cable systems with 20 million households. The industry is now a multibillion-dollar venture with some big operators, such as Westinghouse-Teleprompter, Time-Life, Warner-American Express, and Times-Mirror. Industry analysts believe that were it not for FCC regulatory constraints, the growth of "cablevision" would have been still more spectacular. And there is some substance to this belief, for since the deregulatory actions taken by the commission in 1978–1979 there has been a plethora of new cable systems offering a variety of fare. There are now more than twenty CATV systems in the New York tri-state area (New York, New Jersey, and Connecticut), most coming into existence within the last few years. Industry enthusiasts and detached observers agree that the 1980s will belong to cable television. What explains this sudden spurt in cable? For an answer, a historical perspective is in order.

Up until 1959, the FCC declined to accept jurisdiction over the fledgling CATV industry because it believed that cable television was neither a broadcast facility nor a wire common carrier. But since then things began to change. Because of the rapid spread of microwave relay systems, CATV began import-

---

[42]Details based on Tony Schwartz, "Where Cable Stands after FCC Deregulation," *The New York Times,* Aug. 21, 1980.

ing distant signals (stations); a signal is "distant" if it is imported from a distance of 35 or more miles in small markets. Cable systems literally picked the distant stations "off-the-air" and "piped" them in by cable. As a result, the subscribers of cable began to enjoy more viewing options, which was a definite invitation to new subscribers. Television broadcasters were alarmed by this development, for the importation of distant stations by cable meant fragmentation of the audience and therefore reduction in advertising revenues: They did not mind the cable systems showing the local channels, which in fact would increase the audience for the products they advertised, but showing the programs from imported distant stations was something else.[43]

To counter the new development, television broadcasters launched a double-pronged attack. First, they sued cable systems for violation of the Copyright Act of 1909, contending that the systems imported distant signals without paying royalties to producers of the programs shown on those signals. Second, they pressured the FCC to regulate the cable systems on the ground that without such regulation broadcast television would not be able to show news and other public affairs programs which were not mandated for the cable systems.

Initially, broadcast television had some success in court. In the *United Artists Television v. Fortnightly Corporation* (1966) a U.S. district court held that importation of distant signals without a license was a violation of the 1909 copyright act. But on appeal, in 1968 the Supreme Court overturned the lower court stating that transmission by CATV did not constitute "performance" under the 1909 act, and hence was not a violation of the act.[44]

The broadcast industry had better luck with the commission. In 1962 the FCC assumed control of CATV. In doing so, it seems to have invoked Sec. 303(g) of the 1934 act, which empowered the commission "to promote the wider and more effective use of the radio spectrum." Following this interpretation, the commission issued in 1965–1966 several rules restricting cable systems. First, it required cable systems to carry signals of all local stations in their vicinity. Second, it forbade them to duplicate programs broadcast by local stations during the same day. Thus, if a local station is showing M*A*S*H Tuesday, a cable station serving the area cannot show it that day. Third, the FCC "froze" all CATV systems in the hundred highest ranked markets and also prohibited further importation of distant signals. Finally, it held that cable systems were causing economic injury to broadcast television by importing distant stations without paying royalties for them; implicitly the commission held that the systems violated the 1909 copyright act.[45]

---

[43]By FCC rules, cable systems must carry all local stations.

[44]According to the Court: "Essentially, a CATV system no more than enhances the viewer's capacity to receive the broadcaster's signals; it provides a well-located antenna with an efficient connection to the viewer's television set. It is true that a CATV system plays an 'active' role in making reception possible . . . but so do ordinary television sets and antennas," (*Fortnightly Corporation v. United Artists Television*, 392 U.S. 390, 399 (1968).

[45]For a critical evaluation of these rules, see Alfred E. Kahn, *The Economics of Regulation*, vol. II, Wiley, New York, 1971, pp. 33–43.

Apparently, all these restrictions were within the jurisdiction of the FCC because they were so held (except the copyright matter) in *U.S. v. Southwestern Cable,* 392 U.S. 157 (1968) and *U.S. v. Midwest Video,* 406 U.S. 649 (1972). But these decisions were clearly against the spirit of the Court's earlier decisions. In *FCC v. Sanders Brothers Radio Station,* 309 U.S. 470–475 (1940) the Court had held that:

> Under the Communications Act [of 1934] economic injury to a competitor is not a ground for refusing a broadcasting license. . . . The policy of the Act is clear that no person is to have anything in the nature of a property right as a result of the granting of a license. . . . Plainly it is not the purpose of the Act to protect a license against competition but to protect the public.

Regardless of whether the commission had the power to restrict cable, why did it exercise it? The explanation seems to lie, once again, in the first-in, first-served (FIFS) principle. When a regulatory commission confers some valuable rights (e.g., giving free the frequency channels) on the first group it regulates, it is reluctant to take them back and guards them jealously against another competing group, which may in fact come under its regulatory umbrella later in time.

Although one may not sympathize with the FIFS system, one can very well understand the dilemma facing the commission. As Kahn notes:

> When a commission is responsible for the performance of an industry, it is under never completely escapable pressure to protect the health of the companies it regulates, to assure a desirable performance by relying on those monopolistic chosen instruments and its own controls rather than on the unplanned and unplannable forces of competition. And society must take into account this inherent tendency of regulation when it chooses among alternatives systems of industrial order.[46]

Despite all these restrictions, however, CATV continued to grow. This was, as Owen and Braeutigam note, due to the unconventional, "blue sky" services that cable promised, such as "free public soapbox channels, channels for education, the arts and government, electronic voting, shopping, meter reading, and access to electronic program libraries with limitless possibilities."[47]

In 1971 the CATV industry reached an accord with the FCC as a result of which the 1965–1966 freeze was lifted; the industry had sought the accord following the intiial unfavorable decision in the case of *Fortnightly Corp. vs. United Artists Television,* Inc., (392 U.S. 1968). But in lifting the freeze, the commission imposed some serious restrictions on the industry. First, until 1971, distant signals could be imported, under the "anti-leapfrogging rule," only from the closest markets. But now no more than three nonnetwork signals can be imported in the top fifty markets, no more than two nonnetwork signals in the next fifty markets, and no nonnetwork signals in the remaining smaller markets if there exists a local independent station in these markets. Second, the "exclusivity

---

[46]Ibid., p. 46.
[47]Owen and Braeutigam, op. cit., p. 133.

rule" was imposed, which required the cable systems to black out a nonnetwork syndicated program sold to individual stations if a local station were broadcasting that same program under a contract with a program producer. The exclusivity rule was most severe in the top fifty markets. Third, cable systems could televise sports events that were not generally televised over the air. Finally, pay television, a comparatively recent phenomenon, could not exhibit current motion pictures — in some cases, even 10-year-old movies could not be shown if they had been shown on local stations in the past 3 years.

Because of the Supreme Court's reversal of the *Fortnightly* decision, neither the broadcast television industry nor the FCC could do much about the CATV copyright infringement. But the situation was remedied in 1976 when Congress passed the Copyright Act of 1976. The act accomplished three things. First, it declared that transmission is performance, a provision that was not present in the 1909 act and which caused all the trouble about enforcing copyrights. Second, it granted the cable systems a "compulsory" license to carry all local stations and those distant stations allowed to be imported by the FCC. Third, it established the Copyright Royalty Tribunal (CRT), under which cable systems were required to pay a percentage of their revenue as a fee for importing distant signals. The CRT divides the money among a number of parties, including the movie industry, and public and private broadcast television, based on the percentage of their programing that is used on cable systems.

As a result of the 1976 Copyright Act and the general deregulatory mood prevailing in Washington, in July 1980, the FCC, under its pro-market chairperson Charles D. Ferris, made two significant decisions affecting cablevision, namely, to abolish restrictions on the importation of distant signals and to rescind the exclusivity rule. As a consequence, a cable station need not blackout a syndicated program if the same program is shown on a local station. Thus, if a New York station has exclusive right to the *Mary Tyler Moore* show and if a CATV in the area is carrying a Chicago station that also shows the program, it can now be shown on that cable station in competition with the local station. Note, however, that this concession was not available to programs shown on networks. Thus, CATV cannot broadcast *Dallas,* as it is shown on the CBS network stations. Of course, if the network agrees, the cable systems can show it later. By removing the limitation on distant signals, a Philadelphia cable station, for example, can use all of New York's independent stations by paying a yearly copyright fee. Cable systems can also carry all "superstations," which are simply local stations that have rented satellite space, making it possible for them to deliver their programing to cable stations across the country. Ted Turner's WTBS in Atlanta is the largest such system, reaching more than 1700 stations and 7 million homes with a fare of old movies, reruns, and local sports.

The 1980 relaxation of cable rules still kept intact some previous restrictions. For example, cable systems are still required to carry all local stations and must adhere to the "sports blackout rule," under which a sports event that is blacked out in a local area cannot be shown on a cable station. Thus, if the Washington Redskins do not sell out in Washington and the local station WTOP is required by the Redskins not to carry the game, the cable system in D.C. can be ordered to blackout the Philadelphia cable system that has the Redskins on it.

The deregulatory moves by the FCC did not go unchallenged. Malrite TV of New York, Inc., a small upstate broadcasting company, acting as a petitioner on behalf of the broadcasting industry, brought a suit against the FCC in June 1981 in the U.S. Court of Appeals for the Second District. But the three judges of the court unanimously rejected the suit. Writing for the majority, Judge Newman observed that the deregulatory moves would lift FCC rules that had protected regular broadcasters by restricting cable operators. Then noting that deregulation of the cable television industry had raised serious policy questions, Judge Newman stated that "these questions are best left to the agencies that were created, in large part, to resolve them."[48] He went on to say, "the commission's repeal of the distant signal and syndicated exclusivity rules, after widespread participation of all segments and comprehensive evaluation of technical data, reflects the 'rational weighing of competing policies' Congress intended to be exercised by the agency and to be sustained by a reviewing court."[49]

Unless this decision is challenged in the Supreme Court, it seems that the days of second-class citizenship for cable television are over. There is no question, as pointed out previously, that in the 1980s cable television will give broadcast television a run for its money.

Pay Television: The Home Box Office (HBO) Case[50]

It seems to be a universal law of regulation that the moment a new invention threatens to make inroads in a regulated industry, the established interests and the regulators try their best to thwart it. A good illustration of this is pay cable television. A pay cable system, for a monthly charge of $7 to $10 in addition to the monthly basic charge of about the same amount, will provide a special channel or two that show recently released movies, specialized sports programs, ballets, live and taped concerts, and so on.

Pay cable television is a recent phenomenon, dating since about the late 1970s. This late arrival is not due to any technical reasons, but to the commission's restrictions on pay television. As a matter of fact, as late as 1975–1976, the commission barred cable systems from exhibiting on a per program or per channel pay basis, feature films that were more than 3 years old and specific sports events (e.g., the World Series). The underlying reasoning was to prevent such systems to "siphon off" programs from broadcast television; this was similar to the initial resistance to cable television for fear that it might siphon off audience from the broadcasters.

As Kenneth Robinson points out, these pay cable rules were challenged by the Department of Justice and the cable industry, among others, on "jurisdic-

---

[48] *The New York Times,* June 17, 1981, p. D4.
[49] Ibid.
[50] *Home Box Office, Inc. vs. FCC, No. 75-1280* et al., U.S. Court of Appeals for the District of Columbia Circuit, March 25, 1977

tional, First Amendment, procedural and competitive grounds."[51] (The broadcast television industry, on the other hand, challenged the rules as being too weak.) Home Box Office, Inc., now a leader in pay cable, on behalf of others in the industry, challenged the commission's 1975 pay cable rules in the Court of Appeals for the District of Columbia Circuit. On March 25, 1977, the HBO case was decided. The appeals court ruled that the pay cable rules had far exceeded the commission's jurisdiction over cable and should therefore be rescinded.

The key features of the court decision were these:[52] First, the court found that the FCC has violated the First Amendment when it adopted rules restricting cable's programing content. Second, it rejected the commission's claim that cable television was a secondary or supplementary service to broadcast television. In the court's view, cable television was not a second-class citizen. Third, the court knocked down the commission's theory of "presumptive harm," which implied that, absent the restrictions, "free" television would be harmed economically; in the court's view, specific evidence of actual harm must be shown.

The *HBO* decision was a major victory for the cable television industry. This decision, coupled with the relaxation of the exclusivity and distant signal rules, portends an unbounded future for the industry. Already, there are several pay cable systems in existence since the *HBO* decision. For example, besides HBO, the Movie Channel in the New York tristate area now has a channel that provides nothing but recently released movies. Similarly, Showtime, also in the New York area, now shows recently released as well as classic movies, comedy series, musical and variety specials, programs for children, live and taped concerts and nightclub acts, and taped Broadway plays. There is even a pay cable station (Uptown) which shows action, horror, and foreign movies in Manhattan and Mount Vernon, New York, for about $5 a month. There is no question that these developments will one day fulfill George Orwell's prophesy of a "wired society" made in his famous novel, *1984*. Mike Dann, a leading student of cable television, forecasts that by 1985 cable will have about 40 million subscribers and the 1990s will see as many as 220 different channels compared to the present 5 or 6 channels per viewing area. Established over-the-air broadcasters, such as CBS and ABC, are preparing themselves for this eventually by planning their own cable systems.

15.11 DATA COMMUNICATIONS: A CHALLENGE FOR THE FCC[53]

In the 1950s data processing (by computer) and telecommunications were distinct industries, the former dominated by IBM and the latter by AT&T. Now the distinction between the two industries is blurring so rapidly that the two indus-

---

[51]Kenneth Robinson, "Recent Developments and Predictions about the Future," in the Ford Administration Papers on Cable Deregulation, op. cit., p. 91.

[52]Details provided by Kenneth Robinson, ibid., pp. 92–93.

[53]For a fascinating account, see Vivienne Killingsworth, op. cit.

tries are about to converge into one—the data communications industry. Although such a merger is technically almost inevitable, it has created a serious problem for the Congress as well as for the FCC. The problem put simply is this: The communications industry has been subject to FCC regulation, in various guises, all these years, but the data processing industry is pretty much unregulated. Therefore, if, say, IBM is allowed to enter the communications field, should AT&T be permitted to enter the data processing industry? And if AT&T is so allowed, will it not use its monopoly power in the communications field to cross-subsidize its operation in data processing, which might threaten the survival of others in that field? (Recall the leverage theory of monopoly discussed in Chapter 9 when we discussed the economics of tying contracts.)

These are troublesome questions. As a matter of fact, by a 1956 consent decree, Ma Bell is expressly prohibited from entering the data processing industry by offering products such as computers, computer terminals, and services that process or "change the semantic value of data," for these are provided by the unregulated sector. But AT&T has charged that the joint venture of IBM (with Aetna Life and Casulty and COMSAT General) with Satellite Business System (SBS) is nothing but a foray into the data communications industry—by 1981 SBS planned to put two satellites high into the sky as the linchpin of a computer data and voice service. Considering that in 1980 some twenty-five of the largest telephone users spent $1.3 billion (about 15 percent of all intercity business calling), AT&T cannot look favorably to the SBS entry. To challenge SBS, AT&T has developed a new system, called the Advanced Communications Service (ACS), which is a complex means of allowing dissimilar data processing machines to talk to each other. IBM charges that ACS is data processing, and hence a violation of the 1956 consent decree; AT&T argues that it is not data processing.

Congress has recognized that technologically it is now difficult to tell where communication begins and data processing ends and vice versa. On July 16, 1981, the Senate Commerce Committee, by a vote of 16 to 1, cleared a landmark bill that will lift regulations from much of the telephone industry and allow AT&T to enter new and growing fields of information processing and distribution, although the company will not be allowed to beam classified advertising to homes or to establish its own electronic newspapers. The company will be allowed to provide the above services only through an arms-length unregulated subsidiary. This bill is of academic interest, however, in view of the recent settlement of the antitrust suit against AT&T. As noted before (see footnote 12), Judge Greene has accepted the consent decree worked out by the company and the Justice Department. This decree allows the company to enter the field of data processing but stipulates that for a period of 7 years it cannot start any electronic information service nor can it stop its operating companies when they become independent from selling equipment and publishing the Yellow Pages, a lucrative source of revenue for the company. As noted in footnote 12, as of January 1984, American Bell, a newly established unit of AT&T, will provide data communications and other nonregulated computer services.

15.12   SATELLITE TELEVISION FOR HOMES: ANOTHER CHALLENGE FOR THE FCC[54]

First came the radio, then came over-the-air television, then cable television, then pay cable television, and now comes satellite television, a move approved by the commission in April 1981. In the words of Robert E. Lee, then acting chairperson of the FCC, "the idea of a national station or stations sitting up in the sky nearly boggles the mind."

Satellite television will work like this: A TV signal is beamed to a satellite in the sky and is then relayed from the satellite directly to special dish-shaped antennas on the roofs of individual homes over a vast area. Schematically, satellite television will work as shown in Figure 15.3.

The Satellite Television Corporation, a subsidiary of COMSAT, will operate the proposed system between 12.2 and 12.7 gigahertz, a spectrum now used for internal communication by railroads, some newspapers, and utilities. COMSAT plans to spend $600 million on the new service.

Although the service will be welcomed by consumers, it has sent shivers through the broadcast television industry. The National Association of Broadcasters, the industry trade group, wants the commission to delay final action

---

[54]The following details are based on Earnest Holsendolph, "Satellite Television for Homes: FCC Endorses New Technology in Comsat Plan," *The New York Times,* Apr. 22, 1981, p. D1.

FIGURE 15.3
Tuning in to satellite TV.

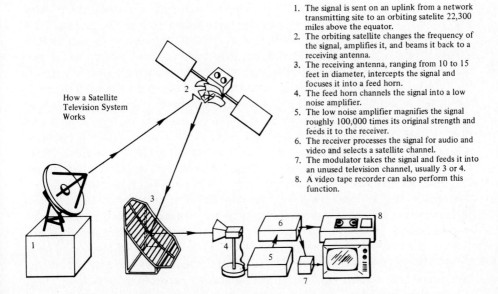

How a Satellite
Television System
Works

1. The signal is sent on an uplink from a network transmitting site to an orbiting satelite 22,300 miles above the equator.
2. The orbiting satellite changes the frequency of the signal, amplifies it, and beams it back to a receiving antenna.
3. The receiving antenna, ranging from 10 to 15 feet in diameter, intercepts the signal and focuses it into a feed horn.
4. The feed horn channels the signal into a low noise amplifier.
5. The low noise amplifier magnifies the signal roughly 100,000 times its original strength and feeds it to the receiver.
6. The receiver processes the signal for audio and video and selects a satellite channel.
7. The modulator takes the signal and feeds it into an unused television channel, usually 3 or 4.
8. A video tape recorder can also perform this function.

pending congressional lead in the matter. The industry is obviously worried about losing advertising dollars. Cable and pay television are less worried about the new competition, since COMSAT will offer only three channels compared to the twenty or more channels provided by many cable systems.

The critical question facing the commission will be this: Will broadcast television, based on the principle of localism, survive purely on the basis of local and regional advertising, since there is no question that national advertising will use satellite television? In that case, how will the FCC protect broadcast television, which following the FIFS principle should have "first" priority? It will be interesting to find out what the commission finally decides when satellite television becomes a widespread reality. However, there are some economists who believe that satellite broadcasting will not affect local broadcasting seriously because the former will be used more in remote areas where cable television does not exist and where broadcast television service is very poor.

15.13   SUMMARY AND CONCLUSIONS

The FCC was created by the Communications Act of 1934 to provide "to all the people of the United States a rapid, efficient, nationwide and worldwide wire and radio communication service with adequate facility at reasonable charges. . . ." To what extent has the FCC accomplished this goal? The primary thrust of this chapter was to provide an answer to this question.

We first considered the communications industry, with special reference to two of its most important sectors, domestic telephone and international communications. Insofar as domestic telephone is concerned, our analysis shows that until very recently the commission generally yielded to the monopoly power of AT&T. This power was both at the production and distribution ends. The production of telephone equipment was dominated by the company by vertical integration with Western Electric, its manufacturing arm. In distribution it had virtual monopoly in the long-distance traffic and monopoly in several major markets via the Bell operating companies. The monopoly power was further enhanced by the company's domination of research via the Bell Laboratories. It was not until the *Above 890,* the *MCI,* and the *Carterfone* decisions that there was a serious challenge to the company's dominance. The *Above 890* decision allowed private users to install microwave communications systems, but only for their private use. This restriction was lifted by the *MCI* decision, which allowed a specialized carrier to be established for the purpose of serving long-distance toll service on a restricted basis in competition with Ma Bell. The *Carterfone* decision practically ended Ma Bell's dominance of the terminal equipment market; before then the user of the company's telephone services had no choice but to install Western Electric–manufactured terminal equipment.

Since these decisions were taken, the evidence is clear that they have benefitted individual consumers as well as private businesses. The specialized carriers have substantially reduced the cost of long-distance transmission for many businesses. Consumers can now install their own terminal equipment produced by non-Western Electric manufacturers, and at substantial savings. The entry of private carriers has also forced Ma Bell to reduce its long-distance telephone rates in several markets. All these developments are clear indications that for a long time the commission did not succeed fully in its objective of providing telephone services at "reasonable charges." In particular, it was slow in recognizing technological changes and in redefining the role of natural monopolies in the face of such changes. This has had the effect of denying the consumer the benefits of lower cost and/or better price-quality; the commission was forced to provide these options by court decisions and public pressure.

The real challenge to Ma Bell's remaining monopoly power will come from the field of data communications. IBM has begun to challenge AT&T's supremacy in the communications field. Sensing that threat, AT&T asked Congress to allow it to enter the data processing field. Congress acted on the request only after the long-standing antitrust suit against the company was settled in August 1982 by a consent decree approved by Judge Greene. Among other provisions, this decree allows the company to enter the unregulated field of data processing. It remains to be seen how Ma Bell handles this challenge. But one thing is clear: Techonologically the fields of communications and data transformation are converging very rapidly.

In the field of international communications, too, Ma Bell has had exlcusive monopoly in voice services, although satellite communications is challenging that monopoly. Even so, the company is using its early start and superb administrative processes to thwart the newcomer; the *TAT-6* decision is a testimony to that. There is no question, however, that in the future those involved with the satellite and underseas cable technologies will have to learn to live with each other.

When it comes to broadcasting, the commission has been in the unenviable position of being the guardian of so many wards — radio, broadcast television, cable television, pay cable television, and now satellite television. And it has not been an easy job.

Although the heydays of radio were over by the 1950s, it was not until the late 1970s that the commission took some actions to relax some of the restrictions on the AM and FM stations. This relaxation has spurred the radio industry and has made it possible for radio to coexist with television.

Insofar as broadcast television is concerned, for a long time the FCC followed a highly restrictive policy in allocating VHF channels. This policy, with its bias for localism, has had the effect of conferring substantial monopoly power on the three networks, ABC, CBS, and NBC, and of earning these networks huge monopoly profits. Although the FCC later opened up seventy UHF channels, they could not compete successfully with the entrenched VHF channels partly because of their technical inferiority and partly because of the commission's policy of intermixing the channels in the same market. It is ironic that there is no network similar to the above three serving the UHF stations only. The alleged logic behind granting monopoly power to the network was the quid pro quo of news and public affairs programing. But the available evidence does not call for such a benefit, for public affairs programing may not only cost less than entertainment programing but may actually be profitable. The net effect has been that the consumer has been deprived of more viewing options.

When cable television made its appearance and promised consumers varied programing, it was difficult for the commission not to succumb to the pressures from broadcast television. In the name of "public interest" (news, public affairs, etc.), the commission imposed the exclusivity and distant signal importation rules, which made cablevision a second-class citizen. It was only after the Copyright Act of 1976 was passed that the commission lifted these rules. Cable television's growth since then has been spectacular.

Soon thereafter came pay cable television. Its growth, too, was stunted by the commission until the 1977 *HBO* decision forced it to relax the stifling restrictions. Since then a plethora of cable systems providing one or more pay channels have come into being, which has made it possible for consumers to vote with their dollars in deciding what kind of programs they want to watch; until now sponsors have decided what programing is best for viewers.

Competition is bound to get "curiouser" when satellite television becomes a practical reality. Whether broadcast television executives like it or not, the new entry is bound to enhance consumers' viewing options. In the end, the real public interest (consumer welfare) may yet be addressed.

It is ironic that despite metamorphic technological changes, the telecommunications and broadcasting industries still are governed by the Communications Act passed in 1934, a time when commercial television was not yet born, let alone cable and computers. There is no question that there is a need for an overhaul of the act; the need has been recognized by Congress, but as yet there is not much concrete action. Antonin Scalia, a respected scholar, suggests that the 1934 act be amended or rewritten with the following objectives in mind.[55]

> (1) The establishment of a framework for open competition in the common-carrier field (including ground rules for competition by A.T.&T.); and the clear delineation of those areas where continued A.T.&T. monopoly will be permitted.
>
> (2) The establishment of a clear and predictable national policy with regard to cable, protecting that medium from constraints designed to subsidize other technologies and ensuring an industry structure that will minimize monopoly characteristics.
>
> (3) Insulation of the fast-growing computer industry from rate-and-entry regulation on the basis of the communications aspects of their services.
>
> (4) At least the beginning of movement towards market allocation, rather than governmental assignment, of spectrum use.
>
> (5) A reduction of government content controls and entry restrictions in the broadcasting field.

Scalia suggests that the administration should establish a presidential advisory commission similar to the Rostow Commission of 1968 (the Presidential Task

---

[55]Antonin Scalia, "Federal Communications Commission," *Regulation*, November–December 1980, pp. 27–28.

Force on Communications Policy headed by Rostow), whose recommendations had great impact.

It remains to be seen what the government does in this regard.

QUESTIONS

15-1 Comment: "In fact, the regulation of the broadcasting industry by the Federal Communications Commission resembles a professional match. The grunts and groans resound through the land, but no permanent injury seems to result." (Ronald A. Coase, op. cit., p. 96.)

15-2 "Many businessmen, especially in regulated industries, tend to look at competition and deregulation much the same way my children do green vegetables. Something that is no doubt healthy, but for others. For themselves, they are much more interested in dessert." (Donald I. Baker, former head of the Antitrust Division, Justice Department, quoted in the Ford Administration Papers on Cable Deregulation, op. cit., p. 95.) Do you agree with the statement? Why or why not? Supply suitable examples from the communications and broadcasting industries.

15-3 According to Paul W. MacAvoy, "the introduction of new technology invariably erodes the position of established firms, but this effect generally benefits the public in terms of new products and competitive prices." (The Ford Administration Papers on Cable Deregulation, op. cit., p. 23.) Give examples of the industries where this has happened.

15-4 Spectrum fee: The commercial radio and television industries are not charged any fee for the use of nation's airwaves. In 1979, Congressman Van Deerlin introduced a bill that would charge a spectrum fee. Under his bill, a television station grossing $20 million a year would pay a fee of $1.2 million annually, whereas a radio station grossing only $500,000 would pay a fee of $1250. What is the logic behind such a scheme? The broadcasters as well as many public interest groups are opposed to the spectrum fee. Why do you think they are opposing it?

15-5 Give arguments for and against the FIFS principle.

15-6 Discuss the effects of cablevision deregulation on free television, cable operators, copyright owners, and consumers.

15-7 Is "free" television really free? Why or why not?

15-8 If pay cable is allowed to show live Broadway plays, what will happen to the theater industry in New York and why?

15-9 What would happen if the "fairness doctrine" were not imposed on the broadcasters?

15-10 During the so-called family hours the FCC discourages the showing of programs involving sex and violence. Does the FCC have the right to do so? Why or why not?

15-11 Writing about the telecommunications industry, Owen and Braeutigam state: "One hypothesis which seems to fit the facts is that the FCC is engaged in performing the role of a cartel manager. In doing so, it is concerned that each member of the industry obtain its fair share of business. The process by which this fare share is determined and implemented turns out to be extraordinarily costly to consumers." (See their book, op. cit., p. 62.) Evaluate the hypothesis critically.

15-12 The TELPAK tariff: In the wake of the *Above 890* decision, Ma Bell filed a new tariff for its private-line service (TELPAK). For some large customers, the new rates were 85 percent lower than charged previously. Earlier, AT&T had complained that the private carriers were charging unusually low rates. Why the change of heart? What does it suggest about the characteristics of private-line service?

15-13 *The Hush-a-Phone* case: The Hush-a-Phone, a cuplike device attached to the mouthpiece of a telephone, permitted more private and more noise-free conversation. Citing that such a device was alien equipment, AT&T forbade its customers to attach the device to their phones. But in 1956 the United States Court of Appeals for the District of Columbia ruled that this type of tariff restriction was not legal as it applied to the Hush-a-Phone device, for it involved an "unwarranted interference with the telephone subscriber's right reasonably to use his telephone in ways which are privately beneficial without being publicly detrimental." (*Hush-a-Phone v. United States*, 238 F. 2d 266, 269.) Do you agree with the decision of the appeals court? What was the logic behind Ma Bell's restriction on the device? Would the company have allowed the device if it had been manufactured by Western Electric?

15-14 Collect data on prices of local stations, their audience sizes, and program rating to find out the effect of the growth of cable on broadcast TV. What do you expect a priori?

PART FOUR

FOUR

SOCIAL REGULATION

From economic regulation we move on to the new breed of social regulation, typified by occupational safety and health regulation (Chapter 16) and environmental pollution control (Chapter 17). The objective of such regulation is usually to better the "quality of life," a phrase difficult to define but probably easy to perceive.

As our discussion in Chapters 16 and 17 will show, in the areas of occupational safety and health, the environment, and many other areas of social regulation (e.g., consumer product safety), a strong case can be made for government intervention in the marketplace to remedy market failures such as lack of perfect knowledge, lack of mobility, negative externalities leading to a divergence between private and social costs, and the public good or collective consumption goods nature of many products and services. The issue at hand is therefore not government intervention versus no intervention, but that of the method and extent of such intervention.

Although there are many ways in which the government can remedy some market failures, such as the tort laws, liability compensation systems, insurance systems, pollution taxes, and freely marketable pollution rights, the government has by and large resorted to direct regulation via engineering-type specification standards. Although the standards approach has the virtue of simplicity, it is generally not as efficient as the incentives approach (taxes or subsidies), the approach generally preferred by most economists. Some case studies presented in these chapters show that the standards established by the Environmental Protection Agency or the Occupational Safety and Health Administration (OSHA) are not cost-effective; that is, the established goals or targets can be achieved

431

by alternative methods at less cost. This does not mean a regulatory agency deliberately chooses the most expensive method of doing things. It is simply that often it does not have the time, the expertise, or the resources to do a thorough cost-effectiveness analysis of the umpteen regulations it promulgates. Under the incentives approach, the task is comparatively simple. Once the level of, say, the emission or effluent tax is announced, it is up to the polluter either to pay up the fine if his or her activities exceed, say, a certain amount of carbon monoxide in the air or to install appropriate pollution control measures. The polluter will install such control measures if the cost of the installation is smaller than the tax payments. Under the incentives approach the polluter is free to choose any method of pollution control he or she wants to employ; an option not available under the standards approach.

Regardless of the method chosen, one thing that should be noted is that the goal of a 100 percent safe workplace or of 100 percent pollution-free air or water is economically not tenable. What one can hope for is the optimal level of safety or air and water purity; that level is reached when the last unit of safety or purity obtained costs as much as it is deemed worth by the worker or the consumer. More technically, at the optimal level, the marginal benefit of the activity is equal to its marginal cost. Very often this commonsensical proposition is lost in the face of rigid engineering-type standards.

CHAPTER 16

OSHA AND OCCUPATIONAL SAFETY AND HEALTH REGULATION

As noted in Chapter 1, beginning in the mid-1960s, Congress passed a variety of laws regarding safety and health in the workplace, product safety, and environmental quality. All these laws, representing the new breed of "social" regulation, were unlike the traditional economic regulation discussed in Part 3 in that their primary concern was not with the determination of prices, quantities, or fair rate of return. Rather, their main goal was to improve the overall quality of life. In this chapter we consider one such social regulation, the Occupational Safety and Health Administration Act of 1970, and its working under the administrative agency created to administer the act, the Occupational Safety and Health Administration (OSHA).[1]

This chapter revolves around questions such as these: What was the need for OSHA? What are the objectives of OSHA? How does OSHA go about its business? Can a strong case be made for government intervention in the workplace? If such a case is established, can this be brought about without the government actually getting deeply enmeshed in it? What have been the accomplishments of OSHA in reducing workplace injuries and in alleviating health hazards, taking into account the cost-benefit aspects? What are some of the criticisms leveled against OSHA? And what are some of the alternatives to OSHA?

16.1 SOME HISTORICAL BACKGROUND[2]

There is no doubt that the workplace exposes workers to many kinds of safety and health hazards. Workers often deal with machines that saw, cut, twist, or

---

[1]The acronym OSHA will be used to denote both the act itself and its administering agency.
[2]For details, see Steven Kelman, "Occupational Safety and Health Administration," in James Q. Wilson (ed.), *The Politics of Regulation,* Basic Books, New York, 1980, ch. 7, pp. 236–266.

flatten human flesh as well as material, should it get in its way. They are also exposed to vinyl chloride, inorganic lead, benzene, inorganic arsenic, and cotton dust, substances that have proved carcinogenic; in most cases, however, there is a long lag between initial exposure and the development of cancerous symptoms, sometimes as long as 30 years. According to the U.S. Public Health Service estimates, about 390,000 new cases of occupational diseases and as many as 100,000 deaths are reported each year on account of one or more of these carcinogenic substances.

Until the late 1960s, safety and health regulation was primarily a state matter; the federal government did some ad hoc research. The first state to take interest in these areas was Massachusetts. In 1867 it established the Department of Factory Inspection and later, in 1877, it required owners of spinning machinery to guard such machinery. Since then most states have passed laws guaranteeing some safety and health protection in workplaces, although there was considerable variation among them in the coverage as well enforcement procedures.

The rising injury rate in manufacturing in the 1960s,[3] and the publication of Rachel Carson's *Silent Spring* in 1962 and of Ralph Nader's *Unsafe at Any Speed: The Designed-in-Dangers of the American Automobile* in 1965 evoked federal interest in work safety and health. But the real impetus to federal action seems to have come accidentally. As Steven Kelman notes, Robert Hardesty, one of President Johnson's speechwriters, had a brother who worked for the Bureau of Occupational Safety and Health [under the Department of Health, Education, and Welfare (HEW)], which did occasional research on occupational safety and health hazards. His obvious interest in these areas found its expression, via the brotherly connection, in the President's Manpower Message of 1968; coincidentally, there was a report in 1967 of high incidence of lung cancer among uranium miners. Quickly, the Labor Department prepared an occupational safety and health bill which, after the usual amendatory process, passed the House by a margin of 384 to 5 and the Senate by 83 to 3 and finally became law on December 29, 1970, during the Nixon administration.

According to Kelman, from initial introduction of the bill to its final passage, the whole procedure was idiosyncratic, for there was none of the usual interest-group politics that precedes any bill. Neither labor nor business was actively seeking federal legislation, although when the presidential interest became evident, labor jumped in with both feet. Despite his book and the attendant fame, Nader did not testify at the 1968 and early 1969 hearings on the bill, although he did so in the late 1969 and the early 1970 hearings. The environmentalists were not yet a potent political force, hence their interest in the bill was limited. Business obviously had no overt interest in the bill.

Why did the bill then become law with such overwhelming support in both houses of the Congress? It must be the emotion-laden nature of the issue — how could one not support a bill that promises to protect the safety and health of workers? It is also possible that business, by its indifference, might have contrib-

---

[3]The injury rate increased from 11.1 lost time injuries per million worker-hours in 1957 to 15.2 by 1970.

uted to the final passage of the bill. Studies made as early as 1933 had established a positive link between asbestos and chronic lung disease (known as asbestosis), but business ignored it. Similarly, although it was known in 1962 that dibromochloropropane, a pesticide, had caused sterility in animals, in 1978 twenty workers at an Occidental Chemical plant in Lathrop, California, were found to have been made sterile by the pesticide.

16.2   THE OBJECTIVES AND PROVISIONS OF THE ACT

Goals of the Act

The primary goal of the act is to "assure so far as possible every working man and woman in the nation safe and healthful working conditions and to preserve our human resources" [Section 2 (b)]. In pursuit of this goal, the general duty clause of OSHA [Section 5(a)(1)] requires every employer to furnish for each employee a job which is "free from recognized hazards that are causing or likely to cause death or serious physical harm"; the recognized hazards are deemed those which can be detected by common human senses, unaided by testing devices and which are generally known in the industry to be hazards.

Although the act does not spell out how much health and safety is to be provided by the employer, the wording above gives the impression that the legal mandate is for absolute worker protection. To what extent this is so and whether such a goal is practically feasible, are matters for later discussion.

Scope of the Act

The act applies to all private establishments in the fifty states, in Washington, D.C., and in Puerto Rico, but not to state, local, and federal government establishments, although federal agencies are required to develop their own laws to match the spirit of OSHA. Presently about 4 million employers and about 57 million employees are covered by the act.

The federal OSHA does not prevent state governments from developing and operating their own occupational health and safety programs provided they are as effective as the federal plan. If a state plan is approved, the federal government may agree to pay up to 50 percent of the cost of operation. By 1974, fifteen states had such plans fully operative, but states such as New York, Illinois, and New Jersey were trying to give up their local plans in favor of OSHA.

Functions

Under the act, the major functions of OSHA are (1) setting of standards to protect workers, (2) inspection of workplaces to find out whether the prescribed standards are put in place, (3) enforcement of standards in cases where the employers are in violation of them, and (4) consultation with business on how it might implement the standards. Details of these functions are considered in the following section.

16.3 THE ADMINISTRATIVE STRUCTURE AND WORKING OF OSHA

The OSHA is an agency within the Department of Labor and is headed by the assistant secretary of labor for occupational safety and health. The administrative structure of the agency is as shown in Figure 16.1.

Setting of Standards

The first major function of the agency is to determine standards, a job done by the Health and Safety Standards Division. As noted in Chapter 4, there are two types of standards, specification and performance. Under specification standards, the standard-setting agency specifies the allowable technologies that may be used, such as equipment design, whereas under performance standards it may state allowable outcomes (e.g., the level of air or noise pollution) and let the affected party determine how to achieve the goal. For example consider noise polution in the workplace. OSHA might prescribe that the noise level may not exceed 90 decibels in a working period averaging 8 hours. This is a performance standard. It leaves it up to the firm to decide how to achieve that level; the firm could ask its workers to wear earmuffs or it could install noise-reducing equipment. But if the agency were to specify that the proposed standard be achieved by wearing earmuffs of a particular type, this would constitute a specification standard.

We have already commented on the pros and cons of specification versus performance standards in a general way in Chapter 4; We will refer to it when we consider some case studies later in this chapter. In passing it may be noted that the wording of the general duty clause of the act gives the impression that Congress meant the agency to use rigid engineering-type (i.e., specification) standards rather than performance standards, although this is not spelled out in the act itself.

To get on with its huge mandate, OSHA initially adopted some 4400 consen-

FIGURE 16.1
The administrative structure of OSHA.

OCCUPATIONAL SAFETY AND HEALTH ADMINISTRATION (OSHA)

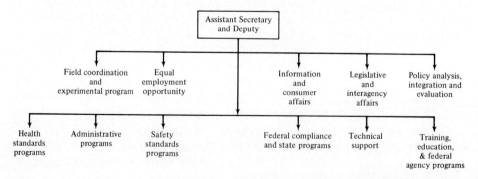

sus standards, which were the standards prevailing at the time of the passage of the act – these standards, meant to be temporary, were recommended by national standard-setting agencies, such as the American National Standards Institute and the National Fire Protection Association. It is important to note that these consensus standards were expedient standards. They were not based on systematic cost-benefit analyses nor did they necessarily protect the workers from the claimed hazards. These interim or temporary standards were to be replaced later by permanent standards after a careful scrutiny and after extensive consultations with the National Institute of Occupational Safety and Health (NIOSH), a federal agency set up in HEW (and, ironically, not in the Labor Department) to do research in occupational safety and health.

Because of the lengthy process involved in developing the permanent standards (discussed later), only a few standards have been issued so far, namely, standards relating to mechanical power processes, asbestos dust, fourteen carcinogens, and vinyl chloride. If in an occupation an interim or a permanent standard does not exist, OSHA may issue an interim standard only when employees in that occupation are exposed to grave danger and some standard is immediately needed to protect them. But it is expected that such temporary standard would be replaced by a permanent one within 6 months. Occasionally, a variance to a permanent standard may be granted if there is a labor or material shortage. But under no circumstance will waiver of a temporary standard be granted simply because it is not economically viable to comply with the standard. The standards, interim or permanent, are published in the Code of Federal Regulations, some 800 pages of it.

In setting the standards, OSHA follows a seven-step procedure. In step 1, a proposed regulation is submitted to OSHA. Such a proposal may come from any source – in the health area, NIOSH makes such proposals. In step 2, an advisory committee is established to consider the proposal. Step 3 consists of publishing the proposed regulation in the *Federal Register.* Step 4 requires the holding of public hearings. Step 5 allows time for posthearing comments by interested parties; usually it is the lawyers who submit extensive briefs. In step 6, the final regulation is published in the *Federal Register,* accompanied by a "statement of reasons," explaining why each provision of the regulation was adopted and the objections made against each. Finally, in step 7, the proposal becomes regulation.

Under the National Environmental Policy Act, any proposed regulation must carry on Environment Impact Statement (EIS) discussing its likely effect on the environment. Concerned that a proposed regulation might add to inflation, Presidents Ford and Carter issued executive orders requiring that each regulation coming from an executive branch agency be accompanied by an Inflationary Impact Statement (IIS) dealing with the costs and the benefits of the advocated regulation. It was the job of the Council on Wages and Price Stability to evaluate each IIS. However, President Reagan has now abolished the council.

Incidentally, the IIS requirement means one has to distinguish between standards that are *technically feasible* (that is, they in fact achieve a particular goal with the recommended engineering standard) and those that are *economically feasible* (that is, the benefits associated with the standard are reasonably related to the costs). But since the IIS is mandated by a presidential executive order and applies only to executive branch agencies and since it is not codified into law by Congress, its legality can be tested only in the courts. And as we will see later, the courts have not always accepted the economic feasibility criterion in deciding upon OSHA standards. It is up to the Congress to legislate the IIS and to decide whether it applies to independent agencies and commissions also. Without such a clear signal from the Congress, it is too much to expect a regulatory commission to apply the twin tests of technical and economic feasibility in each and every case. On the general question of the need or otherwise of cost-benefit analysis in the health and safety area, more will be said later.

Inspection

The law permits OSHA to conduct workplace inspections to see that the promulgated rules and regulations are followed. Such inspections may be made at the urging of a grieved worker or of his or her union, or at OSHA's own initiative as a matter of routine. At first, OSHA inspectors could enter any workplace without advance notice or search warrant, but in May 1978 the Supreme Court ruled that an employer may refuse admission to an inspector who does not have a warrant. But most employers do not insist on such warrants, for they know that OSHA could easily get one and might then be unduly harsh.

Since OSHA has a limited number of inspectors (about 500), it is not possible to inspect some 5 million workplaces. Therefore, to conserve the limited resources, OSHA has followed the "worst-first" approach, concentrating on the industries with severe health hazards or high injury rates. The target industries with high injury rates are: meat and meat products, longshoring, roofing and sheet metal, and miscellaneous transportation equipment (chiefly mobile homes, campers, and snowmobiles). The target health hazards are: carbon monoxide, silica, lead, asbestos, and cotton dust.

If, upon inspection, an employer is found to have violated one or more of OSHA's regulations, the inspector may classify the violation as one of four categories:

1 *De minimis:* Such a violation (e.g., a broken coat hanger in a toilet) does not have direct or immediate relationship to job safety or health. The inspector issues a notice, but no penalties are imposed.

2 *Nonserious violation:* Such a violation has a direct relationship to job safety or health but is unlikely to cause death or serious injury. Such a violation carries a fine of up to $1000 or up to $1000 a day if reinspection shows continuation of the violation.

3 *Serious violation:* Where substantial probability of death or serious physical harm (e.g., no protective guards on saws or punch presses) exists and the employer knows about it, a penalty of up to $1000 is mandatory.

4 *Imminent danger:* A condition or practice that could reasonably be expected to cause death or serious physical harm. The employer is asked to take voluntary steps to remove the danger; if the employer does not take action, a temporary restraining order or an injunction may be obtained from a U.S. district court.

Enforcement

OSHA can only recommend penalties; the actual enforcement, including challenges, is handled by the Occupational Safety and Health Review Commission (OSHRC), a three-member independent agency not connected with OSHA. An employer who is cited for one or more violations has the right to contest before the OSHRC, but if said employer does not appeal the citation within 15 days, the citation and the proposed penalties become the final order without any recourse to the courts. A duly filed appeal is heard by an administrative law judge. The judge's decision becomes final 30 days after the commission receives it, unless a petition for discretionary review by the commission is made. The commission rarely overrides the administrative law judge. The final decision of the commission may be appealed in the Federal Court of Appeals.

16.4 ROLE OF THE FREE MARKET IN THE PROVISION OF HEALTH AND SAFETY

As noted, OSHA was passed without detailed discussion about why government intervention is desirable in the area of workplace health and safety. Also, the wording of the act is so general that employers cannot know how much safety and health they are supposed to provide; safety and health at any cost is obviously not a tenable goal. The question then is: How does one determine the "optimal" level of safety and health in the workplace? To answer this question, what we propose to do is to find out how a purely competitive market would go about determining the optimum level. Having ascertained this, we can then examine the circumstances under which government intervention in this area may be necessary. As the reader can anticipate, such intervention may be called for when one or more of the assumptions of the competitive model may not hold true.

The Market Solution[4]

To fix the ideas, consider safety in the workplace. Given the usual assumptions of perfect knowledge or information, no uncertainty, free factor mobility, etc., how would the free market provide optimum level of workplace safety?

---

[4]The following discussion draws heavily from Edward M. Gramlich, *Benefit-Cost Analysis of Government Programs*, Prentice-Hall, Englewood Cliffs, N.J., 1981, ch. 11. Gramlich's discussion is based on the seminal article of Walter Oi, "On the Economics of Industrial Safety," *Law and Contemporary Problems*, Summer–Autumn 1974.

Consider two hypothetical firms, one "perfectly" safe and the other not so safe, the first paying an hourly wage of w_1 and the second w_2. A priori, w_2 is expected to be greater than w_1, the difference reflecting the *risk* or *safety premium*. How is this safety premium determined?

Assume that jobs in the two firms, apart from the risk-of-injury factor, are identical in all respects. Now let k equal the percent loss of wages as a result of an injury (on account of medical costs, days of work lost, etc.), which is borne entirely by the worker,[5] and let m equal the accident rate in firm 2. A worker who works in firm 2 can earn either w_2 if there is no accident or $w_2(1 - k)$ if there is an accident. Hence the expected or average wages in firm 2 will be:

$$E(w_2) = w_2(1 - m) + w_2(1 - k)m = w_2(1 - mk) \tag{1}$$

where $E(w_2)$ is the mathematical expectation or the average value.

In words, Equation (1) states that the average wage received by workers in firm 2 equals wages if there is no injury [$w_2(1 - m)$] plus wages if the worker is injured [$w_2(1 - k)m$]. [More accurately, it equals w_2 times the probability of not getting injured plus $w_2(1 - k)$ times the probability of getting injured.]

Now for a worker deciding to join firm 1 or firm 2, assuming he considers only expected earnings in the two firms, the wage rate offered by firm 2 must equal that of firm 1, that is,

$$w_2(1 - mk) = w_1 \tag{2}$$

or

$$w_2 = w_1/(1 - mk) \tag{3}$$

Since m and k are both fractions, wages in firm 2 will be higher than those in firm 1, as expected a priori. The risk premium is therefore $(w_2 - w_1)$, which from Equation (3) becomes

$$\text{Risk premium: } (w_2 - w_1) = w_1mk/(1 - mk) \tag{4}$$

Firm 2 will have to pay this amount in additional wages over w_1 to attract workers.

If firm 2 employs L units of labor, the aggregate cost of the risk premium, called the consequence cost (CC) by Gramlich, will simply be

$$CC = Lw_1mk/(1 - mk) \tag{5}$$

To the CC one must add the costs the firm incurs to prevent accidents to begin with, say, by installing proper guards around machines. Call this preven-

---

[5]To keep the discussion simple, we abstract from the workmen's compensation laws, which pay part of the loss borne by the injured worker.

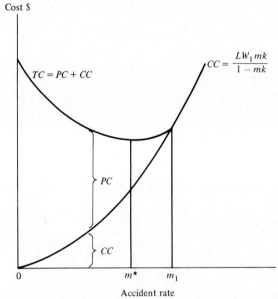

FIGURE 16.2
Injury cost in relation to accident rate.

tion cost (*PC*); of course, there is no guarantee that *PC* will prevent accidents. Hence the total cost of workplace injury is given by (*CC* + *PC*), which can be visualized as shown in Figure 16.2.[6]

What will the profit-maximizing firm do? Obviously, it will try to minimize the total accident cost *TC*, which occurs at m^*, the point at which *TC* is lowest. To the right of m^*, because of increasing *CC*, the *TC* starts increasing. Hence the firm can save on the consequence cost by reducing the injury rate to m^*. To the left of m^*, the *TC* also increases because of the increasing *PC*. Hence, by "allowing" a few more accidents and reaching m^*, the firm can save on prevention costs. The optimum total risk premium is given by the point on the *CC* curve opposite m^*.

Figure 16.2 can be cast in the usual marginal language of economics, that is, in terms of marginal cost and marginal benefit from accident prevention, as shown in Figure 16.3

Notice that the marginal benefit curve *MB* is derived from the *CC* curve, for any reduction in *CC* means that the firm will not have to pay that amount by way of extra wage payments (technically, *MB* is the value of the slope of the *CC* curve at any accident rate). The *MC* curve is derived from the *PC* curve and it represents the incremental cost of accident prevention (technically, it is the absolute value of the slope of the *PC* curve). Also notice that as in Figure 16.2

---

[6]In Figure 16.2 both the *CC* and *PC* curves are drawn on the assumption that there are decreasing marginal returns to accident prevention — initially it is easier to prevent accidents, but the prevention costs increase rapidly as the accident rate increases. Hence they should be read from the right. Notice also that m_1 is the maximum accident rate the firm would have if it spent nothing on prevention.

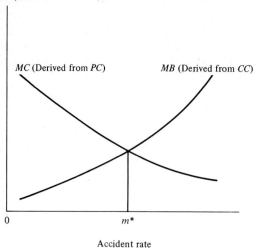

$ Benefits/costs

MC (Derived from *PC*)   *MB* (Derived from *CC*)

0   *m**

Accident rate

FIGURE 16.3
Marginal benefit and marginal cost
curves in relation to accident rate.

these curves are to be read from the right. At the accident rate m^*, $MC = MB$, the incremental accident prevention cost just equals the incremental wages the firm will have to pay by way of additional wages. To the right of m^*, MB exceeds MC. Hence it pays the firm to reduce the accident rate to m^*. By the same token, since MC exceeds MB to the left of m^*, it is economically cheaper for the firm to accept a higher accident rate until m^*.

In short, in a perfectly competitive model "the employer will continue to purchase safety resources until the added savings from injury reduction are just equal to the cost of the resources necessary to generate the reduction."[7] Or, as Nina Cornell, Roger Noll, and Barry Weingast observe:

> Under a caveat emptor market system, any costs of accidents arising from products or employment would be borne by consumers and workers. If it were possible, at little cost, to obtain complete information about hazards, individual economic decisions would force prices of hazardous products to be lower, and wages for hazardous employment to be higher, than those for safer alternatives. The lower prices and higher wages would exactly cover the cost to consumers and workers of assuming the risks. If the cost to producers of preventing a hazard were less than they lost – in lower prices and higher wages – they could increase their profits by taking preventive measures. Thus, with complete and free information, a caveat emptor market would minimize the total cost of prevention plus compensation for hazards.[8]

Of course, the rub is that all this requires a fully operative competitive model. And as we will show in the next section, the competitive model, at least in the area of occupational health and safety, may not be tenable.

[7]Robert S. Smith, *The Occupational Safety and Health Act: Its Goals and Its Achievements,* American Enterprise Institute for Public Policy Research, Washington, D.C., 1976, p. 27.

[8]Nina M. Cornell, Roger G. Noll, and Barry Weingast, "Safety Regulation," in Henry Owen and Charles L. Schultz (eds.), *Setting National Priorities: The Next Ten Years,* Brookings, Washington, D.C., 1976, ch. 11, pp. 464–465.

16.5   WHY REGULATION: THE REASONS FOR MARKET FAILURE

The reason why the idealized market model may not work is that in reality some of its assumptions are not likely to be fulfilled. Let us examine some of the basic assumptions.

Lack of Perfect Information and Uncertainty

How does a prospective worker acquire information about the health and safety hazards associated with various jobs? Or for that matter, how does a consumer know which products are safe to use and which are not? Now one can acquire information from experience or by study. But as Cornell, Noll, and Weingast note, "experience is a costly teacher when it comes to expensive, infrequently purchased products that potentially can do serious harm."[9] A case in point is the potential radiation hazard from microwave ovens. Alternatively, one can acquire information from secondary sources, say, from *Consumer Reports*-type magazines that provide information about various types of products and processes by doing their own testing. But such testing organizations provide information in quantities less than optimally desirable because of the "public good" problem here — the marginal cost of providing testing information is practically zero since it does not depend on the number of people to whom such information is provided once the initial investment is made. Now to cover their fixed cost of investment in testing such agencies may have to charge a price far in excess of the marginal cost (which is practically zero) to an additional consumer, which means the information resulting from testing can be provided only to middle- and upper-income consumers. The upshot is that from society's viewpoint the private market provides safety information that is unlikely to be socially optimal.

The problem of uncertainty is more serious in the area of occupational health hazards; it is often not easy to establish a cause and effect relationship because of (1) the long latency period between initial exposure and final diagnosis, (2) the vast number of toxic substances to which a worker may be exposed (there are about 25,000 known industrial chemicals considered toxic), and (3) the interaction with nonindustrial hazards (e.g., smoking). It is therefore beyond the scope of a single firm or industry to spend resources on research in this complex field.

For these reasons, therefore, there is a definite role the government can play in supplying information in the area of occupational health and safety. It can do so, as in the case of public goods in general, by absorbing the overhead costs (incurred on research) through taxation and charging only the costs of publication and dissemination of the collected information. Alternatively, as suggested by Cornell et al., the government "could require that producers keep workers and consumers fully informed about the hazards of work places and products as a necessary condition for doing business. The government then could assume

[9]Ibid., p. 465.

an enforcement responsibility, checking to see that information was being adequately communicated and spot-checking its quality by performing its own tests."[10]

Lack of Mobility

Even if information is assumed perfect, lack of mobility may also lead to underprovision of safety and health by a purely competitive system. Take, for example, coal mining and the lung diseases associated with it. In exclusively mining areas, workers either work in the mines or do not work at all. Hence they may not get the opportunity wage w_1, the wage rate in work-safe places, because of the monopsonistic (single buyer) power of the mine owner. Regulation may be inevitable in such a case.

Full versus Partial Costs[11]

Even assuming perfect information and perfect mobility, the free market may not guarantee adequate health and safety in the workplace because it does not take into account the full costs of injury or illness. First, the psychic costs of bereavement a family or community may feel for its ill or injured member are not reckoned by the market. It is true that the measurement of the psychic costs is a tall order, yet the importance of those costs cannot be denied. Second, because the various insurance schemes, such as workers' compensation, Medicare, Medicaid, Blue Cross/Blue Shield, bear a substantial cost of medical care, there is divergence between the costs paid by the employer and/or employee and the total costs; consequently the amount of safety and health provided in the workplace may not be socially optimal. For example, knowing that some insurance scheme will pay part of the cost, employers (as well as employees) may not exert themselves fully to remove health and safety hazards (such an attitude toward insurance is called "moral hazard").[12]

Equity Considerations

Assume that all the preceding arguments are taken care of. Will the market-determined amount of health and safety in the workplace be desirable from the viewpoint of equity or on the Rawlsian fairness grounds?[13] Rawls argues that the market-determined optimal amount may require some members of society to bear a disportionate share of the loss resulting from health or safety hazards

---

[10]Ibid., p. 466.

[11]For details, see John F. Morall III, "OSHA and Industry," in Robert F. Lanzillotti (ed.), *Economic Effects of Government Mandated Costs,* Public Policy Research Center, University of Florida Press, Gainesville, 1978.

[12]For a relatively simple discussion of moral hazard problems, see P. R. G. Layard and A. A. Walters, *Microeconomic Theory,* McGraw-Hill, New York, 1978, pp. 382–386.

[13]John Rawls, *A Theory of Justice,* Harvard University Press, Cambridge, Mass., 1971.

so that in the aggregate a greater good can be obtained for the society as a whole.[14] Thus equity considerations may force government intervention in the marketplace.[15]

In short, then, for the reasons just discussed, a strong case can be made for government intervention in the provision of health and safety in the workplace. The question now is about the form or method of such intervention as well as the extent of it, a topic discussed in the following section.

16.6 METHODS OF INTERVENTION

Tort Laws

The simplest form of intervention is via tort or liability laws which permit the injured party to sue for compensation. Thus, a consumer can sue a drug company if he or she is harmed by the products of that company, as was dramatized in the well-known *Thalidomide* case. But in practice this case-by-case approach of the tort laws is time-consuming as well as expensive. An average consumer does not have the energy or the resources to fight a giant drug company. Even under the contingency fee system, under which the lawyer gets a certain percentage of the damage amount (if one is awarded), the litigation may drag on for years.

Liability Compensation Systems

Such a system does away with the case-by-case approach of the tort system by instituting either some type of mandatory insurance system (e.g., workers' compensation laws) or an injury tax rate on the employer (more on the injury tax rate later). The purpose of instituting a liability system is not only to compensate for past damages (which it must do) but also to encourage firms to invest in equipment to prevent accidents or hazards. Now an ideal liability system would be such that "the expected liability of the firm must equal the total expected damage arising from the firm's economic activities."[16] Unfortunately, such an ideal compensation system is just that, for in reality not all damage costs are included (not to mention the uncertainty about the extent of the damage).

In practice, the existing liability systems are limited in many ways. First, the maximum liability cannot exceed the net worth of the firm, otherwise bank-

---

[14]This is not acceptable to Rawls. "In the Rawlsian system of justice, inequalities in the distribution of wealth and income are *just* only when they are advantageous to everyone, especially the lower-income groups in society. Inequalities in the distribution are *unjust* when they are to the disadvantage of anyone, particularly to someone in the lower-income group. Rawls concludes that justice . . . requires that the income of the lower-income people in society be maximized." (Richard B. McKenzie and Gordon Tullock, *Modern Political Economy: An Introduction to Economics,* McGraw-Hill, New York, 1978, p. 368).

[15]For more on this, see Nicholas Ashford, *Crisis in the Workplace: Occupational Disease and Injury,* M.I.T., Cambridge, Mass., 1976.

[16]Cornell et al., op. cit., p. 470.

ruptcy is sure to result. And even such a maximum may fall short of the ideal compensation principle stated above. Second, common law traditionally does not compensate the grieved party for the time spent in litigation, delays in judgment, etc. Third, there are certain legal restraints on the liability systems, such as the Price-Anderson Act limitation on the liability of power companies in cases of accident at a nuclear power plant. One can well appreciate the reason for such a limitation; without it nuclear power as a source of fuel would be economically out of the question. These limitations, although unavoidable in practice, lead to undercompensation of damages and hence reduce incentive to preventive action.

Then there is the additional problem of establishing causal link between a health hazard and its actual impact on the worker. For instance, it takes about 30 years for asbestos-related cancer to appear and 10 years for beryllium-related diseases. As a result, it is quite possible for a worker to develop such a disease well after he or she quits the job. Therefore, it is difficult to determine the appropriate amount of compensation in such cases, a task made all the more difficult by the fact that under the liability system the burden of proof rests upon the person claiming the damages. It is the worker's responsibility to produce evidence to show that the damage was the direct result of a hazard that the employer could have reasonably prevented.

Workers' Compensation Laws[17]   Because the liability system requires that the burden of proof rests on the person claiming the damages, and because of the tenuous link between cause and effect due to the lengthy lags between exposure to a health hazard and the overt appearance of the symptoms, most states have passed workers' compensation laws. The major feature of all the state laws is that the employer provides a guaranteed payment for injuries regardless of who is at fault in exchange for immunity from prosecution from the workers for the full cost of accidents, although there are exceptions which vary from state to state. The level of the benefit payments is usually established by the state government, and the payments are made from the insurance premiums collected from employers — they may pay such payments to a private insurance company or to a state-operated insurance fund, or they may establish an insurance plan of their own. The worker's compensation laws, a compulsory insurance scheme in fact, is in effect similar to the no-fault auto insurance systems, which are now common in many states.

These compensation laws are far from being perfect. Thirty-two of the fifty states limit the weekly compensation payment to 60 percent of the weekly wages in cases of partial disability due to accident or ill health. Moreover, since the premiums employers are required to pay the system are in many cases not

[17]For an interesting discussion of this topic, see James Robert Chelius, *Workplace Safety and Health: The Role of Workers Compensation,* American Enterprise Institute for Public Policy Research, Washington, D.C., 1977.

related to the prior injury rate experience (merit rating), these laws may not exert strong pressure on employers to reduce the risk of injury to the fullest extent. Despite these defects, as Cornell et al. note, ''workmen's compensation, by lowering compensation limits, avoids the relatively high costs of operating the civil liability system, and by lowering the standard of proof, protects more people against capricious loss of income.''[18]

Insurance Systems

Another method of dealing with damages arising out of work-related accidents and health hazards is via the mechanism of the insurance fund. At a small cost (the insurance premium), an insurance fund enables a large group of people to cover an occasional large financial loss. How is such a premium determined? If the probability of sustaining a particular injury and the damage that results therefrom are known, the premium is simply the probability times the damage. Thus, if the probability of an electric saw cutting a human limb is 0.00001 and if the value of the lost limb is placed at $10 million, the expected premium would be $100 a year. If a large number of workers put this amount in the fund, and assuming that the probabilities of accidents are independent, the fund will have enough money to pay the damage.

The rub in the above insurance principle is of course that one can estimate the probabilities of accident or health injury reasonably accurately. But estimation of probabilities, say, of a mishap at a nuclear plant or a young person contracting asbestosis is not easy, to say the least. This is why the insurance principle, although used successfully in life insurance in general, is not practicable in the area of occupational safety and health.[19]

16.7 WHAT CAN THE REGULATORS DO?

Now that we have examined the pros and cons of the market model as well as the alternatives to it, what can the government do? The least interventionist approach is to undertake research in industrial accidents and diseases, either directly or by supporting private research, and simply to announce the information to the public as well as to the various interested parties, such as employers, their trade associations, and workers and their unions, and let them decide how to use the information. But knowing the reality, this approach may not lead to a socially desirable level of accident or health hazard prevention. The realistic alternative seems to be to strengthen the workers' compensation laws by imposing some type of injury tax on the errant employer — whatever money is awarded by Workers' Compensation, the employer pays an additional amount,

---

[18]Cornell et al., p. 475.

[19]For a highly analytical discussion about the inadequacy of the insurance principle in evaluating life and limb, see E. J. Mishan, ''Evaluation of Life and Limb: A Theoretical Discussion,'' in his *Economic Efficiency and Social Welfare: Selected Essays on Fundamental Aspects of the Economic Theory of Social Welfare*, G. Allen, London, 1981, ch. 9.

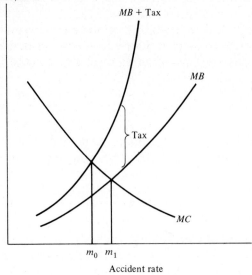

$ Benefits/costs

$MB + \text{Tax}$

MB

Tax

MC

m_0 m_1

Accident rate

FIGURE 16.4
Optimal accident rate with and
without injury tax.

which is some percentage of the award. Progression could be built into such a tax in the manner of the income tax.[20] To see the consequences of the injury tax rate, consider Figure 16.4.

This graph reproduces Figure 16.3 and adds to it the curve $MB + \text{tax}$ — the difference between this curve and the MB curve represents the injury tax rate schedule (it could be made still steeper to reflect steeper penalties). As the figure shows, the optimum accident rate is now reduced from m_1 to m_0: There is a definite incentive for the firm to reduce the accident rate to m_0, for between

[20]For details, see Robert Smith, op. cit., pp. 78–83.

TABLE 16.1
ESTIMATED REDUCTION IN THE MANUFACTURING INJURY
RATE BY SELECTED INJURY FINES

	Estimated reduction in injury rate*	
Fine per injury	Low estimate	High estimate
$ 500	0.34 (2.2%)†	0.48 (3.2%)
1000	0.67 (4.4%)	0.95 (6.2%)
2000	1.34 (8.8%)	1.90 (12.5%)
4000	2.68 (17.6%)	3.80 (25.0%)

*The injury rate is the lost-workday injuries per million worker-hours.
†The 1970 average manufacturing injury rate was 15.2. The figures in parentheses reflect percentage reduction from this figure.
Source: Robert S. Smith, *The Occupational Safety and Health Act: Its Goals and Its Achievements,* American Enterprise Institute for Public Policy Research, Washington, D.C., 1976, table 6, p. 80.

m_1 and m_0 the marginal cost of accident prevention is smaller than the injury tax.

Will the employer react in the manner predicted by the above figure? The empirical research of Robert Smith tends to support the hypothesis that injury tax is conducive to improved safety in the workplace. Smith's statistical results are given in Table 16.1.

The notion of injury tax, although endorsed by economists, has not yet found its way into the workers' compensation systems probably because of the practical problems involved in devising an appropriate injury tax rate schedule. But it should not be difficult to do so, for automobile insurance companies have developed merit insurance premium schedules that are based on prior accident record of the insured.

16.8   WHAT DO THE REGULATORS DO?

In practice, at least in the area of occupational safety and health, the regulators (OSHA) did not choose any of the options discussed in the preceding two sections. Instead, OSHA resorted to the standards approach, setting specification rather than performance standards. In short, OSHA chose a purely engineering approach to health and safety in the workplace, although the enabling legislation did not specifically authorize it to do so.

Why did OSHA choose this approach? One reason is simplicity – once an engineering standard is announced, all that the agency has to do is monitor it. Robert Smith gives two additional reasons. The legislators probably thought that in the safety and health field injury rates would not be responsive to the other methods discussed earlier, perhaps believing that the health and safety market is unlike other markets. Second, specification standards are meant to prohibit the hazards that cause injury, whereas the other approaches would seem to tolerate the presence of injury or illness.[21]

Can a strong case be made for the standards approach? Cornell et al. argue that standards can be efficient in two situations, namely, "when decisions are numerous and information complex, the savings in centralized information processing may be offset by the loss in efficiency that results if prevention is not based on informed, individual market decisions. Second, if the nature of a hazard is uncertain, insurance and the liability system can fail so badly that standards – if kept up to date – may be desirable.[22]

On the basis of these twin criteria, most people prefer the standards approach in the health area. Their application to the safety area, however, may be questionable, save in the area of nuclear power generation, for the following reasons:[23] First, the standards approach is based on a slow-moving process; as noted, a proposed standard has to go through a seven-step procedure before

---

[21]In his empirical work James Chelius found that higher workers' compensation benefits were not associated with lower injury rates. As a matter of fact, there was a positive correlation between the two. See his work, op. cit., p. 46.

[22]Cornell et al., p. 477.

[23]See Smith, op. cit.

it can be adopted. Secondly, because of the protracted nature of establishing standards, they may not reflect the latest available technology. Third, writing precise standards specifications which consider all relevant hazards of a process is a well-nigh impossible task. Fourth, and very important, standards set are not necessarily cost-conscious; that is, they do not necessarily reflect the most economical way of reducing a hazard. For example, as we will show later, OSHA engineering standards concerning noise abatement in the workplace are much more expensive than simple personal protective devices such as earmuffs. Likewise, the requirement that lights at a construction site carry wire guards is more expensive than coating the bulbs with a plastic "skin" which would contain the glass should it be broken. This is why, as we have remarked many times, where feasible it is desirable to resort to performance over specification standards. Finally, even the best established standards (in the cost-effectiveness sense) go awry if proper enforcement and compliance procedures are not established; the OSHA staff of some 500 inspectors is not capable of enforcing even the hastily adopted consensus standards.

Since OSHA has chosen the (specification) standards approach, the question of its adopting the alternatives discussed earlier is now academic. What is open for discussion now is whether the chosen standards can or should be cost-benefit-justified, that is, "Whether the increases in human welfare (the benefits) which arises from compliance with a particular standard is larger than the human welfare foregone because resources which could be used for other goods and services are devoted instead to increased safety and health (the costs)."[24]

Now one may object to cost-benefit analysis in the areas of health and safety. How, the argument goes, can we talk about costs when questions of death or permanent injury are involved? But talk we must, for none of us would be willing to bet all our resources to save life or limb. A moment's reflection will convince us that in our day-to-day behavior we take actions that are not strictly in our best interest, for example, smoking, taking drugs, driving without a seat belt, eating fatty foods, and so on. All these are reflections of the fact that we do not want to go beyond certain limits to protect life from injury or death.[25] All that a cost-benefit analysis calls for is the setting of (broad) limits to the benefits and the comparison of those benefits with the costs. On balance, if the net benefit (i.e., benefits minus costs) is positive, one may opt for that program. How one goes about this exercise can be learned from case studies, a few of which are discussed in the following section.

Should Congress legislate that any standard promulgated by any regulatory agency be subjected to cost-benefit analysis? The executive branch seems to think so, since the IIS requires all executive branch agencies (except the independent agencies and commissions) to provide estimates of the benefits as well as the costs of the regulations they propose. The Occupational Safety and Health Review Commission (OSHRC), an independent agency reviewing OSHA

---

[24]Ibid., p. 34.
[25]Or as Mishan would say, "Only the dead opt out of all risk." (Mishan, op. cit., p. 92.)

standards, thinks, too, that the economic feasibility of a standard should be considered an important desideratum in considering its appropriateness. If Congress goes along, it will be a clear signal to the regulatory agencies that, barring exceptional circumstances, economic feasibility of a standard must be considered as important (if not more) as its technical feasibility. This will avoid unnecessary and costly litigation, as the case studies will soon reveal.

16.9 COST-BENEFIT ANALYSIS: CASE STUDIES

OSHA Noise Standards

Recognizing the cause and effect relationship between workplace noise and hearing loss, OSHA in 1972 proposed an interim noise standard of 90 decibels (90 dBA) in an average working day of 8 hours (a noisy New York subway has a 90-dBA level), with an upper limit of 140 dBA any time.[26] A worker is not to be exposed to more than 100 dBA in any 2-hour period and 95 dBA in any 4-hour period. This was an interim standard because NIOSH had proposed a permanent standard of 85 dBA, with the maximum not to exceed 115 dBA. A reduction from 90 decibels to 85 decibels may not sound like much but a noise level of 85 dBA has less than half the energy and it sounds only 75 percent as loud to the ear as the noise of 90 dBA; at 85 dBA workers standing a yard apart can converse without shouting.

OSHA hired the noise consulting firm of Bolt Beranek and Newman Inc., to estimate the costs of compliance with the 90- and 85-dBA standards; the firm was not specifically asked to estimate the benefits.[27] The consultants considered only direct costs such as the costs of machine enclosure, mufflers, quieter parts, building treatment, and personal enclosures. Indirect costs such as audiometric testing, lost production time during setup, decreased productivity resulting from machine enclosure, and the enforcement costs to achieve complete compliance were not taken into account. The direct costs were initially estimated at $31.6 billion (85-dBA standard) and $13.5 billion (90-dBA standard). But within a year these estimates were revised down to $18.5 billion (85 dBA) and $10.5 billion (90 dBA) for the manufacturing firms through engineering standards alone. It may be added that these cost estimates represent only the one-time cost of capital equipment designed to reduce noise level; they do not include the annual costs of monitoring and record keeping. If estimates of these costs had been made, the final cost figures would have been much higher.

Since the consulting firm was not asked to estimate the benefits of the proposed standards, we have no way of comparing the costs against the benefits. There is no doubt that the benefits associated with noise reduction are real, although they are difficult to gauge quantitatively. Thus, apart from its beneficial

---

[26]A *decibel* is a unit of intensity of sound. It is also a unit used to compare two voltages or currents.

[27]Being an executive brancy agency, OSHA was required to prepare an IIS. It is not known why the consultants were not required to estimate the benefits.

effect on hearing, noise reduction leads to a more pleasant working environment in that it makes personal communication easier; the sheer presence of noise is irritating to most people. There are other negative spillover effects of noise, too. Property values, for instance, near airports are generally lower than in quieter places. The same is true about prices of houses located near factories, mills, and busy highways.

Unfortunately, we have little knowledge about the monetary value of these benefits. The best we have are some educated guesses. The consulting firm in its 1974 study had noted that about 700,000 workers could benefit from a saving of hearing loss from the 90-dBA standard and about 1,300,000 from the 85-dBA standard. Using this figure and the amount of compensation for hearing loss awarded by the New York state workers' compensation of between $2000 to $3000 per person (the only state to award such compensation), Gramlich estimates the benefit of the 90-dBA standard at between $1.4 to $2.1 billion and between $2.6 and $3.9 billion for the 85-dBA standard. Compared with these benefits, the estimated costs of $10.5 billion or $18.5 billion are much higher.

Another indirect estimate of the benefits can be judged from the property value differential due to noise. Robert Smith, after evaluating the several studies made by various authors of the effect of noise on property values, concluded that people would be willing to pay about $130 to reduce noise by one decibel.[28] From this, Gramlich estimates that if the manufacturing sector as a whole were to reduce the noise level to the 90-dBA level, it would cost about $6 billion and an additional $6 billion for the 85-dBA standard.

Collecting all these estimates, the picture that emerges is as shown in Table 16.2. One can conclude that the net benefit of the proposed standard appears negative. Therefore, on the test of economic feasibility, one can make a tentative argument against the proposed engineering standards, tentative because in the area of cost-benefit analysis, especially in the field of social regulation, one can never be sure about the estimates on both sides of the ledger.

One serious objection to the OSHA noise standard is that the agency did not consider alternatives to the engineering standards. Thus, use of personal protective devices such as earplugs and earmuffs, which are comparatively inexpensive, were not seriously considered on the ground that the use of earplugs is unhygenic and that it inhibits communication between workers, which might itself lead to accidents. Then there is the problem of enforcement. Robert Smith reports that in 1968 Employers Insurance of Wausau surveyed 1148 plants which had issued ear protectors and found that only a fifth of the plants maintained the program for longer than 6 months because of the difficulties of enforcement. The situation is very much similar to that of driving without a seat belt: Despite the hazards of driving without the seat belt, many drivers simply don't bother to wear them. One inference that can be drawn is that since many workers are not willing to wear earplugs, the inconvenience of wearing them (the cost) must outweigh the benefits. Apparently, workers are willing to take a change on hearing loss because the loss would probably be marginal; they

[28]See Smith, op. cit., pp. 47–49, for a summary of the various studies.

TABLE 16.2
ESTIMATES OF COSTS AND BENEFITS OF OSHA NOISE STANDARDS (Billions of Dollars)

	Moving to 90-decibel from present system	Moving to 85-decibel from 90-decibel standard
Cost	$13.5*	$18.1*
Benefits		
Home value inference	6.0	6.0
Hearing loss inference	2.1 (high estimate)	3.9 (high estimate)
Net cost		
Home value	7.5	12.1
Hearing loss	11.4	14.2

*These estimates are slightly different from those given in the text.
Source: Edward M. Gramlich, *Benefit-Cost Analysis of Government Programs*, Prentice-Hall, Englewood Cliffs, N.J., 1981, p. 217.

would not hear, say, faint voices. If this is the case, the compulsory engineering standards proposed by OSHA are probably giving employees "undue" protection against hearing loss.

Challenges to OSHA's Noise Standard: The Continental Can Case[29]   The proposed OSHA noise standard did not go unchallenged. In an appeal to the Occupational Safety and Health Review Commmission (OSHRC), the Continental Can Company contended that complying with the 90-dBA standard in three of its plants would require the company to spend $1.23 million on development cost, $32 million on installation, and $175,000 annually on maintenance, whereas it already had a program in place that cost only $100,000 a year and which was generally considered effective. In August 1974 the OSHRC ruled in favor of Continental Can. In the commission's opinion:[30]

[OSHA's noise standard] only requires the implementation of those engineering controls which are economically, as well as technically, feasible. . . .

In determining whether controls are economically feasible, all the relevant cost and benefit factors must be weighed.

In 1978 Continental Can won another victory, this time in the U.S. District Court for Southern Illinois; they stopped OSHA from enforcing its noise standard on plants not covered by the 1974 OSHRC decision on the ground that the standard was economically infeasible.

OSHA Standards on Inorganic Lead

To control occupational exposure to inorganic lead, a carcinogen, OSHA proposed to limit lead content in workplace air to no more than 100 micrograms

---

[29]The following discussion is based on James C. Miller III and Thomas F. Walton, "Protecting Workers' Hearing: An Economic Test for OSHA's Initiatives," *Regulation,* September–October 1980, pp. 31–37. This paper also discusses several other cases on OSHA's noise standards.
[30]Quoted by Miller and Walton, Ibid., p. 33.

per cubic meter during an 8-hour working day. Although health risk occurs largely through the lead entering the body in the blood, the proposed standard involved measuring the level of lead in the air. The primary method of achieving the goal was through engineering standards, namely, by ventilation.

OSHA hired the firm of D. B. Associates, Inc., to do an economic assessment of the proposed standard in a selected number of industries, namely, primary smelting, secondary smelting, nonindustrial storage batteries, and brass and bronze foundaries. The consultants estimated the cost of the proposed engineering standards at around $613 million every 10 years plus annual operating, monitoring, and maintenance costs of more than $115 million.

Do the benefits exceed the costs? Since no direct estimates of the benefits are available, it is hard to answer this question. One can see if there are alternatives which are less expensive, especially in view of the consultants' warning that the estimated costs would create economic hardship for smaller firms. As noted, atmospheric lead levels are not necessarily a good indicator of likely injury to workers from increased blood lead. For example, workers who tap cigarettes on lead-containing benches or machines can develop high blood lead levels even when the level of air lead is low. Likewise, workers living in cities with some degree of lead in the water supply might develop dangerous lead blood levels even when workplace lead level is extremely low. In short, a low level of lead in the air is no guarantee of a low amount of lead in the blood. Hence the expensive engineering controls may not be justifiable. Changes in workplace practices, worker rotation, or the use of respirators which inhibit lead inhalation may accomplish the objective more cheaply.

Yet, OSHA chose to monitor the lead level in the air via the expensive engineering standards simply because that was easier than monitoring the lead level in the blood, which does involve some invasion of privacy of the workers. Whether this consideration alone justifies the enormous costs involved is highly questionable.

The Benzene Case[31]

Benzene is a colorless liquid used in the manufacturing of motor fuel, rubber products, pesticides, and a host of other chemical components. It evaporates rapidly and causes harmful vapors which, at high level of exposure, lead to lukemia, a blood cancer.

OSHA's general attitude toward such substances has been governed by the philosophy that once a substance is found to cause cancer, exposure limits should be reduced to the lowest feasible level without ruining the industries involved. In May 1977 OSHA proposed a permanent benzene standard that provided a reduction in airborne benzene exposure from 10 to 1 parts per million (ppm). To achieve the 1-ppm standard, OSHA established rules relating to dermal and eye contact, exposure monitoring, medical surveillance, methods of

[31]Correctly known as the case of *American Petroleum Institute v. OSHA,* see fn. 32.

compliance, labeling, and record keeping. It was estimated that these measures would cost the concerned industries about $500 million. There were no explicit estimates of the benefits. After hearings on the proposed standard, OSHA made it permanent in February 1978.

The American Petroleum Institute asked a U.S. court of appeals to review the proposed standard on the ground that it was not necessary or appropriate to provide safe or healthful employment. Supporting the petitioner, the court set aside the 1-ppm standard because OSHA had not adduced substantial evidence to show that measurable benefits would be achieved by the standard to justify incurring the half-billion dollar cost. In its decision the court was guided by *Aqua Slide 'N' Dive Corporation v. Consumer Product Safety Commission,* 569 F.2d 831 (5th Cir. 1978), which had held that although the regulatory agency (CPSC here) does not have to conduct an elaborate cost-benefit analysis, it does have to determine whether the benefits expected from the standard bear a reasonable relationship to the costs imposed by the standard. In the court's view, OSHA had failed to show the benefits to balance the costs. This failure ''makes it impossible to assess the reasonableness of the relationship between expected costs and benefits. This failure means that the required support is lacking to show reasonable necessity for the standard promulgated.''[32]

The lower court's decision reached the Supreme Court in the case of *Industrial Union Department, AFL-CIO v. American Petroleum Institute.* Three major issues were involved in the appeal:[33] (1) Whether the OSHA Act of 1970 requires OSHA to consider the cost-benefit of its standards (note: the IIS requires it, but that is not mandated by Congress); (2) whether, before issuing a toxic standard, OSHA must establish that a significant risk of material health impairment warrants the issuance of the standard; and (3) assuming an affirmative answer to (2), whether OSHA may establish the standard on the general presumption that there is reliably no safe exposure level for carcinogens.

Unfortunately, on none of these questions did the Supreme Court provide catagorical answers. On the question of cost-benefit analysis, the vote was 4 against 1 yes and 4 abstentions. On the second issue, the vote was 4 yes, 4 no, 1 not voting; on the third issue, the voting was 4 yes, 3 no, 1 maybe, and 1 absention. Thus, the major issues remained unresolved. But the situation changed on the important question of cost-benefit analysis in the *Cotton Dust* case, as the following discussion will show.

The Cotton Dust Case[34]

Cotton dust is linked to brown lungs or byssinosis, a disabling respiratory ailment. In 1978 OSHA set the level of 200 micrograms of cotton dust as the exposure for workers in cotton mills. This standard was to be achieved by engineer-

[32]*American Petroleum Institute v. OSHA* (5th Cir. Oct. 5, 1978), p. 93.
[33]The following discussion is based on Antonin Scalia, ''A Note on the Benzene Case,'' *Regulation,* July–August 1980.
[34]*American Textile Manufacturers' Institute v. Donovan* (no. 79-1429)

ing controls (ventilation equipment) rather than by performance standards (such as byssinosis-reduction quotas). But the industry immediately challenged the standard on the ground that the compliance costs necessitated by the standard were not justified by the health benefits to the textile workers: The IIS prepared for OSHA by a consulting firm estimated the annualized compliance cost of the standard at a staggering $808 million. This industry argument, unlike in the *Benzene* case, was not accepted by the Supreme Court. In *American Textile Manufacturers' Institute v. Donovan* the Court ruled that OSHA must protect workers from exposure to toxic substances to the greatest extent feasible, without regard to balance between costs and benefits, thus rejecting not only the decision in the *Benzene* case but also knocking down the whole edifice of cost-benefit analysis. Writing for the majority, Justice Brennen said that when Congress passed the act in 1970, it chose to place preeminent value on assuring employees a safe and healthful working environment. Recalling the goal of the act "to assure so far as possible every working man and woman in the nation safe and healthful working conditions," he said that the key phrase in the act was "to the extent feasible." According to Webster's, he went on to say, "feasible" means "capable of being done, expected or effected." Thus cost-benefit analysis is not required by the statute because feasibility is. Commenting further he said:

> The legislative history demonstrates conclusively that Congress was fully aware that the act would impose real and substantial costs of compliance on industry and believed that such costs were part of the costs of doing business. Congress placed pre-eminent value on assuring employees a safe and healthful working environment, limited only by the feasibility of achieving such an environment. . . . The judicial function does not extend to substantive revision of regulatory policy. That function lies elsewhere — in Congressional and excutive oversight of amendatory legislation.[35]

In dissenting from the majority, Justice Rehnquist commented that the phrase "to the extent feasible" reflected a fundamental disagreement in Congress. In his view, Congress unconstitutionally delegated to the executive branch (i.e., OSHA) the authority to make "hard policy choices," in that phrase.

Inorganic Arsenic in the Workplace[36]

In January 1975 OSHA proposed to reduce the permissible level of arsenic in the workplace from 0.5 milligrams of arsenic per cubic feet (0.5 mg As/m^3) to 0.004 mg As/m^3 during an 8-hour working day. Workplace arsenic is linked to respiratory cancer, which is fatal in 95 percent of cases. To achieve the new standard, smelters, herbicide producers, and others were required to install engineering controls.

[35] *The New York Times*, June 18, 1981, p. A1.
[36] The following details are based on Diane R. Levine, "Exposure to Inorganic Arsenic in the Workplace," in James C. Miller III and Bruce Yandle (eds.), *Benefit-Cost Analysis of Social Regulation: Case Studies from the Council on Wage and Price Stability*, American Enterprise Institute for Public Policy Research, Washington, D.C., 1979, ch. 3.

By OSHA estimates, the initial capital cost of the engineering controls was expected to be around $273 million, with annual operating and maintenance costs of $56 million. If the life of capital equipment is estimated at 8 years, and assuming a rate of return of 12 percent per annum, the total annual costs of implementing the new standard would be $111 million. These costs would be augmented by the wage cost of 350 to 380 additional workers that would be required to maintain current levels of output.

To these direct costs of implementing the standard, one must add some indirect costs. Since the industries affected by the standard would try to pass on the increased costs to consumers, the prices of their products would increase. This would generally lead to a reduction in the sales of these products, which would ultimately reduce employment in these industries. By OSHA estimates, nationwide some 3000 to 3700 workers would lose jobs in the affected industries. The earnings loss of these workers is the indirect cost that must be added to the direct cost given previously. OSHA, however, does not provide any monetary figures of the earnings loss.

In any case, the annual cost of the said standard will be much in excess of $111 million. As a matter of fact, the estimated $111 million is itself an underestimation since the estimates were obtained from only a limited number of plants in the affected industries.

To assess the benefits, what is needed, as Levine points out, are "the size of the population at risk, the excess mortality and morbidity experienced by this population, and a monetary measure of life and health."[37] But instead of following this methodology, OSHA relied on five epidemiological studies of very small populations exposed to arsenic levels far in excess of the current 0.5-milligram standard, namely, from 1 to 5.0 milligrams per cubic meter of air. From these studies OSHA concluded that the incidence rate of respiratory cancer among the arsenic-exposed population was likely to be two to ten times that of the general (nonexposed) population. By OSHA's analysis, the number of people exposed to arsenic levels in excess of the proposed standard is about 7400 each year, after allowing for the turnover rate. In the general population the incidence of respiratory cancer among males age 30 and older is about 160 cases per 100,000. Using the multiple of 2 to 10, this would suggest that the crude (unadjusted for age/sex) annual incidence of respiratory cancer for the exposed population is between 320 to 1600 per 100,000. Therefore, under these assumptions, the number of *excess* cases of respiratory cancer resulting from arsenic exposure would be between 12 and 106 annually.[38]

Now it was seen earlier that the annual cost of compliance of the proposed standard was estimated at $111 million. Using the figures of 12 and 106 lives saved, the cost per additional life saved is between $9 million ($111/12) and $1 million ($111/106). Viewed against these "facts," the question is whether society views the value of a life saved in excess of $1 or $9 million. This is a difficult

[37]Ibid., p. 24.
[38]These figures are derived as follows: $(320 - 160) \times 7400/100,000 \doteq 12$ and $(1600 - 160) \times 7400/100,000 \doteq 106$.

TABLE 16.3
ESTIMATED COST OF ALTERNATIVE ARSENIC EXPOSURE STANDARDS
(Millions of Dollars)

Standard		Initial cost	Annual operating cost	Annualized costs
0.1	mg As/m^3	40	10.7	18.4
0.05	mg As/m^3	149	26.3	55.4
0.004	mg As/m^3	273	56.0	111.0

Source: Dianne R. Levine, "Exposure to Inorganic Arsenic in the Workplace," in James C. Miller III and Bruce Yandle (eds.), *Benefit-cost Analyses of Social Regulation, Case Studies from the Council on Wage and Price Stability,* American Enterprise Institute for Public Policy Research, Washington, D.C., 1979, p. 28. (These estimates are made by Arthur Young and Company for OSHA.)

question to answer, what with all the noneconomic value judgments involved.[39] Perhaps there are alternatives which are less expensive. Unfortunately, OSHA did not consider respirators, protective garments, and revised work rules as alternatives to the strict engineering standards. But if OSHA does not want to consider these alternatives, it could at least rethink its proposed standard, because it has not yet been conclusively established that the risk of cancer from arsenic exposure in 1- to 5-milligram range is the same as that in the 0.004- to 0.5-milligram range.[40] Table 16.3 gives some interesting data on cost estimates associated with various arsenic exposure levels.

As the table shows, the annualized cost of the various arsenic standards increases in a nonlinear fashion. Thus, to reduce arsenic by 50 percent from the level 0.1 milligram to 0.05 milligram, the incremental cost goes up by more than 200 percent, but to reduce it by 95 percent from 0.1 milligram to 0.004 milligram, the incremental cost goes up by more than 500 percent. OSHA seems to have realized that its proposed reduction to the 0.004 level was not quite realistic. Hence, ultimately it adopted the standard of 0.01 milligram of arsenic per cubic meter of air, still considerably lower than the current 0.5-milligram standard.

16.10 ACCOMPLISHMENTS OF OSHA

Paul W. MacAvoy contends that the OSHA regulations are not expected to lead to significant and widespread reduction in worker accident rates because "OSHA's activities have been narrowly limited to regulating plant and equipment specifications when worker training, supervision, incentives and plant routine all play an important role in accident prevention as well."[41] There seems to

[39]For an excellent discussion of the problem, see Mishan, op. cit.

[40]In studies of this type there is often the danger of extrapolating the results based on a very high dose of a particular chemical to the levels commonly found in practice. A sufficiently high dosage of milk or water can kill a human being although in moderate amounts these products are highly beneficial, even essential.

[41]Paul W. MacAvoy, *The Regulated Industries and the Economy,* Norton, New York, 1979, pp. 94–95.

be some empirical support for MacAvoy's contention. In his study of the impact of the state agencies enforcing OSHA equipment standards, Paul Sands found that regardless of the severity of enforcement, the states' regulatory activities had little discernible impact on injuries.[42] But this could, as MacAvoy suggests, be due to the generally low level of state operations – the states spent no more than one dollar per year per worker on supervision and enforcement of the control program.

To assess the effect of OSHA's inspections on injury rates, Aldona Di Pietro examined the accident record in companies that had and that had not been inspected by OSHA and found that there was no statistically observable difference in accident rates.[43] As a matter of fact, in some cases there was a positive assoication between inspection and accident rates! In a more detailed study of OSHA-type regulation in California, John Mendeloff found that lost-workday injury rate was not significantly reduced after regulation was instituted in the state.[44]

All these studies were made when OSHA was fairly young. Perhaps more recent data may show OSHA to be more effective. But perhaps not, because, as MacAvoy notes, emphasis on equipment control alone is not enough; one must consider the totality of the factors that cause accidents.

16.11 SUMMARY AND CONCLUSIONS

Concerned with the increasing workplace injury rate in the 1960s, Congress passed the Occupational Safety and Health Act of 1970 to "assure so far as possible every working man and woman in the nation safe and healthful working conditions." After briefly reviewing the history behind the act, its goal, its scope, and its working, we examined in some depth the economic rationale behind the act. It was shown that the free market can provide an optimal level of health and safety in the workplace by making appropriate adjustments in the wages paid the workers in risky jobs. But for this result to occur, the assumptions of the market model must hold true in practice. Alas, this is not the case. Lack of perfect knowledge, lack of mobility, divergence between private and social costs and equity considerations make the results predicted by the market model difficult, it not impossible, to achieve in practice. Hence a case can be made for government intervention in the marketplace.

But government intervention in the marketplace need not be direct. We considered several alternatives, such as tort laws, liability compensation systems, insurance systems, and some type of injury tax rate. We examined the pros and

---

[42]Paul E. Sands, "How Effective Is Safety Regulation?" *Journal of Law and Economics,* April 1968, pp. 165–179.

[43]Aldona DiPietro, "An Analysis of the OSHA Inspection Program in Manufacturing Industries, 1972–1973" Draft Technical Analysis Paper, U.S. Department of Labor, August 1976.

[44]John Mendeloff, "An Evaluation of the OSHA Program's Effect on Workplace Injury Rates: Evidence from California through 1974," report prepared for the U.S. Department of Labor, July 1976.

cons of each alternative and showed that workers' compensation systems modified by the injury tax rate approach can give workers a reasonably adequate level of health and safety in the workplace.

In practice, however, the government chose to intervene in the market place directly via OSHA by mandating specification or engineering standards to alleviate some of the workplace practices. The case studies of OSHA standards on noise, inorganic lead, benzene, cotton dust, and inorganic arsenic showed the nature of the engineering standards prescribed as well as some of their problems. On the basis of cost-benefit analysis, it was shown that in most cases it was questionable whether the claimed benefits exceeded the estimated costs. We also pointed out that very often OSHA did not consider relatively inexpensive alternatives. We also considered the legal view of some of the OSHA standards and found that this view was not always consistent, especially on the role of cost-benefit analysis, in evaluating the prescribed standards. But this is not surprising because Congress did not clearly spell out when it passed OSHA whether economic feasibility (cost-benefit) should be considered as important as technical feasibility in evaluating a proposed standard.

In evaluating OSHA's accomplishments, we discovered that on the basis of the available empirical evidence it is not clear whether OSHA had made any significant dent in workplace injuries. But this is perhaps not surprising, for the engineering standards alone do not necessarily address the real causes behind workplace injuries: worker training, supervision, incentives, and plant routine are perhaps more important than the purely engineering-type standards and should receive more attention from OSHA.

QUESTIONS

16-1 Is the goal of near-absolute safety or health in the workplace socially justifiable? Why or why not? Does OSHA call for such a goal?

16-2 If the answer to the preceding question is negative, how much health and safety should an employer provide? Discuss clearly your criterion or criteria.

16-3 "The decision rule which should guide safety and health policies is therefore exactly the same as the one that is used to decide on how many color television sets and pounds of beef should be produced: are the people who derive benefits from the product willing to pay for it? If not, they are signaling that they would rather spend their income on other things—that the product in question is not worth the cost to them." (Robert S. Smith, *The Occupational Safety and Health Act: Its Goals and Its Achievements,* American Enterprise Institute, Washington, D.C., 1976, p. 24.) Do you agree with the above decision rule? Why or why not? What alternative(s) would you suggest?

16-4 Noting the difference between cost-benefit and cost-effectiveness analysis, which do you think is more appropriate in the field of health and safety? Why?

16-5 "The enormity of the task and the great number of other important social goals and objectives that are competing for our scarce resources require that we as a society pursue our health and safety goals through cost-effective and equitable procedures." [John F. Morall III, "OSHA and U.S. Industry," in Robert F. Lanzillotti, (ed.), *Economic Effects of Government-Mandated Costs*, Public Policy Research Center, University of Florida Press, Gainesville, 1978, p. 61.] Do you agree with Morall's view? If so, can you say that OSHA has followed this principle? You may use the case studies in the text to answer the question.

16-6 "Under the injury tax, firms would compete among themselves to provide safe working conditions and would have incentives not only to modify their equipment and working practices but to provide incentives for their workers to adopt safe practices and use care themselves." (Morall III, op. cit., p. 65.) Do you agree? Explain your answer.

16-7 "If individuals with accurate information about risks show little concern about them, and if we are willing to let people decide important personal issues for themselves, then government bureaucracies (like OSHA) are not justified in pronouncing workers irrational and (by inflating benefits) force more safety upon them than they would voluntarily choose." (Smith, op. cit., p. 57). Do you agree with Smith's views? Why or why not? Do you think that OSHA is requiring more safety and health standards than workers actually need? How would you know?

16-8 In his study of injury rate, Smith obtained the following regression results for the period 1948–1969:

$$I = 24.24 + 0.602A + 0.556H + 0.071C - 16.53W - 0.650T$$
$$ (0.318) \quad (0.247) \quad (0.035) \quad (4.50) \quad (0.229)$$

where I = injury rate frequency in manufacturing
A = the manufacturing accession rate (net new hires),
H = average overtime hours worked per week
C = plant capacity utilization rate
W = wage rate
T = time trend

and where the figures in parentheses are the estimated standard errors. What do these results suggest? Why is the wage coefficient negative?

16-9 Consider the *Cotton Dust* case discussed in the chapter. Do you concur with the majority decision? Was Justice Rehnquist correct in saying that Congress unconstitutionally delegated to the executive branch the authority to make "hard policy choices" by the phrase "to the extent feasible"?

16-10 Given the goals of OSHA and the performance of OSHA reflected in the various case studies and other studies mentioned in the chapter, what can you say about the overall performance of OSHA? Be precise.

16-11 To improve the working of OSHA James C. Miller III (chairperson of the Federal Trade Commission) recommends that, "To the extent possible, change OSHA's primary role from the setting and enforcing of safety and health standards to one of approving or, under extraordinary circumstances, modifying the standards worked out between labor and management. OSHA's function should be consultation and oversight, not command and control." (James C. Miller, "Occupational Safety and Health Administration," *Regulation,* November–December 1980, p. 23.) What problems do you foresee if this suggestion is implemented?

17

THE EPA AND ENVIRONMENTAL POLLUTION CONTROL

Although one hears and reads a lot these days about the deteriorating quality of the nation's physical environment, pollution control as a national issue is of comparatively recent origin. President Eisenhower's Commission on National Goals, in its 1960 report, *Goals for Americans,* did not even mention pollution control among the fifteen major goals it listed for national concern and debate. But since then pollution control has become such a heated topic of public debate that no political candidate, regardless of his or her party, can pay lip service to it. The far-reaching Clean Air Act of 1970, providing for a nationwide program of air pollution control, and the Federal Water Pollution Control Act of 1972 (now known as the Clean Water Act), providing for zero discharge of effluent into the nation's waterways by 1985, are clear indications how things have changed.

The primary purpose of this chapter is to explore the reasons behind the change in the nation's perception of the environmental pollution problem, from one of no concern or benign neglect, to that of compulsive obsession. More specifically, we discuss the following questions: What is the meaning of environmental pollution? What are the factors that cause pollution? Can the free market abate pollution, if not completely get rid of it? If the market cannot do the job, what are the alternatives and what are their relative merits and demerits? What is (are) the alternative(s) chosen by the government and why? What have been the effects of the chosen alternatives? And, in view of the regulatory experience thus far, what should be the rational public policy toward the pollution problem?

It is hoped that answers to these and related questions will help the reader to better appreciate the ongoing public debate about pollution control and to separate the real issues from the mere rhetorical ones.

17.1 THE NATURE OF ENVIRONMENTAL POLLUTION[1]

The term *environment* refers to natural resources such as the air mantle, water bodies, wilderness areas, large landscapes, complex ecological systems (e.g., the mangrove wetlands of Puerto Rico), electromagnetic spectrum, and earth's ozone layers. The term *pollution* literally means "destruction of purity."

Thus, when we talk about air pollution we mean that the inherent quality of the air is so destroyed or diluted by human (and animal) actions that it tends to increase the likelihood of a variety of diseases such as lung cancer, emphysema, tuberculosis, pneumonia, bronchitis, asthma, and even the common cold. For example, carbon monoxide (CO), a colorless and odorless gas formed by incomplete combustion of carbon or any carbonaceous material (including gasoline) in an internal combustion engine (e.g., the automobile), is highly poisonous; in high concentrations it is lethal. Ozone, formed the atmosphere from complex reactions involving sunlight, volatile organic compounds (e.g., those emitted from motor vehicles), and oxides of nitrogen, corrodes, cracks, and weakens materials such as automobile tires and electrical and telephone wires.

In the case of water pollution, the pathogens (disease-causing organisms; primarily bacteria and viruses) present in water bodies break down the organic wastes (or degradable residuals) from domestic sewage as well as industrial wastes from the chemical, food processing, pulp and paper, petroleum refining, and other industries into their component parts. In this process, the bacteria use up dissolved oxygen (DO) in the water. It is common knowledge that most forms of life in water are aerobic; that is, they require free oxygen for survival. Therefore, as the level of oxygen in the water falls, not only fish but eventually the aerobic bacteria themselves die, leaving the water "anaerobic" — the water becomes black, bubbly, and very fetid.[2] Incidentally, biochemical oxygen demand (BOD) is the quantity that measures the amount of dissolved oxygen that is depleted by a specified quantity of the organic waste in a given time (usually 5 days) at a standard temperature (usually 20 degrees Celsius). The degradable pollution content of various kinds of organic wastes can be commonly expressed in terms of the number of pounds of BOD they contain.

There is no question that the problems of environmental pollution, be it air or water, are serious.[3] For a long time it was assumed that the environment was a "free good," a good sufficiently plentiful to satisfy everyone's wants and hence costless. But with the growth of population; the immense increase in industrial production and energy conversion; the new types of exotic material inputs made available by modern physics and chemistry, with complex effects on the world's biological systems; and the increasing expectations of the ordi-

[1]For an overall excellent discussion of the pollution problem, see Allen V. Kneese, *Economics and the Environment,* Penguin, New York, 1977, and Allen V. Kneese and Charles L. Schultze, *Pollution, Prices and Public Policy,* Brookings, Washington, D.C., 1975. This chapter draws heavily from these books.

[2]For most fish, a DO level of 4 to 5 parts per million (ppm) is adequate for survival, but at a 2- to 3-ppm level only carp and other less desirable fish may survive.

[3]Besides air and water pollution, there is noise pollution and pollution due to accumulation of solid wastes such as automobile junkyards and hundreds of millions of tons of discarded bottles, cans, and other trash.

nary citizens that they are ''entitled'' to some minimum standard of cleanliness and safety, what was once perceived a ''free'' good has now become an ''economic'' good, a good which is scarce and hence commands a price. In a growing world this scarcity is bound to increase for two very important features of the environment, namely, the principle of conservation of mass and the common property problem.

The Principle of Conservation of Mass

This principle, one of the basic concepts of physics, states that matter is created or destroyed in the most minute amounts. As Kneese and Schultze note:

> Man uses the materials of nature in various ways — he eats and drinks them, heats them, burns them, extracts metals and chemical compounds from them, and combines them into manufactured goods — but he does not physically destroy them. He consumes the services or utilities that physical objects yield, but not the objects themselves. Materials come from nature, are used, and are returned (usually in different form) to the earth, the air, or the water as ''residuals'' with no loss in their mass.[4]

But, as they warn:

> The return of residuals to nature can damage the environment either because in the process of using original materials man has transformed them into something harmful (toxic chemicals, for example) and has concentrated them in unnatural ways (sewage from a city or a feedlot), or because otherwise harmless residuals react chemically with other substances or with each other in the air or water in a damaging way (as in the reaction of hydrocarbons from auto emissions with sunlight and oxides of nitrogen to form smog).[5]

That is, however, not the end of the story. When one tries to control one type of pollution, another type may emerge. For example, to prevent water pollution from becoming sewage sludge, one may burn the sludge. But that leads to air pollution. Therefore, pollution control is not a one-dimensional problem; one has to think about air, water, and other types of pollution simultaneously and decide upon the ''tolerable'' level of pollution — as we will see, the goal of 100 percent pure air or water is simply not economically feasible.

Common-Property Aspect of the Environment

A better environment is in the nature of a public or collective consumption good. Once it is supplied to one individual, it cannot be withheld from a great many others. Thus, if the air of New York City becomes cleaner, I as a resident

[4]Kneese and Schultze, op. cit., p. 4. The one exception is subatomic reaction, by which mass can be converted into energy.
[5]Ibid.

or worker in the city am entitled to its benefits whether I pay for the cleanup cost or not. That is, I can be a free rider. The free rider phenomenon, as we have already noted, means that no single individual can afford to pay the full cost of such public goods — why should I pay the cost knowing full well that there will be free riders who cannot be denied access to the clean air?

The problem here is that of common property resources. As noted in Chapter 2, common property resources "are those valuable natural assets which cannot or can only imperfectly, be reduced to private ownership."[6] It is very difficult, if not totally impossible, to assign property rights in the nation's air mantle or waterways (more on such rights in Section 17.3). As a result, it is very difficult to prevent people from overusing these resources since everybody's property is nobody's property. Why should a factory owner worry about the smoke her factory emits into the town's air or the effluent it discharges into its river if she regards these commonly held resources as cost-free? As a matter of fact, there is all the incentive in the world for her to exploit the "free" resources as extensively as she can, for she knows that if she doesn't do so, someone else is bound to do it.

Such a situation cannot last for too long if every producer or consumer regards the environment as a free good, since the waste-assimilating capacity of the environment is limited in view of the principle of conservation of mass. Sooner or later, means must be found to conserve the nation's scarce environmental resources, the clean water and clean air.

Ordinarily, the free market can do this job reasonably well for most scarce commodities: Given the demand for and the supply of a scarce resource, the market forces will establish a price (the equilibrium price) at which the quantity sold will be equal to the quantity demanded. But, as we have pointed out in Chapter 2, for the price system to work, the property rights in the scarce resource must be reasonably well-defined. In that case, the market will see that those who cannot or do not want to pay the market price will be denied the use of that resource. In other words, when property rights are well-defined, there will not be free riders.

Alas, that is not the case with common-pool resources, whose very basic feature is that property rights to them are difficult to define. Therefore, the market mechanism which works wonderfully for many a scarce good does not work for common-property resources, such as the environment. Actually, it is not that the price system does not work here. As Kneese and Schultze note:

> . . . it works with marvellous efficiency, but in the wrong direction. When the signals it sends out indicate that air and water are free goods, thousands of firms and millions of consumers bend their efforts to use these cheap resources. And so electric utilities dispose of the sulfur residuals from coal and oil not by scrubbing them from their stacks or by other expensive means, but by pouring them freely into the atmosphere. Paper mills use the rivers as free dumps for noxious chemicals. And consumers avoid

---

[6]Kneese, op. cit., p. 28.

the cost of eliminating hydrocarbon emissions from their automobiles by depositing them in the air.[7]

As a result of the "free" use of air and water as dumps for residuals, there arises the question of negative eternality and the associated problem of the divergence between private and social costs of production. As we discussed in Chapter 2, if the polluting factory in my town does not have to pay for my laundry bill or medical costs, its private cost of production is bound to be less than the social cost, which should include these indirect costs. Then, as Figure 2.2 shows, this results in price-output decisions that are not socially optimal — the negative externality-generating product is overproduced and underpriced. (Later we will show how this situation can be remedied by using appropriate incentive mechanisms; (see Section 17.3).

To sum up:

Clearly, the massive return of residuals to the common-property environmental resources confronts us with a severe problem. The problem arises primarily because the institutions of private property and exchange that we use for determining the value of resources and providing incentives for their efficient allocation cannot function for environmental resources. We thus face a large-scale, pervasive, and unfamiliar problem of collective action and collective management.[8]

Clearly, the government, as that collective agency, will have to play an important role in the provision of the public good, a clean environment. The government can do this in a variety of ways, as we will show in Section 17.3.

17.2 THE ECONOMICS OF POLLUTION CONTROL

Before we proceed to discuss the methods of pollution control, we must be clear about what should be society's overall attitude toward the pollution problem: Do we want 100 percent clean air or clean water or are we willing to live with something less than that? This is an important question because, regardless of the method chosen, pollution control is not costless — some of society's scarce resources that can be used for the production of goods and services will have to be diverted to install pollution control equipment and processes.[9] Therefore, we must decide at the outset how much cleanup we want and how much we are willing to pay for it.

To fix the ideas, let us consider the problem of water quality. Suppose a given body of water is polluted and we want to clean it up. Now as water quality improves, there are definite benefits we can derive in terms of better drinking water or more edible fish or more recreational facilities. The law of diminishing marginal utility states that the larger the number of units of a good consumed

---

[7]Kneese and Schultze, op. cit., pp. 5-6.
[8]Ibid.
[9]Of course, pollution control is a matter of technology as well as economics. As technology improves, the cost of pollution control will decline but it will not go away.

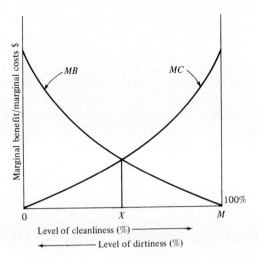

FIGURE 17.1
Cost, benefits, and optimal level of pollution.

in a time period, the less will be the satisfaction yielded by the last or marginal unit. Following this law, the marginal benefit *(MB)* or the demand curve for clean water, an economic good, will be downward-sloping, as shown in Figure 17.1.

To clean up the water, we will have to expend resources. The cost of these resources is what they would have fetched in their best alternative uses (i.e., their opportunity cost). Now as we divert more and more of these scarce resources to pollution control, their opportunity cost is likely to rise faster. Hence the marginal cost *(MC)* curve of cleanup will increase at a faster rate, as shown in Figure 17.1. This is not merely an idle speculation. For example, it has been estimated that the cost of removing an additional pound of BOD is 6 cents when 30 percent of the BOD has been removed from the waste of a large meat processing plant, but it becomes 60 cents when 90 percent of the BOD is removed, and it jumps to 90 cents when 95 percent of the BOD is removed.[10] Similarly, according to Environmental Protection Agency (EPA) estimates, the total 10-year cost of eliminating 85 to 90 percent of water pollution in the United States is estimated at $61 billion, that of eliminating 90 to 95 percent is estimated at $119 billion (an increase of $58 billion), and that of eliminating 100 percent (the goal set by the 1972 act) is estimated at $319 billion (an increase of $200 billion for the last 5 percentage points!)

Now from the geometry of Figure 17.1 it is clear that the goal of 100 percent pure water is economically infeasible, for at that level of cleanliness the *MC* far exceeds the *MB*, which is zero. And since labor, raw material, and capital resources are scarce (relative to the overall demand for them), from an effi-ciency viewpoint it does not make any sense to go that far (sentimentality not-withstanding in favor of 100 percent purity). But how far should we go? Or, to

[10]Ivars Gutmanis, ''The Generation and Cost of Controlling Air, Water, and Solid Waste Pollu-tion: 1970–2000,'' National Planning Association, Washington, D.C., 1972, table 6.1, p. 162.

put it differently, what is the ''optimum'' or ''best'' level of water purity one can aim at? Here the celebrated marginal analysis of economics provides the answer: Water quality (or air quality for that matter) should be improved as long as the benefit of an additional unit of cleanliness (say, 1 percent) exceeds the cost of achieving it. The optimum level of cleanliness occurs where $MC = MB$, or at the point X in Figure 17.1. As the reader can see from this figure, beyond X level of cleanliness the MC of each successive level of cleanliness exceeds the corresponding MB, whereas before X, the MB exceeds the MC. At X, the last unit of clean water confers as much benefit as it costs to achieve it.

In short, it is the commonsensical principle of cost-benefit analysis that will enable us to determine the optimum level of pollution. Keeping this in mind, let us now discuss the various alternatives to pollution control.

17.3   METHODS OF POLLUTION CONTROL

The methods of pollution control that are commonly suggested are: (1) voluntarism, (2) direct control via the standards approach, (3) liability system, (4) pollution or effluent taxes, (5) subsidies, and (6) marketable pollution rights. In principle any of these methods can achieve the optimum level of pollution or cleanliness (X in Figure 17.1), but in practice they differ in feasibility as well as in the cost burden, that is, who bears the cost, as the following discussion will show.

Voluntarism

The mildest and least expensive form of pollution control is voluntarism, that is, appeal to the good sense of the people. Unfortunately, it has proved to be weak and unenforceable because the free rider problem crops up here, too. The tendency is to let someone else practice voluntarism. Of course, in emergency situations voluntarism may be the only quick way to remedy the problem. Thus in the well-known air inversion of 1967 in New York City, which claimed eighty lives, the mayor had to appeal to the citizens not to use their garbage incinerators and drive their cars unnecessarily. And the people responded very well, as they generally do in crisis situations. But barring such circumstances, one cannot guarantee that voluntarism will solve the pollution problem on any appreciable scale.

Direct Control via the Standards Approach

Since voluntarism does not generally work, the government could go to the other extreme and set standards of air and water quality and try to monitor and enforce them through an appropriate agency, such as the EPA. The EPA could establish *ambient* air and water quality standards and prescribe *effluent* or *emission* limits or standards to achieve them. The ambient standards set goals or targets for, say, the amount of DO in a given waterway and the effluent limits specify the amounts of BOD (pounds per day) a particular plant may discharge in that waterway so that the overall ambient limit of DO can be attained when account is taken of all other polluters using that waterway. It is crucial to note that without observing the limits imposed by the effluent standards, it may not be possible to reach the targeted ambient standards because the free rider problem is likely to rear its ugly head here, too; in the absence of supervision and enforcement, one plant may discharge more than the permitted BOD, hoping that some other plant will discharge less than its permitted quota so that on the average the water will contain the overall ambient standard of DO.

In this country, unlike in some European countries, the government has relied almost exclusively on the specification-type standards approach incorporated in the ambient and effluent limits on air and water quality (we will discuss the specifics in Sections 17.6 and 17.7). Although we have commented generally on the standards approach in Chapter 4, here we will discuss it in the context of environmental pollution and some of the problems it poses.

First, underlying the ambient standard is the notion of a *threshold value,* a value below which a pollutant may not pose a serious health hazard but above which it does. Now establishing the critical threshold value is a time-consuming task, since it requires several experimental studies relating the effects of a pollutant to the level of its dosage. Very often the government does not have resources to make such studies for each and every pollutant; some 22,000 primary sources of air pollution and 55,000 major sources of water pollution have been identified. Or, it feels that resources are not worth diverting to such studies because the anticipated benefits are smaller than the anticipated costs: After all, these resources have opportunity costs — what they can accomplish or earn in their best alternative uses. As a result, standards are often set hurriedly and are often unrealistic.

Second, barring situations where nonadherence to the threshold value means a certainty of life or death, the threshold values must consider the costs and benefits of incorporating them into the ambient standard. As Figure 17.1 shows, economically speaking the threshold value should be set at the level X where $MC = MB$. But such cost-benefit analyses of ambient standards are generally conspicuous by their absence.

Third, once an ambient standard is set, it is applied across the board to all polluters. Such an across-the-board application may appear "equitable," but in fact it tends to be inefficient because it neglects to take into account the differing technologies used by the various firms to reduce pollution and hence the associated cost differences (see Table 17.1 and Question 17-15.)

Fourth, and important, the standards approach gives no incentive to the polluter to reduce pollution below the mandated level, whereas, as we will see shortly, the effluent tax or a similar incentive device may do just that.

Fifth, the success of the standards approach depends on the vigilance with which the statutes are enforced, which in turn depends on the resources available to the regulatory agency for that purpose. But as we saw in the previous chapter, regulatory agencies are generally not provided with adequate monies for enforcement purposes; in the case of OSHA the number of inspectors required to do their job effectively was ridiculously low.

Finally, there is the litigious aspect of the standards approach. If a polluter finds a standard ambiguous, he or she can go to court and bottle up compliance for several years, as happened in the case of the auto emissions standards, which are discussed later.

It is for these reasons that economists generally do not favor mandatory standards. To them, the incentive mechanism in the form of compensation for damages, effluent taxes, or *selective* subsidies is the better alternative for the reasons discussed below. (But in some cases subsidies may simply backfire, as shown later.)

Liability System: Compensation for Damages

One can rely on the common-law tradition of suing for damages, be they from pollution or any other cause. Ideally, the amount of compensation awarded should equal the extent of the damage actually done the victim; this amount can be computed with the help of Figure 17.2.

Since the MC curve shows the incremental cost of successive units of cleanliness, the total cost of achieving any level of cleanliness is given by the area under this curve up to that point. Thus, the total cost of cleaning pollution up to the level $0X$ in Figure 17.2 is area B, and that of 100 percent cleanliness is the

FIGURE 17.2
Pollution and compensation under the liability system.

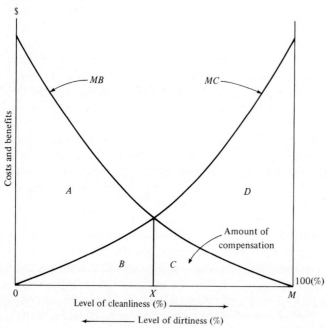

sum of the areas B, C, and D. Reading from right to left, the MB curve shows the damage done by successive units of dirtiness; alternatively, reading from left to right, it shows the incremental benefit of each additional unit of cleanliness. Therefore, the area under the MB curve gives, reading from right to left, the total damage (benefit foregone) done corresponding to a given level of cleanliness. For instance, if the polluter does nothing, the maximum damage is the sum of areas A, B, and C—this is the maximum amount which the court should grant.

From the standpoint of the polluter, she would not like to go beyond X level of cleanliness, for beyond that point the MC of each successive unit of cleanliness exceeds the incremental damage (given by MB) that she will have to pay the victim. Hence, she would clean up to the level X by incurring the cost of B and pay damages of C, her total cost being B + C. But this amount is smaller than the cost of total cleanup of B + C + D by the amount D. A rational judge should not award more than the amount C to the victim of the pollution.

Assuming that the standard is set at the optimum level X, the liability system discussed above is preferable to the standards approach because the polluter bears the entire cost of pollution abatement of B + C,[11] whereas under the standards approach the polluter pays only B and the victim has to pay (implicitly) the remaining cost C.

Although the compensation system is appealing, it has serious drawbacks. First, the system is likely to work when pollution sources (and polluters) are few and identifiable, but not when they are numerous. If air pollution is caused by mobile sources such as motor vehicles and *point* or stationary sources such as residential incinerators and factories, it is not easy to apportion the blame among such diverse sources. Also, because of wind shifts, the pollution in town A may very well have been generated by mobile and stationary sources (e.g., smoke from a factory) in town B and vice versa so that it is difficult to pinpoint the culprits. Second, since damages are awarded by the courts, the liability system is likely to encourage many lawsuits, which, by increasing the burden on the courts, is bound to lead to delays in justice. Third, it is practically difficult for an individual to sue a giant company since he or she may not have the resources to fight it, although class-action suits might alleviate the problem somewhat. Moreover, the burden of proof is with the party claiming the damages, a burden exacerbated by the fact that it is not easy to establish a definite causal link between the claimed damage and the alleged source, especially when more than one source could have caused the alleged damage. This is likely to put a damper even on the best-motivated case.

For all these reasons, the liability system can be a potent method of pollution control only in a handful of highly dramatic cases such as the Love Canal incident in Niagara Falls, New York, where toxic chemicals dumped by the Hooker Chemicals and Plastics Corporation leached into groundwater and migrated into

---

[11] It is likely that the polluter may pass along part of this cost to her consumers in higher prices, the extent of the "pass-along" depending on the price-elasticity of demand for her products.

basements and backyards. Two hundred and forty families were forced to evac-
uate their homes permanently, and some residents were apparently left with
serious illnesses, including neurological disorders, reproductive effects, and birth
defects. Although the company was convicted, the Love Canal case is far from
over, what with the various lawsuits still pending.

Pollution Taxes

Economists by and large agree that a tax on a polluting source, called an emission tax (in the case of air pollution) or effluent tax (in the case of water pollution)
is generally more efficient than direct controls to curb the pollution problem.
Before we see why this might be so, let us see how the tax mechanism would
work. Consider Figure 17.3, which is a slight modification of Figures 17.1 and
17.2.

As we noted in Figure 17.1, $0X$ is the optimal level of cleanliness that society
would want from the polluter. Now if the government institutes a charge or tax
of $0T$ per unit of pollution (say, per 1 percent of dirty water), a charge equal to
the MC of cleanup at the optimal level X, it will definitely pay the polluter to
reduce his effluent discharge to the level $0X$. For up to X the tax of $0T$ per unit
is greater than the MC of abatement; he would rather pay the cleanup cost of
C rather than pay the total tax of $B + C$. Beyond X, however, he would rather
pay the unit tax than cleanup, for the MC of abatement now exceeds the tax
rate; his tax burden beyond X level of cleanliness will be $D + E$, whereas the
cleanup would cost him $D + E + F$, a savings of F.

FIGURE 17.3
Pollution control via effluent or emission tax.

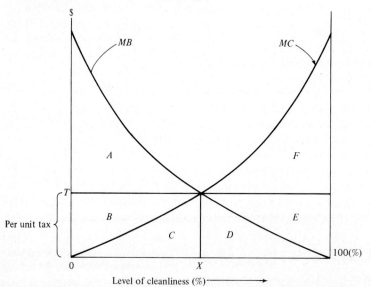

Economists claim these advantages for the emission tax. First, it is self-enforcing. Once the optimum tax rate is fixed, the polluter can either cleanup or pay the tax. As William Baumol and Alan Blinder note: `` . . . pollution taxes are automatic and certain. No one need be caught, prosecuted, convicted, and punished. The tax bills are just sent out automatically by the untiring tax collectors.''[12]

Second, the standards approach, as noted, applies the same standard uniformly regardless of the differences in the pollution-abating efficiency of the various polluters. The tax approach is decidedly better because it allows each polluter the option of choosing between the tax payments and installing appropriate pollution-control equipment. This can be seen from the hypothetical example in Table 17.1. This table shows that under the unified standards approach the total cost of pollution abatement is $460, whereas under the tax system it is only $320. Under the latter, firm A, which is more efficient in reducing pollution, finds it economical to remove all its effluent because its unit cost of pollution reduction is less than the unit tax rate. Firm B, on the other hand, finds it economical to simply pay the tax. Yet the total amount of pollution reduction is the same under both the systems, namely, 4000 gallons a day.

Third, the tax approach offers the incentive to discover new and less expensive ways of reducing pollution, for example, by changing production process or by recycling the waste product. As Kneese and Brown note, a shift from the sulfite to the sulfate process reduces the waste load per ton of product by about 90 percent, and a shift from sulphuric acid to hydrochloric acid can reduce waste production to almost zero in the steel pickling process.[13]

In sum:

> The secret of the efficiency induced by a tax on pollution is straightforward. Only polluters who can reduce emissions cheaply and efficiently can afford to take advantage of the built-in loophole — the opportunity to save on taxes by reducing emissions. The tax approach simply assigns the job to those who can do it most effectively.[14]

Despite its endorsement by economists, the emissions tax has not found much favor with the lawmakers. One of their criticisms is that such a tax requires effective and dependable metering devices to measure effluents at each outfall. But barring some exceptions, it should not be technologically impossible to install metering devices. Besides, these devices are needed under the 1972 Water Pollution Act, which prescribes limits on various effluents that may be discharged in the nation's waterways (more on this later).[15] Moreover, several European countries have successfully implemented such taxes.[16] In Germany,

---

[12]William J. Baumol and Alan S. Blinder, *Economics: Principles and Policy,* Harcourt, Brace, New York, 1979, p. 679.

[13]For details, see Allen V. Kneese and Blair T. Bower, *Managing Water Quality: Economics, Technology, Institutions,* Johns Hopkins, Baltimore, 1968.

[14]Baumol and Blinder, op. cit., p. 680.

[15]In New York State portable testing machines are now routinely used to check the level of auto emissions, and no registration will be issued unless a car passes the minimum prescribed standards.

[16]For details, see Organization of Economic Cooperation and Development (OECD): *Pollution Charges, An Assessment,* Paris, 1976.

TABLE 17.1
THE STANDARDS VERSUS EFFLUENT TAX APPROACH

	Firm A		Firm B	
The standards approach:				
Pollution discharge per day (gallons)	4000		4000	
Effluent limit: goal of 50% reduction	2000		2000	
Cost of reducing pollution, ¢ per gallon	3		20	
Total cost of pollution abatement	$60		$400	$460 (aggregate)
Effluent tax of 5¢ a gallon:				
Pollution discharge per day (gallons)	4000		4000	
Cost of pollution abatement	$120 (3 × 4000)		—	
Tax paid	—		$200	
Total cost of pollution abatement	$120		$200	$320 (aggregate)

since 1973 uniform fees for water pollution have been set throughout the country and small as well as large dischargers are required to pay them, but the choice of pollution control technology is left entirely up to the individual polluter. In France, water pollution charges are based both on the weight of pollutants discharged and on measures of their toxicity. A variety of effluent charges have been in existence in Hungary since 1961. Thus what is needed for the institution of the effluent taxes is not merely technology but political willpower.

Subsidies[17]

Subsidies, the opposite of taxes, can be used as financial rewards for reducing pollution. They may take various forms, such as:[18] low-interest loans to local government units to finance sewer line construction; additional assistance to municipalities in the form of matching grants for construction of waste treatment plants (as is done under the Water Pollution Control Act amendments of 1956); special tax treatment for firms installing pollution abatement facilities; and exemption, especially at the state level, from franchise, property, sales, and income taxes for purposes of installing pollution abatement equipment.

We will comment later on the various subsidy programs instituted by the government (see Section 17.4); for now, we note that, unlike the effluent taxes, subsidies may in fact lead to more rather than less pollution. To understand this paradoxical result, assume that a competitive industry receives subsidies of one type or another to abate pollution. Now consider Figure 17.4. In this diagram S and D are, respectively, the initial supply and demand curves for the pollution-

[17]For a critical view, see James C. Hite, Hugh H. Macaulay, James M. Stepp, and Bruce Yandle, Jr., *The Economics of Environmental Quality,* American Enterprise Institute for Public Policy Research, Washington, D.C., 1972, pp. 98–107.
[18]Ibid.

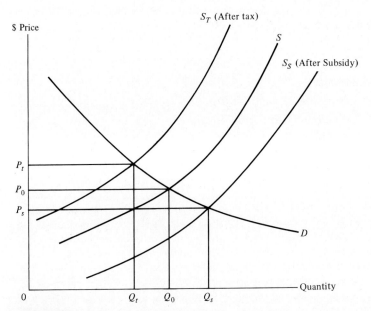

FIGURE 17.4
The effect of pollution tax and subsidies on the price and quantity of the pollution-producing commodity.

producing product of the industry, P_0 and Q_0 being the initial equilibrium price and quantity. If an effluent tax were instituted to abate pollution, the supply curve would shift to the left since the cost of the product would increase on account of the tax. Hence the new equilibrium price would be higher (at the level P_t) and the new equilibrium output would be lower (at the level Q_t). And since the aggregate output would be lower than before, aggregate pollution would likely to be lower too. If, on the other hand, a subsidy were given to the industry, the opposite might be true: The supply curve would shift to the right (because the dollar costs of production are reduced by the amount of the subsidy), leading to a lower equilibrium price of P_s and a higher equilibrium output of Q_s. The higher output is due to the existing firms increasing their output as well as new firms entering the industry to take advantage of the subsidy. Larger output results in more pollution. Although the subsidy helps each firm in the industry to reduce its emissions (after all that is the objective of the subsidy), the aggregate emissions may increase simply because of the added output due to the new entry. Hence the paradox; the subsidies instead of abating pollution may simply backfire.

Of course, this perverse effect of the subsidy is not confined to industrial activities alone. If, for example, the government were to provide a subsidy to install emission control devices on the ubiquitous automobile, it is likely to encourage the use of automobiles still more and thus may lead, unwittingly, to more pollution because of the increased number of drivers. Contrariwise, if the government were to institute an emission tax on automobiles, it might curtail auto travel and reduce pollution in the process, besides helping the struggling mass transportation systems in the country.

Marketable Pollution Rights

As we noted in Section 4.5, the creation of freely marketable pollution rights is another method of pollution control. The idea behind such rights is novel in that they create property rights in the use of environmental resources, rights the marketplace alone cannot determine because of the common-property nature of such resources. We have already discussed the mechanics of such saleable rights and their relative merits and demerits.[19] Suffice it to add that:

> When markets are used by the government to allocate the valuable "right to pollute," there is a real sense in which everybody is treated equitably: everybody has access to the market on equal terms and pays the same price for inflicting approximately the same damage on society. Those who use more of the resource pay more for the privilege, those who spend money to reduce their use of the resource pay less. The economic value of environmental resources can be captured by the larger society which presumably owns them, and need not be given away to particular individuals simply because they have a good technical and economic reason for using the resources.[20]

Methods of Pollution Control: General Comments

Although economists generally favor some kind of incentives approach to pollution control, the government in this country has chosen to rely on direct regulation via the standards approach. There are several reasons for this. First, air and water pollution are extremely complex phenomena and securing consensus in the Congress about what to do, how much to do, and how to do it is not easy; Congress simply does not have adequate staff or technical assistance to thoroughly evaluate all the possible alternatives. As Kneese and Schultz observe, "the staffs of congressional committees are chosen principally for their talent in helping to devise and negotiate legislation that secures a consensus broad enough to assure passage,"[21] and not necessarily for their economic and technical competence. Second, the Congress tends to be dominated by members who are lawyers by training, and lawyers, quite naturally, concentrate "on the specification of rights and duties in law or in regulations and on the case-by-case adjudication of individual situations in the light of the law and the regulations. If it is in society's interest to change social behavior, lawyers go about the task by

---

[19]For a discussion of how such rights can be established, say, in the area of noise pollution, see Donald C. Cell, "Charges to Control Aircraft Noise," in Dean E. Mann (ed.), *Environmental Policy Implementation,* Lexington Books, Lexington, Mass., 1982, pp. 157–171.

[20]Larry Ruff, "Federal Environmental Regulation," prepared for the Senate *Study on Federal Regulation,* vol. I, p. 212.

[21]Kneese and Schultz, op. cit., p. 115.

changing the specified rights and duties."[22] On the other hand, the economic or incentive approach stresses not rights but incentives. Recognizing that people and firms generally follow their self-interest, the incentive approach (taxes or subsidies) motivates people to take actions that are in their best interest — a polluter will install pollution control equipment if it costs less than paying the mandated tax.

Although both regulation and economic approaches have their place, it seems that the economic approach has generally been bypassed in favor of the former in the area of environmental pollution, as it has in many other areas of regulation discussed in this text.

17.4 PRE-1970 REGULATION OF ENVIRONMENTAL POLLUTION

Although the clean air and clean water acts dominate much of the current discussion on environmental pollution, there were pollution control laws even before them.

Pre-1970 Water Pollution Control Laws[23]

The first federal water pollution control law was the 1899 Refuse Act, which required a permit from the chief of engineers for discharge of any refuse (other than from municipal sources) into the nation's navigable waters. This act was pretty much unenforced until 1970. And so were two other minor laws, the Public Health Service Act of 1912 and the Oil Pollution Act of 1924.

The first comprehensive law was the Water Pollution Control Act of 1948, which marked the entry of the federal government into an area which was exclusively a state matter. This act gave the federal government authority to investigate, research, and survey waterways. The act was extensively amended by the Water Pollution Control Act Amendments of 1956, which more or less oversaw the government's water pollution control policies until 1970. The two key features of the act were: federal subsidies for waste treatment plants (municipalities could get 55 percent of the cost of constructing the plants), and the establishment of complex procedures for federal enforcement actions against individual polluters, both intra- and interstate. The act was further amended by the Water Quality Act of 1965, which strengthened the enforcement procedures and also provided for federal approval of ambient water quality standards proposed by the states. The next major, and perhaps radical, law was the 1972 act, which is discussed in the next section.

Working of the Pre-1970 Water Pollution Acts Though the 1948 act, as amended by the 1956 and 1965 acts, recognized the importance of water pol-

[22]Ibid., p. 116.
[23]Ibid., pp. 30–50.

lution, by the end of the 1960s it was believed by many that the act had not really accomplished much. This feeling was shared, among others, by the General Accounting Office (GAO) as well as the Center for the Study of Responsive Law, a Ralph Nader organization. The center published two books, *Vanishing Air* (1970) and *Water Wasteland* (1971), which were highly critical of the pre-1970 legislation.

In the view of Kneese and Schultze, there were several reasons for this dissatisfaction. First, the distribution of subsidies for sewage treatment plants was arbitrary from an economic viewpoint. The program allocated funds among states according to a combination of state per capita income and population, with the result that funds were abundant in some states and sparse in some others, relative to requirements. Where funds were relatively abundant, local officials tended to overdesign public works, which often resulted in excess plant capacity. Second, there was not adequate funding for the maintenance of the plants. The general philosophy behind the grants seemed to be that once the capital funds were provided and the plant built, the water pollution problem was solved; operation and maintenance of the plants was something that the states should worry about. Third, and important, the subsidies "do nothing to remove the perverse incentives with respect to the use of common-property assets like watercourses. They do nothing to bring the private costs of production into line with the costs to society, which include the environmental damages done to other users of the watercourse."[24] Finally, the prime mechanism of enforcement was the Enforcement Conference, a provision made by the 1956 amendments. The administrator of the EPA was empowered to call the conference, at his discretion, to solve an interstate water pollution problem. But these conferences were largely informal convocations and their recommendations never had the force of law.

To sum up:

> . . . the intricate problem of linking subsidies to enforcement was not solved at all; the subsidies were linked to the use of a particular technology — waste treatment — even in the instances when other, more efficient, approaches were available; neither effectiveness nor efficiency played a role in allocating grant funds to particular communities; attention was focused on the construction of treatment facilities and not their operation; and nothing was done to change the economic incentive to overuse and misuse common-property assets.[25]

Pre-1970 Air Pollution Control Laws

The first major federal law was the 1955 Air Pollution Control Act, which was prompted by some studies showing the hazardous effects of air pollution. For example, a 1950 study by the California Institute of Technology established a link between automobile emissions and photochemical smog in the Los Angeles

---

[24]Ibid., p. 37.
[25]Ibid., pp. 37–38.

area. The act authorized, for the first time, a federal program of research, training, and demonstrations relating to air pollution control. But the level of the funding provided for this purpose was a meager $5 million annually for a period of 5 years. The Clean Air Act of 1963 gave the federal government enforcement powers regarding air pollution through the mechanism of the Enforcement Conference. At the behest of a state, the HEW (now Health and Human Services Administration) could call a conference on air pollution in a particular area or air shed and make recommendations, ultimately enforceable by court action. In interstate cases the HEW could act on its own initiative.

Concerned with the growing auto exhaust problem, Congress passed the Motor Vehicle Air Pollution Control Act of 1965, which amended the 1963 act by giving the secretary of HEW the authority to prescribe emissions standards for automobiles as soon as feasible. The first such standards were issued for the 1966 model year, but by some accounts, they were less demanding than those adopted by the State of California, where the auto pollution problem is especially serious.

It seems that public action takes place only when there is some dramatic happening. The 4-day air inversion episode in New York in 1967 lead to the passage of the Air Quality Act of 1967, which authorized the HEW to oversee the establishment of state standards for ambient air quality and the associated enforcement plans as well as to set, for the first time, national standards for auto emissions. The next important federal law was the 1970 act, which we discuss in the next section.

Enforcement of the Pre-1970 Air Pollution Laws   As in the case of water pollution control, the main problem with the various air pollution control laws was one of enforcement. Between 1963 and 1970 eleven Enforcement Conferences were held but they were mostly ceremonial, with little substantive accomplishment. By 1970 not a single state had any well-defined standards for any of the pollutants.

17.5 POLLUTION REGULATION SINCE 1970

Although dramatic events, such as the 4-day air inversion in New York City in 1967 or the spectacular blowout of an oil well in the channels off the coast of Santa Barbara, California, in January 1969 (which killed thousands of fish and much wildlife and covered miles of beach with oil), often prompt quick-fix federal regulation, very often, as Alfred Marcus notes, there are "inventors," "transferers," and "adopters" of a regulatory innovation or initiative.[26] The Clean Air Act of 1970 and the Clean Water Act of 1972, as we will see, are innovative in that they set definite timetables to obtain clearly defined air and water quality levels.

---

[26]Alfred Marcus, "Environmental Protection Agency," in James Q. Wilson (ed.), *The Politics of Regulation*, Basic Books, New York, 1980.

According to Marcus, the inventors were college professors such as Marver Bernstein and Theodore Lowi.[27] The general thrust of their argument was that vague regulatory legislation causes regulatory failure. Therefore, unless well-defined goals and definite timetables to achieve them are set, bureaucratic discretion is bound to dilute the mandate of the law. Hence, define the goals well, set the timetable, and tell the regulatory agency to abide by it.

The idea of forcing the regulatory agencies to abide by the mandate and the timetable developed by the "inventors" was appealing to "transferers" such as Ralph Nader. The publication of *Vanishing Air* and *Water Wasteland* by Nader's Center for the Study of Responsive Law hammered home the theme that ill- or poorly-conceived and politically compromised legislation were the root causes of regulatory incompetence in the area of environmental pollution. The Naderites wanted the Congress to adopt new standards with clearly defined timetables to achieve the designated goals.

Of course, all inventions are for naught if there are no takers. But in Senator Muskie the "transferrers" found an ideal adopter. Muskie was then chairperson of the subcommittee on Air and Water Pollution of the Senate Committee on Public Works as well as a potential 1972 presidential candidate. *Vanishing Air* criticizes him for being lukewarm toward the pollution problem. The 1967 Air Quality Act, which his committee had drafted, came under heavy attack because of its administration and enforcement: The act adopted a purely regional approach to the pollution problem, leaving it to the states to establish standards for particular pollutants; the states were slow to act. The Naderites therefore wanted Muskie to adopt a nationwide approach to pollution control.

All this criticism rattled Muskie, who had prided himself as a friend of the environmentalists. The strategy of the Naderites to accuse and embarrass a key member of Congress (especially one with presidential ambitions) about a politically viable issue in order to secure quick action worked. As Charles Jones notes, "the overall effect put Muskie in the position of having to do something extraordinary in order to recapture his [pollution control] leadership."[28] The final outcome were the 1970 and 1972 air and water pollution control acts.

The government, too, was concerned about the pollution problem. In the wake of the oil well blowout in California, President Nixon, by an executive order of June 3, 1969, established the Environmental Quality Council (EQC), a cabinet-level office, to look into the problem. But Congress was not satisfied with the move and it passed the *National Environmental Policy Act* (NEPA), with the objective of establishing national pollution control policy and required all federal agencies to submit an Environmental Impact Statement (EIS) for all proposed actions. It created a three-person Council on Environmental Quality (CEQ) within the executive office to replace the EQC. Later in 1970 President

---

[27]See their books: Marver Bernstein, *Regulating Business by Independent Commissions*, Princeton University Press, Princeton, N.J., 1955, and Theodore Lowi, *End of Liberalism*, Norton, New York, 1969.

[28]Charles O. Jones, *Clean Air: The Policies and Politics of Pollution Control*, University of Pittsburgh, Pittsburgh, 1975, quoted by Marcus, op. cit., p. 271.

Nixon proposed the EPA to consolidate all governmental efforts in the environmental area; the EPA was to set and enforce pollution control standards and the CEQ was to act as an advisory and policymaking body. The EPA officially came into being on December 2, 1970, as an executive branch agency, a move approved by the Congress. And it was soon entrusted with the formidable task of administering the 1970 and 1972 acts.

17.6   THE CLEAN AIR ACT OF 1970

The primary goal of the act was "to protect and enhance the quality of the nation's air resources" by establishing standards based on health and welfare criteria and not on economic or technical feasibility. In Senator Muskie's words, "the deadline [for automobile emissions standards] is based not, I repeat, on economic or technological feasibility, but on consideration of public health."[29]

Under the act, the EPA was required, among other things, to perform the following tasks so as to achieve healthy air by 1975, a deadline that has been pushed ahead from time to time and now stands at 1982 or 1987 in some cases:

1 To propose National Ambient Air Quality Standards (NAAQs) to protect public health (the primary standards) and welfare (the secondary standards designed to protect property, crops, livestock, and public transportation).

2 Within a year of the proposed NAAQs, to approve state implementation plans (SIPs) relating to pollution-specific emission limits.

3 To set limits on the level of air pollutants emitted from such point or *stationary sources* as power plants, municipal incinerators, factories, and chemical plants and from nonpoint or *nonstationary sources,* specifically from the automobile. It specifically called for a 90 percent reduction in auto emissions in 5 years, as shown in Table 17.2.

The standards established or proposed to be established by EPA fall into the following categories:[30]

Emergency standards.   When air pollution reaches such levels as to pose an imminent and substantial danger to health, the EPA may take emergency actions, including shutting down industrial plants.

National air quality standards.   For the six commonly found pollutants — sulphur oxides, particulates (airborne residuals consisting of heterogenous mixture of suspended solids and liquids), carbon monoxide, photochemical oxidants, hydrocarbons, and nitrogen oxides — primary as well as secondary standards are set.

National emissions standards.   For hazardous pollutants that "may cause, or contribute to, an increase in mortality or an increase in serious irreversible, or incapacitating reversible, illness," the EPA must set national emission standards.

[29]Senate Report 91-1196, 91st Cong., 3d Sess., 1970, p. 32905, quoted in the Senate *Study on Federal Regulation,* op. cit., p. 194.
[30]See Murray S. Weidenbaum, *Regulation By Government,* Prentice-Hall, Englewood Cliffs, N.J., ch. 6, "Managing the Environment."

New plant standards. To encourage new plants to avoid pollution to begin with, the EPA is to require them to use the *best practical technology* (BPT) immediately and the *best achievable technology* (BAT) eventually.

Motor vehicle emission standards. For manufacturers of new or imported cars, the emissions standards set are very specific and are as shown in Table 17.2.

Fuel standards. The EPA can control or prohibit substances in motor vehicles that significantly hinder performance of emission control systems.

The 1977 Amendments to the Act

Realizing that the goals set in the Clean Air Act of 1970 were probably too ambitious to be achieved in the targeted time periods, Congress passed the 1977 amendments to the act. Among other things, these amendments include: (1) postponement of the "healthy" air goals that were to be achieved by 1975 to 1982 and to 1987 in some cases; (2) the 90 percent reduction in automobile emissions to be achieved by 1975 has now been postponed until 1980 (for unburned carbons) and to 1981 (for carbon monoxide); and (3) the EPA is required to give variances for technological innovation as well as to file economic- and employment-impact statements with all new regulations.

Enforcement

The EPA has an extensive monitoring program, developed by the Office of Monitoring and Technical Support. If a violation of any of the provisions of the act is found, the violator is informed and urged to stop the same. If this does not work, the next step is informal negotiations. If that fails, open hearings are held. Ultimately, the agency has the authority to start civil proceedings in the U.S. district courts to force compliance.

Penalties for violation can be severe, up to $25,000 a day for each day of continuance of the violation and 1 year in jail. Subsequent violations can double both the fine and the jail term. A car sold in violation of EPA emissions standards can invite a fine of up to $10,000 for each offending car or engine, and violation of motor vehicle fuel standards can be punished by a fine of up to $10,000 a day.

TABLE 17.2
AUTO EMISSIONS STANDARD (GRAMS PER MILE)

	HC	CO	NO$_x$
1970 emission levels	4.1	34	4.0
Standards to be achieved by 1975–1976 (goal of 90% reduction)*	0.41	3	0.4

Note: The timetables for achieving these goals have been advanced from time to time.

17.7   THE CLEAN WATER ACT OF 1972

The forces that prompted the passage of the 1970 Clean Air Act also propelled Senator Muskie's committee to propose a water pollution control bill. In October 1971 the committee drafted a 120-page bill whose primary goal was to eliminate the discharge of *all* pollutants in the nation's water resources by 1985. Although the bill that finally emerged, the Water Pollution Control Act of 1972, was vetoed by President Nixon because of its impact on the national economy and the burden on the treasury, the House overturned the veto by 247 to 23, the Senate voting 52 to 12. With subsequent amendments, the act is now known as the Clean Water Act.

The Act established two goals for the nation: (1) "fishable" and "swimmable" waters by 1983, and (2) ultimately, no discharge at all of pollutants into waterways.

As in the case of the Clean Air Act, the main feature of this act is the use of specific deadlines to achieve the avowed goals. Among other things, the act mandates the administrator of EPA to do the following:

1 Prescribe effluent standards for individual plants and publicly owned waste treatment plants.

2 Adopt stringent federal standards for toxic discharges, such as carbon tetrachloride, bromodichloromethane, and lead.

3 Issue permits for discharges from municipal and industrial waste; every point source of industrial or municipal pollution must have a permit limiting its discharge. The permits, based on effluent guidelines where they are available, are issued either by the federal government under the National Pollutant Discharge Elimination System (NPDES) or by states that have assumed responsibility for issuing the permits. The permits specify the amount of pollution that may be legally discharged. Incidentally, the permit provision brings back to life the 1899 Refuse Act.

4 Prohibit the dumping of any radioactive waste into the nation's waters.

5 Regulate the disposal of radioactive waste in the ocean.

6 Administer grants to assist states in the areawide waste treatment management planning and make loans to small businesses to help them fulfill water pollution control requirements.

7 Issue grants to state and regional governmental agencies to plan and carry out solid-waste management programs.

8 Control pollution from nonpoint sources (e.g., runoffs from agricultural and silvicultural operations) by requiring the nonpoint polluters to employ "best management practices" which reduce the amount and impact of the runoff.

9 The authority extended by the Safe Water Drinking Act of 1974, to set standards for chemical and bacteriological pollutants in the water systems.

A novel feature of the act was the requirement that by 1977 effluent limitation by point source was to be achieved by the best practical technology (BPT) currently available and that by 1983 effluent limits for categories and classes of point sources be achieved by the best available technology (BAT). But as we will see, these terms are not easy to define.

The 1977 Amendments

Again realizing that the timetables set in the 1972 act were probably unrealistic, Congress passed the 1977 amendments to the act. Among other things, they gave additional time (until April 1979, but again postponed) to industry that acted in "good faith" but did not meet the 1977 BPT deadline, and instead of the BAT standards to be met by 1983, they allowed for the Best Conventional Pollution Control Technology (BCPCT) standards to be met by 1984 in cases where the costs of the BAT technology exceeded the benefits (except for the toxic pollutants).

17.8 CRITICAL EVALUATION OF THE 1970 AND 1972 ACTS

The "energy crisis" following the OPEC oil embargo of October 1973 punctured the almost euphoric zeal for the various environmental pollution laws that were passed in the 1960s and early 1970s when it became clear that the exclusive reliance on health and welfare regardless of the costs involved posed serious trade-offs between clean air and gas mileage and between clean air and clean water and jobs. Under the various acts, electric and gas utilities could not use high-sulphur coal and had to use imported oil. But with the oil crisis, it was a choice, in some cases, between using high-sulphur coal or shut down. Recognizing such trade-offs, Congress passed the Energy Supply and Environmental Coordination Act, extending the deadline for auto emmissions reduction of 90 percent.

Presidents Ford and Carter realized that the costs imposed by the various pollution control laws were a factor in the double-digit inflations of 1979 and 1980 and ordered various governmental agencies to issue the Inflationary Impact Statements of their intended regulatory activities. It soon became apparent that cost-benefit analysis of the various environmental pollution laws was necessary, despite Senator Muskie's contention otherwise. We will refer to this topic shortly, but first we consider some technical problems with the provisions of the various laws as they exist.

Enforcement of the Pollution Control Laws: Some Technical Problems[31]

As noted earlier, to control air pollution, the EPA required industry to use "best adequately demonstrated technology" (BADT) and to control water pollution, the BPT by 1977, and the BAT by 1983, or the BPCT by 1984 in some cases. In developing the BPT and BAT standards, the EPA is supposed to take into account "the age of equipment and facilities involved, the process employed, the engi-

---

[31]For administrative and other problems, see Marcus, op. cit., pp. 281–295.

neering aspects of the application of various types of control techniques, process changes, non-water quality environmental impact (including energy requirements), and such other factors as the Administrator deems appropriate."

Now this is a tall order. To illustrate the difficulty in the prescribed standards approach, consider the problem of automobile emissions. As the 1970 act requires, carbon monoxide (CO), oxides of nitrogen (NOX), and hydrocarbons (HC) are to be reduced simultaneously to the levels shown in Table 17.2. But such simultaneous reduction is very difficult with the internal combustion engine. The technology is such that reduction of CO and HC to low levels increases the emission of NOX and vice versa. Hence new technology must be developed to meet the standards for all three gases simultaneously.

One such technology is catalytic converters. A catalytic converter is a device attached to the car's tailpipe to remove hydrocarbons, carbon monoxide, and nitrogen oxides from the exhaust system (actually there are two converters, one with an oxidizing catalyst for CO and HC and the other with reducing catalyst for NOX). The EPA thought that it would solve the problem without sacrificing fuel efficiency; most other suggested technologies involved low mileage, poor performance, and expensive maintenance. In 1973, however, the Ford Motor Company informed the EPA that the converter emitted sulfuric acid, a health hazard, and later the EPA acknowledged that the health risks from sulfuric acid exposure were greater than the benefits expected from the converter.

As Noel de Nevers correctly notes, the whole notion of BAT or BADT is controversial as well as confusing, to say the least.[32] When the EPA issued standards for fuel-burning power plants, municipal incinerators, and plants that make sulfuric acid or cement, many suits were instituted against the EPA about the BPT and BAT standards and about their economic feasibility. Electric power plants, for instance, that use coal or oil emit sulfur dioxide. To control its emission, the EPA ordered the industry to put exhaust systems containing special aparatus to control the sulfur dioxide. The industry sued the EPA on the grounds that the proposed standard was unreliable, expensive, and troublesome to operate and hence the technology was not "adequately demonstrated." The courts will have to sift out the reality.

The preceding discussion clearly shows that a purely standards approach that neglects the cost side is not practically feasible, especially when the regulator does not have adequate information or adequate resources to acquire one. This brings us to the broader question of cost-benefit analysis of pollution control measures.

17.9 THE COSTS AND BENEFITS OF POLLUTION CONTROL

When it comes to cost-benefit estimates of the pollution control laws, however, one draws a big blank because neither the cost nor the benefit estimates are particularly reliable. This is due to some very difficult measurement problems. As one author notes:

[32]Noel de Nevers, "Enforcing the Clean Air Act of 1970," *Scientific American,* June 1973, vol. 228, no. 6, pp. 14–21.

The problem of estimating the costs and benefits from pollution control cannot be overstressed. First, pollutants must be measured in physical terms and then these must be converted into money values. This is difficult because most involve no market, and hence no market price is available, e.g. damage to recreational facilities. Second, damage can depend very much on environmental influences, such as wind, tides, and location. Third, the occurrence of the damage may be uncertain, as in the case of a leak from a nuclear plant. This places a problem on the decision of when to time the control policy. Fourth, damage and benefits can occur over a period of time and so valuation involves discounting future values, which in turn requires some choice of discount rate. Fifth, pollution may alter probabilities, such as that of catching a certain respiratory disease or even leading to death. This raises the problem of measuring health effects and valuing human life.[33]

The same author adds:

In such a world of poor information two practical procedures can be followed:
　(i) establish the type of information required and begin to obtain it;
　(ii) carry out policies iteratively [i.e., learning by experience] or simply achieve certain prescribed standards (whether optimal or not).[34]

Given the complexity and enormity of its task, the EPA chose the second approach, namely, establishing air and water quality standards. Administratively, too, it was comparatively a simple approach; once the standards are set, all that the agency has to do is monitor and enforce them.

Now that the standards are in place, we can raise two questions: What have been the costs and the benefits of the established standards? and Are the chosen standards optimal or the best ones? Some answer to the first question is provided in the remainder of this section, and the next section discusses the question of optimality of the chosen standards, a question that calls for some cost-benefit studies of specific standards.

Overall Costs of Pollution Control

The National Water Commission (NWC) has estimated that cumulatively it will cost the nation $220 billion between 1972 and 1983 to meet the best-known technology (not BAT) standards of the 1972 Clean Water Act just for stationary or point source pollution; the cost of pollution from such nonpoint sources as runoff from agricultural feedlots, acid mine drainage, and storm water discharges is not known. But even the $220 billion expenditure will not achieve the "zero discharge" goal set for 1985. The 1973 Report of the Council on Environmental Quality (CEQ) estimated that between 1972 and 1983 the cost of achieving the air quality mandated by the Clean Air Act will reach about $130 to $140 billion. According to the Eighth Annual Report of the CEQ pollution control will cost each person in the United States $47 in 1974 and $187 in 1977.

---

[33]Ronald Shone, *Applications in Intermediate Microeconomics,* Wiley, New York, 1981, pp. 283–284.
[34]Ibid., p. 284.

TABLE 17-3
POLLUTION CONTROL OUTLAYS BY BUSINESS, 1975
(Millions of Dollars)

	Pollution control			Pollution control as percentage of all capital expenditures
	Total	Air	Water	
All industries	5,900	3,745	2,155	5.1%
Manufacturing	3,942	2,352	1,590	7.9
Durable goods	1,706	1,162	544	7.4
Primary metals	843	648	196	15.3
Blast furnace, steel works	289	197	92	11.3
Nonferrous	474	375	100	19.6
Electrical machinery	182	70	111	6.3
Machinery, except electrical	85	45	40	1.8
Transportation equipment	134	66	68	3.8
Motor vehicles	107	55	52	4.1
Aircraft	24	11	14	3.5
Stone, clay, and glass	198	175	23	14.5
Other durables	265	157	107	5.1
Nondurable goods	2,236	1,190	1,046	8.3
Food including beverage	168	66	102	5.3
Textile	31	8	23	4.4
Paper	458	262	196	15.8
Chemical	522	215	306	7.3
Petroleum	965	580	385	9.6
Rubber	68	44	24	4.9
Other nondurables	25	16	9	1.8
Nonmanufacturing	1,959	1,393	566	2.9
Mining	43	21	21	1.8
Railroad	36	15	21	1.1
Air transportation	10	7	3	.6
Other transportation	53	18	36	2.3
Public utilities	1,618	1,210	408	7.5
Electric	1,568	1,177	391	8.8
Gas and other	51	33	18	1.4
Communication, commercial, and other	199	122	76	.6

Source: Murray S. Weidenbaum, *Regulation by Government,* Prentice-Hall, Englewood Cliffs, 1979, p. 79. The data are originally from the Bureau of Economic Analysis, Department of Commerce.

Some industry-specific cost estimates for 1975 based on Department of Commerce data are made by Murray Weidenbaum and are as shown in Table 17.3. The table shows that pollution-control expenditures as a percent of total capital expenditures vary considerably from industry to industry. The primary metals, stone, clay, glass, and paper industries spend a considerable amount of their capital expenditure on pollution control, which should not be surprising;

they are among the largest producers of pollution in view of the products they produce.

Overall Benefits of Pollution Control

There is no question that pollution control confers substantial benefits in terms of human health and welfare, the only difficulty being to estimate them and match them up against the costs. Crude attempts at these estimates were made by the CEQ indirectly by estimating the damages from air pollution to health, residential, property, and vegetation that might result in the absence of air pollution control measures. These estimates are as shown in Table 17.4

It is very difficult to compare these benefit estimates with the aggregate 11-year cost of air pollution control of between $130 to $140 billion. On an annual basis, these costs come to about $12 to $13 billion a year. If we compare this cost with the single-year benefit estimates given in Table 17.4, it would seem that the benefits exceeded the costs for the years 1968 and 1977. But it is imprudent to extrapolate from these years and conclude that for the period of 1972 to 1983 as a whole the total benefits exceeded the total costs. And since there are no other aggregate estimates of the costs and benefits of the air pollution laws, it is better to hold judgment on the net cost or net benefit of these laws.

Macroeconomic Effects of Pollution Control Laws

What about the effects of the pollution control laws on macroeconomic variables such as GNP, capital investment, inflation, and employment? The research in this area is rather scanty. A Chase Econometric Associates's forecast prepared for the EPA and CEQ stated that by 1983 GNP would be lower by 2.2 percent than it would have been in the absence of the laws and that inflation would increase at the rate of 0.3 to 0.4 percent more than it would have been in 1983. But again one should use these figures with great caution because they are based on several assumptions and on the particular econometric model used; several well-known econometric models have often given divergent econometric forecasts on many a macroeconomic variable.

Although no numerical estimates are available, employment is expected to

TABLE 17.4
ESTIMATED NATIONAL AIR POLLUTION DAMAGE COSTS WITH NO POLLUTION CONTROL, 1968 & 1977 (Billions of Dollars)

Damage class	1968 (1968 $)	1977 (1970 $)
Health	6 .1	9 .3
Residential property	5 .2	8 .0
Materials and vegetation	4 .9	7 .6
Total	16.2	24.9

Source: "Environmental Quality," *Fourth Annual Report of the Council on Environmental Quality,* September 1973.

increase initially because of the investment in pollution control equipment and then to decline because of the likely price increases in the pollution-producing products and the resulting decline (depending on the price elasticities) in the demand for them.

Capital-intensive materials industries such as electric utilities and chemicals are likely to be adversely affected by the new laws. For the electric utility industry it has been estimated that capital requirements for pollution control will amount to some $25 billion between 1975 and 1985, some 10.5 percent of the projected capital needs of the industry. As a result, it is estimated that by 1985 electricity prices will be higher by 6.6 percent just on account of the pollution control costs. For industries dominated by numerous small production units, such as electroplating and foundry, it will be difficult to raise the needed capital to install pollution control equipment. This might lead to some bankruptcies: Between 1968 and 1974, some 427 foundries, many small, were closed down because, among other things, they could not cope with the compliance costs of the various environmental regulations.

17.10   MICROECONOMIC EFFECTS OF POLLUTION CONTROL LAWS: SOME CASE STUDIES

To find out whether the EPA-prescribed standards are optimal or not, and if not what are the alternatives, one has to consider specific cases. Although case studies are not numerous, there are two very useful publications which will give the reader some insight into the effectiveness of the EPA standards. Lawrence J. White, who served as a senior staff economist on the Council of Economic Advisors, has had the opportunity of examining several regulatory laws at close quarters.[35] He studied photochemical smog (what should be the national ambient air quality standard for the photochemical oxidant ozone?); Ohio coal (should the EPA prohibit electric utilities in Ohio from burning out-of-state low sulphur coal?); heavy-duty truck emissions (what should be the testing and enforcement provisions for heavy-duty truck emissions of hydrocarbons and carbon monoxide?); diesel particulate emissions (what should be the particulate emissions standard for diesel automobiles and light-duty trucks for 1981 and 1983?); fuel economy standards (should the National Highway Traffic Safety Administration revise automotive fuel economy standards for the 1980s?); and Tellico Dam and the snail darter (should the Tennessee Valley Authority (TVA) be allowed to complete construction of Tellico Dam and possibly cause the extinction of the snail darter fish?). These studies are a great source of information on the politics and economics that go into the enforcement of the environmental pollution laws, and they make very interesting reading.

Another book, *Benefit-Cost Analysis of Social Regulation: Case Studies from*

---

[35]Lawrence J. White, *Reforming Regulation: Processes and Problems,* Prentice-Hall, Englewood Cliffs, N.J., 1981.

the Council on Wage and Price Stability, edited by James C. Miller III and Bruce Yandle,[36] provides some interesting data on topics such as emissions standards for new motorcycles, water pollution controls for the iron and steel industries, and reducing airport noise, and is worth reading. So is the excellent article of Robert A. Leone and John E. Jackson, "The Political Economy of Federal Regulatory Activity: The Case of Water-Pollution Controls,"[37] which discusses the economics of the BPT standards applied to the tissue industry.

17.11 SUMMARY AND CONCLUSIONS

Although the health and welfare effects of environmental pollution are real and serious enough, it was not until the 1960s that the environment became a matter of serious public concern, thanks to the environmentalists and other interest groups. For a long time it was assumed that the environment was a "free" good and therefore could be used as a dumping ground for all kinds of pollution. But with the growth of population, the immense increase in industrial production, the new types of exotic materials made by modern science, the once free good has become an economic good, a good scarce relative to the demand for it. This scarcity has been increasing because the waste-assimilating capacity of the environment is limited due to the principle of conservation of mass, which states that matter cannot be made to disappear — it can only be changed into something else.

Ordinarily one can rely on the price mechanism to allocate scarce resources. But this presumes that the property rights in such resources are well-defined. Unfortunately for environment-type resources, which are in the nature of common-property or collective consumption goods, property rights are difficult, if not totally impossible, to define. As a result, some type of government intervention in the marketplace becomes inevitable in order to bring the private and social costs of production into balance. In this chapter we considered several methods of government intervention, from strict voluntarism to direct regulation.

An appeal to people's altruistic feelings, although useful in emergency situations, is generally not a viable method of controlling pollution on any appreciable scale because the temptation of the free rider problem is much too strong.

The next method is to institute some kind of liability system to compensate the victims. The most prevalent of such systems is the common-law tradition of suing the guilty party directly. And although one can always take recourse to this method, it is costly, time-consuming, and generally beyond the reach of common citizens.

Recognizing that people usually react favorably to incentives, economists strongly believe that some type of incentive system will achieve an "optimum"

---

[36]American Enterprise Institute for Public Policy Research, Washington, D.C., 1969.
[37]In Gary Fromm (ed.), *Studies in Public Regulation,* M.I.T., Cambridge, Mass., 1983. This book provides excellent reading in the various aspects of public regulation.

level of environmental pollution at least cost. The method they recommend is the effluent or emission tax on the pollutants. If the tax is set at the level at which the marginal cost of abating pollution is equal to the marginal benefit at that level of pollution, the polluters will reduce their pollution to this optimum level since economically it is in their interest to do. Among many of its advantages, the effluent tax approach is flexible in that it does not hold polluters to any pre-scribed rigid standard, as under the standards approach, but gives them all the incentive to devise new pollution-reducing methods.

Despite the many advantages of the incentives approach and its advocacy by the economists, the government in this country has chosen to rely exclusively on direct regulation via the standards approach, as was seen in our discussion of the pre- and post-1970 air and water pollution laws. The reason for this choice was political expediency. But this political expediency conflicts with eco-nomic efficiency, for an across-the-board application of prescribed standards does not recognize the differences in the pollution-abating efficiencies of the various polluters and therefore does not lead to optimum reduction of pollution. Moreover, as we have seen, the standards approach and the methods of admin-istering the grants and subsidies that have been built into it have led to overde-sign of waste treatment facilities and sheer waste.

Although one can justify the standards approach in the area of highly toxic substances which pose immediate danger to life and limb, it cannot be justified readily in other areas. As a matter of fact, if this approach is continued, then,

> . . . it will, we believe, open a field day for lawyers, incur heavy costs, require a huge bureaucracy to give it any chance of success, impose ad hoc and capricious impacts, and involve far-reaching intrusion of the government into decisions about the design of industrial process.[38]

Granted that the incentive approach is preferable to the standards method, would not a sudden switch to effluent and emission charges which minimize the cost of pollution control be too complex for practical application? As Kneese and Schultz suggest, as a first step a simplified tax schedule can be introduced. This is likely to introduce some inefficiencies and inequities; temporary relief may be sought in some hardship cases. This might necessitate temporary regulatory-type decisions on the part of the government. But with sufficient experience these problems can be gradually resolved. In this regard we can learn a lot from the European countries where effluent and emissions taxes have been imposed for several years now.

QUESTIONS

17-1 In what sense is an improved environment a public good?
17-2 Is it possible to "price" the environment (i.e., bring it under the market system) without government intervention? Why or why not?

[38]Kneese and Schultze, op. cit., pp. 106–107.

17-3 What do you think of the idea of levying a "dangerous substance charge" on the manufacturers of hazardous substances (e.g., chlorinated fluorocarbons)? Discuss the pros and cons of it.

17-4 Consider the billboards you see on the nation's highways. Although they may provide useful information to the traveler (e.g., restaurants, rest stops, etc.,), some travelers object to them as being unsightly. Should the authority leasing out the billboard space charge a "sight right" fee to the advertiser? To the traveler? To both? Discuss the consequences of each course of action.

17-5 Consider a "smog tax" on auto emissions (say, so many cents per gram-mile of CO). In what ways would it be better than the standards approach adopted by the EPA (see Table 17.2)? What problems do you foresee in the implementation of such a tax?

17-6 Refer to Figure 17.2. Suppose that the polluter does not want to incur the pollution control cost of B to achieve X, the optimum level of clean water. Could the users of the water pay the amount B out of thier pockets as a "bribe" to the polluter to induce a cleanup? Should they pay such a bribe? Why or why not?

17-7 Refer to Figure 17.3. At the optimum level of pollution $0(X)$, MX amount of pollution still remains. Can the government compensate the victims of this remaining pollution? How? Where would the government obtain resources for the compensation?

17-8 Again refer to Figure 17.3. What would happen if the government were to set the per unit tax rate at a level higher than the optimum tax rate of $0T$ per unit?

17-9 Refer to Table 17.1. What would happen if the unit abatement cost were 2 cents a gallon? 21 cents a gallon?

17-10 Considering the histories behind the Clean Air and Clean Water acts, what can you say about the lawmaking process in general in the area of environmental pollution? Is it any different from other areas of regulation, say, occupational health and safety?

17-11 In what ways are the Clean Air and Clean Water acts "radical"?

17-12 Considering the provisions and working of the 1970 and 1972 air and water pollution control laws, would you say that those laws are necessarily good laws? Why or why not?

17-13 Recalling the various theories of regulation discussed in Chapter 2, which one (or more) of them best describes the passage of the 1970 and 1972 laws? Explain fully.

17-14 Under the "doctrine of public nuisance" some states prohibit suits brought by individuals against general public nuisances such as air and water pollution. Would you advocate repeal of such laws? And why?

17-15 Consider the following hypothetical data on solid-waste disposal costs of three producers:

	Producers		
	A	B	C
Cost of eliminating first unit	$10	$ 5	$100
Cost of eliminating second unit	20	10	150
Cost of eliminating third unit	30	20	200
Cost of eliminating fourth unit	40	40	250
Cost of eliminating fifth unit	50	80	300
Cost of eliminating sixth unit	60	160	350

a Suppose the government mandates that no more than six units of solid waste in the aggregate can be discharged, each producer discharging no more than two units. What would be the total cost of pollution abatement under this standard?

b What would be the total cost of abatement if the government were to require A and B only to reduce pollution by twelve units and let producer C go his merry way?

c If the cost under item **b** is less than that under item **a,** would you recommend the scheme **b?** Why? Would A and B go along with it?

(For answers to these and other related questions, see Richard B. McKenzie and Gordon Tullock, *Modern Political Economy,* McGraw-Hill, New York, 1978, pp. 352–356; the above data are adapted from this book.)

17-16 *The EPA "bubble" policy:* In 1979, partially in response to complaints against its rigid engineering standards, the EPA introduced the "bubble" policy, underwhich instead of enforcing limits on each source of air pollution within an industrial facility, it allows one overall reduction target for each pollutant type — as if the entire complex were covered by a bubble. The ideal here is to encourage a company to achieve the overall goal through some innovative procedure.

Following this policy, the du Pont Company, at its Chambers Works chemical plant in Deepwater, New Jersey, instead of lowering the emissions of volatile organic compounds (precursors of smog) by 85 percent from each of the plant's 112 stacks, reduced the compounds from the plant's 7 largest stacks by 99 percent through incineration. This not only saved the company $10 million but it also helped the company to achieve better overall pollution reduction, with the average per stack now 90 percent (details based on Steven J. Marcus, "Bubble Policy: Pros and Cons," *The New York Times,* June 30, 1983, p. D2).

What does this episode indicate about EPA pollution control policies? Do you think the "bubble" policy is better than emission taxes? Justify your reasoning.

FIVE

THE NATURE AND SIGNIFICANCE OF REGULATORY REFORM

After discussing the growth, the theories, the structure, and the methods of regulation in general terms in Part 1, we considered in some detail the actual working of the antitrust, economic, and social regulations in Parts 2, 3, and 4, respectively. While discussing these regulations, we pointed out some of their failings and, from time to time, suggested some remedies.

In this final part, consisting of Chapter 18, we consider the various regulatory reform proposals that have been advanced by academic scholars, politicians, practitioners, and the administration. These reform proposals fall into four broad categories: procedural, structural, personnel, and substantive. After a brief discussion of the structural (i.e., the type of regulatory agency) and personnel (the process of recruiting qualified people to run the agencies) reform proposals, the bulk of the chapter is devoted to the discussion of procedural and substantive reforms. The procedural reforms such as *sunset legislation,* the *legislative veto,* the *regulatory budget,* and *congressionally mandated cost-benefit analysis* are discussed in some depth, including their pros and cons and their prospects in the Congress. In the substantive area, we discuss reform proposals in the areas of the environment, occupational safety and health, surface transportation, aviation, energy, and antitrust. Some of these proposals are noncontroversial (e.g., increased air safety) but some are highly controversial when, for example, Richard Posner argues that all antitrust laws other than Sec. 1 of the Sherman Antitrust Act should be repealed or when some economists advocate freely marketable pollution rights.

But controversies are to be expected in any reform battle since any reform is bound to affect adversely some vested interests, be they truckers, milk producers, or owners of TV or radio stations. But from such controversies some reform proposals do ultimately come to fruition, as the history of the Airline Deregulation Act of 1978 or the Motor Carrier Act of 1980 clearly reveals. That generally happens when the inefficiencies or the deadweight losses inflicted on the economy by the existing regulation are far greater than whatever benefits the vested interests might have to give up.

CHAPTER 18

REGULATORY REFORM

As we reach the 1980s, the issue of government credibility — its ability to respond sensibly and effectively, to know when to stay out as well as leap in — has grown larger. Our citizens and businesses feel overregulated. To most Americans regulation is not the president. It is not the secretary of energy or the Department of Health and Human Services. It is not even Washington. It is the energy allocation guidelines no one can understand. It is the government contract officer who puts people through hoops before looking at their applications. It is the inspector from the FAA or the OSHA or the Agricultural Department who may hold life-and-death power over their businesses but who does not seem to understand their operations and acts unwilling to learn. . . .

The mainsprings of the current debate are the high cost of regulation, along with inflation, the general public feeling that government intervenes too much in our lives, and the breakdown of classical rationales for federal regulations. These are the reasons this subject [of regulatory reform] has become more than the preserve of academics and commissions whose reports gather dust on Washington's bookshelves.

Senator Edward M. Kennedy[1]

18.1 THE NEED FOR REFORM

The fact that the preceding statement came from an influential and supposedly liberal politician and not from the University of Chicago economists or President Reagan suggests that all is really not well with the economic regulation practiced since the establishment of the ICC in 1887 and the social regulation carried out

---

[1]"Regulatory Reform: Striking a Balance," in Timothy B. Clark, Marvin H. Kosters, and James C. Miller III (eds.), *Reforming Regulation,* American Enterprise Institute for Public Policy Research, Washington, D.C., 1980, p. 28 (hereafter referred to as *Reforming Regulation*)

since the mid-1960s. The question of regulatory reform — be it deregulation, less regulation, or changes in the way regulation is practiced — is no longer "an issue of Left versus Right with the Left demanding regulation and the Right resisting it."[2]

Our study of economic regulation in the railroad and trucking industries (Chapter 11), the airline industry (Chapter 12), the energy industry (Chapter 13), the securities industry (Chapter 14), and the communications industry (Chapter 15), and social regulation in the areas of health and safety (Chapter 16) and environmental pollution (Chapter 17) has shown that, on the whole, these regulations have not produced the desired results — they have not made the American economy more competitive nor have they necessarily improved the quality of life. And if we apply the test that "regulation is appropriate whenever the aggregate gain in social welfare from regulation exceeds the aggregate social cost of regulation, with all side effects [i.e., externalities] considered,"[3] most economic regulation fails to pass this test, and the available evidence about social regulation suggests that it too has failed.

Consider economic regulation first. The rationale for regulating various industries, such as the railroads, trucking, and the airlines, was that "without controls firms in these particular industries would not sufficiently improve the quality or the volume of service."[4] The means used to accomplish these objectives were price (including rate of return) and entry regulations. But our study of economic regulation in Part 3 has shown that these measures have had adverse economic effects. They have led to economically unjustifiable cross-subsidization (e.g., in the airline, trucking, and railroad industries); protection of a particular industry or firm (e.g., not allowing the railroads to reduce their rates to incremental cost on the long-distance traffic to protect the interests of the truckers although the latter were not ideally suited for long-haul traffic, or the protection of VHF channels against competition from the UHF channels); or retardation of technological innovation (e.g., delayed introduction of the "Big John hopper" or the TAT-5 decision although satellite technology was available and well-developed). All these measures have inflicted serious efficiency or deadweight losses on the economy. They have also lead to conferring valuable property rights on certain individuals or industries (e.g., allocation of the scarce electromagnetic spectrum), thereby transferring large amounts of income to the recipients of the property rights — a transfer that may not be justified on equity grounds.

Turning to social regulation, its justification was primarily on the grounds that "private producers fail to take into account the social harm of unhealthy and unsafe conditions of production"[5]; that is, they fail to take into account the social costs generated by negative externalities on account of air and water pollution and unsafe or unhealthy working conditions. While government interven-

[2]Lester C. Thurow, *The Zero-Sum Society,* Penguin, New York, 1980, p. 128.

[3]Almarin Phillips, "Regulation and Its Alternatives," in Donald P. Jacobs (ed.), *Regulating Business: The Search for an Optimum,* Institute for Contemporary Studies, San Francisco, California, 1978, pp. 165-166.

[4]Paul W. MacAvoy, "Overview of Regulatory Effects and Reform Prospects," in *Reforming Regulation,* Op. cit., p. 10.

[5]Ibid., p. 11.

TABLE 18.1
PERCENTAGE OF GNP IN THE REGULATED SECTOR OF THE ECONOMY

Category	Percentage of GNP under Regulation in 1965*	Percentage of GNP under Regulation in 1975*
Price regulation†	5.5	8.8
Financial markets regulation‡	2.7	3.0
Health and safety regulation§	—	11.9
Total	8.2	23.7

The calculations are GNP originated by industry group as a percentage of GNP originated by all industry. Industries are defined as including those companies or activities accounted for in the Department of Commerce Standard Industrial Classification (SIC).

+ Includes railroads (40), motor freight transportation and warehousing (42), air transportation (45), communications (48), electric, gas, and sanitary services (49), and (for 1975 only) crude petroleum and natural gas (13) (SIC codes in parentheses).

‡ Includes banking (60) and insurance (63) (SIC codes in parentheses).

§Includes metal mining (10), coal mining (11–12), mining and quarrying of nonmetallic minerals (14), construction (15–17), paper and allied products (26), chemical and allied products (28), petroleum and related industries (29), stone, clay, and glass products (32), primary metal industries (33), motor vehicles and equipment (371) (SIC codes in parentheses).

Source: U.S. Department of Commerce, *Workfile* 1205-02-02, 1976 revision; reproduced from Paul W. Mac-Avoy, "Overview of Regulatory Effects and Reform Prospects," in *Reforming Regulation,* p. 12, table 1.

tion is justifiable to abate negative externalities, the methods chosen by the government – the almost exclusive reliance on engineering standards – have inflicted heavy compliance costs on industries. That is why agencies such as the EPA and OSHA are universally detested by all the affected industries; there are very few industries which can escape EPA and OSHA across-the-board compliance standards. As we have seen, economists contend that the objectives of social regulation, such as cleaner environment and safer workplaces, can better be achieved by incentive systems such as the pollution and effluent taxes, which make it in the interest of the affected party to clean up the environment or make the workplace healthier and safer if the cost of doing so is less than the tax payments.

That economic and social regulations affect the American economy is undeniable. As Table 18.1 shows, in 1975 about 24 percent of the GNP was produced in the regulated sector, as compared to only 8.2 percent just 10 years before; the increase is largely attributable to social regulation. Although one may quarrel about the numbers given in the table, one can also argue that "stagflation" (the simultaneous existence of inflation and slow output and employment growth) facing the economy is in no small measure attributable to regulatory constraints imposed on productive activity. The deregulatory initiatives taken by Congress since the Airline Deregulation Act of 1978 are an explicit recognition of that fact. But regulatory reform has a long way to go, for the task is not easy.

18.2 WHY REGULATORY REFORM HAS BEEN SLOW

Despite the many failings of economic and social regulation, regulatory reform has been slow in coming. It was not until the Airline Deregulation Act of 1978 that some visible and durable reform was seen. There are several reasons why the reform has been slow.[6]

Difficult to Change Perception

As Antonin Scalia notes, "The way government goes depends not so much upon the realities as upon the public perception of the realities at the time. And that perception, for many years, has been that 'there oughta to be a law' — that many areas will profit from government control. Changing that public perception takes a long time. . . ."[7]

Income-Distributive Effect of Regulation

According to Sam Peltzman, regulation not only involves deadweight or efficiency losses (i.e., the net value of goods and services not produced because of departure from competitive conditions), but, by conferring valuable property rights, it also transfers income from consumers to owners of these property rights. And as Lester Thurow correctly observes, " . . . whatever the overt objective, the implicit objective [of regulation] is always to alter the distribution of income and this is almost always the real reason for the existence of any regulation."[8] And this is true whether it is the granting of a medallion to run a taxicab in New York City or the acquisition of a lucrative truck route or a VHF channel. As we saw in Chapter 12, the ICC-conferred truck routes gave the operators of those routes substantial monopoly profits.

Now whether the transfer of income from consumers to the recipients of valuable property rights is good or bad is difficult to decide since it does involve some value judgment. But regardless of this controversial question, the point to note is that once granted it is very difficult to take back these property rights because the vested interests will fight tooth and nail to guard these rights by heavy lobbying and political contributions to candidates supporting their position (recall George Stigler's economic theory of regulation). As Robert Samuelson notes, "they are likely to have allies in specialized congressional committees and subcommittees and in batteries of lawyers, consultants, and economists — including, often, ex-regulators and ex-legislators — whose livelihoods and sense of self-esteem are wrapped up in the regulatory process. All these forces become engaged in any effort at "regulatory reform.""[9]

This, however, does not mean that the interest groups will always prevail. In Peltzman's view, if the efficiency or deadweight losses far exceed the income transfer, then some regulatory changes do take place.

In 1970 the CAB investigated the economics of the domestic airfare structure.

---

[6]The following discussion is based on, *Unsettled Questions on Regulatory Reform,* a symposium organized by the American Enterprise Institute for Public Policy Research Washington, D.C., 1978. (Hereafter referred to as the *AEI Symposium.*) The participants were some of the leading scholars in the field of regulation in the country.

[7]Ibid, p. 1.

[8]Lester Thurow, op. cit., p. 123.

[9]Robert J. Samuelson, "The Case-by-Case Approach to Regulatory Reform: Introduction," in *Reforming Regulation,* op. cit., p. 88.

It was revealed that the regulated airfares had lead to large deadweight losses in relation to the income that was being transferred from passengers to the airlines or from one group of passengers to another or from one region of the nation to the other. Once the CAB realized this, and once it had a chairperson like Alfred Kahn, there was some move toward regulatory reform. The Congress soon joined in the reform battle, the final outcome being the Airline Deregulation Act of 1978.

The Asymmetry of the Lawmaking Process

According to John Snow, former administrator of the NHTSA (National Highway Traffic Safety Administration), lawmaking in Washington, D.C., follows the philosophy of regulating "quickly" and then deregulating "eventually"; once Congress passes a law and sets up the regulatory machinery to administer it, it is very reluctant to change it even though in many cases the original need for the law no longer exists. Our study of economic regulation in Part 3 has revealed this tendency time and again. One may even call it the "Washington, D.C., law" of rule-making.

Inadequate Knowledge of the Dynamic Aspects of Deregulation

Although economists generally favor deregulation of many controlled activities, they have not adequately considered the dynamic, that is, the transitional aspects of deregulation — going from the state of regulation to the state of deregulation and what happens to prices, output, employment, and income during the transition phase. As Roger Noll points out, "Virtually all of the economic research comparing deregulated with regulated transportation demonstrates that the deregulated state is more efficient than the other, but price, output, and income distribution during the process of deregulation have not been assessed."[10] The case in point is the energy industry after the 1973 oil embargo. There was no question that the government could not keep the domestic price of crude oil controlled at the price of about $6 a barrel when the world price had gone to $12 a barrel. But it was not until 1978 that some substantial deregulation of crude oil prices took place, the delay being due to the fact that Congress did not have much knowledge about the transitional effect of such deregulation on prices and consumer income; recall the storm over President Carter's proposal to impose a 10 cents a gallon tax on the retail price of gasoline, a proposal ultimately withdrawn. It was not until the windfall profit tax provision was included in the deregulation bill that Congress could vote on the energy bill, although, as we have seen in Chapter 13, no sound economic reasons could be given for the imposition of such a tax.

Inadequate Knowledge of Social Regulation

Economists have studied the effects of economic regulation in considerable depth. But when it comes to social regulation, especially in the areas of health,

[10]Roger G. Noll, *AEI Symposium, op. cit.,* p. 9.

safety, and the environment, their studies have been inadequate. Again to quote Noll:

> . . . economists know almost nothing about the effects of noneconomic regulation, such as regulation of health, safety, or the environment, because our modelling techniques and methods of analysis are based largely on market results. We know very little about how to model qualitative effects, and we have great difficulty inferring things about values that are not transacted in markets. . . .[11]

Lack of Conceptual Framework for Regulatory Reform

In the view of H. S. Houthakker of Harvard, the case for regulatory reform has not been made not because of defects in empirical studies, but because

> What we have not yet done is to give the public a conceptual framework on the whole subject of regulation. What purposes can regulation serve, and how can it best serve these purposes? What activities are outside the proper sphere of regulation? These questions have not been answered, and, as a result, the movement toward deregulation is conceptually on rather thin ice.[12]

18.3 THE ANATOMY OF REFORM

Regulatory reform may be considered under four headings: procedural, structural, personnel, and substantive.

Procedural Reforms

Such reforms revolve around the ways a regulatory agency or a congressional committee or the Congress itself goes about conducting the task of regulation. The overall objective of such reforms is to reduce the costs of regulation, both direct and indirect, to individuals and to businesses. Some of the proposals that have been or are being considered by Congress or by the executive branch are: *sunset review* (to set a definite timetable to terminate a particular regulation or a particular regulatory agency), *legislative veto* (Congress's right to veto the rules promulgated by regulatory agencies), *regulatory budget* (an overall limit to direct and indirect or compliance costs that a regulation can impose on business), and *mandated cost-benefit analysis*. These topics are discussed in the following sections.

Structural Reforms

These reforms refer to the structure of a regulatory agency, whether it is an independent commission, an executive branch agency, or a semi-independent agency. We have already discussed the pros and cons of these structures in

---

[11]Ibid., p. 10.
[12]*AEI Symposium,* op. cit., pp. 12–13.

Chapter 3; little needs to be added to that discussion except to note that very often the talk of structural reform is a smoke screen for avoiding the real problems facing a regulatory agency — making the OSHA an independent regulatory commission is not necessarily going to reduce the workplace injury rate.

Personnel Reforms

As we noted in Chapter 3, very often members of the regulatory bodies are chosen on the basis of the BOGSAT principle, a "bunch of guys sitting around the table" and making recommendations to the President. There is no question that there is vast scope for improvement in the nominating and selection procedures in recruitment for the various regulatory agencies and that qualified people can and do make a difference in the quality of regulation, as Alfred Kahn demonstrated so ably when he became chairperson of the CAB. But the initiative here has to come from the President, who is ultimately responsible for who runs the various commissions and agencies. The Senate *Study on Federal Regulation* strongly recommended that all regulatory appointments should be centralized under the supervision of a single staff member within the White House personnel office and that office should develop and maintain a systematic procedure for recruitment and evaluation of prospective appointees that allows ample opportunity for public involvement.[13]

Substantive Reforms

Useful as the preceding three types of reforms are in increasing the overall efficiency of regulation, the heart of regulatory reform lies in substantive reforms, such as those that have taken place in the airline industry, and, to a lesser extent, in the trucking, railroad, and communications industries. Without considerable deregulation in the area of economic regulation and substantial tightening up of social regulation, it is well-nigh impossible to control regulatory costs. Also, several scholars agree that the all-purpose antitrust laws have been obsolete and need to be revamped. The specifics of these substantive reforms are considered in subsequent sections.

18.4 PROCEDURAL REFORM: THE SUNSET LEGISLATION

As the Senate *Study on Federal Regulation* describes it:

> The essence of the sunset idea is to place a time limit on the existence of Federal agencies and programs. If, for example, at the end of a specified period, a program's continued existence could not be justified, it would terminate; the "sun would set."[14]

---

[13]Senate *Study on Federal Regulation*, Vol I, *The Regulatory Appointment Process*. This volume of about 560 pages goes into the whole question of the appointments process very thoroughly.

[14]Senate *Study on Federal Regulation*, vol. II: *Congressional Oversight of Regulatory Agencies*, p. 129.

In the view of the Senate *Study on Federal Regulation* there are three reasons why sunset proposals have been popular in the Congress, especially in the 95th Congress:[15] (1) the vast number and complexity of federal programs, (2) the dramatic increase in the percentage of federal spending for "uncontrollable" programs, and (3) even more rapid growth in the cost of federal programs with permanent appropriations, those which escape any systematic and thorough congressional oversight.

Therefore, argue the protagonists of sunset legislation, unless Congress undertakes systematic review of the regulatory agencies and gets rid of those which are no longer serving a useful purpose, the regulatory agencies will indeed become the fourth branch of the government, not accountable to the legislative branch that created them in the first place.[16]

On the face of it the sunset idea is very appealing. And yet, despite many bills to that effect in the Congress, not much progress has been made at the federal level, though some sunset measures have been adopted by several states. This is because there are three major hurdles in designing and implementing a sunset procedure.[17] The first concerns the automatic termination feature. In many cases it is an extreme remedy to resort to. The talk of sunsetting an FTC or an FDA would simply be dismissed as nonsense. To mitigate this, Senator Percy, in a bill he has cosponsored, would move toward sunset in stages of three deadlines. If Congress does not take steps to reinstate an agency by the first deadline to sunset it, the agency's authority to issue new regulations would lapse. If Congress still did not act by the second deadline, the agency's authority to enforce existing regulations would lapse. A regulatory agency would cease to exist if Congress failed to meet the third deadline. The second problem with the sunset proposal is the workload it would entail, what with umpteen agencies to evaluate. The third, and perhaps the most critical problem, is a pragmatic one: The strength of the constituency against termination in the Congress, in the agency itself, and in the private sector is very strong. The bureaucrats are reluctant to give up their power, and the forces in the private sector whose incomes are beneficially affected by regulation are not likely to give up that income easily. That this is so can be learned from the fact the recent congressional attempts to sunset the Commodity Futures Trading Commission (CFTC) and the Consumer Product Safety Commission (CPSC) have failed, despite severe criticisms of the working of these commissions in many quarters. As Dennis Avery notes, this is because the strength of the constituency against sunsetting is so much better placed than any generalized reform constituency favoring the termination.[18] Therefore despite its appeal, "sunset remains an idea of promise, not fulfillment."[19]

---

[15]Ibid.

[16]In his book, *Regulating Business by Independent Commissions* (Princeton University Press, 1966), Marver Bernstein argues that regulatory agencies, like human beings, age; these agencies are more vigorous and successful in their earlier years but become less successful as they grow older.

[17]See W. S. Moore, "Sunset Review: Introduction," in *Reforming Regulation* op. cit., pp. 31-33.

[18]Dennis Avery, "The Record on Sunset Review of Two Agencies," in *Reforming Regulation,* op. cit., pp. 41-44. Avery was special assistant to the CFTC.

[19]W. S. Moore, op. cit., p. 33.

18.5   PROCEDURAL REFORM: THE LEGISLATIVE VETO

There is an increasing feeling in the Congress that some of the regulatory agencies, such as the FTC, OSHA, and EPA, have become so powerful that the only way, short of sunsetting, to stop their excesses is to have veto power over the rules and regulations they promulgate. John Snow, the former administrator of the National Highway Traffic Safety Administration (NHTA) sees the legislative veto ``as a way of letting off political pressure when a regulatory agency exceeds political constraints and feels that it does not solve the deeper substantive problems.''[20]

One proponent of the legislative veto argues that the veto will not only curb the bureaucratic excesses of the regulatory agencies but will also force the Congress itself to act more responsibly in delegating authority to these agencies as a result of possessing the veto power. He argues:

> Congress is far too lax, now, in delegating legislative authority broadly and without guidelines. When hard decisions have to be made we pass the buck to the agencies with broadly worded statutes. When our constituents call us to task because of the ensuing regulations it is easy for us to join in the chorus decrying the monster bureaucracy and let it pass at that. If we realize that we have the ultimate responsibility for the administrative rules that flow from these enabling acts, we will be more careful in drafting language and more specific in detailing legislative intent.[21]

Some of the bills introduced in Congress would let either the Senate or the House veto a regulation issued by a regulatory agency during a 60-day period following the issuance of the rule. If one house decided to veto the regulation, the other house would have 30 days to override the veto, thus allowing the proposed rule to become law.

Although Congress recently acquired such veto power over the regulations issued by the FTC, the idea of the legislative veto remains highly controversial. According to Antonin Scalia, the legislative veto over regulatory agencies' actions is unconstitutional on two grounds. First, Article I, Sec. 7 of the Constitution provides for the President's participation in the legislative process. The legislative veto provision would bypass that. Second, and more important, the veto violates the principle of separation of power. Once a law is passed by the legislative branch, its execution is left to the executive branch (and its agencies) and its implementation to the judiciary. Therefore, for the Congress to say, via the legislative veto, that a regulatory agency can issue this regulation but not that, is a sneaky way to violate this separation of power. If Congress does not like a rule, let it pass an explicit law to that effect, which would then involve the executive branch and eventually the judiciary.

Apart from the constitutionality question, the legislative veto has many problems. The Senate *Study on Federal Regulation* believes that it will increase delay in the regulatory process, increase uncertainty in the regulated industries,

---

[20]See *Reforming Regulation,* op. cit., p. 102.
[21]Testimony of Congressman Elliot Levitas, reported in the Senate *Study on Federal Regulation,* vol. II, op. cit., p. 117.

increase pressure on Congress, diminish the usefulness of agency records, encourage the agencies to decrease rule-making and increase adjudication, and generally have an adverse impact on the entire regulatory program. Additionally the legislative veto is "a tool which allows special interests to evade the agency prohibitions against *ex parte* contacts to influence policy," and it defeats "the purpose of delegating rulemaking powers from generalist politicians to independent experts."[22]

The protagonists of the legislative veto, however, feel differently. In their view, ". . . the independence theory of rulemaking is outdated and that political judgements about conflicting societal goals are an essential part of the rulemaking process and should not go unreviewed."[23] They also argue that the possibility of the veto, without its actual use, is often good enough to increase accountability to the public and will make the regulatory agencies more responsive.

The Supreme Court Decision on Legislative Veto

On June 23, 1983, the Supreme Court decided on the constitutionality of the legislative veto. Arguing more or less on the same lines as Scalia, by a majority of 7 to 2, the Court held such vetos to be unconstitutional. In writing the decision, Chief Justice Burger argued that the Constitution permits the enactment of legislation only "in accord with a single, finely wrought and exhaustively considered procedure," namely "passage by a majority of both houses and presentment to the President" for his signature or veto. That procedure, the Chief Justice said, can be "clumsy" and "inefficient." But, he continued, "with all the obvious flaws of delay, untidiness and potential for abuse, we have not yet found a better way to preserve freedom than by making the exercise of power subject to the carefully crafted restraints spelled out in the Constitution."

In the wake of this landmark decision, there is considerable debate in the Congress about viable alternatives to the legislative veto. It will be interesting to see what the Congress does.

18.6 PROCEDURAL REFORM: THE REGULATORY BUDGET

While discussing the costs of regulation in Chapter 5 we observed that it is difficult to measure the compliance costs that many a regulation entails. The question of compliance costs has become especially serious since the mid-1960s when health, safety, and environmental regulations were passed. The compliance costs of these social legislations have far exceeded the direct costs of administering them. Although the regulatory agencies are not directly concerned with the indirect compliance costs, from society's viewpoint one should

---

[22]*Regulation and Regulatory Reforms: A Survey of Proposals of the 95th Congress,* American Enterprise Institute for Public Policy Research, Washington, D.C., 1978, p. 10.
[23]Ibid.

reckon them along with the direct costs of administration to get the total impact of the various regulations on the economy. In short, from society's viewpoint, one should consider the social costs of regulation.

One way to do this would be to pass a *regulatory budget,* which can be described thus:

> Just as Congress authorizes broad fiscal programs but then allocates specific spending budgets for each agency for each fiscal year, Congress could pass broad regulatory programs but then pass annual limits on the costs that each regulatory agency could impose on the sectors it regulates. Thus, each regulatory agency would have its own regulatory budget, and there would be a total regulatory budget for the entire federal government. The legislative process for this new budget could parallel the legislative process for the existing budget.[24]

Thus the regulatory budget would force the government not only to consider the direct costs of regulation but the indirect costs as well. It is indeed a novel concept. As Marvin Kosters notes, ``It would involve assignment of priorities in deciding both the total resources to be devoted to meeting the goals of regulation and how those resources should be divided among competing regulatory objectives.''[25]

The proponents of the regulatory budget claim that it has several advantages. First, Congress would get some definite idea about what the government's regulatory activities are costing the individual citizen or businesses. Second, a regulatory agency would think twice before issuing new regulations, for it would now have to estimate what they would cost the economy. Third, `` . . . it would provide a more accurate picture of the government's total impact on the economy, allowing Congress to determine how much of the nation's output will be directed by government and how much will be directed by the private sector.''[26] Finally, ``It would make possible a better balance between regulatory programs and the traditional methods by which the government has acted in these areas — that is, direct spending on the objectives they want to reach.''[27]

Although a novel weapon to contain regulatory costs, the regulatory budget faces some serious practical difficulties.[28] The first is the problem of collecting and analyzing the vast quantities of cost information that would be needed to estimate and enforce the regulatory budget. Then there is the question of what costs to measure. For example, should it include in costs the benefits consumers would have reaped from a technology that was prevented or was introduced with considerable delay because of regulatory lags (recall from Chapter 5 the ICC prevention of piggybacking for a long time)? This is a difficult question, and

[24]Lawrence J. White, ``Truth in Regulatory Budgeting,'' *Regulation,* March–April 1980, p. 44.
[25]Marvin H. Kosters, ``The Regulatory Budget: Introduction,'' in *Reforming Regulation,* op. cit., p. 70.
[26]Clearance J. Brown, ``Legislating a Regulatory Budget Limit,'' in *Reforming Regulation,* op. cit., p. 74.
[27]Ibid.
[28]For details, see Christopher C. DeMuth, ``The Regulatory Budget,'' *Regulation,* March–April 1980, pp. 29–44.

unless some consensus is obtained on what costs to include in the regulatory budget, this tool is of little practical importance. Another serious problem with the regulatory budget is that it neglects the benefits associated with regulation. Environmental pollution laws, for instance, not only inflict costs on society but also confer benefits. What we need is a measure of the net cost of regulation, that is, costs after subtracting the benefits. But the regulatory budget concept simply bypasses this issue.

In sum, the concept of the regulatory budget is interesting but very difficult to implement. As Ralph Nader states, " . . . the economic tools needed for an analysis of the regulatory process do not exist," and, "the cost of compliance, too, is a whole hornet's nest."[29]

18.7   PROCEDURAL REFORM: COST-BENEFIT ANALYSIS

Before the new breed of social regulation came on the horizon, there was less concern with the overall costs of regulation. But with the passage of health and safety and environmental regulations, the President and Congress began to take note of the increasing impact of these regulations on the nation's economy because of their very broad application to all sectors of the economy.

The Nixon administration was the first to address this problem when it established a Quality of Life Review system. Under it the OMB (Office of Management and Budget) held interagency meetings to comment on health and safety and environmental regulations and possibly modify them to reduce the compliance costs.

President Ford supplemented the Quality of Life Review by requiring the executive branch agencies to issue Inflation Impact Statements, later called Economic Impact Statements, detailing the economic impact of a proposed regulation.

President Carter terminated the Quality of Life Review but continued the Economic Impact Statement and established the Regulatory Analysis Review Group (RARG) to review regulations with substantial economic effects.

President Reagan established a Presidential Task Force on Regulatory Relief to look into procedural reforms and substantive reforms, that is, into the possibility of accelerating the pace of deregulation. The task force has yet to submit its report officially.

All these attempts to introduce some form of cost-benefit analysis of regulation have been essentially by executive orders and cover largely the agencies under the direct control of the executive branch, although the question of bringing the independent regulatory commissions under these orders was also discussed from time to time. The initiative in the latter case had to come ultimately from the creator of these commissions, namely, the Congress. Some bills have been introduced in Congress to that effect. As yet, though, no bill has cleared both the houses.

---

[29]Ralph Nader, "Can a Regulatory Budget Be Calculated," in *Reforming Regulation,* op. cit., p. 79.

We have commented on cost-benefit analysis extensively in Chapter 5 and at various other places throughout the text. One could very well agree with James G. Miller III, chairperson of the FTC, when he writes:

At a conceptual level, few would disagree with cost-benefit analysis as a filter for agency decision making, for all it requires is that agencies engage only in activities that pass the test of common sense. The debate is over whether and how well this concept can be applied in practice. The costs of regulatory proposals are often difficult to measure, and arguably there are biases in the data on which such estimates are based. Benefits are even more difficult, especially in cases involving reduction in the risk of accidental injury or death. Beyond these problems are questions of [income] redistribution. That is, it matters not only how much the benefits and costs are, but who gets the benefits and who bears the costs.[30]

What then is the future of cost-benefit analysis in the regulatory reform movement? Perhaps the reformers may pay heed to what Yale law professor Peter H. Schuk has to say:

... the imperfections and limitations of cost-benefit analysis should be squarely addressed and acknowledged. There is no reason to apologize for them. They are inherent in the limitations of human rationality. Some improvements can be made in cost-benefit analysis, but many shortcomings will inevitably remain, and there will always be incentives to distort and misuse this kind of analysis. . . .
   . . . the real question is not whether cost-benefit analysis can be misused — any tool can be misused — but rather whether it will be used to its full potential.[31]

Another writer expresses a similar view:

Perhaps we are used to thinking of cost-benefit analysis as something which can be precisely worked out and on which decisions can be entirely based. Unfortunately, this is not the case. Particularly with social regulation, problems exist, and will continue to exist in the area of differences of expert opinion on the costs and benefits of improvements in quality of air, water, health, product safety, occupational safety, etc. Yet cost-benefit analysis should present a valuable framework for organizing the disagreements and for determining where differences in expert opinion have originated. If the difference is in the value of human lives saved rather than in the number of human lives saved, at least those making decisions know where the disagreement originates. If the difference is over the number of lives to be saved, more accurate data can be sought.[The advantages of using cost-benefit analysis for organizing debate are great. The advantages of using cost-benefit analysis for making final decision are [may be?] small.[32]]

18.8 SUBSTANTIVE REGULATORY REFORMS

The regulatory reform ushered in by the Airline Deregulation Act of 1978 and continued by the Motor Carrier Act of 1980 and the Staggers Rail Act of 1980

[30]James C. Miller III, "Cost-Benefit Analysis of Social Regulation: Introduction," in *Reforming Regulation,* op. cit., pp. 106–107.
[31]Peter H. Schuck, "A Tool for Assessing Social Legislation," in *Reforming Regulation,* op. cit., p. 121.
[32]An anonymous referee.

are the kind of reforms the reformers have in mind when they talk of substantive reform. While it is impossible to detail the many reform suggestions and proposals that have come from the average citizen, regulatory scholars, the administration, and the Congress, we will consider highlights of some of the reform proposals that have been made by respected scholars in the areas we have studied in this text. In this section we consider these reforms in the area of the environment, health and safety, energy, aviation, and surface transportation. In the next section we consider reforms in the area of antitrust legislation, an area that affects the overall economy significantly but has not received the kind of attention that has been showered upon social regulation.

Environmental Regulation

The EPA is in the unenviable position of being attacked from both left and right for either not implementing the Clean Air and Clean Water acts properly or for enforcing them too strictly and thereby adversely affecting capital formation, productivity growth, employment, and standard of living. According to Robert Crandall, a senior fellow at the Brookings Institution, the EPA finds itself in this bind because it is asked to do too much. He asks:

> How can the agency be expected to determine the "best available control technology," and the "lowest achievable emissions rate" for six or seven different pollutants emanating from each of thousands of sources in hundreds of different industries? Add to all this the requirement for approving 50 state implementation plans for achieving air quality standards — plans that include detailed standards for all existing sources of all major air pollutants — and you have a regulatory task of monster proportions.[33]

Commenting on the future of environmental regulation, Crandall suggests:

> Clearly, it is neither wise nor even feasible simply to abandon the regulatory program that has been worked out by EPA over the past decade. But we should prepare the groundwork for a much more effective program of environmental protection — one that may even work! — with less reliance on detailed standards and intervention in the design of industrial and environmental control systems. Improving the scientific base for decision making, greatly increasing monitoring capabilities, and refining enforcement-penalties system will assist in moving environmental policy in the only direction that holds real promise — toward a decentralized incentive system of pollution taxes or marketable pollution rights.[34]

Occupational Safety and Health Regulation

Perhaps the most despised of the federal regulatory agencies is OSHA. Our review of OSHA in Chapter 16 has shown that it has not made workplaces significantly safer or healthier. As James C. Miller III, the current FTC chairperson,

---

[33]Robert W. Crandall, "Environmental Protection Agency," *Regulation,* November–December 1980, p. 20.
[34]Ibid., p. 22.

notes, OSHA's regulatory failure is due to inadequacies in the enabling legislation and in the agency's own use of its discretion.[35] The Occupational Safety and Health Act is very vague about what OSHA is supposed to do. For example, the act does not say much about conducting a cost-benefit study before a health or safety standard is set. As we saw in the *Benzene* and *Cotton Dust* cases, the courts had a hard time deciding whether such cost-benefit studies were really called for: In the *Benzene* case the lower court held that OSHA must do a reasonable analysis of the expected costs and benefits of the proposed benzene standard, whereas in the *Cotton Dust* case the Supreme Court held that the law does not require it. The agency itself has not always conducted detailed studies before prescribing certain standards, as we have seen in Chapter 16.

Miller suggests that the act be amended as follows: (1) require that all new rules and regulations pass a cost-benefit test and "sunset" all old rules according to a definite timetable. If any of these old rules need to be retained, they too should be subjected to the cost-benefit test; (2) change OSHA's role from that of setting and enforcing safety and health standards to one of approving or modifying the standards worked out between labor and management— "OSHA's function should be consultation and oversight, not command and control,"[36] and where the establishment of enforcement of standards is appropriate, develop an incentive system (taxes or fines) to achieve compliance.

Pending the statutory revision of OSHA, Miller urges the agency itself to take the following initiatives:

1 Issue a directive that personal protective devices, such as earplugs or earmuffs or masks, are acceptable ways to meet performance standards. The potential cost savings here are substantial.

2 As far as possible, resort to performance rather than to specification or engineering standards.

3 Require that all new rules proposed must meet two tests: first, the anticipated benefits of the rule must exceed the anticipated costs and second, the least costly alternative must be chosen.

Surface Transportation

In the area of trucking and railroad regulation, the thrust of some of the reform proposals is toward accelerating the pace of deregulation set in motion by the Motor Carrier Act of 1980 and the Staggers Rail Act of 1980. Thomas Moore, a senior fellow at the Hoover Institute and a scholar in this area, makes the following specific suggestions:[37]

[35]James C. Miller, "Occupational Safety and Health Administration," *Regulation,* November–December 1980, pp. 22-23.
[36]Ibid., p. 23.
[37]Thomas Gale Moore, "Regulation of Surface Transport," *Regulation,* November–December, pp. 34-35.

1 End all operating restrictions on routes and commodities on the trucking industry.

2 Since the Motor Carrier Act prohibits the ICC from investigating, suspending, revising, or revoking any proposed rate on the grounds that it is too low or too high (within certain limits), the commission might simply approve all rates that are proposed by the truckers while reserving the right to know the rate changes 30 days before they become effective.

3 Abolish all barriers to entry into the trucking industry.

4 The Staggers Rail Act introduced only limited flexibility in the rates charged by the railroads, but why not make the rates fully competitive?

5 Considering the fact that the nation's railroads are financially very weak, the Congress should enact guidelines to close down uneconomical rail lines as quickly as possible. Pending this, the commission should be prompt in approving abandonment applications.

One segment of surface transport that did not come under the purview of the Motor Carrier Act of 1980 was the intercity bus industry, which is dominated by two giants, Greyhound and Trailways. This industry has largely been controlled by state regulatory agencies which control prices and routes. The bus industry has been in a decade-long slump and the two giant operators themselves argued for lessening the price and route restrictions. After considerable pressure from various sources, Congress passed the Bus Regulatory Reform Act on August 20, 1982, and President Reagan signed it into law on September 20, 1982. The provisions of the new act more or less parallel those of the Motor Carrier Act. Briefly, the major provisions of the bill are as follows:

1 Any "fit, willing and able" bus operator may enter the business unless it can be proved that the service will be against the "public interest." In the past, as in the case of aviation and trucking industries, the prospective entrant had to prove that the service was needed.

2 Bus companies may withdraw from unprofitable services in most circumstances, although interests of small communities without alternative transportation facilities will be kept in mind before a service is discontinued.

3 In successive stages, the fares will be fully competitive. Immediately, the bus companies can raise fares 10 percent or lower them 20 percent beyond the fare levels a year before the proposed change.

4 Operators of chartered buses can charge whatever they wish, provided the fares are not "predatory."

It is expected by the proponents of the deregulation that consumers will now have price and quality-of-service options which did not exist before, and the bus operators will regain their economic strength by successfully competing with alternative means of transportation. Already the ICC has applications from 950 aspiring entrants — 800 of which are for charter service, according to a July 11, 1983, article in *Business Week*.

Aviation Regulation

The domestic aviation industry is now substantially deregulated, with beneficial effects on consumers but some hardship on some airlines because of the 1981–1982 economic recession and the transitional problems of going from a regulated regime to one of reasonably open and free competition. The reformers are now aiming at fostering competition in international aviation and in improving airline safety.

In the international field, not much can be done without cooperation from foreign governments, some of which own and run international airlines. The best that can be hoped for is for the State Department to emphasize the need for more competition in pricing and routes in its bilateral negotiations with the various countries.

Since airline safety is the responsibility of the Federal Aviation Administration (FAA), an agency with the Department of Transportation, it will have to develop cost-effective methods of aircraft inspection, aircraft maintenance, and approval of new aircraft. It may also have to aid in solving the difficult problem of allocating gate and landing-and-takeoff slots at the nation's busiest airports.

Energy Regulation

In the area of energy the current emphasis of reform is on deregulation of interstate electric power sales, oil pipelines, and some aspects of natural gas pipeline business as well as on acceleration of deregulation of natural gas prices provided under the Natural Gas Policy Act of 1978 (see Chapter 13). For example, a bill introduced by Senator Don Nickles of Oklahoma would end federal regulation of oil pipeline rates but continue to require pipelines to offer their services to all customers on a nondiscriminatory basis.

It is difficult to say how the Congress will react to these proposals since they are controversial; to some extent they pit gas-producing states against the nonproducers. The reaction of consumers to the proposed changes is also likely to be unfavorable for fear of higher prices.

18.9   REFORM OF ANTITRUST REGULATION

The current regulatory reforms are centered on economic and social regulations, but the whole area of antitrust regulation has received scant public attention, except by a few scholars and practitioners in this field. Yet, as we say in Part 2, the omnipresent antitrust laws exert a vast influence on the economy, most of it in a somewhat misguided direction. There is general consensus among respected scholars, both on the right and left, that the antitrust laws need to be substantially revamped. Here is what some of the scholars are saying:

> The thesis of the book has been that modern antitrust has so decayed that the policy is no longer intellectually respectable. Some of it is not respectable as law, more of it

is not respectable as economics, and now I wish to suggest that, because it pretends to one objective while frequently accomplishing its opposite, and because it too often forwards trends dangerous to our form of government and society, a great deal of antitrust is not even respectable as politics.[38]

. . . the entire antitrust system — allegedly created to protect competition and increase consumer welfare — has worked, instead, to lessen business competition and lessen the efficiency and productivity associated with the free-market process. Like many other government interventions, antitrust has produced results that are far different from those that were allegedly intended.
. . . these perverse economic consequences could have been predicted, since antitrust law has continued to rely primarily upon the static models of perfect competition and monopoly.[39]

Antitrust laws were developed to break up man-made monopolies, and regulations were developed to make natural monopolies act as if they were competitive. While both these approaches have had their problems, the time has come to recognize that the antitrust approach has been a failure. The costs it imposes far exceed any benefits it brings.[40]

The body of antitrust doctrine is largely the product of judicial interpretation of the vague provisions of the antitrust laws and thus can be changed by the courts within the very broad limits set by the statutory language and what we know of the intent behind it. What is required is judicial recognition that many of the existing judge-made rules of antitrust are inconsistent with the fundamental, and fundamentally economic objectives of the antitrust laws.[41]

Why this overwhelming dissatisfaction with the antitrust laws? Although we have pointed out some of the specific problems with these laws in Part 2, this dissatisfaction stems from some fundamental and some practical problems associated with the various laws, which can be stated as follows.

At the fundamental level, Richard Posner argues that of the six major antitrust statutes, Sects. 1 and 2 of the Sherman Act, Sect. 2, 3, and 7 of the Clayton Act, and Sec. 5 of the FTC act all but Sec. 1 of the Sherman Act are redundant or superfluous. In his view, "Section 2 of the Sherman Act, with its separate prohibitions of monopolizing, attempting to monopolize, and conspiracy to monopolize, is really three statutes in one."[42] But then Sec. 1 of the act, which forbids contracts, combinations, and conspiracies in restraint of trade "is sufficiently broad to encompass any anticompetitive practice worth worrying about that involves the cooperation of two or more firms,"[43] negating the need for Sec. 2.

---

[38]Robert H. Bork, *The Antitrust Paradox: A Policy at War with Itself*, Basic Books, New York, 1978, p. 418.
[39]Dominick T. Armentano, *Antitrust and Monopoly: Anatomy of a Policy Failure*, Wiley, New York, 1982, p. 271.
[40]Lester Thurow, op. cit., pp. 145–146.
[41]Richard A. Posner, *Antitrust Law: An Economic Perspective*, The University of Chicago Press, Chicago, 1976, p. 7.
[42]Ibid., p. 212.
[43]Ibid.

But what is wrong with superfluity of laws? Posner contends:

The problem of the redundant antitrust statutes is that they have stimulated an uncritical and unwise expansion in the prohibitory scope of antitrust. The courts have tended to reason that, since Section 1 of the Sherman Act is itself so encompassing in its prohibition of anticompetitive practices, any supplementary prohibitions, whether contained in Section 2 of the Sherman Act or in the Clayton or Federal Trade Commission Acts, must have been intended to attenuate the requirements in Section 1 for proving anticompetitive effect — which were never that demanding — still further.[44]

To illustrate his point, Posner cites the Alcoa case (see Chapter 8) He contends:

Were it not for Section 2, the only issue in *Alcoa* would have been whether the defendant had committed any anticompetitive practices, such as mergers or predatory pricing, and the answer to this question — "no" — would have been the end of the case. But on this view the offense of monopolization is simply the commission of Section 1 violations by a monopolist, a view which, . . . hardly gives the concept of monopolization an important place in the statutory scheme. Perhaps that is why Judge Hand read Section 2 to forbid any active efforts to obtain or maintain monopoly power even if the efforts did not violate Section 1, so that Alcoa was guilty of monopolization because it had tried to satisfy as much of the growth in demand for aluminum as possible by expanding its own capacity, instead of sitting back and letting its competitors, or new entrants, provide for the growth of the market.[45]

Posner probably has a valid point, for as we saw in Chapter 8, the *Alcoa* decision dealt a severe blow to Justice White's "rule of reason" enunciated in the *Standard Oil* case, which, in substance, held that a monopolist (either singly or in combination) must have both the power to monopolize and the intent to monopolize; in *Alcoa* the mere possession of power became an offense.
In Posner's view:

There is no place in a rational system of antitrust law for separate doctrine of monopolization. There are unreasonably anticompetitive practices, and whether or not a practice is unreasonably anticompetitive sometimes depends on the market share of the firm or firms employing it. . . . The task of antitrust policy is to identify such practices and forbid them, and it is a task to which Section 1 of the Sherman Act is fully adequate. . . .
    There is equally little reason for having separate offenses of attempting, and of conspiring, to monopolize. If a firm has engaged in a practice unreasonably restrictive of competition, it has violated Section 1 regardless of whether monopoly has been achieved. . . . As for conspiracy to monopolize, any such conspiracy is also a conspiracy in restraint of trade, which violates Section 1.[46]

In short, Posner strongly believes that the antitrust statutes other than Sec. 1 of the Sherman Act should be repealed for they are potentially mischievous.
    Let us now turn to some of the practical objections to the existing antitrust

[44]Ibid., pp. 212–213.
[45]Ibid., p. 214.
[46]Ibid., 216.

laws. At the outset it should be noted that the Sherman Act was passed around the turn of the century and has remained essentially unchanged for well over 90 years. It and the other antitrust regulations simply cannot cope with the changed international economic scene in which the United States now has to operate. As Thurow laments:

> . . . with the growth of international trade it is no longer possible to determine whether an effective monopoly exists by looking at local market shares. Regardless of the share of domestic production held by General Motors, General Motors is part of a competitive industry and must deal with strong Japanese and European competition. In markets where international trade exists or could exist, national antitrust laws no longer make sense. If they do anything, they only serve to hinder U.S. competitors who must live by a code that their foreign competitors can ignore. . . .
>
> If competitive markets are desired, the appropriate policy should be to reduce barriers to free trade. . . . If one measures the potential gains to be made by enforcing the antitrust laws, as opposed to reducing real barriers to international trade, it is clear that the large gains exist in the area of more international competition.[47]

Thurow raises other objections to the antitrust laws. The excessive obsession with monopoly profits or rents is misplaced, for "excessive rates of return attract competitors, and potential competitors have the ability to enter all those markets that are not natural monopolies. . . . Firms with no actual or potential competitors are few and far between."[48] Thurow also questions the economic value of breaking up a corporation such as IBM into three or four large firms. He asks:

> What characteristics of the industry would change? By now we should have enough experience to know that a three- or four-firm oligopoly does not act noticeably different from a one-firm monopoly faced with potential competition (the Japanese) in its main business and actual competition where it is weak (in small computers). . . .
>
> No one questions that IBM has a dominant market position. But this is not to say that it has been able to extract crippling monopoly rents from computer customers. In some ways the [now dropped antitrust] case reads like a government sign saying, "It does not pay to be too efficient." Yet in a larger context, this is certainly a slogan that we do not wish to issue if we are interested in long-run efficiency.[49]

Reforms in Antitrust Laws

If one accepts the general thrust of the preceding comments about the current antitrust laws, what kinds of reforms do these comments suggest? As already noted, Posner would repeat all the antitrust statutes except Sec. 1 of the Sherman Act. Thurow expresses similar sentiment when he writes:

> Given our modern economic environment, antitrust regulations should be stripped back to two basic propositions. The first would be a ban on predatory pricing. Large

---

[47]Lester Thurow, op. cit., p. 146.
[48]Ibid., p. 148.
[49]Ibid., p. 148.

firms should not be allowed to drive small firms out of business by selectively lowering their prices in submarkets while they maintain high prices in other submarkets. The second proposition would be a ban on explicit or implicit cartels that share either markets or profits. Firms can grow by driving competitors out of business or by absorbing them, but they cannot agree not to compete with each other.[50]

A similar theme is echoed by Bork, who would like to see the antitrust laws strike against three classes of behavior:

(a) The suppression of competition by horizontal agreement, such as the nonancillary agreements of rivals or potential rivals to fix prices or divide markets.

(b) Horizontal mergers creating very large market shares (those that leave fewer than three significant rivals in any market).

(c) Deliberate predation engaged in to drive rivals from a market, prevent or delay the entry of rivals, or discipline existing rivals .... [But] care must be taken not to confuse hard competition with predation.[51]

To what extent these reforms will be taken up by the administration or by the Congress is difficult to predict since the constituency for such reforms, unlike that in the area of social and economic regulation, is rather small and not very vocal. However, the Justice Department has eased its attitude toward vertical and conglomerate mergers and vertical price-fixing because they may yield significant efficiencies; consequently it has revised its *Merger Guidelines* (see Section 10.10). This is probably in recognition of the fact that the Reagan administration is convinced of the need for reform in this area. President Reagan's former chief of the Antitrust Division of the Justice Department, William F. Baxter (now a law professor at Stanford), personally believes that "the sole goal" of antitrust is "economic efficiency" and not any social and political aspect. It remains to be seen to what extent the Reagan administration itself or the Congress goes along in espousing such a viewpoint.[52]

18.10 CONCLUDING COMMENTS

To conclude our discussion of regulatory reform, we quote a respected Harvard economist, John Dunlop:

All our institutions have increasingly and in various contexts been called upon to do things that they are not well suited to do, and they make a mess out of trying. Our universities, for instance, have gone through a period in which some students and faculty members thought of them as some kind of all-purpose reform institutions with a mission in society to "straighten things out." Universities are fairly good at training people and at pursuing research. They are not very good at reforming society, and they should stay out of that business. . . .

---

[50]Thurow, op. cit., p. 150.

[51]Bork, op., cit., p. 406.

[52]For a provocative viewpoint, see Fred L. Smith, Jr., "Why Not Abolish Antitrust?" *Regulation,* American Enterprise Institute's Journal on Government and Society, January–February 1983, pp. 23–28.

Similarly, we need to have a more limited view of what government is capable of doing. I deeply admire government, and I have frequently worked with it, but it can help with only a limited number of problems. When it takes on an unlimited agenda of tasks, pushing social reform to the limits under the kinds of general legislation that have been enacted, it will certainly fall into a quagmire, and this will have a very serious adverse impact. . . .[53]

[53]John T. Dunlop, "Setting Priorities in Government Regulation," in *Reforming Regulation,* op. cit., pp. 160–161.

INDEXES

NAME INDEX

SUBJECT INDEX

525

CASE INDEX